CONTENTS

The inseparables:

*with this guide
use the Michelin Red Guide
and maps to Germany
(see page 9)*

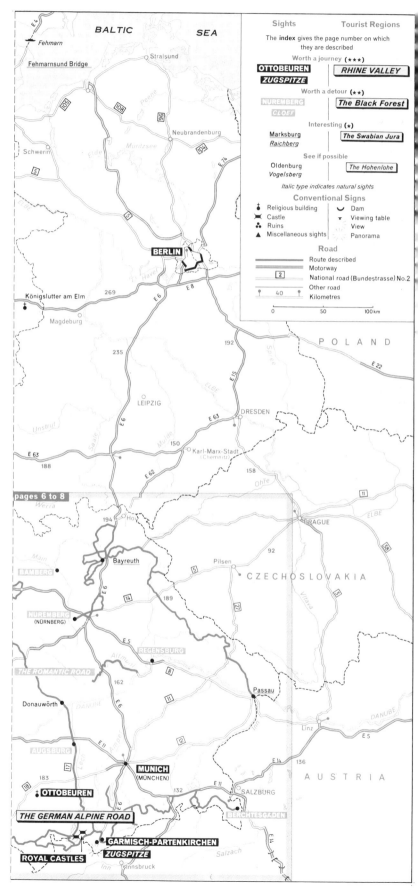

Sights Tourist Regions

The **index** gives the page number on which they are described

Worth a journey (★★★)

OTTOBEUREN *RHINE VALLEY*

ZUGSPITZE

Worth a detour (★★)

NUREMBERG **The Black Forest**

CLOEF

Interesting (★)

Marksburg The Swabian Jura

Raichberg

See if possible

Oldenburg The Hohenlohe

Vogelsberg

Italic type indicates natural sights

Conventional Signs

- ⛪ Religious building
- ⚔ Castle
- ⛰ Ruins
- ▲ Miscellaneous sights
- ᴗ Dam
- ⊤ Viewing table
- View
- Panorama

Road

———— Route described
Motorway
2 National road (Bundesstrasse) No.2
40 Other road
Kilometres

0   50   100 km

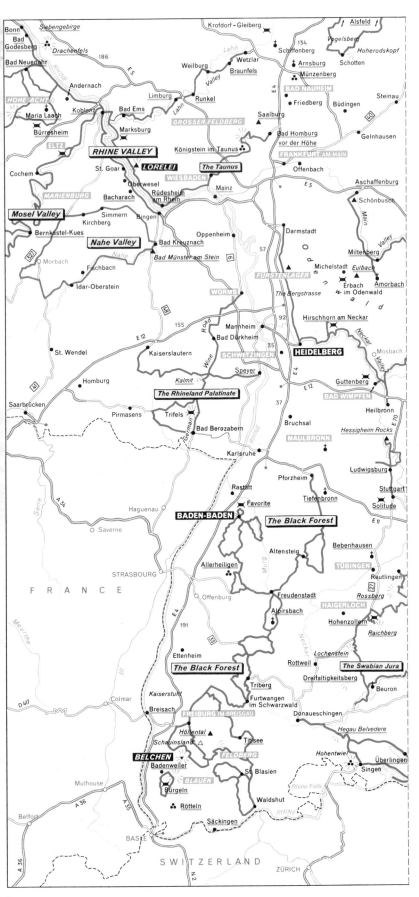

Tipping. – Service is always included on the bill. It is usual, however, to tip hotel staff for personal service, and also, occasionally, the guides to historic monuments. It is customary to round up a bill, leaving the small change for hotel and restaurant waiters, attendants, taxi-drivers, porters and barbers.

Lost property. – In the street – enquire at the local police station.
– on trains – enquire at the local station.
– on municipal transport (trams, underground or buses) – report to the municipal lost property offices.

SOUVENIRS

The visitor from abroad, well aware of Germany's high reputation in the manufacture of precision goods, can also hope to find genuine craftwork in certain regions.

The enforced inactivity of winter formerly encouraged the people of the mountains to take up moneymaking skills. In the Bavarian Alps there developed the arts of wood carving, of making musical instruments (lute making at Mittenwald) and of the making of traditional folk costume (especially at Miesbach and Berchtesgaden). Wood carving is also a speciality of the inhabitants of the Bavarian and the Black Forests, Ivory or bone carving is found at Erbach in the Odenwald.

Candle factories have developed in the devoutly Catholic areas of southern Bavaria. Schongau, Rosenheim and Burghausen, in addition to the traditional religious candles, also produce wax figurines and decorative coloured candles.

The Palatinate, a region which has suffered considerable geological turbulence, contains many mineral deposits particularly in the Idar-Oberstein area, giving it a reputation as the agate and semi-precious stone capital. In this world of adornment the countless pieces of costume jewellery produced at Neugablonz near Kaufbeuren in Bavaria and the gold and silver filigree work of Wyk, Meldorf and Leer in Friesland should not be forgotten. Near Bremen the village of Worpswede thrives as an artists' and craftsmen's centre (handweaving).

Obviously Western Germany produces industrially many articles which can also be designated as "souvenirs" – glassware in the Bavarian Forest area, porcelain at Nymphenburg near Munich, Ludwigsburg and Fürstenberg in the Weser Valley, pottery at Rausbach and Höhr-Grenzhausen near Coblenz, knives and scissors at Solingen, cuckoo clocks in the Black Forest, etc.

RULES OF THE ROAD

Do not forget to equip your car with a nationality plate.

Road Traffic. – Priority must be given to traffic coming from the right, unless otherwise indicated. The **speed limit,** generally, in built up areas is 50 kph - 30 mph and on all other roads it is 100 kph - 60 mph. On motorways and four lane highways the speed limit is 130 kph - 80 mph.

German road traffic regulations provide heavy penalties for exceeding the speed limit, illegally crossing the centre line, not giving way to traffic having priority and being drunk in charge of a vehicle.

Driving on side lights only is prohibited; **dipped headlights** are obligatory when visibility is poor and after sunset (converter lenses are required under Continental regulations).

In Town. – Traffic in towns is strictly regulated by means of underpasses and one-way streets. Trams must be overtaken on the right and never at a stop.

There are two forms of parking in German towns: parking zones requiring a parking disc (can be obtained at the local tourist office or police station) and parking meter zones *(0.10DM)*.

Some service stations in built up areas have coin-operated pumps (Münztank) for the convenience of motorists requiring petrol at night or other times when the pumps are unattended.

Motorways. – Motorways score the contemporary German landscape, their course marked by, sometimes, grandiose civil engineering projects; they have become the favourite routes of communication, drivers preferring the longer motorways (which are free of toll).

The first stretch of motorway or Autobahn was opened in 1932 between Frankfurt and Darmstadt. The great HAFRABA **(Hanse – Frankfurt and Basle)** undertaking was completed in 1962.

6 200 kilometres - 3 850 miles of motorway had been constructed in West Germany by the end of 1976.

From the tourist's point of view, some sections of motorway enable him to see parts of the country better than he might have done in the past. Such roads are the one up the Swabian Jura, the Cologne-Dortmund section which cuts through the rolling woodlands of the Berg Region, the magnificent road through the Spessart Forest, the one over the Rhön mountains between Frankfurt, Würzburg and Bad Hersfeld and the road running alongside the Bavarian Alps and the Chiemsee between Munich and Salzburg.

Safety Measures. – Motorists must be in possession of an officially approved breakdown triangle, a first-aid kit and are urged to carry a fire extinguisher. For Berlin all three are compulsory.

In emergencies call the police (radio patrol cars) by telephone. The number for emergencies is 110, as well as for accident and fire.

ROAD GLOSSARY

Anfang	entrance, start	**LKW**	commercial vehicles
Aussichtspunk	viewpoint	**PKW**	cars
Ende	end	**Radweg kreuzt**	cycle crossing
Engstelle	road narrows	**Rechts, links einbiegen**	turn right, left
Freie Fahrt	no speed restriction	**Rollsplitt**	gravel
Frostschäden } **Frostaufbrüche** }	road damaged by frost	**Sackgasse**	cul-de-sac
Gefährlich	danger	**Schlechte Wegstrecke** } **Schlechte Fahrbahn** }	road in bad condition
Gegenverkehr	two way traffic	**Steinschlag**	danger of falling stones
Geradeaus	straight on	**Verengte Fahrbahn**	road narrows
Glatteis	ice	**Vorfahrt**	priority
Nur für Anlieger } **Anlieger frei** }	residents only	**Vorsicht**	attention, beware
		Wellige Fahrbahn	bumpy road

INTRODUCTION TO THE TOUR

APPEARANCE OF THE COUNTRY

The greater part of Germany is made up of regions, bounded by mountain ranges or rivers. There is also a vast plain, without any natural barriers, which extends eastwards into Poland and Russia. The lack of natural barriers and consequent accessibility to outside influence has had a considerable effect on German history and civilisation.

General Relief Characteristics. – The German landscape reflects in appearance three great geological phenomena described below in the order in which they occurred.

In the north, the vast **German-Polish Plain** reveals an undisturbed horizontal structure, protected by a neighbouring crystalline base, the Scandinavian buckler.

In the centre lies a confused mass of mountains and basins formed originally by the **Hercynian folding** (the name comes from Harz) which also formed the Central and Armoricain Massifs in France. The now worn and wooded mountains with names ending in *Wald* (forest) were shifted by the Alpine folding and broken by the faults which caused subsidences such as the cleft of the Rhine Valley between the Vosges and the Black Forest and volcanic phenomena such as the basalt crust of the Vogelsberg and the peaks of the Siebengebirge. The largest Hercynian mountain chains in Germany are the Rhineland Schist Massif, a continuation of the Ardennes, the Black Forest and the small chains encircling Bohemia (Bayerischer Wald, Böhmerwald, Erzgebirge and Riesengebirge). On the edges of this Hercynian area lie the coal deposits of the Ruhr and Silesia which enabled German industry to develop so rapidly in the 19C.

The largest basin in the Hercynian region lies east of the Black Forest and is the sedimentary Swabian–Franconian Basin, where the unchanging landscape reminds one of the Lorraine Plain, its counterpart on the opposite side of the Rhine. This vast region, drained by the Main and the Neckar and ribbed by hill chains marking the more resistant seams in the terrain, extends in the southeast to the Swabian Jura. This is a limestone plateau which lies at the top of a wall rising 400 m - 1 300 ft – above the basin.

In the south, the German Alpine region consists only of the slender barrier of the **Bavarian Alps** and of the slopes of the Bavarian Plateau, formed from the mass of debris eroded from the mountains and pulverised during the last of the Quaternary Ice Ages.

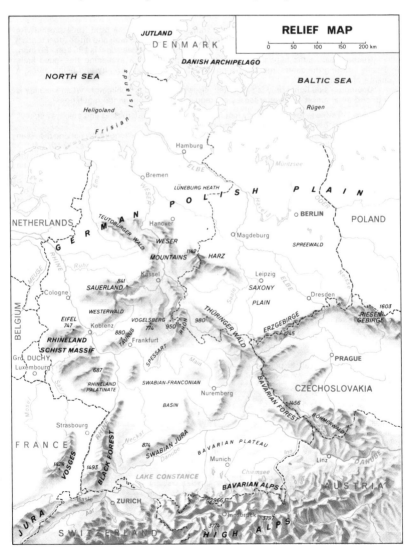

SOUTHERN GERMANY

The Alps and Bavarian Plateau. – The Bavarian and the Allgäu Alps are without glaciers but have a beauty all their own, of dark green forests and contrasting rock escarpments. Their greatest altitude is reached in the Zugspitze – the highest peak in Germany.

The Bavarian Plateau tilts gently towards the Danube, which is navigable below Regensburg. The Iller, the Lech and the Isar, swollen mountain torrents sweeping down infertile debris from the mountainsides, have cut paths across the plateau enabling crops to be grown and such towns established as Augsburg and Munich. The most attractive and fertile area lies in a region never reached by glaciers, between Landshut and Regensburg. West of the River Lech, the hilly landscape of Upper Swabia evens out as it reaches Lake Constance *(p 101)*.

Franconia. – Geologically, Franconia, which corresponds more or less to the Main Basin, is part of the sedimentary Swabian–Franconian Basin. Politically, it is part of Bavaria. The vast, gently rolling and somewhat melancholy plateaus stretch south to the Franconian Jura, a small limestone range where the best stone in Germany for facing buildings is found. In the northeast and the north, the plateaux reach out to the thickly wooded crystalline ranges bordering Bohemia *(p 58)* and Thuringia. Nuremberg is the regional capital.

Swabia. – Swabia corresponds more or less with the former state of Württemberg. It has great variety in its strongly individual landscape; vineyards and orchards adorn the countryside as in the Valley of the Neckar below Stuttgart; elsewhere low wooded hills darken the horizon as does the Schwäbischer Wald between Stuttgart and Schwäbisch Hall. The southern skyline is barred by the blue tinged range of the Swabian Jura *(p 239)*. Over this countryside, the Swabians have scattered a heterogeneous collection of factories and workshops, adding an industrial touch to the smallest towns in the Fils and Rems Valleys and those at the foot of the Swabian Jura. Stuttgart is the foremost local city.

The Black Forest. – The massif has for long been a favourite with visitors *(p 80)*.

CENTRAL GERMANY

The Rhineland Schist Massif. – This ancient mountain range is cut by deep rifts which have been filled by the Rhine, which in itself overcomes many of the most difficult obstacles to internal communications, by the Mosel and the Lahn Rivers. The mountain areas have characteristics in common such as a harsh climate, as may be seen from the slate facing given to the walls of many of the houses. The region rises to its greatest height in the southeast, reaching an altitude of 880 m -2 887 ft – in the wooded Taunus range near Frankfurt.

The Eifel plateau is known for its crater lakes or *Maare (details p 113)*.

Heavy industry has been developed chiefly in the Sieg Valley, by tradition a mining and metallurgical region which is still black with industrial smoke round the town of Siegen.

The Upper Sauerland, thickly wooded and a true mountain area (841 m - 2 759 ft), provides the water and, with its many dams, acts as the reservoir for the Ruhr industrial region *(p 223)*.

The Mountains of Upper Hesse and the Weser. – Between the Rhineland Schist Massif and the Thüringer Wald lies a confused amalgam of basins and heights, some volcanic such as the Vogelsberg and the Rhön. Upper Hesse – the northern area of the *Land* of the same name – is relatively poor, but, since the earliest barbarian invasions, has been used as the highway between northern and southern Germany (Frankfurt–Kassel).

The Teutoburger Wald heights are the best known of the Weser hills. Although low, they form, between the Westphalian and the northern plains, a definite barrier which is breached most importantly at the Porta Westfalica, near Minden, thoroughfare for the greater part of the traffic between the Rhineland and northern Germany.

The Harz Mountains. – This range has been called the Heart of Germany *(p 144)*.

The Upper Rhine Plain. – Between Basle and the Binger Gap, the plain widens out. As in Alsace, its alluvial topsoil is very fertile and its climate of early springs and hot summers favours intensive arable farming (wheat, beet, hops, maize and tobacco) and wine growing.

The whole of this flat area has become one of the great meeting points of Europe and, in consequence, towns of any size such as Frankfurt have acquired international standing.

NORTHERN GERMANY

The Lower Rhine Valley and Westphalia. – The flat green plain of the Lower Rhine, protected from river flooding, is dotted with farms and hamlets, containing the comfortable type of house seen in nearby Holland. The Westphalian Plain area round Münster provides a similar landscape of wooded farms. This region which maintains its tradition of horse breeding, has a noble style with many castles and moated manor houses *(Wasserburgen)*.

The Great Northern Plain. – In spite of its apparent monotony, the North German Plain has a certain variety of landscape.

The Börde country lies in the south, below the last of the Weser foothills and the Harz Mountains and between the Weser and the Elbe – a land covered with an alluvial topsoil known for its fertility. This has resulted in flourishing market gardens as well as farms around Brunswick. The area, where Hanover and Brunswick are near neighbours, is densely populated. It has rich resources, iron at Peine, potash and petroleum at Salzgitter and, more recently, with the establishment of factories at Wolfsburg, a world centre of car production.

Further north is the Geest, a region with little in its favour since the Scandinavian glaciers, which covered this part of Germany as late as Palaeolithic times, retreated, leaving the land either poorly drained or sandy. West of the Lower Weser and in the Worpswede region, north of Bremen, are peat bogs *(Moor)* or very wet pastureland. The *Moore*, formerly so bleak, have been drained by Dutch methods, and are now largely under cultivation.

East of the Weser, the once predominant moorland is gradually disappearing as new methods of improving poor soils are discovered. The nature reserve on Lüneburg Heath *(p 171)*, however, has preserved for all time a typical stretch of the old time moorland.

The North Sea Coast *(details p 128)*. – It is on the northern marshes *(Marschen)* that the Frisians have had to struggle hard to win over to cultivation by polders *(Köge)* the vast mud flats *(Watten)* which used to lie uncovered at low tide. The ports have been built at the inland ends of the estuaries.

Schleswig-Holstein. – There is a striking contrast here between the North Sea coast, beaten by the sea winds and always threatened by storms, and the Baltic shore where the estuaries *(Förde)* cut deeply into the flat coastland, and the sea laps a tranquil beach, a wood or an attractive fishing port. Inland lies Holsteinische Schweiz with its lakes.

THE CLIMATE

The conflict of air currents flowing from the Atlantic and the North Sea with those of the Continent provides the basis in Germany of climatic conditions which are changeable and often turbulent particularly in the northern areas when the winds are strong. The months with the clearest skies are April and May on the coast and June and September, inland.

The air is keen all the year round on the North Sea. On the Baltic it is slightly milder but the west winds prevent much lazing on the beaches.

April often brings brilliant still days to the Rhine Valley and southern Germany which lie decked in blossom. Early May, however, frequently sees the return of icy weather. Spring only reaches the shores of Lake Constance and the Valleys of the Inn and the Salzach when the *Föhn*, the violent and drying south wind, sweeps down in great blasts from the Alps.

Summer is marked inland by a rapid rise in the temperature, especially in basins enclosed by Hercynian ranges such as the Upper Rhine Plain. The air becomes hot, heavy and thundery and visitors will enjoy particularly those resorts which offer bathing and forest walks. The Alps, at this season, vary considerably in climate depending on the orientation of the valley, the way a slope faces and the prevailing local winds.

October and the first two weeks of November may bring an Indian Summer or as the Germans call it, "an old woman's summer" *(Altweibersommer)* when the sun, particularly in the south, highlights the autumn tints. Night, however, falls rapidly.

At the first frost, the Bavarian and Allgäu Alps, the Black Forest, the Sauerland and the Harz Mountains, in spite of their modest altitudes, begin to get their winter covering of snow and to prepare for the winter sports season.

MAN AND NATURE IN GERMANY

The Germans are lovers of nature. The sight of a forest laid waste or a park despoiled, shocks them profoundly. Immediately after the war, when Berlin lay in ruins, the mayor described the devastated Tiergarten as "the most severe wound inflicted on the city by the war".

The Forests. – The once immense forests of Germany are largely gone. The survival of feudal traditions and the difficulty of converting woodland to pasture, however, have resulted in a large number of areas remaining well wooded.

The main forest regions are to be found on the Hercynian mountain ranges in the centre of the country. It is here that the beech forests are thickest, the trees tallest and the carpet of bracken is deepest. The beech woods of the Westerwald, the Thüringer Wald, the Weser Mountains and the countryside around Kassel, are extensive.

The Black Forest, the High Swabian Jura and Harz Mountain forests are darker and seemingly more mysterious, containing mixed groups of beech and spruce.

Magnificent clumps of oaks grow in the Spessart and Reinhardswald.

Pine forests are to be found principally in the Alps.

The Lime Tree. – The lime, in Germany, has poetic and youthful associations. Lime trees shade village squares and busy streets, including the now no longer busy "Unter den Linden" in East Berlin.

Countless commemorative lime trees have been planted to dreaming poets or to honour the philosophies of men of action – Goethe, Schiller, Bismarck. . . .

Fruit Trees. – The fruit trees which line the roads of southern Germany are most attractive. The early plum blossom, followed by cherry, pear and, lastly, apple, bring many thousands of local and also foreign visitors to look at the trees in flower along the Bergstrasse *(p 65),* on the Upper Rhine Plain and in the Altes Land, at the mouth of the Elbe *(p 234).*

The Parks. – German parks and gardens are impeccably maintained, whether they are municipal or spa parks, formal gardens as at Brühl or landscaped gardens as at Munich, romantic parks as at the Linderhof or whole park areas reflecting a modern need for green space, as in the Ruhr.

Every two years (1979: Bonn) the national horticultural exhibition (Bundesgartenschau), which affords a sumptuous display, is held in one of the many large parks of the country.

There are fifty-four **protected wild life parks** (Naturpark) in Germany, amounting to a total area of more than 4 million ha - 15000 sq miles (for their boundaries see Michelin map no 987). These should not be confused with the 900 **nature reserves** (Naturschutzgebiet) which are less extensive and to which access, because of their scientific role, is sometimes strictly controlled.

The wild life parks exist, particularly those in forests, for the enjoyment of walkers. They are provided with car parks, with signposted rides, shelters and belvedere-towers. The largest are those of the Bergstrasse and the Odenwald and the Pfälzerwald in the Palatinate, which is to be further extended to include a part of the northern Vosges in France. The southern Eifel (Südeifel) wild life park, which again straddles the frontier, includes the Luxembourg lake district.

(After a photo from the National Castles)

Linderhof Park.

Even outside the natural parks, all mountain areas of the slightest interest to visitors, and all woods near country resorts are traversed by signposted footpaths, which if designated as *Waldlehrpfad* may well provide the visitor with information on the local forest flora and fauna, for protection of the fauna is included in the nature preservation policy.

One of the most popular winter spectacles is the feeding of big game **(Wildfütterung),** which occurs when snow prevents the animals from grazing. The fodder, placed at set times in special places, attracts a procession of red and roe deer.

THE ECONOMY

The Country and its Population. – The German Federal Republic has an area of 248 500 km² - 95 683 sq miles – as against the United Kingdom's 244 000 km² - 94 059 sq miles. The distance from north to south is approximately 800 km - 500 miles; the population, including that of West Berlin in 1974, amounted to more than 62 million, of which a third live in 62 towns of over 100 000 inhabitants.

Economic Recovery. – Germany owes her rapid post-war economic recovery not only to the outside help she received, principally from the United States, but above all to the industry and sacrifices of all kinds made by her own people, inspired by the thought of creating better times.

The key dates in this economic revival were:
1948: Currency reform;
1952: Creation of the powerful European Coal and Steel Community of which Germany became a member;
1956: Return of the Saar to Germany;
1957: Formation of the Common Market;
1969: Revaluation of the Mark.

EMPLOYMENT

West Germany's labour resources today do not compare favourably with those before the World Wars or even with those of her neighbours. The increase in population during the past years (44% from 1939 to 1974) is due less to the higher birth-rate (as a matter of fact the births have somewhat decreased since 1972) – than to the massive influx of 13 million refugees from East Germany (a number equivalent to the population of the Netherlands). The refugees have been successfully assimilated, but nevertheless war casualties and the extension of compulsory schooling to 15 years forecasts a continuing shortage. Foreign labour continues to be needed – 2 400 000 foreigners entered the country on work permits in 1974. Women represented 36% of the labour force in 1974 in Germany, the highest for any country in the Common Market (GB: 35%).

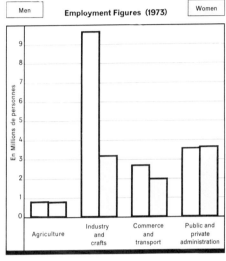

Employment Figures (1973). Men / Women. En Millions de personnes. Agriculture / Industry and crafts / Commerce and transport / Public and private administration

INDUSTRY

The strength of German industry, which used to depend very largely on rich coal resources, now lies in its organisation, rationalisation and modernity.

Industrial Groupings. – German industry has been remarkable for nearly one hundred years for the way it has concentrated into industrial groups. Before the First World War, industry in Germany consisted in the main of powerful family enterprises which undertook all the industrial and commercial phases of manufacture from the raw material to the finished product. Krupp, whose empire continued until 1967, was the most famous example of this "vertical" undertaking.

Between the wars, cartels or *Konzern* (IG Farben Industrie, Vereinigte Stahlwerke, etc.) were formed resulting in "horizontal" groupings of industries specialising in the same enterprises. The cartels were suppressed in 1945 but ten years later were revived in a different form, the establishment of the supra-national European Coal and Steel Community in the intervening period, having allayed fears of the wartime allies in the power of monopolies.

It is noticeable that, with the exception of car manufacture and shipbuilding, which were already flourishing pre-war in the area which is now Western Germany, the industries in which there has been the greatest expansion since 1950 are those which, at the end of the war, moved from the east to the west – namely electrical manufacturing and the "new" industries of man-made fibres, plastics, petroleum, etc.

Sources of Energy. – Germany provides a telling example of what has happened in all the countries of western Europe, namely the reduction in importance of coal in the national economy. In 1974 52% of the power was supplied by hydrocarbons, 22% by coal, 10% by lignite and 15% by hydraulic power and natural gas.

Coal production dropped from 151 million tons in 1956 to 95 million tons in 1974 – 82% going to industry in the Ruhr. Germany is the fifth greatest coal-mining nation in the world.

In contrast to coal, the mining of **lignite**, which is done by opencast methods using machines which extract up to 100000 tons a day, has remained stable; 87% of the total mined (126 million tons in 1974 – third in world totals) comes from the region between Cologne and Aachen. Four fifths is consumed by German thermal power stations.

Even though the German **oilfields** have the highest yield of all those in western Europe, they only produce some 6.3 million tons a year and, therefore, Germany imports the bulk of her oil requirements – nearly 103 million tons in 1974. Pipelines bring the oil to the inland refineries – notably the "South-Europe" (SEPL) – Lavera-Karlsruhe-Ingolstadt line and the "TAL"–Trieste-Ingolstadt line which has a diameter of one metre. The Federal Republic's refining capacity at the end of 1974 was 146 million tons.

Natural gas reserves, which have been estimated to be in the order of 350 thousand million cubic metres, are being fully exploited, but it is thought likely that Germany will soon be calling also on the considerable resources of the Dutch Groningue-Slochteren field.

Electricity production, which is nearly 91% thermal, reached 312 milliard kWh in 1974. Domestic consumption in the same year at 65 milliard kWh represented 12 times the consumption of 1950, although the total national figure had only increased sevenfold.

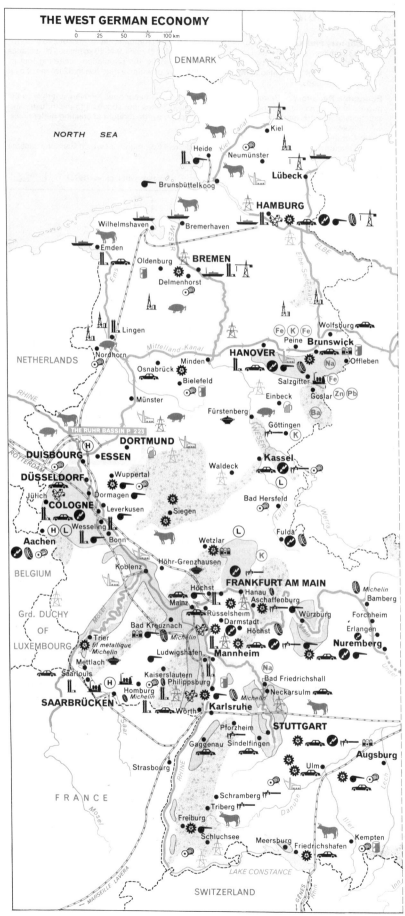

THE WEST GERMAN ECONOMY

0   25   50   75   100 km

DENMARK

NORTH SEA

Kiel

Heide
Neumünster
Lübeck

Brunsbüttelkoog

HAMBURG

Wilhelmshaven
Bremerhaven
Emden
Oldenburg
BREMEN
Delmenhorst

Lingen
Nordhorn

NETHERLANDS

Mittelland-Kanal

Osnabrück
Minden
HANOVER
Bielefeld

Münster

Wolfsburg
Peine
(Fe)(K)(Fe)
Brunswick
Offleben
(Na)
Salzgitter
(Fe)
Goslar (Zn)(Pb)
Einbeck
(Ba)

Fürstenberg
Göttingen
(K)

THE RUHR BASSIN P 223
DORTMUND

DUISBOURG (H)
ESSEN
DÜSSELDORF
Wuppertal
Jülich
Dormagen
COLOGNE
Leverkusen
(H)(L)
Wesseling
Aachen
Bonn

BELGIUM

Waldeck
Kassel
(L)

Bad Hersfeld

Siegen

Wetzlar
(L)
(K)
Fulda

Koblenz
Höhr-Grenzhausen

Grd. DUCHY

OF

LUXEMBOURG

Höchst
Hanau
Mainz
Aschaffenburg
FRANKFURT AM MAIN
Rüsselsheim
Würzburg
Darmstadt
Höchst

Bamberg
Forchheim
Erlangen
Michelin
NUREMBERG

Trier
fil metallique
Michelin
Mettlach
Saarlouis
Bad Kreuznach
Michelin

Ludwigshafen
MANNHEIM

Kaiserslautern
Philippsburg
Homburg
Michelin
SAARBRÜCKEN
(H)
Wörth

(Na)
Bad Friedrichshall
Neckarsulm
Michelin
Karlsruhe

Pforzheim
STUTTGART
Gaggenau Sindelfingen

Strasbourg

AUGSBURG

Ulm

FRANCE

Schramberg
Triberg
Freiburg
Schluchsee

Meersburg Friedrichshafen
Kempten

LAKE CONSTANCE

SWITZERLAND

MARSEILLE LAVERA

16

Agriculture

Major crops (wheat, sugar-beet, potatoes)

Vineyards

Forest regions

Livestock

Cattle

Pigs

Mineral Ressources

(Fe) Iron

(Zn) Zinc

(Pb) Lead

(K) Potash

(Na) Salt

(Ba) Barium oxide

(H) Coal

(L) Lignite

Oil wells

Sources of Energy

Pipeline

Oil refinery

Power station

Hydraulic power station

Walter course channelled to produce electrical power

Power station or nuclear research centre

Chief Navigable Waterways

Rivers

Canals

Industries

Steel (blast furnaces, steelworks)

Metallurgical

Cement and agglomerate industries

Automobile

Electrical equipment

Precision tool

Optical

Chemical

Tyre

Textile

Pottery

Food products

Brewery

Naval dockyard

Large port

BALTIC SEA

BERLIN

Mittelland-Kanal

ELBE

CZECHOSLOVAKIA

Hof
Selb
Kulmbach

Weiden

Amberg

Regensburg

DANUBE

Construction

Neustadt

Ingolstadt

Dingolfing

Passau

Jochenstein

Isar

MUNICH

Burghausen

Inn

Chiemsee

Berchtesgaden

Walchensee

Sylvensteinsee

AUSTRIA

TRIESTE

Nuclear Research. – The nuclear research centres produce approximately 6 milliard kWh, which is constantly increasing. The most highly developed centres are Karlsruhe and Jülich concentrating on nuclear reactors and electric power generators.

Steel and Metallurgical Industries. – German blast furnaces, situated of necessity close to the coal deposits of the Ruhr and the Saar and to a lesser degree by the iron mines of Peine and Salzgitter, produced 50 million tons of smelted metal in 1974. Steelworks producing 53 million tons of raw steel and 40 million tons of sheet steel – nearly a third the production of the European Coal and Steel Community – make West Germany the fourth ranking steel manufacturer in the world after the USA, the USSR and Japan.

The **engineering industry** is one of the advanced industries in West Germany; with its 4 700 factories (more than 73 thousand million DM) located for the most part in Rhineland-Westphalia and Baden-Württemberg, it stands first in the national economy and second in the number of employed – 1 worker in 8. It is the Republic's greatest exporter – more than one third of its products being sold abroad. Machine tools and printing and paper-making machines, the most important of the items exported, are bought principally by France and Italy. Germany ranks third in the world **shipbuilders.**

The German **automobile industry,** which is the third greatest in the world, produced 3 870 000 vehicles in 1976 of which 3 550 000 were passenger cars. Although national demand continues (symbolised in the drawing below) 53% of all production is exported.

The average German driver covers 14 500 km - 8 700 miles – a year.

Tourists interested in visiting car factories are admitted (except on Saturdays, Sundays and holidays) to the following:

– VOLKSWAGEN at Wolfsburg (body work and private cars), Kassel (gear boxes and spare parts), and Hanover (engines, utility vehicles), at 10am and 2pm.
– OPEL at Rüsselsheim (at 8.30 and 10.45am and 2pm) and Bochum (8.15 and 10.30am and 2pm).
– BMW at Munich (at 1.30pm, museum open 9am to 5pm).
– NSU AUDI at Ingolstadt (10am to noon) and at Neckarsulm (at 9.15am and 1pm).
– PORSCHE at Stuttgart-Zuffenhausen (by appointment).
– DAIMLER-BENZ (Mercedes) at Sindelfingen from 7am to 2pm; in addition this firm has an Automobile Museum at Stuttgart-Untertürkheim *(details p 238).*
– FORD at Cologne (groups only by appointment).

The tours usually take between 1 and 3 hours. In most cases it is necessary to book a fortnight in advance. Children must be over 13.

17

The Electrical Industry. – This industry, whose range of 100 000 articles extends from industrial transformers to electric razors, employs the same number of workers, 1 000 000, as engineering. Home demands are primarily for electrical domestic equipment, telephones and television sets *(the ratio of instruments and sets to inhabitants is respectively 1 to 5 and 1 to 4).*

Germany is second in world exports of electrical equipment.

Precision and Optical Industries. – The German reputation for accuracy in measuring and scientific equipment, in glasswork and optical instruments brought her, before the war, a pre-eminence in the precision and optical industries which she has since sought and to a considerable degree regained. One third of all manufactures are exported; the only countries again with a greater volume of trade being the USA and Japan.

Prestige in the optical industry still comes from such long famous specialities as prism manufacture, binoculars and the "24×36" (produced in Wetzlar in 1924); mass production of cheaper equipment is now also undertaken in competition with Japan and America.

Chemical Industry. – Many still think of chemicals with Bayer, BASF and Hoechst as being Germany's primary industry; to the traditional manufactures of dyes, fertilisers, pharmaceutical and photographic products have now been added petrochemicals, manmade fibres, plastics and detergents.

The industry is now third in importance in Germany; more than a quarter of its products are exported.

Construction Industry. – More than one household in two, it is estimated, lives in a house or apartment erected since 1949 (13 million dwellings of the 22.5 million already existing).

TRADE

The prosperity of Germany's **domestic trade** is patently evident in the increasing thundering of its heavy lorries as they travel the main roads and the *Autobahn.*

Most long distance haulage, however, is still by rail; at the beginning of 1974 there were 28 806 km - 17 860 miles – of track of which 9 711 km - 6 020 miles – have been electrified and carry more than half the total railway goods traffic.

River transport and particularly Rhine river traffic *(p 209)* occupies second place in long distance goods haulage in Germany (319 million tons in 1972), being less great than rail and greater than road transport. The canals are among the most modern in Europe but their routing is out of gear with the economy of a country which extends from the North Sea to the Alps. The construction of a new canal was begun in 1968 which will link the Elbe with the Mittelland-Kanal as well as the Rhine-Main-Danube canal.

External trade in 1974 amounted to some 180 000 million DM in imports and 231 000 million in exports; the Republic is, therefore, second only to the USA as a world exporting nation (UK 1974 – £23 115 million imports; £16 490 million exports).

Germany's export trade reflects her high standard of economic development: although a highly industrial country seeking raw materials abroad in ever greater quantities and although not self-sufficient in food, her imports, in value, are principally in manufactured goods – 46% of the 1974 total. As a result the best known German products abroad, machines and equipment, are in keen competition on the home market with imported goods: sheet metal and steel ingots from France, French machines, French and Italian cars, textiles and clothing, chemical products and even photographic equipment.

Germany is France's chief trade partner, in exchange the Netherlands and France are Germany's chief suppliers.

The total import and export trade handled by Germany's seaports (Hamburg, Bremen, Wilhelmshaven, etc.) in 1973 amounted to 142 million tons. It must, however, be remembered that a considerable amount of the Republic's foreign trade is routed through Rotterdam and Amsterdam.

Germany's **trade fairs** – Hanover, Cologne, Düsseldorf, Munich, Frankfurt, etc. – have become international centres of commerce over the years with foreign exhibitors taking one third of the available space.

AGRICULTURE

Although the population living within the borders of what is now the Federal Republic has increased by 50% on the 1939 total and the area under cultivation decreases year by year – one estimate puts the loss of agricultural land in the Land of Rhineland-Westphalia at 20 ha - 50 acres or the equivalent of two smallholdings a day – the country produces the same proportion of its own foodstuffs, namely 74%, as it has always done. Such results have been obtained through greater agricultural productivity, encouraged under a national scheme known as the Green Plan.

In 1975 **wheat** production was 7 013 000 metric tons (UK 4 435 000 tons). **Root crops** (potatoes, beet) occupy the second greatest area, 16% of all arable land – Germany is second in total potato production, on average 18.8 million tons a year. Marked progress has been made since the war in Germany's **viticulture** *(p 33).*

Land usage (1973)

- Agriculture
- Forestry
- Built up and industrial areas
- Non productive areas

0   19.3   38.6   58
In thousands of square miles

Cattle farming supplies 77% of the country's current needs and accounts for three quarters of the agricultural income. Pigs predominate with nearly 20.2 million head (UK 7.5 million) and cattle come second with 14.4 million (UK 14.6 million).

Although the principal **fishing** grounds in the North Sea, Norway, Iceland and Greenland supply more than a quarter of the catch – mainly herring – imports are still needed to satisfy consumption.

HISTORICAL FACTS

The Germans refer to themselves as "Deutsche" – Teutons. This term has come down from the old German *diet* meaning popular, local, and is a reminder of the differences in language which arose between the Latinised tribes such as the Gauls and the Germanic ones who kept their own language.

German history begins in the 10C when the Germanic peoples – Franks from the Meuse and the Rhine Delta, Frisians, Saxons, Thuringians, Franconians, Swabians and Bavarians – came together in the Holy Roman Empire.

ROMANS AND GERMANS

AD 1C	The Roman legions occupy the country as far as the line of the Rhine and the Danube, the territory between the rivers being defended by a fortified line, the **Limes.**
AD 9	Arminius, leader of the Germans *(p 242)*, defeats the Roman General Varus.
314	Founding of the first bishopric in Germania at Trier.
c 375	The Hun invasion. The defeated Germanic tribes settle west of the Elbe; the Slavs east.

THE FRANKISH EMPIRE

Beginning of the 6C	Clovis, King of the Franks (a tribe originally established on the estuaries of the Rhine) is converted to Christianity. With the support of the Church, he vanquishes the Alemanni to the east and colonises the region that later becomes Franconia.
785	Charlemagne conquers the Saxons west of the Elbe, and the Bavarians.
800	Coronation of Charlemagne in Rome by the Pope. The Emperor thus assumes legally the Roman Empire's jurisdiction in the former areas of Gaul and Germania.
911	The Franks in the east choose one of their own men as King of Germania and begin to quarrel with the Franks to the west who eventually become the French nation.
	The Slavs, east of the Elbe, are colonised and converted.

THE CHURCH AND THE EMPIRE

962	The imperial title is revived in Otto I, crowned in Rome "King of the Franks and the Lombards", and marks the beginning of a German Empire.
1073	Opening of the reign of Pope Gregory VII, the great reformer of the Church. The Emperor's intervention in the investiture of the clergy was the start of a period of strife between the two powers which was to shatter Christianity in the 11C.
1152-1190	Reign of Frederick I, Barbarossa. It was while this famous Hohenstaufen dynasty was in power that the term **Holy Roman Empire** was first used.
1180	Dismemberment of the states of the Guelph, Henry the Lion, Duke of Saxony and Bavaria *(pp 90 and 183)*.
1214	Battle of Bouvines, first clash between the French and German armies.
1356	**The Golden Bull,** the fundamental law of the Empire. The King of Germania is elected by a college of three ecclesiastical **electors** (Bishops of Mainz, Cologne and Trier) and four lay electors (the Duke of Saxony, the Margrave of Brandenburg, the County Palatine and the King of Bohemia). He is subsequently crowned King and Emperor of Rome.

MERCHANTS AND HUMANISTS

1358	The organisation of the maritime and commercial **Hanseatic League** which linked more than 200 towns and symbolised the prosperity of northern Germany. Lübeck created the capital of the League.
1386	Foundation of Heidelberg University, the oldest in Germany.
c 1450	The invention of movable type by Gutenberg in Mainz. The flowering of Humanism.

THE REFORMATION AND ITS POLITICAL CONSEQUENCES *(p 20)*

1493-1519	Maximilian I inaugurates the policy of alliances, later extended by the Habsburgs to satisfy their ambitions in Europe. The Habsburgs from this date are elected emperor on a hereditary basis, and the House of Austria becomes the strongest political force in Germany.
1517	Luther nails his "theses", denouncing the traffic in indulgences, to the church door in Wittenberg.
1530	**The Diet of Augsburg** *(p 52)* provides the Protestants with the opportunity of codifying their beliefs (Confession of Augsburg). The majority of German princes impress their subjects to join the Reformation.
1618	The Hohenzollerns, Margraves of Brandenburg, inherit from the Prussian Duchy the former domains of the Order of the Teutonic Knights. Founding of the Kingdom of Prussia.
1618-1648	**The Thirty Years War.**
1689	The ambitions of Louis XIV bring about the "Orleans War" on the left bank of the Rhine and the devastation of the Palatinate.

THE RISE OF PRUSSIA *(p 20)*

1701	Friedrich III Hohenzollern is crowned King of Prussia under the name Friedrich I.
1714	The Elector Georg of Hanover becomes George I of England. The union of the two houses involves England in German politics.
1713-1740	Friedrich-Wilhelm I of Prussia supervises the organisation of the Prussian army.
1740-1786	Friedrich II, Frederick the Great, wins respect throughout Europe.
1792	Start of the Revolutionary wars. French troops on the banks of the Rhine.
1806	The Emperor Franz II (Franz I of Austria) abdicates the now empty title of Holy Roman Emperor and the Empire dissolves.
1814-1815	Congress of Vienna. Establishment of the **German Confederation.**

GERMAN UNITY *(pp 20 and 21)*

1834	A customs union (Zollverein) is set up under Prussian direction.
1848-1849	Meeting at Frankfurt of a German National Assembly.
1862	Bismarck comes to power as minister-president of Prussia.
1866	Prussia, having beaten Austria at Sadowa (or Königgrätz) throws off Austrian domination and establishes herself as a separate state between the Russian Empire and the Middle Rhine.
1871	Victory of Prussia and her allies against France. Proclamation at Versailles of the **German Empire** under King Wilhelm I of Prussia.

GERMANY IN THE 20C

1914-1918	First World War.
1919	Treaty of Versailles. Demilitarisation of Germany. Founding of the Weimar Republic in the midst of popular unrest.
1923	Occupation of the Ruhr by French troops. Devaluation of the mark. Hitler's first *putsch* (at Munich) fails.
1933	Hitler invested as Chancellor of the German Reich, inaugurates dictatorship.
1939-1945	Second World War. Occupation of the whole of Germany by the Allies.
1949	Proclamation of the German Federal Republic, in the zones occupied by the English, the French and the Americans. Bonn made the seat of the Federal Government.
	The German Democratic Republic established in the Soviet Occupation zone.
1961	The erection of the Berlin Wall.
1972	Treaty between West Germany and the Democatic Republic.
1973	Both Germanys become members of the United Nations.

THE HOLY ROMAN EMPIRE

The title Holy Roman Empire, which goes back to the reign of Frederick Barbarossa in the 12C, later had the adjective German added in German and French although not in English. Holy Roman Empire signified, constitutionally, that the Emperor was the heir to the Caesars; that the imperial power was based on legal ties of a feudal nature. Over the centuries the emperors used their power to try and maintain their rule over Italy and dispute the Church's position of pre-eminence (the Investiture Controversy). While these struggles went on, great vassals such as the Wittelsbachs, the Hohenzollerns and the Princes of Saxony each became sovereign rulers within their own territories. German history throughout the centuries was to be marked by the gradual decline of the concept of the Holy Roman Empire.

LUTHER (1483-1546) AND THE REFORMATION

In 1505, Martin Luther entered the Augustinian monastery of Erfurt. A meticulous religious with a burning wish for sanctity, he was tormented by the problem of salvation. He was appointed Professor of Theology and in 1512-3 found in the Holy Scriptures the answer he had been searching for: "Man justifies himself by his faith, not by the workings of the law." He interpreted this as meaning that man plays no part in his own salvation. Faith, therefore, justifies the existence of man.

At the same time, Luther began his attack against the traffic in indulgences. This caused a considerable scandal throughout Germany.

Luther was denounced in the court of Rome but refused to retract his statement. In 1520 he burned the papal bull threatening him with excommunication and published a denunciation of the pretension of priests to primacy in the spiritual domain. He also criticised the sacraments minutely and the institution and hierarchical establishment of the Church. Luther was brought before the Diet of Worms in 1521 which had been convoked by the young Charles V, but he did not give way. He was exiled to the outer domains of the Empire by an edict which also condemned his works to be burnt and instituted an ecclesiastical censorship of all books printed in Germany. Luther accepted the invitation of the Duke of Saxony, Frederick the Wise, to stay in Wartburg Castle above Eisenach in Thuringia. It was while there that he worked on his translation of the Bible into German – a work subsequently considered to have been the first literary work to be written in modern German.

In 1529 after the Edict of Worms had been confirmed and the position further aggravated by the ruling that no innovations were permissible in the Christian faith, six princes and the representatives of fourteen free towns united at Speyer in protest *(p 234)*. From this protest by the believers in the new faith, came the name "Protestant".

In 1530 Charles V invited theologians of the two faiths to meet in Augsburg. It was during this last barren meeting that Melanchthon drew up on behalf of the Lutherans the *Confession of Augsburg* which became the Protestant charter.

THE THIRTY YEARS WAR

The Peace of Augsburg of 1555 laid down the precept, born of the Reformation: *cuius regio eius religio* – the state shall be supreme in its choice of the religious faith of its people. This was a peace made up of compromise and indifference foreshadowing the peaceful conversion to Protestantism of almost the whole of Germany at the end of the 16C. The revival of Catholicism brought about by the Council of Trent (1545-63) and the Counter-Reformation which was strongly supported by the Emperor, the internal dissensions amongst the Prostestants, the confusion which arose in the Empire when the Emperor Rudolph II quarrelled with his brother Mathias, destroyed the balance of power. The Protestant Union, headed by the Palatinate, gathered its forces to oppose the Catholic League which was supported by Bavaria.

The war, which opened with revolt in Bohemia in 1618, continued to spread. It began as a war between the states ruled by the House of Austria; it became a German war at first localised in the west and north of the country; and it ended as a European war with large scale military operations which were less and less connected with religion. After the intervention of Denmark and Sweden, two Protestant states anxious at the threat to national faith, France, under Richelieu, entered the war determined to bring down the Habsburgs who were powerful not only in Germany but particularly in the Low Countries and the Franche-Comté which both belonged to Spain. The war brought glory to several great military leaders: Tilly, Wallenstein, King Gustavus Adolph of Sweden, Turenne, Condé and many others. The campaigns were fought for the most part in Germany; the countryside was laid waste, major towns, some of which were besieged as many as six times, were sacked, and the economy was ruined.

The Peace of Westphalia *(p 191)* re-established the equal rights of both faiths in Germany.

THE RISE OF PRUSSIA

Under the Hohenzollerns, Prussia stood out from the other states within the Empire which, in the 17C, had become weakened internally by the sovereign ambitions of its princes. Friedrich-Wilhelm, the Great Elector, and to a greater extent, the second King of Prussia, Friedrich-Wilhelm I, the King-Sergeant, were the founders of this Prussian strength which was based on the army, bureaucracy and the royal prerogative.

Frederick the Great (1740-86). – On his accession, Frederick II found a state already remarkably well organised and possessing a standing army. Within a few years, he had made Prussia, after Austria, the second most powerful state in the Empire. Reinforced by the Silesian armies and thus completely altering the balance of power within the Empire, he challenged the House of Austria. During the Seven Years War, even the coalition of Austria, France and Russia was unable to put an end to the political and military enterprises of Frederick, who by this time had England as his ally. "Old Fritz", the model of enlightened despotism, fortified Prussia further by instituting a meticulous administration.

TOWARDS GERMAN UNITY

The Napoleonic holocaust broke apart the German princeling states and brought about the final dissolution of the Holy Roman Empire in 1806. This simplified the political map of Europe. The Church's domains were secularised in 1803, the status of the majority of the Free Imperial Cities was suppressed and a number of the principalities, which in many instances were minute, were amalgamated to form medium sized states such as Württemberg.

Prussia became the bulwark of resistance to the French invader and the leading force behind the war of liberation which broke out in 1813 as a battle of the nations and ended in victory at Leipzig.

The German Confederation. – The Congress of Vienna instituted, in place of the Holy Roman Empire, a German Confederation of thirty-five autonomous states and free towns. These states were represented by a *Diet* of eleven members appointed by the state and town governments which sat at Frankfurt-am-Main under the presidency of Austria. Metternich, a Rhinelander who became Chancellor of Austria, became the effective ruler of the federation whose antiquated constitution clashed with the ideas of those liberal Germans dreaming of an independent nationhood. The meeting of a German national parliament at Frankfurt in 1848-9, following the revolutionary flare-up of 1848, produced no result.

The Bismarck Era (1862-1890). – Bismarck, appointed Minister-President of Prussia in 1862, took only eight years by fire and sword to unify Germany (Lesser Germany) under Prussia. All attempts by Austria to regenerate the German Confederation by federating in a Greater Germany the countries between the North Sea and the Adriatic, were brushed to one side. He moved ineluctably towards war, supported, at home, by the loyalty of the newly risen burghers who had emerged from the rapid industrialisation (the Ruhr was then part of Prussia), and abroad by Napoleon III who appeared not unwilling to see Prussia go to war with Austria for the leadership of Germany. In 1866, Prussia launched a lightning campaign against Austria and obtained an overwhelming victory at Sadowa (Königgrätz). Austria's territorial rights were respected, but Prussia removed her rival once and for all from the German Confederation. Bismarck organised north Germany with a free hand, annexing for Prussia, Hanover, Hesse and Schleswig-Holstein and forming from all the states north of the Main, the Northern Confederation.

To crown his ambitions, which were still frustrated by the hesitancy of the southern states, Bismarck took advantage of the mistrust created in those states by the maladroit efforts of Napoleon III who sought territorial gains for France (the Rhineland Palatinate and Luxembourg) in return for his neutrality. Finally after the Hohenzollern candidature affair had been unwisely exaggerated by the French Government, he succeeded in inflaming national pride on both sides of the frontier and France declared war. The southern states united in defence, forming with the rest of Germany a block to Prussia's south.

THE SECOND REICH (1871-1918)

After the German victory at Sedan on 2 September 1870 the southern states opened negotiations with Prussia to forge federal ties. On 18 January 1871, the German Empire was proclaimed in the Gallery of Mirrors at Versailles with Wilhelm I as Emperor. Imperial Germany, increased by the acquisition of Alsace and Lorraine, remained, in theory, a federal state, but was, in fact, under Prussian domination.

Bismarck's diplomacy aimed, from this time, at isolating France and allying Germany with the Austro-Hungarian Empire, Italy and Russia and simultaneously manœuvred to prevent any *rapprochement* between England and France.

But **Wilhelm II,** who succeeded his father in 1888, had little liking for the Iron Chancellor, and Bismarck was dismissed in 1890. The Kaiser found himself at the centre of a crisis caused by over rapid expansion: the population was growing so fast that the 41 million of 1870 had become 61 million by 1913 and industry was developing apace. The need to expand was elevated by Pan-Germans into a philosophy; Wilhelm, stimulated by necessity and ambition, undertook a bold foreign policy. But his interventions in the Balkans, coupled with those of his ally, Austria, conflicted with Russian intentions, his African exploits with France's policy in Morocco and his naval expansion disquieted Britain. By the end of 1913, when increasing tension had resulted in an arms' race, Germany found herself with but one ally, Austria-Hungary and one hesitant supporter, Italy. Opposing the Kaiser were France and Russia, bound by an alliance, and England, who with the *Entente Cordiale*, had openly declared her interests.

The international atmosphere was so tense that the assassination of the Austrian Archduke Franz Ferdinand at Sarajevo on 28 June 1914 was sufficient to unleash the storm; the declaration of war by Austria on Serbia on 28 July enough to bring in all the armies of Europe.

The **Great War** was to last four years and result in the death of more than 9 million men.

In October 1918 the German advance, after one last forward thrust, crumbled before the combined strength of the Allies; while at home, in Germany, revolution burst out, inspired by Socialist revolutionaries, the **Spartacists,** who formed and led military and working men's soviets. It was, therefore, a Council of People's Representatives which signed the Armistice on 11 November 1918. The Kaiser could raise no objections and finally went into exile.

21

THE WEIMAR REPUBLIC (1919-1933)

The Socialist, Friedrich Ebert, Chancellor of the Provisional Government, gave the Spartacists no time to consolidate any power they had; he summoned the army and suppressed the revolution. On 11 August 1919 Germany became a constitutional republic. The Government of the Weimar Republic, whose first parliamentary majority was made up of a coalition of the Social Democrats, the Catholic Centre and the Democratic Parties, determined to re-establish order, peace and prosperity. The task was an arduous one. Public opinion was deeply divided: Bolshevism appealed to many; others turned to a reactionary nationalism. Many small political parties were born.

One of these was the German Workers' Party. In 1919 **Adolf Hitler** joined its Bavarian section and began rapidly to work his way up to the central governing committee of which he was a member when in 1921 the party changed its name to German Workers' National Socialist Party, which abbreviates in German to "Nazi".

The Weimar Republic, at this time, had to pay reparations exacted by the victors, because of the increasing inflation, they were difficult to pay. In 1923, the French, angered by delays in the payment of indemnities, decided to occupy the Ruhr as surety for later returns and the temporary loss to Germany of this industrial centre further disturbed the German economy; extremists, particularly those on the right who had affiliated with the National Socialists, began to agitate. Hitler, by now the party leader, decided to act and on 8-9 November 1923 attempted the first *putsch* at Munich. It failed and Hitler was put in prison.

From 1923 to 1929 Germany knew relative peace politically. The economy revived; in 1925 the French evacuated the Ruhr and in 1926 Germany under Stresemann became a full member of the League of Nations. This economic stability was wrecked by the world economic collapse of 1929. Galloping inflation and ever increasing unemployment, provided extremists of right and left with every excuse to rise in revolt.

After the September 1930 elections, the National Socialists with 107 members in the Reichstag became second only in power to the Social Democrats. From this time onwards, thanks to efficient organisation and the use of violence, they controlled the political life of the country and won the majority of seats (230) in the July 1932 elections; Hitler became Chancellor on 30 January 1933. Given plenary power on 23 March and supported by the Nazi Party, by 1 December the sole political party in the country, he was acclaimed by popular plebiscite on 12 December. The liquidation of his principal opponents and the death of the Reich President, Hindenburg, the following year gave him absolute control – Hitler had become the *Führer*.

THE THIRD REICH (1933-1945)

The Hitler Dictatorship. – Hitler suppressed all opposition and propagated his own racialist mystique.

Lack of interest and action by other governments assisted Hitler's aims – without arousing more than offended protests, he rearmed Germany, violated the Locarno Pact by reoccupying the Rhineland (1936) and annexing Austria (1938). September 1938 brought the meeting in Munich with England and France who thought to buy peace in Europe at the price of the annexation of the Sudetenland. The day of reckoning was only postponed: in March 1939 Hitler invaded Czechoslovakia and emboldened by this success advanced on Poland on 1 September. But this time the Allies honoured their undertakings and war was declared.

The Second World War. – Hitler, allied to Japan since 1936 and to Mussolini's Italy by the Axis Pact of 1939, gained one last trick with the signature of the Non-Aggression Pact with Russia on 23 August 1939, thus ensuring his eastern front against attack. With a massive advance westwards, he overpowered the majority of the armies in the west. The British, evacuating the Continent at Dunkirk, continued the fight alone, returning the blows of the *Luftwaffe* with ever heavier bombing raids by the RAF.

Germany, unable to quell the British, thereupon reversed her policy and turned upon Russia, the eternal ideological enemy in spite of the 1939 Non-Aggression Pact. The attack was launched on 22 June 1941; the Balkans had already fallen, and the Afrikacorps under Rommel was on the offensive in North Africa. By 1942 the Third Reich had reached the height of its power. Nevertheless the German forces had already been halted – before Moscow and Leningrad in the winter of 1941 – and the country exhausted by its gigantic war effort: compulsory military service and forced labour from conquered lands did not compensate for German deaths and losses. In 1943, the Soviet counter-offensive following Germany's defeat in the battle for Stalingrad became ever more difficult to contain, and in the west the vast war machine of the United States, mobilised on behalf of the Allies following the bombing of Pearl Harbor in December 1941, began to turn the tide on the other front. The Allies invaded Sicily in July 1943 and Italy in September, Normandy in June 1944 and Provence in August. Resistance movements everywhere arose against their oppressors – even in Germany itself. Hitler had several narrow escapes from assassination – the narrowest being on 20 July 1944. Violent activity on several fronts proved to be only the death throes of the once mighty Reich, and on 8 May 1945 Germany capitulated in defeat.

GERMANY TODAY

The dissension which soon arose among the victors produced a rift between the occupation zones of, on the one hand, the British, French and Americans and, on the other, the Soviet Union. Crisis point was reached in 1948 with the Berlin blockade *(p 66)*.

The following year the political division of Germany was recognised and on 23 May 1949 the German Federal Republic was proclaimed at Bonn; the Soviet zone was promptly declared the German Democratic Republic.

The Federal Republic, which became a sovereign state in 1955, devoted itself energetically to reconstruction under **Konrad Adenauer** *(p 231)*, Chancellor from 1949 to 1963 – a task rapidly accomplished due to the Marshall Plan and a swift economic recovery *(p 15)*.

Although Germany has been the centre of an ideological and political confrontation (Berlin Wall was erected 13 August 1961) her efforts to normalise relations with her European neighbours and the world over have been fructuous: member of the Common Market since 1958, **Brandt's** open door policy towards the East between 1969 and 1974, entrance into the United Nations in 1973.

The Government. – The Federal Republic of Germany – with the President as chief of state – is composed of ten regions *(Länder, see map p 9)* which enjoy a wide autonomy. The Federal Parliament consists of two chambers; the **Bundestag** or legislative body, with its 500 elected members, from which the government and its leader, the chancellor, are provided; the **Bundesrat** whose 41 members are appointed by the governments of the different *Länder*.

THE ARTS

The German taste for the picturesque is well exemplified in the architecture of tall church towers, Rhineland *Burg* keeps and the sumptuous decoration of Bavarian Baroque abbeys.

Painting and sculpture are characterised by a minute attention to detail and a search for a realism of expression which is sometimes exaggerated. The results, nevertheless, are striking.

In Germany works of religious art (altarpieces, statues. liturgical objects) which survived destruction are often exhibited for their advantage in the sober settings of restored or rebuilt churches. Conversely old but still intact sanctuaries are enhanced with works by contemporary artists.

ROMANESQUE ARCHITECTURE (9-12C)

Pre-Romanesque Architecture. – In Germany, as elsewhere in the west, religious architecture developed from the adaptation of Roman lay basilicas to Christian worship.

The long religious edifices turned towards the east and ending in an apse derive from the meeting halls which were among the buildings surrounding the forum. A vertical section of a basilical building would show a central area raised above the level of the two or four side aisles and lit by a series of tall windows. The nave and aisles are covered with plain wood vaulting.

The Carolingian period, in addition to the somewhat rare type of round or polygonal church such as the Palatine Chapel in Aachen Cathedral, is marked by the erection of churches with two chancels. The west chancel sometimes forms part of the **west end** (Westwerk), consisting of a tall and massive tower of military appearance on to which the nave is firmly anchored. This west end, as for instance at Corvey, frequently constitutes almost a church in itself. A large and tall chapel of several storeys stands upon the low pre-nave and opens, through galleries, on to the nave. Traditionally this chapel was used only by the emperor.

Ottonian Architecture (10C and early 11C). – The restoration of the imperial dignity by Otto I in 962 was accompanied by a revival in ecclesiastical architecture in Saxony and in the Lower Rhine and Meuse regions. The huge churches erected at this period with deeply projecting transepts and wide aisles had as yet no stone vaulting. The alternation of pillars and columns broke the lines of the aisles which were not so far cut up into bays. Flat rounded capitals at the foot and deep square capitals at the head divided the circular columns from the rectangular arch-stones of the larger arcs. The unusual Church of St. Michael at Hildesheim is the best example of a building of this period.

The Rhineland Romanesque style. – This style flourished first in Cologne, the town of relics and pilgrimages.

At Cologne and in the surrounding region, several churches have as a common feature in their plan, a trilobed apse, adorned with blind arcades and a **dwarf gallery** (Zwerggalerie), a motif of Lombard origin.

On the Middle Rhine the Romanesque Rhineland style reached its peak in the majestic "imperial" cathedrals of Speyer, Mainz and Worms. These are characterised in their floor plan, by a double chancel without either an ambulatory or apsidal chapels *(see plan of Mainz Cathedral p 173),* and sometimes by a double transept; in their elevation, by a multiplicity of towers; in their exterior decoration, by the use of galleries of blind arcades and Lombard bands, the latter in low relief and used vertically with small blind arcades as a link at the top. The typical roof to a Rhineland tower was shaped like a bishop's mitre, its sides adorned with a lozenge pattern.

Towards the end of the 11C, the architects of Speyer Cathedral boldly projected groined stone vaulting over the nave.

(After a photo from the German Central Tourist Association)

Rhineland style apse.
Cologne – Church of the Holy Apostles.
1 Blind arcades – 2 Dwarf gallery.
3 Bishop's mitre style roof.

The beginning of the 12C saw the construction of the Abbey at Maria Laach and, nearly a century later, of Worms Cathedral where the refinement of the decoration is a reminder of the great period of the Hohenstaufens.

Marking the transition from Romanesque to Gothic are the churches of Limburg and Andernach which were built with pointed vaulting early in the 13C.

GOTHIC ARCHITECTURE (13-16C)

There are not many great Gothic cathedrals in the country. Cologne, which was not completed until the 19C, is world-famous for its great interior width, the slenderness of the two towers built on either side of the façade in the French manner, and the height of its pointed vaulting.

Also inspired by the French Gothic style are the Cathedrals of Regensburg and Freiburg im Breisgau.

French influence may be seen in the Cistercian monasteries built in such profusion between 1150 and 1250 that they numbered almost one hundred. Through the Cistercians, abbey churches came to be built without either towers or belfries and with flat ended chancels cantoned with rectangular chapels *(see Maulbronn Abbey p 177).*

Impressive brick churches, complete with buttresses and flying buttresses, were erected east of the Elbe – the late 13C church of St. Mary's at Lübeck is typical of this Gothic brick style (Backsteingotik).

Late Gothic Architecture (Spätgotik). – This long period, the 14, 15 and 16C, is marked in Germany by the widespread building of hall-type churches and vaulting divided by purely decorative ribs forming groining or stars in contrast to the bare walls.

Oriel window.
Freiburg.
The New Town Hall.

Hall-type Churches (Hallen-kirche). – This type of building already to be seen in Westphalia at Münster and Osnabrück at the end of the Romanesque period, differed completely in its elevation from churches erected on the basilical plan. The aisles were the same height as the nave and only separated from it by tall columns.

The most famous hall-churches are the very tall constructions erected in southern Germany at the end of the Gothic period – the Church of Our Lady in Munich, St. George's in Dinkelsbühl and the Parish Church in Altötting.

Civil Architecture in the Late Middle Ages. – Commercial prosperity among merchants and skilled craftsmen in the Empire produced a new and powerful middle class in the 14 and 15C. In pride, the burghers erected a great number of town halls and built themselves half-timbered houses. The houses were ornamented with oriel windows (Erker), loggias and corbelled balconies, sometimes two storeys high – true works of art in their painted and sculptured decoration. Examples of civil architecture of the period may be seen today on buildings in Regensburg, Rothenburg, Einbeck, Goslar and Tübingen.

THE RENAISSANCE
(1520-c 1620)

The Renaissance, often eclipsed by the troubles of the Reformation, appears almost episodically in the story of German architecture. Italian influence was always obvious in southern Germany, where, for example, slim Florentine blind arcades were taken as they stood by Fugger the Rich to adorn his funerary

(After a photo by Hirmer Fotoarchiv)

Hall-Church.
Dinkelsbühl – St George's.
1 Nave – 2 Aisle – 3 Groined Vaulting.

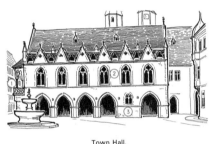

Town Hall.
Goslar.
1 Loggia – 2 Great Hall (Diele) and Council Chamber.
3 Gallery used as a covered market.

chapel at Augsburg (1518) and the Jesuits drew on the Gesù Church in Rome for their design of St. Michael's in Munich.

Palace façades also recall Italian models: the Augsburg town hall by Elias Holl (1623) has only a pediment and the domed towers of its superstructure in typical German style.

Northern Germany was included by Flemish and Dutch design, particularly the Antwerp style known as Floris. In the rich merchants' quarters the multiple storeyed gables such as those of the Gewandhaus at Brunswick, were loaded with ornament in the form of scrollwork, obelisks, statues, pilasters and wreathed statuettes (Hermes), etc. The period's charm is most delightfully seen in the villages round Hanover: Celle, Wolfenbüttel, Bückeburg and Hamelin, heart of the Weser Renaissance *(p 141)*.

BAROQUE ARCHITECTURE (17 and 18C)

The Baroque style was characterised by irregularity of form and infinite variety; it sought above all to give an effect of movement. When pushed to its extreme, it became the Rococo whose fantasies were employed mostly in decoration.

Baroque began to be widely followed in Germany in about 1660. Catholic southern Germany, particularly, was marked by the new style in which the exuberance seemed to answer the Counter-Reformation's exaltation of dogmatic belief in the Real Presence, the cult of the Virgin and the saints and the many manifestations of popular worship.

Enterprising abbots set about rebuilding their abbeys to plans so ambitious that we, today, would find them stupefying. Masons, painters, sculptors and stucco-workers were thus given extraordinary opportunities. Stucco-work, made from a lime, plaster and wet sand mixture suitable for modelling and false relief paintings, which, seen from a distance, give an impression of third dimension, covered all available surfaces.

The Masters of German and Danubian Baroque. – The blossoming of the Baroque style owes much to the **Vorarlberg School** (1680-1750) of which the masters remain largely anonymous so great was the corporative spirit of the school. The architects who worked primarily in Swabia, but also in Bavaria, in Switzerland and even in Alsace were especially interested in the lines of the single aisles in the churches they constructed *(p 25)*.

Baroque was, however, also enhanced in Bavaria by brilliant men, rarely specialising in one technique alone, who often produced great subtlety of design, in plans, for example, using as a focal point a round or oval bay. Johann-Michael Fischer, the Asam brothers and Dominicus Zimmermann were the outstanding virtuosi of this Bavarian school.

The Baroque movement in Franconia, patronised by the prince-bishops of the Schönborn family with residences in Mainz, Würzburg, Speyer and Bamberg, was closely linked with the spreading of similar ideas in Bohemia. The Dientzenhofer brothers decorated the palace in Prague as well as that in Bamberg; they introduced ornate vaulting in pilgrimage and abbey churches *(p 25)*. Balthazar Neumann, who worked for the same prelates, dominated his contemporaries by the breadth of his culture enriched by those French, Viennese and Italian masters with whom he came in contact.

AN ABC TO GERMAN BAROQUE

The Churches

The ground plan (Schönenberg Church – p 116). – In the Vorarlberg School edifices the transept is scarcely advanced and the chancel is unobtrusive.

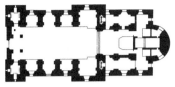

The single aisle is usually enclosed by stone piles attached to the walls.
These piles divide the side chapels (sometimes linked by a passageway) and, on the first storey, the galleries.

The façades (Ottobeuren – p 202). – A sinuous movement, usually convex in line, predominates, whilst the superimposition of two pediments of different design adds vitality to the façades. They are further adorned with twin domed towers, or in the case of pilgrimage churches, with a single tower. The later the façade, the more detached are the towers. The decorative pilasters stand upon raised foundations.

Galleries and Vaulting (Vorarlberg Baroque – Schonenberg Pilgrimage Church – p 116). – Vast galleries stand above the lateral chapels, pilasters with jutting abaci in place of capitals. Chapels and galleries cease at the transept, giving greater depth to the arms (left on the plan). The tall windows, pierced at gallery level, allow ample light to pass. The vaulting above the galleries follows the cradle vaulting above the main aisle including its triangular intersections of "penetrations".

Complex Vaulting (Bohemian and Franconian Baroque – Vierzehnheiligen – p 251). – Round or oval bays are covered with single domes or more complicated vaulting in which the supporting beams bow out in horseshoe shape only to meet in their keystones.

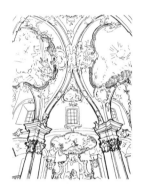

Altarpieces (the main altarpiece at Weltenburg – p 159). – The altarpiece at the high altar, the focal point of the church furnishings, is treated monumentally. Its design is architecturally that of a triumphal arch. This arch, in carved wood or polished stucco, frames either a large picture or a group of sculpture.
The twisted columns, a motif made famous by the baldachin at St. Peter's in Rome, give, in addition, to a vice-like effect, also that of movement which haunted the period.
Back lighting from a hidden source was also much in fashion. The resulting contrast between light and shade was, in fact, one of the principles of Baroque design.

Rococo Decoration. – The typical motif in Rococo decoration was asymmetrical cartouche in a fretted setting (Birnau – p 80).

The Castles

Plan of a small country residence (Monrepos Castle – p 169). – The single storey construction was often given added importance by being on a raised foundation. The focal point was a round central building presenting a convex side to the gardens; small square or rounded porch pavilions were sometimes built on to the ends of the wings.

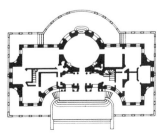

The Grand Staircase in a Great Castle (Pommersfelden Castle – p 58).
The monumental staircases with several flights and considerable theatrical effect are the most typical element often to be found in German palaces of the 18C. The stair well, embellished with arcaded galleries and a painted ceiling, may alone occupy the whole of that front part of the palace which gives on to the courtyard.
The staircase itself will lead to the first floor and the stateroom in which the majestic elevation rises to the level of the ceilings on the second storey.
These pompous ordonnances were often found in the greater abbeys where they were complemented by a second stateroom, the library.

THE ARRIVAL OF NEO-CLASSICISM

Versailles inspired in Germany a new style of court life, particularly in the Rhineland and in the Berlin of Frederick II. French architects such as Robert de Cotte (1656-1735) were consulted by the Electors of the Palatinate, Mainz, Trier and Cologne. They designed or directed the building of town residences and above all of country mansions whose names alone describe them – Monrepos, Monaise, Solitude.

Plain pediments, balustrades running the full extent of the eaves, colonnaded porticoes before main entrances, indicate the desire for unobtrusive elegance outside, while inside, the decoration was done with a light touch, mingling bunches of flowers with by now discrete Rococo motifs (Fredrican and Bayreuth Rococo).

From 1750 onwards, the researches of Winckelmann the German scholar, on the history of Antique art and the excavations at Pompeii, threw new light on Greco-Roman architecture.

In the new fashion of form, architects selected the Doric style, the coldest of all, and the colossal – pilasters and columns of a single order no longer stood one storey high but always two. A purely static line and symmetrical balance became the ideal to such a degree that in some churches a false pulpit was erected to balance the true preacher's desk.

Churches, abbeys, castles and palaces were no longer the only buildings to be erected by craftsmen – museums began to be constructed, a sign of growing interest in the past, particularly in Berlin where Schinkel, master of the colonnade, was at work. Interior decoration showed a preference for sculptured motifs such as garlands, pearl or ovum friezes, vases and urns.

The Neo-Classical movement became sterile by 1830 and gave way, except in Munich, to the Neo-Gothic, which became, for the Romantics, the symbol of Old Germany.

Middle-class interiors and furnishings conformed to the **Biedermeier** style characterised by comfortable, cushioned lightweight furniture with flowing lines and glass-fronted cupboards.

The year 1850 marks the beginning of the **Founders' Period** (Gründerjahre), when wealthy industrialists became enamoured of pretentious reproductions of Mediaeval and Renaissance furniture. Similar pieces were also to be found in public buildings such as the Berlin Reichstag. Commemorative monuments erected in national pride compelled their German architects to compromise design for size.

CONTEMPORARY ARCHITECTURE

Art Nouveau or **Jugendstil,** a solidly constructed style, appeared at the turn of the 20C and enjoyed widespread popularity based on mass production.

Of far greater importance to Germany were the first thoughts on industrial design by such pioneers as Peter Behrens, Mies van der Rohe and Walter Gropius.

After the 1914-18 War, Walter Gropius became head of the **Bauhaus** *(see table opposite).* His influence was felt especially in the United States where, like Mies van der Rohe, he finally went to live and work. Professor at Harvard from 1937 to 1952, he died in Boston in 1969.

Many churches have had to be built in recent years because of war damage and through the continuing spread of urban areas. Dominikus Böhm and Rudolf Schwarz are the architects chiefly involved in this rebirth of sacred art which is to be seen most extensively in the dioceses of Cologne and Würzburg.

The most highly reputed schools of fine arts in Germany today are at the universities of Munich and Stuttgart.

DECORATIVE ARTS

With a long standing tradition of craftsmanship in Germany, certain decorative arts led their fields in Europe.

Porcelain. – The **Meissen** factory (f 1710), the first in Europe to produce white hard-paste porcelain, created a tradition of quality difficult to surpass. In 1747 two other factories were established at **Fürstenberg** (vases, tableware with Rococo decoration, *p 256*) and **Nymphenburg** (statuettes, and the famous Bustelli Rococo figures). The **Berlin** factory (f 1752) produced landscape decorated tableware, figures and flowers in the Vincennes tradition and following a new start in 1761 eventually became the official state factory. The famous Prussian service in Apsley House *(see Michelin Green Guide to London)* comes from Berlin. (Porcelain collections: Berlin Museum of Decorative Arts *p 72*; Frankfurt Museum of Applied Arts *p 124*; Munich Palace Museum *p 188*).

Glass. – The Rhineland was a great glass producing centre in Roman times and a tradition of green glass, *Waldglas,* making was to flourish, till the 17C reaction to Venetian styles. Glass enamelling current in the late 16C produced the wonderfully colourful drinking vessels, *Humpen,* and was followed by enamel painting in Nuremberg. (Glass collections: Frankfurt Museum of Applied Arts *p 124*).

Metalwork. – In Carolingian times the gold- and silversmiths produced exquisite reliquaries, book covers and liturgical plate while bronze workers of the Romanesque period cast bells and monumental doors (Augsburg and Hildesheim Cathedrals, *pp 52 and 150*) and other ecclesiastical objects.

The Renaissance period was the apogee of metalworking: examples in ironwork of the period abound in Augsburg, Nuremberg, Frankfurt and Munich; the first two towns were also great gold working centres.

The **arms and armour** specialisation, closely linked to already established metalworking centres, grew with the transition in the 14C from shirts of mail to plate armour. In addition to the great court workshops of Maximilian I and Henry VIII, the main centres were at Nuremberg, Augsburg, Landshut and Cologne.

The craft demanded great artistic skill (etching, gilding, embossing, damascening, sometimes to designs provided by artists such as Albrecht Dürer) and the German products for quality and elegance were among the foremost in Europe, rivalling those of Italy and England. (Henry VIII established his Greenwich workshop employing German workers).

Bladesmiths flourished in Soligen and Passau and the production of firearms in the 17C created a new outlet for the skilled craftsmen of the above centres. (Arms collections: Château of Dyck *p 111.)*

GERMANY'S GREAT ARTISTS
and their characteristic works

Architects and sculptors

Painters and engravers (in the 16C most painters were also engravers)

15C

Veit STOSS (c 1445-1533). – A sculptor whose tormented genius found greatest expression in wood carving (**Annunciation**, *St. Loren-Kirche, Nuremberg, p 197*).

Stephan LOCHNER (d 1451). – Leader of the Cologne school: golden backgrounds, gentle expressions on the faces of his subjects and fresh colours (**Adoration of the Magi**, *Schnütgen Museum, Cologne, p 98*; **Virgin in the Rose Bower**, *Wallraf-Richartz Museum, Cologne, p 98*).

Tilman RIEMENSCHNEIDER (1460-1531). – A sculptor whose delicately modelled works are intensely expressive and full of gravity (**Heinrich II's tomb**, *Bamberg Cathedral, p 56*; **Adam and Eve**, *Franconian Main Land Museum, Würzburg, p 264*; **Altarpiece to the Virgin** *in Creglingen Chapel, p 217*).

The Master of SAINT SEVERINUS (late 15C). – His sense of intimacy and his iridescent colours display Dutch influence (**Christ before Pilate**, *Wallraf-Richartz Museum, Cologne, p 98*).

The Master of the LIFE OF THE VIRGIN (late 15C). – Delightful portrayer of anecdotes who was influenced by Van der Weyden (**Vision of St. Bernard**, *Wallraf-Richartz Museum, Cologne, p 98*).

Friedrich HERLIN (d 1500). – Picturesque, detailed realist (**Women Donors to the Church at Prayer**, *Nördlingen Museum, p 196*).

16C

Albrecht DÜRER (1471-1528). – Dürer, the most famous artist of the German school and a humanist, painted highly realistic portraits and religious pictures. He also produced a prodigious number of drawings and engravings (**The Four Apostles, Lamentation over the body of Christ**, *Old Pinakothek, Munich, p 186*; **Charlemagne**, *German National Museum, Nuremberg, p 97*).

GRÜNEWALD (1460-1528). – Powerful genius whose works have great tragic intensity (**Crucifixion**, *Fine Arts Museum, Karlsruhe, p 156*; **Virgin and Child**, *Stuppach Church, p 178*).

Lucas CRANACH the Elder (1472-1553). – Cranach the Elder, master of a large studio, painted the portraits of the most famous men of the Reformation. His sense of the mystery of nature brought him into contact with the Danubian school of painters (**The Holy Family**, *Städel Museum, Frankfurt, p 123*).

Albrecht ALTDORFER (1480–1538). – Member of the Danubian school *(p 104)*, he produced a pathetic effect by his use of light. One of the founders of landscape painting (**Battle of Arbeles**, *Old Pinakothek, Munich, p 186*).

Hans BALDUNG GRIEN (c 1485-1545). – Artist with a dramatic sense of light and a preference for unusual colours (**Altarpiece of the Coronation of the Virgin**, *Freiburg Cathedral, p 125*).

Hans HOLBEIN the Younger (1497-1543). – Portrait painter and painter of religious themes of striking realism (**Portrait of Georg Gisze**, *Dahlem Museum, Berlin, p 74*).

17C

Elias HOLL (1573-1646). – Architect of the greatest buildings of the German Renaissance (**Town Hall**, *Augsburg, p 52*).

Andreas SCHLÜTER (c 1660–1714). – The leading sculptor in the Baroque style in northern Germany. Known for his vigorous manner (**Statue of the Great Elector**, *Château of Charlottenburg, Berlin, p 72*; **Heads of the Dying Warriors**, *Berlin Arsenal*).

The MERIANS (17C). – Family of engravers who specialised in depicting German towns and cities.

18C

Antoine PESNE (1683-1757). – French painter at the court of Frederick II, much favoured on account of his use of brilliant colours (**Portraits of Frederick II and his sister, Wilhelmina**, *private apartments of Charlottenburg, Berlin, p 72*).

Dominikus ZIMMERMANN (1685-1766). – Architect of the most perfect Bavarian Rococo style churches (**Churches of Wies**, *p 257* and Steinhausen, *p 235*).

Balthazar NEUMANN (1687-1753). – Architect and engineer whose technical virtuosity combined with the harmony of his work to make him master of the Baroque style (**Vierzehnheiligen Church**, *p 251*).

The ASAM Brothers. – The sculptor Egid Quirin (1692-1750) and his brother the painter, Cosmas Damian (1696-1739), are an example of the close collaboration between artists of the Baroque period (**Asam Church**, *Munich, p 189*).

19C

Caspar-David FRIEDRICH (1774-1840). – Artist from the Romantic school; he discovered and portrayed the tragic in landscape painting (**Monk of the Seashore, Eichwald Abbey**, *private apartments of Charlottenburg, Berlin, p 72*, **Harz Countryside**, *Hamburg Art Gallery, p 140*).

Karl-Friedrich SCHINKEL (1781-1841). – His long colonnades are a characteristic feature of the centre of Berlin (**Neue Wache, the Old Museum and the Schauspielhaus**).

Wilhelm LEIBL (1844-1900). – Leader of the Realist school (**Three Women at Church**, *Art Gallery, Hamburg, p 140*).

Adolf von HILDEBRAND (1847-1921). – His sure taste in monumental sculpture is in contrast with the excesses of the 19C (**Wittelsbach Fountain**, *Munich, p 183*).

20C

Expressionist School. – Expressionism introduced a distorted, violent and tragic vision of the world to German painting in the tradition of Van Gogh and the Norwegian, Edvard Munch (1863-1944), a considerable influence in Germany (**see the works of Emil NOLDE** (1867-1956) *at Seebüll, p 231*). The Brücke or Bridge group united from 1905 to 1913 such painters as Erich Heckel, Ernst Ludwig Kirchner and Karl Schmidt-Rottluff, who recall the French Fauve movement in their passion for pure colour.

Ernst BARLACH (1870-1938). – His massive and tormented works in wood and bronze are examples of the Expressionist school (**The Angel**, *the Antonines Church, Cologne, p 98*; **The Singer** *Ratzeburg, p 205*).

Dominikus BÖHM (1880-1955). – Pioneer of the new style of religious architecture (**St. Mary the Queen**, *Cologne, p 99*).

The BAUHAUS. – Architectural school established at Dessau and directed there from 1925 to 1928 by Walter Gropius. The marriage of art and technique was the fundamental theme inspiring the Bauhaus school which soon attracted a group of advanced painters and sculptors.

The Blue Knight Movement (Der Blauer Reiter). – Artistic movement created in 1911 by Marc and Kandinsky, who were later joined by Macke and Klee. The movement's aim was to free art from the constraint of reality thus opening the way to abstraction (**Deer in the Forest** by **Franz MARC**, *Orangery, Fine Arts Museum, Karlsruhe, p 156*; **The Dress Shop** by **August MACKE**, *Folkwang Museum, Essen, p 117*).

The reference to artists' works cited above are selective only; look also, therefore, at the descriptions of major museums, pp 39-266, for additional works.

MUSIC

PRINCIPAL MUSICAL EVENTS

MIDDLE AGES

12 and 13C *The Minnesänger*, minstrels who included in their number noble knights such as Wolfram von Eschenbach and Walter von der Vogelweide, drew inspiration from French lyric poetry for their songs (*Minnesang*: love song).

14 and 15C The mastersingers *(Meistersinger)* organised themselves into guilds and, most importantly, introduced polyphony to German music (Heinrich von Meissen, Hans Sachs).

LUTHER (1483-1546) AND THE PRECURSORS OF BACH

The Lutheran Reformation brought independence to German music. The liturgy demanded a new musical form – the chorale which was sung in the common tongue. This, in time, inspired further developments – the German cantata and oratorio.

1529 *Ein' Feste Burg Chorale* by Walther.
1645 *The Seven Words of Christ* by Heinrich Schütz shows Italian influence (Monteverdi).
1637-1707 Dietrich Buxtehude *(p 168)* organises the first concerts of sacred music.

JOHANN SEBASTIAN BACH (1685-1750)

Bach excelled, except in opera, with equal genius and ease in every musical form.

1717-1723 Stay at Koethen court. *The Brandenburg Concertos.*
1723 Appointment as cantor at St. Thomas's, Leipzig. Bach's duties included the weekly composition of a cantata to be sung at the Sunday service. He had further to supervise services in four churches, teach Latin and singing, but he nevertheless found time also to compose countless other instrumental and vocal works.
1722 and 1742 *The Well Tempered Clavichord.*

THE BAROQUE PERIOD

1665-1759 **Georg-Friedrich Handel,** the inspired and prolific musician to the Courts of Hanover and St. James's.
1681-1767 **Georg-Philipp Telemann;** developer of descriptive music in which the melody had popular appeal.
Mid 18C The Mannheim school of musicians contribute in perfecting the form of the modern symphony. The sonata becomes popular with the works of **Carl-Philipp-Emanuel Bach** (1714-1788).
Appearance in Germany of the Singspiel, a type of popular operetta in which *lied*, or popular melodies, were interspersed in the dialogue.
1743 Building of the first opera house in Berlin.
1714-1787 **Christoph-Willibald Gluck,** German by nationality although he lived in Paris, roused the enthusiasm of the innovators and the horror of followers of traditional Italian-influenced opera, with his production in Paris of *Iphigenia in Aulis* and *Orpheus.*

HAYDN AND MOZART

Haydn (1732-1809) and Mozart (1756-1791) lived at a time when the classical influence was at its height; the one established the classical form of the symphony and the string quartet; the other brought a perfection all his own to these and other forms, particularly opera.

BEETHOVEN (1770-1827)

Beethoven demonstrated that music could be a means of personal expression.

1808 *Fifth* and *Sixth Symphonies.*
1824 First performance of the *Ninth Symphony.*

THE ROMANTIC PERIOD

1786-1826 **Carl Maria von Weber** defines German operatic form and aims at the triumph of dramatic realism.
1821 Creation of the Freischütz opera in Berlin.
1810-1856 **Robert Schumann**'s music reveals him as a poet, by turn heroic or tender.
1868 **Johannes Brahms** produces his *German Requiem.*
1864-1949 **Richard Strauss** combines audacious harmony on occasion with a floridly imaginative talent.
At the end of the 19C, **Gustav Mahler** (1860-1911), creator of the symphonic *lied*, and **Hugo Wolf** (1850-1903) introduce a new musical language to the German public.

RICHARD WAGNER (1813-1883)

Wagner revolutionised opera in Germany. The music, he believed should serve the actor and had, therefore, to provide atmosphere – the sound décor without which the opera's message could not be conveyed. The orchestra thus became of paramount importance. The singing, like the plot, was made continuous to correspond with dramatic truth. Wagnerian Leitmotivs, musical phrases symbolising characters and situations, became an integral part of the action.

1848 *Lohengrin.*
1868 *The Mastersingers of Nurnberg.*
1869 *The Rhinegold.*
1870 *The Valkyrie.*
1876 Inauguration of the Bayreuth Festival Theatre with a performance of *The Ring.*
1882 *Parsifal.*

THE CURRENT PERIOD

Contemporary music has derived principally from the dodecaphonic Austrian school (Schönberg, Berg and Webern), with Hindemith (1895-1963) retaining a national traditional style.

1921 **Alan Berg**'s *Wozzeck.*
1952 The younger generation's researches produce and develop electronic music (Karlheinz Stockhausen).

The major centres of music in Germany today are Bayreuth for Wagner, Berlin, Hamburg and Stuttgart for opera and ballet, Nuremberg for organ music, Stuttgart for choral work, and Munich for Bach and Richard Strauss. Contemporary music is found particularly at Donaueschingen, Darmstadt and Kassel.

PICTURESQUE GERMANY

GERMAN LEGENDS AND FOLKLORE

German folk tales and legends, whether tragic or burlesque, although they always create a fairy-tale world for children, often given vent to secret adult rancour.

Snow White and the Seven Dwarfs. – Dwarfs, those small genii who live below ground and wear a traditional costume which is, in fact, that of the mediaeval miner, play a large part in German folklore.

The story of Snow White as told by the Brothers Grimm, is now much more widely known through the Disney film.

Rübezahl. – Rübezahl was a good giant who lived in the Riesengebirge – Giant Mountains. He redressed wrongs and was a friend to the poor. Sometimes he appeared as a rich merchant, sometimes as a poor charcoal-burner when he played tricks and vented his anger on the rich and powerful.

The Witches of Brocken. – On Walpurgis night (eve of 1 May), the witches, astride their broomsticks, are said to gather on the summit of Mount Brocken in the Harz Mountains *(p 144)* to hold revels with the devil. This witches' sabbath has been made famous through the scene in Goethe's *Faust*. The legend goes back to the 16C when witches were tried for sorcery and accused of having swallowed potions and then, in a state of hallucination, taken part in demoniacal orgies.

Till Eulenspiegel. – Till Eulenspiegel may or may not have existed as a real person, but his escapades and jests are world-famous. The typical prank finds the perpetrator hoist with his own petard.

The Pied Piper of Hamelin. – *For the historical background to this legend see p 141.*

The Nibelungen. – The tribe of dwarfs of this name were tricked by Siegfried of the treasure they had been guarding. This treasure then became an additional cause for dispute in the heroic family which was torn by quarrels and which itself became known as the Nibelungen *(p 209)*. The secret of its burial place has created many suppositions.

The Loreley. – The most famous of the legends of the Rhine *(details p 209)*.

The Mouse Tower at Bingen. – Another Rhine River legend *(details p 79)*.

Pöppele of Hohenkrähen. – Pöppele was a facetious dwarf. From his castle perched above the highway *(p 101)* he watched travellers pass, amusing himself by discomfiting them, particularly the titled. He made their carriages skid and played other darkly malicious tricks.

The Heinzelmännchen. – These goblins were benign, bestowing their help on the delighted craftsmen of Cologne by night and always with the greatest secrecy. But a woman grew curious to see them at work and the goblins fled back to their hiding place, never to be heard of again.

The Seven Swabians. – This unfair caricature of the Swabians is well known. Seven Swabians joined together to conquer the world, their only weapon, a huge lance with which they rampaged round the countryside. But, at the crucial moment, they were startled and put to flight by a leveret.

Baron Münchhausen. – The famous baron's adventures, told with imperturbable aplomb and a great wealth of detail, transport the reader into a world of fantasy. The tales of the chase, of adventures at sea of unbelievable hardship, journeys to the moon and into the centre of the earth, swamp the true exploits of Baron Münchhausen who really did live adventurously from 1720 to 1797.

GERMANY TODAY

The German Street Scene. – The main shopping streets are often for pedestrians only after 10am, even in small towns present attractive and abundant displays of furniture, furnishings and household goods. The windows stay lit late into the night.

Modern designs predominate and the taste displayed in cutlery and other semi-luxury items is often outstanding.

Buying is simple in Germany for what one hesitated over yesterday may often be seen the next day in another town. This is because many items such as leather goods, chinaware, etc., are supplied by a limited number of well known manufacturers to all specialist shops alike.

Standardisation is widespread in Germany and a German norm (DIN) exists for most items of a practical nature.

The many *Reformhaus* shops and others specialising in naturally grown and special foods serve those who are particular about their diet.

Traditional Costume. – There are strong traditions in Germany governing costume: hunters wear green, the Hamburg Carpenters' Guild travel the roads on their ''German Tour'' in black velvet suits with baggy trousers and master chimney-sweeps must wear top hats. Regional costume has been dying out since the war, although the men of Upper Bavaria may still be seen in leather shorts, the *Loden* short jacket with horn buttons and a felt hat with a chamois tuft or a badger's tail.

Authentic regional costumes may still be seen in the Schwalm countryside (Ziegenhain, Alsfeld and Marburg areas). Some women in this area even wear the short wide skirt and white stockings at work in the fields. At festivals, such as the Salad Fair *(table p 31)* the young girls of Schwalm wear the charming local ceremonial costume: the stiff and heavy dresses, glittering with ornaments, are topped by the minute red hoods and cloaks which gave the Brothers Grimm the title for their famous tale, *Little Red Riding Hood.*

Other costumes, such as those of the Forchheim region, the Black Forest or the Kleinwalsertal *(p 199)* are usually seen at their best at a local festival.

The **Dirndl** skirt and blouse worn by many women in Bavaria, have, in fact, no folklore origin. But the full sleeved blouses and short aprons in gay colours are much in demand as souvenirs.

Young girl from Schwalm.

TRADITIONAL PEASANT HOUSES

There are four principal types of house in Germany: the Alemannian, the central German, the Lower Saxony and the Bavarian. Each has many variations.

The Alemannian House (Black Forest).

Central German House (Hesse).

The Black Forest house is the most impressive of the peasant houses of the Alemannian region.
The huge barn is often accessible from ground level at the back, as in the Jura, since the houses are frequently built on hill slopes. The barn protects the living area from the cold, while below it is raised from the ground by the stables which are built into the stone foundations.

The farmhouse, the cowshed and the barns stand round a yard which is frequently separated from the street by a large gateway (villages around Marburg). The group of buildings are highly decorative when the beams have been left exposed – as in the half-timbered houses of Franconia particularly.

Lüneburg Heath House (Lower Saxony).

Bavarian Mountain House.

The long low house shelters humans and animals under the same roof. The main doorway opens into the *Diele*, a vast open floor serving as hearth and stable. Formerly, the smoke escaped through gaps in the roof.
Note the crossed horses' heads in the small sketch. These are nailed to the gable to ward off bad luck.

Lovely wooden house commonly found in Upper Bavaria (Chiemgau Alps) and in those parts of the Tyrol inhabited by Bavarians.
The low-pitched roof is decorated with a little belfry and often weighted with blocks of stone. Long balconies run the length of the upper storey. *Another type of Bavarian house is illustrated on p 47.*

HOLIDAYS AND LEISURE

The German tourist industry is occupied in large part with the holiday and leisure time travel of the Germans themselves. All workers receive 18-24 days paid holiday a year and now even the smallest towns have a travel agency *(Reisebüro)*.

The tourist season opens on 1 May with school outings, junior rallies, often planned in conjunction with a youth hostel, afternoon café outings *(Kaffeefahrt)* ending in a substantial tea in pleasant surroundings, and fully programmed weekends. The modest charges made by many hotels and inns encourage these outdoor activities. The Mediterranean attracts many Germans for their summer holidays. This is also the period when children often go off on special holidays on their own.

Friendly reunions are frequently organised at an attractive inn or *Lokal* over a tankard of beer or a glass of wine. Spirits rise quickly and the oldest present are by no means always the most staid.

Inns and beerhouses often have large numbers of faithful customers who appear daily to meet and talk around their own tables – these are reserved with the notice *Stammtisch*. In the south, one may go and sit at a beerhouse or restaurant table that is already occupied but, except in the Ratskeller in Bremen *(p 87)*, this is not usually done in northern Germany.

Sport. – With the World Cup victories of the football team in 1954 and 1974, the sport has become a national pastime; due also to the encouragement provided by the football pools known as *Fusball-Totto*. Other national sports include gymnastics – the clubs played an important patriotic role in the 19C – hand ball, swimming and, to a limited degree, gliding. The shooting clubs, which formerly had a high social standing, as in all German-speaking countries, were discouraged by the Allied Powers. Now when you see martial processions of marksmen *(Schützen)* and hear military music or the harsh sound of fife and drum, it is more likely to be a folklore than a shooting club occasion.

Germany has fine racecourses at Aachen, Hamburg, Wiesbaden, Baden-Baden and in Westphalia. The totalisator system does not operate.

Conferences. – The Germans themselves laugh at their national mania for conferences. These congresses *(Tagung)* have a long history and range in subject and size from large religious gatherings (*Katholikentag* or *Kirchentag* – Catholic or Protestant) to technical, scientific, cultural and philanthropic meetings. All illustrate the natural sociability of the German character. Conferences cease in July and August but begin again with renewed enthusiasm in September. This can lead to occasional accommodation difficulties in towns.

After photos by Franckh'sche Verlagshandlung, Hildenbrand, Hans Retzlaff.

FESTIVALS AND HOLIDAYS IN GERMANY

Christmas and birthdays and other family holidays and celebrations are occasions of great importance and sentiment to the Germans.

Christmas. – Christmas is especially beloved. Advent, in accordance with the religious ethic, is celebrated as a period of preparation during which family life is marked by a joyous expectancy. The feast of St. Nicholas – Father Christmas – is celebrated in home and school alike. The Christmas markets open their stalls and on the first Sunday in Advent, the "Advent Crown" made from pine branches bound with red ribbons, appears in the house. The four candles on the crown, which are lit one by one each week, burn all together on the last Sunday before Christmas.

On Christmas Eve, the crown is replaced by a brilliantly lit Christmas tree. Most Germans make every effort to join their families for the celebrations.

PRINCIPAL FESTIVALS

DATE AND PLACE		PAGE (1)	NATURE OF EVENT
Sunday before Shrove Tuesday	Munich	183	Carnival processions.
Monday before Shrove Tuesday	Mainz	172	Rosenmontagszug: great carnival procession.
	Cologne	95	
Night of 30 April/1 May	Marburg	175	Students' festival: town and gown fraternise.
One Sunday each month, from Easter to September	Rothenburg	218	Shepherds' historical Danse.
Friday after Ascension	Weingarten	255	Blutritt: procession on horseback in honour of the Precious Blood.
Whit Sunday	Schwäbisch Hall	229	Kuchenfest: dance of the Salt-Boilers in 16C costume.
Whit Saturday, Sunday and Monday	Rothenburg	218	Performance of the quaffing of the Magisterial Bumper of Wine (Meistertrunk); Monday: great
2nd Sunday in September			commemorative festival with everyone in fancy dress.
Last Saturday in May	Merfelder Bruch	193	Catching of wild horses and rodeo.
Corpus Christi	Munich	183	Solemn procession through the decorated city.
—	Cologne	95	Boat procession on the Rhine.
—	Hüfingen	205 7	Processing through flower decked streets.
1st Saturday in June, July and September	Heidelberg	146	Castle floodlit; fireworks.
2nd Sunday after Whitsun	Schwalmstadt	31	Salatkirmes (Salad Fair): festival commemorating the introduction of the potato to Hesse; Schwalm local costume (p 33).
End June – beginning July (1978 and 1981)	Landshut	164	Fürstenhochzeit (the princes' marriage): grandiose historical festival.
Sundays from Whit Sunday to the end of September	Hamelin	141	Rattenfängerspiel; performance of the Pied Piper legend.
2nd weekend in July	Speyer	234	Brezelfest: popular *bretzel* festival.
3rd Monday in July	Dinkelsbühl	106	Kinderzeche: commemoration of the saving of the town through the children's appeal.
Next but last Monday in July	Ulm	250	Schwörmontag (the Monday of the oath); boat procession on the Danube.
End July	Kaufbeuren 987	36	Tänzelfest: great historical procession by schoolchildren.
2nd Saturday in August	Koblenz	160	"The Rhine in Flames": floodlighting of the Rhine Valley from Braubach to Koblenz with bonfires and fireworks.
Saturday after 24 August	Markgröningen	169	Schäferlauf: shepherds' race, barefoot in a field of stubble.
2nd and 3rd Sundays in September	Bad Dürkheim	108	Wurstmarkt (sausage fair): large wine festival.
3rd Saturday in September	St. Goar	225	Floodlighting of the Rhine and castles.
End of September to early October	Bad Cannstatt	238	Cannstatter Volksfest: folklore festival.
—	Munich	183	Oktoberfest: October festival.
6 November (St. Leonard's day)	Bad Tölz	244	Leonhardifahrt: pilgrimage to the protector of horses and cattle; procession of horses and decorated peasant carts.
Sunday after 6 November	Benediktbeuren	62	
10 November	Düsseldorf	109	Feast of St. Martin: procession of children bearing lanterns.
Three weeks before Christmas	Nuremberg	197	Christkindlesmarkt: (Market of the Infant Child): sale of Christmas tree decorations and gifts; children's festivities on the illuminated Hauptmarkt.
Christmas Eve	Berchtesgaden	63	Weihnachtsschützen: shots fired in the mountains.

(1) The Michelin map number and fold are given where the town is not described in the guide.

THE GERMAN CARNIVAL

The Germans have a reputation, amply borne out in their secular carnivals, for playing as hard as they work. The festivals are marked by a variety of displays and a length and scale of rejoicing unknown elsewhere.

The traditional carnival centres are found particularly in the Rhineland (Cologne, Mainz, etc.) and also in the Black Forest and the Alemannian regions of the south, when wild processions revert, in their terrifying masks, to their age-old purpose of frightening away the evil spirits of winter. Finally, there is Munich, where *Fasching*, a whirl of balls and masquerades involves everyone in the local frenzy. Carnivals in the Rhineland are large undertakings, involving the local notables in good natured rivalry. The carnival period begins on 11 November. In Mainz, a year's preparation goes into producing a programme of satire and burlesque which is also televised and broadcast throughout the country.

LITERATURE AND LETTERS

PRINCIPAL LITERARY EVENTS
Great philosophers appear in bold type

Place reference
quoted in
the Guide

MIDDLE AGES

9C	*The Lay of Hildebrand.*	Fulda *(p 129).*
Late 12C	National and folk saga of the Nibelungen.	Rhine Valley *(p 209).*
13C	Wolfram von Eschenbach writes the epic poem *Parsifal*, the knight in quest of the Holy Grail.	
1170-1228	Walter von der Vogelweide, knight and troubadour, raises mediaeval lyric poetry to its greatest heights.	Würzburg *(p 263).*
Early 16C	Chronicle of the buffoon Till Eulenspiegel.	Brunswick *(p 90).* Mölln *(p 180).*

THE REFORMATION AND THE THIRTY YEARS WAR

Only at the end of the Reformation and after the disastrous Thirty Years War, were German letters able to develop freely.

1534	Luther completes his translation of the Bible, the first great literary work to be written in modern German.
1669	Grimmelshausen publishes his picaresque novel *Simplizissimus*.

THE RATIONALISTS' CENTURY (Aufklärung)

1646-1716	**Leinitz** writes his *Theodociea* in French and Latin; and invents differential calculus.	
1729-1781	Lessing, the creator of the principles of modern German drama (Hamburg Dramatic Theory), writes bourgeois plays with rationalist leanings.	Wolfenbüttel *(p 260).*
1724-1803	Klopstock composes the Christian inspired epic, *The Messiade*.	
1724-1804	**Kant** defines the balance between liberty and morality; man finds liberty in submission to the categorical imperative.	

"STURM UND DRANG" AND CLASSICISM

Sturm und Drang, in reaction to the rationalism of Aufklärung exalted sentimentality, nature and titanic liberty. Goethe (1749-1832), a universal genius – in drama, poetry, science and philosophy – tempered the fashionable enthusiasm with a proposal of the classical ideal of a harmonious and triumphant humanity.

Frankfürt *(p 120).*

1759-1805	Schiller, poet and playwright, writes historical dramas *(Don Carlos, Wallenstein* and *William Tell)*, which are hymns in praise of liberty.	Marbach am Neckar *(p 239).*
1774	*Werther*, the novel in letter form, is widely acclaimed.	Wetzlar *(p 257).*
1788	Goethe, on his return from Italy, publishes his great classical dramas: *Iphigenia in Tauris, Egmont* and *Torquato Tasso*.	
1796-1821	*Wilhelm Meister*, an educational novel in two parts.	
1808 and 1832	Faust, the quintessence of Goethe's message to mankind.	

THE ROMANTIC MOVEMENT (1790-1850)

The Romantic Movement, reflecting an essential element in the German character, was the soul's quest of the infinite in all forms. It influenced not only literature but also the arts, philosophy and even religion and politics. Heidelberg, Jena and Berlin were the main centres.

1770-1831	**Hegel** defines the historical conscience and dialectic.	
1772-1801	Novalis, poet and mystic, exalts mediaeval art and religion; he defines the Absolute by means of the Blue Flower theme (Heinrich of Ofterdingen).	
1805	A series of poems inspired by popular tradition, *The Child with the Enchanted Horn* is published.	Heidelberg *(p 146).*
1810	Heinrich von Kleist writes *The Prince of Homburg*, a play about a man of action led away by his dreams.	
1812	First edition of *Grimms' Fairy Tales*.	Kassel *(p 156).*
1776-1822	E T A Hoffman explores the supernatural in his *Tales*.	Bamberg *(p 56).*

POETIC REALISM AND NATURALISM

The disillusion following the idealism of the Romantic Movement was succeeded by a search for realism and, after 1848, by philosophic materialism and social literature.

1797-1856	Heinrich Heine, the "unfrocked Romantic" poet of the Loreley, mingles bitter irony with the swept away emotions of a liberal "Young Germany".	Düsseldorf *(p 109).*
1788-1860	**Schopenhauer**, the pessimistic theorist of the will to live and the urge to pity.	The Loreley *(p 211).*
1813-1863	Hebbel composes forceful tragedies *(Agnes Bernauer)*.	
1848	**Karl Marx** and **Friedrich Engels** publish their *Manifesto*.	
1862-1946	Gerhart Hauptmann presents realistic drama *(Die Weber)*.	

THE CURRENT PERIOD

1844-1900	**Friedrich Nietzsche** denounces, in lyrical phrases, the decadence of man and praises the man of the future freed from the morals of the feeble *(Thus Spake Zarathustra)*.
1868-1933 Circum	Stefan George publishes formally perfect poems.
1900-1930	The Austrians Rainer Maria Rilke and Hofmannsthal achieve the peak of poetic impressionism.
1875-1955	Thomas Mann, the novelist, writes *Buddenbrooks, Dr. Faustus*.
1883-1924	Franz Kafka, symbolic novelist of the absurd *(The Trial, The Castle, The Metamorphosis)*.
1898-1956	Bertolt Brecht, social dramatist *(The Threepenny Opera, Mother Courage, Galileo)*.
1920-1950	Existential movement (**Husserl, Heidegger, Jaspers**).
1945 onwards	Group 47 formed by writers (Weiss Grass, Böll) who embraced political beliefs. The Nobel Prize for literature given to novelists Hermann Hesse (1946) and Heinrich Böll (1972).

Lübeck *(p 167).*

FOOD AND DRINK

German cooking whets the appetite, less by its subtlety than by its careful presentation and plentiful wholesomeness.

Potatoes are a staple item in the German diet but, contrary to general belief, pickled cabbage *(Sauerkraut)* is not.

The Gastronomic Regions. – Southern Germany offers rather fat food, with, in particular, a wide range of sausages *(Wurst)* and pork butchers' meats. Potatoes are sometimes replaced by dumplings known as *Knödel* or *Klösse*, little balls of liver or paste, and *Spätzle*, a kind of freshly made noodle.

The River Main forms an approximate demarcation line, gastronomically speaking, between north and south. Northern Germany, especially in the more favoured regions of Brunswick and the Hanseatic towns, consumes far more green vegetables and fresh meat, including mutton. Salt-water fish are also, naturally, to be found on the menu.

The Rhine Valley and Westphalia have their own traditions: the Rhine for its many types of rolls and bread, cakes, fritters and biscuits which are to be seen in every baker's shop, and Westphalia for its hams.

Meals. – Lunch *(Mittagessen)* can be ordered *à la carte*, but most restaurants also offer fixed price menus *(Gedecke)*. The meal usually begins with soup; a thick cream of vegetable or noodles, clear soup with an egg, dumplings or pancake flakes. The main dish comprises garnished meat with a portion of chopped green salad, red or white cabbage, or with game, cranberry jam *(Preiselbeeren)*. The meal may end with a prepared dessert or tinned fruit.

To be served quickly at either lunch or dinner in a hotel or restaurant, it is advisable to arrive punctually at noon or 7pm.

Afternoon tea – generally called **Kaffee** – consists of coffee (or tea) and cakes. The Germans enjoy it and for tourists it makes a pleasant break.

The **evening meal** *(Abendessen)* is frugal. Many Germans are satisfied with a plate of cold meats *(Aufschnitt)* and then linger over a glass of beer, wine or *Schnaps*.

Non-alcoholic drinks. – Germans seldom touch the local water. With a few rare exceptions *(Fachinger)* mineral waters are highly aerated. Non-alcoholic fruit juices, especially apple-juice *(Apfelsaft)*, make refreshing drinks.

Coffee, which is served with a small jug of milk or cream, is usually weak, except when made in the *espresso* machines to be found in the popular coffee and ice cream shops.

BEER

Beer, the national drink – consumption in Bavaria is estimated as $46\frac{1}{2}$ gallons per person per year – is made from barley, which is soaked, allowed almost to germinate, then baked to form brewer's malt. This is added to the hops, which give it flavour and aroma, and fermented.

Light Beers *(Helles Bier)* are brewed from malt which has only been dried and baked; **dark beers** *(Dunkles Bier)* are made from darkly roasted malt which is fermented over a longer period. The larger quantity of malt in the dark beers makes the taste sweeter.

The light *Pils* or *Pilsener* beers, which have become a speciality of Dortmund, contain more hops; they are recognisable by their clarity and slight bitterness.

In Germany, the stock beer *(Vollbier)* which you get when you order "ein Bier" is 4% proof, *Export* is 5% and *Bockbier*, about 6%.

Beer drinking is one of the attractions of a tour of Bavaria where a wide variety of locally produced beers may be found. Beer drinking in Munich takes place in enormous cellars, often on a Gargantuan scale. It is consumed at such speed that it is not pulled under pressure, but served direct from the barrel.

WINES

The German vineyards, which extend over 69 000 ha - 150 000 acres – lie between Lake Constance and the Siebengebirge and between Trier and Würzburg *(see map in Michelin Red Guide Deutschland)*. They produce principally white wines (80% of production) which can be agreeably tasted in the half light of local inns and taverns *(Weinstube, Weinhaus)* or in the impressive cellars beneath town halls, the *Ratskeller*.

The **hocks,** now commonly available in England, are white table wines produced in the Rhine Valley, and derive their English name from Hochheim.

The Vintages. – **Riesling,** one of the most famous white grape stocks in the world, produces a vigorous, elegant and true wine. **Sylvaner,** which is the most widely grown, has a high yield. The wine, which is delicate and sweet, is consumed when young and cold. **Traminer** are not in the least dry and have a full bouquet. **Ruländer,** which is the equivalent of French *rosé* wine, can be quite potent in good years.

There are few red wines. The vineyards lie in the middle reaches of the Neckar (Württemberg vineyards) and in the Ahr. The best is the **Spätburgunder** (a late red Burgundy).

The most recent "good" years for German wines are: **1967, 1969** and **1971**.

Terms to know. – **Auslese** is applied to wines produced from a harvest from which every poor quality grape has been removed. **Spätlese** means that the grapes were ripened to the limit before cutting. German wines are produced with the greatest care. Those requiring no preservation or sweetening treatment are known as **naturrein**; the terms *Wachstum, Kreszenz* or *Gewächs* on the label also apply to *naturrein* wines. "Château bottled" wines *(Originalabfüllung)* are of the same quality.

Wine and Spirit Drinking. – In Germany wine is drunk mostly outside meal times. The typical long necked bottles are tinted green in the Mosel Valley and brown in the Rhine. The curious Franconian wines, which are potent and very dry, are bottled in pot-bellied flagons known as **Bocksbeutel.** Stock wines are served by the glass (open wines: *offene Weine* or *Schoppenweine*). **Sekt,** a sparkling wine produced mostly in the Mainz and Wiesbaden districts, is served at many functions in place of champagne.

Spirits are consumed in different ways according to their origin. Grain spirits or *Korn* are drunk in northern Germany and gentian in the Alpine regions, as chasers to beer. Fruit based spirits or *Schnaps* and the glory of the Black Forest, often end a meal.

For further details on food and drink, look at the introduction in the Michelin Red Guide Deutschland.

TOURING PROGRAMMES

RHINE AND MOSEL REGIONS (1381 km)

0   40 km
Key p 35

- ★ Zons
- ★ Burg an der Wupper
- p 94
- Altenberg ★
- 108
- ▲ *Attahöhle* ★
- Bigge Dam ★
- p 226
- Olpe ★
- 98
- 62
- 24
- 70
- E 5
- 13
- **COLOGNE** ★★★
- Brühl ▣
- **★★ MARBURG**
- **AACHEN** ★
- 61
- Bonn ★
- p 213
- Monschau ★
- *Eifel Massif* ★
- p 113
- Bad Neuenahr ★
- 148
- Wetzlar
- 147
- 149
- *Lahn Valley*
- p 163
- *Hohe Acht* ★★
- **KOBLENZ** ★
- Runkel ★
- BELGIUM
- 258
- ★ Nürburg
- Limburg ★
- ★★ Eltz ▣
- 6
- *Loreley* ★★★
- Cochem ★
- 49
- **WIESBADEN** ★★
- ★★ *Marienburg*
- *Rhine Valley* ★★★
- p 209
- 110
- *Mosel Valley* ★★
- p 181
- 131
- Mainz ★
- Bernkastel-Kues ★
- Rüdesheim ★
- 53
- 6
- **★★ TRIER**
- 60
- RHINE
- LUXEMBOURG
- p 224
- 107
- 51
- ★★ *Cloef* ▲
- ★★ Worms
- p 65
- Merzig
- Kaiserslautern
- **★★★ HEIDELBERG**
- 93
- 40
- 68
- p 216
- 106
- Schwetzingen ★★
- ▲ *Kalmit*
- Speyer ★
- Saarbrücken
- F R A N C E

BLACK FOREST
BADEN-WÜRTTEMBERG (1084 km)

0   80 km

- Pforzheim
- Neckar
- ✝ Tiefenbronn ★
- 77
- **★★★ BADEN-BADEN**
- Hirsau ★
- ★ Solitude ▸
- **STUTTGART** ★
- Yburg ★
- p 81
- Altwindeck
- 101
- 41
- E 70
- 60
- 463
- ✝ Bebenhausen Abbey ★
- ★ Allerheiligen
- Nagold ★
- Tübingen ★★
- 28
- Freudenstadt ★
- FRANCE
- ★ Alpirsbach
- ★★ Haigerloch
- 95
- *Grossengstingen*
- *The Black Forest* ★★
- p 80
- Hohenzollern ★
- 312
- Zwiefalten ★
- 33
- 124
- Neckar
- ★ Triberg ★
- **★ SIGMARINGEN**
- 66
- Breisach ★
- 294
- Danube
- 42
- **FREIBURG IM BREISGAU** ★★
- ★ Beuron
- ★★ *Feldberg*
- Titisee ★
- 129
- 317
- 107
- *Hegau Belvedere* ★
- ★★★ *Belchen* ▲
- p 84
- 101
- 51
- p 101
- Überlingen ★
- **ST. BLASIEN**
- 500
- ★ *Hohentwiel*
- ★★ *Mainau*
- Meersburg ★
- 35
- 311
- 40
- Waldshut
- ★ Constance
- ★★ *Lake*
- **LINDAU** ★★
- RHINE
- *Constance*
- S W I T Z E R L A N D
- AUSTRIA

34

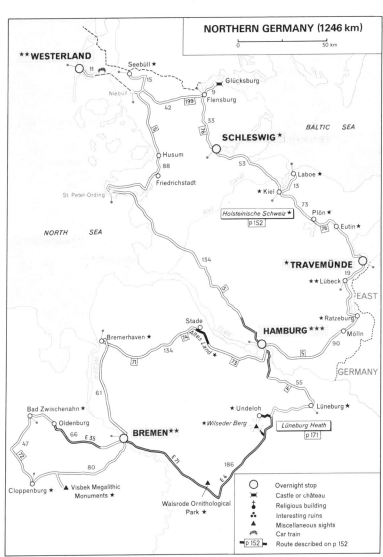

NORTHERN GERMANY (1246 km)

0   50 km

** WESTERLAND

Seebüll ★

11

15

Niebüll

42 199

Glücksburg

9

Flensburg

33

76

SCHLESWIG ★

BALTIC SEA

Husum

88

Friedrichstadt

53

Laboe ★

13

★ Kiel

73

Holsteinische Schweiz ★
p 152

Plön ★

76

Eutin ★

St. Peter-Ording

NORTH SEA

134

5

★ TRAVEMÜNDE

19

★★ Lübeck

EAST

Stade

Bremerhaven ★

74

Altes Land ★

75

HAMBURG ★★★

★ Ratzeburg

Mölln

90

134

71

ELBE

55

5

4

GERMANY

61

Bad Zwischenahn ★

Oldenburg

66 E 35

★ Undeloh

★ Wilseder Berg

Lüneburg ★

Lüneburg Heath
p 171

47

72

BREMEN ★★

E 71

186

E 4

80

Cloppenburg ★

▲ Visbek Megalithic
Monuments ★

Walsrode Ornithological
Park ★

○   Overnight stop

Castle or château

Religious building

Interesting ruins

▲ Miscellaneous sights

Car train

p 152   Route described on p 152

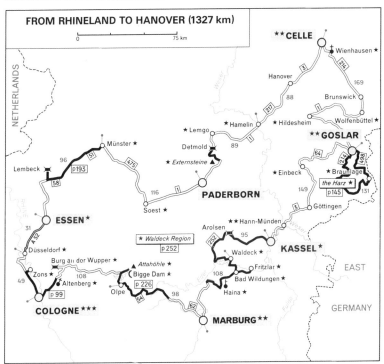

FROM RHINELAND TO HANOVER (1327 km)

0   75 km

★★ CELLE

Wienhausen ★

3

214

NETHERLANDS

Hanover

217

88

Brunswick

169

1

Hamelin

★ Hildesheim

Wolfenbüttel ★

★ Lemgo

Detmold

★★ GOSLAR

64

214

898

★ Braunlage

96

51

Münster ★

p 193

475

89

★ Externsteine

★ Einbeck

the Harz ★
p 145

131

Lembeck

58

116

1

PADERBORN

149

3

Soest ★

Göttingen

ESSEN ★

31

A 52

Hann-Münden

Arolsen

Waldeck Region
p 252

252

95

Düsseldorf ★

Burg an der Wupper ★

▲ Attahöhle ★

Waldeck ★

KASSEL ★

Zons ★

108

▲ Bigge Dam ★

Fritzlar ★

EAST

49

Altenberg ★
p 99

Olpe ★

54

108

Bad Wildungen ★

Haina ★

GERMANY

COLOGNE ★★★

98

62

MARBURG ★★

35

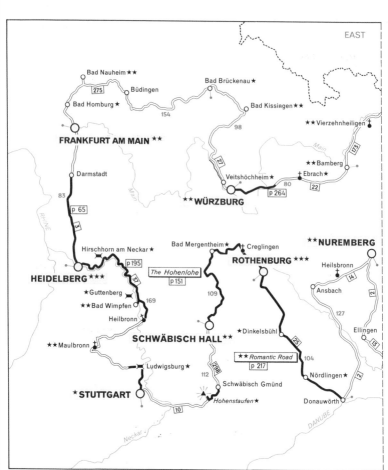

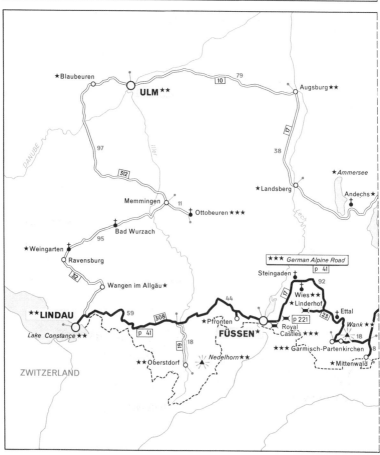

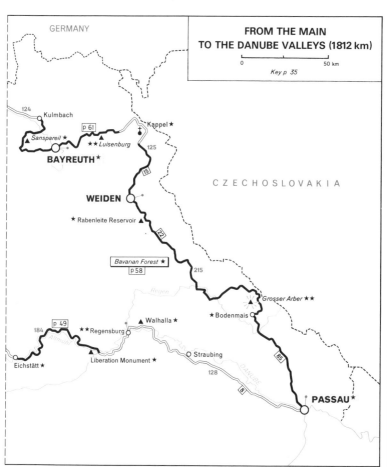

FROM THE MAIN
TO THE DANUBE VALLEYS (1812 km)

0   50 km

Key p 35

GERMANY

124 Kulmbach

Kappel ★

p 61

Sanspareil ★   125

★★ *Luisenburg*

BAYREUTH ★

15

CZECHOSLOVAKIA

WEIDEN

★ Rabenleite Reservoir   22

Bavarian Forest ★

p 58

215

Grosser Arber ★★

★ Bodenmais

184   p 49

★★ Regensburg   ▲ Walhalla ★

Eichstätt ★   Liberation Monument ★   ○ Straubing

85

128   8

PASSAU ★

MUNICH AND THE BAVARIAN ALPS (1132 km)

0   50 km

Schleissheim ★

15

MUNICH ★★★

304   ○ Wasserburg am Inn

76   127

Chiemsee ★

Bad Tölz ★   88   SCHLIERSEE ★   126   E 11   ○ Ruhpolding ★   Bad Reichenhall ★★

Benediktbeuern   p 44   ▲ *Wendelstein* ★★   p 47   305   26   18

★★ Bad Wiessee   p 46   ★ Reit im Winkl   45

Walchensee ★   ★★ BERCHTESGADEN

A U S T R I A

37

CONVENTIONAL SIGNS

OTTOBEUREN / *LORELEY*	} Worth a journey (★★★)
Marburg / *Königssee*	} Worth a detour (★★)
Bacharach / *Höllental*	} Interesting (★)
Kallmünz / *Teufelshöhle*	} See if possible

Wittlich	Reference point
Rtn	Return, Round trip
(2)	Reference no. common to plans of towns and to Michelin maps
Pop 14 280 : Population	
987 **204** ⑫	No of Michelin map and section

Urban Network

AUTOBAHN	Motorway		Sightseeing route
	Dual carriageway through route		Tree lined street
	Through route		Street under construction
	Dual carriageway		Street closed or impassable or subject to restrictions
	Wide street		Steps
	Fairly wide street		Footpath
	Narrow street	Karlstraße	Shopping street

Landmarks

	Railway crossings : level crossing, road crossing rail, rail crossing road		Trolleybus
	Street passing under arch, tunnel		Tram
	Gateway		Rack-railway, funicular
	Railway, station		Teleferic, cableway, chair-hoist

Roads

	Route described		Motorway (*Autobahn*)
	Alternative route or excursion	*19*	National road (*Bundesstrasse*) no 19
	Walk	*E 14*	European road no 14
	Other sightseeing route described	*12*	Distance (in kilometres)
	Other roads		Pass

Miscellaneous

	Interesting Catholic church, chapel		Catholic church, chapel - for reference only
	Interesting Protestant church, chapel		Protestant church - for reference only
	Place of interest (with main entrance)		Other church - for reference only
	Interesting castle		Public building (with main entrance)
	Interesting ruins		Castle - for reference only
	Miscellaneous sights		Ruins - for reference only
	Viewingtable		Monument, statue, tower
	Panorama, View		Ramparts
	Best place to park the car when going sightseeing		Main Post Office with poste restante
	Start of sightseeing tour		Telephone number
	Frontier { German Customs / Foreign Customs		Covered market
	Public garden (with main entrance)		Hospital } with
	Private garden		Cemetery } main
	Woods		Jewish cemetery } entrance
			Local Tourist Office

POL.	Police : in large towns : police H Q (*Polizeipräsidium*)		Golf course	
R	Town Hall (*Rathaus*)		Racecourse	
J	Law Courts		Airport	
M	Museum		Fountain	
L	Provincial Government office (*Landesregierung*)		Water tower	
T	Theatre		Calvary	
U	University		Tower	
			Factory	
			Gasometer	

Dam	
Mine, pit	
Lighthouse	
Landing stage	
F Car ferry (*Fähre*)	
Windmill	
AZ B { Reference letters locating sights on a town plan.	

TOWNS, SIGHTS
AND TOURIST REGIONS

AACHEN ★

Michelin map **203** 11 – Pop 242 000

Aachen (Aix-la-Chapelle) is, first and foremost, the town of Charlemagne, the heart of the Frankish Empire of the 8 and 9C. It is also an industrial centre closely linked to nearby brown coal mines; a centre of higher technical learning (engineering, electricity, mining, etc.); a shopping centre, where the neighbouring Belgians and Dutch do their errands, with a bustle of activity in the pedestrian zone surrounding the town hall, and a spa of long standing.

The Emperor Charlemagne. – Charlemagne, King of the Franks, after wandering like his ancestors before him, holding his court wherever war and the chase led him, settled finally in 794 in Aachen. He became Emperor of the west in AD 800.

By overpowering the Saxons and the Bavarians, and by consolidating his conquests to the north of the Pyrenees, he grouped together, for the first time in history, the peoples and territories of what were later France and Germany. He brought to the west treasures of the Latin civilisation and the advantages of centralised government. His palace became a fountain-head of civilisation from which culture spread throughout his vast Empire.

Charlemagne died at Aachen on 28 January 814 and was buried in the octagon of the Palatine Chapel. In the 12C he was canonised.

The Imperial City. – Between 936 and 1531, thirty princes were crowned King of Germania in the cathedral. But in 1562 the town lost the status of coronation city to Frankfurt.

Two treaties were signed at Aachen: that of 1668 terminated the War of the Spanish Devolution between France and Spain and that of 1748 ended the Austrian War of Succession.

■ **SIGHTS** tour: 1½ hours

Cathedral** (Dom). – Shortly before AD 800 Charlemagne ordered the construction, on similar lines to the churches in the eastern Roman Empire, of a domed octagonal basilica. The Gothic chancel, begun in 1355, was consecrated in 1414, the 600th anniversary of the death of the Emperor.

AACHEN

0 ————— 300

Alexanderstraße	CY 3
An der Schanz	AZ 4
Büchel	BY 7
Buchkremerstraße	BZ 8

Driescher Gäßchen	BY 10	Kleinmarschierstraße	BZ 25
Eilfschornsteinstraße	BY 12	Kockerellstraße	BY 26
Friedrich-Wilhelm-Platz	BZ 13	Komphausbadstraße	BZ 27
Großkölnstraße	BY	Krämerstraße	BY 29
Hartmannstraße	BZ 15	Kurhausstraße	CY 30
Kaiserplatz	CZ	Markt	BY
Kapuzinergraben	BZ 19	Peterstraße	BCY
Karmeliterstraße	BZ 20	Ursulinerstraße	BZ 32
Kleinkölnstraße	BY 23	Zollernstraße	CZ 34

39

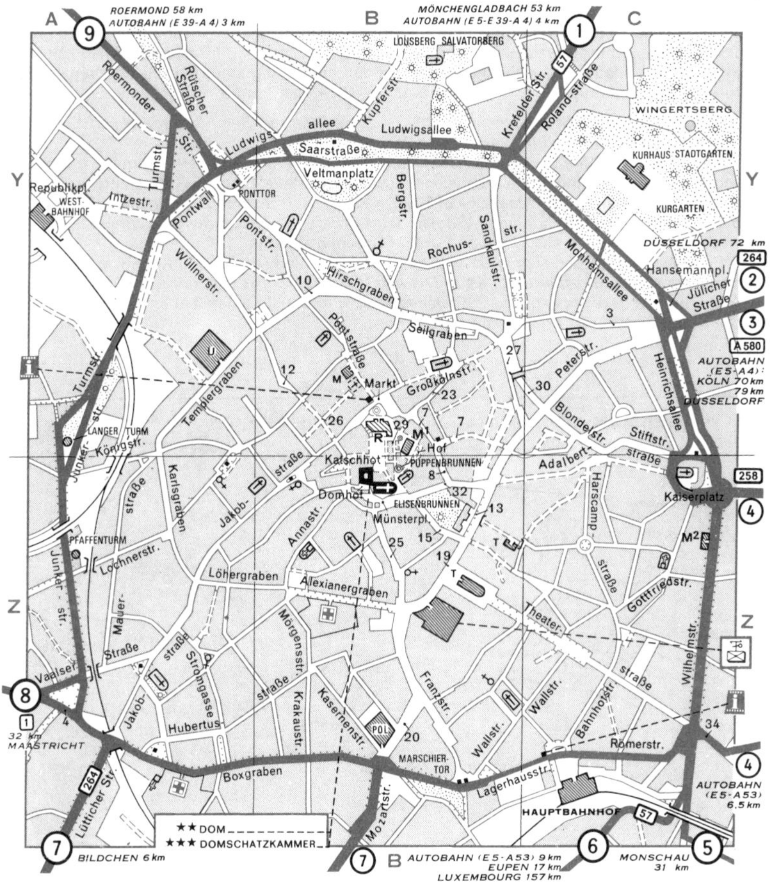

Exterior. – As you bear left round the cathedral you see the Chapel of St. Nicholas, the Chapel of Charlemagne with its Flamboyant doorway, and the chancel, adorned, between its tall Gothic windows, with 19C statues – that on the seventh buttress is of St. Bernard of Clairvaux. From the Münsterplatz there is a good view of the upper part of the Carolingian building crowned with a strange 16-sided dome dating from the 17C. The Gothic Chapels of St. Matthias and St. Anne and the Hungarian Chapel obstruct the view of the lower part.

The portal on to the Domhof, is closed by two 9C bronze doors embossed with lions' heads.

Interior. – A two-storey ambulatory circles the octagon, at whose centre hangs a magnificent bronze **chandelier★★** (Radleuchter). Against one of the pillars of the octagon before the chancel may be seen a statue of the Virgin, believed to be miraculous.

The chancel is lit by modern stained glass windows. The **ambo** (small pulpit) **of Henry II★★★** made of copper and decorated with precious stones stands to the right of the communion table. **The Pala d'Oro★★★**, a gorgeous altar frontal painted with scenes from the Passion and an 11C Crucifix adorn the Carolingian high altar. The Emperor's relics were placed in a **gold shrine★★** (Karlsschrein) at the end of the chancel, at the time of the coronation of Frederick II in 1215. Only by going on the guided tour *(suspended during services and confessions – apply to the keeper of the treasure for details; 1DM.)* can you see Charlemagne's still undamaged throne made of plain marble slabs, the fine bronze grilles which close the octagon, and, in the upper Chapel of St. Michael, a 2C marble sarcophagus decorated with a low relief of the abduction of Persephone.

Treasure★★★ (Domschatzkammer).– *Domhof 4a. Open 15 April to 15 September 9am to 1pm and 2 to 6pm (5pm 16 September to 14 April) Sundays 10.30am to 1pm and 2 to 5pm; 2DM.*

This is one of Germany's richest treasures. Note: to the right of the entrance, the 13C arms chest of Richard, Earl of Cornwall (1209-72; younger brother of Henry III of England); in the centre of the room, the gold cross of Lothair dating from 990 encrusted with precious stones, adorned at its centre with a fine cameo of the Emperor Augustus. Also in the centre is a reliquary bust of Charlemagne, cast in gold and silver in 1350 and presented by Karl IV together with the crown worn by the Emperor when he was King. At the back on the left is an altarpiece whose central panel depicts the Crucifixion (1510) and in the centre the Shrine of the Virgin (13C).

Go up the Krämerstrasse, east of the cathedral, to the **Fountain of Dolls** (Puppenbrunnen) where children as well as adults will spend a happy moment moving the dolls anyway they wish.

Town Hall (Rathaus) (BY R). – *Open 10am to 1pm and 2 to 4pm (1pm weekends); 1DM.*

The town hall was built in the 14C, on the site of Charlemagne's palace of which the low Granus Tower may still be seen at the corner of the Krämerstrasse. Slightly back in the same street is the Postwagen Inn (Post Inn) of 1657. On the other side of the square, the Haus Löwenstein, a restored Gothic house, is now the tourist information bureau.

The tower façade, ornamented with statues of the kings and emperors crowned at Aachen, overlooks the Market Square (Markt) with its fountain dedicated to Charlemagne.

The Peace Treaty of 1748 was signed in the reception chamber to the right of the entrance which is ornamented with Italian stuccowork of 1725. On the left is the Council Chamber with 1727 panelling. On the second floor the Coronation Chamber with ogive vaulting has 19C frescoes by Alfred Rethel of the life of Charlemagne.

Couven Museum★ (BZ M¹). – *Open 10am to 5pm Tuesdays to Fridays (1pm weekends); 1DM.* At one time a pharmacy, a dispensary has been arranged as it was in the 18C (ground floor), this bourgeois residence is now a museum with a collection of household furnishings from the 17 and 18C upper class homes. On the first floor there is a large room with a chimney decorated in sculptured wood. The diversity of the collection is further exemplified, on the second floor, by the furniture, the manger with a multitude of figurines and the children's toys. Returning to the ground floor one admires the faience tiles from the Netherlands.

Suermondt-Ludwig Museum★ (CZ M²). – *Open 10am to 5pm; Saturdays and Sundays 10am to 1pm; closed Mondays and holidays.*

On the ground floor are **sculptures** of the Lower Rhine and southern Germany up to the Baroque period, including a locally carved altarpiece to St. Peter, graceful Gothic Virgins, among which are a Swabian *Robed Madonna* of 1420, a *Virgin of the Crescent Moon* and a 14C *Virgin and Child*. *Jesus and the Samaritan Woman* dates from 1530. In a showcase, admire the richly carved ivories, especially the *Virgin and Child* (School of Tournai, 14C).

Primitive German and Flemish as well as 17C Flemish and Dutch paintings are displayed on the first floor. The oldest work of art is *The Arrestation of Christ* (School of Cologne, 1460).

On the 2nd floor are exposed 20C **stained glass windows** illuminated at the end of the week and a rich collection of ecclesiastical art.

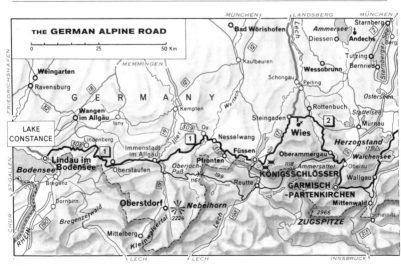

The road runs from Lindau to Berchtesgaden, from Lake Constance to the Königssee, along the foot of the Allgäu and the Bavarian Alps for the entire length of their frontier with Austria. It passes through mountain scenery and beside such famous sights as the Royal Castles near Füssen and the Church of Wies, but is still incomplete, necessitating detours into the lowlands.

TOURS

Tourists should allow three days for the drive along the Alpine Road between Berchtesgaden and Lindau. Numerous alternatives can be added such as:

– **a family drive,** between Schliersee and Rosenheim: arriving at Schliersee from Lindau, turn north to Miesbach to come to the Irschenberg entrance to the Munich–Salzburg motorway (**belvedere★** facing the Alps). Continue towards Salzburg along the motorway from which there are repeated **views★** of the Bavarian Alps to the south. Leave the motorway by the Rosenheim exit if you wish to visit this town. If not, then continue along the motorway according to route ⑤;

– **a mountain drive,** avoiding the lowlands as much as possible by incursions into Austria, but through them missing the Church of Wies and the Chiemsee. Between Lindau and Garmisch follow successively the alternative routes by the Oberjoch Pass and the Ammersattel. However, do not miss the section between Reutte and Hohenschwangau with a visit to the Royal Castles. From Bayrischzell go on to Kufstein by way of the Ursprung-Pass, Walchensee *(see Michelin Green Guide Austria)* and Reit im Winkl, where you join route ⑤.

① ★FROM LINDAU TO FÜSSEN by Oberstaufen and Nesselwang

105 km - 65 miles – about 2½ hours – Local map pp 42 and 43

The landscape during this stage is not particularly Bavarian in character: it is the **Allgäu,** whose quietly industrious farmers, of Alemannian strain, have made their mountain countryside into the great cheese manufacturing area of Germany.

Lindau★★. – *Description p 166.*

Leaving the banks of Lake Constance with their many orchards, the road, which is wide as far as Immenstadt, passes over an undulating countryside, the last spurs of the Bregenzerwald. Drivers should slow down while taking the beautiful sweeping **curve★** of the road as it crosses the Rotach Valley, passing to one side of Lindenberg (major German centre for hat-making industry) and Weiler.

Paradies. – Engineers have given this name to the part of the road, laid out as a viewpoint, whose sharp curve above the Weissach Valley gives a view of the distant Appenzell Alps (Säntis and Altmann) in Switzerland.

Oberstaufen. – This township, which is a holiday spot among the most charming of the Allgäu, stands on undulating ground. The road skirts south of the wooded Kapf hump (alt 1 032 m - 3 386 ft) which appeals to walkers who can see from its summit the Säntis and the Altmann in the Swiss Appenzell Alps. In winter, the slopes of the Hündlealpe and its surrounding heights offer skiers good practice slopes. Snowfalls are often heavy.

Immenstadt im Allgäu. – This little town, lying in a basin at the opening of the Iller Valley, manufactures stockings and string. It is dominated by the Grünten, the Guardian of the Allgäu, on whose summit is a television relay station.

The road next winds round to the north of the Allgäu Alps, across a region of hilly morainic deposits to reach more open country in the region of Pfronten and Füssen, where the beautiful pointed summit of Säuling dominates the wooded slopes.

Nesselwang. – The approach to Nesselwang from the west (the direction of our description) shows up the situation of the village whose church belfry stands out against the background of the Säuling and the Zugspitze.

Pfronten★. – Pfronten is separated from the Alpine Road by the crest of the Falkenstein. On this stands a ruin which Ludwig II of Bavaria wanted to replace with a colossal structure in the style of Neuschwanstein Castle. The resort extends 2½ miles along the road: Pfronten-Berg, Pfronten-Ried, Pfronten-Heitlem, Pfronten-Dorf, Pfronten-Osch and Pfronten-Steinach. All are equallly attractive with inns freshly renovated and painted. The cable-car hoist of the Breitenberg, set up for skiers using the snowfields of the Hochalpe, in summer shortens the ascent of the Aggenstein, a fine Dolomitic, jagged summit of the Tannheim group. From the Alpine Road, 400 m to the east of Pfronten-Kreuzegg, near a Cross, the view extends across the Pfronten Valley with the church belfry of Pfronten-Berg.

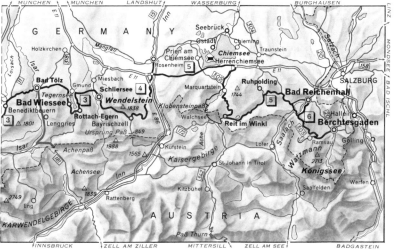

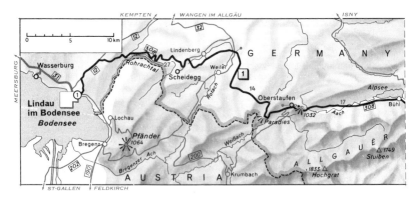

Alternative route* by the Oberjoch Pass and Reutte (passing through Austria). – *Extra distance: 23 km - 14 miles.*

Hindelang*. – Hindelang, a large flower decked village, rejoices in a delightful **setting*** in a bend of the Ostrach Valley. With its neighbour, Bad Oberdorf, is a holiday centre and spa (sulphur waters) from which mountain walks can be made in summer and skiing enjoyed in winter on the slopes of the Horn, facing the resort or on the snowfields of the Oberjoch.

Above Hindelang, along the **climb**** of the "road of 106 curves", famous in Germany but not difficult, there are varied views over the small pointed summits of the limestone Allgäu Alps.

Kanzel*. – From the Kanzel belvedere which stands on a steep slope, there is a good **overall view*** of the Ostrach Valley and the surrounding mountains.

On the eastern slope of the Oberjoch, the Tannheim Valley presents rough looking Tyrolean villages and the curious rock formation, above the Haldensee, of the bases of the Rote Flüh and the Gimpel. The road then descends the steep Gaicht Pass towards the Austere Valley of the Upper Lech.

Reutte (Austria). – *Description in Michelin Green Guide Austria.*

The road passes along the foot of the Säuling rock wall, a magnificent sight at sunset.

Lech Waterfall (Lechfall). – *Description p 43.*

Füssen*. – *Description p 130.*

---

② *FROM FÜSSEN TO GARMISCH-PARTENKIRCHEN
by way of Wies and Oberammergau
75 km - 47 miles – about 6 hours – Local map below

Royal Castles*** (Königsschlösser). – *About 3 hours walking and sightseeing. Description p 221.*

After passing Hohenschwangau, the route comes out in a region strewn with the deposits of the old Lech Glacier. From the ridges of this rolling countryside, often accentuated by a line of fir trees, rise the rounded belfries of the village churches. The final descent before Steingaden, with glimpses of solitary pools, is characteristic of the rural charm of Bavaria.

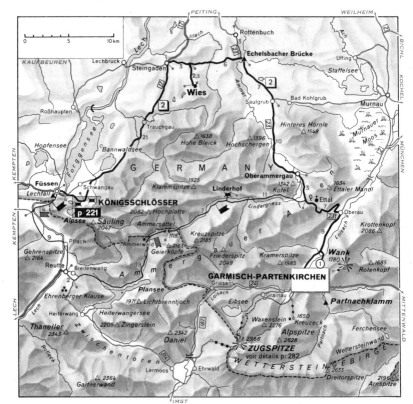

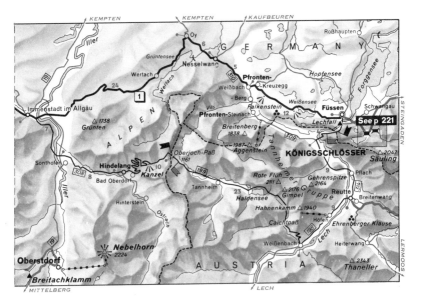

Steingaden. – The former Abbey of the Premonstratensians of Steingaden, founded in the 12C, still possesses its remarkable **minster*** (Klosterkirche), transformed, however, in the 18C into Baroque style. Only the outside has preserved the thick-set Romanesque appearance, with massive towers and Lombard arcades.

The nave is very wide. The sobriety of the stuccoes decorating the chancel is in sharp contrast to the lightness of those in the nave which are outlined with richly painted motifs. The Rococo furnishings – the pulpit, organ-loft, altarpieces and statues – triumphantly complete the scene.

Church of Wies ** (Wieskirche).** – *Description p 257.*

Rottenbuch. – *3 km - 2 miles – excursion from the Echelsbach Bridge.* The **Church of the Nativity of the Virgin*** (Mariä-Geburts-Kirche), first built as an Augustinian monastery, was entirely remodelled in the Baroque and Rococo styles in the 18C, except for the transept, which remains complete and original late 15C Gothic. The stuccoes show the talent of the Wessobrunn school *(details p 256)*, among whom was Joseph Schmuzer. The frescoes by Matthäus Günther harmonise with the exuberantly sculptured decorations. The pulpit and altars are overburdened with statues and gilded works. The monastery has not been in use since 1803.

Echelsbach Bridge* (Echelsbacher Brücke).** – Since 1929 this structure of reinforced concrete has crossed the 250-foot deep cutting made by the River Ammer. Before this, motorists had to resort to the help of oxen belonging to the local peasants – a situation recalled by the commemorative monument on the left bank.

South of the Echelsbach bridge, the region, known as "the parsons' corner" (Pfaffenwinkel) because of the unusual number of monasteries, is open and peaceful. The road avoids the Ammer Ravine but becomes uneven – its undulating character, however, offers good views of the clearly outlined Ammergebirge range.

Oberammergau*. – *Description p 199.*

Alternative route* between Füssen and Ettal by Reutte and Linderhof Castle (passing through Austria). – *This alternative route by way of the Ammersattel Pass (alt 118 m - 3 688 ft) is not longer, but involves crossing the frontier (customs at Ammerwald and Linderhof) which is only possible between 6am and 11pm (10pm 1 November to 31 March). Allow 2 hours for the visit to Linderhof Castle.*

Lech Waterfall (Lechfall). – About 500 yds north of the Austrian frontier, on the Füssen–Reutte road, the manmade Lech Falls tumble noisily to the bottom of a little rock gorge: this, the Step of St. Magnus (Magnustritt), is crossed by a footbridge, the Maxsteg. The bridge enables pedestrians to return to Füssen by an alternative route.

The Lech Valley, which is followed as far as Reutte, passes between the rocky Tannheimer mountains and the Säuling escarpments.

Reutte (Austria). – *Description in Michelin Green Guide Austria.*

The road from Ammersattel then climbs above the wooded ravine which runs into the outlet of the Plansee (good views of the Tannheimer Gruppe).

Plansee* (Austria). – *Description in Michelin Green Guide Austria.*

The road passes beside the lake and enters small deserted valleys, which become a little less austere and more richly wooded on the Bavarian side of the Ammersattel.

Linderhof Castle*. – *Description p 167.*

Ettal. – The size of Ettal Abbey is astonishing when one considers the setting of Alpine solitude given to it by its founder, the Emperor Ludwig the Bavarian, in 1330. The veneration of a statue of the Virgin, attributed to Giovanni Pisano, and the blossoming of Benedictine life explain the dimensions of these buildings of which the church alone has preserved anything of archaeological interest. It is unique in Germany in having a Gothic polygon as foundation.

18C Baroque architects gave it its present aspect: Enrico Zuccalli, the façade and chancel (1710-26) and Joseph Schmuzer, stucco-master of the Wessobrunn school *(p 256)*, the cupola when the church was rebuilt after devastation by fire (1744). The cupola paintwork is by Johann-Jakob Zeiller.

The road drops rapidly on leaving Oberammergau into the Valley of the Loisach, some 200 m - 650 ft – below the Upper Basin of the Ammer. The Wetterstein chain now comes into view to the south with the summits of the Zugspitze, the Alpspitze – recognisable by its pyramidal shape – and the Dreitorspitze.

Garmisch-Partenkirchen*.** – *Description p 131.*

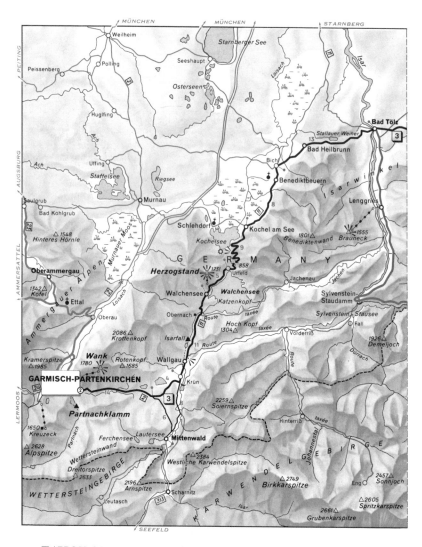

③ *FROM GARMISCH-PARTENKIRCHEN TO SCHLIERSEE
by way of the Walchensee and the Tegernsee
106 km - 66 miles – about 4 hours – Local map above

Leaving the mountains again, from which you have a good view of the Karwendel range, the road passes through the lake area. The Tegernsee and the Schliersee in the Alpine foothills, attract crowds of holidaymakers in contrast to the wild solitude of the Walchensee.

Garmisch-Partenkirchen*. – *Description p 131.*

Between Garmisch and Mittenwald a remarkable gorge in the Limestone Alps opens the way for a long straight road. The different chains of the Wetterstein, seen here from the side, present the unmistakable outlines of the Waxenstein and the Alpspitze. A wide shelf opens the way to the Mittenwald Plain, which is dominated by the jagged crests of the Karwendel (known as Westliche Karwendelspitze: alt 2 385 m - 7 825 ft), from which the whole massif between the Upper Isar and the Inn takes its name.

Alternative route* by Mittenwald. – *Extra distance: 10 km - 6 miles. Description p 180.*

After the pretty village of Wallgau, there is a wide **view*** from the top of a steep hill, to the south from left ro right, of the Karwendel, the Reitherspitze (seen through the Scharnitz gap), the twin summits of the Arnspitze, the regular crests of the Wettersteinwand, and the two blunted horns of the Dreitorspitze.

Isar Waterfall (Isarfall). – A road runs beside this cascade forming an alternative route to the modern road. The waterfall is made by a diversion of the waters of the Isar to the Wallgau Plain to increase the Walchensee hydro-electric reserves *(see below)* and my be dried up during periods of low water.

The **drive*** beside the Walchensee, cut by the Katzenkopf promontory, affords a view of the delightful village of Walchensee along the water's edge.

Walchensee*. – This intensely blue **lake*** framed by woods is one of the beauties of the Bavarian Alps on a sunny summer's day. Some isolated hotels at Urfeld and Walchensee, as well as camping sites along the banks attract nature lovers. Away from the excursion route, a small toll road runs along the southern bank *(3DM per car)* to Jachenau.

Since 1924 the Walchensee has served as the reservoir for the power station built along the Kochelsee, some 200 m - 600 ft – lower down. This arrangement, which makes use of a series of stepped installations, is one of the Federal Republic's most outstanding engineering constructions (installed power: 114 300 kW). It necessitated the diversion of the Isar by the little Valley of Obernach *(see Isar Waterfall)*, and in 1949, an underground diversion of the Rissbach whose works stand beside the Karwendel road near the Austrian frontier.

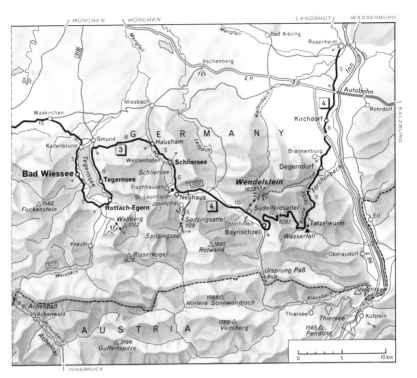

Herzogstand★★. – *Excursion of about 2½ hours Rtn, including 30 minutes in a chairhoist and 45 minutes walk (the hoist operates in season at least every ½ hour). Rtn fare: 6DM.* The Herzogstand chairhoist gives the visitor a view of the magnificent scenery of the Walchensee, the Karwendel and the Wetterstein.

From the upper station a ½-hour walk along an easy path brings you to the Herzogstand summit (belvedere) from where there is a **panorama**★★ over the Tauern heights (snowy summits of the Grossglockner and Gross Venediger, in clear weather), the Karwendel, the Tyrolean Alps of Stubai, and rock wall of the Wetterstein culminating in the Zugspitze on the extreme right. To the north, the view drops to the Kochelsee and the other great lakes in front of the Bavarian Alps, which are often shrouded in mist.

The far-off peaks of the Arnspitze and the Wetterstein can be seen rising in the distance above Urfeld. The road climbs to a small pass before descending through woods to the Kochelsee. During this winding descent, the Kesselbergstrasse, a bend furnished with a belvedere, some 1 500 yds from the pass, offers a view of the lake and Schlehdorf Abbey.

Kochelsee. – Originally the lake stretched as far as Benediktbeuern, as may be seen from the marshes which still extend from it northwards. A series of alternating bays and promontories at the foot of the wooded slopes of the Herzogstand account for its popularity with the holidaymakers who come to stay at Kochel am See. The Walchensee power station is on the shores of the lake (Walchenseekraftwerk – *details below*).

From Kochel to Benediktbeuern the road passes the buttresses of the Benediktenwand.

Benediktbeuern Abbey. – *Description p 62.*

The countryside is still pre-Alpine where it shelters the little spa of Bad Heilbrunn.

Bad Tölz★. – *Description p 244.*

Between Bad Tölz and the Tegernsee, the road passes the rising land of the Tegernsee, last foothills of the Bavarian Alps to the north of the chain. The rural countryside with birchwoods is not without charm.

The road circles the Tegernsee beside which are a number of holiday spots. The best views of the lake are to be had at the junction of the road with the west bank between Kaltenbrunn and Bad Wiessee. To the south, the massive summit of the Walberg blocks the view.

Bad Wiessee★★. – The thermal establishments and many hotels and pensions stand on their own beneath the shade of the avenues of Bad Wiessee which lies in cultivated green surroundings. The resort has developed exceptionally rapidly; it was only in 1909 that prospectors boring for oil, quite by chance struck iodised sulphur springs in what, until then, had been a quiet peasant village on the shores of the Tegernsee. The constant progress in spa equipment, particularly that for the treatment of rheumatism, heart and circulation disorders, together with the attraction of the semi-Alpine surroundings and the sporting and fashionable amusements have contributed to the expansion of the resort which is now one of the most elegant in Germany.

Rottach-Egern★. – The twin towns of Rottach and Egern have combined to take advantage of the tourist trade at the southern end of the Tegernsee, where the Weissach Valley starts – the usual way to and from the Austrian Achensee.

Tourists can add to the pleasure of a stay at this lakeside resort by ascending the Wallberg (alt 1 722 m - 5 814 ft). The summit (belvedere) can be reached either by cable-car or on foot from the end of a 4-mile mountain toll road.

Tegernsee Resort★. – The Benedictine monks, established in the 8C, possessed one of the richest abbeys of Bavaria. Tradition has it that the fathers of this monastery were from the original foundation of the same name in Munich. The Abbey, secularised in 1803 and partly transformed at that time into a pleasure residence by Maximilian I Joseph, has been known since then under the name of "Schloss". The north wing contains the "Bräustüberl", a branch of the Hofbräuerei of Munich. The castle walk (Schlosspromenade) affords tourists peace from the crowds.

Schliersee★. – *Description p 228.*

4 *FROM SCHLIERSEE TO ROSENHEIM by the Sudelfeld Road
50 km - 30 miles – about 1½ hours – Local map p 45

A gap in the Alpine Road between Tatzelwurm and Degerndorf compels the motorist to take a surfaced mountain road – not suitable for heavy traffic (toll: 2 DM per car). A single-lane tunnel in which the roadway has a gradient of 1 in 5½ needs considerable care. Tourists wishing to avoid this can follow the "family" route outlined on p 41.

Schliersee★. – *Description p 228.*

The traveller soon loses sight of the Schliersee, as the road passes into the Upper Valley of the Leitzach, dominated to the north by the hump of the Wendelstein surmounted by the antennae of the Bavarian television transmitter.

Neuhaus. – The 17C church, dedicated to St. Leonard, stands under its shingle roof alone at the side of the Alpine Road in a shaded site which enhances its rustic charm.

Spitzingsee. – *5 km - 3 miles – about ½ hour – from the Alpine Road.*
The road, climbing by a steep ramp up to the Spitzingsattel Pass, offers below the summit a **general view★** of the Fischhausen-Neuhaus Plain and of the Schliersee. The road ends shortly afterwards at the Spitzingsee, a small lake around which a mountain resort is developing. 3 km before Bayrischzell the road leads down to a station from where there is a cable-car up to Wendelstein.

Bayrischzell. – This attractive medium sized resort in a somewhat enclosed setting is well equipped to entertain winter and summer visitors.

Road to the Ursprung-Pass★. – *From Bayrischzell to Kufstein (customs formalities at the frontier), 28 km - 16 miles. Description in Michelin Green Guide Austria.*

The modern mountain road goes round Bayrischzell and rises by easy gradients above the town, clustered at the bottom of the valley. On the east side of the pass, known as the Sudelfeldsattel (alt 1 097 m - 3 599 ft) the road goes through a bare valley, which in winter is a popular skiing centre equipped with mountain hotels and mechanical hoists. Close by tower the crests of the Wilder Kaiser.

Tatzelwurm Waterfall. – *15 minute walk Rtn.* Leave the car in the Naturdenkmal Tatzelwurm car park 200 m before the temporary end of the new route of the Alpine Road. Take the wide scored path below the park, and, as you come out of the wood, a path to the right which leads to the falls.

Downstream from Tatzelwurm the road avoids the Förchenbach Gorges and descends by tunnel towards the Valley of the Inn. A little before Degerndorf, a road leads off to the left to the station from which there are trains up to Wendelstein.

Wendelstein★★. – *Excursion of about 4 hours Rtn, of which 2 hours is by the rack-railway and ¾ hour Rtn on foot starting from the lower station at the entrance to Brannenburg. Departures from the lower station between 9am and 3pm. Last train from the upper station at 5pm. Rtn fare: 18DM. Access to the summit of the Wendelstein also possible by cable-car (9am to 5pm) on this side of Bayrischzell. Rtn fare: 13DM. Combination train-cable-car-bus: 19DM.*
The rocky summit of the Wendelstein familiar to habitual users of the Munich–Salzburg motorway, is a popular viewpoint. Battling its way pluckily up a track that becomes steeper and steeper, the little train achieves an altitude of 1 738 m - 5 643 ft – near the Berghotel (not a hotel) and the Wendelsteinhaus (café-restaurant with limited sleeping accommodation). One can reach the summit by climbing steep footbridges past the Bavarian television buildings. On the summit are a solar observatory and a chapel built in 1718.

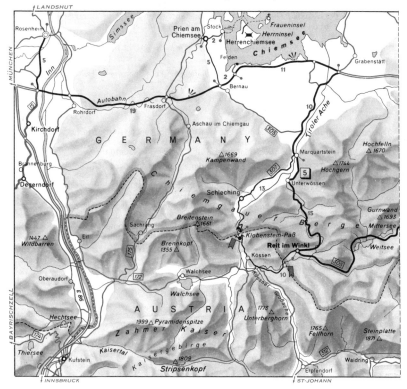

The **panorama**✶✶ is immense: from east to west are the mountains of the Chiemsee and the Berchtesgaden Alps, the Loferer and the Leoganger Steinberge, the Kaisergebirge and their lacework of stone, and the glacier crests of the Tauern Heights. In the plain below lies the Chiemsee.

Degerndorf. – At the entrance to the village, coming along the road from Tatzelwurm, are the fine two-storey country houses with wooden balconies common to the Inn valley.

Between Degendorf and Rosenheim lies the **Inn valley**, well farmed and dotted with slender church spires offering such attractive scenes as that of the church at Kirchdorf, surrounded by ornamental trees. To the south, the Kaisergebirge bar the horizon.

Degerndorf country house.

5 *FROM ROSENHEIM TO BAD REICHENHALL
by the south bank of the Chiemsee and the Alpine Road

110 km - 69 miles – about 3 hours – Local map below

On the Munich–Salzburg motorway is a view of the rocky slopes of the Kampenwand and the Chiemsee. This still lake, with its immense sheet of blue water, lies directly in front of you at the start of the **descent**✶✶. On a fine summer's day the whole countryside takes on a southern aspect. Out in the water are the two islands of Herrninsel and Fraueninsel.

Chiemsee✶. – *Regular boat services for Herrninsel, the most popular of the lake's islands, leave from the pier at Prien-Stock (Bernau exit from the motorway, 7 km by car). P 93.*

Leave the motorway at the Grabenstätt exit in the direction of **Marquartstein**, an attractive resort.

Travelling south towards the mountains, one comes to the beginning of the plain which marks the final opening out of the Tiroler Arche Valley, which runs down from the Kitzbühel Alps. Between Marquartstein and Reit im Winkl, leaving the main valley and therefore missing the beautiful countryside of the Schleching region *(recommended alternative route)*, the Alpine Road passes through a series of small winding valleys to come out just above the Reit Basin which widens out at the foot of the Zahmer Kaiser (the Kaisergebirge range).

Alternative route✶ by Schleching, the Klobenstein Defile and Kössen (through Austria). – *Extension of drive: 8 km - 5 miles.*

Klobenstein Defile. – *Description in Michelin Green Guide Austria.*

Reit im Winkl✶. – This attractive town includes some large modern **mountain houses✶**. The traditional Chiemgau Alpine farmhouse with a shingle roof weighed down with heavy stones and surmounted by a bell-turret may often be seen still in the surrounding countryside *(illustration p 30)*. The distinctive outline of the Zahmer Kaiser mountains stands out in the distance, and, further over to the left, the first cliff faces of the Wilder Kaiser.

Towards the east, the route follows a stark valley, with shallow pools of green-black water.

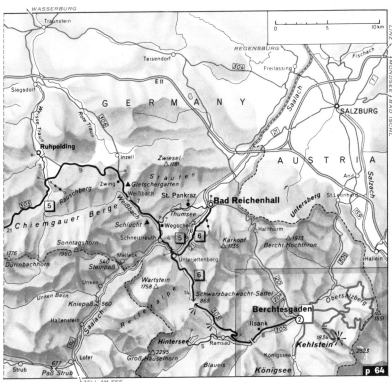

Ruhpolding★. – Ruhpolding, the most popular holiday centre in the Chiemgau Alps, is a place of stylish houses set in flower gardens, small waterfalls, a cableway to the Rauschberg, and walks in the "enchanted" forest (Märchenwald). The life of the town which has many associations with folklore and art, centres round the parish church of St. George.

Between the Valleys of the Weisse Traun and the Rote Traun the road comes to the open grazing lands of Aschenau, where there are views of the Ruhpolding Basin and the Hochfelln group, and on the other side, the Staufen chain whose highest point is the Zwiesel.

Gletschergarten. – $\frac{1}{4}$ *hour on foot Rtn from the Alpine Road.* This "garden of glaciers" forms a museum of glacial erosion. Below Gletschergarten, the waters of the Weissbach fall in graceful cascades.

Beyond the green Weissbach Basin lie the imposing **Weissbach Gorges**. The **steep parts★** of the road are especially impressive; right, of the bridges at Pfannloch and Höllenbach; downstream, of the Watzmann to the left of the Reiteralpe cliffs. The River Saalach, which you rejoin at Schneizlreuth, becomes steeply embanked before flowing out into the Reichenhall Basin.

Thumsee. – The lake, which lies off the main route, on the short cut from Wegscheid to Bad Reichenhall, is a favourite local spa. Downstream lies a marsh which has been transformed into an aquatic plants reserve and, perched high up, the Church of St. Pancras of Karlstein.

Bad Reichenhall★★. – *Description p 208.*

6 ★★FROM BAD REICHENHALL TO BERCHTESGADEN
by the Alpine Road
29 km - 18 miles – about 1 hour – Local map pp 46-47

Begin by taking road no 21 to get on to the Alpine Road, no 305. The road up to the Schwarzbachwacht Pass (alt 868 m - 2 848 ft) introduces a striking contrast between the severe wooded Valley of the Schwarzbach, dominated to the west by the escarpments of the Reiteralpe and pastures dotted with maples and the chalets on the Ramsau side. It is on these beautiful southern slopes that the road comes to an end. Several parking places by the roadside allow one to enjoy the **panoramas★★**: 1 400 m - 4 500 ft – below the pass (fountain) with its view of the saw edge of the Hochkalter framing the white patch of the Blaueis. This and the Höllentalferner in the Zugspitze Massif are the only glaciers in Germany whose crossing presents real dangers to climbers. To the left the Watzmann raises its heavy shape. 1 200 m further on, from a new belvedere set on a terrace in a curve, one can see as far as the Upper Ramsau Valley, dominated by the rock humps of the Reiteralpe. Two bends in the road bring one to the bottom of the valley.

Hintersee★. – *5 km - 3 miles – from the Alpine Road.* The lake, framed by the jagged peaks of the Reiteralpe and the teeth of the Hochkalter, is enjoyed for the beauty of its meadows and woods. The east bank and the "enchanted forest" (Zauberwald), which runs along its edge, and downstream, the shady river banks, are much appreciated by walkers.

Ilsank. – In the old pumping station, Brunnhaus, recognisable by its barrel-roof, the venerable machine constructed by the engineer, Georg von Reichenbach, worked from 1817 to 1927 pumping salt water through the special conduit from Berchtesgaden to Bad Reichenhall by way of the Schwarzbachwacht Pass. This monument to German technical achievement is today on view in the salt mines of Berchtesgaden *(p 63).*

ALSFELD ★
Michelin map 987 25 – Pop 17 800

The charm of Alsfeld lies in its many wooden houses and its picturesque Marktplatz.

■ SIGHTS *time: $\frac{1}{2}$ hour*

Marktplatz★. – The northeast corner of the square is picturesque with the Rathaus, the Weinhaus, recognisable by its stepped gable, and the church tower overlooking all. The surprising **town hall★** (1516), half-timbered above stone arcades that once served as market alleys, is decorated with twin turrets. Diagonally opposite stands the solid stone house with the double-storey corner oriel window (1565), which is known as the Wedding House (Hochzeitshaus). Its two gables, set at right angles, are a prime example of the height to which First Renaissance decoration in festoons and scrolls went in Germany.

Rittergasse. – This street, which opens into the square on the side facing the town hall, contains two of the most interesting **old houses★** in Alsfeld. The Neurath-Haus at no 3 is a very fine example of Baroque half-timbering, while the Minnigerode-Haus at no 5, built of stone, contains its original spiral staircase. This masterpiece of carpentry rises without any support from the walls, round a tall twisted tree trunk.

Church (Stadtkirche). – The church is early Gothic and has preserved its ancient furnishings. There are wooden galleries and, behind the altar on the left, a fine carved and painted panel of the Crucifixion between four scenes from the Life of Jesus.

The small square to the north of the church is made attractive by a house decorated with modern graffiti and a fountain above which stands a goosegirl in Schwalm costume. This costume was seen by the Brothers Grimm *(p 29)* around Alsfeld and

(After a photo by Erich Müller)

Alsfeld – The Marktplatz.

described by them as being worn by Little Red Riding Hood.

Behind the town hall, follow the Obere Fulder Gasse continuing on Untere Fulder Gasse, an amusing narrow street with crooked half-timbered houses; note also numbers 2-4 and 15-17.

EXCURSION

The Vogelsberg. – *Round tour 148 km - 98 miles – about 5 hours.* Leave Alsfeld by route no 62 (direction Bad Hersfeld) exit at Niederjossa and continue to Schlitz.

Schlitz. – This small town perched on a hill, has (16, 17 and 18C) half-timbered houses and four castles. From the keep of Hinterburg castle *(lift: 1DM, April to September, 9am to noon and 2 to 6pm)* is a splendid panorama of the verdant region.

Take the road through the charming town of Lauterbach, a pleasant town where large cattle markets are held.

Leave Lauterbach by the Frankfurt road. Soon, on the right, in the park in the valley below, the outlines of the majestic 16C **Eisenbach Castle** can be seen rising out of the trees. *To reach the castle, bear right into the avenue which crosses the railway and climbs the hill; visit the park, chapel and courtyard.*

Continue on road no 275 to Herbstein.

Herbstein. – *Extra distance: 5 km - 3 miles.* Fortifications surround this charming village made up of half-timbered houses as well as homes, commonly seen in the area, with façades covered with wood in the shape of fish scales.

Return towards Eisenbach, take a left turn upon reaching the railway line. The road climbs to the top of the Vogelsberg range, which is volcanic in origin and now much flattened.

Ulrichstein. – $\frac{1}{2}$ *hour on foot.* To reach the ruins follow the signs "Kriegsgräberstätte". A viewpoint affords a **panorama★** of the Wetterau Plain on whose horizon may be just seen the wooded slopes of the Taunus. To the east, the Mileseburg spur can be identified as the characteristic landmark of the Rhön heights *p 216).*

Turn and follow the signposts first to Schotten and then Hoherodskopf.

Hoherodskopf. – $\frac{1}{4}$ *hour on foot Rtn.* This hillock, one of the highest points of the massif (alt 763 m - 2 503 ft), affords a view of the plain and the Taunus. The tower is the Grosser Feldberg telecommunications tower.

Turn again: leave the approach road to the Taufstein-Hütte and drop sharply downhill on the left into a well designed panoramic road leading to Schotten.

Schotten. – On the square is a typical 16C town hall: with a turret and, on the façade, an oriel window. The 14C church houses, above the north portal, a lovely sculptured Adoration.

Turn right for Laubach. The hilly **drive★** through pastoral country is enchanting.

Laubach. – *Extra distance: 3 km - 2 miles.* Town enveloped by greenery. The 17 and 18C castle contains fine rooms with vaulted ceilings which have been arranged as a museum. *Closed temporarily.*

Return to Alsfeld by road no 276, then no 49 on the right.

ALTMÜHL Valley (ALTMÜHLTAL)

Michelin map **987** south of 26, 27

The Altmühl, 180 km long - 112 miles – is one of the few large tributaries entering the Danube on its left bank in Germany. It flows across the limestone plateaux of the Franconian Jura (Fränkische Alb) and joins the Danube at Kelheim. The valley, with its wide curves, affords a pleasant drive to the leisurely traveller well away from heavy traffic. The final section, which is more enclosed and sombre, will soon provide access to the large navigable waterway connecting the Rivers Main and Danube *(details p 104).*

FROM EICHSTÄTT TO KELHEIM
81 km - 50 miles – 2½ hours

Eichstätt★. – *Description p 112.*

The Altmühl Valley, scarcely noticeable at first, deepens beyond Arnsberg as it skirts castle crowned promontories.

Arnsberg. – The town lies massed at the foot of a cliff crowned by castle walls which, seen from a distance, appear almost to be part of the rock face.

Kipfenberg. – A huge fortified castle, rebuilt in 1925, is the village's main feature.

Riedenburg. – Marking the entrance to the last defile is the most developed resort in the valley, Riedenburg.

Hexenagger and **Altmannstein.** – *10 km - 6 miles from Riedenburg.* Hexenagger Castle appears as a solid white mass within its fortifications at the top of a mound commanding the Schambach Valley. The chapel belfry rises in slender silhouette above the main buildings. Continue to Altmannstein, an old picturesque village with moss-covered roofs, steep and winding streets crowded round a truncated keep.

Prunn. – 1½ *hours walking and sightseeing if one tours the castle, starting from Nusshausen.* The castle stands in a remarkable **setting★** on a promontory above vertical faces. *Castle interior open 9am to 6pm in summer (4pm in winter); closed Mondays in winter; 1DM.*

Kelheim. – *Description p 159.*

ALTÖTTING

Michelin map **987** 37, 38 – Pop 11 000

Altötting is the oldest and best known goal of pilgrimage in Bavaria. Veneration of the Virgin which has been fervently practised since the Middle Ages, brings 500 000 pilgrims each year to the town. The parish church, the Holy Chapel, and the Church of St. Mary Magdalene stand in the vast square where processions are held.

■ **SIGHTS** *time:* $\frac{1}{2}$ *hour*

Holy Chapel (Heilige Kapelle). – At the end of the 15C an oblong building was added to the existing Romanesque octagonal chapel; a little later arcaded galleries were built right round the church. Thousands of painted ex-votos cover the walls and ceilings of these arcades – the oldest dates from 1517 – to form a highly coloured background.

The miraculous Virgin stands in a silver niche on the altar in the octagonal chapel.

ALTÖTTING

Parish Church (Stiftskirche). – The **treasury** (Schatzkammer) of this late Gothic church is visited separately *(guided tours 1 March to 31 October, 10.15am, 1.30pm and 2pm; Sundays 9.30am to noon and 1 to 4pm; 0.50DM)*. The two most important exhibits are a very fine Flemish ivory Crucifix dating from 1580 and a masterpiece of French goldsmiths' work of 1392, a small gold horse. King Charles VI of France had been given the horse by his wife Isabel of Bavaria, but had pledged it for a loan to his brother-in-law, Ludwig the Bearded, Duke of Bavaria-Ingolstadt, who brought it back to Bavaria in 1413. The horse was added to the Altötting treasury in 1509.

Johann Tzerklaes, Count of Tilly (1559–1632), a general on the side of the Catholic League in the Thirty Years War *(p 20)*, lies buried in the crypt *(entrance through the cloisters)*.

AMBERG

Michelin map **987** 27 – Pop 50 000

Amberg has evolved around a beautiful old town which lies tightly packed within ramparts, still well preserved in their green setting. The town areas beyond the walls have developed from the important industrial undertakings associated with the nearby iron mines.

The most popular town sight is the **Stadtbrille** (town's pair of spectacles) which may be seen from the south from the Ring Bridge and from the north from the path alongside the Arsenal (Zeughaus): the twin arches of the fortified bridge, when reflected in the river below, form two perfect circles, evocative of a pair of spectacles.

Salesian Church* (Deutsche Schulkirche). – *Apply to the convent on the corner of the Deutsche Schulgasse.*

This Rococo church is covered with most graceful decoration largely executed by Amberg master craftsmen (1738-58). Original features of the church include the peculiar position of the altar niches flanking the triumphal arch and the organ loft in the shape of a shelf.

AMMERSEE *

Michelin map **987** 36, 37 – *Local map p 40*

This lake, at an altitude of 533 m - 1 749 ft – and of glaciary origin, lies 35 km - 22 miles – southwest of Munich in a beautiful setting surrounded by wooded slopes. Pleasant resorts such as Diessen and Herrsching border its shores and are extremely popular during the season with Munich citizens who come to enjoy the fishing, sailing and swimming.

You can go round the Ammersee by car. The road along the eastern shore passes through woodland and affords attractive glimpses of the green waters of the lake.

Visit Andechs Abbey *(description below)* from Herrsching.

AMORBACH *

Michelin map **987** 25 – *Local map p 217* – Pop 4 400

Two pairs of belfries rise above Amorbach as it stands, built on the eastern slope of the Odenwald at the meeting place of green tributary valleys of the River Main. The white towers with red masonry courses belong to the former abbey church. A visit to this church with its satisfactory proportions and relatively plain decoration will provide a pleasant surprise for those who criticise Baroque art as being too fanciful and ornate.

Former Abbey. – *Guided tours (every ½ hour) in English. Open 1 April to 31 October, 8am to noon and 1 to 6pm (5pm 1 November to 31 March). Sundays and holidays 11am to 6pm; 2DM.*

Abbey Church* (Abteikirche). – *Enter through the abbey buildings on the Schlossplatz.*

The church was built between 1742 and 1747 deferring in plan to the Romanesque church which had preceded it. The architect left standing the twin towers of the old façade but, nevertheless, covered the latter with a Baroque facing of sandstone.

The best view of the building as a whole inside is from below the organ loft. The absence of galleries and the pierced cradle vaulting (painted, as were all the upper parts of the church, by Matthäus Günther) make the roofing seem unusually low. A light and simple cornice runs beneath the glass bull's eyes that take the place of the usual tall windows. The most important church furnishings are the **chancel grille*** (Chorgitter), the Rococo pulpit and the organ, built in 1782 and well known for its rich tone *(concerts on Sundays during the season)*.

Abbey Buildings (Klostergebäude). – Of the original buildings, dating from the end of the 18C, there still exist the library and the green room (Grüner Saal), the more revealing example – and rare especially in a German abbey – of a chamber decorated in the Neo-Classical style *(p 26)*.

ANDECHS *

6 km - 4 miles – south of Herrsching (Michelin map **987** west of 37) – *Local map p 40* – Pop 1 128

Crowning the hill of the Holy Mount (Heiliger Berg), the Benedictine Abbey of Andechs dominates the wooded shores of the Ammersee from an altitude of some 200 m - 600 ft.

In the 12C the Counts of Andechs chose this precipitous place to build a fortress; during the struggle between the last of the counts and the Dukes of Bavaria, the fortress was almost completely destroyed, but the discovery in 1388 of important relics in the castle's chapel prompted the counts to invite the Benedictines to the site. The abbey prospered and the church became one of the most frequented pilgrimage centres of Upper Bavaria.

A brewery set up in the outbuildings of the abbey produces over 400 000 gallons of excellent beer each year.

Abbey Church* (Klosterkirche). – *Tour: ½ hour.* The architectural sobriety of the exterior gives no hint of the fine decorations inside. The originally Gothic church was Rococoised to its present form from 1751 to 1755. J B Zimmermann (1680-1758), then at the full height of his talent, was the artist of both the frescoes and the stuccoes – many details remind one of the Church at Wies. An elegant gallery, decorated with painted panels evoking the history of the abbey, goes entirely round the nave.

The lightness of the gilded and painted stuccoes counterbalance the impression of heaviness which the high altar and the altars of the chapels, crowned with statues and gilded Rococo woodwork, might give. The pastel tones of the stuccoes on the vaulting show the artist's skill in the arrangement of his colours. The Virgin in gilded wood standing above the high altar dates from 1500. St. Nicholas and St. Elizabeth of Thuringia, patrons of the Abbey, stand on either side. A second Baroque Virgin of 1609 stands at the upper high altar.

ANDERNACH

Michelin map 204 southwest of 13 – *Local map p 213* – Pop 29 000

Andernach, on the Rhine, is a mixture of the strongly mediaeval and the modern, epitomised in the viaduct built to carry road no 9 along the cliffs to the north of the town.

Old Quarter. – Leave the car outside the walls on the road beside the Rhine.

Enter the old town through the **Rheintor**, a fortified double gateway whose inner door is 12C; follow the Rheinstrasse (Baroque house on the left at no 4) and then bear left into the Hochstrasse. The street, which passes beside the Gothic church originally Franciscan and now Protestant, leads to the **castle ruins**. This was built in the 14 and 15C at the edge of the old quarter to defend the south entrance to the town. Go round the **ramparts** by the left to return to the car.

Parish Church (Pfarrkirche). – The beautiful twin towered façade is a fine example of the early 13C Rhineland style (transitional period from Romanesque to Gothic).

Round Tower. – Former watch-tower with an octagonal top.

ANSBACH

Michelin map 987 26 – *Local map p 217* – Pop 38 900

Ansbach, half mediaeval, half Baroque, is a peaceful Frankish town which owes its fame to the Hohenzollerns.

The margraves of the Frankish line of the House of Hohenzollern settled in Ansbach and Bayreuth as early as the 13C. Since then the two towns have often been associated in history as for example when the Ansbach-Bayreuth Dragoons fought under Frederick the Great.

The cultivated margravines of the 18C, one of whom was the sister of Queen Wilhelmina *(p 62)*, made the court life of Ansbach almost as brilliant as that of Bayreuth.

■ **SIGHTS** *time: 1 hour*

Castle* (Residenz). – *Open in summer, 9am to noon and 2 to 5pm; in winter, 10am to noon and 2 to 4pm; 1.50DM.*

This 14C castle was enlarged and transformed in the Frankish Baroque style by Gabrieli, architect to the Court of Vienna, and Retti, at the behest of the Margrave Wilhelm-Friedrich who reigned from 1703 to 1723.

The façade is impressive, having plain lines and simple decoration. The interior, which is symmetrical like most German Baroque palaces, is particularly remarkable for the princes' apartments (Fürstenzimmer): the **Porcelain Gallery**** (Fayencenzimmer) with some 2 800 Ansbach pottery tiles, lightly and delicately designed with rural motives; the **Room of Mirrors*** (Spiegelkabinett) with its exuberance of china ornaments and gilded woodwork; the Red Saloon with portraits of the Hohenzollerns; and the Gobelin Gallery with three tapestries woven after cartoons by Charles Le Brun.

The castle park extends away on the far side of the esplanade.

St. Gumpert's (St. Gumpert-Kirche). – This church, with its 16C Gothic chancel, was transformed in the 18C into a vast hall for preaching. Its particular feature is the Chapel of the Knights of the Order of the Swan (Schwanenritterordenkapelle – door on the left behind the altar), a lay order founded by the Elector of Brandenburg in 1440. Through the grille are the emblems and funerary monuments of the knights and a fine late 15C altarpiece of the Virgin in Glory.

AROLSEN

Michelin map 987 south of 15 – *Local map p 252* – Pop 16 000

Arolsen, formerly the residence of the Waldeck princes, is a small town whose regular plan testifies to its aristocratic origin. Lining the main street, cut halfway by the shaded church square, are houses each with a small gable in which the owners once used to be compelled to lodge a soldier, since the town had no barracks.

The Baroque castle stands at the eastern end of the main street.

Castle (Schloss). – *Open 1 May to 30 September, 9 to 11.30am and 2 to 4.30pm; 2DM.*

The palace, inspired by Versailles, was built between 1714 and 1728, although the decoration of the apartments was to continue until the beginning of the 19C. The result, inevitably, is that some of the rooms are in the Empire style.

A vestibule and double staircase, which with the Baroque Garden Chamber (Gartensaal) and Great Hall (Grosser Saal) form the state apartments, lead to further apartments decorated with stucco and painted ceilings (1715-19).

The Grosse Allee walk extends away from the castle and parallel to the main street.

ASCHAFFENBURG *

Michelin map 987 25 – *Local map p 217* – Pop 54 900

Town plan in Michelin Red Guide Deutschland

Aschaffenburg, which has grown up at the foot of the wooded Spessart hills above a bend in the River Main, has enchantingly beautiful parks, so that one well understands the Electors of Mainz in the 17C making it one of their residences.

■ **SIGHTS** *time: ½ hour*

Castle* (Schloss). – This huge Renaissance palace (1605-14), built for the Bishops of Mainz and known as the St-Johannisburg, is in the form of a hollow square quartered by lantern towers. The appearance of the inner courtyard is even more impressive with corner turrets matching the massive outer towers. Heavy Renaissance pediments with characteristic shell niches and the old castle keep, which was preserved, mask to some degree the steeply sloping roofs.

The interior *(open April to September, 9am to noon and 1 to 5pm; October to March, 10am to noon and 1 to 4pm; closed Mondays; 2DM; brochure in English)* consists of a picture gallery, a gallery of liturgical objects and the local museum.

Cross the castle garden (Schlossgarten) to reach the Pompeianum, a reconstruction of the house of Castor and Pollux at Pompeii, built by Ludwig I of Bavaria, on the bank overlooking the Main.

ASCHAFFENBURG★

Schöntal Park★. – The Electors established this park as a zoo in the 15C.

Church (Stiftskirche). – *To see the cloisters, the Chapel of Our Lady of the Snows and the treasury, apply to the sacristan and, if he is not in the church, to Stiftsgasse 1; 0.50DM.*

Well sited at the top of a monumental Baroque stairway, this Gothic church has a curiously asymmetrical appearance from the outside, due to the overshadowing peristyle which flanks the façade and north aisle. The tower was only completed in the 15C. The Romanesque west door with an interesting plant motif decoration is dedicated to Christ in Judgement. The nave with its rounded arches remains Romanesque in character but the major interest lies in the works of art – a painting, in a glass case, of *Christ's Sorrow* by Grünewald (1525), the praedella of an altarpiece now lost; a *Resurrection* by Cranach the Elder (1520) in the south transept; a *Crucifixion* of the same date in the north transept; a copy in the Chapel of Our Lady of the Snows of Grünewald's famous painting of the Virgin which was taken from the church in the 16C and is now at Stuppach *(p 178).*

The Romanesque cloister has 64 columns with a wide variety of deeply carved capitals.

EXCURSION

Schönbusch Park. – *3 km - 2 miles – off the Darmstadt road (branch off this and make for the park restaurant on the left), plus 1 hour sightseeing.*

In the centre of this shaded 18C park, laid out with ornamental pools, canals, islands and follies (Temple of Friendship), there stands a country house built in 1780 for the archbishops. It is decorated in the Empire style. *Open April to September, 8am to 1pm and 2 to 6pm; October to March, 10am to noon and 2 to 4pm; closed Mondays; 1DM.* The Chamber of Mirrors on the first floor affords a distant **view★★** of Aschaffenburg Castle and further off, of the Spessart.

AUGSBURG ★★

Michelin map 987 36 – Pop 250 000

Tacitus wrote of Augsburg that it was "the most outstanding colony in all the province of Rhaetia". Today this town on the Romantic Road *(p 217)* and near the Stuttgart–Munich motorway, reminds one attractively of life in the Renaissance period.

HISTORICAL NOTES

A Roman City. – The city, founded in 15 BC by a kinsman of the Emperor Augustus, is, with Trier and Cologne, among the most ancient in Germany. It became a trading centre on the highway to Italy, and, at the fall of the Roman Empire, an episcopal see. By the end of the 13C it was a Free Imperial City and the seat of the Diet.

The Fuggers. – At the end of the 15C, Augsburg which already counted 50 000 inhabitants became a centre of high finance and banking. This was due to the Fuggers and the Welsers, two local dynastic families who, it was said, shared the then known world between them, so far as money and trade were concerned. History has preserved the name of Jakob Fugger the Rich (1459-1525), renowned as the Empire's banker and even more as the financier of the Habsburgs. Charles V himself was even rebuked by this high personage: "It is well known that without my advice, Your Majesty would no longer wear the crown of the Holy Roman Empire." The debt of the Habsburgs to their Ausburg bankers has been estimated at 4 million ducats.

The Confession of Augsburg. – In 1530, Charles V, anxious at the growing strength of the Reformation in many of the states of the Empire, called an Imperial Diet at Augsburg in the hope of dissipating the religious disturbances. The Protestants, inspired by Luther, thereupon proclaimed in their Confession a statement of their belief. It has become the classic statement of Lutheran belief but was rejected at the time.

Only in 1555 under the Peace of Augsburg did the Protestants win freedom of worship. In 1686 the town again gave its name to an historical event: the Augsburg League, directed by Prussia and Austria against Louis XIV following the Revocation of the Edict of Nantes.

The Pine Cone. – This fruit, which appears on the city's arms, is an ancient symbol of fertility. The town flowered with artists and humanists: Holbein the Elder (d 1525), Hans Burgkmair (1473-1541), Martin Schongauer, and Konrad Peutinger. The "town of the German Renaissance" was created, so to speak, by the architect Elias Holl (1573-1646). The glory of Mozart, whose father came from Augsburg, has also left its imprint.

The 19C was marked by the production of the first Diesel engine (1893-7).

■ MAIN SIGHTS *tour: 1½ hours*

Cathedral (Dom). – The church was rebuilt in Gothic style in the 14C. Outside, look at the Gothic south door to the chancel or **Doorway to the Virgin★★** (Südportal des Chores) and the Romanesque bronze **panels★** (Türflügel) decorated with 32 low reliefs depicting scenes and characters from the Old Testament and mythology.

Inside, the tall nave is supported by double side aisles. The chancel on its east side has a double ambulatory with appended Gothic chapels; the four altars in the nave are adorned with **paintings★** (Gemälde) by Holbein the Elder (on the left: *Birth of the Virgin Mary* and *Entry into the Temple*). 12C **Windows of the Prophets★** (Prophetenfenster), rigid in style and surrounded by panes of alabaster, have been placed in the tall lights on the south side of the nave.

Follow by car the itinerary marked on the plan. After Müllerstrasse the route goes along an avenue which runs beside the moat and parallel to the old ramparts.

Fuggerei★. – This name was given to the quarter – a sort of enclosure – founded in 1519 by Fugger the Rich to house the town poor. The eight streets in the Fuggerei are lined by 66 gabled houses. It also has its own church and administration. Every evening the four gateways to the quarter are closed as they always have been. This social settlement, the first of its kind in the world, still receives citizens in need as it did in the 16C, charging them only a token rent but placing on them the moral obligation of praying for the souls of the founders.

Town Hall (X R). – This huge Renaissance building is by Elias Holl. Two towers frame the pediment adorned with a pine cone; that on the left, the Perlach Tower (X A) was originally a Romanesque watch-tower. It was re-modelled in the 17C. When the Alps can be seen from its summit a yellow flag is flown.

Maximilianstrasse*. – This street, lined by private houses and mansions built by the richer burghers of Augsburg during the Renaissance, provides one of the most majestic vistas today of old Germany. Decoration is provided by three bronze Renaissance fountains.

St. Ulric and St. Afra*. – This former Benedictine abbey on to which has been built the Protestant church of the same name, was founded at the end of the 15C by Maximilian I and refitted in the 17C. The high central part of the building, separated from the three aisles by a fine Baroque grille, strikes one immediately on entering. The caissoned vaulting is well lit by large windows at whose base stand three Baroque altars: in the chancel, the Altar of the Nativity; to the right, the Altar of the Resurrection and to the left the Pentecostal Altar. At the transept crossing is a bronze group of the Crucifixion dating from 1607.

Among the north side chapels that to St. Simpert has a balcony topped by **statues of the saints*** in terracotta and a Gothic baldachin. Note also, above the pulpit the sounding board supported by the two angels.

The juxtaposition of two churches, one Catholic the other Protestant, both with the same name, is characteristic of Augsburg. The churches of the Holy Cross (X D) are another example.

AUGSBURG
CENTRE

0 ___ 300 m

Afrawald	Y 2	Katharinengasse	Y 22	
Annastraße	XY 3	Königsplatz	Y 23	
Bahnhofstraße	Y 4	Lechhauser Straße	X 25	
Barfüßertraße	X 5	Leonhardsberg	X 26	
Bürgermauer-Fischer-Straße	Y 6	Ludwigstraße	X 28	
Dominikanergasse	Y 8	Margaretenstraße	Y 29	
Franziskanergasse	X 10	Maximilianstraße		
Fuggerstraße	Y 12	Milchberg	Y 31	
Grottenau	X 13	Mittlerer Graben	X 32	
Haunstetter Straße	Y 14	Mittlerer Lech	X 33	
Hoher Weg	X	Müllerstraße	X 34	
Jakoberstraße	X 15	Oberer Jakobermauer	X 35	
Karlstraße	X	Pilgerhausstraße	X 37	
Karolinenstraße	X 18	Rathausplatz	X 38	
		Stephingerberg	X 40	
		Unterer Graben	X 41	
		Vorderer Lech	X 42	
		Volkhartstraße	X 43	
		Weite Gasse	X 44	
		Wintergasse	Y 45	

ADDITIONAL SIGHTS

St. Anne's (X B). – This church was formerly part of the Carmelite monastery in which Martin Luther found sanctuary when he came to Augsburg in 1518. The Flamboyant Gothic architecture contrasts with the Rococo stucco work and frescoes.

The **Fugger funeral chapel*** (Fuggerkapelle), dating from 1518, is considered as the first example of the Italian Renaissance style in Germany. Blind arcades at the back of the chapel frame four sculptured scenes (centre, above the recumbent figures: the Resurrection and Samson Wrestling with the Philistines after Dürer, and on the sides, the Fugger arms from which the fleur-de-lys is reproduced on the pavement). There are two paintings by Cranach the Elder – *Jesus, the Friend of Little Children* at the high altar and a portrait of *Martin Luther*.

The Goldsmiths' Chapel (Goldschmiedekapelle), on the north side of the chancel, has kept its Gothic plan and late 15C wall paintings.

Fine Arts Gallery (Städtische Kunstsammlungen). – *Entrance Maximilianstr. Open 1 May to 30 September 10am to 5pm (4pm 1 October to 30 April); closed Mondays; 1 DM.*

The Schaezler Palace galleries, through which one passes first, display the master works of the German Baroque period (Deutsche Barock-Galerie) (Y M¹). The vast **banqueting hall**** (Festsaal) has a ceiling lavishly decorated with Rococo frescoes and similar wall panelling.

Communicating with the first, a gallery (Staatsgalerie Augsburg) (Y M²) contains works by the 15 and 16C Swabian and Augsburgan masters including a votive painting of the *Schwarz family* by Hans Holbein the Elder and the famous portrait of *James Fugger the Rich* by Dürer.

Maximilian Museum (X M³). – *Same times of opening as the Fine Arts Gallery.*

Reconstructions of olden times in Augsburg; Swabian sculpture and Augsburg gold and silversmiths' work.

Mozart's Father's House (Mozarthaus) (X M⁴). – *Open weekdays 10am to noon and 2 to 5pm (4pm Fridays); closed Saturday and Sunday afternoons and Mondays; 0.50DM (free Sundays and holidays). Guided tours in English every hour.*

Exhibits emphasise the Swabian origins of the Mozart family and the artistic heritage which was to benefit the young prodigy.

Red Gate (Rotes Tor) (Y). – A fortified 16C group of buildings with two vaults and a central courtyard which was remodelled by Elias Holl in 1622. The tower overlooking the town is circled by bands of decoration between the engaged pillars. An open air theatre has been laid out at the foot of the tower (opera).

BACHARACH ★

Michelin map **204** 15 – *Local map p 212* – Pop 2 900

Bacharach, one of the most famous villages in the Rhine Valley, is still overlooked by picturesque towers which rise above the surrounding vineyards.

Leave the car on the road beside the Rhine, outside the ramparts and opposite the landing quay, and enter the town through a gateway. From the gate, go up on the right to the covered parapet walk which leads to the houses. The view from the level of the railway lines is unusual.

Markt★. – The square is a delight with its flower decked half-timbered houses.

The Blücherstrasse, on the right of the Protestant Church, is lined with picturesque half-timbered houses, among them the baker's house with maxims carved into the beams.

St. Peter's (Peterskirche). – *Open June to September, 8.30am to 6pm*. The Romanesque nave, one of the last to be built in Germany, already reflects French Gothic design. The aisles are unusual, having hanging keystones. Follow the stepped path which runs beside the ruins of the Gothic Chapel of St. Werner to the Burg Stahleck.

Burg Stahleck. – This old fortress has been rebuilt. Go past the youth hostel and bear left into a rocky path which leads to a belvedere tower from which you get one of the best **views★★** of the Valley of the Rhine. Return by the same path bearing right for the post office.

Post Office Square★ (Posthof). – Charming group: view of the St. Werner Chapel.

BADEN-BADEN ★★★

Michelin map **205** 3 – *Local map p 81* – Pop 48 000

Baden-Baden, which lies in a sheltered area in the Oos Valley between the Black Forest and the Baden vineyards, is one of the most luxurious resorts in Germany. International conferences are often held in the town which is also a meeting place for statesmen and politicians.

Spa and Casino. – In Roman times the Emperor Caracalla came to Baden-Baden to cure his rheumatism; in the 12C the town became the seat of the Zähringen branch of the Margraves of Baden; in the 16C the great Paracelsus, one of the first to use chemical products and so a founder of modern pharmacy, came to look after the Margrave. In the 19C the town became the summer capital of Europe: a casino was opened by the Frenchman Jacques Bénazet, a born businessman; opera was inaugurated in 1862 with Berlioz's *Beatrice and Benedict* conducted by the composer; the Iffezheim racecourse, in the plain, was organised by the Paris Jockey Club.

The **Kurhaus** (AY), built in 1821 and typical with its portico and white Corinthian columns, contains rooms where glittering balls and concerts are held and gaming rooms. The other building in the spa park (Kurgarten) is the **Pump Room** (Trinkhalle) with a gallery (1842) with decorative wall paintings of the legends of the Baden-Baden countryside.

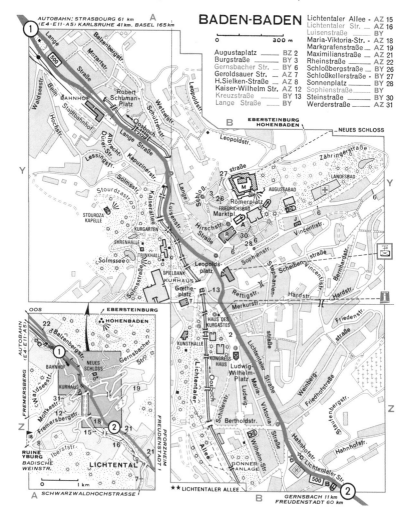

BADEN-BADEN

Augustaplatz	BZ 2
Burgstraße	BY 3
Gernsbacher Str.	BY 6
Geroldsauer Str.	AZ 7
H.Sielken-Straße	AZ 8
Kaiser-Wilhelm Str.	AZ 12
Kreuzstraße	BY 13
Lange Straße	BY

Lichtentaler Allee	AZ 15
Lichtentaler Str.	AZ 16
Luisenstraße	BY
Maria-Viktoria-Str.	AZ 18
Markgrafenstraße	AZ 19
Maximilianstraße	AZ 21
Rheinstraße	BY 22
Schloßbergstraße	BY 26
Schloßkellerstraße	BY 27
Sonnenplatz	BY 28
Sophienstraße	BY
Steinstraße	BY 30
Werderstraße	AZ 31

■ **SIGHTS** *time: 2 hours*

Lichtentaler Allee**. – This, the most beautiful promenade in Baden-Baden, runs beside the Oos which here flows over an artificial bed. The history of this promenade, scene of many major international political encounters, is spiced with many strange incidents: a Duke of Hamilton, to win a bet, led a calf along it on a blue riband; Edward, Prince of Wales, draped in sheets rode along it, to attend a ghost party. Queen Victoria and Bismarck, Napoleon III and Eugénie rode along it. The attempt on the life of the King of Prussia in 1861 took place within its shades.

The promenade, originally planted with oak trees, has since acquired azaleas, magnolias, maples and silver poplars, tulip trees, Chinese ginkgos, etc. On the left, beyond the swimming pool, is the **Gönneranlage** (BZ), where pergolas and fountains flank a rose garden.

New Castle (Neues Schloss). – Access by car from the Gernsbacher Strasse and then the Zähringerstrasse (east on the plan). *Apply in advance to the castle administration.* ☎ 2 55 93. *Open Mondays to Fridays; 0.30DM.*

The castle, built by the Margraves of Baden at the time of the Renaissance, has been partly transformed into the **Zähringen Museum***. *Guided tours Easter to 31 October at 3pm, closed Saturdays; 3DM. Brochure in English.* The collections include paintings – Cranach and Stimmer – porcelain and china, gold and silver plate and mementoes of Ludwig the Turk *(p 205)*.

From the terrace overlooking the town, view with the Stiftskirche in the foreground.

Church (Stiftskirche) (BY A). – The funerary monument of Ludwig the Turk, overloaded with trophies (1754), stands in the chancel.

St. Joseph's (BZ B). – This church (1961), is oval in plan with a separate campanile.

Roman Baths. – *Beneath the Römerplatz. Guided tours April to October, 10 to 11.30am and 2.30 to 5pm; closed Mondays; 1DM.* The underground heating system is interesting.

EXCURSIONS

Yburg Ruins. – *6 km - 4 miles – about ½ hour – by the Fremersbergstrasse* (AZ) *and the Yburg road (fork left after the bus stop Golf-Hotel) plus ¼ hour to climb the tower (115 steps).*

Vast **panorama**** over the Rhine Plain with the Baden vineyards in the foreground.

Hohenbaden Ruins (or Altes Schloss) (AZ); **Ebersteinburg Castle.** – *Round tour of 13 km - 8 miles – about ½ hour. Leave by the Zähringerstrasse* (BY) *and the Hohenbaden road, north on the map. Return from Ebersteinburg directly by the Gernsbach road.*

The parapet walk of the old castle of Hohenbaden commands the town and valley. Climb the Ebersteinburg keep *(access: 0.30DM)* next to see the Black Forest foothills.

Tour of the Baden Vineyards and the Black Forest Heights*. – *Round tour of 75 km - 47 miles – about 3 hours (the roads through the vineyard villages are winding and require careful driving).*

Leave Baden-Baden by the Fremersbergstrasse (AZ) and follow the signposts of the Baden Wine Road (Badische Weinstrasse) with its many turns as it leads from village to village through the vineyards of the first foothills of the Black Forest.

At the bottom of a hill at Altschweier, leave the Wine Road to turn first right then left, to approach Bühl. At the entrance to the town bear left to climb, by way of Kappelwindeck, to Altwindeck Castle.

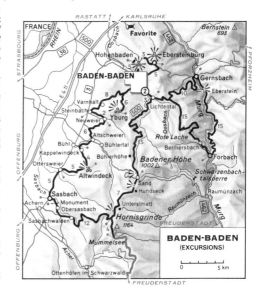

BADEN-BADEN (EXCURSIONS)

0   5 km

Altwindeck Castle. – This old castle, built on a circular plan, has been transformed into a restaurant with panoramic views. From its precincts (go towards the commemorative monument) there is a wide **view*** of the plain.

Turn the car and immediately bear left, dropping down steeply towards Ottersweier where you take road no 3 on the left as far as Sasbach.

Sasbach. – *¼ hour on foot Rtn.* Leave the car opposite the Linde Hotel and walk into the park which surrounds the Turenne monument. An obelisk and stele with inscriptions in French, German and Latin mark the spot where a fatal bullet ended Turenne's career in 1675.

Turn round and after 200 yds bear right for Obersasbach, then left to reach the delightful village of Sasbachwalden. The road, which is picturesque, then climbs towards the crest of the Black Forest. Turn right into the Hochstrasse and follow it as far as Mummelsee *(p 81)*. Return from there to Baden-Baden along the Hochstrasse *(description p 80)*.

Murg Valley. – *Round tour of 46 km - 29 miles – about 2 hours – local map above.* Leave Baden-Baden by ②, the Gernsbach road, which you later leave on your left to reach the Rote Lache Pass – an outing popular with people taking the cure.

The road, which is very hilly, drops down from the pass to Forbach in the Murg Valley.

Forbach. – The 18C covered wooden bridge is the pride of the town.

Gernsbach. – *Tour ¼ hour.* Go into the old town on the left bank of the Murg. The old **town hall*** (Altes Rathaus) stands in the quiet Marktplatz, a 17C building crowned with gables ornamented in German Renaissance taste with volutes and pinnacles. To return once more following the river upstream, but without crossing it, take the uphill road on the right laid out above the valley skirting the promontory, and crowned by Eberstein Castle.

55

BADENWEILER ★

Michelin map **205** 18 – *Local map p 84* – Pop 4 000

Badenweiler is built on a hillside within sight of the Rhine Plain and the Vosges, where a valley in the southern part of the Black Forest opens out finally. The spa's open **setting★** is embellished with orchards and vineyards. Rheumatism, circulatory and respiratory disorders are treated.

Leave the car at the entrance to the town (obligatory car parks).

Spa Park★★ (Kurpark). – The rolling parkland abounds in beautiful trees – cedars and cypresses encircle the music pavilion, enormous sequoias stand beside the pool. Within the park also are important remains of Roman baths and the castle ruins.

Castle Ruins (Burgruine). – From the ruins there is a **panorama★** of the resort and also of the Rhine Plain and the Vosges.

EXCURSION

Blauen★★; Bürgeln Castle★. – *Round tour of 43 km - 27 miles – about 2½ hours.* Leave Badenweiler by the Blauenstrasse; after 5 km - 3 miles – turn right towards Blauen.

Blauen★★. – ¼ *hour on foot Rtn.* From the belvedere-tower *(0.30DM)* rising out of the woods at the top of the hill, there is a remarkable **panoramic view★★** of the Rhine Plain – the two parallel ribbons of the Rhine and the great Alsatian Canal can easily be distinguished – and the rounded Vosges Mountains. The bare round summit to the northeast is the Belchen. The Swiss Alps can be seen on a clear day. Turn and make first for Marzell and then Kandern. At the entrance to the latter, bear right towards Badenweiler, turning a further twice to the right. Three miles beyond Kandern leave the Obereggenen–Müllheim road on your left; at the crossroads one mile further on, turn right into the Bürgeln Castle road.

Bürgeln Castle★. – *Guided tours, 1 February to 30 November 10.15am (10am Sundays) to 11am and 2.45pm (2pm Sundays) to 5pm; closed Tuesdays; 2DM. Brochure in English.* This gentleman's residence, set in a carefully tended terrace garden, was built in 1762 for the abbots of St. Blasien. It overlooks the last undulations of the Black Forest enclosed in the elbow formed by the Rhine at Basle and also several stretches of the river and the city of Basle itself.

Inside are beautiful stuccoes in the Rococo style.

Turn and take the road that goes through Sehringen to return to Badenweiler.

BAMBERG ★★

Michelin map **987** 26 – Pop 73 400

Bamberg is a beautiful cathedral city whose art treasures have been spared by war. The most brilliant of those who helped to create it were the sculptor Riemenschneider and the Dientzenhofer Brothers, architects of the Baroque area of the town.

Among Bamberg's gastronomic specialities are carp prepared to a local traditional recipe, small Frankish sausages and "smoky beer" (Rauchbier).

General view. – Go up to the former Benedictine Monastery of St. Michael at the top of the hill; walk left round the buildings to the terraces for a **view★** (Y E) of the episcopal quarter overlooking the lower town where the burghers lived and traded.

HISTORICAL NOTES

Bamberg was founded as early as the 10C by the Counts of Babenberg, who gave them their name. It owes most to the Emperor Heinrich II, the Saint (1002-24), who added to its status of imperial residence that of a flourishing episcopal town.

From the 12C onwards, as with all episcopal towns, the clergy, established in the upper town, pressed their authority and came into conflict with the burghers who had settled in the valley, on the island round the Grüner Markt and in the Sand quarter. The quarrel ended in the 16C with the bishops prevailing. Gradually the division healed and the 18C found both quarters building impartially in the new Baroque style.

Cathedral – The Knight.

■ **MAIN SIGHTS** *tour: 1½ hours*

Old Residence (Alte Hofhaltung). – *The courtyard closes at nightfall.*
This former episcopal and imperial palace has a façade which includes carved gables, oriels and corner turrets and a doorway dating from the Renaissance. The beautiful **inner courtyard★★** (Innenhof) is encircled by half-timbered Gothic buildings with steeply pitched roofs cut by dormer windows, and picturesquely ornate wooden balconies.

Walk down a covered passage facing the entrance to reach a small square surrounded by the old houses of former canons. The Domstrasse on the left brings you back to the Domplatz.

Cathedral★★ (Dom). – The cathedral, Transitional Gothic in style, is characterised by two apses: the one to the east, the oldest, stands raised upon a terrace with a fine balustrade, its cornices worked in a chequered pattern; the western apse is entirely Gothic.

The finest of the cathedral's entrances is the Princes' Doorway on the Domplatz. Ten recessed orders rest alternately on fluted, ribbed or squared columns or on telamones representing the prophets and the apostles.

Enter the church by the north transept door. Inside from left to right note the evolution from Romanesque to Gothic architectural styles. At either end of the church the two chancels are raised appreciably through crypts having been built beneath them.

The cathedral contains many masterpieces of German Gothic sculpture.

(1) Equestrian statue of the "**Knight of Bamberg**"*** (Bamberger Reiter). This 13C representation of a knight-king symbolises an idealised Middle Ages *(illustration p 56)*.

(2) Famous statue group of the Visitation; note the face of St. Elizabeth.

(3) The **tomb***** of Heinrich II, the Saint, and Kunigonde (St. Heinrichs-Grab) stands in the centre of the nave. Tilman Riemenschneider *(p 263)* took fourteen years to complete the tomb.

The following scenes may be identified: Kunigonde's ordeal by fire under suspicion of adultery; Kunigonde's dismissal of dishonest workmen; the death of the Emperor Heinrich II; the weighing of Heinrich's soul before St. Lawrence; the Emperor being operated on miraculously for gall-stones by St. Benedict.

(4) Altarpiece of the Nativity (1523) by Veit Stoss *(p 197)*.

(5) Funerary statue of a bishop.

(6) Statue representing the Church.

(7) Statue of a blindfolded older woman symbolising the Synagogue.

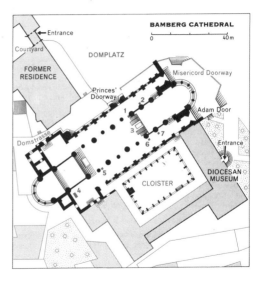

Leave the cathedral by the Adam Door, decorated with diamond and dog-tooth carving (the statues are in the diocesan museum). Go along the Karolinenstrasse to the old lay town.

Old Town Hall* (Altes Rathaus). – This strange building which stands alone on an island was remodelled in the 18C. In addition to the town hall proper, with its façades painted with *trompe l'œil* frescoes, there is, on the left, a monumental Rococo doorway and the Häuslein, a small timbered house balanced on one of the bridge's pierheads. From the Untere Brücke, the bridge at the lower end of the island, there is a good view of the old fishermen's houses bordering the Regnitz.

Returning to the Domplatz, notice the statues of the Virgin on house corners.

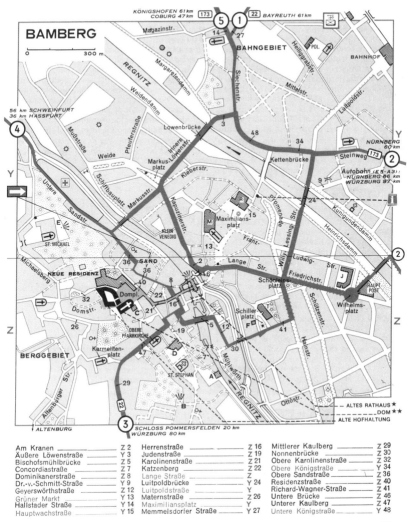

■ ADDITIONAL SIGHTS

Upper town

Diocesan Museum★ (Z C). – *Open May to October, 10am to noon and 3 to 6pm; Sundays and holidays, 10am to 1pm; 1DM.*

The collections include lapidary remains (statues of Adam and Eve which gave their name to one of the cathedral doorways – *see above*) and the pontifical vestments.

New Residence (Z). – *Open 9am to noon, 1.30 to 5pm (4pm 1 October to 31 March); 2DM.*

The palace, the largest edifice in Bamberg, consists of four main buildings; two, lining the Obere Karolinenstrasse, were constructed at the beginning of the 17C and are Renaissance, and two around the Domplatz are Baroque, built by Leonard Dientzenhofer in 1695.

The Imperial Apartments on the second floor overlook the square and are amongst the finest in the Residence with beautiful parquet floors, Baroque furniture and authentic Gobelin tapestries. The Emperors' Hall is outstanding for its allegorical frescoes and portraits.

View of the 4 Churches★ (**Vierkirchenblick**) (Z B). – This viewpoint embraces in a single glance the spires and belfries of four typical churches: St. Michael, the Cathedral, the Parish Church (Obere Pfarrkirche) and St. Stephen.

Along the banks of the Regnitz

Böttinger Palace★ (**Böttingerhaus**) (Z D). – This, the finest Baroque mansion in the town, was inspired by a Venetian palace and built in 1713. The overpowering decoration of the windows, cornices and doorways is amazing in this quarter of narrow streets. The terraced gardens can be reached from any storey of each of the three wings.

Concordia House★ (Z A). – This mansion was built on the banks of the Regnitz in 1716 as the summer residence of the Councillor Böttinger. The elegant façade, together with its reflection, can best be seen from the quayside (Mühlwörth).

ETA Hoffmann's House (Z F). – *Open 1 April to 31 October from 4.30 to 5.30pm on weekdays and from 9.30 to 10.30am on Saturdays, Sundays and holidays; 1DM.*

This house occupies a special position in the places with which Hoffmann was associated, and which his tales of fantasy have made famous. He lived here from 1808 to 1813, in two small rooms one above the other, communicating through a square opening. This allowed the poet, sitting beneath the eaves, to talk and joke with his wife in the room below. It was here that he composed one of his most successful tales, the *Golden Pot (der Goldene Topf)*.

EXCURSIONS

Pommersfelden Castle★ (or **Weissenstein Castle**). – *20 km - 12 miles – about 1 hour – (Guided tours 1 April to 31 October 9, 10, 11am and 2, 3, 4pm; 3DM. Brochure in English).*

Leave Bamberg by ③, the Würzburg road. After 7.5 km - 5 miles – turn off road no 22 for the Pommersfelden Castle road on the left. It goes by way of Oberndorf.

The castle is one of Germany's outstanding examples of a Baroque palace. A rapid tour *(1.50DM)* includes the **well★** of the three storey staircase *(illustration p 25)* – the painting on the ceiling shows the Olympian Gods (Apollo's chariot) and the four quarters of the globe.

On the ground floor a room opening on the garden perpetuates a Renaissance tradition in its Rococo "grotto decoration". To the right a room has false relief paintings of Samson destroying the Temple. The marble hall on the first floor with stuccoed pillars has two gilded medallions on the chimney breasts showing the Forge of Vulcan and the Siege of Troy.

A longer tour *(time: 1 hour; 3DM)* includes, in addition, the Elector's Apartments (Bishop of Bamberg and Archbishop of Mainz) with their small painting gallery and room of mirrors.

Altenburg. – *2.5 km - 1½ miles – by the Altenburger Strasse (southwest on the plan).* Former castle of the bishops of Bamberg *(open 1 April to 30 September 9am to 6pm; 1 October to 31 March 10am to 3pm, closed Mondays)*; the keep *(access: 0.50DM)* commands a good **view★** of Bamberg and the surrounding countryside.

BANZ Abbey

Michelin map **987** 26 – 31 km - 19 miles – north of Bamberg

Banz is the holy mountain of Franconia. The abbey towers which look down the Valley of the Main are balanced by Vierzehnheiligen Church, built on the opposite slope.

The Franks, having subdued the Thuringian tribes at the Battle of Unstrut in 531, settled in the region and introduced it to the **cult of St. Denis,** protector of the Merovingian dynasty and patron of the French abbey near Paris.

In 1120, Bishop Otto of Bamberg declared the martyr-saint patron of the abbey.

Abbey. – *Tour: ½ hour.* The monumental Baroque buildings of Banz are best seen as a group from the edge of the woods on the slopes above the abbey. Today part of the buildings constructed between 1698 and 1772 have been converted into an old people's home.

Abbey Church (Klosterkirche). – *Open 8am to 6pm (7pm 1 April to 30 September).*

The building was completed in 1719 to the plans of Johann Dientzenhofer. Among the statues adorning the façade is that of St. Denis. Inside, the complexity of the roofing is bewildering: the principal dome ends in two niches framing a central spindle-shaped space. The massive beams, also out of true and ending in keys, emphasise the virtuosity of design.

The pierced baldachin above the high altar frames, 45 ft away, at the end of the former chancel, an 18C picture of St. Denis setting out from Montmartre on his miraculous march.

Terrace. – This affords a **view★** of the Main Valley and Vierzehnheiligen Church *(p 251)*.

The BAVARIAN FOREST ★ (BAYERISCHER WALD)

Michelin map **987** 27, 28

Along the border of Bavaria and Bohemia (Czechoslovakia), the crystalline massifs of the Bavarian Forest (Bayerischer Wald) and Oberpfälzer Wald darken the horizon with their endless fir and spruce trees. The region, whose highest point, 1 456 m - 4 777 ft – is at the Grosser Arber, attracts visitors with simple tastes who enjoy solitude. The frontier, being part of the Iron Curtain, should be approached circumspectly, or better still, avoided until excursions to Czechoslovakia are again possible *(border posts: see Michelin map no* **987***)*. For car drivers there is the great crosscountry road, the **Bayerische Ostmarkstrasse★** between Bayreuth, Marktredwitz and Passau which also allows one to make the excursion to the summit of the Arber.

FROM BAYREUTH TO WEIDEN

110 km - 68 miles – about 2½ hours drive – Local map p 61

Approaching Weiden from the north, an indirect route from Bayreuth would be, along the Fichtelgebirge road (no 303), and at Marktredwitz – starting point of the Ostmarkstrasse – road no 15 with detours to Luisenburg *(p 169)*, Waldsassen *(p 253)* and Flossenbürg.

Flossenbürg. – *Excursion of 14 km - 8 miles – starting from Neustadt an der Waldnaab – about 1 hour.*

At the top of Flossenbürg town, turn left at a pass and leave the car near a hut where the wide road to the castle begins. The Flossenbürg ruins lie in separate groups on a granite **rock***. The upper town *(steps up)* commands a **view*** of the low hills of the Oberpfälzer Wald.

A concentration camp existed on the plateau during the 1939-1945 War (memorial chapel).

FROM WEIDEN TO PASSAU by the Ostmarkstrasse and the Grosser Arber

215 km - 134 miles – about 1 day – Local map below

The climb, which begins after Weiden, affords a vast panorama of the Waldnaab Valley.

Leuchtenberg. – *Excursion of 2 km - 1 mile – from the Ostmarkstrasse.*

Leave the car at the church approach and walk up to the castle *(apply to the caretaker – Winter, house no 3 in town – 0.40DM)* – apartments, the chapel which still has its roof, the keep (restored) on massive foundations. **Views** of the rolling countryside.

The approach to Tännesberg, particulary the **view*** of Leuchtenberg crowded round its castle is picturesque.

Alternative route* by Trausnitz. – *Extra distance 12 km - 7 miles – see map below*

Rabenleite Reservoir* (Hochspeicher). – This strange hollow at the top of a hill holds water for the Reisach power station. When not naturally full water is piped from the Reisach dam (Reisach Stausee), partly visible 180 m - 600 ft – below. Views from the circular dyke and the belvedere tower of the tiered village of Tännesberg and Leuchtenberg Castle.

Trausnitz. – A remarkably situated village and castle overlooking a bend of the Pfreimd.

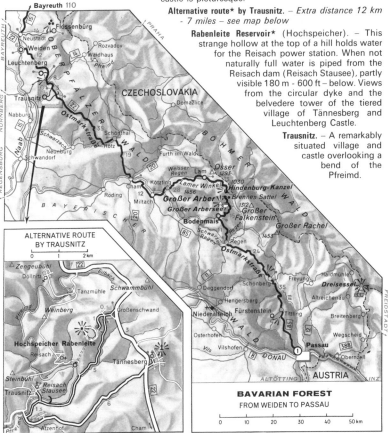

BAVARIAN FOREST
FROM WEIDEN TO PASSAU

Tännesberg. – From the top of the hill against which the village is built *(access: ½ hour on foot Rtn from the church, along a difficult path cut as a Stations of the Cross ending in a Calvary)*, a good view of Leuchtenberg castle and the Rabenleite reservoir. The Oberpfälzer Wald around **Oberviechtach** is green with birches and pines. The road circles the Arber range by the north, going up the Weisser Regen Valley, overlooked ahead by the Osser spikes.

Lam. – Lam is an attractive mountain resort set in an open valley. The road rises through the Lamer Winkel combe to the mountainside and ends at the Brennes Sattel (1 030 m - 3 379 ft).

Hindenburg-Kanzel*. – **Belvedere*** over the Lamer Winkel and the Arber.

Grosser Arber. – *About 1 hour Rtn from the lower chairhoist station and ½ hour on foot Rtn (services 8am to 5.45pm in summer, 4.45pm in winter). No service 15 October to 20 December; Rtn fare: 5DM.* Continue on foot to two rock spikes. The one on the left, above a chapel, overlooks the Schwarzer Reger and the frontier to the southeast; the one on the right (Cross), a **view*** of the Lamer Winkel and the Bayerischer Wald.

Grosser Arbersee. – Pine trees stand reflected in the dark lake. The descent of the Arber south face affords **views*** of the Zweisel basin, the Falkenstein and the Rachel.

Bodenmais*. – The resort lies surrounded by pasture in a basin at the foot of the Arber. Road no 85 along the crest overlooks the Bayerischer Wald; Fürsterstein can be seen in the distance, stepped at the foot of its castle.

Passau*. – *Description p 203.*

BAYREUTH ★

Michelin map **987** 26, 27 – Pop 68 700

This Franconian town, built near the wooded heights of the Fichtelgebirge, existed peacefully for hundreds of years before suddenly in the 18C knowing hours of glory which have been repeated at intervals ever since. From being the residence of the Margraves of Brandenburg-Bayreuth and one of the European capitals of Baroque and Rococo architecture, the town has now become the goal of Wagnerian pilgrims the world over.

Princess Wilhelmina. – Margravine Wilhelmina, one of the most cultivated women of the 18C, the daughter of the King-Sergeant *(p 66)* and sister of Frederick the Great, King of Prussia, might have pretended to a throne, but instead married the Margrave of Brandenburg-Bayreuth, a somewhat dull person. Her lifetime, from 1709 to 1758, marked the most brilliant period of the town's history. She was a talented artist, writer (memoirs, drama), composer, decorator, architect, dilettante and patron; she inspired Bayreuth Rococo to ornament with flowers and garlands – a personal and original style very different from the rustic Rococo of France.

Wagner and Liszt. – Wagner and Liszt, the two innovators of musical expression who were stimulated by mutual admiration and drawn close together by family ties (Wagner married Liszt's daughter, Cosima, in 1870), both died at Bayreuth. The tomb of Liszt, who died during one of the first festivals in 1886, is in the cemetery (Stadtfriedhof) (Z) while Wagner's tombstone can be seen from the castle park (Hofgarten) (Z) standing in the garden of his house, Wahnfried.

The Festival. – With the support of Ludwig II of Bavaria, Wagner had the festival theatre (Festspielhaus) built to his own design. The theatre, which was inaugurated in 1876 with *The Ring*, was intended to focus attention on the dramatic action. Even the music, rising from a camouflaged orchestra pit, was only intended as a flowing background.

Festspielhaus; guided tours in English 1 April to 30 September 10am to noon and 1.30 to 3.30pm; closed Mondays; 1.50DM.

The tradition established by Wagner has been perpetuated since his death in 1883 through the tenacity of Cosima; his son, Siegfried; and with renewed and reinvigorated inspiration by his grandson, Wieland (d 1966), and now by Wolfgang Wagner.

■ **SIGHTS** *time: 2 hours*

Margrave Opera House★ (Markgräfliches Opernhaus). – *Open 1 April to 30 September 9am to noon and 1.20 to 5pm; 1 October to 31 March, 10am to noon and 1.30 to 5.30pm; 1.50DM. Guided tours in English (20 min.).*

Wilhelmina had this private theatre built between 1745 and 1748.

The arena contained no seats but was reserved for dancing; the three galleries were divided into boxes. The whole building complete with stage and proscenium, which was of a remarkable depth (72 m - 236 ft), was in the Baroque style and constructed entirely of wood.

New Castle (Neues Schloss) (Z). – Wilhelmina, in her desire to make Bayreuth into another Potsdam, had the castle completed in two years, 1753-4.

The apartments. – *Guided tours in English 1 April to 30 September 10am to noon and 1.20 to 5pm (1.30 to 3.30pm the rest of the year); closed Mondays; 1.50DM.* The interior decoration has an attractive elegance in a flowery and light Rococo style. One discerns Wilhelmina's taste and influence on the stucco-master, Pedrozzi, who was chiefly responsible.

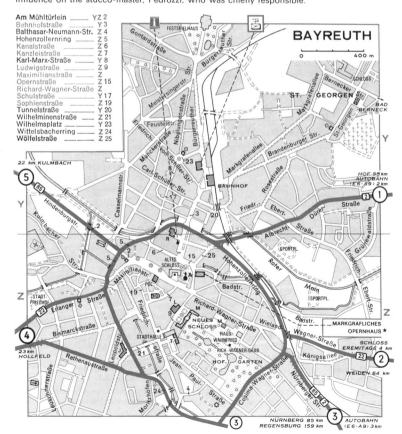

Am Mühltürlein	YZ 2
Bahnhofstraße	Y 3
Balthasar-Neumann-Str.	Z 4
Hohenzollernring	Z 5
Kanalstraße	Z 6
Kanzleistraße	Z 7
Karl-Marx-Straße	Y 8
Ludwigstraße	Z 9
Maximilianstraße	Z
Opernstraße	Z 15
Richard-Wagner-Straße	Z
Schulstraße	Y 17
Sophienstraße	Z 19
Tunnelstraße	Y 20
Wilhelminenstraße	Z 21
Wilhelmsplatz	Y 23
Wittelsbacherring	Z 24
Wölfelstraße	Z 25

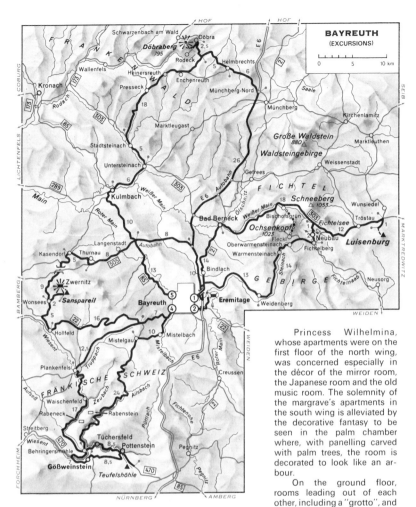

Princess Wilhelmina, whose apartments were on the first floor of the north wing, was concerned especially in the décor of the mirror room, the Japanese room and the old music room. The solemnity of the margrave's apartments in the south wing is alleviated by the decorative fantasy to be seen in the palm chamber where, with panelling carved with palm trees, the room is decorated to look like an arbour.

On the ground floor, rooms leading out of each other, including a "grotto", and bathroom, open directly on to the garden and also lead to the residence of Margrave Friedrich's second wife, the Italian Palace, where the decoration is far less interesting.

Richard Wagner Museum (Z M). – *Open Mondays to Fridays 9am to 5pm; 3DM.*

The ground floor contains personal souvenirs of Wagner (death mask, cast of his hand); the first floor, the story of the festival and famous Wagnerians.

Castle Church (Schlosskirche) (Z A). – The single aisle (1756), painted rose-pink and decorated by Pedrozzi with stuccowork, is a visual feast. A closed oratory beneath the organ contains the tombs of the Margrave Friedrich, Wilhelmina and their daughter.

EXCURSIONS

Hermitage Castle★ (Schloss Eremitage). – *4 km - 2⅓ miles – by ② on the plan and the Schlossallee (Castle Avenue) on the left – plus 1 hour sightseeing.*

The **park★** (Schlosspark) particularly enhances the beauty of the property; it is romantic and, beyond the informal flower gardens, full of the unexpected fantasy of the English gardens which were a novelty at this period; Wilhelmina's touch can be seen everywhere. *Fountains play daily in the park from 1 May to 15 October at 10 and 11am, 2, 3 and 4pm.*

The **Old Castle** (Altes Schloss) was built in 1715 and remodelled by Wilhelmina in 1736. *Guided tours 1 April to 30 September, 9am to noon and 1 to 5pm; 1 October to 31 March, 10am to noon and 1 to 3pm; closed Mondays; 1.50DM.* Note the curious grotto opening on to the inner courtyard and the cells in which the guests could make believe that they were hermits.

A little further on is a theatre built as an artificial ruin in 1743.

The **New Castle** (Neues Schloss), built on a semicircular plan, was rebuilt in 1945. Mythological scenes may be seen in the Sun Temple in the centre.

Tour in Swiss Franconia★★ (Fränkische Schweiz). – *Round tour of 95 km - 57 miles – about 4 hours – Local map below.* Leave Bayreuth by ④, the Bamberg road. Turn off left, half a mile beyond a lower roadway, in the direction of Behringersmühle.

The road first crosses a wide rolling plateau, then drops into the steeply enclosed Valley of the Ailsbach. At Behringersmühle turn left for Pottenstein.

Tüchersfeld. – The houses of the village are scattered amongst the rounded rock points that make up its bizarre setting.

The valley winds between pillars of rock, some of which rise vertically from the ground.

Pottenstein. – An old castle, perched on a rounded rock, marks the town site. Nearby are such natural phenomena as gorges, caves, etc.

Teufelshöhle. – *Tour (time: ¾ hour); 1 April to 31 October, 8am to 5.30pm; 2.70DM.*

The caves, particularly the one known as Barbarossa's Cathedral, contain fine concretions. The exit is picturesque through a maze of chaotically piled rocks. Turn, and just before Pottenstein, bear left for Gössweinstein.

Gössweinstein★. – *Description p 134.*

Take the Muggendorf road along the bottom of the green wooded Wiesenttal Valley.

Turn right and, at Behringersmühle, bear left to Waischenfeld. The stretches of water on the now smoothly flowing river, the wooded slopes with occasional rock escarpments and former mills, make up a lovely countryside – fit inspiration for any angler.

The return from Plankenfels to Bayreuth is direct.

Sanspareil★. – *Round tour of 72 km - 45 miles – about 3½ hours – Local map p 61.* Leave Bayreuth by ④, the Bamberg road.

Turn right as you come out of Hollfeld for Kulmbach. Turn off in front of the Wonsees Rathaus, bearing right into the Sanspareil road. Leave the car at the foot of Zwernitz Castle.

The Gardens★ (Felsengarten). – *See times of opening of the castle below.* The Sanspareil rock garden was conceived by Princess Wilhelmina. Taking advantage of a beech wood strewn with large rocks, the margrave, inspired by Fénelon's *Télémaque* added further adornments marked by a theatricality which was typically Baroque in taste.

Follow the arrows from a Baroque pavilion to the monuments scattered in the wood. Calypso's Grotto opens on to the Ruined Theatre.

Zwernitz Castle. – *Open in summer 9am to noon and 1.20 to 5pm; closed Mondays; 1DM.* Wilhelmina reconstructed this fortified castle. The chief feature is the **panorama** from the keep. Darkening the horizon are the Fichtel and Frankenwald Mountains.

Return to Wonsees and take the Kulmbach road again, 9 km - 6 miles – further on turn right into Thurnau. Do not enter the town but bear right just before coming to the railway. Turn left to reach road no 505, which leads to Bayreuth.

Döbraberg★; Kulmbach. – *Round tour of 104 km - 65 miles – about 5 hours.* Leave Bayreuth by ① and take the motorway in the direction of Hof. Leave the motorway at the Münchberg-Nord exit and follow the road first to Helmbrechts and then towards Schwarzenbach am Wald. Within sight of the houses of Döbra village, turn left back into the Rodeck country road and 450 m further on leave the car where a wide path climbs through woodland to the Döbraberg summit.

Döbraberg★. – *¾ hour on foot Rtn.* Climb to the belvedere tower. The majestic **panorama★** extends as far as the mysterious depths of the Thuringian Mountains in the north and the Fichtelgebirge in the south. These two massifs enclose the Hof Basin.

Turn and again make for Helmbrechts. After 2.5 km - 2 miles take the Enchenreuth road on the right. A pleasant run across the plateau is marked by the villages of Enchenreuth and Heinersreuth and brings you to Presseck and finally, Kulmbach.

Kulmbach. – *Description p 162.*

Fichtelsee; Luisenburg★★. – *Round tour of 88 km - 55 miles – about 5 hours – Local map p 61.* Leave Bayreuth by ①, and, after crossing the motorway, drive straight ahead to Weidenberg. The road follows the Steinach Valley, penetrating deeply into the pine covered granite massif of the Fichtelgebirge. At the entrance to Warmensteinach you can see the television tower erected at the top of one of the highest of the Fichtelgebirge peaks, the Ochsenkopf (alt 1 023 m - 3 356 ft – *access from the north by teleferic from Bischofsgrün, or the south from the hamlet of Fleck).*

Fichtelsee. – *½ hour on foot Rtn.* Turn right for the lake, a peaceful stretch of water.

Turn right into the Marktredwitz road. After 12 km - 7 miles – turn right towards Luisenburg.

Luisenburg★★. – *Description p 169.*

Return to Bayreuth by road no 303 through the pleasant resort of Bad Berneck.

▐ BEBENHAUSEN Abbey ★

Michelin map ▐206▐ 14 – 6 km - 4 miles – north of Tübingen

This ancient Cistercian abbey which was founded in the solitude of Schönbuch Forest at the end of the 12C has accumulated over the centuries several half-timbered annexes which harmonise with buildings in the village.

Guided tours (time: ½ hour): 1 April to 30 September, 9am to noon and 2 to 5pm; the rest of the year, 10am to noon and 2 to 4pm; 1DM. Ring at stone post left, going up to main building.

Church. – Built to the classical Cistercian plan *(p 23)*, but heavily restored.

Cloister. – The gallery with its fan vaulting surrounds a peaceful close. On the south side, where a lavabo abuts on the gallery, the tracery on the vaulting and filling the windows becomes even more elaborate. The cloisters are topped by a half-timbered single storey.

Facing the lavabo is the summer refectory; on the west side is the winter refectory (now a small museum) with wooden ceiling with exposed beams, and the lay brothers' refectory. Above, the monks' cells lead off a corridor which still has 15C paving.

▐ BENEDIKTBEUERN

½ mile south of Bichl (Michelin map ▐987▐ 37) – *Local map p 44* – Pop 2 500

The imposing buildings of Benediktbeuern, most ancient Benedictine monastery of Upper Bavaria, stand with their backs to the first spurs of the Bavarian Alps at the foot of the Benediktenwand. Since 1930 these buildings have been occupied by Salesian fathers.

To visit not only the church and the chapel described below, but also the new and the former banqueting halls, apply to the porter: 10 July to 15 September at 10.30am and 2.30pm; Wednesdays and Saturdays at 2.30pm only.

Abbey Church (Klosterkirche). – The present church, built from 1681 to 1686, is a massive edifice with lateral chapels going far back beneath low galleries. On the barrel vaulting not covered with stuccoes, Hans Georg Asam – father of the celebrated Asam brothers *(p 26)* – carried out the first complete and great cycle of frescoes to date from the beginning of the Bavarian Baroque period: the *Birth, Baptism, Transfiguration* and *Resurrection of Christ,* the *Descent of the Holy Spirit* and the *Last Judgment.*

Chapel of St. Anastasia★. – To the north of the church, behind the chancel, Johann Michael Fischer constructed a separate chapel (1751-8). It was decorated by artists, who, like the architect, were to become famous a few years later for their work at Ottobeuren *(p 201)*. The elegance of its frescoes and its stuccoes make it a charming example of Rococo art.

Berchtesgaden enjoys so intense a tourist trade in summer that the village streets are sometimes completely blocked. Journey's end on the German Alpine Road and departure point for the well known excursion to the Königssee, the village has still retained much of its old character. In the background rises the pincer-like summit of the Watzmann, the dominating landmark of the countryside, the centre of what was once known as the "Bavarian redoubt".

The Basin of Berchtesgaden is surrounded on three sides by the chains of the Watzmann, the Steinernes Meer and the Hagengebirge. Natural barriers separate Berchtesgaden from the Basin of the Salzach, but it is above all an historical evolution that explains this strange situation. The origin of Berchtesgaden is linked with the development of a priory of Augustinian monks, who became the pivot of the Bavarian political machine in the face of the grasping Archbishops of Salzburg. The House of Wittelsbach alone provided Berchtesgaden with three of its most powerful commendatory prince-priors between the 16 and 18C. Secularised in 1803, the priory and its possessions passed into the possession of the King of Bavaria in 1809.

■ SIGHTS *tour: 2½ hours*

Schlossplatz★. – Most of the old buildings are grouped round the Schlossplatz, a picturesque square whose western side, composed of the wheat granary and the tax collector's office, transformed and given an arcaded gallery in the 16C, makes it the best architectural group in the town. The façades of the church, the former monks' priory and the castle, complete the picture.

Church (Stiftskirche) (A). – The church with its Romanesque foundations is interesting for its links with St. Zeno of Reichenhall. The Lombard influence is seen in the façade with stones of alternating colours making for a decorative effect. The towers were rebuilt during the last century after a fire. Early 16C network vaulting in the nave and a chancel some 200 years older, much higher and of a purer Gothic style, characterise the interior.

Castle (Schloss). – *Open 10am to 1pm and 2 to 5pm; closed Saturdays all the year round, Sundays and holidays 1 October to 31 May; 3.50DM.*

This former monks' priory became a sumptuous palace at the time of the commendatory priests. A possession of the Bavarian crown since 1810, it became in 1923 the residence of Crown Prince Rupert, former C.in-C. of the Bavarian troops in the First World War and head of the House of Wittelsbach until his death in 1955. Through his mother, Maria Theresa, Archduchess of Austria, he was descended from the Stuart kings of England. The prince greatly enriched the building with furniture and art treasures and opened to the public his collections which show a particular taste for German wood carvings of the 15 and 16C and for Oriental art.

Cloister. – 13C. The Romanesque galleries remain on three sides of the cloister which delights in the variety of its columns, capitals with foliated scrolls, latticework and plant design and examples of stonework which include lions used, in the Lombard manner, to support the columns at the church's main entrance.

Dormitory★. – The fine Gothic hall with two aisles, contemporaneous with the church's chancel, contains an excellent selection of German religious art dating from the end of the Gothic period; altarpieces, wood carvings of the Swabian-Franconian school (Virgin by Gregor Erhart, 1500, works by Veit Stoss, Tilmen Riemenschneider), and twelve magnificent busts coming from the stalls of the abbey church of Weingarten (1487), etc.

Other Rooms. – Two fine Renaissance rooms on the first floor in the former council chamber and refectory (Italian furniture of the 15 and 16C); on the third floor, eight rooms *(Herrenzimmer)*, leading off one another and facing south towards the Steinernes Meer Massif, offer an attractive glimpse into the romantic 19C and its Biedermeier style (p 26).

Salt Mines (Salzbergwerk). – *Access by the Bergwerk-Strasse. Open 1 May to 15 October, 8am to 5pm; 16 October to 30 April, 1 to 4pm except Sundays and certain holidays; time: about 1 hour; 7DM, children, 4DM. Brochure in English.*

The exploitation of the Berchtesgaden salt mines has, since 1517, been the source of the priory's prosperity and, through it, of the whole region which up to then was very poor. Practising methods traditional in the eastern Alps, the salt rock is washed by fresh water and the resulting brine (Sole), with a concentration of 27%, is sent by pipeline to Bad Reichenhall, where it is refined *(p 208)*. The 600 000 m³ of brine produced annually at Berchtesgaden average 150 000 tons of refined salt.

The organised tour includes, besides the traditional phases of the work – dressing in miners' clothes, a trip along galleries in a small train and the crossing by raft of an illuminated subterranean lake and a documentary film show in a room arranged as a salt museum.

BERCHTESGADEN

Angergasse	2
Franziskanerplatz	3
Griesstätterstraße	4
Hanielstraße	6
Hasensprung	7
Königseer Straße	8
Locksteinstraße	9
Marktplatz	10
Metzgerstraße	12
Ramsauer Straße	13
Schiesstätt-Brücke	15
Weihnachtsschützen	17

EXCURSIONS

Königssee★★. This lake with its steep and often inaccessible banks provides the most romantic scenery of Upper Bavaria.

5 km - 3 miles – plus about 2 hours boat trip (electric power) for the complete tour. Tourists with little time can stop at St. Bartholomä. All-year service: in summer, departures every 10 minutes from Königssee pier from 6.40am to 7pm. Fare: 8.50DM for complete tour, 7DM for St. Bartholomä Rtn. Leave Berchtesgaden by the Königsseer Strasse (south on the map) and park your car in the large space marking the end of the roadway.

Then walk to the pier through the little township of Königssee. The boat slips silently through the sombre waters of the lake, dominated to the east by the great escarpments of the Watzmann and to the south by the base of the Steinernes Meer. There are some attractions that appeal to all tourists – evoking an echo

by sounding a bugle and identifying the Watzmann Family (the sharp outline of each crest looks like a person) – before the **Chapel of St. Bartholomä** comes into view. This original building has a triple apse like three overlapping ninepins. The stop at St. Bartholomä permits a view of the **site★** and a visit to the hamlet where houses nestle under thick maples. By way of the Sallet pontoon, ten minutes walk is enough to reach the Obersee at the circular end of the valley below the Teufelshörner (Devil's Horns), where the Röthbachfall rushes down.

Obersalzberg and Kehlstein★★. – There is a magnificent view of the Berchtesgaden country from the top of the Kehlstein.

4 km - 2½ miles – plus about 2 hours Rtn, of which ¾ hour is by bus. The bus shuttle-service for Kehlstein runs from mid-May to mid-October, leaving Obersalzberg every half-hour between 8.30am and 6pm. No bus runs at 12.30pm. Rtn fare (bus and lift): 11DM. Leave Berchtesgaden by the Schiesstatt-Brücke (east of plan) and follow the road for Obersalzberg (no 319), a very steep gradient (sometimes 1 in 5). Park your car on the great Hintereck esplanade, near the bus station for Kehlstein.

The Lords of Obersalzberg. – After his abortive *Putsch* of 1923 and the end of his prison term, Adolf Hitler, settled in Obersalzberg. This locality had, between 1850 and 1914, already attracted members of high society, scholars and artists, charmed by its pastoral plateau.

After Hitler seized power in 1934, the chalet (Berghof), which he had acquired, was enlarged on an increasingly ambitious scale. Martin Bormann, Nazi Party Chief of Chancellery, took on the execution of a huge and, at times, frenzied, building programme, aimed at making the Domain of the Führer the high place of the regime. The sanctuary of the Lonely Man of Berchtesgaden, evidence of Hitler's love of ceremony, was the scene of some cleverly staged diplomatic receptions such as that of Dr. Schuschnigg, Chancellor of Austria, on 12 February 1938, and that of Neville Chamberlain on 15 September of the same year.

The greater part of the Obersalzberg buildings were destroyed in an air attack on 25 April 1945, which preceded by only a short time the occupation of the area by a detachment of the French 2nd Armoured Division operating with the 101st US Airborne Division.

Obersalzberg. – The buildings of the Platterhof – a People's Hotel – have been restored by the American Army. The ruins of the other buildings of this Nazi sanctuary have been completely razed. Only a few basement walls mark the site of Hitler's Berghof.

Kehlstein★★. – Take your place in the postal bus, the only vehicle authorised to drive along the small sensational **road★★★**, blasted in the rocky spur of the Kehlstein. The hairpin bend by which the road leaves the Scharitzkehlalm ravine, confined by the cliffs of the Hoher Göll, is the high spot of the drive. At the end of the road *(on arrival reserve a place in the bus in which you wish to descend)* a lift takes you up the last 400 ft to the summit. At the summit (alt 1 834 m - 6 017 ft), a detached spur of the Hoher Göll, is the Teehaus (tea-room) which was never a military installation, despite the name Eagle's Nest. Hitler himself only went there about five times. Today, it is a mountain inn, the Kehlsteinhaus.

The **panorama★★** (go up a little on the crest) spreads out to the right of the Hoher Göll: Steinernes Meer (part of the Königssee in the foreground), Watzmann, Hochklater, Reiteralpe, Untersberg and, beyond Salzburg, the low rounded Pre-Alps of Salzburg and the Dachstein mountains where small glaciers glint.

Rossfeld Road★★ (Rossfeld-Ringstrasse). – *Round tour of 29 km - 19 miles – about 1½ hours – making use of a toll road (for cars: 1.50DM per person). This excursion can be combined with that of Kehlstein, described above.* Start from the Hintereck esplanade. At the crossroads after passing under the bridge of the Kehlstein road, turn sharp right and follow the road uphill. The road comes to the edge of the crest and runs above the Austrian Valley of the Salzach, dominating the Golling Basin, hollowed out at the foot of the Tannengebirge, and the steep ridge linking the Hoher Göll with the Kleiner Göll. The Dachstein, recognisable by its little glaciers, fills the background. Continuing northwards, the **view★★** extends over the Salzburg Plain. From the "Hennenköpfl" car park, it is only a few minutes climb to the beacon and the Hennenkopf Cross. The road leaves the crest at the Rossfeldhütte (inn) and winds through the charming and wooded valley region of Oberau in view of the Berchtesgaden mountains (Watzmann and Hochkalter). Turn to the left on leaving Oberau to return to Berchtesgaden via Obersalzberg.

BERGEN-BELSEN Memorial

7 km - 4 miles – southwest of Bergen (Michelin map **987** 15)

The memorial raised to the victims of the Bergen-Belsen Concentration Camp stands in solitude in a clearing on the Lüneburg Heath on which grow a few pine trees and birches.

The Monument. – *¾ hour on foot Rtn from the car park which you reach from Bergen by following the "Gedenkstätte" signs.*
After passing the mounds that mark the sites of the common graves, one reaches the obelisk of light tufa with its inscriptions in thirteen languages honouring the memory of the victims of the Nazi policy of extermination.
Anne Frank, the schoolgirl who kept a diary while she and her family were in hiding in Amsterdam, is buried somewhere near here.

The BERGSTRASSE

Michelin map **204** 7, 8, 9

The Bergstrasse, a route going back into history, runs at the foot of the low Odenwald mountains covered in scrub and woodland. It has also given its name to the sunny hillsides which slope towards the Rhine Plain between the Neckar and Main River gaps. Orchards flourish on these exposed slopes and the fruit and almond blossom is a picture. Apples are in bloom by 10 April – ten days before those of the Upper Rhine Plain.
The Bergstrasse, with its typical Rhineland scenery of commercial centres and small towns with uneven pavements and half-timbered houses, is attractive at all times of the year.

FROM HEIDELBERG TO DARMSTADT

58 km - 38 miles – about 3 hours

Heidelberg***. – *Description p 146.*

Weinheim. – *Tour: ¾ hour.* Make for the castle at the top of the town. The two main buildings (now the town hall) are set in **gardens*** (Schlosspark) planted with rare trees.
Walk down from the gardens to the arch of the Obertor below, the Marktplatz and then straight ahead, to the floor of the small valley. The Stadtmühlgasse leads to an old tanners' quarter from which you can see the perched houses of the upper town.

Wachenburg. – *Excursion of 3 km - 2 miles. From Weinheim take first the Schlossbergstrasse then the Wachenbergstrasse.*
Go to the terrace of this entirely reconstructed castle: **view*** of Weinheim and the Rhine Plain as far as Mannheim.

Heppenheim an der Bergstrasse. – The **Marktplatz*** or Grosser Markt owes its charm to two wooden buildings, the 16C town hall and the Liebig pharmacy with their corner oriel windows. A vast Neo-Gothic **church**, the "Bergstrasse Cathedral", dominates the square.

Lorsch. – *Excursion of 4 km - 2½ miles – plus 1 hour sightseeing, from Bensheim. Open 10am to noon and 1 to 5pm (4pm 1 November to 28 February); closed Mondays and some public holidays; 1DM.*
Of the great abbey founded in 774, there now exist at the east end of the town only the church narthex and the **Königshalle***. This triumphal gateway is Carolingian in style: above the composite style columns rises a wall adorned with blind, cowled bays and red and white ceramic marquetry. From behind the church: view of the Rhine Plain.

Fürstenlager Park**. – *Tour: 1 hour.* Starting from the centre of Auerbach (Hotel Krone crossroads), drive towards the mountains. Leave the car at the start of the Fürstenlager rise. This park in a sheltered valley is planted with tropical trees and studded with pavilions and symbolical monuments in the late 18C style. Go from the car park to the Princes' Pavilion (Herrenhaus) and then follow the numbering on the more remarkable trees.

Auerbach Castle. – *Excursion of 3.5km - 2 miles – plus ¼ hour sightseeing (0.40DM) from the Bergstrasse (at the fork).* Restored castle whose north tower commands a **view*** of the Rhine Plain.

Darmstadt. – *Description p 105.*

THE BERGSTRASSE
0   10 Km
NECKAR VALLEY

Car lights in Germany

Drive with dipped lights when crossing towns any time from dusk to dawn and also whenever visibility is poor in the daytime – in thunderstorms, fog, etc. Never drive on your parking lights alone

BERLIN ★★★

Michelin map **987** 17, 18 – West Berlin: Pop 1 964 000

For conditions of entry into West Berlin, particularly by car, from the Federal Republic refer to the current Michelin Red Guide Deutschland.

Berlin, where partition has disrupted normal communications, is a cruel example of the division of the world into two opposing camps. Unavoidably it has not been able since 1945 to fulfil its former function as the capital of Germany. In spite of one third of the city being destroyed during the war, the 1948 blockade and, since 1961, the Berlin Wall dividing the city in two, the former Reich metropolis is vigorously alive.

HISTORICAL NOTES

Cölln and Berlin emerge in the 13C as towns situated respectively on a sandy island and on the right bank of the River Spree, inhabited by travelling merchants and fishermen. Berlin's evolution as a capital city was to be the political undertaking of the Hohenzollern Electors of Brandenburg. The first castle to be built on Cölln was completed in 1451; in 1470 it became the permanent residence of the Hohenzollern family *(details p 152)*.

The Great Elector (1640–1688). – Friedrich-Wilhelm of Brandenburg found Berlin largely deserted at the end of the Thirty Years War.

The great commander, who had succeeded at Fehrbellin in 1675 in beating the Swedish Army, was also a considerable administrator. Emulating the Dutch – he had passed his youth in Holland – he constructed quays along the banks of the Spree and promulgated many ordinances designed to make Berlin into a healthy and well governed town. The construction of a canal between the Spree and the Oder stimulated commerce, but his most important act was to open Berlin to the French Huguenots after the Revocation of the Edict of Nantes in 1685. The arrival of a massive contingent – approximately one Huguenot to every five established Berliners – transformed the city and strengthened its influence on its neighbours through the increased number of its craftsmen, theologians, doctors, learned men and others.

City Life in Berlin in the Age of Enlightenment (18C). – The first King of Prussia, Friedrich I, built for his wife, Sophie-Charlotte, the Château of Charlottenburg. He entrusted the work to an architect and sculptor of genius, Andreas Schlüter *(c* 1660-1714), who worked primarily at the Royal Palace and the Arsenal.

Friedrich was succeeded by **Friedrich-Wilhelm I** (1713-40), who is known in history as the **King-Sergeant** by reason of his punctilious administration and his policy of systematic recruitment which became the basis of Prussian military power. He was less interested in embellishing Berlin than in making it more powerful. He had a new town, Friedrichstadt, laid out beyond the old town bastions. Commanding access to it were three monumental squares, the Quarré (Pariser Platz) (GUV), the Oktogon (Leipziger Platz) (GV) and the Rondell (Belle Alliance, and later the Mehringplatz) (GX). Draconian measures accelerated the development and peopling of this quarter which is cut by such wide arteries as the Leipziger Strasse, the most lively street of pre-war Berlin, the Friedrichstrasse and the Wilhelmstrasse (now the Otto-Grotewohl-Strasse), the Reich Whitehall.

Frederick II, the Great (1740-86) continued this effort, bestowing monuments along both the famous Unter den Linden and the Forum Fredericianum (Bebelplatz) (GHUV). To fulfil his purpose he called on Knobelsdorff (1699-1753), an architect as happily inspired by the Rococo tradition (Sans Souci) as by the Antique (the Opera).

The evolution towards Neo-Classicism continued until 1835. The monuments of Berlin were completed by the Brandenburg Gate (1789) and Neue Wache (1818), etc.

Towards Bismarck's Berlin. – Berlin found its soul for the first time when the high patriotism called into being by the professors of the University, founded in 1810 by Wilhelm von Humboldt, was allied to the call to arms by the King of Prussia in 1813 when he joined the Allies against Napoleon. The city benefited from the growing prestige of the Kingdom of Prussia and, as a favoured subject, began its industrial life under the forceful direction of such great advisers as August Borsig "the locomotive king" and Werner von Siemens (1816-92), the pioneer electrical engineer.

By 1871, Berlin became the capital of the Empire and numbered nearly a million inhabitants.

Greater Berlin. – In 1920 the city united under one administration 6 urban suburbs, 7 towns, 59 villages and 27 domains to form a unit of 4 million inhabitants.

In spite of the upheavals which Germany was still undergoing, "the twenties" were an exciting period in Berlin, particularly intellectually and artistically. Berlin newspapers set the tone for all other German papers.

Films made in Berlin won international acclaim thanks to such directors as Ernst Lübitsch, Fritz Lang, Carl Mayer, Georg-Wilhelm Pabst and the actors Emil Jannings and Marlene Dietrich (*The Blue Angel, Maidens in Uniform,* etc.). The theatre, brought back to life by Max Reinhardt (1873-1943), also flourished brilliantly. In 1928 Bertolt Brecht produced his *Threepenny Opera (Die Dreigroschenoper)*.

The Hitler regime, with its persecution of the Jews and others, smothered this artistic flowering in the so-called fight against "degenerate art".

The Taking of Berlin. – The final communiqué of the Yalta Conference in February 1945 announced that Berlin would be occupied by the major powers.

From 21 April to 3 May Berlin was a battlefield – the Red Army commanded by the Generals Zhukov and Koniev against the German Army. The Soviet troops advanced through the defence lines, destroying everything above ground – 120 of Berlin's 248 bridges were destroyed. Finally able to crawl out of their hiding places, the inhabitants learnt of the capture of the Reichstag and the suicide of Hitler (30 April).

Divided Berlin. – After the capitulation of Germany had been signed in Berlin on 8 May 1945, two four-power organisations came into being: the Allied Control Commission, in which was vested responsibility for the supreme government of Germany, and the Kommandatura, under the Control Commission, which was responsible for Berlin.

The eastern sector of Berlin, which was considered by the Russians as the potential kernel of a future people's democratic republic, began to evolve politically in such a way as rapidly to bring the city's administration to a halt. Pressures, vetoes and various incidents brought increasing tension. The municipal councillors who were not members of the Socialist Unity Party (Communist) left the city hall and formed a new council at Schöneberg. The Russians withdrew from the Allied organisation and from 1948 the eastern sector became a separate entity.

The blockade, provoked by Russian opposition to the currency reform introduced in the western sectors, and beaten by the Berlin Airlift (26 June 1948–12 May 1949), the proclamation in 1949 in the east of the German Democratic Republic, the popular uprising of 17 June 1953 and its suppression, innumerable incidents, the influx of refugees into West Berlin, have all aggravated the split. On 13 August 1961 the eastern authorities prohibited communication between the two parts of Berlin and a few days later the "Wall" was set up. With the Quadripartite Agreement in 1971 communication between the two parts of the city was strictly regulated. West Berlin is not constitutionally part of West Germany, although it is tied to the latter economically, judicially and financially. The supreme authority, however, is still in the hands of the western powers; and air traffic is still under their jurisdiction.

LIFE IN BERLIN

Berlin the largest city in Germany occupies an area of 883 km² - 341 sq miles. A unique city, due to its political and geographical insularity – now with the Wall the city is completely isolated – it has become a pole of opposing forces. Badly destroyed during the last months of the war, the former capital lost most of its historical quarter. Reconstruction was done by such famous architects as Le Corbusier, Scharoun and others; out of their plans a modern city with main thoroughfares appeared. In the west, residential districts (Märkisches Viertel to the north, Hansa-Viertel on the north side of the Tiergarten, Gropiusstadt to the south) alternating with parks and open spaces complement each other.

Before the war the centre of the city's life was concentrated around the Potsdamer Platz and Friedrichsstrasse. In West Berlin the liveliest part of the city is now along the Kurfürstendamm and memorial church – its shops, cabarets, restaurants and night-clubs; in East Berlin it is around the amazing urban complex of Alexanderplatz.

Many visitors come to Berlin because of the quality and diversity of its cultural life. Programmes are presented all year round not forgetting the festivals (The Theatrical and Musical: *Berliner Fest-*

Berlin – The Kurfürstendamm.

wochen in the fall). The most important theatre and concert halls in West Berlin are: the Philharmonie *(p 77),* the Opera (Deutsche Oper, founded in 1961) (BV), the Academy of the Arts (Akademie der Künste) (EU), the Schiller-Theatre (CV) and the Westen Theatre (Theater des Westens) (DV). In East Berlin there are the State Opera, the Berliner Ensemble (GU) and the Deutsches Theater (GU) made famous, respectively, by Bertolt Brecht and Max Reinhardt. The museums are no longer just on the "Isle of Museums" in East Berlin. They have now been distributed among the two "cities".

Because of Berlin's situation light industries tend to dominate – electrical industry, mechanical engineering, chemical and optical industry and clothing. With Munich and Düsseldorf, Berlin is also a centre of fashion – located primarily around the Kurfürstendamm. East Berlin produces basically the same light industries as its western counterpart.

Berlin is the melting pot of Central Europe because for the past 300 years immigrants from all over (6000 French Huguenots, after the Revocation of the Edict of Nantes; Poles and Bohemians) have settled. This has, thus, played a major part in the development of the Berlin character: tolerant and vivacious with a sardonic sense of humour. This "character" was portrayed by Theodore Hosemann, who sketched in the Biedermeier style *(p 26)* and Heinrich Zille (1858-1923) who depicted Berlin street life.

Also due to this blending of cultures – Berlin has a large variety of international restaurants. There are two types of beer preferred in the city *Berliner Molle,* a "chope" of lager beer, and *Berliner Weisse mit Schuss* a wheat based beer with a dash of raspberry syrup or woodruff.

■ GENERAL VIEW

Kreuzberg (GY). – This mound, which has been made into the Victoriapark is the highest "natural" point (66 m - 216 ft), in the centre of Berlin. At the top there is a monument honouring the memory of the wars of "liberation". View to the north of the centre of East Berlin and to the south of the Tempelhof military airfield.

Victory Column (Siegessäule) (EV). – The column is the landmark to look out for when travelling along any of the roads which, under a variety of names, lead 12 km - 8 miles from the shores of the Havel to the centre of Berlin. It is 67 m - 222 ft high (The Monument in London – *see Michelin Green Guide to London* – overall height is 62 m - 202 ft; 311 steps) and is topped by a Victory commemorating the campaigns of 1864, 1866 and 1870. From the top (285 steps) an aerial view of the Spree, the Tiergarten and the Hansa quarter.

Radio Tower (Funkturm) (AV). – Known to Berliners as "the lump" it has become the city's mascot, 138 m - 453 ft high the tower has a wide but confusing **panorama★** of the whole of Berlin from the gallery *(access by elevator open 10am to 11.30pm, 2DM).*

Europa Center (EV). – 86 m - 282 ft. From the platform *(on the 22nd floor and up some stairs; 2DM)* a plunging **view★** on the lively Kurfürstendamm area, the Kantstrasse and the Tiergarten. At night, with the neon lights, the "Ku-Damm" becomes a kaleidoscope of colour.

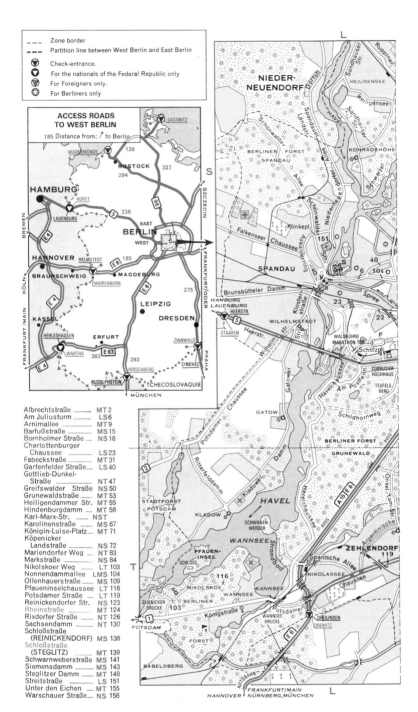

PRACTICAL INFORMATION

Tourist and Reception Bureaux, Automobile Clubs

Berlin Tourist Office (Verkehrsamt Berlin): Fasanenstrasse 7/8, ☎ 240111. *Open Mondays to Fridays 8am to 4pm.* Hotel reservations can be made before arrival in Berlin.

Information bureau at Zoo station: Hardenbergstrasse 20, ☎ 317094/95. *Open every day 7.30am to 10.30pm.*

Tourist Information Bureau at Tegel Airport: ☎ 41013145. *Open every day 8am to 10.30pm. Air traffic information:* ☎ 41011.

ADAC: Bundesallee 29, ☎ 86861, at Checkpoint Dreilinden, ☎ 8686238. *Open 8am to 8pm.*

AVD: Schöneberger Ufer 83, ☎ 2617048.

Banks are usually open Mondays to Fridays 9am to 1pm furthermore Tuesdays and Thursdays 3.30 to 6pm. The Post Office at the Zoo station is open round-the-clock.

Urban Transportation

West Berlin has an underground (Untergrundbahn) – sign "V" white on a blue background – and buses. There is an S-Bahn (Stadtbahn): sign "S" white on a green background.
Lines 6 (Tegel – Alt - Mariendorf) and 8 (Gesundbrunnen – Leinestrasse) cross East Berlin *only* at "Friedrichstrasse" – the correspondence station for the "S-Bahn" and serves as a checkpoint to East Berlin *(bring your passport). For further information concerning East Berlin, see p 77.*

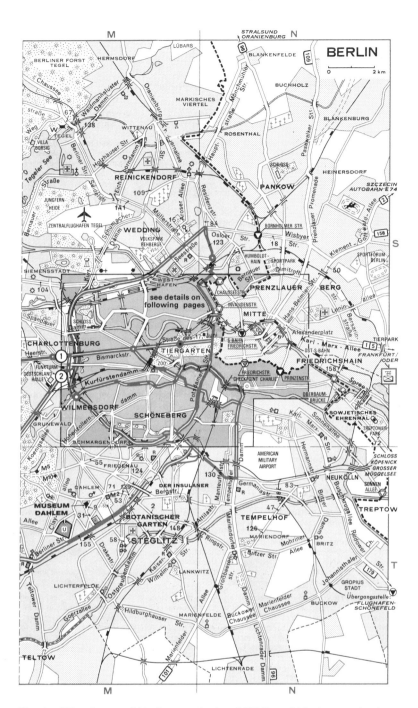

There is a **BVG tourist pass** valid for 2 consecutive days: 7.50DM or valid for 4 consecutive days: 14DM for unlimited travel on all Berlin (West) public buses, the underground and the Kladow-Wannsee boatline (excluding excursion buses marked with a triangle). It can be obtained at the BVG Ticket Offices: in Kleistpark Tube Station or the BVG Kiosk at Zoo/Hardenbergplatz.

TOURING PROGRAMME

Because of the variety and distance between sights, the tourist will find it necessary to establish an itinerary.

For tourists who have not much time we suggest below a 3-day programme (which will enable them to see the buildings and essential scenes of Berlin).

Day 1 **Morning** – The memorial church quarter, the Kurfürstendamm, the Zoo.
Afternoon – Dahlem Museums.

Day 2 **Morning** – Charlottenburg Palace.
Afternoon – The Reichstag, Brandenburg Gate, the Wall, Potsdamer Platz.

Day 3 **Morning** – New National Gallery, Philharmonic, Berlin Museum.
Afternoon – Excursion on the Havel, a stroll through the Grunewald Forest.

Berlin has much to offer to the night owl: the Philharmonic, the Opera, and the excitement of the cabarets, theatres, and pubs or simply a stroll along the Kurfürstendamm.
1 day can be for touring East Berlin *(p 77)*.

WEST BERLIN

■ **THE INTERNATIONAL CENTRE** *time: about 3 hours*

Kurfürstendamm★★. – During the 16C, the Kurfürstendamm was but an alleyway, giving access to the Prince-Electors Hunting Lodge in Grunewald *(p 71)*. Opened and enlarged in 1871 on Bismark's initiative, this prestigious thoroughfare which ripples with neon lights as night falls has become the centre of international life in Berlin.

The view is closed on the side of the Zoological Gardens by the broken tower of the Neo-Romanesque **memorial church** of 1891-5, built in memory of Kaiser Wilhelm I (Kaiser Wilhelm-Gedächtniskirche (EV **A**). This ruin, kept as a reminder of the destruction of war, has been strangely incorporated in the modern group (1961) of pierced polygonal buildings which are the new church and its separate campanile.

The stained glass windows, in blue tonalities, were done by Gabriel Loire and made in Chartres.

The *Ku-Damm* as the Berliners call it, with its 3.5 km - 2 miles of luxury hotels, car showrooms, cafés, cinemas, nightclubs, international restaurants, art galleries, antique shops, and boutiques is the centre of luxury trade and of entertainment in the city.

Adjacent streets. – The **Tauentzienstrasse** (EVX) is the shopping street where the large department store: "Ka De We" (abbreviation for Large Store of The West) is located.

At the beginning of the street is **Europa-Center** a multi-purpose centre where pubs, restaurants, cinemas, shops and panorama *(p 67)* are to be found, sports enthusiasts are also attracted to the centre with its skating rink and swimming pool.

Continue along Wittenbergplatz where Berlin's first tube station was inaugurated. Enter the disused Nollendorfplatz tube station, now the Flea Market with its 16 rail carriages and stalls. *(Open every day except Tuesdays 11am to 7.30pm)*.

The **Hardenbergstrasse** (DV) opens on to the Ernst-Reuter Platz lined with office buildings. Bookstores abound, with the clientele mostly from the universities across the way: the Technical University, Fine Arts University and the Music Conservatory.

Conference Centre (Kongresshalle) (FU). – *John-Foster-Dulles-Allee Avenue. Guided tours 10am to 5pm (when a conference is not in session); 1DM*.

This rather unique building, built by the American Hugh A. Stubbins, for the International Architecture Exposition in 1957 ("Interbau"), with its folding concrete roof, resembles an open oyster shell.

Exhibition Grounds (AV) (MS). – Lying at the foot of "the lump" *(p 67)* is the site of large international fairs and exhibitions: International "Green Week" (agricultural exhibition) and the German industrial Exhibition. The Deutschlandhalle is a conference hall, with a capacity for 14 000 people.

Berlin is now building *(opening in 1979)*, near the exhibition grounds, a large international conference centre (AV).

■ **THE DIVIDED CITY**

Ever since the construction of the wall on 13 August 1961, Berlin has been cut in two.

This concrete construction 3.50 to 4 m - 10 to 13 ft high and 160 km - 99 miles long is impassable. It is lighted up at night by powerful projectors, doubled by wire entanglement, guarded by observation posts and firing stations. In spite of it, life continues. The East Berliners try to ignore the curious tourists, who try to catch a glimpse of life on the "other side", from observation posts, arranged specifically for that purpose.

When visiting the streets and monuments near the Wall, obey the instructions indicated on the signs. Anticipate ½ day walking tour.

Brandenburg Gate★★ (Brandenburger Tor). – The gate stands in the eastern sector, separated from the West by the Wall. A triumphal arch which was once the city emblem, has, in recent years, become the symbol of the city's and even Germany's division. Six Doric columns forming part of the stone arch walls support an Antique-style coping. The gate inspired by the Propylaea of the Parthenon, was built by Langhans in 1789 and is surmounted by a reconstruction (after the war there was a contest between the two Berlins) of the famous Victory Quadriga by Schadow (1793).

The Soviet Army Memorial at the section of 17 Juni street which is closed to traffic, except tourist buses, was built with what was left of the marble from the former Reich Chancellery. Two Russian sentries, stand guard. They are "protected" by the British Army.

Reichstag (GU). – *Platz der Republik*. The Parliament building was destroyed in a fire in 1933 and badly damaged in 1945 during the last Allied offensive. Since restored (except the dome) this heavy Renaissance pastiche, was opened in 1894 for meetings of the Imperial Diet, a body elected by universal suffrage.

The exhibition "Questions Addressed to German History" is in the west wing of the building *(enter at Paul-Löbe-Strasse; open Tuesdays to Sundays 10am to 5pm)*. It deals with Germany since 1800.

Bernauer Strasse Quarter (G-U). – Before 1945, the south side of the Bernauer Strasse was the boundary between the Wedding and the Mitte quarters; but after the war it became the division between the French and Soviet occupied zones. In 1961, the Bernauer Strasse section of the Wall became the most guarded. Numerous crosses and wreaths remind us of the past dramas which have taken place in this street. At the end of Huessitenstrasse, the church known as "Reconciliation" is, ironically, enclosed on all sides by the Wall.

On the other side of the Bernauer Strasse near the old buildings of the last century are modern buildings such as the Ernst-Reuter urban complex with its splashes of blue and grey.

Potsdamer Platz Quarter (GV). – The Potsdamer Platz, the octagonal Leipziger Platz and the Leipziger Strasse, which before the war were filled with the noise of traffic and the bustle of pedestrians, are now desolate. To the northeast the Television Tower in the eastern sector can be seen and in an undefined area that used to be the Reich Chancellery gardens, a mound marks the site of an air-raid shelter where Hitler committed suicide (30 April 1945).

Not far from the Wall on Askanischer Platz there are the remains of the façade of the old Berlin train station: Anhalter Bahnhof.

Checkpoint Charlie (GV). – On the Friedrichstrasse is the famous Allied checkpoint where foreign motorists are obliged to pass to enter East Berlin.

The Wall Museum (Haus am Checkpoint Charlie) (GV M¹). – *44 Friedrichstrasse. Open 9am to 8pm; 1DM. Brochure in English.* Here evoked are the political events and tragedies which occurred during and after the construction of the Wall.
Although dispersed throughout the city the following sites are concerned with the divided city.

Airlift Memorial (Luftbrückendenkmal) (GY B). – *At the entrance to the American Military Airport at Tempelhof.* The three arcs shooting towards the sky and facing west symbolise the three air corridors used in the Allied Airlift to break the Soviet blockade *(p 66)*. The monument commemorates the Allies and 5 Germans who lost their lives for the city.

Town Hall (Rathaus) of Schöneberg (EY R¹). – It houses, since the administrative schism of the two Berlins in 1948, the West Berlin Chamber of Deputies and their Senate. At noon every day rings the Liberty bell given to the Berliners in 1950 by the Americans. A bronze plaque reminds us of President Kennedy's famous speech, dear to Berliners, in July 1963.

Theodor-Heuss-Platz (AV). – The square is named after the first West German president. Since 1955 a flame has burned that is to be extinguished when Germany is reunited.

Plötzensee Memorial (Gedenkstätte von Plötzensee) (DU C). – The Plötzensee prison where a large number of political prisoners were held, became a memorial to the German Resistance to Hitler after a hundred victims were hanged there following the unsuccessful coup of 20 July 1944, the execution chamber may still be seen.

Church of Maria Regina Martyrum★ (BU D). – Built in 1962 by Hans Schädel and Friedrich Ebert, this Catholic church is on the Heckerdamm. It is a memorial to all victims of the dictatorship. Inside is a large mural by **Georg Meistermann** which gives off splashes of colour in an otherwise austere interior.

■ THE GREEN CITY

Berlin is a green city, especially West Berlin, which includes most of the more elegant residential quarters of the Former Reich capital. The Havel has formed several lakes amidst the forests (Tegeler See, Stössensee, Grosser Wannsee). The forests, parks and rivers covering more than a third of the total area make Berlin an outdoor city with a variety of leisure pursuits *(for excursions on the lakes inquire at the Pavilion of the Zoo station, p 68)*. With the debris, after the war, several hills were made, one of which, the Teufelsberg (115 m - 378 ft) (LS) is used for skiing and tobogganning in winter. From north to south the forests of Tegel, Spandau and Grunewald have become a favourite place for citizens and visitors to the city. Berlin is also the city of farms (about 100); more than a fifth of the total surface is devoted to agriculture – the villages of Lubars, Gatow and Mariendorf to name but a few.

Tiergarten★ (EFV). – *About 2 hours on foot.* The oldest public park in Berlin extends from Ernst-Reuter Square in the city, to the Brandenburg Gate, about 3 km - 2 miles. It was a park for royalty only; after P. J. Lenne's (1789-1885) marvellous landscaping it became a splendid park in the English fashion, with brilliant flower beds, broad walks, and lakes. Badly destroyed during the war it was completely rewooded and arranged. In the centre, at "Grosser Stern" Square is the Victory Column *(p 67)*. To the north is the Hanse residential complex **(Hansaviertel)** (EU), an example of a modern urban programme, rebuilt in 1957 by 14 famous architects.

Zoological Park★★ (Zoologischer Garten). – *Main entrance: Hardenbergplatz, opposite the train station. Open 1 April to 30 September, 8am to 7pm; 1 October to 31 March, 9am to 7pm; 4DM; combined ticket zoo and aquarium: 6DM; time: 1½ hours.*
This perennial attraction, for all Berliners with time to spare, has been rebuilt. The environment of each species has been respected, thus to the joy of the visitors, numerous births occur each year. The animals are known by name to adults and children alike: Knautschke (the father hippopotamus) and Knorke (the oldest gorilla) are unique in their eyes.
The **aquarium** (EV E) *(open 9am to 6pm, 7pm Sundays; 3.50DM. Enter by the zoo or directly by Budapester Strasse)*. Many species (1 400) are housed here. On the first floor next to the aquarium is a terrarium renowned for its crocodiles.

Botanical Gardens★★ (Botanischer Garten) (MT). – *Königin-Luise-Strasse 6-8. Open 8am (10am Sundays and holidays) to sunset. The hothouses are open 8am (10am Sundays and holidays, 9am in winter) to 6pm; 1.50DM; time 1½ hours (garden and museum).*
There is an arboretum where rare flora and gardens are topographically arranged. In the large hothouse (Grosses Tropenhaus) are admirable orchids and carnivorous plants.

Botanical Museum (Botanisches Museum) (MT M²). – *Leave the garden by the main entrance and take a right turn. Open 10am to 5pm (7pm Wednesdays); closed Mondays.*
There is a section concerning the evolution of flora and a herb garden as well. Plants used for decoration, found in Ancient Egyptian tombs, are also on display. In the entry is a slice of sequoia tree, more than 800 years old!

Grunewald Forest (Grunewald) (LS T). – On the Havel★ the largest of the Berlin forests (3 100 ha - 745 acres), where the Prince Electors in the 16C would hunt, is the Grunewald forest. The boundary to the east is a series of little lakes interspersed with residential areas. The beautiful Havelchaussée road, runs to the south along the **Wannsee★★** (LT) beach, very popular with Berliners in the summertime. Deer and boar roaming freely among the oak, birch and pine trees create a typical Brandenburg landscape.

Peacock Island★ (Pfaueninsel) (LT). – *Access by boat leaving from the landing-stage at the end of Nikolskoer Weg (service by demand – 0.30DM). Château open 1 April to 15 October, 10am to 5pm; closed Mondays; 1DM; time: 1½ hours.*
A perfect example of the 18C landscaped garden with its little pavilions or temples dispersed about the park, beside small ponds, provides the setting for a peaceful shaded walk.
The chateau (1796) exhibits souvenirs of Queen Louisa in its panelled saloons.

Olympic Stadium★ (Olympia-Stadion) (LS F). – From the top of the campanile (77 m - 286 ft; *lift: 0.50DM, 9am to sunset)*, there is an overall view of the former "Reich sports centre" which extends along 66 acres. The stadium evokes the pomp of the 1936 games. The Marathon Gate *(access west, nearest the campanile)* houses the cup, which held the Olympic flame and commemorative plaques of the different contests.

THE CHÂTEAUX

Château of Charlottenburg★★. – The Charlottenburg was the favourite home of Queen Sophie-Charlotte, wife of Frederick I. With Leibniz, the Queen, in 1700, encouraged the formation of a scientific society which later became the Royal Academy of Science and Fine Arts. With the disappearance of the Royal Berlin Palace, the château, which is largely restored, has become the most accessible place in which to see mementoes of the Prussian Royal House.

The original castle which was begun in 1695, was small but was immediately enlarged and topped by a dome in 1710. Charlottenburg was abandoned by the King-Sergeant but it attracted the attention of Frederick II, who then had a new east wing added by Knobelsdorff. This had as its only decorative motif a forefront preceded by a peristyle. Fame was again attached to ·the château, when Queen Louisa, wife of Friedrich-Wilhelm III, would stay there.

In the Court of Honour stands the **equestrian statue of the Great Elector★★** (Reiterstandbild des Grossen Kurfürsten). The bronze statue by Andreas Schlüter (1703) is a masterpiece – one of the most vigorous and lifelike of Baroque sculptures.

There is a combined ticket (valid 1 month) to tour the interior of the château, the apartments and the outbuildings (3.50DM); ½ day tour. Brochure in English. The apartments and the galleries in the Knobelsdorff wing are open 9am to 5pm (last entry at 4pm); closed Mondays.

Nering-Eosanderbau. – This central part of the château was built (1695-1707) by the architects, Arnold Nering and Eosander von Götha, for the Princess Sophie-Charlotte.

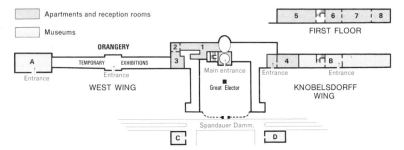

Apartments of Frederick I and Sophie-Charlotte★ (Historische Raüme) (**1**). – *Guided tour 1 hour; 2.50DM.* One is led through several sombre galleries lined with portraits of the Royal Family by the official Painter to the Prussian Court, **Antoine Pesne** (1683-1757).

The apartments of Frederick I consist of his study with the portrait of the Polish King, Stanislas Leszczynski by Pesne, a room decorated with red damask and gold braiding and the large main gallery. In the apartments of Sophie-Charlotte tapestries from Berlin and richly carved furniture evoke the memory of the ''Queen-philosopher''.

Porcelain Room★★ (**2**). – On entering one is immediately captivated by the rich vases, figurines and plates, mostly of Chinese origin, covering the walls.

Chapel (**3**). – A large royal baldachin faces the altar. Decorated pilasters frame medallions *(closed, restoration in progress).*

1st floor. – Take the elegant staircase by Eosander von Götha. In the large oval gallery, looking onto the garden, insignia of the Prussian Crown (sceptres, swords, globe) is on display (behind plate glass) in the south-east arcade.

Knobelsdorff Wing. – The eastern or new wing (Neuer Flügel) was built between 1740-9 as a counterpart to the Orangery.

Summer apartments. – *Ground floor.* Friedrich-Wilhelm II's apartments on the garden side are made up of two rooms decorated in the Chinese style and one room in the Etruscan style. On the street side are the apartments of Friedrich-Wilhelm III, note the mortuary mask of Queen Louisa.

Painting Collection★★ (**5**). – *1st floor.* The 18C French collection was assembled by Frederick the Great. It contains Watteau's *Embarkation for Cythera* and **Shop Sign**, which was bought in 1745 to decorate the **concert hall** (**8**) of the château. There are also several representative works of Chardin, Beauvais tapestries with motifs by François Boucher are also exhibited. Elegant furniture (bed and sideboard for flowers) by Schinkel can be seen in Queen Louisa's bedroom.

Beyond the vast stairwell, two magnificent reception rooms, designed by Knobelsdorff and decorated by Nahl, have kept their original aspect – the ''Frederick Rococo'' so famous and admired in Potsdam.

Banquet Hall★ (**6**). – The walls are clad with pink marble stucco. The reliefs above the doors represent the seasons. The ceiling fresco, painted by Hans Trier, in 1973, over the destroyed Pesne fresco, expresses abstractly the ethereal atmosphere of Olympus.

Golden Gallery★★ (**7**). – A superb example of Prussian Rococo. Knobelsdorff emphasises creative art expression. On entering one is struck by the mass of sparkling gilt ornament on a background of light green marble stucco. The scrolls, foliage, garlands, and mirrors blend – expressing movement, illusion, light and colour – springtime reigns.

Frederick the Great's memory is recalled in his private quarters: the room decorated with landscapes done by Italian masters, the study with a medallion by Knobelsdorff and the library with books from Sans-Souci.

Museum of Decorative Arts★ (Kunstgewerbemuseum) (**B**). – *On the ground floor of the Knobelsdorff wing. Open 9am to 5pm; closed Fridays.* The museum contains 1 500 European works of art from the Middle Ages to the 18C.

In the first room the **Guelph treasure★★** (Welfenschatz) is exposed: the reliquary, in the form of a Byzantine church with a dome (Cologne 1175) which held the head of St. Gregory brought back from Constantinople in 1173, the cross of Guelph and Elbertus' portable altar, completing the collection are gold and silver plate, ceramics and porcelain, exemplifying the perfected technique of the Saxe manufacturers.

West Wing. – This wing, the Orangery, was built in 1701-7 by Eosander von Götha. The theatre, at the far end was built by Langhans in 1788-91.

Museum of Pre and Proto-history (Museum für Vor- und Frühgeschichte) (**A**). – *Open 9am to 5pm; closed Fridays.* Pre-history of Brandenburg to the Bronze Age.

Castle Park★ (Schlosspark) (BU). – The park was landscaped, with English taste, by Friedrich-Wilhelm II, and is an oasis of tranquillity. To the west, yews and cypresses cast their shadows over the small temple **mausoleum** (BU G) built in 1810 by H. Gentz. It contains the royal tombs, among which are those of Friedrich-Wilhelm III and Queen Louisa, Emperor Wilhelm I and Empress Augusta. The remains of the King-Sergeant and Frederick II have been transferred from Potsdam to Hohenzollern Castle.

The Schinkel Pavilion *(at the far end of the Knobelsdorff wing)* was built in 1824 for Friedrich-Wilhelm III. Inside the furniture was created by Schinkel. This summer pavilion is in the Pompeian style, very popular in Berlin in the 19C. It displays biscuitwares by **Schadow** and paintings by **Caspar David Friedrich** *(The Monk and the Sea, The Cross on the Mountain).*

North of the lake, the **Belvedere** (BU K), was designed by Langhans and built facing the Spree. It houses a historical **exposition★** of the Royal Berlin Porcelain Manufacture, founded in 1751 by Frederick the Great. *(Start the tour on the 3rd floor. View of the Château.)*

Opposite the château. – The two buildings by Stüler, facing the Court of Honour were used as barracks for the royal guards.

Antique Museum★ (Antikenmuseum) (BU M³). – *Open 9am to 5pm (noon to 8pm Wednesdays); closed Fridays.* Ancient Crete, Etruria and Greece are illustrated by ceramics, bronze ware, arms and everyday utensils.

Down in the basement is the fabulous **ancient treasure★★★** (in the Schatzkammer). Contributions from princely collections and archaeological find make up this treasure which contains: millenial jewellery from the Mediterranean basin, Scythian gold and silver ware (exemplified by a gold fish weighing more than 600 grammes), silver dishware, dating from the Romans, discovered in 1868 near Hildesheim, arresting portraits painted on wood from mummies (when Egypt was a Roman colony), and a multicoloured cameo depicting the Triumph of Hadrian.

Egyptian Museum (Ägyptisches Museum) (BU M⁴). – *Open 9am to 5pm; closed Fridays.* This collection traces the artistic and cultural evolution of Ancient Egypt from 4 BC to AD 3.

The painted **bust** (plaster over limestone, 1350 BC) **of Queen Nefertiti★** is exquisite. There are also terracotta vases, bronze statues, sarcophagi, funerary masks, musical instruments as well as other examples of Egyptian life.

Nefertiti.

Hunting Lodge in Grunewald★ (Jagdschloss Grunewald) (MT M⁵). – *Access by Clay-Allee, Pücklerstrasse, then 15 min. walk through the forest. Open 10am to 6pm (5pm March and October and 4pm November to February); closed Mondays; time: ½ hour; 1.50DM.*

This graceful Renaissance pavilion was built in 1542 for Joachim II by the architect, **Caspar Theyss**. The main section with its two storeys and hexagonal tower, date from that time (the two wings, on the lake side, were added in the 18C). Within the pavilion are nine scenes of the Passion from the **School of Cranach the Elder** (room 1), 17C, Flemish and Dutch paintings (Jordaens, Jan Steen, Caesar by **Rubens**) and a series of portraits. In rooms 6, 7 and 8 are works and various objects illustrating the history and function of the pavilion as a hunting lodge. The last royal hunt was held in Grunewald in 1907.

The harmony between the architecture, interior decoration and scenery is what makes this visit so pleasant.

Château of Bellevue (Schloss Bellevue) (EU N). – *Amspreeweg. Telephone in advance: 391051, for guided tour (1 hour), organised by group. Park open 8am to sunset.*

The palace was built in 1785 in the Neo-Classical style by Boumann as the summer residence for Frederick the Great's younger brother, Prince Augustus-Ferdinand. Since 1959, it has been the official residence of the President of West Germany.

In the entrance hall (ground floor), the vase is the only object left of the original château (badly damaged during the last war). All the other works of art, tapestries and paintings have been since acquired. On the 1st floor, in the oval room, designed by Langhans, in 1791 – eight marble pilasters support the elliptical ceiling.

Stroll in the lovely 50 acre park (behind the château); the weatern section is fashioned after an English landscape garden.

The Spandau Citadel (Spandauer Zitadelle) (LS S). – *Access by "Am Juliusturm" Avenue. Open in summer Tuesdays to Fridays 9am to 5pm, Saturdays 2 to 5pm, Sundays 10am to 1pm and 2 to 5pm (guided tours); 1DM. Duration of the tour of the citadel and church: 1½ hours.*

At the confluence of the Havel and the Spree, the citadel demonstrates the "newer" Italian system of fortification. It is a square, where each of the four angles are right-angled bastions. It is on the former 12C castle built by Margrave Albert the Bear and enlarged under Joachim II. The citadel has been assulted by the Swedish, French, Russian and Prussian troops and has served as the state prison. After 1945 it held the accused of the Nuremberg trial. Rudolph Hess, the last prisoner is now kept in the military prison of Wilhelmstrasse.

Take the drawbridge to the 16C portal. Represented on its pediment are the polychrome coat of arms of the Prussians with the blue ribbon of the Order of the Garter in front.

Julius Tower (Juliusturm). – *Go around the brick edifice.* This keep, the representative symbol of the citadel is the only remaining vestige of the old 12C fort. In front of the entranceway is an impressive locking system, 145 steps lead up to a terrace with a vista on the industrial section of Spandau. A local history museum *(access by the footbridge)* is in the Palas.

St. Nicholas★ (Nicolaikirche) (LS V). – *On Reformations platz on leaving the citadel, take a right turn on to "Am Juliusturm", after having crossed the Havel, take the second street on the left.*

This is the last Gothic church (end of 14-15C) in brick remaining in West Germany. It is a hall-church *(p 24)*. The entrance to the northern chapel, in the polygonal chancel is surmounted by a handsome **Crucifixion** group (1540), in polychrome carved wood. The magnificent Renaissance **altar★**, more than 8 m - 26 ft high is in painted limestone and stucco, the **baptismal fonts** cast in bronze are the oldest works of art in the church (1398).

Château of Tegel (Humboldtschloss) (MS W). – *Gabrielenstrasse. Guided tours 15 April to 15 October on Wednesdays, Saturdays, Sundays and holidays 2 to 6pm; 2DM. The park is open everyday until sunset; ¾ hour.*

A manor house under Joachim II, it was transformed into a small Neo-Classical château (1821-3) by Schinkel for Wilhelm of Humboldt. The inside contains mementoes of the Humboldt family and ancient sculpture (collected by Wilhelm while Ambassador to Rome 1801-8 and after). In the park, an alley of lime trees leads to the family vault.

BERLIN
CENTRE

0   500 m

■ COLLECTIONS AND MUSEUMS

DAHLEM MUSEUMS★★★ (MT)

Open 9am to 5pm; closed Mondays, 1 May, Tuesdays after Easter and Whitsun, 24, 25 and 31 December; time: ½ day.

The amount and vast contents of these collections can make the visit difficult to follow, buy the brochure "Itinerary" (plan and explanation in English) at the entrance.

Painting Gallery (Gemäldegalerie)★★. – *Enter at Arnim-Allee. This department takes up two floors in the right wing of the old building.*

This important collection displays European painting from its beginning (13C) to the Rococo period.

Ground floor. – All the schools, to the end of the 16C are exhibited.

German painting (to the right) begins: the 14C Madonna of Glatz from the School of Bohemia. German Renaissance paintings are in the side galleries, **Dürer**'s *Jerome Holzschuher* (this portrait is also on the German 100 mark note) and *Jacob Muffel*; the admirable portrait of

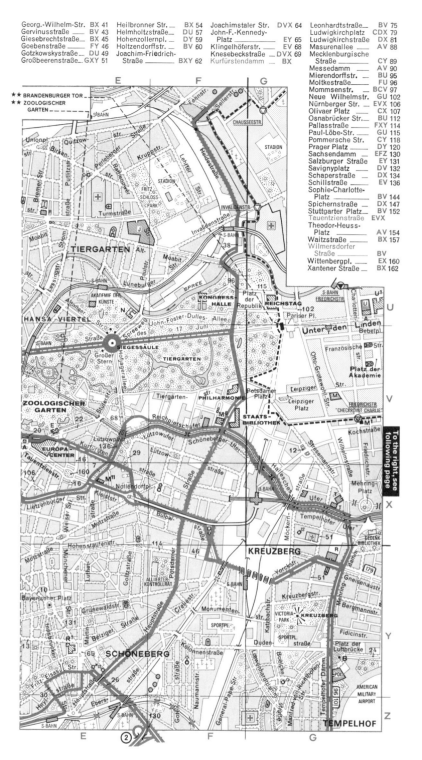

the *Merchant Georg Gisze* by Hans **Holbein the Younger**; the luminous *Rest on the flight out of Egypt* by Albrecht **Altdorfer** who founded the Danube School *(p 27)*, and **Cranach the Elder**'s *Portrait of the wife of Dr Johann Reuss*.

The Dutch and Flemish Primitives: **Van Eyck**'s famous *Virgin at Church,* Petrus **Christus**' delicate *Portrait of a Young Girl*, several portraits of gentlemen by the **Master of Flemalle,** by his student Roger **van der Weyden**, *Young Girl in a Wimple*, the animated *Adoration of the Shepherds* by Hugo **van der Goes** and the fantastic *Proverbs* by **Brueghel the Elder** can all be seen in this section.

The *St. John The Baptist* by **Geertgen tot Sint Jans** and *St. John at Patmos* by Hieronymus **Bosch** demonstrate the richness of religious inspiration in the Dutch Primitives. Jean **Fouquet**'s masterpiece *Etienne Chevalier* represents 15C French painting.

18C French painting is exemplified by the graceful *Dance* by **Watteau**, **Chardin**'s *Young Boy Drawing* and *Frederick II* by Antoine **Pesne**.

Displayed left of the entrance is Italian painting from 13 to 16C: the School of Florence illustrated by **Giotto**'s *Death of Mary*, **Botticelli**'s *Choir of Angels*, the School of Padua illustrated by **Mantegna**'s *Virgin and Child*, **Raphael**'s *Colonna Madonna*, and the School of Venice with **Titian**'s *Young Girl holding a basket*.

1st floor. – 17C Flemish and Dutch paintings preponderate. In the main gallery are: *Portraits of a Genoan Couple* by **Van Dyck** and *Andromeda attached to the Rock* by **Rubens**. In the side galleries genre and landscape paintings are exhibited: *Man and Woman Beside a Pitcher of Wine* by **Vermeer**, *The Mother* by Pieter de **Hooch** as well as works by van Goyen, Ruysdael, Jan Steen *(The Inn Garden)*. Livliness exudes from *Malle Babbe* a portrait by **Frans Hals**. A large section is devoted entirely to **Rembrandt**: *Portrait of Hendrickje Stoffels* and especially *Man with the Gold Helmet* a remarkable work – the warmth and luminosity contrasting so well with the severe expression of the man.

Revealed in the stairwell are: Georges de **La Tour**: *Peasants Eating*, as well as masters of the Italian Baroque: **Caravaggio, Caracci**, the 18C Venetian School represented by **Tiepolo, Canaletto**, and **Guardi** *(Views of Venice)*. The two French Classical landscape painters: **Poussin** and **Lorrain** *(Italian Landscape)* are also presented.

Sculpture Department* (Skulpturengalerie). – *Enter by Lansstrasse on the right, on the ground floor and 1st floor.*

This department contains Byzantine and European sculpture from the 3 to the 18C.

In the Primitive Christian and Byzantine sculpture section the 4C Pyxidus of Berlin in ivory and the glass mosaic Christ of Misericordia are displayed.

The Swabian and Franconian Schools demonstrate the quality of German Mediaeval sculpture: the group *St. John, The Virgin of Dangolsheim*, and two superb works by **Riemenschneider** the *Four Evangelists* and the *Choir of Angels. Luxure* (1320) typifies French Gothic sculpture. Works of the Quattrocento, representing the Italian Renaissance, are shown: **Donatello**'s *Pazzi Madonna*, Luca and Andrea della Robbias' Virgins in terracotta and the small bronzes by Giovanni of Bologne.

The Baroque and Rococo section is well represented with the 18C German masters Martin **Zürn** *(St. Sebastian* and *St. Florian)* and **Feuchtmayr** *(Assumption)*.

Drawings and Prints Department (Kupferstichkabinett). – *Enter to the right at Arnim-Allee. On request one can consult the works more closely in the study room.*

Featured here are a large collection of 14 to 18C drawings, from the European Schools (**Dürer, Brueghel the Elder, Rembrandt, Botticelli,**), lithographs, 15 to 20C illustrated books and sketch books (Knobelsdorff).

Ethnographic Museum** (Museum für Völkerkunde). – *Enter to the right at Lansstrasse on the ground floor, 1st and 2nd floor.*

Coming from all over the world this is one of the most complete collections of its kind.

Precolumbian Art*. – This section deals with the Central and South American civilizations – with the carved **steles** from the Mayan civilization (Guatemala) sacred and secular **statues** (cup for human sacrifice) from the Aztecs, and Peruvian multicoloured material and anthropomorphic **ceramics**.

The Gold Room* is devoted to exquisite engraved objects (7 BC to AD 11): jewellery and cult objects.

South Seas Section (Südsee). – Among the collection assembled by Captain Cook, in the 18C, are **carved wood** objects, **painted masks** from New Guinea and a **boat section** (canoes, sailing ships); on the 1st floor the King of Hawaii's elegant multicoloured feather coat is shown.

African, Southern Asian and Far Eastern Sections. – Note the **terracotta** from Ife, the **bronze work** from Benin (now known as Nigeria) and the carved and painted **wood** from Bali.

Museum of Oriental Art. – *Enter to the left on Lansstrasse, on the ground floor and 1st floor.*

These collections give a general idea of the various types of art from the East.

Indian Art (Museum fur Indische Kurst) with its carved stone sculpture and painted miniatures, **Islamic art** (Museum für Islamische Kunst) with its rich ornamentation, as seen in its bronzes with silver inlay and **Far Eastern Art** with its collection of porcelain and Chinese, Japanese and Korean **lacquer ware** (an intriguing 12 BC ceremonial axe in bronze).

German Folklore Museum* (Museum für deutsche Volkskunde). – *Am Winkel, 6-8.*

The museum contains varied forms of handicrafts from German speaking countries as early as the 16C.

The diversity of the furniture (chest of drawers, beds, chairs) shows the evolution of ornamentation more abundant in Bavaria and Austria than in Northern Germany. **Traditional costumes**, mostly feminine, vary according to the region, age, and use (work or holiday). The pictures hung in the "Herrgottswinkel" (God's corner) show the piety of the people. The different kitchen and table ware: in wood, copper, stone, and porcelain (rediscovered in Germany in 1709 by Böttger) is presented in a separate section.

OTHER MUSEUMS

National Gallery* (Neue Nationalgalerie) (FV M⁶). – *Potsdamer Strasse 50. Open 9am to 5pm (noon to 8pm Mondays); closed Fridays and some holidays.*

Within this glass and steel structure built by Mies van der Rohe in 1968 *(p 26)* is a diverse 19 and 20C painting and sculpture collection. An interesting parallel can be made between the French Impressionists (Manet, Renoir, Monet, Pissaro) and their German contemporaries (Liebermann Slevogt). Other artistic styles shown are: German Romanticism with **C D Friedrich** *(Man and Woman Looking at the Moon)* and K. Blechen *Greenhouse Interiors on the Isle of Peacocks*; Realism with Liebl and Adolph von **Menzel** *(Frederick II's Flute Concert)*; the vitality of Lovis Corinth *(Trojan Horse)* foresees the Expressionism of Nolde, Kokoschka *(Portrait of Adolph Loos)*, the "Brücke" style of Schmidt-Rottluff, Kirchner and Heckel, the technique of Bauhaus shown by Schlemmer, Kandinsky and finally the Surrealism of Paul **Klee** *(Departure of the Boats)* and Max **Ernst**.

Sculpture is displayed inside and on the terrace – note especially Renoir's *Washerwoman*, Calder's *Heads and Tails*, and Gerhard Marcks' *Maja*.

The graphic collection devoted to Max Beckmann and Edvard Munch is being rearranged.

Berlin Museum* (Berlin-Museum) (HX M⁷). – *Lindenstrasse 14. Open 11am to 6pm; closed Mondays; 1.50DM. Restaurant with Berlin specialities in a typical locale (Attberliner Weissbierstube).*

The former Court of Justice built in 1735 by P. Gerlach, late Baroque style, in ochre colour now holds the Berlin Museum. The modern interior houses different aspects of Berlin as a city and the life of its citizens (from 17C to early 20C).

Musical Instruments Museum★ (Musikinstrumentenmuseum) (DX M⁹). – *Bundesalle 1-12, on the 2nd and 3rd floors. Open 9am to 5pm; Wednesdays 11am to 9pm and Sundays 10am to 2pm. Guided tours (call in advance 889 78 35) Saturdays at 11am; closed Mondays.*

The former Joachimsthal secondary school, with its attractive Neo-Classical façade contains a collection of keyboard, chord, wind and percussion instruments used in Europe since the 16C. Especially interesting are (on the 3rd floor) Far Eastern (set of gongs from Java and a Burmese harp) and African musical instruments with their marvellous colours and forms.

Quite moving are the instruments used by the illustrious: Frederick the Great's flute and Edvard Grieg's piano.

Bauhaus Museum (Bauhaus-Archiv-Museum für Gestaltung) (BU M⁹). – *Schlosstrasse 1, near the Antiques Museum. Open 11am to 6pm (2 to 9pm Wednesdays); closed Tuesdays; 1.50DM. The ground floor has temporary exhibitions (1.50DM) and on the 1st floor is a permanent exhibition.*

A school of architecture, design and craftsmanship was founded by **Walter Gropius** in 1919. The aim was to create a complete homogeneous physical environment in which all the arts have their place – an end to the schism between art and technical expert craftsmanship. The beginning of modern "design" can be seen in the sculptures of Oskar **Schlemmer,** the paintings and watercolours of Lázló **Moholy-Nagy** and Georg Muche.

Brückemuseum (MT M¹⁰). – *Bussardsteig 6. Open 11am to 5pm; closed Tuesdays; 1.50DM.*

Die Brücke (The Bridge) was an organisation of Expressionist artists founded by four students: **Karl Schmidt-Rottluff** (who gave the group its name), **F. Bleyl, E. Heckel,** and **E. L. Kirchner,** in Dresden in 1905, installed in Berlin in 1911 and dispersed in 1913. The style encompassed all varieties of subject matter in a simplified style that stressed bold outlines and strong colour planes influenced by the expressive simplifications of German Gothic woodcuts and by Primitivism. Where French Fauvism treated form and colour in a lyrical manner, the art of "the Bridge" as is seen in the sculpture, watercolours and drawings shown, expressed a certain anxiety. Other members of the group were **Max Pechstein** and **Otto Mueller.**

Berlin Postal Museum (Berliner Post-und Fernmeldemuseum) (EX M¹¹). – *An der Urania 15. Open 10am to 4pm, Saturdays and Sundays 10am to 1pm; closed Mondays and holidays.*

This small museum contains documents, models and costumes relative to the development of communications in Berlin covering the past 300 years.

Transport Museum (Verkehrsmuseum) (EX M¹¹). – *Same address as Berlin Postal Museum. Open 10am to 5pm; closed Mondays and in July; 1DM.*

The first cycles, as well as models of trams, trains, boats (Christopher Columbus's *Santa Maria*), aeroplanes and spacecraft exhibit the diversity and importance of transportation. A display concerning the Berliner Otto Lilienthal (1848-96), aeronautical pioneer, whose studies on gliders and "flying models" influenced the Wright Brothers, can be seen.

Der Insulaner (MT). – West Berliners have adopted this nickname "the islanders" for themselves. This artificial hill, built up from rubble accumulated from war damage, is the site of the Wilhelm Foerster Observatory. It has a high powered telescope for seeking out satellites. There is also a planetarium *(open at 8pm; Sundays 5 and 8pm; closed Mondays; 2DM).*

Philharmonie (FV). – *Kemperplatz. Guided tours 1.15 to 3pm (2 to 3pm Sundays). Call in advance 269251; time: 20 minutes.*

This bold asymmetric construction built by H. Scharoun (1963), whose roof appears like a great wave from the sea, houses the Berlin Philharmonic Orchestra directed first by Furtwängler then by Herbert von Karajan. The orchestra plays, surrounded on all sides by the audience.

To the south is the second work by Scharoun the **National Library** (Staatsbibliothek) (FV).

EAST BERLIN

Access. – Foreign (non-nationals of the Federal Republic) motorists must enter through Checkpoint Charlie in Friedrichstrasse. *Open until midnight. Duration of control: 15 min. to 1 hour.* Bring visa, valid passport, car papers, including the international insurance green card. Without a car it is possible to reach the Eastern Sector by the underground, use line no 6 or the S-Bahn leaving from Zoo Station. Arrival point: Bahnhof Friedrichstrasse station.

To return to the west you must go through the same checkpoint.

Currency (MDN) *(mark deutscher notenbank)*: the exchange rate is 1 East German mark to 1 West German mark; the taking in and out of West German marks and currency coin is not restricted but should be declared. No East German marks may be taken in or brought out. *(Foreign exchange office is always open at the Friedrichstrasse station.)*

This information is given without any guarantee of its continuing validity.

Visit. – East Berlin, the capital of the German Democratic Republic, is a constantly expanding metropolis. Its 18C Neo-Classical buildings (restored), its rich artistic collections, its newly built up areas attract tourists, mostly from Eastern Europe, all year round.

Tourist coaches leave West Berlin *(addresses p 68)* and East Berlin *(Information Bureau at the foot of the Television Tower and Berolinastrasse 7)* for tours in East Berlin and Potsdam.

We suggest you leave your guide or any printed material in West Berlin and prepare your itinerary according to the suggested sites mentioned below.

Left Bank of the Spree

Brandenburg Gate★★ (Brandenburger Tor). – Built by Langhans, as seen from the east.

Unter den Linden★ (GUV). – This famous avenue, beneath the lime trees is lined by 18 and 19C monumental buildings.

Humboldt University (GU U¹). – Built by J. Boumann between 1748 and 1753.

Old Library (Deutsche Staatsbibliothek) (GU A). – In Viennese Baroque (1774-80) style.

St. Hedwige Cathedral (GHV B). – Catholic church (1747-73) restored in 1963.

State Opera House★ (Deutsche Staatsoper) (GHUV C). Knobelsdorff designed the Opera House in 1743. It reopened in 1955.

Neue Wache★ (GHU D). – In the form of a temple with Doric columns it was designed by Karl Friedrich Schinkel in 1818.

Arsenal★★ (Zeuhaus). – The most impressive Baroque building in Berlin (1695-1706) houses the Museum of German History. **Masks★★** of the dying warriors to be seen in the inner courtyard, by A. Schlüter.

BERLIN
CENTRE

0 _____ 500 m

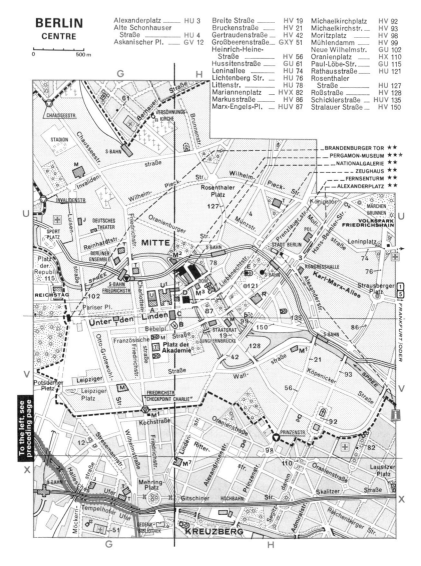

BRANDENBURGER TOR ★★
PERGAMON-MUSEUM ★★★
NATIONALGALERIE ★★
ZEUGHAUS ★★
FERNSEHTURM ★★
ALEXANDERPLATZ ★★

Platz der Akademie★ (Ex-Gendarmenmarkt) (GV). – Two churches – the French Reformed Church *(Huguenot Museum)* and the Evangelical Lutheran Church – surround the Schauspielhaus, a theatre rebuilt by Schinkel in 1821.

March Museum (Märkisches Museum) (HV M¹). – History of Berlin and the Brandenburg march.

Treptow Park Soviet Memorial★ (Sowjetisches Ehrenmal) (NS).

Köpenick Château (Schloss Köpenick) (NS). – In the Baroque style, it holds the Museum of Decorative Arts.

Grosser Müggelsee (NS). – The largest of Berlin lakes; at Müggelturm is panoramic terrace.

Museum Island

Pergamon Museum★★★ (Pergamon-Museum). – The department of Oriental and Greco-Roman Antiquities is marvellous: **Pergamon Altar★★★ Market Gate★★** from Miletus, Babylonian **Processional Way★★**

National Gallery★★ (Nationalgalerie). – Painting and sculpture from the 19C.

Bode Museum★ (GHU M²). – Egyptian Antiques as well as Byzantine and Paleochristian collections.

Old Museum (Altes Museum) (HU M³). – A fine colonnade by Schinkel. 20C painting and sculpture.

Marx-Engels Platz★ (HU). – Where the Royal Palace used to stand, the square is the site of the Ministry of Foreign Affairs, the State Consul and the Palace of the Republic.

Right Bank of the Spree

Alexanderplatz★★. – Centre of life in East Berlin: stores, restaurants and the "Universal Clock".

Television Tower★★ (Fernsehturm). – The 365 m - 1 197 ft high tower has a revolving sphere (restaurant and observation terrace).

Karl-Marx-Allee★ (HU). – Considered the prestige avenue of the Eastern Sector it is embellished by international hotels, restaurants, cafés and cinemas.

St. Mary's (Marienkirche) (HU E). – A Flamboyant Gothic hall-church.

Town Hall (Rathaus) (HU R). – This brick building was built between 1861 and 1870.

Friedrichshain Park (HU). – Fountains play in the Fairy Basin (Märchenbrunnen).

BERNKASTEL-KUES ★

Michelin map 𝟐𝟎𝟑 6 – *Local maps pp 115 and 181* – Pop 7 800

Bernkastel-Kues is, in fact, two towns, lying on either side of the Mosel where a ravine cut through the Hunsrück schist opens into the main river. It is a well known wine growing centre which becomes very gay at the time of the wine festivals in the first week in September. Besides wine, which can be tasted in many cellars, the local speciality is Mosel smoked eel.

The **vineyards** cover the land flanking the bend in the Mosel and continue in closes in Graach and Zeltingen. It is the largest single vineyard in Germany: 95% are Riesling vines producing a dry white wine, of which the most sought after is the fruity *Bernkasteler Doktor*.

Markt★. – In the centre of this small sloping square which is surrounded by colour-washed half-timbered houses, stands a 17C angel fountain. In the Karlstrasse, to the right of the town hall, note the curious little pointed house with the tapering gable.

St. Nicholas' Hospital (Cusanusstift) at Kues. – *Open all the year round. Guided tours Mondays and Fridays in summer at 10am.*

The hospital was founded by Nicholas of Kues or Cusanus (1401-64), humanist, theologian and artist, who was born at Kues and wished to heal the sick poor; his work continues to this day. The number of boarders is kept symbolically at 33, the age of Christ when he died.

The chapel has an attractive 15C altarpiece depicting scenes of the *Crucifixion*. Note the bronze copy of the Cardinal's tombstone, the original is in Rome (San Pietro in Vincoli), on the left of the entrance is a 15C fresco, the *Last Judgment* and to the right a **tombstone** of Clara Cryftz, the prelate's sister. Mementoes of the founder are in the library.

EXCURSION

Landshut Castle (Burg Landshut). – *3 km - 2 miles – by the Longkamp road and the narrow uphill road to the castle on the right.* The castle standing on a promontory can be seen by anyone visiting the valley. From the 11C the castle belonged to the bishops of Trier; it was not spared by war and since 1692 has been a ruin. The **view★★** of the Mosel bend enables you to see the extent of the vineyard stretching from gentle to the most abrupt slopes.

BIELEFELD

Michelin map 𝟗𝟖𝟕 14 – Pop 322 000 – *Town plan in Michelin Red Guide Deutschland*

Bielefeld is spread out along the edge of the Teutoburger Wald, halfway between the Ruhr and Hanover, not only the linen industry which dates back to the 16C, but also the engineering industry (cycle manufacturer's, sewing machines, printing houses) created in the past century has made Bielefeld the major economic centre of East Wesphalia.

Badly damaged during the last World War, Bielefeld offers a group of old houses on the Old Market Square (Alter Markt), note particularly the **Crüwell-Haus** (1530). On a hill to the south stands the castle of the Earls of Ravensberg who founded the town in 1214: **Burg Sparrenburg** (restored – *closed Mondays*). *Access to the keep and the dungeons: 0.60DM and 0.80DM.*

Fine Arts Museum (Kunsthalle). – *Arthur-Ladebeck-Str. 5. Open Tuesdays to Saturdays 11am to 6pm (Thursdays 8pm); Sundays 10am to 6pm; 0.50DM.*

A selection of valuable works of art carefully displayed, provides an interesting display of German and European art in the first half of the 20C: paintings by Beckmann, Kandinsky, Nolde and Max Ernst; sculptures by Barlach and Richard Heizman (Big Black Car, Eagle).

Farm Museum (Bauernhaus-Museum). – *Dornberger Str. 82 (follow the indication signposted in front of the Kunsthalle). Open 10am to 1pm and 3 to 6pm (2 to 5pm October to March); closed Mondays; 0.50DM.*

This large north German farm *(p 30)* houses collections of utensils, costumes, jewels as well as traditional instruments used for the working of linen. A mill covered with wooden tiles and other outlying buildings complete the picture.

EXCURSIONS

Enger. – *17 km - 10 miles – plus ½ hour sightseeing.* Leave Bielefeld by the road to Bünde, north. Just before reaching Enger, you can see to the right of the road a beautiful windmill (Liesberg-Mühle) of 1756. The town is proud of possessing the remains of **Widukind** (or Wittekind), the leader of the Saxon resistance (778-85) against the Frankish King Charles (the future Charlemagne), and hero of several German historic legends.

The **collegiate church** (Stiftskirche) presents an unusual steeple and on the south portal an interesting Romanesque tympanum. Above the high altar an altarpiece in painted wood depicts the Passion of Christ. Behind the altar the sarcophagus of Widukind is covered by a carved recumbent figure (11C). At the east end of the church a small **museum** (Gedächtnisstätte) commemorates the Saxon hero and shows a replica of the former collegiate church treasure (8-13C) which is now kept in the Museum of Decorative Arts of Berlin-Charlottenburg *(p 72)*.

Herford. – *16 km - 10 miles.* Leave by ① on the plan. Among several Gothic churches, you should not miss the 17C carved and painted **woodwork★** of **St. John's** (Johanniskirche), a Protestant church: the galleries, the pews and the pulpit were offered by different guilds, whose crests are recognisable. In the chancel, note the 15C stained glass windows.

BINGEN

Michelin map 𝟐𝟎𝟒 16 – *Local maps pp 211 and 212* – Pop 26 900
Town plan in Michelin Red Guide Deutschland

The Rhine changes direction at this spot, heading north as it cuts a narrow passage through the Hercynian massifs *(p 209)*. This passage which is taken cautiously by navigators is known as the Binger Loch; it is guarded at its entrance by the **Mouse Tower** (Mäuseturm) which got its name from a legend. Archbishop Hatto of Mainz, to put an end to the plaints of a people half starved after a hard winter, had the beggars rounded up and put in a barn which was then set on fire. "Listen to my mice squeaking" said he in satisfaction, but a host of mice came out of the barn, chased him to the Bingen Tower and devoured him.

Burg Klopp. – At one time it was the fortress of the bishops of Mainz. From the town hall terrace there is an extensive **view★** of left, the twin town of Bingerbrück, an important railway marshalling yard; then the Binger Loch between the Hunsrück heights and the Rheingau hills; halfway up the hillside, surrounded by vines, the Ehrenfels ruin and, on the Germania plateau *(p 222)*, the Niederwald monument. Further over to the right are the St. Hildegarde Convent towers and, in the background, above Rüdesheim, the wooded peaks of the Taunus.

BIRNAU ★

Michelin map 206 18 – 5 km - 3 miles – southeast of Überlingen – Local map p 102

The Birnau pilgrimage church stands in one of the most open sites★★ on Lake Constance in full view of the Swiss Alpstein Massif (Säntis), often snowcapped far into the spring.

Church★ (Wallfahrtskirche). – Tour: $\frac{1}{2}$ hour. The present Rococo church was built from 1746 to 1750 by Peter Thumb, master of the Vorarlberg school, who was entrusted with the construction by the Cistercians of Salem (p 226).

The single aisle, lacking pillars, affords an uninterrupted view of the sombre narthex and light chancel. The Rococo charm can best be seen in the architectural design and painted decoration of the pierced roof above the aisle, the flattened dome above the chancel and the cupola over the apse. Halfway up the walls a delicate gallery is supported on corbels whose bosses are decorated with Rococo cartouches (illustration p 25).

The right altarpiece dedicated to St. Bernard of Clairvaux, has on its left the famous statuette of the Honey-Taster (Honigschlecker), a cherub sucking the finger he has just pulled out of a bees' nest. This theme, repeated in the picture, recalls the title, "doctor whose words are as sweet as honey", which was given to St. Bernard, founder of the Cistercian Order. The statuette is but one of the many works made for Birnau by the brilliant sculptor and stucco worker, J A Feuchtmayer. His talent is shown to greater advantage in the statue of St. Wendelin with a somewhat effete expression (at the top of the south niche in the nave), the two St. Johns – especially St. John the Baptist – on the altars marking the entrance to the apse, and the group of the Virgin's kinsmen round the high altar. Typical of Rococo decoration is the altarpiece encrusted with a hundred small mirrors.

Pilgrims come to venerate the 15C Virgin and Child above the tabernacle on the high altar.

The BLACK FOREST ★★ (SCHWARZWALD)

Michelin map 205 2 to 8, 14 to 19

The Black Forest stretches for 170 km - 106 miles – from Karlsruhe to Basle – long lines of dark crests facing across to the Vosges.

Between the two ranges, which bear a remarkable resemblance, lies the subsided Plain of the Rhine, a consequence of the Alpine fold. The crystalline base which rises in the south, drops gently towards the north in both the Black Forest and the Vosges, each having a limestone topsoil at its northern end. The two ranges approximate in altitude – the Feldberg reaches 1 493 m, the Grand Ballon 1 424 m – 4 899 and 4 674 ft; both are densely wooded and drop steeply towards the Rhine Plain and more gently on the opposite slopes, in one case towards the Swabian Plateaux of the Upper Neckar, and in the other to the Lorraine Plateau.

The Black Forest is a massif in its own right, however, and is both denser and vaster than the Vosges – 7 860 km² - 3 035 sq miles (Norfolk and Suffolk, 3 143 sq miles). The range, 60 km - 37 miles across at its widest point has no marked north–south line of crests or east–west passes. The generously rounded summits rarely afford good local viewpoints but observation towers fill the need. The Alps are most clearly seen in October and November.

The Forest is crossed by large valleys, particularly in the north where the Murg and the Kinzig gaps play an essential part in the country's economy as communications' channels.

The freshness of the woods and streams, the curative powers of the springs, the sight in a quiet valley of a typical house sheltering beneath an immense roof, all go to make the Black Forest popular with tourists even in winter. Cuckoo-clocks symbolise the area's rustic charm.

Traditional costume may be seen sometimes at local festivals, particularly that of the women of the Gutach Valley headdress (Bollenhut), loaded with huge black or red pompoms.

The Northern Black Forest. – The area, drained by the Murg, the Enz rivers and the Nagold, is sandy and covered with conifers. The vineyard and orchard fringe which spreads over the last foothills south of Baden-Baden, and the upper parts of the Grinde moors which are crossed by the Hochstrasse in the Zuflucht area, are in marked contrast and yet are only a few miles apart.

The Central Black Forest. – The region's main axis is formed by the Valleys of the Kinzig and the Gutach through whose gap the road and rail routes cut diagonally towards the Upper Danube and Lake Constance. The patchiness of the limestone topsoil is reflected in the way the pines grow in groves. A variety of contour and, on the horizon, an intermingling of fields and pastureland, compose an inviting and attractive region.

South of the Elz and the Breg Valleys the mean altitude increases: this is the **Upper Black Forest**, the Freiburg hinterland where the countryside from being pastoral becomes almost mountainous around the Feldberg where gentians grow. With the exception of the Belchen, the most sharply defined massif height, and the Feldsee rock amphitheatre, which is of glacial origin, the relief is seldom abrupt. Mountain excursions, sometimes rewarded by a view of the Alps, and bathing in the Titisee, draw crowds of tourists to this area.

The Southern Black Forest. – This region drops progressively towards the German-Swiss course of the Rhine and the waters of the Wehra, the Alb and the Schlücht bound through wild gorges before flooding into the river. This area leans economically towards Switzerland – particularly the Hotzenwald (St. Blasien and Todtmoos districts). The climate, favourable to mountain cures, makes the area, now a health resort, much frequented.

The Baden Vineyards. – The vineyards, forming a pendant to those of Alsace but smaller, outline with vines the contours of the last foothills of the Black Forest. The land is rich along the tourist route "Badische Weinstrasse-Oberrhein" (a typical section of this road starting from Baden-Baden is described on p 55). In addition to the vines, fruit is grown: cherries, Bühlertal strawberries and early Bühl quetschen (plums) which are often fermented to make schnapps.

South of the Kinzig, the lonely volcanic **Kaiserstuhl Massif** (p 154) provides both soil and climate favourable to vine growing.

1 ★★FROM BADEN-BADEN TO FREUDENSTADT
by the Crest Road (Schwarzwald-Hochstrasse)

60 km - 39 miles – about 2 hours – Local map p 81

The Black Forest Crest Road, the Hochstrasse, an excellent tourist road amply provided with belvederes and car parks approaches many winter ski slopes with mechanical hoists.

Baden-Baden★★★. –Description p 54. The road serves only large Kurhäuser and isolated hotels. The views over the Rhine Plain are outstanding in the corniche sections above the start of the Bühlertal and Laufbach Valleys. The chief belvederes signposted are:
– between Sand and Hundseck: Bühlertal – Rheinebene;
– $\frac{1}{2}$ mile south of Unterstmatt: Blick durch das Laufbachtal.

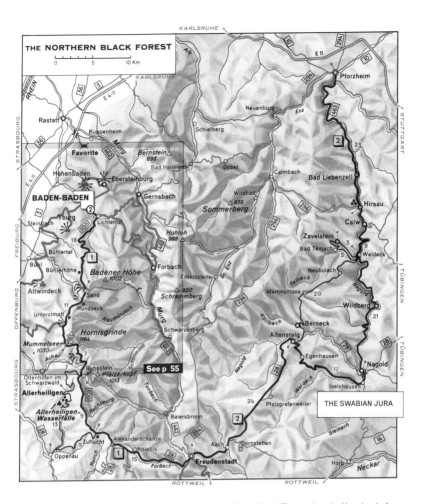

Mummelsee. – This small dark lake is a classic halt on the Crest Road. The road to the Hornisgrinde, the highest point in the northern Black Forest, starts from the Mummelsee.
Further south, between the Mummelsee and Ruhestein, the road circling the upper reaches of the Seebach Valley is very beautiful, particularly when the cherry blossom is out.

Alternative route from Ruhestein to Zuflucht via Allerheiligen and Oppenau.** – *Extra distance: 20 km - 12 miles. Allow an extra hour (twisting and hilly roads).*
Soon after leaving Ruhestein, the road drops towards the lonely Allerheiligen Combe, reaching the valley floor at the base of the Büttenstein Waterfall.
The suggested route from Oppenau, which is the most impressive of the Black Forest, climbs abruptly along steep slopes to join the Crest Road at Zuflucht.

Allerheiligen*. – The ruins of a church built in the latter half of the 13C for a Premonstratensian monastery add a romantic touch to the remote Allerheiligen **combe***.The roofed porch and the transept walls are still standing together with a polygonal Gothic chapel which leads off the transept. The three stepped fishponds date back to the 18C. A pleasant walk is downstream (*about ½ hour Rtn*) to the bottom of the Allerheiligen Falls.

Allerheiligen Waterfall*. – *Excursion of ¾ hour on foot Rtn from the road bridge at the bottom of the fall.* A stepped path gives a good view of the fall, the steep rock walls and huge trees. Above the upper fall the path becomes a road which leads to the Allerheiligen ruins.

Between Ruhestein and the built-up area of Kniebis, the road crosses a plateau region, which, as you approach Zuflucht, appears in the swampy moorland typical of the Grinde.

Freudenstadt*. – *Description p 127.*

② FROM PFORZHEIM TO FREUDENSTADT by the Nagold Valley
94 km - 58 miles – about 4 hours – Local map above

The drive along the twisting Nagold Valley, the natural frontier between the Black Forest and the Swabian plateaux to the east, would be very monotonous without the small wayside towns.

Pforzheim. – *Town plan in Michelin Red Guide Deutschland.* Pforzheim, has come alive again thanks to its economic revival which is based on the production of gold jewellery, wrist watches and costume jewellery. An attractive **jewellery museum** (Schmuckmuseum) has been established in the Reuchlinhaus, the new cultural centre in the Stadtgarten at the southern exit to the town.
Open weekdays 10am to 5pm; Sundays 10am to 1pm and 3 to 5pm; closed Mondays.

Bad Liebenzell. – This spa's **Kurpark** is a pleasing feature of the Nagold Valley.

Hirsau. – *Free visit of the ruins. Guided tours of the ruins and of St. Mary's Chapel: apply in advance to the Bath Administration (Kurverwaltung) ☎ 1896.*
Enter through the monumental doorway on the Wildbad road. The old Abbey of Hirsau, which has been in ruins since the Palatinate War of 1692 *(p 146)*, was the mother-house of an 11C reformed Benedictine congregation, which, under Cluny's influence, greatly changed monastic life and architecture in mediaeval Germany. The only parts of the abbey still standing are the elegant Romanesque Owl Tower (Eulenturm), decorated on three sides with a frieze roughly

carved with human and animal figures, the square cloister with Flamboyant windows and the Protestant Chapel of St. Mary whose upper storey now houses a historical and lapidary museum. The first monastery stood on the left bank of the Nagold. Its 11C Romanesque Church of St. Aurelian has been restored *(signposts from the car park: "Aureliuskirche")*; the patron saint's relics are kept in a modern bronze reliquary within the church.

Calw. – The centre of the town is reached over a mediaeval bridge, which supports a Gothic chapel on one of its piles. There are fine half-timbered houses, including **no 29 Lederstrasse** (bear right after crossing the bridge) with its huge pointed gable and stepped roof.

Wildberg. – *Tour: ¼ hour.* On your way to the upper town, which is encircled by a bend of the Nagold, you pass by the Rathaus, pierced by a covered alley, and the Marktbrunnen. This 1554 fountain is surmounted by a figure in 16C dress bearing the city's arms. At the end of the spur rise a few of the walls of the *Burg* whose approaches are public gardens.

Nagold. – The town, well situated in a wide basin at the head of the Nagold Defile, has an interesting half-timbered Post Hotel dating from 1697.

> **Alternative route★ by Zavelstein and Berneck.** – *Reduction of run: 10 km - 6 miles.* Two points are outstanding: the entry into the small Bad Teinach Valley dominated by the Zavelstein Burg, and the sudden appearance of Berneck.
>
> **Zavelstein.** – The village stands perched in a picturesque, almost romantic setting, where undulating woodland is punctuated by the silhouette of a castle whose restored tower now serves as a belvedere *(access March to September: weekdays 9am to 5pm; 0.30DM)*. The crocuses attract many visitors in early spring.
>
> **Berneck.** – The road, as it drops down from the plateau, affords a good **view★** of the village which is curiously built along a hill ridge at the foot of the castle. This, in its turn, abuts on the high defensive wall of the old feudal castle.
>
> 3 km after Berneck, take the suggested route to Altensteig.

Altensteig. – The best view of this small town in its **setting★** is from the Egenhausen road: before you, on the opposite hillside, their gables all pointing towards the valley, the houses rise one above the other until they reach the church and the foot of the castle.

③ ★ FROM FREUDENSTADT TO FREIBURG

by Triberg and Furtwangen

124 km - 76 miles – about 5½ hours – Local map adjoining

This route across the Central Black Forest, the "kingdom of the cuckoo-clock", keeps to good roads along the valleys. Some are quiet, such as those in the Upper Kinzig and Simonswald Valleys; some, such as those in the Gutach Valley, are noisy with heavy traffic. The itinerary passes through attractive towns, some old and seemingly moribund, others reinvigorated by the watch and clock industry.

Alpirsbach★. – *Tour: ½ hour.* The **old abbey★** (Ehemaliges Kloster) church is the most important late 11, early 12C Romanesque building in the Black Forest.
Before entering the church, go into the gardens at the east end to see the unusual lines of the apse. The main west door, beyond a porch with three arches, is surmounted by a 12C tympanum carved to show Christ in Majesty surrounded by angels and two church donors. The interior simplicity is typical of the ascetic leanings of the Hirsau school *(p 81)*.

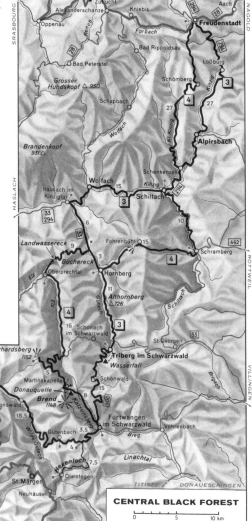

CENTRAL BLACK FOREST

0   5   10 km

Three niches hollowed out at the lower level of the apse contain traces of 12C wall paintings. To visit the cloisters come out of the church and go through the former abbey buildings by way of a door with a pointed arch which opens opposite the *Burg.*

Schiltach. – The town hall square is irregular, sloping and picturesque with wooden gabled houses and old inns.

Wolfach. – The town, which is confined between the mountain and a bend in the Kinzig, lies on either side of a curved street and so provides an unusual vista. The main road enters the town from the south through a passageway cut through a building attached to a castle once owned by the Fürstenbergs. This castle almost blocks the valley.

Triberg*. – *Description p 244.*

Furtwangen. – *Description p 130.*

④ ****FROM FREUDENSTADT TO FREIBURG**
by the Kleine-Kinzig Valley, Schramberg and the source of the Danube
141 km - 88 miles – about 5½ hours – Local map p 82

The preponderantly minor roads demand constant vigilance, particularly in the Kleine-Kinzig Valley, throughout the Rohrhardsberg sector and at the source of the Danube (forest roads cut by sharp and steep rises – watch the crossroad signposts carefully).

Schiltach. – *Description above.*
The crossing of two passes in succession, the Büchereck and the Landwassereck, halfway between Freudenstadt and Furtwangen, and the Rohrhardsberg summit provide good **views*** of the rolling country of the Central Black Forest.
Before Oberprechtal there is a delightful **run*** beside the small cascades of the Elz.

Rohrhardsberg. – ¼ *hour on foot Rtn.* The Gasthaus Schwedenschanze path goes to the Rohrhardsberg's rounded summit from where one can see pastureland dotted with chalets.

Source of the Danube or **Donauquelle.** – ¼ *hour on foot Rtn.* Below a chapel and the Gasthaus Donauquelle, lies the source of the Breg; this is now called "the source of the Danube". A plaque describes the journey undertaken by this spring before flowing into the Black Sea. *See p 104.*

Katzensteig. – A series of large mountain farms is strung out along a cradle shaped valley.

Furtwangen. – *Description p 130.*

Hexenloch*. – *Excursion of 7.5 km - 4½ miles – about ½ hour.* Deep wooded gorge with waterfalls (turn back at the Dreisteige Inn in Dreistegen hamlet).
The watch and clock industry, which provides a living for Schramberg and Furtwangen, also prospers in the Upper Simonswald Valley – at Gütenbach for example.

Waldkirch. – A small industrial town with castle ruins and a Marktplatz with a fountain. The tranquil shaded quarter of the Church of St. Margaret at the beginning of the Kandel road is charming. Lovely 18C houses surround the old Baroque collegiate church.

Freiburg im Breisgau**. – *Description p 125.*

⑤ ****TOUR THROUGH THE UPPER BLACK FOREST**
starting from Freiburg im Breisgau
162 km - 101 miles – a day's drive – Local map p 84

The main attraction of the Freiburg-Todtnau stage is the Schauinsland road, famous in the motor world for the annual hill race held at the end of July around its wicked bends.

Schauinsland. – *Excursion of ½ hour on foot Rtn to the viewing table. Description p 127.*

Todtnauberg*. – This, the highest situated resort in the Black Forest (1 019 m - 3 300 ft), is in a delightful **setting*** with its pine shingled chalets dispersed in a combe.
Below the village, the stream cascades in two series of **waterfalls*** through a wooded rock fault *(1 hour on foot Rtn).* This can also be reached directly from the valley by leaving the car on the itinerary road between Schauinsland and Todtnau.

Alternative route*** by the Belchen. – *Extra distance 25 km - 16 miles – reckon 1½ hours.* This itinerary includes the Belchen with its splendid viewpoint.

Staufen. – This small town, sheltering in one of the last of the Black Forest recesses, has a smart Marktplatz with a fountain and a brightly painted Rathaus (1546).
The Staufenburg ruins are reached *(¾ hour on foot Rtn)* from the Schlossgasse which branches off the town's encircling road. The castle **site*** at the summit of a vine-covered spike commands an extensive view of the Rhine Plain, the Kaiserstuhl and the Vosges. The climb to the rounded Belchen is through the Münstertal which is embellished by the St. Trudpert Abbey group of buildings and, higher up, by the Rehfelsen rocks.

Belchen***. – *From the Belchenhaus Hotel, at the end of the road, it takes ½ hour on foot Rtn to reach the viewing table on the summit.* This rounded mountain with its steep, bare flanks dominates the Wiesental and valleys such as the Münstertal which interlace the west side of the Black Forest. It is the perfect **observation point*****, close to the Rhine Plain, and facing the rounded High Vosges. The Alps can be seen to the south ranging from the Säntis, in the Appenzell Swiss Alps, to Mont Blanc.
The descent is by a small mountain road which is interesting but very narrow. It comes out on road no 317, between Utzenfeld and Schönau.

The lovely Feldberg road leads near to the highest point in the Black Forest.

Feldberg**. – *About 1 hour Rtn from the Feldbergpass including ¼ hour in a chairhoist and ¼ hour walking to the Bismarck's statue and the television tower.*
The chairhoist *(service: 9am to 5pm; Rtn fare: 2.50DM)* takes you to the Bismarck's statue, from which there is a bird's-eye **view**** of the **Feldsee****, a small lake enclosed in a ring of hills. The walk can be extended by climbing to the nearby television tower *(lift: 0.50DM)* where the **panorama**** of the horizon is not quite circular as the Feldberg summit hides the Vosges.

Schluchsee. – A dam has raised the level of the water, altered the setting and so enlarged the lake that it is now the most extensive in the Black Forest. The climb above the town of Schluchsee going towards Fischbach provides one of the best general views of the lake.
A somewhat austere wooded countryside lies between the Schluchsee and Neustadt. The undulating run, however, holds surprises – the sudden appearance of the Schluchsee, the heights looking down on the town and the Kappel sector.

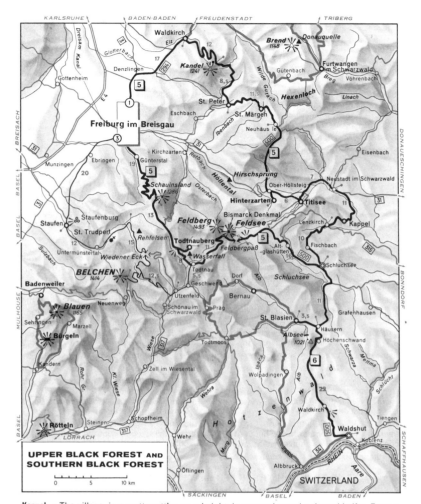

UPPER BLACK FOREST AND
SOUTHERN BLACK FOREST

0   5   10 km

Kappel. – The village, in a pretty **setting** on a height, is grouped round a domed belfry. From a terrace, there is a view across a series of terraced woods to the distant Feldberg tower.

Titisee*. – Thanks to the lovely **lake*** formed by the moraine barrage, it attracts holidaymakers who enjoy water sports and excursions into the Black Forest. It is in fact from Titisee that the network of roads spreads out to serve the southern end of the massif and the best known sights. Leave Titisee by road no 31 towards Freiburg. At Ober-Höllsteig, turn left to reach Hinterzarten.

Hinterzarten*. – Stylish mountain resort, fairly quiet and dispersed over the shelf dividing the Höllental and the Titisee.

The **road****, which climbs continuously, runs along the mountainside between Ober-Höllsteig and Neuhäusle, to reach the wide plateau pastureland. Here the belfries of St. Peter and St. Märgen rise to face the Feldberg which can be recognised by its tower.

St. Märgen. – A country market town built in a sunny setting high on the plateau. The rebuilt Baroque **church,** contains a Romanesque Virgin which is venerated by pilgrims.

St. Peter. – St. Peter, whose abbey towers are a landmark throughout the north of the Höllental, has become a resort. The Baroque **church** (1727) is the burial place of the Dukes of Zähringen.

Kandel*. – $\frac{1}{2}$ hour on foot Rtn. Go from the hotel at the end of the road to a pavilion, which you can see, containing a viewing table: **panorama*** of the Vosges, from the Ballons to the Donon; in the Rhine Plain, note the Breisach Rock and the lonely Kaiserstuhl Massif; on the Black Forest side the towers of St. Peter and the Feldberg and Belchen heights.

Waldkirch. – *Description p 83.*

⑥ *FROM SCHLUCHSEE TO WALDSHUT by St. Blasien
40 km - 25 miles – about 1½ hours – Local map above

The Hotzenwald plateau, whose even slopes sweep down to the Rhine, succeeds, south of St. Blasien, a hilly forest region cut by deep valleys, such as the Schwarza Valley (Schwarzhalden).

St. Blasien. – *Description p 225.*

The route runs across the plateau, affording for long periods far-away views of the Swiss lowlands. In clear weather the Swiss Alps and Jura can be seen on the horizon.
Suddenly as you come out of a wood and pass beneath a high-tension cable, you see a bend in the Rhine with, above it, the houses of Waldshut all crowded together.

Waldshut. – The town, within sight of the Swiss plateau and the Alps, is pleasantly situated halfway up a wooded semicircular slope.
Waldshut retains its two fortified gateways and its **Kaiserstrasse** whose ordered lines are broken by gables with overhanging eaves reminiscent of Bernese country houses. Walk, if the morning is fine, beside the Rhine: take the bridge above the Oberes Tor (Upper Gate) across a ravine on the Koblenz road, then bear right, walking down the ravine to the ferry landing stage. The old town is reached by the Bernhalde rise.

84

BONN ★

Michelin map **203** 2 – *Local map p 213* – Pop 283 000

Bonn, the "federal village" as it is sometimes called by the West Germans, has been the seat of the Federal Government since 1949.

The disparity between its size as a German town and its present governmental function in a land of 58 million inhabitants emphasises the temporary nature of its current status and the desire to see Berlin as Germany's capital once more.

Political life has, however, temporarily concentrated in Bonn, entailing a sharp increase in population, the erection of new buildings and improvements in communications.

Since 1969, Bonn, Beuel and Bad Godesberg are for administrative purposes one town.

Beethoven's Youth. – Ludwig van Beethoven (1770-1827), the precursor of romantic music, was born and grew up in the quarter round the Church of St. Remigius (CY).

At sixteen he was already a distinguished musician, attached to the chapel of the brilliant court of the Elector. At this time he joined the von Breuning family who liked and encouraged him. At twenty-two, a great admirer of Mozart and Haydn, he left Bonn finally for Vienna, arriving with only his virtuosity at the piano as baggage.

The **Beethovenhalle** (CY), a bold example of modern architecture and the finest concert hall in the town, is the setting for the biennial Beethoven Festival.

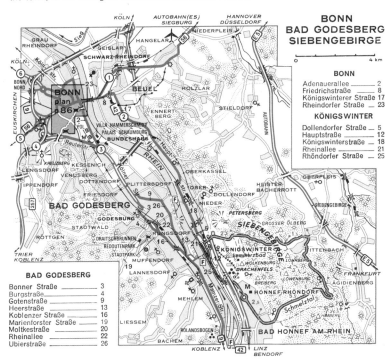

■ **MAIN SIGHTS** *time: 2 hours*

Government Quarter★ (Regierungsviertel). – *Plan p 86.* This has developed southeast of the town, between the Rhine and the Koblenzer Strasse, in a residential district.

The **Hammerschmidt Villa** and the **Schaumburg Palace**, the Presidential Residence and the Federal Chancellery respectively and both white, stand surrounded by parkland.

The **Bundeshaus★**, where Parliament (Bundestag) and the Federal Council (Bundesrat) both sit, is a modern complex building facing the Rhine. *Guided tours of the chamber when no plenary sessions are in progress: weekdays 9am to 4pm (2pm Fridays); Saturdays and Sundays, 1 March to 31 October, 9am to 4pm; entrance V, Rhine façade.*

Beethoven's Birthplace★ (Beethovenhaus). – *Open April to September, 9am to 1pm and 3pm to 6pm; October to March, 9.30am (10am Sundays) to 1pm and 3 to 5pm; closed Sunday afternoons; 1.50DM.*

The house where Beethoven first lived stands in a court in the old town. A family tree may be seen in the hall; at the end of the garden is a bronze statue of the composer by a student of Rodin. On the second floor, the room where he was born is ornamented only with a marble bust. In the larger room next door are personal Beethoven mementoes: ear trumpets, a viola, grand piano and a cast of his face at 42. In the small rooms on the first floor are a few pieces of furniture, the organ on which he played when 10 years old, original scores and souvenirs of his friends and great Beethoven interpreters.

The house next door, Zum Mohren, contains Beethoven archives.

■ **ADDITIONAL SIGHTS**

Collegiate Church (Münster) (CZ A). – The eastern end of the chancel and the towers are 12C Rhineland Romanesque, whereas the nave, by its height, is already transitional Gothic. The transepts end in semicircular apses. The 11C crypt has been restored.

The greater part of the furnishings are Baroque. Note the altars (1735) at the beginning of the chancel and the bronze statue of St. Helen (1620) in the nave.

Cloister★ (Kreuzgang). – *Open weekdays 10am to 6pm.*

The collegiate church has a delightful 12C cloister on its south side.

Town Hall (CY R). – Pleasant Rococo building with a pink and grey façade.

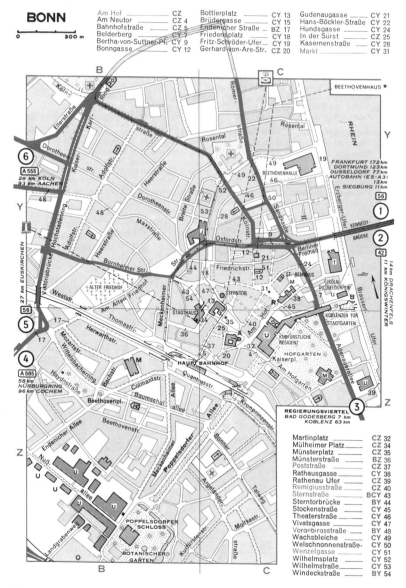

BONN

0 ___ 300 m

University (CZ U). – The University is in the Electors' Castle, a long Baroque building whose charm is greatly enhanced by the Hofgarten lawns which surround it.

Alter Zoll (CY B). – There is a **view★** from the bastion top of the Rhine and the Siebengebirge range. The Rhine embankment at the foot of the terrace makes a pleasant walk.

Poppelsdorf Castle (Poppelsdorfer Schloss) (BZ). – The Elector Clement Augustus entrusted the design of this building in 1715 to the architect Robert de Cotte *(p 26)*. It is linked to the electoral castle by the **Poppelsdorfer Allee,** a long avenue of chestnut trees which provides the town's finest vista. The façade with three gables shows French influence, whereas the inner courtyard, bordered by a semicircular colonnade is Italian in style. At the back, on the now level ground where the moat once flowed, are the University botanical gardens.

Rhineland Museum (Rheinisches Landesmuseum) (BZ M). – *Open 10am to 5pm (9pm Wednesdays); closed Mondays; 1DM.*

The prehistorical collection includes the skull of Neanderthal man *(p 112)*.

The department of **Roman Antiquities★★** (Römische Abteilung) is the most interesting, containing altars, funerary monuments, terracottas, glass, etc. Note the altars to the Matrones, evidence of a cult of benignant deities which was widespread among landowners in the Rhine Valley in Roman times. The fine votive stone found beneath Bonn Cathedral in 1928 shows clearly the distinguishing physical characteristic of the Matrones – a huge round headdress.

The Frankish period is represented by pieces of gold and silver plate.

Mediaeval art is to be seen in the Romanesque section (Euskirchen Virgin).

19C paintings and engravings of the Rhine Valley landscape have been collected in an annexe *(Neubau)* added to the museum in 1967.

EXCURSION

Schwarz-Rheindorf★. – *Local map p 85. 3 km - 2 miles – by the Rhine bridge (Kennedy-Brücke) and the Rheindorfer Strasse on the left through the Beuel suburb, plus ⅓ hour sightseeing.* This two storey Romanesque **church★** was consecrated in 1151. The upper part gives directly on to the palace and was reserved for the archbishop and his immediate circle; his attendants occupied the ground floor. The walls of this lower floor are decorated with most expressive Romanesque frescoes illustrating the Book of Ezekiel.

BAD GODESBERG ★

Detailed plan in Michelin Red Guide Deutschland.

Godesberg, with its comfortable villas, parks and modern buildings, serves as a residential suburb to Bonn and as the seat of some diplomatic missions, ministries and international organisations. Diplomats, senior civil servants and industrialists meet in this pleasant setting before the Siebengebirge mountains on the banks of the Rhine for conferences and social exchanges.

The Godesburg and Drachenfels ruins, on either side of the river, are characteristic of the legendary Rhine scene.

The Rhine Promenade★ (Rheinufer). – The walk along the Rhine between the ferry landing stages is popular especially at sunset when the **view★** is at its best. The Petersberg Hotel and the Drachenfels ruins look down on an endless flow of river traffic.

Godesburg. – The castle ruins which have been restored and are now part of a hotel, stand in the centre of the town upon a basalt rock. The castle, built in the 13C by the Electors of Cologne, was destroyed in 1583.

There is a **panorama★** from the terrace and an even better one from the keep *(access 1 April to 31 October, 10am to 6pm; 0.30DM)* of the town and its surrounding hills, the Bonn depression northwards as far as Cologne and to the east over the Siebengebirge and the Rhine (right to left – the Drachenfels ruins, Drachenburg Castle halfway up a slope, and the Petersberg).

The Parks. – A continuous green area between the station and the forest (Stadtwald) is formed by the **Municipal** (Stadtpark), the **Redoute** and the **Draitschbrunnen Parks.** The small and elegant 18C **Redoute Castle** is a social centre for those taking the cure and a diplomatic conference centre.

BRAUNSCHWEIG See Brunswick p 90

BREISACH ★

Michelin map **205** 16 – Pop 9 200

Breisach and its rock, crowned by a large church, stand towering above the river facing the fortified town of Neuf-Brisach in France which was built in the 17C on the left bank of the Rhine. The rock at Breisach was the heart of a system of fortifications which was among the most redoubtable in Europe. Breisach's exposed position made it, after the Westphalian Treaties, sometimes a French bridgehead, sometimes an Imperial advance post and resulted in its overrunning by French Revolutionary troops in 1793 and again by the Allied armies of 1945.

Church. – Approach from the south up a rise which still has two fortified gateways.

The church **site★** commands the Rhine Valley. Of the Romanesque church built on the basilical plan *(p 23)* there remains the nave, the transept and the two Clock Towers flanking the apse, as at Freiburg. One hundred years later, between 1300 and 1330 a new Gothic chancel was constructed resting on the roof of a lower church with pointed arches still visible at ground level.

The church's most important work of art is the carved **altarpiece★** on the high altar (1526). The style is far advanced on the Gothic original: from an incredibly complicated decoration of leaves, flowing hair and draperies blowing in tempestuous winds and an avalanche of cherubim, emerge uneasily the figures of the Eternal Father and Christ crowning the Virgin. The panels are dedicated, on the left, to St. Stephen and St. Lawrence, and on the right to St. Gervase and St. Protase.

In addition there are a Gothic roodscreen and, in the transept crossing, a group of late 15C mural paintings of the *Last Judgment* by Martin Schongauer of Colmar.

Terrace (views★). – Viewing tables enable you to pick out the Black Forest heights to the south, the Sundgau and Lomont peaks, the Vosges, from the Grand Ballon to Upper Königsburg Castle and, quite close, the Kaiserstuhl.

In the foreground the frontier bridge across the Rhine leads to the lock gates and the Vogelgrün power station which mark the end of the main reach of the Great Alsatian Canal *(p 209)*.

BREMEN ★★

Michelin map **987** 14, 15 – Pop 572 000

Built up area plan in Michelin Red Guide Deutschland

Bremen, at the end of the long Weser Estuary, and Bremerhaven its outer harbour 59 km - 37 miles downstream, together form a remarkable port system. Bremen itself is the oldest German maritime city; from 965 it had market rights; in 1358 it joined the Hanseatic League; in 1646 it was declared a Free Imperial city; in 1783 it began to trade with America.

By tradition it is a cotton and a coffee town: its cotton exchange stands beside Liverpool as a world authority.

But Bremen is also a cultured town where the Weser Renaissance style flowered *(p 141)*.

For those who enjoy good food, in addition to overseas specialities, there are many typical Bremen dishes: chicken stew *(Kükenragout)*, Vegesack herring *(Vegesacker Matjeshering)*, cabbage and black pudding sausage *(Braunkohl mit Pinkelwurst)*.

■ THE PORT

The port of Bremen provides 40% of the townspeople with their living. It ranks second to Hamburg as a German commercial port with 26 million tons of traffic in 1973; in addition there are more than 7 million tons of river traffic.

It has specialised in handling tropical raw materials – principally cotton, wool, coffee, tobacco, cereals and wood. About 10% of Germany's foreign trade, including exports (industrial and engineering products), passes through Bremen.

The free ports of Überseehafen and Europahafen, and, on the left bank, Neustädterhafen, are among the most active of the dock basins. The medley of flags, variety of merchandise and modern equipment – transporters and containers – are symbolic of modern Bremen.

Tour. – *A motorboat service starting from the landing stage near St. Martin's Church* (**BY K**) *tours the port. Time: 1¼ hours: departures from 10am to 4.30pm (end March to end October); fare: 5DM.*

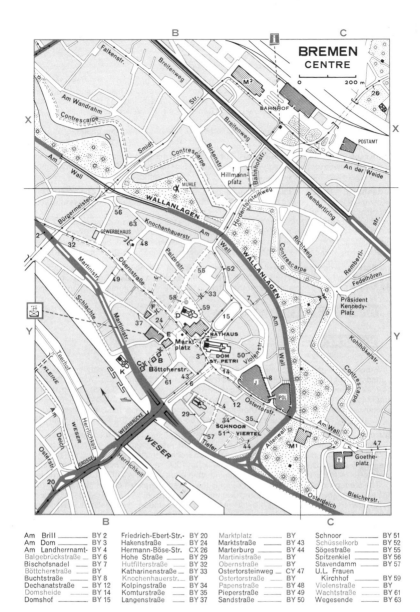

Am Brill	BY 2	Friedrich-Ebert-Str.-	BY 20	Marktplatz	BY	Schnoor	BY 51
Am Dom	BY 3	Hakenstraße	BY 24	Marktstraße	BY 43	Schüsselkorb	BY 52
Am Landherrnamt-	BY 4	Hermann-Böse-Str.	CX 26	Marterburg	BY 44	Sögestraße	BY 55
Balgebrückstraße	BY 6	Hohe Straße	BY 29	Martinistraße	BY	Spitzenkiel	BY 56
Bischofsnadel	BY 7	Hutfilterstraße	BY 32	Obernstraße	BY	Stavendamm	BY 57
Böttcherstraße	BY	Katharinenstraße	BY 33	Ostertorsteinweg	CY 47	U.L. Frauen	
Buchtstraße	BY 8	Knochenhauerstr.	BY	Ostertorstraße	BY	Kirchhof	BY 59
Dechanatstraße	BY 12	Kolpingstraße	BY 34	Papenstraße	BY 48	Violenstraße	BY
Domsheide	BY 14	Komturstraße	BY 35	Pieperstraße	BY 49	Wachtstraße	BY 61
Domshof	BY 15	Langenstraße	BY 37	Sandstraße	BY 50	Wegesende	BY 63

■ **MAIN SIGHTS** *tour: 1½ hours*

Marktplatz★★ (BY). – The Market Square lies in the heart of the old town. A giant 30 ft **statue of Roland** (1400), beneath a Gothic canopy, marks the centre. The knight bears the sword of justice and a shield adorned with the imperial eagle.

The **Schütting** (**E**), a restrained but elegant building of the 16C, formerly housed the guild of merchants. The decoration of its façade shows a Flemish influence.

Town Hall★ (BY). – The main building is Gothic with decorative gables, a transformation made in the Weser Renaissance style. The main façade is divided into three storeys: the arcaded gallery is emphasised by a balustrade, the middle storey alternates tall windows and Gothic statues of Charlemagne and the seven Electors, the top is crowned with three gables.

At the corner of the west wing stands the modern statue of the Street Musicians of Bremen (a pyramid of an ass, a dog, a cat and a cock) from the popular story by the Brothers Grimm.

Interior. – *Tours at 10am (except Sundays), 11am and noon when no session; closed Sundays November to February.*

The state room on the first floor is adorned with a splendid carved wood spiral **staircase★★** (Treppe – 1620). The Renaissance decoration recalls the connection with the law courts (the *Judgment of Solomon*) and the sea (ships). The *Ratskeller* serves German wines only.

Cathedral★ (Dom St. Petri) (BY). – The cathedral generally has the same massive appearance as it did in the 11C but in detail the effect of the rebuilding of the 16 and 19C is clearly apparent.

Inside from the nave, the development in mediaeval architecture can be traced from Romanesque to late Gothic and is at its best in the fan vaulting above the north aisle.

The last chapel in the south aisle contains the remains of some Gothic stalls. Against the first pillar on the left of the raised chancel stands a fine 16C **Virgin and Child★**. Among the 16C carvings on the organ balustrade can be seen, in the centre, the figures of Charlemagne and Willehad, first bishop of Bremen, carrying a model of the cathedral. Beneath the organ loft is the 11C crypt with Romanesque capitals and a magnificent 13C bronze **font★★** (Taufbecken).

In the southeast corner is an ancient chapel, the *Bleikeller* (lead cellar), which contains mummies. *Open May to October, 9am to noon and 2 to 5pm; closed Saturday afternoons, Sundays and holidays; 1DM. Brochure in English.*

■ ADDITIONAL SIGHTS

Rampart Walk★ (Wallanlagen) (BY). – The walk includes lovely green spaces where the old bastions used to be; also a working windmill.

Böttcherstrasse★ (BY). – This narrow street which runs from the Marktplatz to the Weser was built from 1923 to 1933 by the industrialist Roselius. The tall brick houses with gables, whose peculiar design was influenced by the Jugendstil *(p 26)*, house art galleries, museums, theatres, bookshops, inns, etc.
The porcelain **carillon**, set between two gables, chimes at noon, 3 and 6pm.

Roselius (no 6) **and Paula Modersohn-Becker Houses★** (no 8) (BY B). – *The houses inter-communicate and are open at the same time: Mondays to Fridays 10am to 4pm (Mondays, Tuesdays, Wednesdays 7 to 9pm), Saturdays 10am to 2pm, Sundays 11am to 1pm and 3 to 6pm; 1DM.*
 The Paula Modersohn-Becker House is dedicated to the woman painter who lived sometimes in Bremen but more often in Worpswede *(see below)*. The room on the first floor shows her most important works: *Young Girls in a Pastoral Setting (Elsbeth), Still Life with an Egg and Bread, Peasantwoman with a Bottle* and self-portraits.
 Roselius House, an authentic 16C merchant's mansion, contains mediaeval furniture and art objects collected by Roselius.

Atlantis House (no 2) (BY C). – This 1932 block, decorated with signs of the zodiac, has a curious spiral staircase of glass and concrete.

Schnoor★ (BY). – The cottages in this quarter were formerly occupied by fisherfolk. Illuminated restaurants, craft and antique shops provide a centre of attraction for tourists in the evening.

Church of Our Lady (Liebfrauenkirche) (BY D). – The church's bare interior is distinguished by 13C rounded ogive vaulting.

Municipal Weights and Measures Office (Stadtwaage) (BY F). – A lovely 16C building with alternating use of brick and embossed stone.

St. Martin's Church (BY K). – This 13 and 14C hall-type church has transverse gables on the side facing the Weser.

Art Gallery★ (Kunsthalle) (BCY M¹). – *Open 10am to 4pm (2pm Saturdays and Sundays) Tuesdays and Fridays also 7 to 9pm; closed Mondays; 0.50DM.*
 19 and 20C German and French schools are outstanding in this gallery. Detailed commentaries describe the place of the Worpswede School *(see below)* and in particular of Paula Modersohn-Becker and of such French artists as Delacroix, Courbet and Daumier.

Focke Museum★★. – *In Schwachhausen. Open weekdays 10am to 4pm (6pm Wednesdays); Sundays and holidays 10am to 2pm; closed Mondays and some holidays; 0.50DM.*
 The quality of the objects and the way they are presented make the visit particularly attractive. In the entrance hall the model of an 18C convoy-ship and the wooden chest decorated with wrought iron symbolise navigation and trade, traditional activities of Hanseatic towns and the affluence of these merchants.
 In the main gallery are evoked the power and the wealth of Bremen during the Middle Ages and the Renaissance through original statues from the façade of the Town Hall, church furnishings, crockery and works of art from aristocratic houses. The first floor *(staircase at the back on the right)* typifies the art of the 17C and 18C: engraved cups, portraits of merchants, stained glass windows, silver and gold objects and ceramics.
 Return to the ground floor. There is a gallery with Prehistoric, Roman and Saxon antiquities from the region of Bremen. Another gallery illustrates the history of navigation from the Middle Ages with a model of a cog, a broadly built ship with bluff prow and stern. The original is to be seen in Bremerhaven *(p 90)*. Other examples of a town whose history is linked to the sea include whaling (instruments, carved whalebones), the transport of emigrants to the United States, the famous steamers of the Norddeutscher Lloyd and the shipbuilding yards. A small tobacco museum recalls that the port of Bremen has been one of the major importers of "Nicot's plant" since the 17C. In the park, do not miss the typical Lower Saxony farm, its barn and well.

Overseas Museum (Überseemuseum) (BX M²). – *Scheduled to reopen in 1979.*
 The museum is both ethnographic and commercial and exhibits the chief products of tropical countries.

EXCURSION

Worpswede. – *24 km - 15 miles – about 2 hours.* Leave Bremen by the Lilienthaler Heerstrasse (northeast of the built up area plan – *See Michelin Red Guide Deutschland*).
 This village, lying at one time at the centre of a peat-bog, attracted a colony of artists who were tired of living in Munich and Berlin at the end of the 19C. Since then galleries, studios and craftshops have multiplied.
 Odd, asymmetrical buildings such as the Worpswede Café and Niedersachsenstein (1914-18 War Memorial) illustrate the ambitious ideas of the colony's architects.

■ BREMERHAVEN ★

Michelin map **987** 4 – Pop 144 000 – *Town plan in Michelin Red Guide Deutschland*

 Bremerhaven, a city with no past history, was founded at the mouth of the Weser Estuary in 1827 as Bremen's deep sea port; its life is directed towards the North Sea.
 Since the disappearance of the luxury liners, cruise ships and ferries berth at the ship terminal of **Columbuskaje**, which was for a long time one of the starting points for the transatlantic crossings. The port is still alive with the bustle of passenger traffic.
 To the north of the town, the cargo ships which carry containers and ore and link Germany to the Americas and Far East, use a large container terminal **(Container-Kreuz)** protected from the tides. Loading and unloading time is reduced to a minimum.
 The odour of fish permeates the southern part of the town where the fishing port **(Fischereihafen)** is located. Half the West German fishing fleet is based on Bremerhaven. Each trawler brings in, on the average, 170 000 tons of fish a year.
 The most interesting sight is the fish auction, held at 7am on weekdays in the Fischauktionshallen sheds.

■ **SIGHTS** time: 2 hours

National Maritime Museum★★★ (Deutsches Schiffahrtsmuseum). – Old Port Basin. Open 10am to 6pm; closed Mondays; 2DM. The ships of the open air museum are only open from 1 April to 30 September.

Facing the sea and built by the architect Scharoun, this museum was inaugurated in 1975. It traces the history of the German merchant service since ancient times (the Navy has its own museum in Kiel-Laboe – p 160).

Basement. – Liners after 1900 (luxury cabin of the Cap Polonia, deck and bridge of the paddle-boat Meissen, mementoes and bell of the Bremen); description of the (modern) traffic of the ports of Bremen and Bremerhaven (basin with models operated by visitors).

Ground floor. – The age of the great sailing ships (18C-1918) and whalers (cabin of a whaler captain); the different types of fishing; the shipbuilding yards.

First floor. – Models of old European boats; pleasure boats; navigation in the mouth of the Elbe and the Weser (old charts, instruments, light of a lighthouse). Note a 1944 pocket submarine with part of its hull removed.

At the back of the museum is a special hall **(Koggehalle)** immersed in an artificial mist in a Hanseatic **cog** (1380) discovered in the port of Bremen in 1962. This one-sailed and shallow-draught ship was very common during the Middle Ages, it could transport up to 120 tons of goods and call at small ports. In the nearby galleries German navigation is traced prior to the 12C: flat-bottomed skiff used on the Rhine, Roman bireme and Viking ships.

Boat shed (Bootshalle). – River and sea boats: pleasure boats, lifeboats, etc.

Open air museum (Freilichtmuseum). – Seven original ships are moored in the Old Port: the sailing ship Grönland which accomplished the first German polar exploration to the Arctic; the three-masted Seute Deern (last German wooden sailing ship, 1919); the lightship Elbe 3 (1909); the ocean-going tug Seefalke; the small Antarctic whaler Rau IX; the fast patrol boat Kranich and a boat (1953) said to be the prototype of the hydroplane.

Deichpromenade. – From the top of the breakwater on the south side of the mouth of the Geeste, one can see the Weser Estuary and the cargo ships waiting their turn to go up to Bremen.

Zoological Caves (Tiergrotten) and North Sea Aquarium (Nordsee-Aquarium). – Open 8am to 7pm (5pm 1 November to 30 April); 2.50DM.

The aquarium makes a special feature of the edible fish of the North Sea. The caves in the open air house bears, monkeys and seals.

BRUCHSAL

Michelin map **205** 1 – Pop 38 000

Bruchsal, on the right bank of the Rhine, has inherited, as residence of the last four prince-bishops of Speyer, a pompous Baroque castle. This was virtually a seignorial town consisting of 50 or more dwellings or annexes; like the rest of the town it was badly damaged in 1945 but is gradually being restored.

Castle (Schloss). – Open 10am to 5pm; closed Mondays. Brochure in English.

Its builder, the Cardinal of Schönborn, constructed this vast group of buildings from 1720 onwards. The Heidelberg road which passes through the St. Damian Door (Damianstor) cuts right across the enclave.

In the main building there is a magnificent **staircase★★** (Treppe) with an oval well designed by Balthazar Neumann (p 26) in 1731. The dome is decorated with Rococo stucco.

At the west end a room with a vaulted ceiling and marble floor (Gartensaal) opens on to the park.

Park. – When it was at its best, there were formal flowerbeds and a view which extended to the Rhine, ten miles away.

Public Gardens (Stadtgarten). – The Belvedere Pavilion built also by the Cardinal of Schönborn in 1738, crowns agreeably planted garden slopes.

BRUNSWICK (BRAUNSCHWEIG)

Michelin map **987** 16 – Pop 270 600
Town plan in Michelin Red Guide Deutschland

Brunswick has restored the monuments to its past. It stands in the centre of "the Lower Saxony vegetable garden", a plain where the alluvial soil provides good crops of sugarbeet and allows market gardening (asparagus) to be carried on successfully. The town's current prosperity is linked with the swift development of several industries: buses and utility vehicles, food canning (more than half the German total) and photographic equipment.

HISTORICAL NOTES

The Lion of Brunswick. – Early in the 12C, **Henry the Lion,** Duke of Bavaria and Saxony, made the House of **Guelph** the most politically powerful in Germany (p 183). His second marriage to Mathilda, daughter of Henry II Plantagenet, assured him of support at the English court. In 1166 he chose Brunswick as his permanent residence, and had the castle built and the lion monument erected.

Frederick Barbarossa took offence at Henry the Lion's increased power and after Henry's refusal to appear before the diets to which he had summoned him, stripped the Lion of all his possessions except his own domains which lay between the Upper Weser and the Lower Elbe. Henry the Lion died at Brunswick in 1195 an was buried in the cathedral. The Battle of Bouvines in 1214 when his son Otto IV and King John of England were beaten by Philippe-Auguste of France marked the end of the sovereignty of the House of Guelph.

Till Eulenspiegel Land. – The jester, Till Eulenspiegel, whose fame was spread far and wide from the 16C onwards by chroniclers, was German through and through. His memory is kept alive in Brunswick (monument in Bäckerklint Square) and the local countryside. It is supposed he was born in about 1300 in the town of **Schöppenstedt** (14 miles southeast of Brunswick) where a small museum has been devoted to him.

A Cultivated Court. – After the fall of Henry the Lion, the Guelphs were represented by many branches in Brunswick, Lüneburg, Wolfenbüttel and elsewhere.

Brunswick ceased to be a princely residence but remained a ducal city while Hanover, Göttingen and Lüneburg progressed.

In 1753 a younger member of the House of Brunswick left Wolfenbüttel *(p 260)* to re-establish the court at Brunswick. One of the dukes, **Karl-Wilhelm-Ferdinand** who commanded the Prussian troops at Valmy in 1792, was the famous "Brunswick" whose "manifesto" inflamed Revolutionary France. In 1807, after being taken by Napoleon, the Brunswick area was joined to the ephemeral kingdom of Westphalia. It was at this time that the young Stendhal (Henri Beyle) passed nearly two years in the town first as War Commissioner then as Steward of the Emperor's Domains.

Some of the Brunswick princes were patrons of the arts: Karl II invited Goethe to give the first performance of *Faust* at Brunswick in 1828.

■ MAIN SIGHTS *tour: $\frac{1}{2}$ hour*

Burgplatz. – The square stands at the heart of the old ducal town: round it are the cathedral, the Neo-Romanesque Dukes' Burg and two half-timbered houses.

In the centre is the **Lion Monument★** (Löwendenkmal), a masterpiece of mediaeval heraldic sculpture (1156) in bronze and a symbol of the Guelph pretension to supremacy.

Cathedral★ (Dom). – *Open 10am to 1pm and 3 to 5pm; closed Sundays.*

The characteristic feature outside is the west end *(p 23)* where the base supports two octagonal towers joined right to their top by a Gothic bell gable (1275). This design was subsequently copied in other Brunswick churches.

The Romanesque church built by Henry the Lion has lightly broken cradle vaulting whose weight has been considerably reduced by large cut-outs. The two original aisles were replaced in the Gothic period by four new aisles; those on the north side in the Flamboyant style have columns turned in alternate directions.

Among the works of art are, in the chancel a massive seven branch **candelabrum★** (Bronzeleuchter), in the north aisle the impressive mid-12C Imerwald **Christ Clothed★★** (Imerward-Kruzifix), in the nave the tomb of Henry the Lion and Mathilda of England. Their Romanesque sarcophagi can be seen in a modern crypt. The vast main crypt beneath the chancel, contains the tombs of the Guelph princes.

The chancel and the transepts are adorned with 13C wall paintings in reds and blues.

■ ADDITIONAL SIGHTS

Altstadtmarkt. – The ensemble formed by this square makes it an island in time, recalling the municipal institutions of the Brunswick merchant quarter. A lead fountain with three basins stands in the centre.

Altstadtrathaus (A). – The two main buildings of this old 13-15C town hall stand at right angles and its gables are stepped. The sides on the square are pierced by two superimposed galleries; the bays of the upper gallery are set in stepped gables. Pillars support mid-15C statues of Saxon and Guelph princes.

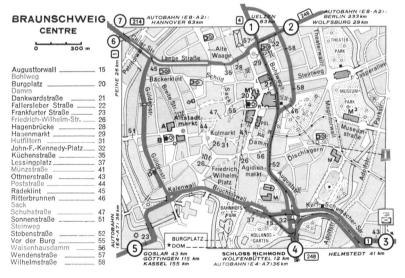

BRAUNSCHWEIG CENTRE

0 — 300 m

Linen Hall (Gewandhaus) (D). – The most decorated of the gables on this long building faces the centre of the Poststrasse; it is late Renaissance and rises four storeys and above that four pediment levels high. The divisions of the gable proper are marked by massive double cornices. The architect used every artifice known at the time to soften the steps of the gable: inverted brackets, statuettes, balls topped by stone pinnacles, etc. Beneath the statue of Justice which crowns the building is a large medallion with the Brunswick Lion.

St. Martin's (B). – *Open 10.30am to 12.30pm; closed Mondays.*

This late 13C church was much influenced by the cathedral. Gables with Gothic motifs form a delicate coronet at the base of the eaves. A happy 14C addition is the statuary on the transept gables – on the north: the Wise and Foolish Virgins; on the south: the Virgin, the Magi and the Saints.

Inside, the Gothic Chapel to St. Anne – first chapel in the south aisle – contains a Romanesque font with a Baroque cover. At the entrance to the chapel the statues facing each other are of the Virgin and St. Anne. St. Martin in the uniform of a 17C officer, rides on horseback at the foot of the pulpit.

BRUNSWICK

Mediaeval Art Treasures* Exhibition (Ausstellung ''Ausgewählte Kostbarkeiten mittelalter-licher Kunst'') (M¹). – *Open 10am to 4pm; closed Mondays and holidays.*
This display of church plate in the ducal castle includes a reliquary of St. Blaise's arm (patron saint of the cathedral and protector of the Guelphs) and the imperial coat of Otto IV.

Herzog-Anton-Ulrich-Museum (M²). – *Open 10am to 4pm; closed Mondays.*
Pride of place in the picture gallery is taken by the 17C Dutch and Flemish masters.

Richmond Castle (Schloss Richmond). – *Access by ④ on the plan. The castle may be visited only on application to the ''Kulturamt der Stadt Braunschweig'', Steintorwall 3, ☎ 470 441.*
This square Louis XVI style building is not set squarely so that it is seen cornerwise on. The arrangement inside is determined by the staterooms which follow the building's diagonal line. Stendhal spent the summer of 1808 in the castle.

BÜCKEBURG

Michelin map 987 15 – 10 km - 6 miles – southeast of Minden – Pop 21 000

Bückeburg retains some Renaissance buildings from the time when it was a princely seat. The Schaumburg-Lippe princes reigned over this small state until 1918.

Castle. – *Guided tours from April to September, 9am to noon and 1 to 6pm (5pm October to March); 3DM.*
Before visiting the castle, we suggest you walk to the right of the state entrance, into the park. From the lawns beyond the moat you will see a true example of German First Renaissance architecture in the **façade*** with gables and semicircular pediments. The overall effect is majestic.
Go next through an early 17C monumental gateway to the court of honour and then to a small inner court – 16C and the earliest part of the castle. This inner court is adorned on three sides with a Renaissance balcony.
On the tour you see reception rooms and the chapel with late Renaissance woodwork. A stand with blind arcades and decorative pediments supports the pulpit placed, in accordance with the Lutheran tradition, in the centre of the building. It faces the Princes' Gallery.

Church (Stadtkirche). – *Open 1 May to 30 September, 10.30am to noon; closed weekends.*
This church was one of the first large German religious buildings to be designed for the Lutheran sect (1615). The overwhelming façade is symmetrically divided according to the Renaissance tradition but several elements – the false bull's eye windows for example – are already Baroque. There is a fine 1615 font inside.

BURGHAUSEN ★★

Michelin map 987 38 – Pop 19 000

The Burghausen fortress, whose ramparts are half a mile round, crowns a long spur and looks down on the town stretched round a bend in the Salzach River which here forms the boundary between Bavaria and Austria.
In the 12C the castle became the property of the Dukes of Bavaria who, taking advantage of the **site****, made it the biggest fortress in Germany. It reached its present size in about 1480; early in the 16C it was further reinforced in face of the menace of a Turkish invasion.

Castle**. – *Open in summer from 9am to noon and 1 to 5.30pm (4pm in winter); closed Mondays in winter; 1DM; about 1½ hours walking and sightseeing.*
Leave the car on the Hauptplatz and follow the road which circles the base of the spur. After passing beneath the **Mühlturm**, one walks briefly beside the waters of the Wöhrsee before climbing a steep path and gaining the castle's outer perimeter. The line of ramparts which climbs on the far side, up the Eggenberg Hill comes into sight. There is a bird's-eye view of the lower town and the Salzach from a wooden footbridge which crosses a moat and leads to the **St. George's Gate** (Georgstor) through the innermost perimeter wall.
The full strategic value of Burghausen becomes apparent: the lower town with its main square (Hauptplatz) lined with brilliantly coloured house façades, onion domed churches and the fortifications linking the castle with the Eggenberg, and, as far as the eye can see, the Salzach Valley winding through the hills. An interesting collection of paintings on wood is outstanding for a *Baptism of Christ* and a *Christ on the Mount of Olives*, both from the late 15C Bavarian school. The Gothic chapel has elegant star vaulting.
Descend directly to the Hauptplatz by the ramp between the castle and St. George's Gates.

EXCURSION

Raitenhaslach. – *6 km - 3 miles – by the Salzburg road (no 20), plus ½ hour sightseeing.* An old Cistercian church, now reduced to a long single aisle, contains Baroque decorated red marble tombstones. The beautiful main courtyard is planted with chestnuts.

CELLE ★★

Michelin map 987 15 – Pop 74 000 – *Town plan in Michelin Red Guide Deutschland*

Celle was the residence of the Lüneburg branch of the Guelph princes (*p 90*) from 1378 to 1705, when these had been banished from their ducal town by the freed burghers. The town has retained the atmosphere of an aristocratic seat. Its ancient heart of wooden 16 and 17C houses escaped war damage. Celle is known as one of Europe's major centres of orchid growing.

The Three Ladies of Celle. – Eléonore d'Olbreuse, a beautiful Huguenot from Poitou, seduced Georg-Wilhelm, the last Duke to live in Celle and, by 1676, had virtually become the town's chatelaine. She opened the small court to French influences; the beautiful French garden on the south side of the town stands as her memorial.
Sophie-Dorothée (1666-1726). Eléonore's daughter, was married, for reasons of state, to her cousin George I of England (*p 143*); she had a son, George II, and a daughter, the future mother of Frederick the Great. Sophie's love affair with Count Philip of Königsmarck was discovered and she was repudiated and banished for the rest of her life to Ahlden Castle, whilst her lover disappeared in mysterious circumstances.
From 1772 to 1775 another unfortunate lover lived out her life in Celle Castle: she was Caroline Mathilda, sister of George III of England and wife of the eccentric Christian VII of Denmark, who thus paid for her affair with Struensee, the all powerful minister and king's favourite. Her monument stands in the French garden.

■ **THE OLD TOWN★★** *tour: ¾ hour*

The local half-timbered house is characterised by the stepping of certain gables and more generally by roofs being notched to correspond with the corbelling of each successive storey.

Go into the quiet and narrow Kalandgasse at the foot of the church tower. A recess on the left allows extra space to the **old college** (Lateinschule), a building dating from 1602 and remarkable for the rich decoration of its posts and wood traverses carved with Biblical sayings.

Turn right into the Kanzleistrasse. From the next crossroads there is an attractive view on the right towards the town hall gable. The lantern turret on the church tower rises above the quarter.

Town Hall. – This rough-cast building in light colours pleasantly blends several Renaissance architectural features. The graceful north gable, built in 1579 by craftsmen who came from the banks of the Weser *(the Weser Renaissance, see p 141)*, has a top entwined with serpentine decoration and bristling with fantastic pinnacles.

Bear left before the town hall entrance into the Neue Strasse, then right into the Rabengasse (lovely corner house at no 27). A typical house with stepped gables stands at the corner of the Zöllnerstrasse. Walk along the Zöllnerstrasse to get a good idea of the development of the local architecture. Before returning to the town hall go and see the Hoppener House, 1532, the most ornate house in the town, in the Poststrasse, a continuation of the Markt.

■ **ADDITIONAL SIGHTS**

Castle. – *Guided tours 9am to noon (11am Saturdays) and 2 to 4pm; closed Saturday afternoons; 1DM.*

This castle, flanked by corner towers is overwhelmed by roofs like ribbed helmets. The east façade overlooking the town has an uninterrupted series of pedimented dormer windows – a characteristic, in north Germany, of architecture of the First Renaissance.

Chapel★ (Hofkapelle). – It was built at the end of the 16C to the design of the Flemish painter, Martin de Vos, who painted the Crucifixion. With open or glassed-in galleries and bizarre ornaments hanging from the ceiling, the chapel is a strange Renaissance assemblage.

Theatre (Schlosstheater). – Charming Baroque auditorium built for Eléonore d'Olbreuse.

Church (Stadtkirche). – This dark and originally Gothic church was considerably renovated in Baroque style by Italian stucco-workers between 1676 and 1698. The chancel monuments indicate its function as necropolis of the Celle branch of the Guelph dukes.

Blumlage. – On either side of alleys leading off this street, are delightful 17 and 18C houses.

EXCURSION

Wienhausen Convent★. – *12 km - 7½ miles – by ③ in the Michelin Red Guide Deutschland, the Brunswick road (no 214). After 6 km - 4 miles – bear left into the Wienhausen road – plus about 1½ hours sightseeing.*

Tours 1 March to 30 November: weekdays 9, 10, 11am, 2, 3, 4, 5pm; Sundays 11.30am, 1, 2, 3, 4, 5pm; after 11 October tours cease at 4pm; closed 1 December to 28 February; 3DM.

This Cistercian abbey, founded in 1233 by Henry the Lion's daughter-in-law *(p 90)*, has been occupied, since the Reformation, by a small community of Protestant canonesses.

Among the piously preserved art objects are the 13C Wienhausen Virgin and the stone statue of the founder (1280). The nuns' chancel is in fact a gallery decorated with early 14C mural paintings (restored). In the centre a large Gothic wooden shrine constitutes a Holy Sepulchre. In the course of restoration work in 1953 a harvest of trinkets was gathered – minute notebooks, penknives and spectacles mounted on wooden frames such as may be seen in Primitive paintings – which must have been dropped by the nuns through the floorboards more than 500 years earlier. The trinkets are on display in a small museum.

The convent holds an exhibition once a year for 11 days only, starting from the Friday after Whitsun of its mediaeval tapestries. Admission: 4DM.

The CHIEMSEE ★

Michelin map **987** 37 – *Local map p 46*

Known as the "Bavarian Sea", the Chiemsee (pronounced Keemzay) is the largest of Bavaria's lakes. It spreads its calm waters over 82 km² - 32 sq miles between, on one side, gentle banks bordered by rushes and, on the other, the first foothills of the Bavarian Alps whose crests may be seen clearly in the south. Two islands, not far from the western bank, the Herrinsel and the Fraueninsel, are worth a visit.

Many summer resorts lie spread out along both sides of the lake and are popular with water-sports enthusiasts in particular **Prien,** most lively of the resorts, and **Seebruck.**

The Salzburg–Munich motorway runs close to the lake's flat and marshy southern bank *(route ⑤ p 47)*, but it is on the northern bank, between Rimsting and Seebruck, that one comes across the most interesting viewpoints, with the Alps as a backcloth.

The Islands are usually reached from the western side. From the motorway (the Bernau exit) make for the Prien-Stock landing-stage. Allow ¼ hour for the trip to Herrninsel and ½ hour for Fraueninsel (Rtn fare: 4DM for Herrninsel, 5DM for the two islands).

Herrninsel. – The island, which is largely wooded, is famous for its castle.

Herrenchiemsee Castle. – *Tour: 2 hours. Open 1 April to 30 September, 9am to 5pm; in winter 10am to 4pm; 3.50DM.*

The whole island was bought in 1873 by the young King Ludwig II of Bavaria *(p 183)*, who not only wished to save its trees but also to build a sumptuous castle. His visit to Versailles in 1867 had quickened his admiration for the Sun King: Herrenchiemsee would therefore be the replica of Versailles. Work began in 1878 and continued until 1885 by which time 20 million marks had been spent and the treasury's coffers were empty. The king had only lived a week in this palace when his death put an end to the dream.

The similarity between the original and the copy is striking: the Latona fountain is surrounded by gardens whose style is French; the façade is decorated with columns and covered by an Italian-styled roof behind a balustrade; the apartments include a Room of State and Hall of Mirrors, which are magnificent.

In summer, concerts of chamber music on Saturdays by candlelight in the Hall of Mirrors.

Fraueninsel. – Although small, the island has a charming fishing village and an ancient Benedictine monastery whose 13C church was rebuilt in Gothic style in the 15C.

CLOPPENBURG ★

Michelin map 987 14 – Pop 20 000

The thriving market town of Cloppenburg in the flat and humid Oldenburg region is known to tourists for its open air museum.

Museum Village★ (Museumsdorf). – *Open 1 March to 15 October, 8am (9am Sundays and holidays) to 6pm; 16 October to 28 February, 9am (10am Sundays) to 4pm; 2.50DM.*

16 to 19C farmhouses and outbuildings, craftsmen's studios and windmills stand round a pond and a church in an area of 15 ha - 37 acres.

The peasant houses are arranged inside with great care in the Lower Saxony style (*p 30*). The lord's house (Burg Arkenstede) is richer and contains a very fine collection of ornaments and furniture. The Dorfkrug house still serves as an inn.

COBURG ★

Michelin map 987 26 – Pop 47 000 – *Town plan in Michelin Red Guide Deutschland*

Coburg, whose fortress can be seen from afar, is rich in dynastic memories.

The Saxe-Coburgs, who lived in the town from the 16C onwards, established themselves in many of the courts of Europe: by the 19C, when they were related to the English, Belgian, Portuguese and Bulgarian royal families, they could be said to "reign over half the world".

The centre of the town, between the Marktplatz, the Church of St. Maurice and Ehrenburg Castle, bears a late Renaissance imprint. This was given it by the most enterprising member of the family, Duke Johann Casimir. Note the corner "Coburg oriels".

■ **SIGHTS** *time: 2 hours*

The Fortress★ (Veste). – Set out by car from the square in front of the theatre and take the Festungsstrasse to the roundabout beyond the castle where you leave the car.

Open 1 April to 31 October daily 9am to 1pm and 2 to 5pm; the rest of the year 2 to 5pm; closed Mondays in winter; 2DM. Brochure in English.

This is one of the largest fortresses in Germany with a double ring of fortified walls. The original castle was 12C but the present structure is 16C (the time of Johann Casimir). The approach ramp leads to the south doorway. The buildings with high roofs, broken by dormer windows, enclose an inner garden.

The half-timbered **Princes' Palace** (Fürstenbau) holds memories of Luther's stay in 1530. The Music Room, in the apartments, contains four paintings by Lucas Cranach the Elder.

The wing at right angles **(Kemenate)** is now an art museum (Kunstsammlungen). On the first floor Luther's Room contains a collection of autographs and pictures by Cranach; on the second floor are furniture and glass.

The **Duchess' Building** (Herzoginbau) has a vehicle museum on the ground floor, including curious 17-18C sledges and 17C wedding carriages. Collection of armour in the attics.

Hofgarten★. – This vast shaded grassland, on the flank of the hill between the fortress and Ehrenburg Castle, invites the visitor with plenty of time, to walk up to the castle.

Casimir School★ (Gymnasium Casimirianum). – The school facing the Church of St. Maurice which is topped by a Baroque turret, is the finest civil Renaissance (1605) building in Coburg. The statue of the founder, Johann Casimir, stands at the corner nearest the church.

Natural History Museum (Naturwissenschaftliches Museum). – *In the Hofgarten. Open 9am to 6pm (5pm 1 October to 31 March); 1DM.*

There are bird, fossil, taxidermy and mineral collections and an ethnological department.

Ehrenburg Castle. – *Open 9am to noon and 1 to 4pm; closed Mondays; 1.50DM.*

Prince Albert, who later married Queen Victoria, passed his childhood in the castle. It is a Renaissance building remodelled in the 19C on the side facing the Schlossplatz in the English Neo-Gothic manner. The most original rooms are the Giants' Hall with its heavy Italian stuccoes and the Throne Room in the Neo-Baroque style. The Gobelin Room is adorned with rich French tapestries. The Baroque chapel, which has heavily carved galleries in the Italian style, was designed and has remained Lutheran as is shown by the vertical positioning of the altar, the pulpit and the organ.

COCHEM

Michelin map 203 5 – *Local maps pp 115 and 181* – Pop 7 000

Cochem's **setting★**, distinguished by its castle crowning a mound covered with vineyards, is one of the most famous in the Rhineland. The town's position on the left bank of the Mosel and within easy reach of the chief tourist centres of the Eifel, makes it a popular stopping place and a winetasting centre. Cochem and its valley can be seen downstream from a viewpoint in a bend in the new route taken by road no 259 south of the town.

Burg. – *½ hour on foot Rtn from the Marktplatz via the Schloss-Strasse.* Only the keep and the base of the walls remained after the destruction of 1689 *(p 146)*. In the 19C the ruins were rebuilt in 14C style with many turrets and pinnacles. *The interior, furnished in a richly feudal manner, is open from Easter to 30 October, 10am to 5pm (9am to 6pm July to September); 3DM.*

Pinnerkreuz★. – *About 1¼ hours Rtn: 1 hour is by chairhoist (lower station in the Enderstrasse, the street along the bottom of the ravine which ends at Cochem – 9am to 6pm in summer. Rtn fare: 3DM) and ¼ hour on foot Rtn.* Overall view upstream of the town and the valley.

(After a photo by Robert Cornely Verlag)

Cochem.

COLOGNE ★★★ (KÖLN)
Michelin map 202 16 – Pop 982 800

Built up area plan in Michelin Red Guide Deutschland

Cologne is the capital of the Rhineland and one of the largest cities in Germany. The Rhine frontage, almost rhythmic with its belfries, bold cathedral spires and group of bridges, is majestically attractive.

The city is built for the most part on the left bank of the river and spreads out towards the west; the right bank (Deutz) is largely industrial. Cologne was rebuilt after the war in fifteen years around the cathedral, which was damaged but not irretrievably.

The principal industries are metal processing (metal cables, motor cars), chemical (rubber), petrochemical and pharmaceutical. Chocolate and especially perfume are among its luxury industries. Cologne has given its name to the famous toilet water *(Eau de Cologne)*, first made by the Italian chemist, Giovanni-Maria Farina, who settled in the town in 1709.

In addition to tourists a great many businessmen visit Cologne especially at the time of its specialist fairs and exhibitions.

General View. – The best general view of the cathedral is from the vast **Rhine Park★** (DU) on the right bank of the river. Use the cable-car, for preference, which leaves from near the zoo and crosses high over the Rhine to get to the park *(service: Good Friday to end of October, 10am to 8pm; closed Fridays – Rtn fare: 4DM).*

HISTORICAL NOTES

Colonia. – Once the Romans had extended their empire as far as the Rhine, General Agrippa, the coloniser of the region, allowed in 38 BC, the Ubii, a Germanic people, to occupy the east bank of the Rhine, known as Oppidum Ubiorum. Agrippina, the wife of the emperor Claudius, acquired for her native town the official title of Roman colony, Colonia Claudia Ara Agrippinensi (CCAA) in AD 50. Thus the town developed rapidly in urbanism, commerce, industry and art *(see Roman-Germanic Museum p 97).*

Roman ruins still stand: The Zeughausstrasse (restored), also in the same street is a section of the old fortifications, the north gate which is in front of the cathedral, and the **Praetorium**. The ruins of a 1-4C Roman palace, which extend under the new town hall (DX R) *(entrance Kleine Budengasse)* were uncovered in 1953. The central octagon, the well and the drainage system are now all visible *(open Tuesdays to Sundays 10am to 5pm; 1DM).*

The 11 000 Virgins. – Legend has it that **St. Ursula**, the daughter of a 4C King of Britain, was murdered by the Huns when returning with 11 000 companions from a pilgrimage to Rome. But history discounts the number of her companions; the Latin manuscript contains the inscription XIMV which could equally well mean 11 virgin martyrs as 11 000 virgins.

St. Ursula is the patron saint of Cologne and the city's arms bear 11 flames symbolising the martyrs, beneath the crowns of the Magi Kings whose relics were brought to the town in 1164. By popular tradition, St. Gereon, a Roman soldier and martyr of the 3C, is also associated with the city's patronage.

"Holy" Cologne. – Cologne flowered in the Middle Ages when it was the largest city in all Germany – 40 000 people lived within its fortified walls. Its political power derived from the Church. The bishopric founded by the Emperor Constantine in the 4C was raised to an archbishopric by Charlemagne. The archbishops, of whom several were canonised, remained powerful until the 13C. Churches – of which the cathedral was one – monasteries and collegiate churches – more than 150 in all – rose quickly. The city became the enlightened religious, intellectual and artistic centre of the Rhine Valley. Eminent men came to preach between 1248 and 1327: Albert the Great, the teacher of Thomas Aquinas, and Master Eckhart, both Dominicans and Duns Scotus, a Franciscan.

Cologne's economic strength was no less great: rivalling Lübeck in the Hanseatic League, it imposed its own system of weights and measures over northern Germany. The first Cologne Fair was held in 1360. It became a Free City in 1475.

■ THE TOWN

Cologne has the most extensive "old town" in Germany. It is in the shape of a semicircle, the two mile long diameter running along the left bank of the Rhine and the perimeter being formed by the four mile "Ring" which follows the line of the 12C fortifications and is bordered by a green belt. Two intersecting roads provide the main thoroughfares: the **Hohe Strasse** (DX) (north to south) and the **Schildergasse** (CDX) (east to west). Now pedestrian, these streets are lined by shops, large stores, bars and restaurants and much frequented.

The remainder of the town forms concentric circles around this kernel: the "new town", now nearly a hundred years old, extends to the second green belt (Universitätsstrasse, Innere Kanalstrasse) and includes the University and the parks. Beyond lie the suburbs.

The quarter round the cathedral and the station is cosmopolitan with luxury hotels, blocks of flats and offices and is not really characteristic of the city. Traffic has been diverted, under a recent city plan, away from the cathedral area.

The Ring, a noisy, lively boulevard-promenade is the banking and insurance quarter, the area of luxury shops and smart cafés. It is also the entertainment and night-life area.

The **"Veedel"** (dialect word) are parishes in the old town which have kept their local autonomy and traditions (St. Pantaleon, St. Gereon, St. Cunibert, etc.). The most original is St. Severinus with its provincial-type street lined with local shops and cafés.

Near the Rhine, in the Alter Markt and Heumarkt quarter are the Weinhäuser where the people of Cologne come to drink and eat.

A popular attraction on Wednesdays, Saturdays, Sundays and holidays *(1 May to 15 September)* is the **Dance Fountain** (Tanzbrunnen) (DU) in the Rhine Park.

Cologne Carnival, one of the most famous in Germany, reaches its height in a processional pageant parodying topical themes and celebrities.

From the Thursday before Shrove Tuesday the Women's Carnival with its clown processions begins to disorganise all business life; the following Sunday each quarter organises its own masked procession: "Rose Monday" is when the fun reaches its climax with dancing, fanfares and the giants' procession.

The Corpus Christi procession, held in addition to these secular festivities, is known as the "Gottestracht"; it is solemn and at the same time popularly sumptuous in character. The procession winds round the cathedral and embarks by boat on the Rhine between Mülheim (DU) and St. Cunibert (DU).

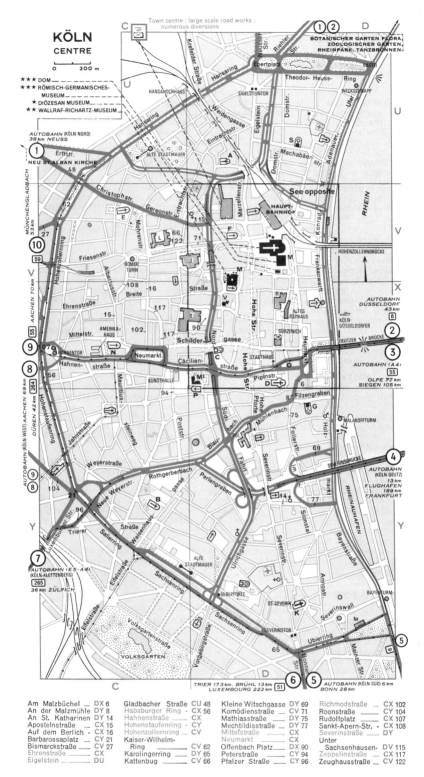

KÖLN
CENTRE

0   200 m

★★★ DOM
★★★ RÖMISCH-GERMANISCHES-
        MUSEUM
  ★ DIÖZESAN MUSEUM
★★ WALLRAF-RICHARTZ-MUSEUM

■ **MAIN SIGHTS** *time: 4 hours*

Cathedral★★★ (Dom). – *Brochure in English.* It took more than 600 years to complete this gigantic edifice. In 1164 when Frederick Barbarossa offered relics of the Magi Kings brought back from Milan to the archbishopric of Cologne, pilgrims flocked to the town. By 1248 a new cathedral was needed and thus the first Gothic church in the Rhineland came to be built, its design influenced by buildings in Picardy. The chancel was completed in the 14C. Work on the front south tower however stopped in 1437. The gap between the two parts of the building was not to be filled until after 1842 when Neo-Gothic fever took hold of Romantic Germany. In 1880 the cathedral was at last ceremoniously inaugurated.

The visitor finds himself overwhelmed by the size of the building and the ornateness of the decoration.

The façade is characteristic of a full Gothic style with stepped windows and gables mounting slimly in line with spires which rise to a height of 157 m - 515 ft (Salisbury 400 ft).

Go left round the cathedral and step back on the car park in the Domplatz to appreciate the bold lines of the apse and its multitude of pinnacles and turrets.

Note the bronze doors by Mataré in the south transept doorway (Celestial Jerusalem above; Cologne in flames, on the right).

Go into the church by the west door. In a single glance one takes in the sweep of the nave, but, until one reaches the transept, one has little idea of the size of the building.

The five **stained glass windows★** (Glasmalereien) in the north aisle (c 1500) depict the lives of the Virgin and St. Peter. In the north transept there is a Vigin and Child of the period of the Beautiful Madonnas and in the south transept a large Flemish polyptych of 1520 known as the *Altarpiece of the Five Moors.*

The 10C **Cross of Gero★** (Gerokreuz), a unique example of Othonian art, hangs in the first northern chapel off the ambulatory. Further on note the **Magis' Shrine★★★** (Dreikönigenschrein) in a glass case behind the high altar. This magnificent 12C work is attributed to the goldsmith Nicolas of Verdun. The axial chapel has a fine 13C window. In a south chapel off the ambulatory is the **altarpiece★★★** (Altarbild) by Stefan Lochner of the Adoration of the Magi.

Treasure★ (Domschatzkammer). – *Open 9am (12.30pm Sundays and holidays) to 5pm; 2DM.*
The treasure contains liturgical gold and silver plate and episcopal accoutrements.

Chancel Furnishings. – Only on the guided tours *(10 and 11am, 2.30, 3.30 and 4.30pm in summer except Sunday mornings; time ¾ hour)* can one see the **stalls★** (Chorgestühl); the frescoes symbolising the Church and the Empire high up on either side of the chancel and the 14 **statues★** (Chorstatuen) against the pillars, of Christ, Mary and the Apostles.

Diocesan Museum★ (Diözesan Museum) (   ). – *Open Tuesdays to Saturdays 10am to 5pm, Sundays 10am to 1pm; 1DM.*

This museum is devoted to precious religious objects: vases, statues, sacerdotal vestments, paintings, chalice cups and crucifixes. The most unique work of art is the Persian silk dating from the Sassanian era (the dynasty reigning between 3 and 8C), found in St. Cunibert's shrine, bishop of Cologne in 6C. This weave, divided symmetrically by a palm tree, illustrates a hunt. The Romanesque Virgin and Child, sculpted in wood, and Stefan Lochner's Virgin with Violets, where the flowers represent her virtues enrich this collection. Note in a glass showcase the admirable 11C crucifix with the head of Christ (Roman 1 BC) set in lapis-lazuli, representing Livia, the wife of Augustus, and a ciborium cup in vermeil (end of 12C).

Roman-Germanic Museum★★★ (Römisch-Germanisches Museum). – *Open daily 10am to 8pm; 1DM.*

Public monuments, a port, a system of drainage, villas, tombs and works of art have been discovered throughout the centuries.

In the basement, the **Dionysos Mosaic** was found here in 1941. The medallions, set against a background of geometrical designs, depict the world of Dionysos, god of wine and pleasure. The vividness of the scenes and colour

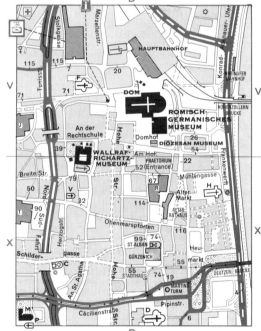

KÖLN

CATHEDRAL QUARTER

0   300 m

Am Leystapel	DX 4
Am Malzbüchel	DX 6
An den Dominikanern	DV 7
Augustinerstraße	DX 19
Bahnhofstraße	DV 20
Bechergasse	DX 22
Bischofsgartenstraße	DV 26
Breite Straße	DX

Brückenstraße	DX 32
Drususgasse	DV 39
Glockengasse	DX 50
Große Budengasse	DX 52
Große Neugasse	DV 54
Gürzenichstraße	DX 55
Hohe Straße	DX
Kleine Budengasse	DX 67
Komödienstraße	DV 71
Martinstraße	DX 74
Minoritenstraße	DX 79
Offenbach Platz	DX 90
Quatermarkt	DX 99
Schildergasse	DX
Unter Goldschmied	DX 114
Unter Sachsenhausen	DV 115
Unter Seidmacher	DX 116

harmony are remarkable. The continuous rooms evoke domestic life: games, pottery, sewing, keys, surprising mosaic of swastika, tombstones.

Overlooking the Dionysos Mosaic, the **tomb to Lucius Poblicius** (a veteran who retired in Cologne), which formerly stood on the road to Bonn, illustrates private monumental art. From above one can determine the carved foliage and mythological scenes.

The visitor is introduced, by the different floors of the museum, to architecture and statuary (note the door with the inscription CCAA), travelling (four-wheeled cart), traffic of the port (pillars of the Rhine Bridge), cults, amusements, coins.

The wealthy owners did not hesitate to order works of art from Egypt and Greece as is seen by the Philosopher's Mosaic dedicated to the Seven Greek Sages, the Pompeian frescoes and the variety of multicoloured marbles.

Among the precious collection of **glassware**, is a splendid 4C diatrites or transparent glass, with an outer tracery of coloured glass and a Greek inscription in colour. Also exhibited are bottles with coloured twisting motifs applied in relief and vessels in the shape of animals.

The Roman jewels and the Barbarian ornaments in engraved gold and cloisonné enamel form an invaluable archaeological treasure.

COLOGNE★★★

Wallraf-Richartz and Ludwig Museum★★★. – *Open 10am to 5pm (10pm Tuesdays and Thursdays); 1DM.*

The first 12 galleries on the 1st floor contain **14-16C pictures by Cologne Masters** (Alte Meister der Kölner Schule). Painting in Cologne belongs to two periods: at the beginning of the 15C it drew inspiration from French art, particularly Burgundian; about the middle of the same century Dutch influence became widespread in Northern Germany. Simultaneously the mystical idealism of the Gothic period gave way to the gracious realism of the Renaissance. The constant traits are the refinement and suavity with which subjects are treated and the delicacy of colour.

Exemplifying this style is the early 15C triptych of *The Holy Family* by the Master of St. Veronica (gallery C). In *The Virgin and The Rose Bush* (gallery E) by Stefan Lochner note the delicate yellows and golds and the serenity of the faces. In gallery F is *The Annunciation* and *The Vision of St. Bernard* by the Master of the Life of the Virgin (the Annunciation appears on the back of the wing panels). On display in gallery I is *The Annunciation* and *St. Francis Receiving The Stigmatas* by the Master of St. Severinus. The portraits of Gerhard Pilgrim and Heinrich Salsburg (gallery J) confirm the reputation of Barthel Bruyn the Elder (1493-1555) as the portrait painter of the bourgeoisie of Cologne. In gallery L are exhibited German masters: Dürer *(Fife Player and Drummer)* and Cranach the Elder *(Virgin and Child)*. Dutch and Flemish masters with such famous names as Rubens (gallery R – *Holy Family* and *The Stigmatas of St. Francis)*, Ruysdael *(View of the River)* and Frans Hals (gallery S – *Fisherman's Daughter)*, Rembrandt *(Self-portrait* – gallery U). Completing the collection are works by the Italian, French, Spanish and German schools of the 17-19C with such examples as Boucher: *Young Girl Resting* (gallery V), Munch *Girl on the Bridge* and in gallery X French impressionists and Leibe *Portrait of Heinrich Pallenberg.*

The 2nd floor, in contrast, contains an important collection of modern and contemporary art. In the west wing are artists of the Brücke *(p 27)* – Kirchner *(Five Women in the Street)*, Nolde, Klee (*Main Street with Secondary Streets*, 1929). Kandinsky and Max Ernst demonstrate the quality of expression perfected in the Der Blaue Reiter *(p 27)*, with the Ludwig Collection (he donated his "Sacred art" collection to Suermondt-Ludwig Museum at Aachen, *p 40*), many contemporary forms of expression are displayed.

The 1960s **Pop Art movement** was iconoclastic, sceptical of conventional esthetic attitudes and values and tended to break down established art categories, producing works that spanned painting, sculpture and objects of daily use. There is Rauschenberg with his combine-paintings: Odalisk and Allegory. Andy Warhol where the form of expression is deeply rooted in our mechanised, standardised, mass-production culture has created Pepsi-Cola, Jackie Kennedy, Marilyn Monroe as well as death and riot scenes: demonstrating the new generation of German artists is Joseph Beuys (*Princess seeing Iceland*, 1960).

Returning to the ground floor do not miss the Black Nana by Niki de Saint-Phalle.

Schnütgen Museum★★ (DX M¹). – *Open Tuesdays to Sundays 10am to 5pm; 1DM.*

The museum which is in the former Church of St. Cecilia contains a rich collection of ivory carvings and religious art: monstrances, reliquaries and particularly rich mediaeval sculpture: the Madonnas of Cologne. In these Gothic virgins, with their gracefully slim hips and their scarcely discernible smiles, mysticism is replaced by a certain religious sentimentality.

Close by the museum stands the Kunsthalle, a vast building erected in 1966 to house the major temporary Rhineland exhibitions.

■ ADDITIONAL SIGHTS

Churches

Two types of churches are distinguishable in Cologne: the old Romanesque churches, which during the centuries, have been remodelled, according to the architectural trends and the modern churches. Three men stand out among the architects of the new religious buildings: Dominikus Böhm (1880-1955), his son Gottfried, and Rudolph Schwarz. For the most part they have emphasised space, texture, and lighting to enable the congregation to take an increased part in the service. Ernst Barlach *(p 26)*, Ewald Mataré (1887-1965) and Elmar Hildebrand are well known masters associated with the religious art of Cologne.

Church of the Antonines (DX C). – Bronze **angel** by Barlach (1938).

St. Andrew's (St. Andre) (DV F). – This Romanesque church with a very tall octagonal lantern tower and widely projecting west transept was transformed by the addition of a chancel in the Gothic period. The sarcophagus of Albert the Great (an illustrious philosopher and theologian of the Middle Ages) lies in the crypt.

St. Cunibert (DU S). – The last uniformly Romanesque church in Cologne: the two towers flank the chancel. On the pillars at the intersection of the nave and transept is a larger than life size Annunciation group in stone (1439). The folds of the robes and the personages' gestures show the artist's search for reality. Left of the chancel, in a small chapel, are murals representing the life of the Virgin. **Stained glass windows★** in the chancel (1230) depict scenes of courtesan life. In the south aisle the bell clapper originates from the west tower which is today in ruins.

(After a photo by the German Tourist Office)

Cologne – The Cathedral and the quays on the Rhine

St. Gereon (CV E). – *Entrance by the Christopherstrasse*. The unique construction of this church is shown by its elliptical plan and, in 1220, the adding of a decagon, between the two towers. Descend into the crypt, which has mosaic flooring (11C), and contains the coffins of St. Gereon and the other martyrs of the Theban legion. The frescoes are of the 13C and the Renaissance altarpiece, above the altar, has Gothic characteristics. In the church, one's attention is drawn to the north side where there is an Aubusson tapestry (17C) and a tabernacle with a bas-relief depicting the Last Supper (1608) and on the south side a polychrome Virgin and Child (1400). The door of the sacristy is decorated with an Ecce Homo and a Mater Dolorosa.

St. Maria Lyskirchen (DY G). – A basilica, with three aisles and galleries, built in 1220. On the ceiling in the central nave are frescoes (1250) exemplifying 13C Rhineland painting: parallel scenes with at the north the Old Testament and at the south the New Testament. Above the west portal, in the same style, is the 1230 Adoration of the Magi. There is also the remarkable polychrome Virgin and Child (1420), the patron saint of the Rhine boatmen. This large statue with its intricate detail creates a powerful and moving sculpture.

Gross St. Martin (DX H). – Seen from the Rhine the imposing square tower rising out of the transept and the four smaller towers evoke a fortress-like quality in the church. The three apses, trefoil shape, recalling St. Mary of the Capitol demonstrate the late Romanesque style in Cologne.

St. Pantaleon (CY B). – The church was built in the 10C and is an example of Ottonian architecture. The **roodscreen★** (Lettner) inside is Flamboyant Gothic. In the crypt is the 10C tomb of Archbishop Bruno of Cologne.

St. Peter's (DXY P). – Upon entering there is the celebrated Crucifixion of St. Peter by Rubens. Note also the late 14C **stained glass windows★** (Glasgemälde).

St. Severinus' (DY K). – *Open 9am to noon and 3 to 7pm; closed Sundays.* This, the oldest Christian foundation in Cologne, has, **inside★**, a fine Gothic nave. In the south aisle is a triptych of the Crucifixion, on the right of the central altar, the Cross of St. Severinus. The saint's 4C shrine, restored in the 19C, is behind the high altar and, in the south chapel is a 14C Crucifixion. St. Severinus' tomb was discovered in the crypt.

St. Mary of the Capitol (DX D). – A church in which the transept is to the Rhenish trefoil plan. Beneath a Renaissance roodscreen which closes the west end of the nave, on the left, are a 12C standing Madonna and Child and left of the altar, the Madonna of Limburg (1300). In the south aisle are splendid carved 11C **wooden doors★★** (Holztüren).

St. Ursula (DU A). – The **treasure★** (Goldene Kammer) located in the south aisle consists of bones, which have been arranged to spell out maxims, 14-17C reliquary busts and the Aetherius shrine (1170): repoussé in copper with gold and enamel. *Open Tuesdays to Saturdays 10am to noon and 3 to 5pm. Ask for the key at the sacristy or telephone in advance: 13 28 23.*

Holy Apostles (St. Aposteln) (CX N). – This 11C Romanesque church is partly Rhenish in style with a trefoil plan chancel and transept. Outside, the 13C **apse★** (Chorabschluss), which is flanked by two octagonal lantern turrets, is decorated with a beautiful 13C Romanesque gallery *(illustration p 23).* Inside, look at the chancel and the transept.

St. Alban the New★ (CU). – This sombre modern brick church has unusual vertical architectural lines. The ciborium on the right is by Hillebrand.

St. Columbia★ (St. Kolumba) (DX V). – On the ruins of a Gothic church, destroyed during the war, Gottfried Böhm built in 1950 St. Columba. There is a particular luminosity in the chancel with its blue stained glass windows. Note the 15C Virgin saved from ruin. In the chapel on the left is a Stations of the Cross with carved intaglio on a basalt slab.

St. Mary the Queen (St. Maria-Königin). – *Entrance by the Mainzer Strasse, southeast of the plan* (DY), *and the Goldsteinstrasse.* This modern church, designed by Dominikus Böhm in 1954 in a residential quarter in the southern part of the city, is lit by a **wall of glass★** (Glaswand).

Miscellaneous

Metropolitan Historical Museum (Kölnisches Stadtmuseum). – *In the Arsenal* (CV M²). *Open 10am to 5pm (8pm Thursdays); closed Mondays, 24, 25 December and 1 January; 1DM.*
The life of the city is depicted on the ground floor with exhibits of arms and armour, battle pictures, weights and measures, bishops' tombstones and portraits of eminent personages.

Old Town Hall (DX). – The building has two distinct architectural periods: the main part is Gothic and 14C, while the wing, which forms a porch, is Italian Renaissance. The 15C tower has a pleasant peal of bells *(noon and 5pm).*

Flora Park (DU). – *Open 9am to 8pm (4pm September to April).*
Tropical plants grow in a vast **hot-house★**.

Zoo (DU). – *Open May to August, 8.30am to 6pm; September to April, 9am to 5pm; 3.50DM.* Important collection of birds.

EXCURSIONS

Altenberg★. – *20 km - 12 miles – about 1½ hours.* Leave Cologne by ② and take the Berliner Strasse on the right. At Dünnwald turn right towards Altenberg. As you pass, note the curious modern church at Schildgen, bristling with concrete pinnacles. "Altenberg Cathedral" *(admission: 0.30DM – closed Fridays and from 3.30pm on Saturdays)*, still known locally as the Bergische Dom (Berg Region Cathedral), stands in a green agricultural valley much loved by the citizens of Cologne. The building, a 14C Cistercian abbey in which Protestant and Catholic services are now held alternately, is in a very pure Gothic style. The monochrome windows are 13C and the magnificent **stained glass window★** with figures above the west door, is 14C.

Zons★. – *24 km - 15 miles – about 1½ hours.* Leave Cologne by ①, road no 9, which you follow to Dormagen before bearing right to the delightful fortified village of Zons on the Rhine *(irregular boat service: apply to the Tourist Office, Cologne).*

Brühl Castle. – *13 km - 8 miles – about 1¼ hours. Closed last weekend each month.* Leave Cologne by ⑥, road no 51. The castle, called the Augustusburg after its builder the Elector Clement-Augustus, was erected in the main from 1725 to 1728. Inside, the Rococo **staircase★** (Treppenhaus) peopled with telamones and caryatids (pillars in the form of male and female figures) is attributed to Balthazar Neumann *(p 27).* The **gardens★** (Schlossgarten) are formal.

CONSTANCE ★ (KONSTANZ)

Michelin map **206** 19 – *Local map p 102* – Pop 71 000

Constance, a German enclave on the left bank of the Rhine, lies in a pleasant **setting**★ at a place where the lake which bears its name narrows and divides into two quite distinct basins: the Bodensee, a true inland sea, to the east, and to the west the Untersee, which is the more picturesque with steep, indented shores.

The foundation of a new university at Mainauwald brought even more people to the town.

HISTORICAL NOTES

The founding of Constance, which has long been attributed to the Roman Emperor Constantius Chlorus, played a prominent part in the Great Schism of the West (1378-1429).

Constance as the Capital of Christianity. From 1414 to 1418 a council made it the hub of the Christian world. Sigismund, Emperor of Germany, and many princes, abbots and bishops settled in the town.

What was afoot was no less than the re-establishment of the unity of the Church, compromised for nearly forty years by the conflicting claims first of two, then of three ecclesiastical dignitaries, all elected in due form to the papal throne. The confusion was such that the rival popes each found supporters not only among temporal princes but among church people of their time – St. Catherine of Siena and St. Vincent Ferrer were in opposing camps – and mutually excommunicated one another. After prolonged negotiations the work of the Council achieved tangible results: two of the three rival Popes (Gregory XII and John XXIII) agreed to resign. Only Benedict XIII, who had taken refuge in Spain and was abandoned by all his followers, remained obdurate. In 1417 the election of Martin V, who was recognised everywhere as the only pope, put an end to the Schism for a time.

A Precursor of the Reformation. – **John Hus,** an eminent member of the Bohemian clergy hostile to German influence and Rector of Prague University, was summoned before the Council at Constance to expound his doctrines which were opposed particularly to the current rites of confession and the Eucharist and to the apostolic primacy.

He received a safe-conduct from the Emperor Sigismund to attend the council, but on breaking the "suspension" clause by which he was forbidden to celebrate mass or to preach, he was arrested and thrown into prison. On being declared a heretic by the ecclesiastical court he was expelled from the priesthood and handed over to the secular arm. On 6 July 1415, he was burnt alive (commemorative stone known as the Hussenstein on the Alter Graben – access by ⑤ on the map) and his ashes scattered on the Rhine. But his disciples kept up the struggle, where necessary by force of arms, so establishing Hus, the reformer, as one of the precursors of Protestantism and a hero of the Czech nation.

■ SIGHTS *time: 2 hours*

The Lake Shore★ **(Seeufer).** – The shores of Lake Constance (Bodensee) form an attractive scene with the port, the shady gardens, the casino (Spielbank), the quays – especially the Seestrasse – and the old defensive towers such as the Rheintorturm and the Pulverturm. There is a terrace belvedere in the Stadtgarten. A flotilla of pleasure-boats and steamers plies the lake offering excursions.

Basilica★ **(Münster) (A).** – The old cathedral looking down on the quiet and old-fashioned Münsterplatz, has no unity of design for it was built over a period of 600 years, from the 11 to the 17C. The **panels**★ (Türflügel) of the main façade doorway are decorated with low reliefs of the life of Christ (1470).

Enter by the north door. The 17C vaulting in the nave rests on the sanctuary's 11C arcades; the decoration of the organ loft and the organ case anticipate the Renaissance yet the overall impression of the huge building remains Romanesque. The side chapels are closed by grilles giving an effect of perspective common in 18C Swabia – those on the north side being the more remarkable. Go up the Schnegg in the north transept, a spiral staircase turret worked in the French Flamboyant style.

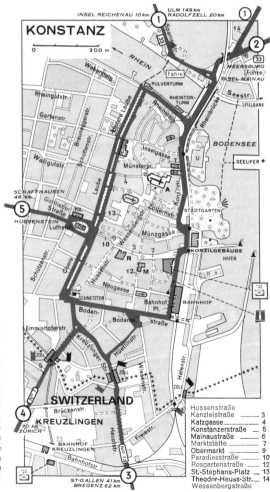

Hussenstraße	
Kanzleistraße	3
Katzgasse	4
Konstanzerstraße	5
Mainaustraße	6
Marktstätte	
Obermarkt	9
Paradiesstraße	10
Rosgartenstraße	12
St.-Stephans-Platz	13
Theodor-Heuss-Str.	14
Wessenbergstraße	

Above the south doorway four gilt copper plaques dating from the 11 to 13C depict respectively Christ in Majesty, the symbolic Eagle of St. John, St. Conrad and St. Pelagius, patrons of the diocese.

A staircase to the right of the main door leads to the tower platform *(open 1 May to 30 September, 9am to 5pm; 0.50DM)* from which there is a view of the town and the various arms of the lake.

City Hall (R). – The façade of this fine Renaissance building is decorated with paintings depicting the history of the town. In the inner courtyard – a quiet spot in the tourist season – is an elegant 16C dwelling house between two round towers.

Rosgarten Museum (M). – *Open 9am to noon and 2 to 5pm (4pm October to March); closed Mondays and Sunday afternoons.*

This regional museum of the areas surrounding the shores of Lake Constance is in a former corporation building. It contains a well known engraving of the Palaeolithic period of a reindeer grazing and a copy of the chronicle by Ulrich Richental, illustrated with vivid pictures of council meetings and daily life in Constance at that time.

Konzilgebäude. – *To visit the so-called Council Chamber, which occupies the whole of the first floor, apply to the Couicl inn (Konzil Gaststätten).*

This former warehouse, built at the end of the 14C, was used by the Conclave of 1417 which proclaimed the election of Pope Martin V. A monument to Count Zeppelin (1838-1917), the famous airship inventor, stands in the garden opposite, bordering on the pleasure harbour.

EXCURSION

Mainau Island★★. – *7 km - 4½ miles – plus 2 hours sightseeing. Boats on Lake Constance also visit the island.* Leave Constance by ②, the Staad landing-stage (Meersburg Ferry) road and bear left towards Mainau.

Leave the car in the car park *(1DM)* at the end of the footbridge to the island *(admission: 4DM)*. Brushwood and tropical plants were successfully collected by the Baden princes and members of the Royal House of Sweden and still grow on Mainau. Palm, orange and lemon trees stand at the approaches to the south wing of the castle and church; a hibiscus flourishes in the rose garden. Below in the foreground in a protected spot near the lake, banana trees open wide their immense fragile leaves and Mexican daturas display huge trumpet flowers.

Magnolias and daturas also grow on the castle esplanade, while in the background the oldest trees on the island cast their shadows on the grass – a tulip tree, a silver poplar and a lime. The tour ends with a walk through conifers planted over the remainder of the plateau facing the mainland (signposts "Koniferen-Rundgang").

CONSTANCE, Lake ★★ (BODENSEE)
Michelin map **206** 9, 18, 19

Lake Constance, so vast that its horizons are lost in the summer haze, might be thought of as one of the "inland seas" of Central Europe. Fleets of boats, the good nature of the lakeside people and a climate which, in certain places such as Mainau Island, enables tropical vegetation to flourish, engender a Mediterranean air and attract hosts of German holidaymakers.

The "Swabian Sea". – Lake Constance with a maximum depth of 252 m - 827 ft – and an area of 53 800 ha – 208 sq miles – is only a little smaller than Lake Geneva, the biggest of the Alpine Lakes, but lies at a higher altitude (394 m - 1 295 ft). Next to the main part of the lake, which is known as the **Obersee** and has a maximum width between Friedrichshafen and Romanshorn of 12 km - 7 miles – lies the arm of the lake known as **Überlingersee** with its steep and frequently wooded banks, and beyond, the **Untersee**. This sheet of water, linked to the main lake only by the Constance Channel, has much indented low-lying shores.

The lake's size moderates the local climate without, however, ensuring warm winters. It has frozen over some thirty times since the year 1000 – most recently in 1830, 1880 and 1963. Water from below a certain depth is pure enough to be used in the towns; a 150 km – 93 mile – pipe starting opposite Sipplengen brings water to the particularly needy industrial region of Stuttgart at the rate of 660 gallons per second.

TOUR

A tour right round the lake lacks interest in places. The Constance-Meersburg Ferry *(departures every 15 minutes during the day, hourly at night, in summer; time for crossing: 20 minutes; fare: 4 to 9DM)* makes it possible to go from Donaueschingen to Lindau in one trip.

The Engen-Meersburg route allows one to see the somewhat wild shores of the Überlingersee. Boat services provide many more excursions; the most frequent run from Constance, Überlingen, Meersburg, Lindau and the Austrian town of Bregenz.

★ FROM DONAUESCHINGEN TO LINDAU
by way of Constance and the Meersburg Ferry
121 km - 75 miles – 1 day – Local map pp 102-103

Donaueschingen. – *Description p 107.*
From Donaueschingen to Geisingen the road follows, at a distance, the course of the newly born Danube across the widely undulating Baar plateau. The Randen hill range, an extension of the Swabian Jura to the southwest, divides Geisingen from Engen.

Hegau Belvedere★ (Hegaublick). – The terrace, a little below the highest section of the road, on the southern slope of the Randen chain, looks out over the volcanic Hegau region, spiked with such rock hillocks as the Hohenkrähen, and the wide table summit of the Hohentwiel in the Singen range. To the left of the Hohenkrähen can be seen a stretch of Lake Constance, the Untersee. In clear weather Säntis and the jagged ridges of the Churfirsten in the Swiss Alps appear on the horizon. The road drops steeply to the plain all the while affording expansive views.

Singen. – *Description p 232.*
The journey from Singen to Radolfzell is dull but in the reverse direction the sudden appearance at a bend in the road of the Hohentwiel rock is impressive, especially at sunset.
Between Radolfzell and Constance the Untersee shores are low lying in contrast to the wooded escarpments of the Swiss shore to the south. The large island is Reichenau – the two towers belong to Niederzell Church, the massive abbey is Mittelzell and the single belfry, Oberzell.

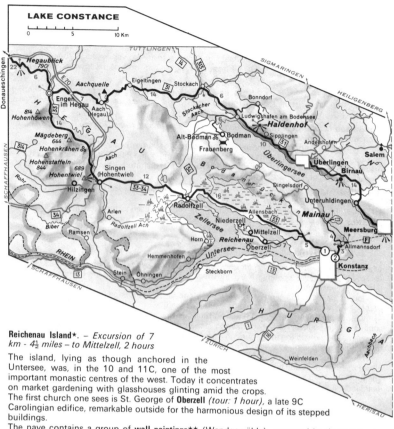

LAKE CONSTANCE

0   5   10 Km

Reichenau Island★. – *Excursion of 7 km - 4½ miles – to Mittelzell, 2 hours*

The island, lying as though anchored in the Untersee, was, in the 10 and 11C, one of the most important monastic centres of the west. Today it concentrates on market gardening with glasshouses glinting amid the crops.

The first church one sees is St. George of **Oberzell** *(tour: 1 hour)*, a late 9C Carolingian edifice, remarkable outside for the harmonious design of its stepped buildings.

The nave contains a group of **wall paintings★★** (Wandgemälde), executed in about the year AD 1000 and concerned uniquely with Christ's miracles. As in miniatures of the period, the figures are painted against a background of stripes of different colours.

The **old abbey★** (Münster) at **Mittelzell,** the chief town on the island, was built from the 8 to the 12C. The robust Romanesque tower at the west end of the building *(p 23)* is lightened in appearance by a decorative band of Lombard pilasters and friezes. Inside *(tour: ½ hour)*, the Romanesque main part has a timbered vault and the Gothic apse is much pierced with windows. A Rococo grille with perspective effect stands in the centre. The **treasure★** *(1DM)* includes an early 14C reliquary of St. Mark of beaten silver enriched with enamels.

Constance★ (Konstanz). – *Description p 100.*

    Mainau Island★★. – *Excursion of 4 km - 2½ miles – from Allmannsdorf, plus 2 hours sightseeing. Description p 101.*

Take the ferry across the Überlingersee and you reach Meersburg on the north shore of the Obersee.

Meersburg★. – *Description p 178.*

The coast road begins as a minor *corniche* above the lake, passing through orchards and vineyards. As you come out of **Hagnau** to the east, a **belvedere★** with a car park enables you to stop and enjoy the scenery which includes the village church, vineyards, the great stretch of the lake with the Swiss towns of Romanshorn and Arbon on the shore and, above, the jagged outlines of the Säntis Massif.

The road between Immenstaad and Lindau ceases to follow the curving shoreline which is flat and rural. The quay promenades of Friedrichshafen, Langenargen, or Wasserburg, therefore, make the best stopping places.

Friedrichshafen. – Friedrichshafen, first a transit and entrepôt port for trade between Swabia and Switzerland and later a construction base for zeppelins, was severely bombed in 1944. The town, now rebuilt, is particularly attractive on account of its wide and pleasant promenade quays. The lake is at its widest between Friedrichshafen and Romanshorn.

Wasserburg. – This much visited village, within sight of Lindau, is squeezed on to a narrow tongue of land which juts out into the lake. Walk down to the church and the presbytery built at the tip of the cape.

Pfänder Mountain, which overlooks Bregenz in Austria, can be recognised by its television masts, from the outskirts of Lindau.

Lindau★★. – *Description p 166.*

FROM ENGEN TO MEERSBURG

51 km - 32 miles – about 3½ hours – Local map above

On leaving Engen, follow road no 31.

Source of the Aach (Aachquelle). – *Tour: ¼ hour.* The waters of the Danube, "lost" 12 km - 7 miles – away, reappear on this Rhine slope as a powerful spring breaking the surface of a shaded pool.

    Haldenhof★★. – *Excursion of 7 km - 4½ miles – from road no 31 by the Bonndorf road, then in the last bend before the village, right, by the Haldenhof road.*
From this natural terrace (restaurant) there is an **end on view★★** across the Überlingersee to Mainau Island. Sipplingen is in the foreground and Bodman, overlooked by its two castles, on the far shore.

Bodman. – *Excursion of 6 km - 3½ miles – from Ludwigshafen.*

It is believed the lake, Bodensee, took its name from this town, where the remains of Neolithic, Celtic, Alemannian and Roman civilisations can all be seen. The peace of this end of the lake, where there are no busy through-roads, attracts holidaymakers. They can wander in the castle park and visit the two old fortresses, Frauenberg (chapel, collection of arms, dolls' houses) and Alt-Bodman, which overlook the town.

After Ludwigshafen, the road skirts the Überlingersee, a lake more remarkable for its steep and often wild shores, which even include a few cliffs, than for its views. The far bank, well wooded, appears deserted.

Überlingen*. – *Description p 249.*

As you approach Birnau church you can see right along the southwest shore of the Überlingersee from Bodman to Mainau Island with its distinctive castle.

Birnau*. – *Description p 80.*

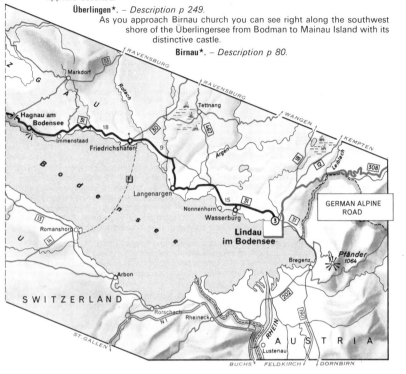

Unteruhldingen. – Two groups of prehistoric dwellings were reconstructed here on piles in the lake in 1922 and are known as the "Freilichtmuseum Pfahlbauten" (open air palafitte museum *burnt down in April 1976*).

Meersburg*. – *Description p 178.*

CUXHAVEN *

Michelin map **987** – 4 – Pop 63 000 – *Town plan in Michelin Red Guide Deutschland*

Cuxhaven is the second fishing port of Germany and the maritime port responsible for navigation in the Elbe Estuary. It lies in a slightly protected site at the mouth of the River Elbe and is therefore also developing into a seaside resort, utilising the new installations at Döse and Dühnen, two well arranged beaches on a narrow strip of wind-driven sand facing the open sea. The frequent passage of ocean liners draws many spectators to the quays.

Cuxhaven is also the port for the many ships crossing the Atlantic and passengers embarking for Heligoland *(p 149)*. A small ferry runs three times a day during the season from Cuxhaven to Brunsbüttelkoog on the right bank of the Elbe *(1 May to 30 September every two hours; time: ¾ hour; fares: 9-17DM for the car plus 6DM per person).*

■ SIGHTS *time: ½ hour*

Alte Liebe Pier* (Landungsbrücke). – The gallant tag "Old Love" derives from the mispronunciation of the name of a boat the "Olivia" which sank in these waters in 1732, thus producing a primitive pier. Today the pier is used by the Heligoland boats. The Alte Liebe, which is known to sailors the world over, makes an excellent **observation point*** from which to watch the shipping. Nearby are pilot and shipping controls including the old lighthouse of 1803.

Kugelbake. – This great beacon, which is no longer in use but remains the emblem of Cuxhaven, stands at the end of a breakwater marking the geographic, if not the hydrographic, mouth of the Elbe – a river born 1 145 km - 712 miles away – in the Riesengebirge Mountains on the borders of Bohemia and Silesia. From near the beacon there is a **view*** of the river mouth (Elbmündung) and the open sea.

EXCURSION

Lüdingworth. – *10 km - 6 miles plus ½ hour sightseeing.* Leave Cuxhaven by ①, the Hamburg road. In the Altenbruch bypass bear right for Lüdingworth. The **church*** furnishings *(open April to October, 9am–noon Sundays–to 6pm; 0.50DM; if closed apply at the sacristy)* reflect the taste of a prosperous peasantry. Many items, collected from the 14 to the 18C, have remained undamaged. Note the pews fitted with painted doors, the 17C pulpit in the form of a covered gallery supported by a statue of Moses, the north gallery, the 14C bronze lectern eagle standing on an immense Baroque credence.

DACHAU Concentration Camp

Michelin map **987** 37 – 22 km - 14 miles – northwest of Munich

The name Dachau, which since 1933 has evoked only horror, used to be charged with poetry for the people of Munich of an older generation who were charmed by the town built in terraces below a castle belonging to the Wittelsbachs and by the infinitely delicate light of the often painted Dachauer Moos, the misty nearby heath.

This camp was the first to be set up by Himmler in March 1933, received 200 000 prisoners or deportees; no one knows the number of those who died or disappeared.

Camp Relics, Memorial and Museum. – *Follow the signposting "KZ – Gedenkstätte". Open 9am to 5pm; time: about 2 hours; closed 24 December and the afternoons of 31 December and Shrove Tuesday. Brochure in English.*

Within the camp perimeter a Catholic expiatory chapel in the form of an open tower has been built and named Christ in Agony (Todesangst-Christi-Kapelle) and on either side a Protestant commemorative chapel and a Jewish memorial. Behind stands the Carmelite Convent, completed in the autumn of 1964, where the chapel is also open to all.

The **museum,** which is in the former administrative buildings, gives an idea of the Nazi concentration camp system. The original prison barracks were razed but two have been faithfully reconstructed and are on view.

Outside the perimeter stand four of the cremation ovens – the surroundings have now been turned into a park necropolis. Tombstones mark where ashes have been buried. The bodies of other victims have been buried in the cemeteries of Dachau (Waldfriedhof) and Leitenberg.

The DANUBE ★ (DONAU)

Michelin map **987** 35 to 40

The Danube is the longest river in Central Europe, with a course of 2 826 km (647 km in Germany – 1 756 and 402 miles respectively), and the second longest in Europe, after the Volga, which is 3 895 km – 2 292 miles long. The outflow is by far the greatest in Europe, deriving as it does from a catchment area of 817 000 km – 320 000 sq miles or nearly 3½ times the area of Great Britain. It forms a link between Germany and southeast Europe; it crosses or skirts seven states, and three capitals, built on its banks, bear witness to its international importance. But if it is a link between peoples, it has also often been an obstacle to their coming together.

The Danubian School (early 16C). – The countryside and forests along the Danube below Regensburg have inspired a number of painters, mainly Swabians, who had in common a keen sense of nature, conceived not simply as a setting but tingling with hidden life. The artist then made a point of depicting the secret countrysides in which the legendary spirits, inseparable from German imagination, might roam.

Albrecht Altdorfer (1480–1538), a citizen of Regensburg, is the master in whom this poetry is most clearly visible. In the panels of the Passion painted for the monks of St. Florian in Austria, the *Battle of Arbèles, St. George,* and the *Danube Valley* shown at Munich, Altdorfer handles contrasting light in a way so striking as to make him one of the founders of landscape painting, as well as a forerunner of Romanticism.

A Franconian painter, Lucas Cranach the Elder (1472-1553), is also among the Danubian masters. The mysterious depths of water, rocks and woods which form the backgrounds of his works show his affinity with the "forest painters".

GEOGRAPHICAL NOTES

The Danube in Germany. – Rising at an altitude of 1 078 m - 3 537 ft – on the eastern slopes of the Black Forest, about 100 m from the actual watershed between the Danube and the Rhine basins, the Danube is really formed at Donaueschingen *(p 107).* Approaching the Swabian Jura, the river almost comes to a stop in the deep limestone fissures. Emerging finally through the Source of the Aach *(p 102),* it flows from Tuttlingen to Sigmaringen between the steep cliffs of a picturesque defile. Below Ulm, the Danube takes on the characteristics of an Alpine river: in summer the stream is swollen, in autumn depleted. This variation it owes to the tributaries on its right bank: the Iller, the Lech and the Inn which bring down thaw-waters from the Bavarian and Tyrolean Alps. Their large volume – the Inn at Passau has a flow almost as great as the Danube itself – make it, by the time it reaches Austria, a powerful river, able to carry shipping.

Navigation on the Danube. – After passing Ulm, where the Iller waters increase the main flow, the Danube becomes navigable. Clumsy craft called "Ulm boxes", as well as rafts of logs, used to float down as far as Vienna. They had a draught of only about 2 ft, and, being unable to go upstream, they were broken up at the end of the journey.

In 1829 steamships appeared and the passenger and freight traffic grew. The Danube made trading possible between the industrial districts of the upper valley and the agricultural lands downstream. None the less, international use of a river is no simple matter and free navigation remained dependent upon the vagaries of Balkan politics. The 1856 and 1919 Treaties of Paris

made the Danube an international waterway. Although this statute has never been abrogated by law, since the creation of a new European Commission for the Danube under the Belgrade Convention of 1948, only the riparian countries enjoy free trade and navigation rights on the river. In effect today only the Danubian states – including Germany although she was not admitted to the Commission – profit from the free flow of navigation and commercial rights on the river.

Other reasons make the Danube a much less frequented river than the Rhine: there are large variations of flow and moving sandbanks which are dangerous to navigation and have often to be marked afresh; winter freezing may hold up traffic for several weeks; the river flows into an inland sea; the whole area is sparsely populated and little developed industrially.

River Engineering. – For two centuries important civil engineering works have been undertaken to improve the navigability and usefulness of the river. The greater part of the current programme (dams and hydro-electric stations) is being undertaken on the one hand by Austria, on the other by Yugoslavia and Rumania who have undertaken jointly the construction of an immense dam in the Iron Gate defile. Work was completed in 1972.

Small seagoing ships can, at present, go up as far as Budapest and 1 000-1 200 ton barges can reach Regensburg. Ultimately the Rhine-Main-Danube connection will enable, in 1985, 1 500 ton Rhine barges and 3 000-3 500 ton convoys to go from Rotterdam to the Black Sea. The Forchheim-Nuremberg section is already completed.

THE DANUBE IN GERMANY

The map below indicates with a cross-reference to the descriptive page, the towns on the Danube in Germany, the chief belvederes and parts of the valley most frequented by tourists.

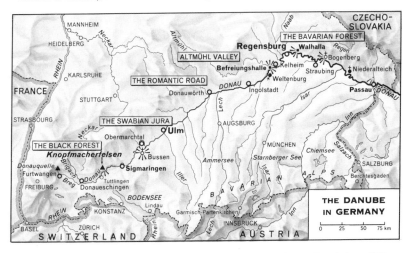

Knopfmacherfelsen**. – Belvedere overlooking the Upper Danube Gorge. *Description p 239.*

Bussen. – From the pilgrimage chapel *(access by car by Offingen, 10 km - 6 miles – east of Riedlingen)* which can be seen from afar off, there is an immense **panorama** from the southern foothills of the Swabian Jura to the plateaux of Upper Swabia.

Liberation Monument* (Befreiungshalle). – There is a **view** from the monument gallery of the Danube and Altmühl Valleys. *Description p 159.*

Walhalla*. – **View** of a bend in the Danube and the Regensburg belfries. *Description p 253.*

Bogenberg. – There is a bird's-eye **view** from the pilgrimage church terrace and the churchyard of the river where the barges begin to ply.

Passau*. – There is a **view**** from the Oberhaus of the town crowded together at the confluence of the Inn, the Danube and the Illz. *Description p 203.*

DARMSTADT

Michelin map **204** 6, 7 – Pop 138000 – *Town plan in Michelin Red Guide Deutschland*

The former capital of the Grand Duchy of Hesse-Darmstadt, now a thriving industrial centre (machine tools, unbreakable glass for car windscreens, electronic equipment) lies close to the Odenwald Massif.

Darmstadt has long been renowned as a cultivated city, thanks to the endeavours of its princes who were enlightened amateurs and who at the turn of the century made it a home of Art Nouveau or Jugendstil *(p 26)*. Several institutions continue the tradition – the Academy of Language and Poetry, the Institute for Industrial Design (Rat für Formgebung).

Hesse Museum* (Hessisches Landesmuseum). – *Open 10am to 5pm (Wednesday evenings also 7 to 9pm); closed Mondays and some holidays.*

The picture galleries (2nd and 3rd floors) contain German masters of the 15 and 16C (Lochner, Cranach the Elder) and the Romantic period, 17C Flemish and Dutch pictures (Rembrandt, Rubens, Brueghel) and works by Stuck, Böcklin, Corinth, Marc, Hofer and others.

The ground floor is devoted to religious art, including stained glass and to Jugendstil.

Mathildenhöhe. – In about 1900 a colony of artists, including architects, painters and sculptors, who had come at the invitation of the Grand Duke Ernst-Ludwig, to work together in the search for "total art" in accordance with Jugendstil's ideal, settled on Mathildenhöhe hill. Outstanding were the architect Josef Olbrich and the sculptor Bernhard Hoetger.

The group of buildings near the Russian chapel have a somewhat disparate appearance with their terraces and pergolas, but are typical of the period.

The **wedding tower** (Hochzeitsturm), erected on Ernst-Ludwig's marriage in 1905, overlooks all. Inside there is an allegorical mosaic on Love.

Castle. – *Open 10am to 1pm and 2 to 5pm; closed Fridays, Saturday, Sunday and holiday afternoons; 1DM.*

The former landgraves' residence, in the centre of the town, consists of two main buildings. The new, 18C, castle is plain with a wide symmetrical façade on the Marktplatz.

The old castle (Altschloss) is adorned with voluted gables and the richly decorated doorway through to the courtyard, the family coat of arms. The Hesse-Darmstadt family collections (Schlossmuseum), which are on view, include carriages, furnishings, silver and, in the picture gallery, Holbein the Younger's *Darmstadt Virgin.*

Prince George's Palace (**Prinz-Georg-Palais**) – *Open 10am to 1pm and 2 to 5pm; closed Fridays, Saturday and Sunday afternoons; 1DM.*

The early 18C former summer residence of the dukes now houses a fine **porcelain collection** ★ (Porzellansammlung). Almost all the pieces were given by members of the royal or imperial families of Europe: services and ornaments bear great names – Nymphenburg, Berlin, Frankenthal, Ludwigsburg, or Meissen or the grand-ducal factory of Kelsterbach.

Prince George's Garden. – Symmetrical beds planted with clipped yews adorn the formal gardens round the palace. Alleys afford pleasing vistas of scattered pavilions.

EXCURSION

Kranichstein Castle (**Jagdschloss Kranichstein**). – *5 km - 3 miles – plus ¾ hour sightseeing (10am to 1pm and 2 to 5pm – closed Mondays – 1.50DM).* Leave Darmstadt by the Kranichsteiner Strasse *(see Michelin Red Guide Deutschland)* and enter the courtyard by the road on the right. The **hunting museum** ★ (Jagdmuseum) contains weapons, hunting trophies and pictures.

DETMOLD

Michelin map **987** 15 – *Local map p 242* – Pop 65 500
Town plan in Michelin Red Guide Deutschland

Until 1918, Detmold was the capital of the Lippe Principality, cradle of the family of Prince Bernard of the Netherlands. It is a pleasant small town, enlived by students of the Academy of Music, and the usual departure point for the Arminius monument and Teutoburger Wald *(p 242).*

Castle. – *Guided tours: 1 April to 15 October, 9am to noon and 2 to 5pm; the rest of the year, Tuesdays to Saturdays at 10 and 11am, 3 and 4pm; 3DM.*

The special features of this fine rectangular 16C building are, on the façade, dormer windows ornamented with semicircular pediments in the First Renaissance style and, particularly in the inner courtyard, a very elegant corbelled gallery linking the corner towers.

Souvenirs given by foreign royalty enrich the interior: outstanding are a porcelain service presented by the Empress Josephine in the Empire Room and a Delft porcelain stove.

Fine 17C tapestries woven in Brussels after cartoons by Charles Le Brun and illustrating the history of Alexander the Great are also on view in the final rooms of the tour.

DIESSEN AM AMMERSEE

Michelin map **987** 36, 37 – *Local map p 40* – Pop 6 200

Pleasantly placed on the southwest bank of the Ammersee, Diessen draws many people from Munich during the summer because of its sailing school and other water sports.

Abbey Church ★ (**Stiftskirche**). – *Tour: ½ hour.* Johann-Michael Fischer, one of Upper Bavaria's most famous architects in the Baroque style, rebuilt the collegiate church from the old monastery of the Augustinians on a hill in the suburb of St. George from 1732 to 1739.

From the fine iron grille wrought in 1738 and placed below the organ loft, one can take in the nave and the chancel together and admire the general perspective, emphasised by the side altars, which focuses attention on the high point of the altar.

The quality of the rose, gold and white stuccoes and the remarkably decorated paintwork of the dome, the vault and side altars contrast with the slightly theatrical character of the high altar by François Cuvilliés. On either side of the altarpiece, on which is painted the Assumption, gigantic statues of the Fathers of the Church are set in pairs; the Holy Trinity crowns all.

DINKELSBÜHL ★

Michelin map **987** south of 26 – *Local map p 217* – Pop 10 500

Dinkelsbühl, an attractive stop on the Romantic Road, is a mediaeval looking town still complete with surrounding ramparts and watch-towers. It is a curious example of early town planning with houses stepped along wide roads with no pavements.

Every year the town comes very much alive in mid-July when, with great costumed displays and fanfares, the *Kinderzeche* or children's festival is celebrated to commemorate the city's salvation in the Thirty Years War *(p 20).*

St. George's ★. – The church still has its Romanesque tower. The interior takes the form of a Gothic hall *(illustration p 24)* and is a remarkable sight with its three aisles covered with skilfully designed fan vaulting. Note the altar to the Trinity, an instance of 15C Franconian art, in the south aisle. Against the pillars marking the entrance to the chancel are a fine ciborium of 1480 and on the right a Virgin of the Riemenschneider school. Against three apsidal pillars are 15C statues, from left to right, of St. Bartholomew, the Virgin and St. George.

From the top of the tower *(open 8am to noon and 1.30 to 6pm or 4pm in winter; 0.50DM)* there is a **view** of the town crowded within the ramparts.

Deutsches Haus ★. – This fine 15C house in the Martin-Luther-Strasse stands out from the other gabled houses, through the richness of the Renaissance decoration on its painted and carved façade. The small Virgin over the entrance is late 17C.

Old houses. – Go down the Segringer Strasse where among the flower decked houses adorned with picturesque signs stands, near the church at no 7, the **Hezelhof.** This house is remarkable for the long double balconies hung with flowers in its inner courtyard.

Go in the opposite direction, down the Nördlinger Strasse, where the houses are out of line. Take the third turning on the left to reach the foot of the ramparts which you follow to the right, via the Bauerlinsturm, to the Nördlingen Gate. Outside, against the gate, stands the Stadtmühle, the fortified town mill, which one can ask the miller to let one enter to get a view of the ramparts.

DONAUESCHINGEN

Michelin map **205** 7 – Pop 18 200

The small town of Donaueschingen stands at the source of the Danube in the centre of the Baar, a fertile basin with a harsh climate lying between the Black Forest and the Swabian Jura. Its industries are brewing and tourism. The annual music festival specialises in the most modern works.

■ THE SOURCE OF THE DANUBE *tour: ¼ hour*

The monumental fountain, known as the "Donauquelle" which was constructed in the castle park in the 19C is the official source of the Danube.

In fact two streams, the Breg and the Brigach, meet at Donaueschingen, hence the catch-phrase "Brigach and Breg bringen die Donau zuweg" roughly the equivalent of "large streams from little fountains flow". The geographical source of the Danube is actually the source of the Breg *(p 83)*.

■ ADDITIONAL SIGHTS

Princely Collections (Fürstlich-Fürstenbergische Sammlungen). – *Open 9am to noon and 1.30 to 4.30pm; closed Mondays and in November; 2DM.*
The collections are in a building on the Karlsplatz.

The **picture gallery★** (Gemäldegalerie) on the 2nd floor is the most interesting. In the large gallery on the right are works by 15 and 16C Swabian masters such as Bartholomäus Zeitblom and an outstandingly fine **altarpiece of the Passion★★** (Passionsaltar) by the Elder Holbein: note Christ's stance. There are two appealing paintings of *St. Elizabeth* and *St. Lucia* by Grünewald. The left gallery is devoted primarily to the Master of Messkirch (Wildenstein altarpiece).

Castle. – *Open Easter and Whitsun to 15 September, 9am to noon and 2 to 5pm; closed Mondays; 2.50DM. Guided tours in English.*
The Fürstenberg residence, which was remodelled in the 19C, retains the luxurious amenities of the period further enriched by pieces of porcelain, gold and silver plate, Beauvais tapestries, uniforms, etc.

Church (Pfarrkirche). – 18C. In the first bay on the right is the 1522 Virgin of Donaueschingen.

DORTMUND

Michelin map **202** 8 – *Local map p 223* – Pop 620 000
Town plan in Michelin Red Guide Deutschland

This, the most easterly of the Ruhr industrial towns is where 20% of the steel of the Land of North Rhine-Westphalia is produced. It is also a thriving centre for the machine tool industry.

Dortmund, an old Hanseatic town, keeps up its commercial tradition: it is the biggest sugar market in the Federal Republic and the biggest wheat market of northwest Germany. But for the visitor it is, above all, the beer capital. Seven breweries produce more than 10% of the country's total output. *To visit a brewery apply to the Verband Dortmunder Bierbrauer, Karl-Marx-Strasse 56 (☎528973).*

Television Tower★ (Fernmeldeturm). – *Time: ¼ hour.* The tower, including the 47 m - 154 ft antenna, is 220 m - 722 ft high. The width at the base is 12 m - 39 ft (lift: 2DM). (GPO tower: 620 ft; restaurant at 520 ft).

138 m - 453 ft up, on a platform which revolves 2-6 times an hour, there are a restaurant and a terrace with an impressive **panorama★** of the Ruhr and the Sauerland.

Westphalia Park★. – *Entrance charge.*
The park makes an outing for the people of Dortmund: there are a rose garden with 2 600 varieties from all over the world, playgrounds for children with a miniature railway and a cablecar and attractions such as the water-borne open air theatre.
Nearby the Westfalenhalle, an immense hall seating 23 000, is used for congresses, exhibitions and sporting events.

St. Reynold's (Reinoldikirche). – This and the neighbouring Marienkirche are among the last examples of old architecture in the centre of the town which has been extensively rebuilt.

The design is Gothic, the interesting furnishings include 14C statues of Charlemagne and St. Reynold on either side of the chancel and a 15C carved high altarpiece of the Crucifixion.

St. Mary's (Marienkirche). – *If closed apply at the presbytery, Kleppingstrasse 5 (except Sunday afternoons).*
This Romanesque basilica with a Gothic chancel contains one of the finest works by Konrad von Soest, 1420, the **altarpiece of Our Lady★** (Marienaltar) with remarkably expressive face and hands.

Ostwall Museum. – *Ostwall 7. Open 9.30am to 6pm; Sundays 10am to 2pm; closed Mondays and holidays; 1DM.*
Works by the greatest modern European, and particularly German, painters are displayed: Paula Modersohn-Becker, Jawlensky (8 canvases), Macke, Kokoschka, Müller, Nolde, Rohlfs and amongst the sculptors, Barlach, Käthe Kollwitz, Kolbe. Works by younger generations are constantly being added to keep the museum up to date.

DREISESSEL Rocks ★ (DREISESSEL-FELSEN)

Michelin map **987** south of 28 – *Local map p 59*

A drive to the Dreisessel Rocks close to the meeting point of the German, Austrian and Czechoslovakian frontiers *(the Czech frontier is closed – keep to the road!)* northeast of Passau, takes you to the heart of one of the wildest forest regions of Bohemia *(p 58)*.

Drive to the Hochstein★. – *8 km - 5 miles – about 2 hours – by the Dreisesselstrasse which branches off the Altreichenau-Haidmühle roads.*
The Dreisessel Inn at the foot of the granite Dreisessel Rocks, worn away into horizontal ridges by erosion, is soon reached from the end of the road. Continue through the underbrush along the path marked by white-bordered green triangles. Go past a first group of rocks and up the steps to the summit and the Hochstein Rock belvedere. The **panorama★** from the Crucifix extends over an immense forestland.

DUISBURG

Michelin map **202** 5, 6 – *Local map p 222* – Pop 598 000
Town plan in Michelin Red Guide Deutschland

Duisburg, at the confluence of the Ruhr and the Herne – Rhine Canal with the Rhine, occupies a key position in the German economy. It is the largest European inland port and serves the greatest industrial area in Germany.

In addition, abundant local supplies of raw materials and sources of energy have concentrated industry in the area. Duisburg is the greatest iron town in Germany; it produces one third of the country's crude steel.

Far from the red and purple smoke poured out from the blast furnaces and chemical works, Duisburg offers its citizens a peaceful stretch of water in the Wedau sports park and, to the east of the Mülheim road, the Kaiserberg Zoo.

The Port*. – Duisburg-Ruhrort-Meiderich with an area of 1 020 ha - 2 500 acres (Liverpool and Birkenhead: 647 acres; lineal quayage: 37¼ miles) and 20 basins, has modern equipment for transhipment and warehousing: along the 44 km - 28 miles of quays are 100 mobile and other cranes, 2 coaltippers and a mixer, oil-storage tanks with a capacity exceeding 1 000 000 m³ - 176 million gallons and cereal warehouses and silos capable of storing 150 000 tons of cereals.

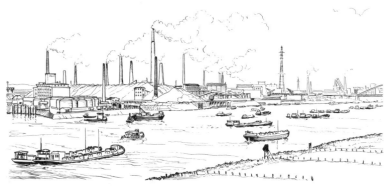

(After a photo by Fritz Rotgans)

The Rhine at Duisburg.

Traffic in 1975 amounted to 22 million tons. Iron ore is basic freight (35%, coal 19%, petrol 19%). Scrap iron and non-ferrous minerals, sand, salt, fertilisers, cereals, etc. make up the balance.

Trade is particularly with Rotterdam, Amsterdam and Antwerp and the Middle-Rhine ports, although small ocean cargo ships also trade direct with North Sea, Baltic and even Atlantic ports as far as Spain.

Port Problems. – The level of the Rhine drops an average 1½ ins a year (7 ft since 1900) as a result of the natural dredging of the river bed. The depth of the bottom of the basins, however, remains constant. To maintain sufficient depth therefore for the larger ships, the dock basins have to be repeatedly deepened. Two methods are used: dredging and the mining of coal seams beneath the port.

Tour of the Port by Motor Boat* (Hafenrundfahrt). – *The motor boats run from April to October. Departures from the Schifferbörse for Ruhrort and from the Schwanentor for Duisburg. Time: 2 hours. Fare: 5DM. Timetables at embarkation points and at the Tourist Office (Stadtinformation) Friedrich-Wilhelm-Strasse 94 (▊ on the plan in the Michelin Red Guide Deutschland).*

Leaving from the Aussenhafen, which handles mostly cereals and sand and also has repair yards, you move down the Rhine as far as the mouth of the Ruhr opposite Homberg before going into the northern part of the port, visiting Basin B which lies between the scrap iron island with its huge press and the coal island where you see tippers and mixers at work.

DÜRKHEIM, Bad

Michelin map **204** 8, 9 – *Local map p 215* – Pop 18 500

Bad Dürkheim, a spa protected by the Pfälzer Wald and lying at the centre of the vineyards crossed by the German Wine Road, is the setting in September of a monster wine carnival known as the Sausage Market *(see list of principal festivals, p 31).*

The **spa park** flourishes from the locally mild climate which makes almond, fig and chestnut trees all flower early.

EXCURSIONS

Ringwald-Teufelsstein. – *Leave from the square where the Sausage Market is held. Cable cars Easter to October, 9am to 5pm; November to March, Saturdays, Sundays and holidays, 11am to 5pm; 5DM (round trip).*

In the "Naturpark" Palatinate Forest, the tourist will discover the leisured world with its well conceived network of paths through the pine forest; and the fantastic Celtic ring wall (Heidenmauer), impressive by its size, dating back to 500 BC. James Fenimore Cooper *(The Last of the Mohicans)* used the beauty of the scenery as the setting for his book *The Heidenmauer.*

Limburg Abbey. – *4 km - 2½ miles – by the Schillerstrasse and the Luitpoldweg going west, plus ½ hour sightseeing.*

The ruins lie amid picturesque greenery *(serenade concerts in summer);* there are pretty views westwards of the Isenach Valley and the Hardenburg ruins and eastwards of the Rhine Plain.

Düsseldorf, once a fishing village on the right bank of the Rhine, where it is joined by the Düssel, is today, with its industrial suburbs, one of the commercial metropolises of Germany. Since 1946 been created capital of North Rhine-Westphalia.

HISTORICAL NOTES

Düsseldorf first acquired city status in the 13C when it became the residence of the Dukes of Berg. In the 17C there settled in the city the family of the Electors of the Neuburg-Palatinate whose most famous member was Johann Wilhelm known as Jan Wellem (1690-1716). Patron and apostle of the Baroque, he surrounded himself with a brilliant court of musicians, painters and architects and made a city of the arts. A large part of his collection of paintings is now in Munich in the Old Pinakothek. After the French Revolution, the town became a little Paris; Napoleon made it the capital of the Grand Duchy of Berg, and first Murat then Jerome Bonaparte were its rulers. In 1815 it became Prussian.

Heinrich Heine (1797-1856). – Heine, the son of a small tradesman in the Bolkerstrasse, lived in Düsseldorf throughout his youth, deeply influenced by the presence of the French and the personality of Napoleon. In his *Memories of Childhood* he expressed his admiration of France with characteristic verve, at once biting and melancholy. A poet who was also a willing pamphleteer, everlasting traveller, defender of liberalism, a European and a Francophile, he described himself as a "German nightingale which would have liked to have made its nest in Voltaire's wig".

DÜSSELDORF-NEUSS

BUILT UP AREA

0   2 km

Auf 'm Hennekamp	T 2	Kettwiger Straße	S 58	Werstener Straße	T 124	
Brehmstraße	S 7	Kevelaerer Straße	S 59	Witzelstraße	T 126	
Brüsseler Straße	S 8	Kölner Straße	S 61	**NEUSS**		
Burgunder Straße	S 10	Lindemannstraße	S 66	Bahnstraße	ST 3	
Danziger Straße	S 13	Ludenberger Straße	S 67	Düsseldorfer Straße	S 16	
Dorotheenstraße	S 14	Luegallee	S 68	Further Straße	ST 28	
Düsseldorfer Straße	S 15	Mecumstraße	T 74	Gielenstraße	T 30	
Eckenerstraße	S 18	Morper Straße	S 75	Kaarster Straße	S 51	
Erasmusstraße	T 22	Münsterstraße	S 77	Nordkanalallee	T 80	
Eupener Straße	S 23	Nördlicher Zubringer	S 81	Oberstraße	T 85	
Grafenberger Allee	S 36	Nordring	S 82	Rheydter Straße	T 88	
Hans-Böckler-Straße	S 37	Oberrather Straße	S 83	Schorlemerstraße	T 97	
Heerdter Landstraße	S 38	Pariser Straße	S 86	Selikumer Straße	T 98	
Heinrich-Ehrhardt-Straße	S 40	Pöhlenweg	S 87	Stresemannallee	T 100	
Heinrichstraße	S 42	Siegburger Straße	T 99	Venloer Straße	T 120	
Jägerstraße	T 45	Uerdinger Straße	S 105	Viersener Straße	S 121	
Johannstraße	S 48	Vautierstraße	S 107	**BUDERICH**		
Kaiserswerther Straße	S 52	Völklinger Straße	T 122	Düsseldorfer Straße	S 17	
Karl-Geusen-Straße	ST 54	Werdener Straße	S 123			
ennedydamm	S 57					

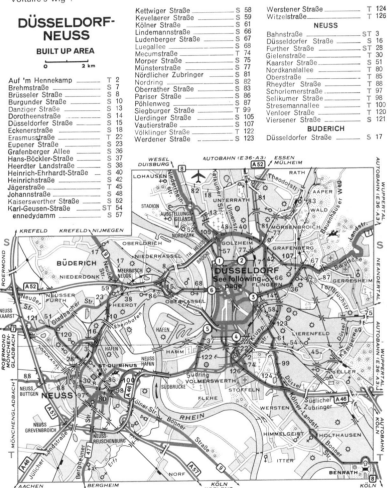

Musical Chronicle. – Schumann and Mendelssohn are among the musicians who have given Düsseldorf its musical reputation.

Robert Schumann (1810-56), appointed conductor of the municipal orchestra in 1850, lived for four years in a house in the Bilker Strasse (**BX**). He was already seriously ill mentally and attempted to commit suicide in the Rhine in 1854. **Felix Mendelssohn** (1809-47), who was his friend, brilliantly directed the town's Rhine Festival. He made his first journey to England in 1829, conducting his Symphony in C Minor at the London Philharmonic Society.

LIFE IN DÜSSELDORF

The Business Centre of the Ruhr. – Düsseldorf, the seat of one of the largest stock-exchanges in Germany, is also the banking capital and administrative centre of many of the major Rhineland industries (iron, steel, chemicals, electrical engineering and precision tools, cars, etc.). Almost all the commercial transactions of the Ruhr and the nearby towns could be said to take place in the area between the Kasernenstrasse, the Breite Strasse (**CX**) and the Berliner Allee.

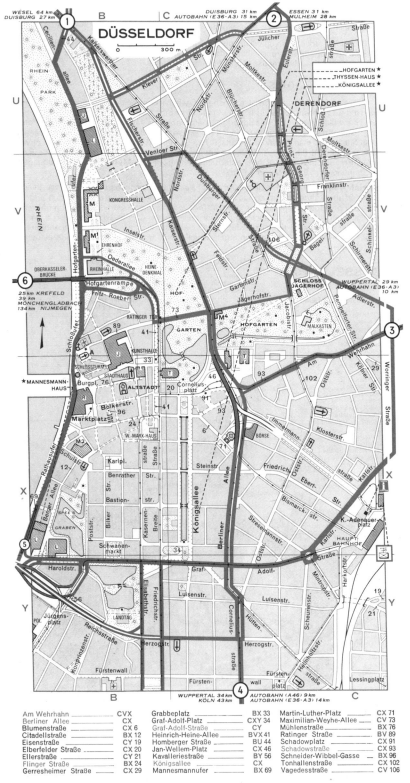

Am Wehrhahn	CVX	Grabbeplatz	BX 33	Martin-Luther-Platz	CX 71
Berliner Allee	CX	Graf-Adolf-Platz	CXY 34	Maximilian-Weyhe-Allee	CV 73
Blumenstraße	CX 6	Graf-Adolf-Straße	CY	Mühlenstraße	BX 76
Citadellstraße	BX 12	Heinrich-Heine-Allee	BVX 41	Ratinger Straße	BV 89
Eisenstraße	CY 19	Homberger Straße	BU 44	Schadowplatz	CX 91
Elberfelder Straße	CX 20	Jan-Wellem-Platz	CX 46	Schadowstraße	CX 93
Ellerstraße	CY 21	Kavalleriestraße	BY 56	Schneider-Wibbel-Gasse	BX 96
Flinger Straße	BX 24	Königsallee	CX	Tonhallenstraße	CX 102
Gerresheimer Straße	CX 29	Mannesmannufer	BX 69	Vagedesstraße	CV 106

Fashion. – Düsseldorf has still another title as a setter of sartorial fashion. Linger on the Königs-allee, meeting place for the elegant, or in the Berliner Allee or the Schadowstrasse (CX). Fashion shows and special exhibitions are held at different times of the year.

Food. – The taverns of the old town propose regional specialities: a black pudding with onions, *Halve Hahn*, a caraway cheese eaten with mustard, and *Röggelchen*, small rye loaves. On Friday evenings *Reibekuchen* or a kind of potato cake is eaten. A brown beer, *Alt-Bier*, is popular.

The Future. – The desire to preserve the residential character of the town without impeding its industrial expansion has encouraged town planning and the construction of such office blocks as the Mannesmann and Thyssen buildings. A first solution to the traffic problem has been found in the construction of road viaducts (Berliner Allee, Immermannstrasse). A third bridge over the Rhine, the Kniebrücke, was opened in 1969 (Oberkasseler Brücke) (CX).

■ MAIN SIGHTS *tour: 1½ hours*

Königsallee*. – The Königsallee, commonly known as the "Kö", has been laid out along a section of the moat which formerly surrounded the old town. Elegant and lively, it is the heart of modern Düsseldorf with large banks up the west side and big cafés and restaurants, complete with terraces, and luxury shops over on the east side beyond the moat declivity. It is round this part that one is especially likely to see the *Radschläger* or urchins doing handstands to amuse the tourists and gain a tip. The Königsallee ends at the Corneliusplatz, a busy crossroads-square. The newer **Berliner Allee** nearby is more commercial with airline offices, the Chamber of Commerce and the Stock Exchange.

Mannesmann and Thyssen Offices*. – The office of the **Mannesmann** steel firm is an aluminium and glass building 23 storeys high, set on the Rhine embankment, in a peaceful quarter south of the old town. From it there is a good view in the foreground of the lake, Spee's Graben, with the Poststrasse bordering its far bank.

The **Thyssen building,** on the other hand, erected in 1957 and still called "the three slabs" (Dreischeibenhaus), stands surrounded by bustling traffic, rising 26 storeys above a wide crossroads. The best place from which to see it is at the junction of the Schadowstrasse and the Berliner Allee.

Hofgarten*. – The Hofgarten forms a continuation of the Königsallee northwestwards towards the museum quarter and eastwards towards the delightful Jägerhof Castle. The park is well shaded and attractive with unexpected fountains such as those of the Fairies and the Young Man (Jröne Jong). The small monument to Heine, *Harmony* by Maillol, stands on Napoleon Hill.

■ ADDITIONAL SIGHTS

The **old town** (Altstadt) (BVX) beside the Rhine is distinguished by the castle's solitary keep (Schlossturm) and the twisted belfry of St. Lambert's Church which stand out against a background of modern blocks. A stroll round the quarter is enjoyable, especially in the evening.

Bolkerstrasse (BX). – Two events in history occurred in this street. Heine was born in the house at no 53 and the tailor Wibbel, immortalised in a popular rhyme, also lived there. It is said that the tailor was present at his own funeral after an exchange of identity which he made to avoid imprisonment – the anecdote is commemorated in the Schneider-Wibbel-Gasse clock with the striking figure of the tailor *(11am, 1, 3, 6 and 9pm)*.

Marktplatz (BX). – An early 18C equestrian statue of Jan Wellem stands in the centre of this square which is separated from the Rhine by the town hall.

St. Lambert's (Lambertikirche) (BVX A). – The church, whose originality lies in its twisted belfry, is of the 14C hall-church type. It is spacious with Baroque furnishings and modern stained glass windows. The bronze door is by Ewald Mataré.

Jägerhof Castle (CV). – *Open 10am to 5pm (8pm Wednesdays); closed Mondays: 1DM.* The castle is the former hunting lodge of the Electors. It was partly constructed in the 18C by the French architect Nicolas de Pigage.

On the ground and first floors are the **Rhineland-Westphalia Collection** of 20C paintings including works by Picasso, Braque, Léger, Chagall, Ernst, Kandinsky and a group of 90 pictures by **Paul Klee** exhibited in rotation.

In an exquisite setting, on the second floor, may be seen the private collection of Dr. Schneider: Aubusson carpets, Augsburg gold and silver work.

Land Economic Museum* (Landesmuseum Volk und Wirtschaft). – Ehrenhof (BV M¹). *Open Mondays to Fridays 9am to 5pm; Saturdays 9am to 1pm; Sundays and holidays 10am to 6pm; closed 1 May, Easter, Whitsun and Christmas; 0.50DM. Guided tours and film showing.*

Illustrated comparative tables, photographs, moving models, and up-to-date maps, show the current state of the economy both nationally and internationally, taking full account of co-operative organisations, particularly the Common Market.

Hetjens Museum* (Deutsches Keramikmuseum) (BX M²). – *Open 10am to 5pm; closed Mondays.* The museum has a collection of 10 000 **ceramic** objects from all over the world which illustrate 7 000 years of art.

Fine Arts Museum (Kunstmuseum). – Ehrenhof (BV M). *Open 10am to 6pm; closed Mondays.* The museum contains a large collection of paintings, principally Romantics from the Düsseldorf School (Cornelius, Schirmer, Achenbach, Rethel) and 20C German Impressionists and Expressionists (Corinth, Kandinsky, Jawlensky, Macke, Klee, Kirchner, Nolde, etc.).

In addition the departments of graphic art, sculpture and glass can also be seen.

Goethe-Museum* (CV M³). – *Open 10am to 5pm; closed Mondays; 0.50DM.* Goethe manuscripts, engravings and autographs, first editions of his works, pictures and busts of the writer at different times of his life are displayed.

Neuss. – Leave the centre of Düsseldorf by ⑤ and after turning right beyond the racecourse, follow the tramlines to the quarter of Neuss.

The 13C **St. Quirinus*** is stylish Rhenish with a trefoil apse *(p 23)*, dominated by a domed octagonal tower and four small square flanking turrets. The very high interior is unusual for its mingling of round and pointed arches and fanlights above tall windows which, in Germany, mark the transition to the Gothic style. From the raised chancel there is a good view of the aisles.

EXCURSIONS *see map p 109*

Château of Dyck*. – *20 km - 13 miles. (Park open 10am to sunset: 1.50DM; museum guided tour every hour 10am to noon and 1 to 6pm, in winter Sundays and holidays, 11am to noon and 1 to 4pm; 2DM; 3DM for the park and the museum; closed Mondays).* Leave Düsseldorf on route no 230 to Glehn, then a left turn in the direction of Damm. In the village follow the road sign.

The castle, rebuilt on the ruins of a mediaeval castle, is surrounded by a moat. The towers, at each corner of the inner courtyard, are capped by characteristic High Baroque domes. On the ground floor, are exquisite Chinese silk hangings, ordered in the 18C by the Empress Maria Theresa of Austria depicting commercial life in China at that time. There is, as well, a rich collection of **weapons,** many are from the gunmakers of the Counts of Dyck – chiefly wheel and flintlock sporting guns of the 16C and the 18C.

The large informal **garden** offers marvellous walks among the many rare flowers and trees.

Château of Benrath. – *10 km - 6 miles – plus 1 hour sightseeing (1 March to 30 November, 10am to 5pm; 1 December to 28 February, 10am to 4pm; closed Mondays; 1DM).* Leave Düsseldorf by ④ and then road no 8 going southeast. The château, built in 1768, is pure Louis XV. A sheet of water on the town side mirrors the central part of the building framed on either side by the lower wings of the annexes. The rooms are in their original state of Rococo decoration which by this time was already classically formal. The **park★**, which is densely wooded, extends to the Rhine, its vista elongated by rides laid out formally in the shape of a star. The west end, however, was landscaped and planted with trees in the English style of the early 19C.

Neandertal. – *14 km - 8 miles – about 2 hours.* Leave Düsseldorf by ③. Turn off right from road no 7 for the Pöhlenweg which continues as the Torfbruchstrasse and brings you out of the built-up area by the Morper Strasse *(east on the map, p 109).*

The green Valley of the Düssel, which the road ascends, is named Neandertal after the 17C Calvinist poet, Neander, who liked to use it as a retreat. The site of the cave in which the famous 60 000-year-old skeleton of Neanderthal man was discovered in 1856 is marked on the right of the road one mile beyond the motorway underpass by a plaque on a triangular rock.

The **prehistorical museum** stands beside a wild animal reserve (aurochs). *Open 10am to 6pm (5pm 1 October to 30 April); closed Mondays and all December and January; 1DM.*

Only a few original bones are on view – the Neanderthal skull is in the Bonn Museum. Displays show life in prehistoric times and prehistoric man's place in history.

Château of Rheydt. – *24 km - 15 miles. Open 15 March to 15 October Mondays to Saturdays 11am to 1pm and 3 to 6pm; Sundays 10am to 1pm and 2 to 6pm; 16 October to 14 March Wednesdays and Saturdays 11am to 1pm and 2 to 5pm; Sundays 10am to 1pm and 2 to 5pm. 0.50DM.* Follow route no 230 to Schelsen, turn right to Neerbroich, where at the entrance of the village turn left.

A Renaissance château surrounded by a moat, Rheydt was constructed with four wings of which only two have weathered the years. Upon entering the courtyard note the basalt columns. Inside the château is the Manor House Museum (collection of arts and crafts).

EBRACH ★

Michelin map **987** 26 – 34 km - 21 miles – west of Bamberg – Pop 2 400

Ebrach shelters a Cistercian abbey (now a prison) at the end of a small valley.

Former Abbey★★ (Ehemaliges Kloster). – This Cistercian abbey, founded in the 12C and completed in the 13C, underwent a drastic Baroque transformation at the hands of Balthazar Neumann *(p 26).* The church, among this great conglomeration of buildings, foreshadows the Neo-Classical leanings of the late 18C.

Church★. – *Tour: ¼ hour. Admission: 0.30DM.* The Cistercian plan persists with the flat-ended chancel and square ambulatory taken straight from Cîteaux. The exterior is more or less intact; the rose window, 7 m - 23 ft – across, is the main decorative feature of the façade.

Inside, the Gothic plan can be perceived beneath the plaster decoration and stucco. Among the works of art are the Renaissance altarpiece of alabaster depicting the vision of St. Bernard in the north transept and the Baroque organ in the chancel.

EICHSTÄTT ★

Michelin map **987** southeast of 26 – Pop 13 000

Eichstätt, a small episcopal city, is dominated by the Willi-baldsburg, St. Willibald's Castle, standing on a promontory in a bend of the Alt-mühl Valley.

The houses are roofed with limestone tiles which here and there show white, giving an unexpected wintry aspect to some quarters of the town.

■ **EPISCOPAL QUARTER★**
(Bischöflicher Residenzbezirk)
tour: ¾ hour

Cathedral (Dom). – The building as a whole is 14C, but parts are Romanesque, others Gothic or Baroque. On the north side, facing the Dom-platz, a Romanesque door opens into the transept but the main entrance is through a second Gothic door decorated with multicoloured statues. The west face is Baroque.

The most interesting work of art is the **Pappenheim altarpiece★★** (15C) in the north aisle. In the west chancel, which is dedicated to St. Willi-bald, there is a seated statue of the saint as an old man, the major work of a sculptor of Eichstätt, Loy Hering (1514).

Go through the south transept to the mortuarium.

EICHSTÄTT

0 _____ 300 m

Aumühlbrücke	2
Aumühle	3
Domplatz	
Gabrielistraße	4
Kapuzinergasse	7
Leonrodplatz	10
Linden Allee	11
Luitpoldstraße	

ANSBACH 76 km
WIESSENBURG 26 km
HILPOLTSTEIN 38 km
AUTOBAHN (E6-A9) 32 km
BEILNGRIES 38 km
INGOLSTADT 27 km
MÜNCHEN 105 km

★★RESIDENZPLATZ
DOM

Marktgasse	12
Marktplatz	
Ostenstraße	
Pater-Philipp-Jeningen-Platz	13
Pfahlstraße	15
Spitalbrücke	17
Walburgiberg	20
Weißenburger Straße	23
Westenstraße	
Wiesengäßchen	24

Mortuarium*. – This funeral chapel, which forms a wing to the cloister, appears as a late 15C Gothic hall with two aisles paved with gravestones. Groined vaulting rests on columns twisted at either end; the ''beautiful pillar'' is skilfully carved. The Crucifixion on the east wall is 16C.

Cloister* (Kreuzgang). – The cloister, built in the 15C, has a complicated tracery in some bays. Leave the cathedral through the mortuarium and come out on to the Residenzplatz.

Residenzplatz**. – Stand in the southeast corner to get a general view.

The square is irregular in shape but has a striking unity: in the centre are lawns, round the outside, Rococo palaces. On the south side are four large houses with pediments and entrances guarded by atlantes; facing them is the south wing of the Residence; on the west side is the former vicar-general's house. In the foreground, the **Virgin's column*** (Mariensäule) rises from the centre of a fountain surrounded by cherubs.

Bear right, round the Episcopal Residence.

Former Episcopal Residence (Fürstbischöfliche Residenz) (**A**). – *Apply to the caretaker between 9am and 4pm.* The entrance opens on to a fine staircase with a Baroque banister and painted ceiling.

■ ADDITIONAL SIGHTS

Hofgarten. – This park was designed in the style of an English garden by Eugène de Beauharnais, the son-in-law of Napoleon and Maximilian I of Bavaria who created him Prince of Eichstätt in 1817. It extends before the summer residence of the prince-bishops. Three delightful pavilions adjoin the **south wall**; the **Shell Pavilion*** (**B**) in the centre, with its fountain and stuccoes, is a true shrine to Rococo.

Capuchin Church (Kapuziner-Kirche) (**C**). – In a chapel of this 17C church is a 12C copy of the Holy Sepulchre of Jerusalem.

St. Walburg (**D**). – The Baroque church of the Benedictine convent is discreetly decorated inside with Wessobrunn stuccoes. From the balcony facing the main doorway there is an attractive **view** of the old roofs of the town and the Altmühl Valley.

EIFEL Massif ★
Michelin maps **203** 2 to 6, 11 to 16 and **204** 14

The Eifel Massif, the most extensive of the four Rhineland schist massifs, has the most complex structure and the most varied rural scenery. The wide undulations and vast forest areas do not afford really spectacular views but impress with a sense of space and calm in contrast to the bustle of the valleys and countryside on the edge of the range.

It is a healthy area. Fishing, walking and photography are the most popular recreations to which must be added car racing on the Nürburgring.

GEOGRAPHICAL NOTES

The Eifel is an undulating plateau (average altitude 600 m - 1 969 ft) deeply cut by the Ahr, the Kyll and the Rur which wander through picturesque wooded valleys.

The **Hocheifel** (Upper Eifel), in the centre, bears traces of volcanic origin with basalt crests (Hohe Acht, 747 m - 2 451 ft), tufa deposits, lakes (Maare) and hot springs.

The **Schnee-Eifel** is the roughest and most lonely area. It runs northwest of Prüm along the Belgian frontier, forming a sombre 700 m high - 2 300 ft – barrier.

The **North Eifel**, a countryside of moors and forests, cut by deep valleys, is romantic and most attractive. The tourist Seven Lakes area reaches out in the northwest to the Upper Fagnes (Hohes Venn), a swampy plateau, no longer part of the Eifel region but of the Ardennes.

The **South Eifel** borders Luxembourg and has picturesque valleys.

The Maare. – *See map p 116.* These are lakes, which mark the upheaval which took place in the volcanic areas of the Upper Eifel in the Tertiary Era. Gas pressure forced up craters without cones. These exploded, producing no lava but a circle of cinder; water collected to form still, circular lakes. The largest and most recent is the Maria-Laach.

The Ahr Wines. – The Ahr vineyards, planted with Burgundian stock on rock slopes, produce deeply coloured red wines late in the season. They are drunk almost warm in the valley's wine centres: Walporzheim, Ahrweiler, Dernau, Mayschoss and Altenahr.

① *FROM MONSCHAU TO SINZIG
by way of the Rur Lakes and the Ahr Valley
138 km - 83 miles – about 6 hours – Local map pp 114-115

Monschau**. – *Description p 180.*

Road no 258 rises rapidly above Monschau, on which you look down from a **belvedere**** on the right after one mile. From Imgenbroich onwards, particularly between Strauch and Schmidt, there are attractive glimpses, on the right, of the Rur lake region. As you come out of Schmidt, the Nideggen ruin lies straight ahead. Rock outcrops appear. The approach to Nideggen is hilly and allows one to see the eagle's eyrie where the *burg* was constructed.

Nideggen. – The 12C *burg*, an outstanding pink limestone barrier, was the residence of the counts and dukes of Juliers until the 15C, falling into ruin in the 16C. Now partially restored, it commands an extensive **view**, particularly from the keep to the south, of the Rur Valley cutting into the Eifel plateau and to the north of the distant Aachen Basin. The restored 12C church has a Romanesque chancel decorated with frescoes and attractive statues.

A wide road leads from Heimback to Schwammenauel from which one can reach the Rur Dam.

Rur Dam* (Rurtalsperre). – *Car parks near the dam. Motorboat services April to October from Schwammenauel, Woffelsbach, Rurberg and Einruhr, 10am to 6pm; services on the upper part of the lake (Lake Urft), Saturdays, Sundays and public holidays only, leaving from Gemünd.*

The **artificial lake***, the Stausee, known also as the **Schwammenauel**, is, with the Ufrt Lake to the south, the largest stretch of water in the Eifel. The road crosses the dam to enter the Kermeter Forest, affording, at the second hairpin bend, a brief good view of the lakes.

North of Roggendorf make a detour to Kommern.

Kommern. – *Museum open April to October, 9am to 6pm; November to March, 10am to 4pm; 1DM*. Delightful village with half-timbered houses lining the winding streets. An **open air museum** (Rheinisches Freilicht-museum) stands west of the village and represents the everyday life of the rural population. In the pine forest are windmills, peasant cottages, stables, water and barns and artisans' workshops from different regions and a complete Eifel village. Follow the numbers on the buildings as given on the plan obtainable at the entrance.

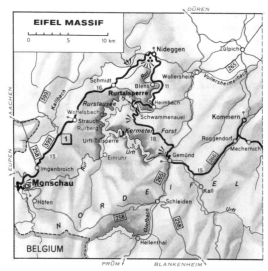

Bad Münstereifel★. – *Tour: ¾ hour. Description p 193.* The road, looking down upon the world's largest fully steerable radiotelescope, meets the Ahr east of Münstereifel at Kreuzberg and follows the river's enclosed bends. The Teufelsloch (Devil's Hole), a pierced rock which dominates the River Ahr level with Altenburg, indicates the approach to Altenahr.

Altenahr. – Altenahr, built between two enclosed river bends, is an excursion centre. The 12C **Burg Are** is now only a ruin scattered over the rock spur commanding the resort. The church terrace and upper terminal of the chair-hoist afford beautiful **views.**

Mayschoss, at the foot of the Saffenburg, overlooks a picturesque river bend of vineyards amidst rock outcrops. The valley's romantic section, punctuated by wine villages – Rech with its Roman bridge, Dernau its wine fountain, Marienthal its monastery ruins – ends at Walporzheim.

Bad Neuenahr-Ahrweiler. – To the west the picturesque old town of **Ahrweiler★ has kept its** mediaeval fortifications and gates. The tourist will find himself strolling through the charming little streets bordered with half-timbered houses.

Bad Neuenahr is a spa for diabetics. The park beside the Ahr, is famous for its dahlias and its gushing hot water fountain, the Grosser Sprudel *(Sundays at 11.45am, Mondays 11.30am)*. The park and casino are the centres of tourist life in the town. The Apollinaris spring, at the town's eastern exit, produces a gaseous mineral water.

The valley opens out, the vines disappear. A last spur, the Landskron, raises its individual beheaded cone directly in front in the valley as this makes its way towards the Rhine.

Sinzig. – *Description p 213.*

---

② ★FROM AHRWEILER TO BERNKASTEL-KUES
by way of the Nürburgring and the Maare
145 km - 90 miles – about 4½ hours – Local maps pp 115 and 116

This itinerary crosses the High Eifel and takes the visitor by beautiful plateau roads to the Ahr and Mosel Valleys, well known for their red and white wines respectively.

Starting from Ahrweiler the road climbs towards the forest; at the fourth bend you get a bird's-eye **view** of the Ahr Valley and, in the distance, of the Siebengebirge.

From Kempenich to Daun the road rises and falls gently and repeatedly with the contour of the mountains or cuts across picturesque valleys.

Alternative route★ by Maria Laach. – *Extra distance: 41 km - 25 miles – about 2½ hours.*

Bad Neuenahr-Ahrweiler. – *Description above.*

The first part of the trip by way of Niederzissen and the Brohl Valley is much the same scenically as the itinerary above, although the road is narrower and more winding. Maria Laach, the crater lake, appears in all its beauty at the foot of the abbey.

Maria Laach★. – *Description p 177.*

Mayen. – An austere, though original, appearance is given to the town buildings and the castle by the blackish basalt. The 13C castle (Genovevaburg) was reconstructed in the 18C for the Electors of Trier. It now houses the Eifel geological and folklore museum.

Bürresheim Castle★. – *Open 1 April to 31 October, 9am to 12.15pm and 2 to 5.15pm (4.15pm 1 November to 31 March); closed Mondays; time: ¾ hour; 1.50DM.*

The north wing and round tower of this elegant castle date from the 14 and 15C; the south wing with a pretty formal garden surrounding it was completed in the 17C. Graceful Baroque gables encircle the inner courtyard. Furniture and furnishings are displayed in the apartments which are now a museum.

The road rises again to the plateau, affording a pleasant **view★** backwards of Bürresheim.

The climb suggested to the Hohe Acht starts from the Adenau road which forks to the right.

Hohe Acht★★. – *2.5 km - 1½ miles – by the Adenau road, then left by a road to the foot of the mountain, plus ½ hour on foot Rtn.*

From the belvedere tower erected at the highest point of the Eifel (alt 747 m - 2 457 ft) there is a **panorama★★** of a wide valleyed region where arable land alternates with wooded ridges. The only heights to stand out are those of Nürburg Castle in the southwest, and Olbrück ruin in the northeast in front of the Siebengebirge.

Road no 412 first skirts and then crosses the Nürburgring circuit.

Nürburg★. – *1 km - ½ mile – (leave road no 412 before skirting the Nürburgring stands and passing under the circuit), then ½ hour on foot Rtn.*

This much restored ruin is set majestically in a hilly **countryside★** which is best appreciated after you have passed the two perimeter walls and climbed to the top of the keep.

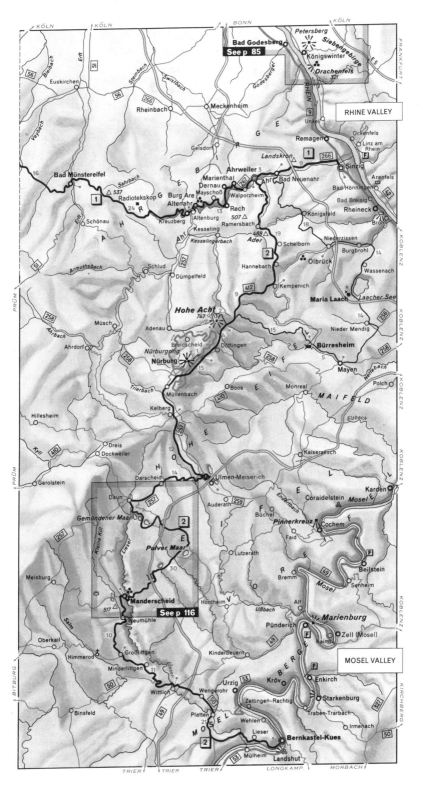

Nürburgring. – *Description p 196.*

On arriving at Ulmen from the north bear left off road no 257 towards the station and once there turn right to enter the town.

Ulmen. – Bear sharp left at the town's central crossroads towards Cochem and stop in the car park. Take the path along the bank to enjoy the delightful scene created by the Ulmen crater lake (Ulmener Maar), the town and the castle ruins.

Turn and leave Ulmen by the westerly road no 257 going to Daun.

The landscape is Jurassian, with alternating meadowland and pinewoods. The Maare volcanic region begins at Daun. Two kilometres - 1 mile south of the town, follow the oneway road to the Gemündener Maar.

Gemündener Maar. – The small dark green lake lies in a wooded hollow. Swimming and boating in summer.

Weinfelder Maar and Schalkenmehrener Maar. – The lakes occupy wide craters on either side of the crest along which the road has been laid. This unusual double **setting*** is given added character by a small chapel overlooking the Weinfelder Maar on the right.

Pulver Maar*. – Follow the sign which takes you to the north shore. This almost perfectly circular lake in a dark and romantic setting is the most beautiful in the area.

Holz Maar. – This is the smallest of the lakes on the route.

After passing beneath the motorway, you leave the plateau for the lovely enclosed valley which leads to Manderscheid. The ruins of Niederburg Castle suddenly appear on the right as you circle the last downhill bend.

Manderscheid.* – *Description p 174.*

After crossing a final hill barrier, the drive ends in the Mosel vineyards.

Bernkastel-Kues*. – *Description p 79.*

MAARE REGION
0   4 km

EINBECK *

Michelin map **987** 15 – Pop 31 000

Einbeck was known in the Middle Ages for its 600 breweries which provided the whole of Germany with Einpöckisches Bier from which Bocksbier derives its name. The town still has a part of its fortified perimeter walls, but a prouder heritage are the 16C **wooden houses**, grouped particularly round the Marktplatz, and decorated with carvings naïvely touched with colour.

Marktplatz.** – Among the wooden houses near the church, note first the two corner houses on the Münsterstrasse: the Brodhaus (1552) and especially the impressive Ratsapotheke building (1590) where the attics, ventilated by weather boards, served, as did those of most of the houses in the town, as barley and hop barns. Opposite, side by side, are the town hall and the weights and measures building.

Town Hall. – Two frontal buildings topped with pointed roofs, give the edifice an unusual outline.

Weights and Measures Building* (Ratswaage). – The carefully designed façade enables one to see decoration typical of the bourgeois architecture of Einbeck: fan motif of palm leaves, beaded and twisted mouldings, traverses and door frames festooned with garlanded friezes.
In line with the Marktplatz, beyond the Marktkirche tower, is the Tidexerstrasse.

Tidexerstrasse.** – The façades and roofs of the houses are aligned to form a pleasantly uniform vista (note no 16 particularly).

Return to the Marktplatz and bear right in front of the church into the Marktstrasse where there are several interesting buildings: no 26 and no 13 especially, the **house** at the corner of Knochenhauerstrasse. This house was built in about 1600 in wood not in traditional style but in imitation of the stone mansions of the Renaissance. A whole symbolic drama (the Virtues and the Arts) is played out on the carved panels separated by expressive masks.

ELLINGEN

Michelin map **987** 26, 51 km - 32 miles – south of Nuremberg – Pop 2 393

Ellingen is an 18C Baroque creation. It owes its monumental air to the Teutonic Knights (*details p 178*) whose Franconia commander resided in the town from the 13C until 1809 when Napoleon dissolved the Order.

Castle. – *Open 9am to noon and 1 to 5pm (10am to noon and 2 to 4pm, 1 October to 31 March); closed Mondays; 1DM.*
The castle, built between 1708 and 1721, stands on the edge of the town. Four impressive wings, one of which is a church, surround an inner courtyard.
The double flight of the **grand staircase*** links the coldly solemn apartments. A small museum is devoted to the Teutonic Order.

ELLWANGEN

Michelin map **987** south of 26 – *Local map p 217* – Pop 23 000

Ellwangen is a calm and pleasant town, dominated by the white buildings of the castle of the former prior-princes and Schönenberg Church. In the valley round the collegiate church are grouped the apartments once lived in by canons.

Church (Stiftskirche). – The church adjoins a former Jesuit church with a Baroque façade. The collegiate church was transformed to Baroque in about 1740. Of the Romanesque building there remain the small south doorway which is well preserved but has modern bronze doors, the low west porch adorned with fine knights' tombs, and the crypt. This last rises strangely above ground on either side, and is lit through arcades buttressed by carved stone animals.

Schönenberg Church. – *2 km - 1 mile – plus ½ hour sightseeing.* Leave Ellwangen by the Dinkelsbühl road which you turn off at the foot of the castle to go straight up the Schönenberg hill. A bend to the right avoids the Stations of the Cross path. The church, well situated at the top of Schönenberg hill, was built in 1682 and is one of the first of the Vorarlberg school (*illustrations and commentary p 25*).

The graceful interior decorations are made up of delicate stuccoes and pale frescoes between a number of medallions. Note especially the Assumption painted on the chancel vault.

A door on the north side of the chancel leads to the galleries and the upper parts of the Chapel of Mercy (Gnadenkapelle), the pilgrims' particular place of worship.

EMDEN

Michelin map **987** 13, 14 – Pop 53 900. *Town plan in Michelin Red Guide Deutschland*

In the 16C the silting up of the Ems estuary struck a blow at the port of Emden. However, the embanking of the river and the opening of the Dortmund-Ems and Ems-Jade canals have enabled Emden to be today the main maritime port of Westphalia, specialising in car exports. Large vessels sail into the inner harbour to tranship iron ore destined for the Ruhr Basin.

The regular ferry service to the island of Borkum leaves from Emden.

East Frisian Museum* (Ostfriesisches Landesmuseum). – *In the Rathaus. Open 10am to 1pm and 3 to 5pm; Sundays 11am to 1pm; closed Mondays October to April; 1DM.*

The excavations of peat bogs, the models of the harbour and the fishing boats (Emden is the oldest German port for herring fishing) and the works of Dutch School painters evoke a colourful history. From the bell-tower there is a view of the harbour and surrounding countryside.

A place of honour is given to the old burghers' arsenal, the **Rüstkammer****. Accompanying this splendid display of 16-18C side arms and armour, are old reproductions illustrating the history of the armoury.

From Emden there is a daily passenger service to the Island of Borkum; it is also a point of departure for the touring of the East Frisian Islands *(information p 128)*. Approximately 15 km - 9 miles – northeast are two villages, exemplifying Frisian characteristics: the old village of **Pilsum** (in the church there is a striking bronze baptismal font of the 15C) and the picturesque fishing port of **Greetsiel**, with its boats filled with large nets.

ERBACH IM ODENWALD

Michelin map **987** 25 – Pop 10 300

The market town of Erbach appears almost as only a dependant of its huge castle.

Castle. – *Guided tours, 1 March to 31 October, 8.30am to noon and 1.30 to 5pm; 3DM.*

The exhibits are the chief interest in the 18C castle.

Trophies of the chase assembled in the entrance hall and in greater number in the **Stag Gallery*** (Hirschgalerie) on the first floor, are described in detail by the guides.

The Roman apartments (Römische Zimmer) contain ancient busts and statues.

The Knights' Hall (Rittersaal) on the ground floor, decorated in the troubadour style (13 and 14C stained glass windows), contains foot soldiers' and knights' armour and rare harnesses – the Ortenburg ceremonial saddle is early 17C Milanese work.

ERLANGEN

Michelin map **987** 26 – Pop 101 000 – *Town plan in Michelin Red Guide Deutschland*

Erlangen was one of the cities in which the French Huguenots settled. Its uniform buildings make it look, even today, like a residential town of the Baroque period. The Protestant church marks the centre of the quarter built for the refugees. The town, which was the birthplace of the physicist George Ohm (1789-1854) who discovered the laws of specific resistance of electric circuits, now shares with Nuremberg the functions of a university city and has also become an important electrical engineering and electronics centre.

Park (Schlossgarten). – A late 18C English garden behind the castle contains, as well as flowerbeds, a strange **Huguenot Fountain** (Hugenottenbrunnen) erected by the French in 1706 in gratitude to their protector, the Margrave of Bayreuth.

ESSEN *

Michelin map **202** 6 – *Local map p 222* – Pop 685 000.
Detailed plan of the city centre in Michelin Red Guide Deutschland

The capital of the Ruhr is not a black city as many persons might suppose. It has elegant shops, a lovely art gallery and pleasant residential suburbs in green surroundings. A permanent exhibition of industrial design (Haus Industrieform – *open 10am to 6pm – Sundays 11am to 5pm for special exhibitions – closed Mondays*) occupies a site in the centre of this altogether surprising town. No blast furnaces or steelworks have been restarted in the town's immediate vicinity since the end of the war; instead machine workshops of all kinds have been established. The woods, which extend south, border the tranquil Baldeneysee. One of the oldest Rhineland churches stands in the centre of the town, in the heart of the business quarter.

■ **SIGHTS** *tour: 3 hours*

Folkwang Museum** (R). – *Open 10am to 6pm; closed Mondays; 1DM.*

In the first galleries are portraits of women by Feuerbach and Trübner; there follow galleries containing French Impressionists (Signac) and a warm toned Rohlfs; Van Goghs and Gauguins, the Blue Knight group (Marc, Kandinsky), the Cubist school (Léger, Delaunay, Miro), the *Fashion Shop* by Macke, a good Braque, and in Room XI, a fine group with some lovely Renoirs, Daumiers and Gaugins. The last galleries have works by Müller, Kirchner, Kokoschka, Rohlfs, Chagall, Nay, Manessier, Ernst, Beckmann, and others.

Minster Treasure** (Münsterschatzkammer). – *Displayed in a museum south of the cathedral* (P M). *Open 10am to 4pm; closed Mondays; 1DM.*

The treasure proper includes four splendid 10 and 11C **processional crosses***** (Vortragekreuze) once owned by abbesses, the crown of the Gold Madonna, monstrances, gospels and the sword of the martyr saints Cosmas and Damian.

Another gallery displays the 16C altarpiece from the cathedral by Marthel Bruyn.

Villa Hügel* (S). – *Access by the Haraldstrasse. Admission to park: 0.50DM.*

The villa, now a museum, belonged to the Krupp family from 1872 until recently. The **park** is distinguished from the surrounding woods by the variety and rarity of the trees.

Villa. – *Open 10am to 6pm.* This residence is an excellent example of the pompous style of the Bismarck period. The immense rooms, darkly panelled, have witnessed memorable meetings of industrial leaders and sumptuous receptions.

Krupp Collections** (Historische Sammlung Krupp). – *Same times as for the villa.* This museum in an annexe illustrates the rise of the famous industrial family. It is a story which epitomises the development of heavy industry in Germany – 150 years of technical progress which began in about 1815 with the first crucible cast steel of Friedrich Krupp.

ESSEN

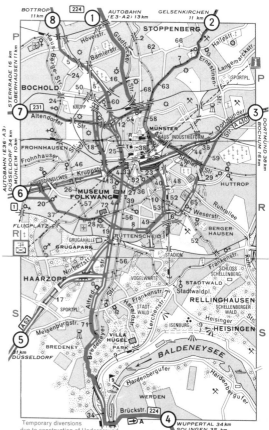

Temporary diversions
due to construction of Underground

Gruga Park★ (R). – This vast rolling green space, extended still further by the botanical gardens, begins behind the Grugahalle, a large exhibition and conference hall.

Minster (P). – The 10C west chancel, with three angled side walls, was directly influenced by the chancel at Aachen and is the oldest part of the building. The nave, a Gothic hall, has a certain elegance; the crypt has stained glass windows by Manessier.

The most precious work of art, a **Gold Madonna★★★** (Goldene Madonna) of 980 is in the north side chapel. This statue of the Virgin is thought to be the oldest in the West.

Essen-Werden. – *South of the plan* (**A**). *8 km - 5 miles – from the centre of Essen – plus ½ hour sightseeing.*

Abbey Church. – This 13C building, which is still Romanesque, nevertheless shows signs of early Gothic design, particularly in the pointed arches of the nave. The transept crossing is covered by a **dome★** (Vierungskuppel) on pendentives.

An 11C bronze **Crucifix★** with very pure lines stands in the sacristy.

The crypt contains one of the few German pierced galleries from which pilgrims could venerate the tomb of St. Leger, lying in a central vault.

ESSLINGEN AM NECKAR

Michelin map ▨ 13 – Pop 98 600 – *Town plan in Michelin Red Guide Deutschland*

An old and prosperous Swabian town with the charm of the Neckar's vine covered slopes surrounding it, Esslingen is distinguished by belfries, the *Burg* tower, and the last remains of the 13C fortifications. It is an important centre of mechanical engineering.

The quarter on the right river bank, at the foot of the vineyards, still retains the bourgeois atmosphere of a one-time Free Imperial City.

Marktplatz. – This irregularly shaped and picturesque central square was built in the 19C. The Kielmeyer house is its finest ornament. All the roads leading into the square are interesting – old houses, usually of wood, line the streets.

Former Town Hall★. – This 15 and 16C building combines the severe charm of the old half-timbering with the grace of decorated Renaissance façades.

The corbelled gable overlooking the Rathausplatz is topped by a double lantern tower (carillon) and is brilliantly coloured. The south gable is outstanding and typical of half-timbering in Swabia, with heavy corbels and obliquely crossed beams.

St. Denis's (Stadtkirche). – The Gothic building, with its towers linked unusually by a footbridge, overlooks the Marktplatz. The church's name recalls that Esslingen began as a hermitage which was given in the 8C to the great Frankish Abbey of St. Denis. The church interior is divided by a rood-screen; a 15C *pietà* adorns a lintel on the right beyond the screen; fine 13 and 14C stained glass is to be seen in the chancel.

Church of Our Lady (Liebfrauenkirche). – This Gothic church has beautiful architectural unity. It stands on a hillside and may be reached from the Marktplatz by the Untere Beatau rise. From the west there is a good view of the ornate tower flanked by slender staircase turrets. The church decorations are rich particularly round the doorways: the southeast door depicts the Life of the Virgin (1350), the southwest, the Last Judgment (1430).

ETTENHEIM

Michelin map **205** south of 15 – Pop 7 500

The Baden town of Ettenheim, which until 1803 was part of the Strasbourg bishopric, still recalls Cardinal de Rohan and the unfortunate Duke of Enghien.

Old Kirchberg Residential Quarter. – The quarter lies at the foot of the large parish church, separated from the rest of the town buildings by two 18C gates. Facing the outer staircase of the Rathaus is the gable of **Cardinal de Rohan**'s former palace. It was in this long edifice that the notorious protagonist in the diamond necklace affair lived out his exile with dignity (1790-1803).

Higher up, where the Rohanstrasse rise bends towards the church, is the house, with arms above the door, where the Duke of Enghien lived. It was here that the duke, the fiancé of Charlotte de Rohan, the cardinal's niece, was arrested on the night of the 14-15 March 1804 on the orders of Napoleon and in violation of the sovereignty of the State of Baden. Six nights later the duke was executed by firing squad in the castle moat at Vincennes.

Cardinal de Rohan's tomb lies beneath the chancel in the church.

FEHMARN Island

Michelin map **987** 6

The coastal Island of Fehmarn, which is fertile and inhabited, has been on the international route map of Europe since the inauguration, in 1963, of direct ferry services, the Vogelfluglinie ("as the crow flies"). The forward position of the island allows road and rail connections to be pushed north close to the Danish archipelago.

Fehmarnsund Bridge★ (Fehmarnsund-Brücke). – The bridge, 964 m - 1 054 yds long, across the sound separating Fehmarn from the mainland, is the largest civil engineering undertaking (road and rail) on the Vogelfluglinie route.

FLENSBURG

Michelin map **987** 5 – Pop 95 600 – *Town plan in Michelin Red Guide Deutschland*

The port of Flensburg lives principally from its naval yards and on its rum and spirit trade. It lies at the end of the **Flensburger Förde★**, a sinuous arm of the sea where pleasure craft – Glücksburg harbour can accommodate 500 – sail up inlets whose banks are shaded by beech trees. The town, the most northern in Germany, has certain Danish features as one can see from the signs and newspaper kiosks along the Holm, the town's commercial artery, and on the quays.

Boat services from Flensburg enable you to take a trip round the bay and to visit the small neighbouring Danish ports (Sönderborg, Ærösköbing, etc.).

■ **SIGHTS** *time: 1 hour*

Municipal Museum★ (Städtisches Museum). – *Open weekdays 10am to 1pm and 3 to 5pm; Sundays 10am to 1pm; closed Mondays.*

Attractive antiques are on view from Schleswig-Holstein, and the part of Schleswig which is now Danish. The furniture includes wedding and travelling chests and Gothic and Renaissance cupboards. Look at the carefully reconstructed peasant and bourgeois interiors in the lower rooms where brass and copper gleam. Ships' models recall the town's connection with the sea.

St. Nicholas' (Nikolaikirche). – The church overlooks the bustling Südermarkt (market). The massive 15C Gothic brick building contains an **organ★** (Orgel) dating from 1609.

Northern Gateway (Nordertor). – The plain late 16C brick doorway has two stepped gables.

EXCURSION

Glücksburg. – *9 km - 5½ miles – about 1 hour.* Leave Flensburg by the Bismarckstrasse and the Mürwiker Strasse (northeast on the plan) and continue, via Mürwik and a road affording glimpses of the Flensburger Förde to Glücksburg. Glücksburg Castle suddenly comes into view, apparently floating on a lake. Every advantage was taken of the **site★** to construct the block (1587) of the three main buildings flanked by corner towers. The whole, which is said to have been inspired by the Loire Castle of Chambord, has the decorative sobriety typical of northern Renaissance architecture.

Open 15 May to 15 October, 10am to 4.30pm; the rest of the year 10 to 11.45am and 2 to 4.45pm (Sundays 11am to 4.45pm); closed Mondays; 2.50DM.

Exhibits recall the House of Oldenburg-Schleswig-Holstein to which the Danish Royal Family is related.

In the great Banqueting Hall or Rote Saal, on the first floor, the segmented vaulting is delicately adorned with coffering, stars, rosettes and small busts, the walls with strange leather hangings embossed in gold and silver – Malines (Belgium) work of 1670.

FORCHHEIM

Michelin map **987** 26 – 24 km - 15 miles – southeast of Bamberg – Pop 23 700

Forchheim lies at the entrance to the Wiesent Valley, the main road of entry from the east into Swiss Franconia *(p 61)*, and makes an interesting stop. To the pleasure of walking round the old quarter may be added that of eating the local carp.

On certain occasions such as Corpus Christi, women from the surrounding villages – particularly Effeltrich, 8 km - 5 miles – to the southeast – wear the traditional costume with its typical crown or a heavy white widows' headdress.

Church (Pfarrkirche). – The 14C church stands surrounded by ·impressive half-timbered buildings, one of which forms the corner block of the town hall. Inside look at eight 15C **pictures★** (Tafeln) taken from an ancient altarpiece and now placed against the pillars. Seven of the panels relate the story of St. Martin.

The cult of St. Martin was one of the spiritual links of Carolingian Europe: the Christian saint was then the patron of warriors and high officials of the crown. St. Martin's Day (11 November), a holiday for German children in Catholic countries, is celebrated in style in Forchheim.

Palace (Pfalz). – This rough 14C castle facing the church and surrounded by a moat has two main buildings linked by a beamed gallery.

FRANKFURT AM MAIN ★★

Michelin map **204** 5, 6 – *Local map p 242* – Pop 631 000

Frankfurt is a prosperous, cosmopolitan town, a mixture of new and old. It was a Free Imperial City until 1866; today it has all the attractions of a metropolis and could be said to offer a true replica of the Germany of the seventies. According to Goethe it was "the secret capital".

The **An Der Hauptwache** Square (CX), the heart of Frankfurt, lies at the junction of two of its busiest streets, the **Zeil** and the Rossmarkt.

Visitors to the town should go to the taverns in the Sachsenhausen quarter on the left bank of the Main and drink the famous Appelwoi (a somewhat dry cider).

A Breeding Ground for Financiers. – In the 16C Frankfurt was granted the right to mint money. The money market flourished and the exchange was founded.

Banking dominated the economy in the 18C and attained worldwide fame in the 19C, thanks to such financiers as **Bethmann** and more especially **Rothschild** (1744-1812), whose sons, "the five Frankfurters", founded houses in London, Paris, Vienna and Naples. Industry was able to develop successfully in such a favourable climate: a somewhat specialised chemical industry grew up associated particularly with dyestuffs, pharmaceutical and photographic products. Machine tool and electrical apparatus industries are the two other pillars of the city's prosperity.

Besides the two annual commercial fairs and the Motor Show, which define Frankfurt's economic activities, there are also the special Fur and Book Fairs.

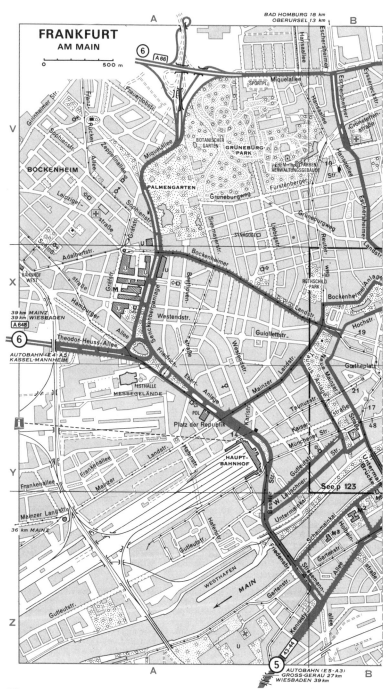

HISTORICAL NOTES

When the Emperors Ruled. – Frederick Barbarossa's action in having himself elected King of Germania in 1152 at Frankfurt inaugurated a tradition which was to be ratified by the Golden Bull *(p 19)* of Karl IV in 1356; in 1562, under Maximilian II, Frankfurt superseded Aachen and became the coronation city of the Emperors of the Holy Roman Empire – a privilege it retained until 1806.

Goethe describes in great detail in *Poetry and Truth*, the sumptuous ceremonies and the popular exuberance he witnessed as a boy and enjoyed when Josef II was crowned in 1764.

Goethe's Youth. – Johann Wolfgang von Goethe was born on 28 August 1749, the son of a solemn imperial counsellor and a delightful and lively young woman. The great writer frequently described what he owed to his parents: to his father his serious attitude to life; to his mother, his happy temperament and his love of telling stories.

Frankfurt gave Goethe the unforgettable experiences he recalled with pleasure in his memoirs. At 15 he fell in love for the first time with a girl called Gretchen – the model for Marguerite in *Faust.* Not long afterwards he left for the University of Leipzig. Frankfurt, nevertheless, remained his home town and when he fell ill in 1768 he returned there, undergoing a religious conversion during convalescence. After the Wetzlar episode *(p 257)* he returned again, and between 1772 and 1775 passed the most fruitful years of his career in the town: *Werther,* written in just four weeks, dates from this period.

FRANKFURT AM MAIN★★

GENERAL VIEW

The old town is now only a kernel reconstituted round the Römerberg. Beginning on the left bank of the Main at the end of the bridge, the Untermainbrücke, it gains architectural unity from its Gothic silhouette. Between the east end of the old church of the Carmelite Convent and the cathedral may be seen, from left to right, the lantern-tower of St. Paul's Church, the Römer, St. Leonard's Church on the river bank, the pointed belfry of St. Nicholas and, at the end of the iron bridge (Eiserner Steg), the Baroque Saalhof, once an imperial palace with a Gothic corner tower (Rententurm). From the Henninger Turm *(open 10am to 11pm; lift: 1.50DM)*, south of Sachsenhausen, one has the best overall **view**★ of the city with the skyscrapers of the business district, the Main River, the Stadwald forest and the Taunus mountains.

■ MAIN SIGHTS *time: 3 hours*

Goethe's House (Goethehaus)★★. – *Open weekdays 9am to 5.30pm (4pm 1 October to 31 March); Sundays, 10am to 1pm; closed on some holidays; 1.50DM.*

Goethe described it as a spacious house, light and gay, with freestanding staircases, large vestibules and pleasant views of the garden. An atmosphere lingers of ease and serenity, of a taste for the good things of life, a love of Italy transmitted by the father to his son, the family friendships as seen in paintings on the walls and details of day to day life.

The house was faithfully reconstructed after the war. The room in which the poet was born, has been turned into a memorial. The room in which he wrote is as it used to be: his old marionette theatre is in its place near the desk. The memory of Charlotte Buff haunts the room. The window may still be seen which Goethe's father had constructed in the library so that he could watch his children's comings and goings without leaving what he was doing.

Goethe Museum★ (CY M¹). – *Same times of opening as for Goethe's House.*

The museum, adjoining the poet's birthplace, displays documents on Goethe's life and work, pictures and sculpture by well known artists (Tischbein, Füssli, Graff, Friedrich).

Cathedral★ (Dom). – *The chancel, the Electors' Chapel and the treasure can only be seen on guided tours of at least 10 people from 11am to 3pm; time: 1 hour; no tours Sundays or Mondays; 0.30DM. Open 9am to 12.30pm and 3 to 6pm (5pm November to February).*

The cathedral's outstanding feature is its tall 15C Gothic **tower**★★, ornamented with a gabled polygonal crown surmounted by a dome and lantern tower. The transept is wide.

The interior which rises high was built in the 13 and 14C in the form of a Gothic hall with three aisles. The 14C **choir-stalls**★ (Chorgestühl) show fine workmanship. Note the tombstone, on the right, of Count Günther von Schwarzburg (14C), the unsuccessful rival of the Emperor Karl IV for the Kingdom of Germania. The next door leads to the 15C Chapel (Wahlkapelle) where the seven Electors of the Holy Roman Empire *(p 19)* made their final choice.

A *Deposition from the Cross* (School of Van Dyck), hangs in the north transept.

Treasure★ (Domschatz). – The treasure contains sumptuous ornaments worn by the ecclesiastical Electors at their coronation; the oldest is 14C.

Römer and Römerberg (CY F). – The Römer, a diverse block of reconstructed 15C burghers' houses, was once the town hall and coronation palace. The most characteristic façade gives on to the Römerberg Square. The Zum Römer house in the centre which has given its name to the whole group and, since 1405, has been used by the municipality is the most ornate: the four statues of Emperors guarded by imperial eagles were added in the 19C above the balcony with the carved balustrade. The small inner courtyard is ornamented by a graceful pierced Renaissance stairway (entrance via the Limpurgergasse).

Imperial Hall (Kaisersaal). – *Open 1 April to 30 September, 9am to 6pm; the rest of the year, 9am to 1pm and 1.30 to 5pm, Sundays and holidays, 10am to 4pm; closed during receptions; 1DM.*

The walls, hollowed out with niches, were fitted in the 19C with portraits of the 52 Emperors from Charlemagne to Franz II (1806) – a graphic personalisation of the Holy Roman Empire.

South of Römerberg Square, the **Church of St. Nicholas,** built in red sandstone of the region, is crowned by a gallery with turrets at each corner, from where the town officials and their families would observe the large popular celebrations. On the other side of the square, the contemporary buildings contiguous to the **Steinernes Haus**, a restored mediaeval home, blend well, in spite of the old quarter. In front of the cathedral, excavations have revealed walls of different epochs which are grouped under the name of **Historic Garden** (Historisches Garten). Other Roman excavations are at the **House of the Teutonic Order** (Deutschordenshaus) (Brückenstrasse 3-7).

Zoo★★★. – *Open 8am to 7pm (6pm in spring and autumn, 5pm in winter); 4.50DM with Exotarium.*

The Zoo is famous for its rare species, which are encouraged to reproduce. The animals live in their natural habitat. The bird section is filled with colour and in the large free-flight Aviary, the visitor is not separated from the occupants, that fly about freely. Penguins, reptiles and insects live in the **Exotarium** *(open 10am to 10pm; 3DM)* where the climatic conditions and landscape have been re-created. There is an amazing beehive with its thousands of bees busily at work.

■ ADDITIONAL SIGHTS

Churches

St. Leonard's (Leonhardskirche) (CY B). – This 15 and 16C Gothic church has a composite appearance, especially on its north side. From an earlier Romanesque basilica, there remain the octagonal east towers and the 13C doorways carved by Master Engelbert. These can now be seen only from inside as aisles were subsequently added on either side.

The nave, which is square, is surrounded on three sides by a gallery which gives an original touch to the plain design. Fine bits of old stained glass can still be seen in the windows in the chancel. Left of the chancel is a finely carved altarpiece representing scenes of the life of Christ. The baptismal chapel in the north aisle has an enormous hanging keystone.

St. Catherine's (Katharinenkirche) (CX A). – Goethe was baptised in this church. The 14C building was rebuilt in the 17C in a near-Gothic style which accorded with Lutheran taste. The modern **windows**★ (Glasfenster), dating from 1954, form a uniform group on Biblical themes.

St. Michael's (Michaelskirche) (EV C). – This church was built in 1953 by Rudolf Schwarz *(p 109)*. It is severe in design, elliptical in shape and interesting in its bold silhouette which resembles a ship's prow. There is balance in its interior proportions.

Museums

Senckenberg Museum* (Naturmuseum Senckenberg) (AX M). – *Open 9am to 4pm (8pm Wednesdays, Saturdays and Sundays); 2DM. Brochure in English.*

This is the largest natural history museum in West Germany.

The **palaeontology department**** (ground floor) has a remarkable collection. Displayed left of the entrance are crinoids, which in spite of their plant-like appearance are considered sea animals (related to the starfish and sea urchins). In gallery 5, the skeletons of the Diplodocus and Ichthyosaurs, illustrating the fauna of the secondary era and the Mastodone skeleton, discovered in New York State, are on display. In gallery 6 are fish and reptiles: note the remarkable Placodus (secondary era) whose gigantic stone-like teeth were for mashing into shellfish; mineralogy, geology and fossilised invertebrates are exhibited in gallery 7. The duck-billed dinosaur (trachodon or aratosaunis) in gallery 9 led probably an amphibious life – in shallow water and on land. In galleries 10 to 13 large mammals (whales, bisons, "Irish elk") and the evolution and prehistory of man are shown.

The 1st floor has a collection of stuffed animals from the five continents: reptiles and mammals (anaconda swallowing a "water pig") and a great variety of birds representing all sizes and colours.

Städel Museum* (Städelsches Kunstinstitut) (BZ M²). – *Open 10am to 5pm (8pm Wednesdays); closed Mondays and holidays; 2DM.*

The picture gallery on the 2nd floor is famous for its collection of **Flemish Primitives and German Masters of the 16C****. Gallery A: Van der Weyden, Hieronymus Bosch *(Ecce Homo)*, Hans Memling *(Man with a Red Hat)*, Jan van Eyck *(Lucca Madonna)*. Gallery C: Pieter Brueghel the Elder *(Vase of Flowers)*. Gallery 2: Hans Baldung Grien *(Nativity and Baptism of Christ)*. Gallery D: remarkable altarpieces which came, in large part, from churches in the town: altarpiece from the church of the Dominicans by Hans Baldung Grien, *Genealogy of Christ* by Hans Holbein the Elder.

Also displayed are works of the Italian School: Fra Angelico, Botticelli *(Portrait of Simonetta Vespucci)*, Tintoretto, Veronese and contemporary Baroque works: Rembrandt, Brouwer, Jordaens, Rubens.

The 1st floor is devoted to German masters of 18 and 19C, including Johann Heinrich Wilhelm Tischbein, whose *Goethe in the Roman Countryside* (1789) immortalises the writer in meditation; French Impressionism: Cézanne, Renoir *(The Lunch)*, Manet and 20C painters: Matisse, Picasso *(Portrait of Fernande Olivier)*, Braque, Liebermann (influenced by French Impressionism), Beckmann and Kirchner (German Expressionists). Feininger, Marc and Klee are members of the Cubist and Realist Schools.

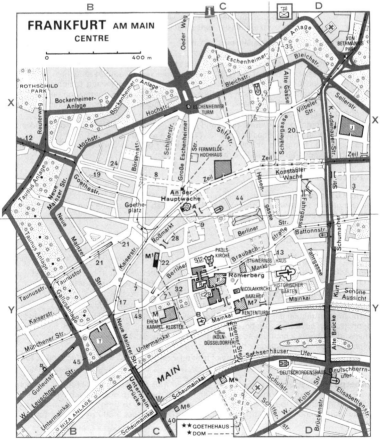

FRANKFURT AM MAIN
CENTRE

0   400 m

Liebieg Museum of Sculpture (Städtische Galerie Liebieghaus) (BZ M³). – *Open 10am to 5pm; closed Mondays.*

This museum holds an admirable variety of sculpture from different civilisations and epochs – Egypt: head of a dignitary (middle Kingdom); Greece and Rome: statuettes, small bronze horse (8 BC), head of a woman (460), Tanagra figurines and copies of great Roman sculpture: Torso by Polyclitus and Satyr by Praxiteles. Also represented are works of art of the Middle Ages, Renaissance and Baroque in Europe – Germany: Madonna (11C), Riemenschneider's Madonna and Child; Italy: statues from the cathedral in Florence (14-15C), ceramic altarpiece by Della Robbia; France: Madonna and Child (14C), and bust of the Count of the Tour d'Auvergne by Lemoyne (18C).

Museum of Applied Arts★ (Museum für Kunsthandwerk) (CY M⁴). – *Open 10am to 5pm (8pm Wednesdays); closed Mondays. Brochure in English.*

Only parts of this rich collection are exhibited on a given theme, at a time. When seen together, European and Oriental art reveal their common influences.

The European furniture, Gothic to modern style, demonstrates the different approaches in the conception of a piece: 15C folding chair, a richly carved Renaissance cupboard, as well as the intricate detail in the inlay of the Baroque-Rococo cabinets. Note also the variety of glassware and porcelain (18 to 20C) from such famous houses as Meissen, Berlin, Nymphenburg, Vienna and Sevres. The book and manuscript department is worth noticing, including the **Stammbücher** collection (Stammbüchersammlüng), with personal notebooks, illustrated with miniatures, poems and mottoes.

Oriental and Far Eastern art is revealed by splendid material and carpets (Persia, Turkey), as well as faience, Iranian ceramics and India ceremonial arms in silver or gold, encrusted with precious stones.

Postal Museum (Bundespost Museum) (CYZ M⁵). – *Open 10am to 5pm (8pm Wednesdays); closed Mondays.*

The transportation of mail and travellers is illustrated from the mail coach to the aeroplane including the first bus. In the stairway are postal signs indicating the great variety of posting houses in Germany in the past.

On the 1st floor papyrus letters, a signal drum (New Guinea), pictures of the mounted courier to telephone, telex and radio, which all give evidence of the progress in mass communication. The 2nd floor is of special interest to the philatelist: stamps from different countries, stamp printing machines and postmarks; there is also an interesting collection of post-boxes and the reconstruction of an 1890 post-office.

Museum of Ethnography (Museum für Völkerkunde) (CY M⁶). – *Open 10am to 5pm (8pm Wednesdays); closed Mondays.*

Temporary exhibitions explain the life and customs of primitive people in the various continents: collection of masks, utensils, cult objects and jewellery.

History Museum (Historisches Museum) (CY M⁷). – *Open 10am to 5pm (8pm Wednesdays); closed Mondays. Arrows indicate the itinerary.*

The origins and the development of Frankfurt in the context of the country are explained through: ecclesiastical works of art (statues, altarpieces from Frankfurt churches), objects of everyday life (reassembled interiors, costumes and utensils), commerce (colonial products, modes of transportation), politics and justice (paintings), war (arms and armour), industrialisation (early printing presses, spinning wheels, and models of steam machines) as well as engravings, and reproductions.

Upon returning to the ground floor, and crossing a reconstructed goldsmith's workshop, enter the **Chapel of Saalhof** (Saalhofkapelle, 1175); the only building left from the Emperor's Palace as well as being the oldest remaining vestige of old Frankfurt. The visit terminates at Gartensaal: religious art and a 1912 model of the town.

Parks and Walks

Tropical Garden★ (Palmengarten) (AV). – The park has rose and alpine gardens, many species of trees and greenhouses where rare tropical plants flourish including the palms which give the garden its name.

EXCURSIONS

Plan of Frankfurt's Built up Area (Innenstadt) in the Michelin Red Guide Deutschland.

Offenbach. – *7 km - 5 miles – plus 1 hour sightseeing.* Leave Frankfurt by the southeast along the Offenbacher Landstrasse which continues as the Frankfurter Strasse into Offenbach.

The **Leather Museum★★** (Deutsches Ledermuseum) is at no 86.

Open 10am to 5pm; closed at Christmas, on 1 January and 1 May; 1DM.

The most attractive departments are those recording the history of the handbag (15-20C) and on leather coverings (embossed and gilded Venetian, Spanish, French and German leatherwork) among which are such rare items as Marie de' Medici's casket, Louis XV's toy elephant and one of Napoleon's briefcases.

The shoe museum presents a history of fashion in all its fantasy, from Coptic sandals to 18C court shoes and 19C button boots.

Lohrbergpark. – *9 km - 7 miles – plus ¼ hour on foot Rtn.* Leave Frankfurt by the Berger Strasse, east on the plan. Continue up the hill, beyond the suburb of Seckbach which has kept its village atmosphere, to the large crossroads at the entrance to Bergen-Enkheim where you take the first turning on the left, the Klingenweg. The park lies 1 500 m - 1 mile further on to the left.

From the terrace there is a **view** of Frankfurt's conglomeration of buildings (except for the historical central area) and the mountains (Spessart, Odenwald, Taunus) which make up its familiar skyline.

To find a town, a sight or setting,
a historical or geographical reference described in this guide,
consult the index.

Freiburg, one of the most attractive cities of southern Germany, was founded in the 12C by the Dukes of Zähringen.

The town was badly damaged during the war and has not returned to its former glory, but the cathedral, with its pierced spire rising before the wooded slopes of the Schlossberg, remains the Catholic metropolitan church of the German Upper Rhine.

Marie-Antoinette's Farewell. – After the Zähringens had died out in 1388, Freiburg passed under the rule of the Habsburgs.

It was from Freiburg on 4 and 5 May 1770 that the Archduchess Marie-Antoinette who had been born in Vienna in 1755, the ninth child of Maria Theresa and the Emperor Franz I, bade farewell to Austria and set out for Strasbourg. There she was greeted by Cardinal de Rohan in the name of France as the bride of the future Louis XVI.

She remained in France as queen until her execution in 1793.

LIFE IN FREIBURG

The pleasant tenor of life, a shade easy-going, which the city perhaps acquired through five centuries of Austrian rule and which was only ended by Napoleon, has helped to make Freiburg a favourite retreat for both students and the retired.

Though the town may often be scorching, the nearby Upper Black Forest affords running streams and the refreshing Höllentaler breeze which blows gently from the mountain of the same name at nightfall. The streets between the cathedral and Swabian Gate are continuously cleansed by large streams – the Bächle – which run in deep gullies *(park carefully!).*

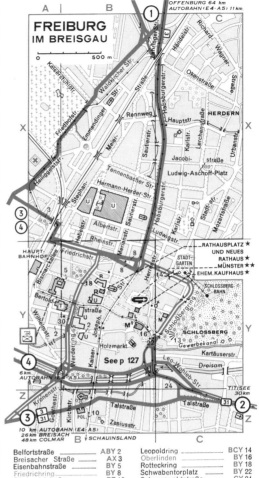

Belfortstraße	ABY 2	Leopoldring	BCY 14
Breisacher Straße	AX 3	Oberlinden	BY 16
Eisenbahnstraße	BY 5	Rottecking	BY 18
Friedrichring	BY 8	Schwabentorplatz	BY 22
Günterstalstraße	BZ 10	Schwarzwaldstraße	CY 24
Kanonenplatz	CY 13	Werthmannplatz	BY 27

■ MAIN SIGHTS *tour: 2 hours*

Start from the Münsterplatz.

Cathedral ★★ **(Münster).** – Of the original Romanesque building begun in about 1200, there remains the transept crossing flanked by the Cock Towers, octagonal towers with Gothic superstructures. Construction was continued slowly westwards, reflecting the technical progress which took place in the Gothic period. This stage was concluded with construction of the splendid west tower, one of the few in Germany to be completed in the Middle Ages.

The construction of a new chancel began in 1354 but the size of the building programme and harshness of the times only enabled this huge edifice to be consecrated in 1513. The ambulatory, utterly German in appearance, has fan vaulting in keeping with its late Gothic style.

Exterior

North Side. – The tympanum above the north door leading to the chancel was carved in about 1350 and illustrates Original Sin; on the archivolt is the Creation of the World according to Genesis – note the rare representation of the Creator resting on the seventh day (right).

Tower ★★★. – On the plain square base stands a pierced octagonal belfry surmounted by a delicate openwork spire of stone. At the base of the belfry is the Sterngalerie – a gallery of four sharply jutting points in the form of a star.

South Side. – The south side is particularly ornate with statues of the kings of the Old Testament and the Apostles on the buttresses.

Enter the church through the Renaissance porch and the south door. Make for the main façade door beneath the west porch.

West Porch and Doorway (Vorhalle). – The porch is crowded with late 13C figures: on the left wall, facing the door, the procession is led by Satan, beguilingly disguised as the Prince of this World, and his victim sparsely clothed in a deerskin; Biblical personages and the Wise Virgins follow.

On the right wall, the Foolish Virgins with bitter expressions are followed by statues of the liberal arts, St. Margaret and St. Catherine, the patron saints of Christian wisdom.

The doorway itself, flanked by statues of the Church (left) and the Synagogue with eyes covered (right), is entirely occupied by the mystery of the Redemption – note the Last Judgment.

Interior

FREIBURG CATHEDRAL

The Nave. – *Free entry.*

Sweeping only moderately high, the nave is adorned with graceful galleries with trefoil blind arcades decorating the aisle walls from end to end. The statuary and furnishings of especial note are:

(1) The Virgin before the pillar (1270-80), worshipped by two angels (Ile de France art).
(2) Pulpit with rustic themes (1560). The sculptor portrayed himself in a window beneath the stairs.
(3) Statue (originally recumbent, remodelled in 17C) of Berthold V, last Duke of Zähringen.
(4) Holy Sepulchre (1340) behind a delicate Gothic grating.
(5) Stained glass medallions, 13C and the oldest in the cathedral, probably originally in the old Romanesque chancel and now in the three windows of the south transept.
(6) Group sculpture of the Adoration of the Magi (1505).

The Chancel. – *Open 1 July to 30 September, 10am to noon and 2.30 to 5pm (closed Saturdays, Sundays and holidays); 1DM. Brochure in English.*

When visiting the well lit chancel note the skilful design of the vaulting in the ambulatory combined with that of the widely open side chapels. Look also at the many works of art.

(a) **Altarpiece★★** (Hochaltar) at the high altar by Hans Baldung Grien (1512-6). *Coronation of the Virgin* on the central panel.
(b) Stürzel Chapel: Rococo baptismal font by J. C. Wenzinger.
(c) University Chapel: Oberried Altarpiece (1521). The two side panels, *The Nativity* and the *Adoration of the Magi* are by Hans Holbein the Younger.
(d) Second Imperial Chapel: Altarpiece carved by Schnewlin depicting the *Holy Family at Rest.* The paintings are from the Baldung Grien studio.
(e) Reverse of the large altarpiece by Baldung Grien: painting of the Crucifixion.
(f) Böcklin Chapel: Romanesque Crucifix in beaten silver by Böcklin.
(g) Locher Chapel: altarpiece (1521-4) by Sixt von Staufen: the carved part depicts the Virgin, her cloak shielding humanity held by cherubim.

Ascent of the Tower

Access 1 April to 31 October, 9am (1pm Sundays) to 5pm; 1 November to 31 March, 10am to 4pm (Sundays 1 to 5pm) except Mondays; 1DM. Brochure in English.

One reaches first the star-shaped gallery and then, after a further climb, the upper platform beneath the beautiful pierced spire. There are **views★** of Freiburg, the Kaiserstuhl and the Vosges.

Münsterplatz. – Buildings, whose pomp declares them to have been built for municipal or ecclesiastical prestige, face across the square to the south side of the church.

Archiepiscopal Palace (Erzbischöfliches Palais). – The palace, built in 1756, has a fine wrought iron balcony.

Kaufhaus★. – This Gothic building dashed with red, flanked by watch-towers with pointed roofs, covered with glazed tiles and supported by an arcaded gallery, gives a picturesquely mediaeval air to the square. It contains the town's reception halls and staterooms. The large emperors' statues dating from 1530, on the first floor, recall the rule of the Habsburgs.

Wenzingerhaus. – The mansion the great painter and sculptor Christian Wenzinger had built for himself in 1761 completes the square's layout. It still has its Baroque staircase.

Make for the Rathausplatz by the Eisenstrasse on the left, then, on the right, the Schusterstrasse which continues as the Eisenbahnstrasse, a narrow street bustling with the comings and goings of townsfolk and travellers.

Rathausplatz★. – This square is a pleasant sight with its flowered balconies and its scent from the chestnut trees which encircle the statue of Berthold Schwarz, a Franciscan who is said to have invented gunpowder in about 1350.

New Town Hall★. – The two 16C burghers' houses, heart of the old Freiburg University, were linked to 1901 by a central arcaded building to become the town hall. The oriel window at the corner of the square and the Eisenbahnstrasse *(illustration p 24)* still has its carved decoration of the *Lady and the Unicorn.*

Go down the Franziskanerstrasse, to the left of St. Martin's Church.

Whale House (Haus zum Walfisch). – Of the original building (1516) there remains an oriel window forming a canopy over a doorway decorated richly in late Gothic style.

Where the Franziskanerstrasse comes out into the Kaiser-Joseph-Strasse there is a striking view of the cathedral with its herringbone-effect tower.

Return to the Münsterplatz by way of Münsterstrasse.

■ ADDITIONAL SIGHTS

Augustine Museum★ (BY M¹). – *Open 1 April to 18 December, 10am to 5pm (1pm Sundays) except Mondays; 19 December to 31 March, 10am to noon and 2 to 4pm except Saturdays, Sundays 10am to 1pm; 1.50DM.*

The collections of religious art are enchanting, particularly the **section on Mediaeval Art★★** (Mittelalterliche Kunst) housed in the church of the former Augustinian monastery and the nearby ground floor rooms. The works displayed were originally made for the abbeys and churches of the Upper Rhine and come mostly from the Baden region, Alsace and the Lake Constance area. Statuary especially is represented by valuable 14 and 15C pieces.

A wing from the Grünewald altarpiece, originally at Aschaffenburg *(p 51)* showing the St. Mary of the Snows' Miracle (1519) is among the museum's treasures together with a striking **crucifix★★** dating from the 14C (Adelhauser Kreuz).

Swabian Gate (Schwabentor) (BY). – Remains of the mediaeval fortifications.

One can go down from the Swabian Gate to the quays beside the Gewerbekanal, the poor but picturesque quarter of the Insel where at one time fishermen and tanners lived. There is a view of the cathedral spire from a small bridge over the canal.

EXCURSIONS

Schlossberg★ (CY). *About ½ hour, of which 6 minutes are in a cable-car starting from the Stadtgarten (CY) – service from Easter to end of October, 10am to nightfall; Rtn fare: 2.80DM.*

This last foothill of the Black Forest is wooded. The climb, which can also be undertaken on foot starting from the Swabian Gate, affords unexpected views of the cathedral.

Schauinsland Road★. – *19 km - 12 miles – about 1½ hours.* Leave Freiburg by the Günterstalstrasse, south on the map. After Günterstal, the mountain road, which is well surfaced but extremely winding, becomes a redoubtable part of one of the mountain car rally courses.

Leave the car on coming out of the woods at the upper teleferic station fork. Make for the station before following the wooded crest to the Erzkasten viewing-table (alt 1 286 m - 3 619 ft). From this point there is a **view** across the meadows to the distant Feldberg tower.

Höllental★; Titisee★. – *30 km - 16 miles – about 1½ hours.* Leave Freiburg by ② and follow the Höllental road (no 31).

The Höllental only justifies its name of Hell Valley in the defile in which a bronze stag appears poised on a rock – the **Hirschsprung★** *(car park and facilities for a walk beside the stream)*. Higher up the road climbs in wide curves to a pass.

Titisee ★. – *Description p 84.*

FREIBURG CENTRE

Franziskanerstraße -	7
Friedrichring	8
Gerberau	
Greiffeneggring –	9
Herrenstraße	
Kaiser-Joseph-Str.	
Münsterstraße –	15
Oberlinden	16
Rathausgasse	17
Salzstraße	19
Schiflstraße	20
Schusterstraße	21
Schwabentorplatz -	22
Schwabentorstraße-	23
Turmstraße	26
Universitätsstraße -	27
Unterlinden	29
Werthmannplatz —	30
Bertoldstraße —	4
Eisenbahnstraße –	5
Eisenstraße –	6

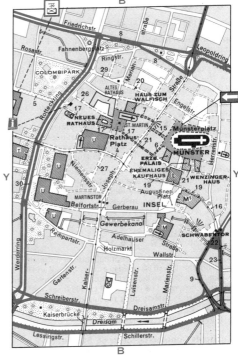

FREISING

Michelin map **987** 37 – Pop 32 000

Freising which was formerly a Bavarian episcopal city and whose title is still borne by the Archbishop of Munich, groups impressive religious buildings on the **Domberg★** hillside.

Cathedral★ (Dom). – *Open 8am to noon and 2 to 6pm (5pm in winter); closed Monday afternoons.*

The present cathedral is a vast 12C Romanesque building masked inside by numerous Gothic, Renaissance and Baroque re-stylings.

The inner Gothic porch with two bays and numerous bishops' tombs leads to the nave through a Romanesque doorway. The tall windows were cut into the walls of the nave in the Baroque period. The Asam brothers *(p 27)* adapted a Baroque decoration to the somewhat rough Romanesque architecture, to produce a dignified overall effect.

The chancel is rich: the **stalls★** (Chorgestühl) shaded by Flamboyant canopies are carved with the busts of the early prince-bishops. The impressive high altarpiece in gilded wood is adorned with a copy of a most animated Rubens: *The Woman of the Apocalypse* (the original is in the Munich Old Pinakotek). Note the dome above the chancel with the false relief painting of the *Virgin and Child*.

Crypt. – The crypt is the only visible part left of the Romanesque building. In the centre stands the Bestiensäule, a strange column entirely covered with carvings of fantastic beasts. Maximilian's Chapel is octagonal and adorned with light 18C Wessobrunn stuccowork.

Cloister. – At the end of the south aisle a side door leads to a cloister which has been finely decorated with stuccoes by J. B. Zimmermann and adorned with funerary medallions. Walk round the cloister to see the **St. Benedict Chapel★**, originally Gothic but later given a light Baroque flavour (Wessobrunn stuccoes).

FREUDENSTADT ★

Michelin map **205** 4 – *Local maps pp 81 and 82* – Pop 19 700
Town plan in Michelin Red Guide Deutschland

Freudenstadt stands amid pine trees on a high plateau at the meeting point of all the main roads of the northern Black Forest. It has the appearance of a new town, for although built originally in the 17C by order of the Duke of Württemberg, it was burnt down in April 1945. The **Marktplatz★** is the showpiece of the new Freudenstadt, whose swift, methodical reconstruction caused something of a sensation.

Church (Stadtkirche). – *Open 8am to noon and 2 to 6pm.*

The 17C church with identical domed belfries, has the unusual feature of two aisles being set at right angles. The 12C Romanesque carved **lectern★★** is said to come from Alpirsbach *(p 82)*. The pulpit is borne by the four Evangelists whose symbols decorate the sides.

FRIEDBERG (HESSEN)

Michelin map **204** east of 4 – Pop 25 000

Friedberg is an attractive example of a mediaeval community with two distinct centres: the town enclosed within the imperial castle and the bourgeois town grouped at the foot of the church, at either end of the main street, the Kaiserstrasse.

■ SIGHTS time: ½ hour

Leave the car in the castle courtyard at the north end of the Kaiserstrasse.

Imperial Town (Burg). – The castle erected by Frederick Barbarossa in 1180 together with its outbuildings still has the atmosphere of a small self-sufficient town. The ramparts, now a promenade, have been made still more attractive with bays of greenery and belvederes. **Adolphe's Tower★** (Adolfsturm), erected in 1347, looks down on the assembled buildings. *Open 10am to noon and 1 to 6pm; closed Mondays and November to March; 0.50DM.*

Walk by the Kaiserstrasse and the Sandgasse on the left to the Judengasse on the right.

Jewish Bath★ (Judenbad). – *20 Judengasse. Open 9am to noon and 2 to 5pm; Saturdays and Sundays, 10am to noon; closed Fridays; 0.50DM.*

This deep square 13C well beneath a dome is arranged for the ritual ablutions prescribed by Jewish Law. Columns with Gothic capitals support the arches over the steps *(74 difficult stairs)* which lead down 80 ft to the water.

Return to the car and go to the church in the centre of the town.

Church (Stadtkirche). – The 13 and 14C building has a typically Hessian exterior with separate gables jutting from the roof above the aisles. The façade is unusual, its towers resting on Gothic arches. Inside, an unusually long **ciborium★** of 1482 stands in the chancel. Three 15C stained glass windows light the apse.

FRIESLAND

Michelin map **987** 3, 4, 5, 14, 15

Friesland is that single geographical region stretching from the Zuider Zee (Ijsselmeer) to the Danish frontier, which is united in a single culture and in its exposure to the sea. Nothing impedes the winds as they sweep along this flat countryside of large brick farmhouses, sheep and windmills, not even the dykes and canals break the monotony. A soft clear light or lowering clouds, endlessly circling gulls, plovers and the short sharp cries of the tern complete the picture.

GEOGRAPHICAL NOTES

A Difficult Conquest. – Since 5C BC, the line of dunes which marks the coastline from the Escaut to the Weser, has been battered by storms and eroded into islets: these are the Frisian Islands.

In the 13C new tide-races swept the coast creating the Zuider Zee in Holland, the mud covered Dollart Bay at the mouth of the Ems and the similar Jade Bay at the mouth of the Weser. The last disastrous inundations were in 1362 and 1634 when northern Friesland suffered the brunt and certain islands were reduced to groups of islets, the Halligens.

The consolidated mudflats, divided by dykes and put under cultivation, are now known in Friesland as the **Marschen**. These former polders are even more fertile than the **Geest** which has a more sandy soil, is slightly higher and gently undulating.

The Frieslanders. – These big men, fresh complexioned, blond, blue-eyed, placid seeming but stubborn, who raise cattle and fish for herrings, have, on either side of the Dutch frontier, fought bitterly to win their land. "God", they say, "made the sea, the Frieslanders made the shore." Many of them are Calvinists. They drink a lot of tea, live in low-lying brick houses which are often thatched and speak a dialect, deriving from Anglo-Saxon which they jealously preserve.

THE FRISIAN ISLANDS

East Frisian Islands. – *Look in the Michelin Red Guide Deutschland under the name of the island to be visited for the embarkation port. The boat service times vary with the tides except to Borkum and Norderney.*

The islands between the Ems and Weser Estuaries are really dunes which rise 20 to 30 m - 70 to 100 ft above sea level. Winds and coastal currents constantly modify their shape, eating into the coast, pushing the land eastwards and southwards: the western shores are rounded, the eastern attenuated. A dyke system mitigates erosion. The fine sand beaches are gay with hundreds of brilliantly coloured bathing tents, often rounded like wagon hoods, set up in sheltering hollows.

The islands are a bird-watcher's paradise while on and offshore live several hundred seals, particularly in the area between Borkum and Sylt.

Not only **Borkum**, the largest and the most easterly island and **Norderney** the nearest to the coast are very popular summer resorts but also **Wangerooge, Langeoog** and **Juist,** where cars are forbidden.

Riding or walking *(guide essential)* for miles at low tide across the firm mudflats are the most popular pastimes here as on the mainland shore. Shells of every colour, starfish, seaweed abound.

The North Frisian Islands. – These islands divide into two geological groups: the three northern islands, Sylt *(description p 241)*, Föhr and Amrum, land masses from the Geest region which escaped submersion when the level of the sea rose with the melting of the glaciers in the Quaternary Era, and the **Halligen** Archipelago, one time Marsch area which was battered in 1634.

As in east Friesland, the water sports, the air rich in iodine, nudism, salt-water and sulphur cures, mud-baths have made **St. Peter Ording** (on the coast) and **Wyk** reputed climatic health resorts and spas.

*If you intend combining your tour of Germany with journeys through Austria or Switzerland remember to take the **Michelin Green Guides Austria, Switzerland.***

FRITZLAR ★

Michelin map **987** north of 25 – *Local map p 252* – Pop 15 000

The mediaeval towers and belfries of Fritzlar rise above the placid Eder.

General View. – The town and its fortified walls overlooked by the towers of the collegiate church may be seen from the south end of the bridge leading to the station on the right bank of the main stream of the Eder.

Nearly all the towers are still standing on the **ramparts** (Stadtmauer), including the impressive 13C spur tower, known as the **grey tower★** (Grauer Turm).

■ SIGHTS *time: 1 hour*

Marktplatz★. – The half-timbered gables in all their variety – some are covered with wooden shingles – have been preserved. Note the small and elongated 15C Kaufhaus ("Reformhaus" – shop), crowned with a turret.

The fountain stem (1564) supports a statue of Roland, the symbol of public liberty here as at Bremen.

Collegiate Church★ (Dom). – This church was built in the 13C on the site of an earlier church of which only the west face, the lower parts of the towers and the crypt remained. A typically Rhineland feature may be seen round the apse in the decorative dwarf gallery *(p 23)* adorned with blind arcades. The church's individuality appears in the many encased eaves and the graceful beaming of the chapter-house, built on to the north side of the apse.

Enter the building by the main door on the west side.

Interior. – *Guided tours, 10am to noon and 2 to 5pm (4pm 1 November to 30 April); no visit during offices; 2.50DM.*

The Gothic ciborium is outstanding as are, on either side of the chancel opening, the two Romanesque column statues carved in wood, of the Virgin and St. John. The crypts below ground are vast; the main one has three aisles and fine square cut Romanesque capitals with simple ribbed decoration.

Am Hochzeitshaus	2
Brüdergasse	4
Burggraben	5
Dr.-Jestädt-Platz	6
Flehmengasse	7
Fraumünsterstraße	
Gießener Straße	
Kasseler Straße	9
Marktplatz	10
Martinsgasse	12
Meydeweg	
Nikolausstraße	14
Roßmarkt	15
St.-Wigbert-Straße	16
Schildererstraße	17
Schladenweg	18

FULDA

Michelin map **987** 25 – Pop 60 000 – *Town plan in Michelin Red Guide Deutschland*

The imprint of its religious past remains on Fulda. From the time of the prince-bishops, guardians of the tomb of St. Boniface, the town still possesses a Baroque heart of palaces, towers, flights of stairs, monumental doorways and balustrades. A good overall view may be obtained from the top of the steps leading to the Frauenberg Church.

St. Boniface, the Apostle of Germany. – In the 8C, Winfrid, an English missionary monk associated with Exeter and Nursling in Hampshire, was sent to preach the gospel in Germany. Anointing Pippin the Short king in 751, he established, for centuries, the union of the church with the Frankish monarchy. Winfrid, who had changed his name to Boniface, was on a mission to Friesland when he was murdered at Dokkum in 754. He lies buried in a monastery, founded on his orders at Fulda.

The Benedictine abbey, particularly under the rule of Abbot Raban Maur (822-42), became a centre of religious devotion, art and learning and it was to it that Germany owed its first literary works (*The Lay of Hildebrand* was copied by two monks in about 820).

■ SIGHTS *time: 1½ hours*

Cathedral (Dom). – The architect Johann Dientzenhofer rebuilt the church at the beginning of the 18C in a style inspired by Italian Baroque.

Pilgrims make for St. Boniface's tomb which lies in a crypt (Bonifatiusgruft) beneath the high altar. Note especially, at the base of the **funerary monument★** in the form of an altar (Bonifatiusaltar), an 18C alabaster low relief depicting Boniface, in his priestly vestments, raising his tombstone on Judgment Day.

The Boniface reliquaries (the saint's head and sword) and the codex with which the saint tried to protect himself against his murderers' swords (a book half cut through is the saint's symbol), are the most precious items in the cathedral **treasure★** (Domschatz) which is in the **Dom-Museum.** *Access by the crypt. Guided tours, 1 April to 31 October, 9.30am (12.30pm Sundays) to 5pm; 1 November to 31 March, 9.30am to noon and 1.30 to 4pm, Sundays 12.30 to 4pm; 1DM. Brochure in English.*

St. Michael's Church★ (Michaelskirche). – This church, built round an early 9C rotunda and possessing a stout square tower, looks down on the cathedral forecourt. The crypt, whose vaulting rests on a single pillar, is Carolingian. The rotunda itself is supported on eight columns which mark the outline of an impressive well-head.

Castle. – Only the minor buildings are interesting. Walk through the park (Schlossgarten), surrounded by terraces or balustraded walls, to the main staircase to the Orangery (1724). Halfway up is a monumental **floravase** (1728), a superb Baroque masterpiece.

EXCURSIONS

Petersberg Church (Kirche auf dem Petersberg). – *4 km - 2½ miles – plus ½ hour walking and sightseeing.* Leave Fulda by the Petersberger Strasse and road no 458, east on the map; follow the "Petersberg" signposts to the foot of the rock on which the church stands, and park the car.

The top of the rock commands a vast **countryside***: east lies the Rhön Massif with the Milseburg spur and the rounded Wasserkuppe; southwest behind Fulda is the Vogelsberg Massif.

The Romanesque church built on this **spot*** was largely rebuilt in the 15C. It contains five 12C **low reliefs**** (Steinreliefs) fixed on either side of the triumphal arch (Christ in Glory and the Virgin) and on the north transept wall (St. Boniface, Carloman and Pippin the Short). The Carolingian crypt has four niches decorated with 9C wall paintings.

Pheasant Castle (Schloss Fasanerie or Adolphseck). – *6 km - 4 miles – by the Frankfurt road (exit ② on the map) and the castle avenue on the left, plus 1 hour sightseeing. Guided tours, 1 April to 31 October, 10am to noon and 2 to 6pm; closed Mondays; 3DM. Guided tours in English.*

The Baroque castle, which was completed by a prince-abbot of Fulda in 1756, owes to landgraves from the Electoral House of Hesse its interior style which today appears as a panoply of decoration and furniture from 1740 to 1860. Special items include Marie-Antoinette's mirror and a *Portrait of the Landgrave Anne* (1859), a masterpiece by Winterhalter, painter of beauties of the Second Empire.

The **park** (Schlosspark) is left more or less in a natural state.

FURTWANGEN
Michelin map **205** 6 – *Local maps pp 82 and 84* – Pop 11 000

Furtwangen, which lies in a hollow close to the source of the Danube *(p 83)*, is a busy Black Forest watch and clock centre with workshops and an advanced precision industries' school.

Historical Horological Collection (Historische Uhrensammlung der Staatlichen Ingenieurschule). – *Open 1 April to 31 October, 8.30am to 5.30pm; the rest of the year, 9am to noon, 2 to 4pm; 2DM. Brochure in English.*

The exhibition acquaints the visitor with the traditional Black Forest skill of clockmaking (reconstruction of an old workshop; cuckoo-clocks and other clocks with good casings display). Many of the valuable exhibits, which come from all parts of the world, were selected because of their ingenuity, artistry or their gay nonsense: Baroque clocks, clocks with singing birds, astronomic clocks, mechanical organ clocks, etc.

EXCURSION

Brend*. – *5.5 km - 3½ miles – by a road which branches off the Freiburg road on the right as it leaves Furtwangen.*

The belvedere (alt 1 148 m - 3 765 ft) tower commands a **panorama*** to the south and a view which drops straight down into the Simonswald Valley.

FÜSSEN *
Michelin map **987** 36 – *Local map p 42* – Pop 11 600
Town plan in Michelin Red Guide Deutschland

Füssen stands on the gorge where the Lech river cascades out of the Alps *(see Lechfall description p 43)* and owes its intense vitality to its position as an approach to the Tyrol as well as to the nearby Royal Castles *(p 221)*. Downstream lies the **Forggensee**, one of a number of small lakes in the area, but in this case manmade – a reservoir formed by the Rosshaupten dam. It provides visitors with motorboat services, sailing and bathing.

The historical part of Füssen is best seen from the Schwangauerstrasse, on the right bank of the Lech between the two bridges. The castle rises high above the roofs of the old town.

■ **SIGHTS** *time: 1 hour*

Former Abbey of St. Magnus (Ehemaliges Kloster). – On this spot, where St. Magnus (or St. Mang), the Apostle of the Allgäu, died in his hermitage in 750, the daughter of St. Gall set up a Benedictine foundation. The Abbey was rebuilt during the 18C in the Baroque style, secularised in 1803 and the church given over to the parish.

Parish Church (Stadtpfarrkirche). – The church, which was rebuilt from 1701 to 1717, has a remarkable unity, for Johann-Jakob Herkomer, born in the district, was not only the architect but also the stucco-worker and the painter. The Romanesque crypt was rearranged in 1950.

Chapel of St. Anne. – *The last door on the left before the church porch.* Inside the chapel there is a curious **Dance of Death*** (Totentanz), painted by a local artist about 1600, and a group in Gothic style of The Holy Family.

The Abbey Buildings. – The main quadrangle (Klosterhof), also attributed to Herkomer, is a good example of Baroque architecture with its three ante-chapels with scrolled gables. In the so-called **Heimatmuseum** may be seen the former state rooms of the abbey – the Room of the Princes, the library and the Pope's Room *(guided tours: 11 June to 30 September, 10.30 to 11.15am; the rest of the year only on Wednesdays; 1DM).*

Castle (Hohes Schloss). – The slope leading to the entrance starts behind the parish church. The castle was the late 15C summer residence of the Bishops of Augsburg. The surrounding land, which is picturesque and peaceful, has been made into a public park, the **Baumgarten**, from which one suddenly comes across views of the Säuling. The apartments and, in particular, the Knights' Hall (Rittersaal), which has a rich octagonally coffered ceiling, contain religious paintings of the 15-18C Swabian school.

*Don't use yesterday's maps
for today's journey.*

Michelin map **987** 36, 37 – *Local maps pp 42 and 44* – Pop 27 500

Garmisch-Partenkirchen's setting is worthy of its renown as the metropolis of the Bavarian Alps and a great international winter resort. It lies in an open mountain basin at the foot of the Wetterstein range from which two silhouettes stand out: the Alpspitze and the axe shaped Waxenstein, masking the Zugspitze. The fourth Olympic Games of 1936, which were held at Garmisch, were a decisive event in the resort's development where the brilliant high season is undoubtedly during the annual winter sports' period.

THE RESORT

Germany's Snow Stadium. – Winter sports enthusiasts may be surprised that a ski resort should have been developed at an altitude of only 700 m - 2 363 ft – but, in fact, meteorological conditions in the eastern Alps assure Garmisch-Partenkirchen of an almost certain snowfall of between 30 and 50 cm - 12 to 20 inches – in January and February. Between 1 200 and 2 000 m - 3 900 and 6 560 ft – that is to say the part served by the mechanical lifts and hoists, the snow is often deeper than six feet.

Winter sports take place towards the base of the Wetterstein, facing northwards. The Kreuzeck cableway (upper station alt 1 652 m - 5 420 ft) was the first built in Bavaria, when completed in 1926, and offers to the skier several classic descents. Many skiing competitions are held here. From the cableway start the Olympic Standard and Kandahar downhill runs (Garmisch is one of the resorts where this race is held). Further to the east, towards Partnachklamm, the teleferic leaves the exercise slopes of Hausberg and takes the skier to the beginning of the Horn (women's Kandahar) and the less redoubtable Kochelberg and Partnachalm runs. The Eckbauer cable-car, running at the back of Olympic stadium, has opened the way to new skiing grounds.

Finally, on the far side, there are pleasant ski-runs down the sunny slopes of the Wank and Kreuzwankl.

Thanks to the Zugspitze railway, Garmisch provides skiing facilities throughout autumn and spring on the Zugspitzplatt snowfields at an altitude of 2 300 to 2 800 m - 7 500 to 9 200 ft.

But it is the Olympic skiing and skating stadia that are the outstanding features of Garmisch. Built for the 1936 winter games, they recall the feats of the games and the ostentatious ceremonies put on by the Nazi regime.

The ski stadium (Skistadion) at the edge of Partenkirchen has two ski-runs for competition and two for training. Here, ski-jumping and slalom events can take place before 80 000 spectators. All the best-known skaters have been seen at Garmisch's ice arena. Consisting of three artificial skating rinks with a total ice surface of nearly 6 500 m² - 4 800 sq yds, the arena (Olympia-Eisstadion) holds 12 000 seated spectators for figure skating championships and ice hockey matches. Nearby is a complex of six swimming pools (five indoor and one outdoor).

Between seventy and eighty competitions are held every winter: toboggan races, curling and others (as well as skating and skiing). Often the competitions are grouped to form the "International Winter Sports Week".

The Summer Season. – In summer, life in the resort is much quieter. Visitors, searching for the sunniest slopes, make for the lower inclines of the Wank and the Kramerspitze, facing the Wetterstein and criss-crossed by "Höhenwege", or easy paths such as the Kramer-Plateau-Weg and the Philosophenweg. Strolling at leisure, they will also discover the individual characteristics of Garmisch and Partenkirchen: Garmisch is the more fashionable, while Partenkirchen's simple village atmosphere is centred round the little Church of St. Sebastian, where Bavarians in national costume sit calmly smoking their long pipes. Garmisch, however, also maintains her traditions: at about 6 pm the village herds are brought down from the mountain pastures and, under the kindly eye of the police, hold up all traffic as they wander down the main road.

■ SIGHTS *time: ¾ hour*

The Old Church (Alte Kirche). – *At Garmisch.* This old parish church stands on the left bank of the Loisach, in a picturesque district whose chalets have been carefully preserved. The interior is formed by two equal aisles, with 16C Gothic vaulting with liernes and tiercerons (subordinate vaulting ribs) is supported by a single centre column. A large number of 14 and 15C mural paintings have been uncovered and restored as far as possible, in particular on the north wall (a huge effigy of St. Christopher and scenes from the Passion).

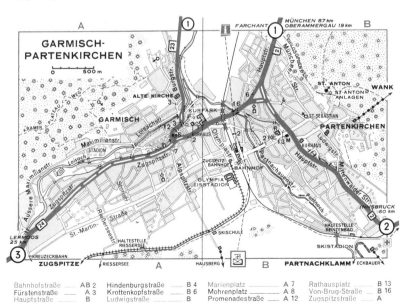

St. Anthony's (St. Anton). – *At Partenkirchen.* This gracious pilgrim's sanctuary, built in 1708, is formed by two aisles, one octagonal and the other oval (enlarged in 1739), and both covered by domes.

The nearby slopes, steep but shaded, make up the **St. Anton-Anlagen** park from which the Philosophenweg path, cut horizontally on the mountainside and affording panoramic vistas, leads to Farchant – the region, in fact, abounds in full **views★** of the Zugspitze standing out clearly behind the Waxenstein.

EXCURSIONS

The Zugspitze★★★. – *A half-day excursion in fine weather (take warm clothing). Departures from Garmisch (Zugspitzbahn station) every hour from 8am to 4pm (3pm in winter); Rtn from the Schneefernerhaus terminus every hour from 10.20am to 5.20pm (6.20pm mid-July to mid-August, 4.20pm in winter). Time of one-way journey: 1 hour. Rtn ticket (Zugspitzgipfel cableway not included): 25DM.*

The electric rack railway (Bayerische Zugspitzbahn) goes to the Eibsee, an attractive lake in the middle of a forest.

As the lake is accessible by car, the train to the Zugspitze can be boarded at Eibsee *(30 minutes after departure from Garmisch).*

Tourists can reach the summit of the Zugspitze directly from Eibsee by cableway (details p 266).

The winding tunnel of over 4 500 m - 2½ miles – bored through the mountain marks the end of the railway.

The rest of the climb to the summit of Zugspitze is described on p 266.

Wank★★ (alt 1 780 m - 5 840 ft). – *About 1½ hours Rtn, of which 20 minutes are spent on the cableway from Partenkirchen, leaving every hour (summer service) from 8.30am to 5pm; Rtn fare: 11DM.*

Extremely sunny viewpoint summit offering a complete panorama of the Wetterstein chain and an aerial view of the Garmisch Basin.

Partnachklamm★★. – *1 hour on foot Rtn (mackintosh useful); 1.50DM. Winter visits in a setting of icicles are also possible.*

We strongly advise including the route through the gorge in the following short tour. Leave the Partenkirchen ski stadium by the road to Partnachklamm (cars not allowed). Take the Graseck cable-car, whose lower station is reached in 20 minutes *(from 8am to 8pm. Fare: 2DM).* From the charming Forsthaus Graseck Inn, the path leads up the valley, following the sides of the slope. Do not take the path on the right leading to the Hohe Brücke but continue past the Wetterstein-Alm Inn and down to the right to the foot of the gorge which you follow downstream. The path, cut out of the rock, crosses the gorge in two spectacular, narrow places where the spray of the falls vaporises above the heads of the walkers. At the Gasthof Partnachklamm rejoin the path taken on the way out.

Ettal; Oberammergau★; Linderhof Castle★. – *30 km - 17 miles – about 3 hours.* Leave Garmisch by ①, the German Alpine Road.

After visiting Ettal church *(p 43),* continue to Oberammergau *(p 199),* from where you briefly retrace your drive to turn right up the valley to Linderhof Castle which was built by Ludwig II *(p 167).*

Return to Garmisch by the same road, omitting Oberammergau.

GELNHAUSEN

Michelin map 👁987 25 – 40 km - 25 miles – northeast of Frankfurt – Pop 18 400

Gelnhausen was built on a sunny slope of the Kinzig Valley by the Emperor Frederick Barbarossa as a military foundation, and to this day is encircled by fortifications.

The most easily seen building is the Church of St. Mary whose towers overlook the village-type square, the Untermarkt, at the highest point of the town.

■ **SIGHTS** *time: ½ hour*

St. Mary's★ (Marienkirche). – Enter through the small south door that looks out over the valley. This stout red limestone building with its spires and gables is typical of the Rhineland Romanesque style *(p 23).* Inside, the **chancel★★** (Chorraum), with its adornment of trilobed blind arcades and heavily worked consoles, is considered to be one of the masterpieces of 13C decorative architecture.

Imperial Palace Ruins (Kaiserpfalz). – *Open 10am to 1pm and 2 to 5pm (4pm October to March); 0.50DM.*

The ruins, which are not extensive, stand on a green island in the Kinzig. They consist of an entrance hall with two aisles, a colonnade with sculptured capitals, traces of the old perimeter wall, the chapel and watch-tower – all remarkable for the perfection of their Romanesque decoration.

EXCURSION

Büdingen. – *17 km - 10½ miles – plus 1 hour sightseeing.* Leave Gelnhausen by the Frankfurt road; branch off right after 4 km - 2 miles along the Büdingen road.

Pass the first road on your right going to the centre of Büdingen and go on to the large roundabout where you bear right into the Bahnhofstrasse.

The 15 and 16C **fortified perimeter★** (Stadtmauer) has fine decorative details. Coming from the Bahnhofstrasse note the Jerusalem Gateway (1503) and its squat towers with Gothic decorative motifs.

The Ysenburg Princes' **Castle** *(open 1 April to 31 October at 2, 3 and 4pm; closed Mondays; 3DM. Guided tours)* is one of the few Staufen fortresses which are still inhabited. It consists of a polygonal kernel with an inner courtyard. The age of the buildings decreases from the 12 to the 17C in a clockwise direction starting from the entrance arch. The 15C chapel contains **choir-stalls★** (Chorgestühl) decorated with saints' effigies and coats of arms.

GOSLAR ★★

Michelin map 👁👁👁 16 – *Local map p 145* – Pop 52 000

Goslar, which is a mining town near the Harz Mountains, was the favourite residence of the Salian Emperors (1024-1125), particularly Heinrich III, Heinrich IV and Heinrich V. In its old quarter there is a singular grouping of half-timbered houses and monuments.

From the **Georgenberg** (B) promenade (viewing table at the foot of the Bismarck statue) there is a good **view** of the town built up against the Harz Mountains.

The Goslar Mines. – Goslar, a former Free Imperial City, owed its prosperity to the mineral wealth of the Harz Mountains and particularly to the Rammelsberg mines worked during the Middle Ages for lead and silver. The city's rise reached its apex at the beginning of the 16C when profit accrued from the vast forests whose timber was used to fire the metal refineries. From this time date the houses typical of the burghers of the Bakers' and Brusttuch Guilds.

After 1550 religious controversy brought discord between the Free City and the Dukes of Brunswick, who owned the mines. Goslar's brilliance waned. In the 19C the town, by now under Prussian domination, revived and prospered to a limited extent commercially as the regional centre. The Rammelsberg lead and zinc mines are still worked.

■ **OLD TOWN★★★** *tour: 3 hours*

Marktplatz★★. – The square is surrounded by houses with façades, many protected by slates. In the centre stands a **fountain** (Marktbrunnen) with two bronze basins (1230) surmounted by the crowned imperial eagle with outspread wings. The square's prestige rests on its two Gothic buildings, the Rathaus, with behind it the spires of the Marktkirche, and the Kaiserworth.

On the fronton of the house, opposite the town hall, is an interesting **chiming clock**. There are four different scenes representing the history of mining in the Harz Mountains from the Middle Ages to the present day; the clock can be seen functioning at *9am, noon, 3 and 6pm*.

Town Hall★. – *Illustration p 24.* In the mediaeval tradition an arcaded gallery (Lauben) opens on to the Marktplatz. A balustrade with decorated gabling masks the roof cornice.

Go up an outside staircase (left) to the state room (Diele) on the first floor.

Chamber of Homage★★ (Huldigungssaal). – *Open June to September, 9am to 5.30pm; October to May, 10am to 4pm; 2 DM.*

This small room was painted in about 1510 by a master artist who adorned the walls with a procession of kings from the Old Testament and sibyls in Renaissance costume. A minute chapel, hidden in a corner, contains paintings of the Passion. Gold and silver plate are on display.

Kaiserworth (B X). – This Gothic building (1494) now a hotel, has an oriel with a turret and Baroque statues of emperors beneath canopies. On a gable ridge, at the foot of the statue of Abundance, a grotesque figurine of the Ducat Man (Dukatenmännchen) demonstrates scatologically Goslar's right to mint coins.

Carved, timber-fronted houses★★ (Fachwerkhäuser). – Go northwest out of the Marktplatz past the Rathaus to the **Schuhhof**, a square entirely surrounded by timber-fronted houses, those on the right resting on arcades. At the end of the square go through a passageway to the Münzstrasse on the left. Follow this on the right to the old staging inn, **Am Weissen Schwan** (A) – go into the yard – and to the **Old Mint** (Alte Münze) of 1500 (Z), now a restaurant.

Turn round and return towards the Marktkirche. The towers of this church can be seen at the end of the Münzstrasse which is always narrow and, where it runs into the Marktstrasse, is overhung by the corbelling of the corner houses. The right-hand corner house (no 1 Marktstrasse) (V) dates from 1526 and has a superb two-storey oriel window.

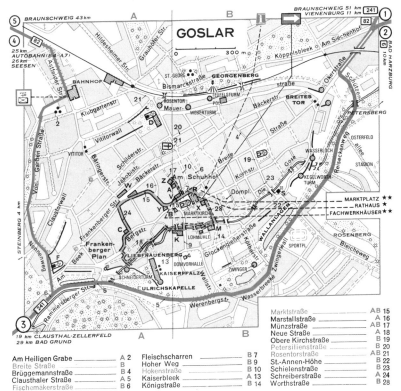

Turn right and walk the length of the church to see the tall gable of the 16C **Bakers' Guild House** (Bäckergildehaus) (**Y**). Facing the Marktkirche, is the immense pointed roof of the **Brusttuch** (''the shawl'') (**B**) dating from 1526. A rich mine owner had it decorated, in accordance with Renaissance taste, with a host of mythological, Biblical and buffoon motifs.

Return to the Marktstrasse; at the Bäckerstrasse crossroads, a line of **Renaissance houses** are adorned with the fan motif often seen in Lower Saxony (no 2 Bäckerstrasse), or a cellular frieze (no 3 Bäckerstrasse) (**W**). Turn left into the Schreiberstrasse.

Siemens' House (**C**). – *Open May to September, 9am to 1pm; closed Wednesdays.*

This striking half-timbered house on the right corner of the Bergstrasse was built in 1693 by Hans Siemens, the ancestor of the famous Berlin industrialist. Go inside to see the beautiful **Däle**, an entrance hall paved with small tiles, and the old courtyard with its ancillary buildings.

Follow the Bergstrasse to a lovely small square in which a lime tree stands. Turn left and after following the Gose stream, you will come to the Liebfrauenberg quarter. Go along the Neue Strasse; cross the Gose opposite a flourmill and wander down the right bank of the stream which has given its name to a well known Continental beer – *Gosebier*.

Hospice of St. Cross Major (Stift zum Grossen Heiligen Kreuz) (**B K**). – *Open daily 9am to 6pm.*

The hospice, founded in 1254, raises its Gothic gable, protected by an overhanging roof, above the Hoher Weg. Inside, a 17C hall with galleries leads to the unadorned chapel.

Continue downstream. After an old mill (Lohmühle) and the museum *(description overleaf)*, turn left into the Worthstrasse to return to the Marktplatz.

■ ADDITIONAL SIGHTS

Neuwerk Church★ (**A D**). – This Romanesque church, alone in a garden, has tall polygonal towers and an exceptionally elaborately decorated apse.

Inside, the building has heavily ribbed pointed vaulting. In the central bay, the small columns bearing the beams are hollowed out in their upper parts into a curious stone ring motif.

The organ loft balustrade is decorated with six low reliefs which came from the old rood-screen (Christ, the Virgin and four apostles) and are already elegantly Gothic.

Frankenberg Church (**A F**). – *Entrance on Frankenberger Plan.*

A visit to the church brings you to the peaceful Frankenberger quarter, and particularly to the Frankenberger Plan, a square formerly lived in by miners. The 12C church was extensively remodelled and received, in the 18C, a Baroque roof and a lantern tower.

Inside, note the west gallery known as the Nonnenempore (nuns' gallery), where the blind arcades rest on capitals ornamented with acanthus leaves topping small columns with a plaited decoration derived from those at Königslutter *(p 162)*. On the church's north and south walls are traces of vast mural paintings dating from the early 13C.

St. Anne's Chapel (St. Annenkapelle) (**B S**). – *Guided tours; offering.*

The chapel, which is attached to a small hospice (founded in 1494), is unusual for its close and 17C wooded galleries. Among the works of art is a precious veil embroidered in the 14C.

Imperial Palace (Kaiserpfalz) (**A**). – *Open 1 May to 30 September, 9am to 6pm; March, April and October, 10am to 4.30pm; November to February, 10am to 3.30pm; 2DM.*

The palace, which was rebuilt in 1879, is reminiscent in outline and plan, if in nothing else, of the old 11C palace of Goslar. The ambitious historical paintings in the Reichssaal on the first floor depict Germany's hours of glory when the Emperors resided at Goslar. The Reichssaal communicates with the early 12C Palatine **Chapel** of St. Ulrich, in which the plan passes in elevation from Greek cross to octagon. Inside are the tomb of Heinrich III, which contains the Emperor's heart, and his recumbent effigy dating from the 13C.

Wide Door★ (Breites Tor) (**B**). – The building was almost a fortress in its own right with round towers, two doors (only the inner door still stands) and barracks.

Rampart Walk★ (Wallanlagen) (**B**). – Green bays and stretches of water have been laid out between the Wide Door and the Imperial Palace.

Goslarer Museum (**B M**). – *Open June to September, 9am (10am Sundays and holidays) to 1pm and 2.30 to 5pm; October to May, 10am to 1pm and 3 to 5pm; closed Sunday afternoons, Christmas Day and 1 January; 1.50DM.*

There are particularly interesting exhibits of old Goslar – models of the town. There is also a large 11C bronze reliquary, the Crodo Altar, unfortunately stripped of its precious stones, and miscellaneous objects from Goslar Cathedral which was demolished in 1819 and of which only a secularised chapel, the Domvorhalle, remains on the original site.

EXCURSION

Church of Grauhof★. – *3 km - 2 miles.* Leave Goslar by ① on the map, road no 82 to Schladen, then turn left towards Grauhof. The Augustinian friars of Grauhof monastery had this church built in 1717 by an Italian architect. The interior is striking for its dimensions and the restrained use of colour. Note particularly a 1721 pulpit in the form of a boat, the rare choir-stalls where are represented 56 scenes of the life and philosophy of St. Augustine and the 1737 organ loft.

▨ GÖSSWEINSTEIN ★ _____

Michelin map **987** east of 26 – *Local map p 61* – Pop 3 300

This market town of Swiss Franconia is known for its gallery-like site above the Behringersmühle Basin and its pilgrimage church dedicated to the Holy Trinity.

The best approach is from the west by the road which climbs out of the Wiesent Valley.

Church (Wallfahrtskirche). – The church was built in 1739 by Balthazar Neumann *(p 27)*. Inside, attention is immediately drawn to the pyramid shaped high altar, supporting at the top a glass cage in which may be seen the early 16C Gothic group, venerated by pilgrims, of the Three Figures of the Trinity Crowning the Virgin.

The belvederes. – If possible, starting from the castle entrance, go round the Burg rock *(follow the signs: Marienfels – Schmitt-Angalen)* by way of the **Marienfelsen** *(about ¾ hour walk)*. Amidst the boulder strewn woods are **belvederes★★** affording views of the deep Wiesent Valley.

The **Wagnershöhe** pavilion (take the path behind the Heimatmuseum) which is nearer the centre of the town *(¼ hour on foot Rtn)* affords a more extensive but less striking **view★**.

GÖTTINGEN

Michelin map 987 southeast of 15 – Pop 125 000
Town plan in Michelin Red Guide Deutschland

Göttingen, Tübingen and Marburg are the German towns most deeply dyed in the university tradition. Students impart a vivacity which is often noisy and highly coloured, particularly at examination time and on foundation days (Stiftungsfest). The background to the bustling streets – squads of students cycling to dispersed lecture halls and libraries – is an old town of Gothic churches and Neo-Classical university buildings which suffered little in the war.

Two Centuries of University Life. – Göttingen University, founded in 1737 by George II, King of Great Britain and Ireland and Elector of Hanover, tended at first to be an aristocratic institution frequented by the sons of minor Hanoverians, and of English or Russian families. While lawyers and philologists studied, famous equestrians practised their art in the monumental riding-school.

The nomination, in 1807, of **Karl-Friedrich Gauss** (1777-1855) as Director of the Observatory and Professor of Astronomy marked the opening of a period of high scientific learning for Göttingen. Gauss, who, it has been stated, was a mathematician of the calibre of an Archimedes or a Newton, was extraordinarily precocious and at the age of 16 had conceived the possibility of non-Euclidean geometry. His name was given to an international unit of the field of magnetic intensity and to a learned society which is trying even now to extract the quintessence from his scientific testament which consists of 145 enigmatic pronouncements condensed into 19 pages.

Since the war Göttingen has become the headquarters of the Max Planck Society (successor of the Kaiser-Wilhelm-Gesellschaft) which groups some 50 scientific research societies in Germany. Max Planck himself (1858-1947), the author of the Quantum theory in the Law of Radiation (1900), is portrayed on the 2DM coin and is buried in Göttingen.

■ **SIGHTS** *time: 1½ hours*

Town Hall. – Students, tourists and the citizens of Göttingen have made the nearby neighbourhood (Marktplatz) and the cellars (Ratskeller) of this building into the heart of the town. The 14 and 15C building was constructed on the classic mediaeval plan *(p 24)*.

A modern **fountain** of a goosegirl (Gänselieselbrunnen) stands before the town hall and is the goal for processions of students when examinations are over.

Viewpoint for four churches (Vierkirchenblick). – A church can be seen at each point of the compass from the southeast corner of the Markt: east, the country church dome of St. Alban's; south, St. Michael's; west, the two octagonal towers of St. John's; and north, the lofty belfry of St. James', the tallest tower in the town at 72 m – 236 ft.

Half-Timbered Houses (Fachwerkhäuser). – Most of the half-timbered houses are in the east part of the old quarter. The old **Junkernhaus★** inn, which is near the Rathaus, on the corner of the Barfüsserstrasse and the Judenstrasse, is Renaissance and half-timbered; medallions adorned with portrait heads are surmounted by Biblical characters (Adam and Eve, Samson and Delilah, etc.). The master and mistress of the house are depicted on the corner post.

Municipal Museum (Städtisches Museum). – *Open 10am to 1pm and 3 to 5pm; closed Sunday afternoons, Mondays and holidays.*

The museum, which is largely devoted to the regional religious art, also possesses a historical department showing the development of the town and the university. A **collection of miniature weapons of war** is interesting, also the exhibition of diaries of young ladies and gentlemen illustrated with miniatures, poems and mottoes.

HAIGERLOCH ★★

Michelin map 206 15 – *Local map p 240* – Pop 6 300

Haigerloch, a tiny town on the northern edge of the Swabian Jura has an extremely curious **setting★★** between two steeply enclosed wooded bends of the Eyach River. When the lilac is in flower at Whitsun it is delightful.

■ **SIGHTS** *time: 1 hour*

Start from the Marktplatz in the lower town; go up by the slope or staircase which both rise to the castle. This is built along the clifflike promontory of the downstream bend of the Eyach.

Castle Church★ (Schlosskirche). – The early 17C church, built at the end of the spur, is enchanting with its radiant Rococo furnishings (1748).

Continue up the rise, cross the castle court obliquely and follow the marked path to the Kapf.

Kapf. – From the belvedere behind the rock (Cross) there is a view of the Eyach bend which, on the far side, encloses the upper town, looked down upon by the Roman Tower (Römerturm).

Return to the Marktplatz and the car. Go up the Hauptstrasse, the road to the upper town, and leave the car at the top of the hill in the car park facing St. Anne's Church.

St. Anne's Church. – St. Anne's stands on a shaded esplanade, overlooking the Eyach Gorge and facing the Castle Church. To get an uninterrupted **view★**, walk back a little down the approach road.

The pilgrims' church, built by Johann-Michael Fischer in 1755, with the chaplain's house (Kaplaneihaus) before it, forms a remarkably elegant Rococo group. Inside note the enveloping altarpieces by Johann-Michael Feichtmayr on the side altars.

HAIGERLOCH

0   200 m

Bahnhofstraße ———— 2
Hauptstraße
Hechinger Straße ———— 3

Hohenbergstraße · 4
im Haag
Klosterstraße ———— 6
Marktplatz ———— 7
Pfleghofgasse ———— 9
Pfluggasse ———— 12
St. Annaweg ———— 13
Schloßsteige ———— 15

HAMBURG ★★★

Michelin map 987 5 – Pop 1 698 000

Hamburg, Germany's second city after Berlin, is one of the largest European ports. Its old title of "free and Hanseatic" town, its status of "city state" (Stadtstaat) testify to its longtime importance. Its business transactions and day and night activity derive from the ever increasing size of the port, which is situated on the River Elbe – 110 km - 68 miles – from the open sea.

Two other rivers flow into the Elbe at Hamburg, the Alster and the Bille.

From the shores of the Alster you have a good view of the old city's silhouette with the spires of its churches and town hall *(illustration p 140)*.

The Hamburg skyline is marked by the Television Tower *(p 140)* and especially by the imposing **Köhlbrandbrücke★★**. This 1975 suspension bridge, 3 975 m - 2.5 miles long, is suspended over an arm of the Elbe, from two pylons 135 m - 443 ft high.

The road tunnel **Elbtunnel** (1974), 27 m - 88 ft under the surface of the Elbe, allows an uninterrupted north-south traffic through the town.

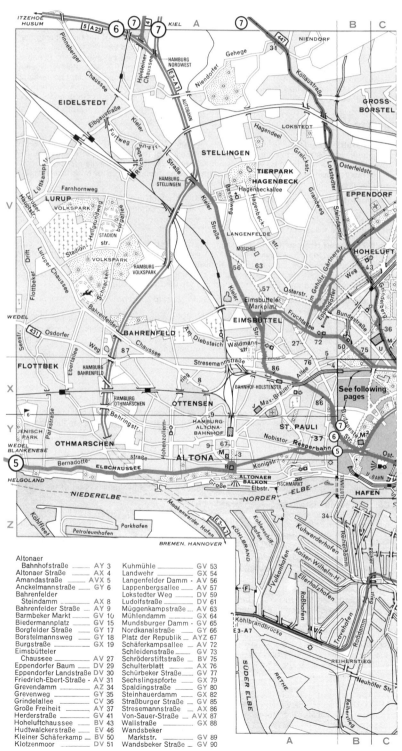

HISTORICAL NOTES

On 7 May each year Hamburg celebrates Overseas Day (Übersee-Tag) in commemoration of the concession granted by Frederick Barbarossa in 1189 of the right to navigate freely on the Lower Elbe. The town authorities had to be constantly on guard in order to preserve this right, which was challenged by pirates and the feudal ambitions of the riparian powers, particularly Denmark. They could safely relax their vigilance only in the 17C.

The Hanseatic Town (13-15C). – Hamburg, which began as a modest group of buildings on the banks of the Alster, a small tributary of the Elbe, had its first period of prosperity on entering the Hanseatic League *(p 167)*, which was headed by Lübeck (a town founded by Adolf II, count of Holstein). Merchants took courage and began to organise the banks of the Elbe for berthing ships and warehousing.

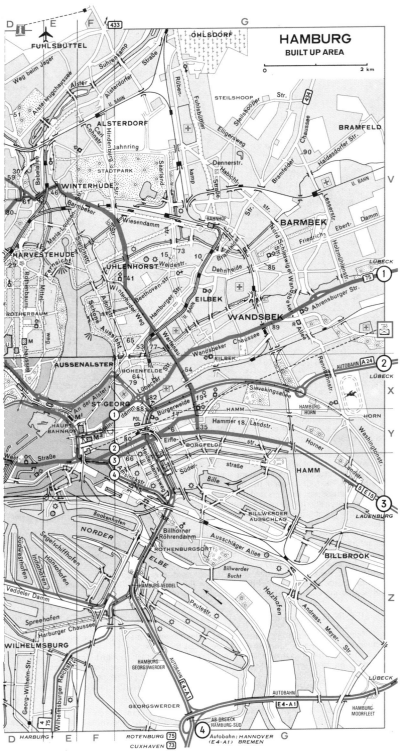

HAMBURG
BUILT UP AREA

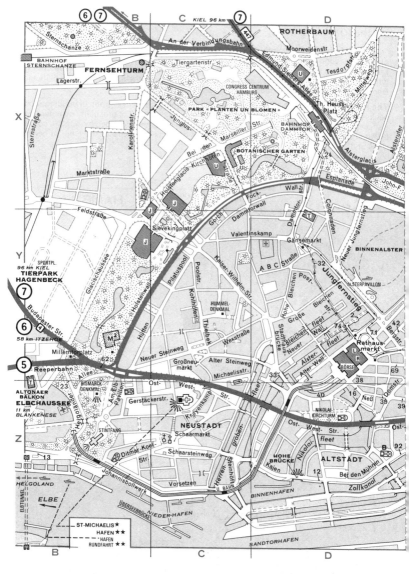

The town profited from the peculiar conditions of the Baltic and North Sea trade. At that time only heavy grain and timber vessels went by open sea, via the Kattegat and the Skagerrak. Valuable cargoes were landed at Lübeck, carried by land to Hamburg and reloaded.

Liberty and Neutrality. – The discoveries of new lands in the 16C upset existing trading patterns and dislocated the Hanseatic trade. Spanish, Portuguese and later British navigation monopolies compelled the Hamburg traders to become intermediaries in warehousing and distribution. The foundation of the Stock Exchange in 1558 was a manifestation of the town's intense business activity. This trading was favoured by a policy of strict political neutrality and thus, exceptionally, the town stayed out of the Thirty Years War.

In 1618 Hamburg became a Free Imperial City. The Bank of Hamburg was founded one year later.

American independence and the emergence of Latin America gave an impetus to the extraordinary expansion of the 19C. In 1913 the Hamburg-Amerika-Linie steamship company was the largest in the world. The Hamburg flag was seen on every sea. Shipbuilding, mostly for export, became a key industry.

In 1975 Hamburg's turnover reached the record total of 48 million tons.

Fuhlsbüttel airport, north of the town, saw the beginning of German commercial aviation and is now the engineering base of Lufthansa, the German airline.

LIFE IN HAMBURG

Members of the old Hamburg families, some of whom are of the "big blond type", are imbued with the independent spirit and power of their city.

In business dealings this consciousness is manifested in their caution before agreeing to any economic proposal which might modify certain traditional commercial arrangements.

Hamburg is the biggest centre in Germany of printing and publishing, especially of weekly newspapers and illustrated papers and magazines. It is also the headquarters of the German Press Agency (DPA).

Amusements. – Hamburg, like many other large sea-ports, has a reputation for night-life. This is mainly in the St. Pauli quarter (AY) where the **Reeperbahn** and the Grosse Freiheit are lit by coloured neon signs, and shooting galleries, a *Panoptikum* (waxworks), a racecourse, a dance hall and some 300 *Lokale* or bars, foreign restaurants, etc. line the streets.

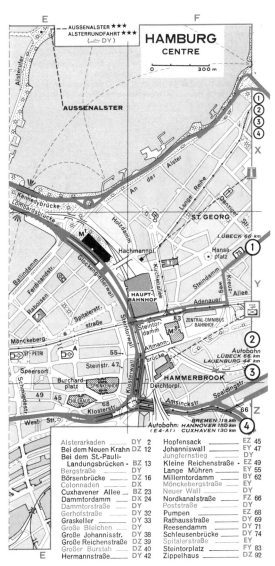

HAMBURG
CENTRE

0   300 m

Wandering in the streets of Hamburg by daylight can also be a pleasure, there being many bars and wine shops where, in summer as in winter, one can enjoy a skilfully prepared grog.

The antique shops round the Gänsemarkt (DY) display objects from the East: lacquer work, ivory, jade, porcelain, etc. Collectors of maps and engravings will find specialist bookshops between the station and the town hall. Philatelists and lovers of tobacco will go to the small shops in the printing and counting house quarters *(see below)*. Tobacco manufacturers are amongst the most prosperous of Hamburg's businessmen.

Food Specialities. – These draw on local produce and on Eastern spices, sometimes combining in one dish, meat, fruit and sweet-sour sauce.

Among the most typical dishes are *Aalsuppe* – eel soup – and *Labskaus* – a sailors' dish of minced meat (usually corned beef), herring, mashed potato, chopped gherkins, all mixed together and topped with a fried egg.

■ **MAIN SIGHTS**

The central quarters

tour: 4 hours

Rathausmarkt (DY). – The square, which was replanned after the disastrous fire of 1842, is dominated by the 1897 town hall's high campanile.

The bridge (Schleu-

senbrücke), which forms part of the lock controlling the level of the Alster, crosses the Alsterfleet, and is a last relic of the canal system which was characteristic of old Hamburg *(see p 140 – Hohe Brücke)*.

At the end of the bridge is the 1914-18 War Memorial, a stele with a carving by Barlach. On the far bank, an arcade, known as the Alsterarkaden, shades elegant shop windows.

Jungfernstieg (DY). – This well known road, running along the end of the Binnenalster Basin, is the town's cosmopolitan artery: the crowded Alsterpavillon (café-restaurant) terraces, the basin crossed and recrossed by craft using the Alster, all add to the general animation. Shipping and air companies' offices line the Ballindamm on the east quay of the Binnenalster.

Aussenalster***. – *Take a trip on the Alsterrundfahrt boats: in season 10am to 6pm; time: 50 minutes; 5DM.*

This lovely sheet of water makes sailing and canoeing possible in the centre of the city. A fleet of Alsterschiffahrt motorboats calls regularly at the landing stages.

A **trip by boat***** (Alsterrundfahrt) on the Alster enables one to get far enough away to see together the outline of the five towers of the principal churches and the town hall campanile all over 100 m - 300 ft tall *(illustration p 140)*.

Tourists preferring to go round the Alster by car should go clockwise, following the long shaded avenues bordered by blocks of luxury flats. Their use as **viewpoints** has given the quays the literal meaning names of **Fernsicht** (EV) and **Schöne Aussicht** (FV) – view and beautiful vista.

Counting Houses (Kontorhäuser) (EYZ). – The counting houses stand, colossally massive in glossy brick, in the printing and business quarters round the Burchardplatz. The Chilehaus, built in 1924, is still an amazing landmark against the sky; the Sprinkenhof (1930) is a town of offices with thoroughfares and 6 000 people in the one building (Shell Centre, London, 5 000 people).

St. Michael's* (Hauptkirche St. Michaelis). – The church was built in brick in 1762 by the architect Sonnin, one of the best representatives of the Baroque tradition in northern Germany. It was designed for the Lutherans and is light, spacious and has many inner amenities.

The famous **tower** (1786) "Michel", which is the town's popular symbol, rises beside the Elbe, its roof a lantern turret in the form of a rotunda.

HAMBURG★★★

From the platform *(access: weekdays 9am to 5.30pm – Sundays and holidays 11.30am to 5.30pm; November to 15 March, 10am to 4pm – Sundays 11.30am to 4pm – closed Wednesdays; lift: 2DM; or 450 steps: 1DM)*, there is a **panorama★** of the centre of the town with the larger church towers and square modern blocks, the Alster Lakes and especially the Elbe, criss-crossed by ships' wakes, docks, warehouses and port installations.

Near the east end of the church, pass through the porch at no 10 Krayenkamp. This blind alley is lined with astonishing timber and brick houses **(Krameramtswohnungen)** which were built in 1670 as almshouses. The area has now become an artists' colony.

Hamburg – The city spires as seen from the Aussenalster.

(1) St. James' (St. Jakobi). – Height 124 m - 417 ft (rebuilt). Details p 141.
(2) St. Catherine's (St. Katherinen). – Height 112 m - 367 ft (rebuilt). Details p 141.
(3) St. Peter's (St. Petri). – Height 133 m - 436 ft. Rebuilt as a Gothic hall-church after the 1842 fire.
(4) St. Nicholas' (St. Nikolai). – Height 147 m - 482 ft (third highest Belfry in Germany after Ulm and Cologne). Only the pierced Neo-Gothic tower remains; it is to be converted into a memorial.
(5) Town Hall (Rathaus) campanile. – Height 112 m - 367 ft.
(6) St. Michael's (St. Michaelis). – Height 108 m - 354 ft. Details p 139.

The port★★

One of the best **viewpoints★**, other than the St. Michael Tower, from which to see the port is the Stintfang hill (BZ) (terrace below the youth hostel).

A few figures. – The port of Hamburg consists of 62 dock basins with 64 km - 40 miles - of quays, plus a great many mooring buoys. The 38 basins for maritime vessels able to come up the Elbe (drawing 12 m - 39 ft – and 65 000 tons) have no need of locks since the tide makes a difference, on average, of less than 2.50 m - 8 ft. The port has built its reputation on its speed of handling and the wide variety of its equipment, warehouses and transport.

Two hundred and ninety lines call regularly (about 650 departures a month) to carry cargo to 1 100 ports all over the world.

Boat trip round the port★★ (Hafenrundfahrt). – *Time: 1 hour; HADAG boat departures every $\frac{1}{2}$ hour from 9am to 6pm during the season; fare 7DM. Embarkation from the St. Pauli river station landing stage no 2 (St. Pauli-Landungsbrücken)* (BZ).

The size of the dockyards – 5 undertakings, 26 floating docks – is striking and also the activity of the Elbe where every type of boat is built: cargo ships, tankers, lighters, tugs, launches, customs and police patrol boats, pleasure boats, refrigerator ships, etc. Motor-ferries ply all day and in the evening bring home workers from the left bank.

On Sunday morning, before 10am, explore the St. Pauli-Fischmarkt (AZ), a lively food market on the St. Pauli quays.

Hagenbeck Zoo★★ (Tierpark Hagenbeck) (AV) *tour: about 1 hour*

Open 8am to 7pm (4pm in winter); 6.50DM; children: 3.25DM.
The zoo was founded in 1907 and to a degree keeps up the Hagenbeck tradition of capturing, selling and training wild animals for circuses.

■ ADDITIONAL SIGHTS

The old fortifications to the west and north of the town between the Elbe and the Alster have been laid out as gardens.

Television Tower★★ (Fernsehturm) (BX). – *Lift: 3DM.* This concrete needle with its antenna climbs 271.5 m - 890 ft. On the top an observatory *(open until 11pm)* and a revolving panoramic restaurant *(noon to midnight)* afford a fine **view★★** of Hamburg.

Planten un Blomen Park★ (Erholungspark) (CDX). – *Open 7am to nightfall. Fountains play from 16 April to 1 October every 2 hours starting at 2pm. Floodlighting and musical accompaniment to the fountains at 9.30pm (8.30pm out of season).*

The gardens, which were laid out geometrically in 1936, serve as a proving ground for new species of flowers and trees. An artificial cascade flows into the main pool (Grosser Parksee), where, at nightfall, the fountains are accompanied by a *Son et Lumière* performance.

Hohe Brücke (DZ). – The bridge, which crosses the Nikolaifleet, lies parallel with the Binnenhafen, a basin reserved for river traffic and tugs. Decrepit warehouses lining the bend of the canal, which is cluttered with lighters and small boats, present a picture of old Hamburg.

Museums

Art Gallery★★ (Kunsthalle) (EY M¹). – *Open 10am to 5pm (7pm Wednesdays); closed Mondays; 1DM (free Wednesdays).* Among others, the following pictures are on the first floor.

In the **Grabow Altarpiece** (1379) executed by Master Bertram for St. Peter's of Hamburg, the museum possesses one of the largest and well executed examples of North German Primitive painting. The 24 door panels depict Salvation and display both lively and naïve scenes with beautiful colour effects and attitudes. Compare this polyptych to the Buxtehude Altarpiece by the same artist and to the Altarpiece of Thomas of Canterbury by Master Francke.

19C German painting is illustrated by Feuerbach, von Marées, Böcklin, Philipp-Otto Runge (1777-1810), a Hamburg painter by adoption who was gifted as a portraitist and painter of allegorical figures. Caspar-David Friedrich is well represented by his Romantic compositions *(The Seasons, Harz Countryside, Hope Disappointed)* and Wilhelm Leibl from the Realist school, *Three Women at Church.*

Together with paintings by Max Liebermann *(Portrait of Eva),* Louis Corinth and Edvard Munch *(Madonna),* the museum also possesses an outstanding collection of works illustrating the Brücke group and Blue Knight movement *(p 27)*: triptych of *St. Maria Aegyptica* by Nolde, *Artist and his Model* by Kirchner, *Frieze with Monkeys* by Franz Marc. One gallery is illuminated by Paul Klee's fascinating **Goldfish.**

Historical Museum* **(Museum für Hamburgische Geschichte)** (BY M²). – *Open 10am to 5pm; closed Mondays; 1DM.*

The models of Old Hamburg are interesting as is the large department concerning the port and navigation (more than 100 ships' models including the impressive *Wappen von Hamburg* dating to 1720; central part of a 1909 steamer) and the scale model of the railway system.

Decorative Arts and Crafts Museum* **(Museum für Kunst und Gewerbe)** (FY M³). – *Open 10am to 5pm (7pm Wednesdays); closed Mondays; 1DM (free on Wednesdays).*

Among thousands of objects exhibited by epochs, particularly remarkable are the mediaeval statuary gold and silver plate (shrine of St. George by Berndt Notke), the sumptuous Renaissance furniture, the precious clocks from Northern Germany as well as delicate 18C china and porcelain. Also full display of Jugendstil *(p 26)*: ornaments, furniture and works of art.

Churches

St. James' (St. Jakobi) (EY A). – The 13-15C Gothic hall-church possesses several works of art (St. Luke and the Brotherhood of Fishermen altarpieces) saved from war damage. The famous organ of 1693 has been rebuilt.

St. Catherine's (St. Katherinen) (DZ B). – This Gothic church, which was built in brick in the 14 and 15C, looks down attractively from its rounded and pierced Baroque tower on the old quarter in the port.

EXCURSIONS

Altona (AZ); **Wedel.** – *20 km - 12½ miles – about 2 hours.* Leave Hamburg by ⑤.

Altona and Northern Germany Museum★★ (Norddeutsches Landesmuseum) (AY M). – *Open 10am to 5pm; closed Mondays.*

The Lower Valley of the Elbe and the Schleswig-Holstein are illustrated through the housing, costumes, everyday life and traditional activities of the region. Note the exceptional collection of **figure-heads** (room 6), the models which explain the different sorts of fishing and boats to be found in the North Sea (room 7), the astonishing variety of old Toys (room 13) and the delicate Frisen embroidery (rooms 22-23). An authentic cottage from the Vierlande, a region located southeast of Hamburg, houses a small restaurant. The third floor of the museum is devoted to the history of Altona.

Altona Balcony (Altonaer Balkon) (AZ). – There is a **view**★ from the terrace south of the Altona Rathaus, of the confluence of the two arms of the Elbe, which mark the limits of Hamburg's industrial and port area. The shipping is fascinating!

Ride down the **Elbchaussee**★ which is lined with handsome properties established from the early 19C onwards by the great Hamburg shipowning and banking families.

Wedel. – Follow the Willkomm-Höft signposts to the large café-restaurant beside the Elbe where a greeting dais has been set up for passing ships (Schiffsbegrüssungsanlage). The ceremony consists of saluting the colours in accordance with maritime practice and playing the national anthem of the ship's country of origin (the sounding of the siren and the anthem alert those not on the dais). Many come for the **spectacle**★

Friedrichsruh. – *29 km - 18 miles – 2 hours.* Leave Hamburg by ③, the Lauenburg road; in Bergedorf bear left into the Schwarzenbek road. At the Kröppelshagen crossroads turn left to go through a wood and reach the Friedrichsruh estate.

The **Bismarck Museum** *(open 1 April to 30 September, 9am to 6pm, closed Monday mornings, 1 October to 31 March, 9am–10am Sundays–to 4pm, closed Mondays; 2.50DM)* gives a picture of the Iron Chancellor's career (1815-98), his honours, and his family retreat at Friedrichsruh. A Neo-Romanesque mausoleum chapel contains the family vault.

HAMELIN ★ (HAMELN)

Michelin map 📘 15 – Pop 66 700 – *Town plan in Michelin Red Guide Deutschland*

Hamelin is built on the right bank of the Weser and glories in some fine old houses, of which the most typical belong to the **Weser Renaissance** or late 16, early 17C period. This architectural style is characterised by ram's horn scrollwork and pinnacles on the gables, delicately worked stone bands encircling the buildings, forward wings (Utlucht) treated as reduced examples of the main façade and aedicules (Zwerchäuser) with decorated gables advanced at the base of the roof as with dormer windows.

Hamelin is also a city with a special place in German folklore: it is the town of the famous ratcatcher who was immortalised by Goethe and, in English, by Robert Browning. *The Pied Piper of Hamelin.* A dramatic version of the legend is performed every Sunday at noon in the summer on the town hall terrace.

The rats are to be seen in many shop windows in the form of souvenirs and sweets.

The Pied Piper of Hamelin. – In 1284 a mysterious man in multicoloured clothes promised the townspeople of Hamelin that for a good reward he would free the town of rats and mice. He played his pipe and the rats came out and followed him to the banks of the Weser where they were drowned. But the reward was not forthcoming, so the man returned one Sunday when everyone was at church, and in revenge, played his pipes again, this time summoning the children out of the houses. There were 130 children and they followed him only to disappear forever; two only did not go but one was dumb and the other blind.

The historical version is that, in the 13C, over-population was such that a troop of young people were sent by the authorities without hope of return, to colonise faraway lands to the east.

■ **SIGHTS** *time: 1 hour*

Ratcatcher's House★ (Rattenfängerhaus). – This large well designed house dates from 1603. The symmetrical decoration of the façade is made up principally of differently sculptured bands of stonework further ornamented with carved busts and masks. The gable bears the typical Weser scrolls and pinnacles.

Marriage House★ (Hochzeitshaus). – The house, built between 1610 and 1617, acted as a reception building for burghers' weddings. Three elegant gables break the horizontal line of the building which is emphasised by cornices and bands of stone.

Dempter House (Demptersches Haus). – *On the Markt*. This house, which was built in 1607, is outstanding on account of its typically Weser Renaissance *Utlucht (see above)*.

Canonry (Stiftsherrenhaus). – *Osterstrasse no 8*. This remarkable mid-16C half-timbered house is adorned with corbels carved as gargoyles.

Wichmann House. – *Wendenstrasse no 8*. This is a rich half-timbered mansion of 1638 with a rounded doorway in the centre of a rectangular recess.

Rattenkrug. – *Bäckerstrasse no 16*. The Rattenkrug, built in 1568, includes an *Utlucht* and a tall five-storey gable in its design.

Collegiate Church (Münster). – From the public gardens to the south, the church appears to be protected by the massive polygonal tower above the transept which formed part of the 11C Romanesque basilica and was transformed in the 13C into a Gothic hall-church. Inside, the placing of the columns and the capitals, carved with palm-leaves or chequered, again make the raised transept the most interesting part of the building.

EXCURSIONS

Hamelschenburg★. – *11 km - 7 miles*. Leave Hamelin by ③, road no 83, and turn right in Emmern.

This **castle★**, with a moat and a pool, was built between 1588 and 1612 in the shape of a horseshoe and is one of the masterpieces of the Weser Renaissance *(p 141)*. The wing overlooking the road is the most ornate, with typical alternating smooth and embossed bands, an oriel immediately above the moat and four decorative gables.

Inside collections of pieces of furniture, arms and trophies. *(Open 1 April to 15 October, 10am to 1pm and 2 to 5pm; closed Mondays; 2.50DM.)*

The Abbey of Fischbeck. – *7 km - 4 miles*. Leave Hamelin by ⑤, road no 83 towards Rinteln. *Guided tours April to September Tuesdays to Saturdays, 9 to 11.30am and 2 to 5pm (Sundays only 2 to 5pm); 2DM*.

The Abbey, founded by Dame Helmbourgis, was officially recognised by Otto I in 955 (photocopies of original documents in the church). It is still used as a home for elderly Protestant women. The church is of the 12C with boxes, added in the 19C, on the 1st floor, allowing the women to participate in the service. The **crypt** is pure Romanesque: all the columns are topped by capitals decorated with different motifs. In the church itself, at the high altar, is a Gothic statue of Dame Helmbourgis. Left of the chancel is a moving Ecce Homo in sculpted wood while at the right of it is a 16C tapestry depicting the legend of the founding of the abbey. The cloister is also of the 12C.

HANN. MÜNDEN ★★

Michelin map **987** 15 – 24 km - 15 miles – north of Kassel – *Local map p 256* – Pop 28 000 *Town plan in Michelin Red Guide Deutschland*

Hannoversch Münden, or as it is commonly known, Hann. Münden or even H. (pronounced Ha) Münden, is situated where the Fulda and the Werra meet and flow on as the Weser. Towers and remains of the ramparts surround the old town with its more than 450 half-timbered houses built in various styles.

The River Confluence. – A stone, the Weserstein, was erected to commemorate poetically in a four-line inscription, known to all Germans, the union of the two rivers.

■ **SIGHTS** *tour: ¾ hour*

Leave the car near the château (Welfenschloss) a picturesque Renaissance building with scrolled brackets and corner posts, which houses the local museum (faiences, models of half-timbered houses). Take the Marktstrasse and left on Lange Strasse; at no 34, Doctor Eisenbarth, miracle doctor of the period, died; there is a commemorative wooden statue. By the Ritterstrasse and Ziegelstrasse return to St. Blaise's church.

St. Blaise's. – The hexagonal tower stands crushed beneath its steep slate roof.

Inside the building, which was transformed into a hall in the 15C, look in the south aisle at the tomb of Wilhelm of Brunswick, who died in 1503; his son's epitaph to the north of the chancel and, at the entrance to the chancel, a 14C font.

The Gothic façade on the square is the back of the town hall.

Town Hall★. – The town hall's main façade is typical Weser Renaissance *(p 141)* with three gables adorned with scrollwork, pyramids and statues.

The Old Houses★★ (Fachwerkhäuser). – Start at the Markt in front of the town hall, take a left turn on Lange Strasse as far as the 14C bridge over the Werra, turn round. There is a good view up the street.

Turn round and take the second alley on the left, the Sydekumstrasse. Walk round a bend to the right and you see the **Duchess Elizabeth Convent** (Herzogin-Elisabeth-Stift) and the château. Continue along the Vord Burg and return to the château by the Schulstrasse.

The times given after the distance for drives and excursions allow the visitor to see and enjoy the scenery.

HANOVER (HANNOVER)

Michelin map **987** 15 – Pop 565000 – *Built up area plan in Michelin Red Guide Deutschland*

Hanover is the capital of Lower Saxony and one of the principal economic centres of northern Germany. The rubber, automobile and record industries are among its most highly developed undertakings; the annual International Fair, its pavilions erected southeast of the built up area (Messegelände), is highly successful.

The town centre has been rebuilt to a plan which allows traffic to move freely and includes a traffic free shopping centre near the station. On the periphery, residential areas are developing, and stretches of water (Maschsee) and green spaces – first thought of in the 17C and even inaugurated with the laying out of the famous Herrenhausen Gardens (Herrenhäuser Gärten) – are now to be seen.

HISTORICAL NOTES

The House of Hanover. – In the 17C the Principality of Hanover fell to a branch of the House of Brunswick and Lüneburg *(p 90)*. The court moved to Hanover. Herrenhausen bestirred itself and became transformed; a period opened under the aegis of Princess Sophia, when the arts and letters she loved flourished. Handel, who wrote his first operas in Hamburg, was frequently invited to give concerts.

In 1676 the philosopher Leibniz arrived to take up the post, which he was to hold for forty years, of librarian to the court. In 1692 the principality became the Electorate of Brunswick and Lüneburg, the ninth in Germany.

From the Hanoverian Court to the Court of St. James's. – The marriage in 1658 of Duke Ernst-Augustus with the Princess Palatine Sophia, grand-daughter of James I, established a Hanoverian claim to the throne of England.

In 1714 the Elector Georg of Hanover, son of Princess Sophia, became King George I of England. The court left Herrenhausen and did not return until 1837 when the union of England and Hanover under one sovereign lapsed because of the application of the Salic law in Hanover. In England Queen Victoria mounted the throne; in Hanover it was her uncle Ernst-Augustus who did so.

The new Hanoverian king resided in the town and restored its former glory. But 1866 saw the downfall of the House of Hanover and the annexation of the kingdom by Prussia.

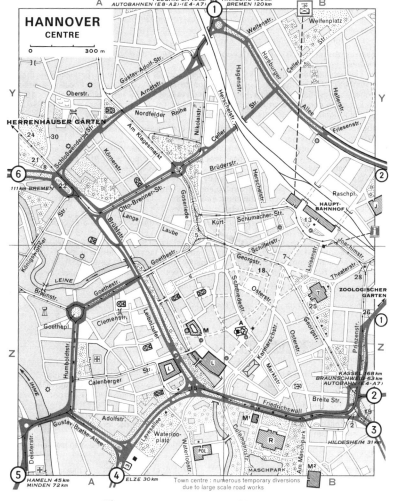

Aegidientorplatz	BZ 2	Friederikenplatz	AZ 15	Königsworther Platz	AY 22
Am Marstall	AZ 4	Georgstraße	BZ	Nienburger Straße	AY 24
Am Steintor	AY 5	Große Parkhofstraße	BZ 18	Opernplatz	BZ 25
Bahnhofstraße	BZ 7	Hildesheimer Straße	BZ 19	Schiffgraben	BZ 26
Bremer Damm	AY 8	Jägerstraße	AY 21	Thielenplatz	BZ 28
Ernst-August-Platz	BY 13	Karmarschstraße	BZ	Wilhelm-Busch-Straße	AY 30

- # MAIN SIGHTS *tour: 1½ hours*

Herrenhausen Gardens★★ (AY). – The Herrenhausen Gardens on the northwest side of the town consist of four quite different and separate gardens: the Grosser Garten, the Berggarten, the Georgengarten and the Welfengarten. They are linked by the Herrenhäuser Allee, an avenue of limes first laid out in 1726 (cars should come along the Nienburger Strasse).

Grosser Garten★★. – *Open from 8am to nightfall.*

The garden was begun in 1666; between 1696 and 1710, Princess Sophia remade it, transformed it and enlarged it for, as she wrote repeatedly, "that garden is my very life".

It forms a rectangle nearly 800 m - 900 yds long, surrounded, in the Dutch style, by a moat. The oldest part is a formal French pleasure garden divided into flower borders punctuated by statues of allegorical figures or Roman gods; in the centre a fountain plays, its waters falling in a liquid dome; on the left is an open air theatre, on the right a maze.

The intervening area is filled with fountains and is almost a model of garden design.

Finally at the southern end a mosaic of clipped hedges is cut by alleys linking small pools. The powerful central fountain (Grosse Fontäne) has a plume of 82 m - 269 ft (Nelson's Column 170 ft).

Southeast of the park, the small **Wilhelm Busch Museum** *(open 10am to 5pm – 1pm Sundays – 4pm 1 October to 31 March – closed Saturday afternoons and holidays; 0.50DM; brochure in English)* is devoted to the poet, illustrator and humorist (1832-1908) who was considered as the precursor of the comic strip. His *Max and Moritz* was very popular among the 19C German youth.

Berggarten★. – *Open from 8am to nightfall.*

This botanical garden, which was founded about the same time as the Grosser Garten, is smaller. It is known for its wealth of flowers, particularly rare ones *(tour of the orchid houses: 0.50DM)*. At the end of the main vista is the mausoleum of the Royal House of Hanover.

- # ADDITIONAL SIGHTS

Market Church (Marktkirche) (BZ A). – This 14C church is dominated by a four-gabled tower topped by a pointed bell turret. The bronze doors are by Marcks (1959).

Inside, in addition to tombs and epitaphs, there are a 15C carved and multicoloured **altarpiece**★★ (Schnitzaltar) depicting the Passion at the high altar, 14C stained glass windows in the chancel and, in the north aisle, a 15C bronze font.

Town Hall (BZ R). – This huge building draws tourists for the view from its dome *(ascent by lift March to November every hour from 10am to 5pm; ticket: 0.80DM)*. In the grand hall are models made of the town at different periods in its history – 1689, 1939, 1945 and at some future date when the present plans have been completed.

Kestner Museum★ (BZ M¹). – *Open 10am to 6pm (8pm Wednesdays); closed Mondays and holidays.*

This rich museum, which was founded by the son of Charlotte Kestner, better known, thanks to Goethe *(p 257)* as Charlotte Buff, displays on the second floor one of the finest collections in Germany of Egyptian antiquities. Four thousand years of history are recalled in galleries 15-20.

European decorative art is amply represented on the first floor; glass – gallery 6; German porcelain – galleries 7-9; pottery – galleries 11-13.

Museum of Lower Saxony (Niedersächsisches Landesmuseum) (BZ M²). – *Open: weekdays, 10am to 4pm; Sundays, 10am to 2pm; closed Mondays.*

This vast regional museum with early history, natural history, ethnography and fine arts departments has a special **prehistorical department**★ (Urgeschichtliche Abteilung) on the first floor, which shows the evolution of primitive civilisations in northwest Germany.

On the floor above is a **picture gallery** (Niedersächsische Landesgalerie) with several collections including those of the Guelph and Land Museums – German and Italian Primitives and 17C Dutch paintings – and the municipality, rich in 19 and 20C works, particularly German paintings. Modern sculpture completes the displays.

Historical Museum (AZ). – *Open 10am to 4pm (6pm Saturdays and Sundays, 8pm Tuesdays); closed Mondays.*

The museum has a section showing the history of the town and of Lower Saxony: mementoes of the Hanoverian Royal House and a collection of harnesses and carriages; in the ethnology section, note the beautiful cupboards and chests from Lower Saxony as well as peasant interiors, which have been reconstructed with their stoves and faience tiles.

Zoological Gardens (BZ). – *Open April to October, 8am to 7pm (5pm November to March); 3.50DM.*

The most attractive area is that of the antelopes, kangaroos and giraffes.

The HARZ Mountains ★

South of Goslar – Michelin map 987 16

The wooded Harz Mountains, covering an area of some 2 035 km² - 785 sq miles, stand as the most advanced of the bastions of northern Europe between the French Central Massif, the Rhineland Schist Ranges and the mountains of Bohemia and a Hercynian massif thrust upwards *(p 12)* in the Primary Era.

The range which provides a first obstacle to the west winds which sweep across the north German-Polish plain, together with the additional humidity of the forests, is consequently an area of high rainfall and much snow.

The Harz region is old, with a strong mining tradition once associated with gold and silver, today with zinc, lead and barium oxide.

The Upper Harz Mountains (Oberharz). – The Upper Harz lie for the most part in West Germany, although the highest point, the legendary Brocken (alt 1 142 m - 3 747 ft), scene of the Witches' sabbath *(p 29)*, is in the East Zone.

Streams, partially draining the upper areas which have been abandoned and become peat bogs, rush down through picturesque ravines, some of which have been drowned by dams.

The western Upper Harz Mountains with its excellent road network attracts many visitors. Danes, among others, enjoy the mountain surroundings where the villages have painted wooden houses and the green of the pine forests is, in turn, made brilliant or blotted out by rain and mist.

★ROUND TOUR STARTING FROM GOSLAR

137 km - 86 miles – about 4 hours – Local map below

Goslar★★. – *Description p 133.*
Leave Goslar by ③. The road rises as it goes through the Gose Valley and, after two large hairpin bends, reaches the plateau.
Continue to **Hahnenklee** where on entering, you can see a small church standing on an eminence. Built entirely of wood in 1908, it has a strong resemblance to Scandinavian churches (Stabkirche) *(open 10.30am to 12.30pm and 1.30 to 5.30pm; 2.50DM).*

Clausthal-Zellerfeld. – The former mining capital of the Upper Harz Mountains consists of two towns. At Zellerfeld is the **Museum of the Upper Harz Mountains** (Oberharzer Museum – open 9am to 1pm and 2 to 5pm; 2DM) where strange local mining methods which were practised until the last mine was closed in 1931 are displayed.

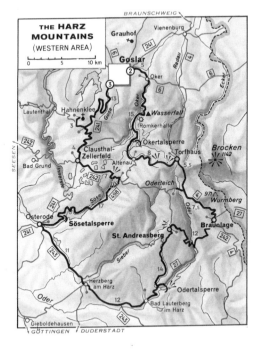

The **Church** (Marktkirche zum Hl. Geist) at Clausthal is built entirely of wood and so designed that the galleries appear majestically positioned and the light falls obliquely from windows placed just below the panelled vaulting *(open 16 May to 15 September, 9.30am to 5.30pm – Sundays, 2 to 5pm; 16 September to 15 March, 10am to noon and 3 to 4pm – Sundays, 2 to 4pm; the rest of the year, Saturdays 10am to noon and 2 to 4pm – Sundays 1 to 4pm).*

Follow the Upper Harz Road (Harz-Hochstrasse – no 242) which, once past an area dotted with ponds, affords, as it descends, wide **views★★** across the Altenau Depression towards the Tofhaus television masts and the Brocken.

At the foot of a tall embankment, turn right towards Osterode.

Söse Dam★ (Sösetalsperre). – Drinking water is piped from the dam to Bremen, 200 km - 124 miles – away. The banks of the reservoir have been abundantly planted with spruce firs and other decorative trees *(water sports allowed only in the basin immediately below the dam). No traffic on the south bank.*
The valley ends in the lowland area south of the Harz Mountains.

Osterode. – This picturesque town centred on the **Kornmarkt**, a wide square framed by half-timbered houses, was claimed as his home town by the sculptor Tilman Riemenschneider *(p 263).*

Oder Dam (Odertalsperre). – From the crest of the dam which controls the flow of the Oder, there is a pretty view of the artificial lake, the Oderstaussee, tapering away between wooded banks. Turn and after the lower dam basin, bear right to go deep into the mountains.

St. Andreasberg★. – *Tour of the mine: weekdays at 2.30pm; time: 1 hour; 1.50DM.*
The road leads first to the former silver mine (Silberbergwerk), the Samson, which lies in the valley bottom and was closed in 1910 but has since been reopened for tourists. The "Fahrkunst", an engine of ingenious simplicity which brought miners to the surface can be seen working: two poles side by side, with steps cut into them and a steady backwards and forwards movement. All the miner had to do was mark time on the two poles.
The town's **site★** at the top of a hill gives St. Andreasberg a wide horizon.

Braunlage★. – Braunlage, the most developed of the Upper Harz resorts, lies in an attractive plateau distinguished by the Wurmberg's wooded mass (alt 971 m - 3 186 ft), and delightful parks.
The road rises through the woods to Torfhaus. Turn left to make a detour to Oderteich.

Oderteich. – This small artificial lake was created in this romantic setting in 1721.
Turn and continue along the road towards Bad Harzburg.
On reaching the hotels of Torfhaus, the busy tourist centre of the Upper Harz within view of the Brocken, which can be identified by its observatory, bear left into the Altenau road.

From the second car park, the **view★** extends to the right over the Altenau Depression. Go down the road to the bottom; north of Altenau follow the course of the Oker Valley until it becomes submerged.

Oker Dam (Okertalsperre). – The dam holds a widely dispersed reservoir.
Below the dam, the valley narrows sharply. Beyond the Romkerhalle power station (right of the waterfall), the boiling torrent rushes past granite rocks, bizarrely polished, cut, fractured, balanced on high or standing like pinnacles raised to the sky.
When you come out on to the plain at Oker, take ② on the map to return to Goslar *(see map above).*

*If you would rather
plan your own itinerary
look at the map in this guide
of the principal sights and tourist regions (pp 4–8).*

HEIDELBERG ★★★

Michelin map **204** 9 – *Local maps pp 65 and 195* – Pop 130 000

Heidelberg, heart of the Romanticism celebrated by German writers, pleases many visitors with its translucent skies and the outline of its ruined castle. As the oldest university town in Germany, it has become a cultural centre of considerable influence.

General View★★★. – From the quays on the right bank of the Neckar – **Neuenheimer Landstrasse** and **Ziegelhäuser Landstrasse** – both above and below the picturesque **Old Bridge** (Alte Brücke or Karl-Theodor-Brücke), there are captivating views of the old town clustered at the foot of the Church of the Holy Spirit, and of the gaping red walls of the castle, against the green forest background: the German colours of the Romantic period.

HISTORICAL NOTES

The Rhineland Palatinate, of which Heidelberg was the political centre, owes its name to the title "palatines" given to the highest officers in the Holy Roman Empire who were in the sovereign's confidence. These functions and dignities disappeared in the 14C, except in the hereditary family ruling a group of territories whose approximate centre was the confluence of the Neckar with the Rhine. Through the wise government of these **palatine-electors** (Kurfürsten), the Electoral Palatinate (Kurpfalz) became one of the most advanced states of Europe.

The "Orleans War" (1688-97). – In the 16C, the electors, who had become Protestant, were continually reinforcing and embellishing their castle at Heidelberg. The Elector Karl-Ludwig restored his states in an exemplary manner after the Thirty Years War. In the hope of ensuring peace in the Rhineland and extending the influence of his house he married his daughter, Liselotte **(Elizabeth-Charlotte)** to "Monsieur", Philip of Orleans, brother of Louis XIV. The **Palatine Princess** did not pass unnoticed at the Court of France. Saint-Simon in his *Memoirs* returns frequently to her loud voice, her endless chatter and her intractable dislike of Mme de Maintenon.

When the son of Karl-Ludwig died without an heir in 1685, the marriage alliance, which was invoked by Louis XIV to assert his claim to the territories on the left bank of the Rhine, proved disastrous to the Palatinate and to Heidelberg. The town was laid waste, the castle sacked in the brutal campaign of 1689. Total disaster followed in 1693, when the town, was completely destroyed by fire. This catastrophe led to the rebuilding of the town in an uninspired Baroque style on the same foundations and with no new thoroughfares. Soon the electors abandoned the ruined castle, turning their attention instead to their residences at Mannheim and Schwetzingen.

■ ASCENT TO THE CASTLE★★★

access and tour: about 2 hours – excluding the interior

Take the car up the Neue Schlossstrasse to the castle.
The castle gardens and courtyard are open all day.

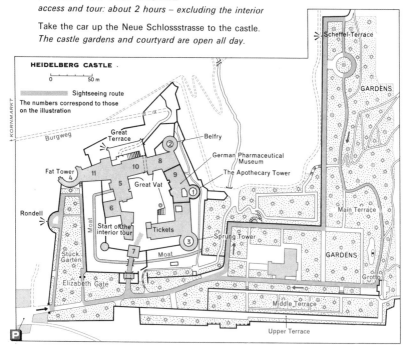

HEIDELBERG CASTLE

Rondell. – This promontory, which was once occupied by a battery of guns, now serves as a **viewpoint★** from which to see the town, the Neckar Valley with its wooded slopes and, in the distance, the Rhine Plain and the mountains of the Palatinate.

Fat Tower (Dicker Turm). – This tower is now an empty shell without even its upper part.

Elizabeth Gate (Elisabethentor). – Friedrich V had this graceful gateway erected in a single night in 1615. The gate, which forms a triumphal arch adorned with rustic motifs, was intended as a surprise for his wife, Elizabeth Stuart, daughter of James I.

Sprung Tower (Gesprengter Turm). – Since the end of the 16C this defence tower has included gun embrasures.

Continue along the terrace so as to see, close at hand, the castle's east side which is flanked by the Apothecary (Apothekerturm) and Clock Towers (Glockenturm), the first rounded and evenly pierced by windows, the second crowned with a polygonal coping.

The Gardens★ (Schlossgarten). – The gardens were terraced by Friedrich V between 1616 and 1619. The east side of the castle with its three towers can be seen best from the Scheffel terrace to the north. In the background, there is a **view★★** of the town lying on either side of the Hauptstrasse and the Old Bridge bestriding the Neckar.

THE COURTYARDS AND BUILDINGS

Cross the fortified bridge defended by the Gate Tower (Torturm). Immediately on the right is the fine Gothic hall of the Well Building.

Library (Bibliotheksbau). – This meticulous Gothic building which is not aligned with the façades on either side, has windows on all four sides. It contained the personal library of the princes, their collections of art objects and their treasure. The loggia is attractive.

Friedrich's Wing (Friedrichsbau). – This wing with its two festooned gables was added by Friedrich IV. The façade design remains somewhat rigid, marked by the superimposition of the classic orders of Antiquity – Doric, Ionic and Corinthian – rediscovered at the time of the Renaissance. But the repetition of certain motifs such as the intersection of pilasters and cornices, creating contrasts of light and shade, presaged the Baroque style which was to follow. The large statues (restored) honour the House of Wittelsbach, the electors' forbears.

The entrance to the passageway leading to the Great Terrace is to the right of the palace.

Great Terrace (Altan). – This great terrace, contemporary with Friedrich's Wing, which presents, to this side, the castle's only ornamented façade, looks down on to the roofs of Old Heidelberg, affording a **view★** of the town, the Neckar and the Old Bridge.

Return to the courtyard.

The Mirror Room Wing (Gläserner Saalbau). – Only a shell remains of this building, which, however, retains a series of galleries in tiers in the Italian Renaissance manner.

Otto-Heinrich Wing (Ottoheinrichsbau). – This palace was built by the Elector Otto Heinrich, who in the three years of his reign (1556-9) opened wide the Palatinate to new ideas particularly on religious and artistic matters. The building marks a point in the history of civil architecture in Germany, inaugurating as it did the fertile late Renaissance period.

Horizontal lines predominate; the ornament, in accordance with contemporary taste, is a mixture of Biblical and mythological symbols. The doorway, in the form of a triumphal arch and in which the well known sculptor of that time, Alexandre Colin of Malines (1526-1612), collaborated, displays the electors' fine armorial bearings: the Palatinate lion and the lozenges of the House of Wittelsbach surround the globe surmounted by a cross which symbolised the Empire. Crowning the edifice was the effigy of the builder in a medallion and, above the helmets topping the blazons, his initials OHPC (Otto-Heinrich, County Palatine).

End of the Feudal Period (and later rebuilding)

1) The Apothecary's Tower (14C) – 2) Belfry (14C) – 3) The Broken Tower (15C)

Gothic-Renaissance Transitional Period

(Ludwig V – 1508-44)

4) The Fat Tower (1533) – 5) The Women's Wing – 6) The Library – 7) The Gate Tower

Renaissance Period

8) The Mirror Room Wing (1549) – 9) Otto-Heinrich Wing (1566)

Renaissance-Baroque Transitional Period

10) Friedrich's Wing (Friedrich IV – 1592-1610) and below the Great Terrace – "Altan" – 11) The English Wing (Friedrich V – 1610-32)

(After the aerial photo by Strähle no. 3460)

Heidelberg Castle.

INTERIOR *tour: 1 hour*

Guided tours: 1 April to 31 October, 9am to noon and 1 to 5.30pm (6pm Sundays and 4pm in winter); 2DM; brochure in English.

Of all the rooms, the Great Vat is worth while and can be visited separately.

Great Vat (Grosses Fass). – *Same times; 0.70DM.* The enormous vat, which dates from the end of the 18C, has a capacity of 2 200 hl - 49 000 gallons – and supports a platform where wine-tasting or dancing can take place. This Bacchic curiosity and the memory of its guardian, the jester-dwarf Perkeo, who is recalled in a figurine and was known for his hair-raising alcoholic capacity and his ingenious clock, are part of Heidelberg folklore.

■ ADDITIONAL SIGHTS

In the Castle

German Pharmaceutical Museum★ (Deutsches Apotheken-Museum). – *Open 10am to 5pm (Saturdays and Sundays only 1 December to 31 March from 11am); 1DM. Entrance beneath the steps of the Otto-Heinrich Wing (see above).*

Fine 18 and 19C apothecaries' furniture. The most curious sections are the collections of ancient prescriptions whose ingredients are enough to make weak stomachs turn! An alchemist's laboratory has been reconstituted in the Apothecary's Tower.

In Town

Marktplatz (Y). – The square, which lies between the Church of the Holy Spirit and the Rathaus, is filled, on certain mornings, with market gardeners' stalls. From the east end of the church you get a good view of the castle.

Church of the Holy Spirit (Heilig-Geist-Kirche) (Y E). – The church is an example of the late Gothic style. As in earlier times covered stalls stand against the walls between the buttresses. The central part of the building and the chancel are in the hall style *(p 24)*, but galleries above the aisles reduce the height on the sides. The well lit **chancel** was formerly the palatine electors' sepulchre but since 1693 only the tomb of Ruprecht III remains.

The Knight's Mansion★ (Haus zum Ritter) (Y N). – This glorious mansion, which was built in 1592 and is a late Renaissance masterpiece, owes its name to the bust of St. George in knightly armour which crowns the rich, scrolled pediment.

University Library (Universitätsbibliothek) (Z A). – *The exhibition gallery (Ausstellungsraum) is open from 11am to noon; closed Saturdays, Sundays and holidays.*

Books and manuscripts★ (Buchausstellung) are displayed, including a facsimile of the early 14C Manesse manuscript (Manessische Liederhandschrift), a jewel of mediaeval poesy and illumination. Another important work is the *Desk Knaben Wunderhorn* or *Child with the Magic Horn* by Achim von Arnim and Clemens Brentano which was published in Heidelberg in 1805 and marks the advent of popular verse in German literature.

Electoral Palatinate Museum★ (Kurpfälzisches Museum). – *Hauptstrasse 97* (Y M¹). *Open 10am to 1pm and 2 to 5pm; closed Mondays; 1DM.*
The museum is partly in a Baroque palace. The galleries displaying the history of the Palatinate exhibit a cast of the jaw of the prehistoric "Heidelberg man" (500 000 BC). In the German Primitives department may be seen the **altarpiece of the Twelve Apostles★★** (Windsheimer Zwölfbotenaltar) by Tilman Riemenschneider (1509). The second floor, on the Hauptstrasse side, is devoted exclusively to **works from the Romantic Period★★** (Gemälde und Zeichnungen der Romantik), particularly iconography of the town and castle.

Students' Gaol (Studentenkarzer) (Y B). – *To visit apply to the caretaker, Augustinergasse no 2.*
Between 1778 and 1914 the gaol was occupied by too-uproarious students. Many passed their enforced leisure in carving inscriptions, coats of arms and outlines upon the walls commemorating their incarceration which was considered by many a mark of distinction.

EXCURSIONS

Philosophers' Walk★ (Philosophenweg) (Y). – *About 1 hour on foot Rtn.*
This, the best known Heidelberg walk, starts from the Bergstrasse in the suburb of Neuenheim (right bank of the Neckar) and, rising up the Heiligenberg slopes, affords enchanting **views★** of the town and castle *(direct access from the old bridge).*

Molkenkur (Z); Königstuhl. *– 5 km - 3 miles – about ¾ hour.* Leave Heidelberg by the castle rise (Neue Schlossstrasse) which continues as the Molkenkurweg.

Molkenkur. – The restaurant terrace affords a **view★** of the castle towers and walls below.
Continue the climb through the woods by way of the Gaiberger Weg. After crossing a valley, bear diagonally left towards the Königstuhl summit.

Königstuhl. – From the television tower platform *(lift: 1DM; October to March, Saturdays and Sundays, 10am to 5pm)* a **panorama** unfolds of the Neckar Valley opening out on to the Rhine Plain on emerging from the Odenwald.

Military Cemetery (Ehrenfriedhof). *– 3 km - 2 miles – plus 1 hour sightseeing.* Leave Heidelberg by ③, the Rohrbacher Strasse. 800 m - ½ mile from Seegarten, bear left into the Steigerweg. After two hairpin bends, turn right and park the car at the main gate.
The 1914-18 cemetery is formal; the 1939-45 one, landscaped. From a memorial rotunda, shaded paths radiate through silent woodlands.

HEILBRONN

Michelin map **206** 11 – *Local maps pp 151 and 195* – Pop 117 000
Town plan in Michelin Red Guide Deutschland

The town, which has been rebuilt, is a wine growing basin in the Neckar Valley.

St. Kilian's. – The Gothic church (13C nave – 15C chancel) rises above the Kiliansplatz now restored to look much as it did formerly. The church's Renaissance **tower★**, which is highly ornate, has an octagonal upper part with superimposed pierced lantern turrets. Inside is a 15C carved altarpiece.

Weinsberg; Wartberg. – *Excursion of 8 km - 5 miles – plus ½ hour on foot Rtn.* Leave Heilbronn by ②, road no 39. Leave the car at **Weinsberg** in a car park at the back of the church and climb to the Weibertreu ruins *(½ hour on foot Rtn)*. Popular tradition relates how in 1140 the women in the besieged castle were told by the enemy outside that they could leave but only with what they could carry. The women came out carrying their husbands on their backs.

Turn; but before the final descent into Heilbronn, bear right into the **Wartberg** vineyard road. From the observation tower, there is a **panorama** of the Heilbronn Basin.

HEILSBRONN

between Nuremberg and Ansbach (Michelin map **987** 26) – Pop 6 600

Heilsbronn Church, which was once the abbey to a Cistercian monastery and is now a Protestant institution, contains attractive works of art.

Church (Ehemalige Klosterkirche). – *Open 8.30am to noon and 1 to 6pm (5pm in winter); Sundays, 11am to noon; 0.50DM.*

There remain of the first Romanesque building, founded in 1132, the austere nave and the north aisle. In 1263 the apsidal chapels were pulled down to allow the chancel to be extended to the east in the Gothic style. In the 14 and 15C, the church was enlarged to contain the tombs of the Nuremberg branch *(p 165)* of the Hohenzollern princes.

The altarpiece, *The Three Magi*, at the high altar, was carved and painted in about 1520 by Nuremberg painters (School of Wolgemuth and Dürer) and the delightful **altarpiece of the Saints of Intercession★** (Nothelferaltar) of the same period is from the Veit Stoss school of sculpture *(p 30)*.

HELIGOLAND ★★ (HELGOLAND)

Michelin map **987** 4 – Pop 2 500

Thousands of tourists each year, attracted by the short sea cruise, make for the red limestone cliffs of the Island of Heligoland. It lies 70 km - 43 miles – out from the mouth of the River Elbe and was for a long time held by the English who, however, exchanged it for Zanzibar in 1890.

A Fantastic Rock. – The island, which for centuries has been undermined by the sea (its actual area is less than 1 km² - ⅓ sq mile), was very nearly wiped off the map in 1947 by the British who tried unsuccessfully to blow up what had been a submarine base during the war with 7 000 tons of explosives. It was returned to Germany in 1952 and is once more a tourist centre. The built up area which is divided by the cliff-face into two levels (Unterland and Oberland) has been entirely reconstructed. An aquarium, an ornithological observatory and a marine biology station give to this site great scientific importance.

Heligoland has many attractions to offer the visitor: cliff walks, sea bathing from the lonely but sheltered Düne sand beach as well as tax-free tobacco, sweets and spirits.

Access. – There is a daily service from Cuxhaven and, in summer, the more comfortable Hapag-Hadag vessels which sail from Hamburg (St. Pauli boat station, stage 9 – *map p 138*). A day excursion allows only about 4 hours on the island *(leave Hamburg about 7.30am; Rtn about 11pm)*. Rtn fares: 48DM from Hamburg; 40DM from Cuxhaven. Disembarkation at Heligoland is in the roadstead by tender. Other boat services ply to Heligoland during the season from the coastal ports and the Frisian Islands.

HERSFELD, Bad ★

Michelin map **987** 25 – Pop 30 000

The hydromineral spa, Bad Hersfeld, offers visitors all the charm of a bustling small town surrounded by one of the most undulating forest regions of Hesse.

Its July Drama Festival is well known for the majestic décor provided by its ruined abbey which stands between the main square, the Marktplatz, and the spa area proper.

Abbey Ruins★ (Ruine der Abteikirche). – *Open 15 March to 31 October, 10am to noon and 1 to 5pm; 0.50DM. Brochure in English.*

The ruins reveal the noble proportions of a church which dated back to the Ottonian period *(p 23)* and whose length was more than 100 m - 300 ft.

The pronounced transept formed an unencumbered transverse chamber. In the 11 and 12C, the abbey, while keeping its general plan, was transformed to the Romanesque style with two chancels. The building was destroyed by French troops in 1761.

The western apse, built upon a rectangular base and flanked by a solitary Romanesque tower, is impressive, particularly when seen from inside.

The Romanesque tower of St. Catherine (1120), standing apart northeast of the church, was formerly part of the abbey buildings. It contains the 900-year-old convent clock.

Old Quarter. – The blunt tower of the parish church emerges from a picturesque group of burghers' houses with wooden walls near the Marktplatz. Note the sacristan's house (1480) and the pastor's Baroque house (1714) with its beautiful door.

Town Hall. – There is a good **view★** of the church from the town hall forecourt. This building was erected in 1600.

EXCURSION

Rotenburg an der Fulda. – *21 km - 13 miles.* Take road no 27 into Bebra, on leaving the town take road no 83. The village situated in a narrow part of the Fulda Valley has preserved its ancient charm. From the bridge, the view of the houses huddled against the cliff, which drops vertically to the Fulda, is remarkable. The centre of town, filled with stone and half-timbered houses, has a town hall with a Rococo staircase which takes you to the Renaissance doorway. The château, now a School of Finance, recalls the time of the Landgraves of Hesse.

Hildesheim remains the capital of Ottonian Romanesque art *(p 23)* in Germany thanks to the reconstruction of the buildings damaged during the war.

The Thousand Year Old Rose Tree. – On an evening in 815 Ludwig the Debonair returned tired after the chase and, so the legend goes, hid his personal shrine in a rose bush before going to sleep. The following morning he could not find it. Taking this as a sign from heaven he founded first a chapel and then a bishopric on the spot; round this Hildesheim developed.

In the winter of 1945, the rose tree, although apparently burnt in an air raid, suddenly burst into flower; the town also has returned to life.

■ SIGHTS *time: 1½ hours*

Cathedral★ (Dom). – *Free visit or guided tours, 10am (11.30am Sundays) to 1pm and 3 to 4.30pm (4pm in winter); closed Saturday afternoons; 0.50DM.*

The present building is a reconstruction of the 11C basilica, except that the side chapels were rebuilt, as they once were, in Gothic style and the transept dome is modelled on the cupola added in the 18C.

The interior has kept the original basilical simplicity. In the nave the alternate use of single pillars and double columns is typical of the Old Saxony school of architecture.

There are fine **works of art★** (Kunstwerke) in the church.

An immense 11C chandelier hangs at the transept crossing. On the north side, in the last side chapel, is a rare carved font dating from the 13C, borne aloft by four figures symbolising the rivers of the Apocalypse. An 11C bronze column depicting the Life of Christ lies in the south transept.

The two-storey Romanesque **cloister★** *(guided tours only)* lies at the east end of the cathedral. The thousand year old rose tree is at the foot of the apse.

The bronze west doors *(guided tours only)*, which are an example of primitive Romanesque sculpture, depict scenes from the Old and New Testaments.

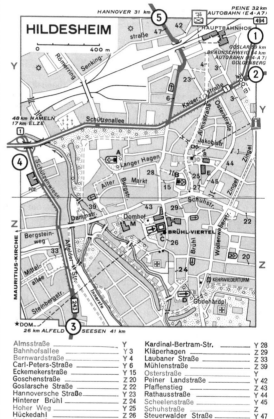

HILDESHEIM

Almsstraße	Y
Bahnhofsallee	Y 3
Bernwardstraße	Y 4
Carl-Peters-Straße	Y 6
Eckemekerstraße	Y 15
Goschenstraße	Z 20
Goslarsche Straße	Z 22
Hannoversche Straße	Y 23
Hinterer Brühl	Y 24
Hoher Weg	Y 25
Hückedahl	Y 26
Judenstraße	Y 27
Kardinal-Bertram-Str.	Y 28
Kläperhagen	Z 29
Laubaner Straße	Z 33
Mühlenstraße	Z 39
Osterstraße	Y
Peiner Landstraße	Y 42
Pfaffenstieg	Y 43
Rathausstraße	Y 44
Scheelenstraße	Y 45
Schuhstraße	Z
Steuerwalder Straße	Y 47
Zingel	Y

Roemer-Pelizaeus Museum★ (Z M). – *Open 10am to 4.30pm (1pm Saturdays); closed Mondays, Christmas and 1 January; 1DM.*

The collection of Egyptian Antiquities, which is among Germany's richest, is the main feature of the museum. In Gallery II are the coffin tomb of the officer Uhemka and a number of funerary statues going back to the Antique Empire in the 3rd millennium BC, including those of Prince Hem On (3rd chamber) and the scribe Heti (1st chamber).

St. Michael's★ (St. Michaelis-Kirche) (Y A). – The church, early 11C but rebuilt since 1945, is typical of early Romanesque Ottonian art in Old Saxony in its aged basilical plan with two apses and also in its elevation. In the nave, where the 13C painted ceiling has been re-erected, note the alternate single pillars and double columns *(see above)*, and in the transepts the two tier galleries and rough square capitals, a first essay in the Romanesque style. Of the original decoration an Angel screen remains to the right of the west chancel – on your left as you enter. Above is a balustrade decorated on its inner side with thirteen angels in the corners.

The Brühl (Z). – The southern area of this quarter escaped damage during the war and has some fine old houses. Typical of old Hildesheim is the Hinterer Brühl with ancient houses (nos 9, 15, 17, 20, and no 12a round the corner) and a good view of St. Gothard's Church.

St. Gothard's (St. Godehardkirche) (Z D). – This 12C church has an elegant silhouette marked by the slender pointed roofs of its three towers.

St. Andrews' (St. Andreaskirche) (Y B). – This late 14C church is the only original building still standing in the mediaeval quarter. It has an outstanding **façade★** pierced by great Gothic windows and an asymmetrical tower bearing a spire which rises to 118 m - 367 ft.

St. Antony's Chapel (Antoniuskapelle) (Z C). – *South of the cathedral cloisters; enter from Hückedahl Street. Open daily 6.30am to 5.30pm. Guided tours above include chapel.*

A lovely Renaissance **rood-screen★** (Lettner) has been installed in the chapel.

Templars' House (Y E). – A fine 15C house with a Gothic façade adorned with a Renaissance oriel window.

Church of St. Maurice (St. Mauritius-Kirche). – Located in the Moritzberg section west of Hildesheim, the church and monastery were built in 11C. St. Maurice has a Romanesque exterior: three naves and a large transept. The interior was transformed during the Baroque period. The Romanesque cloister, however, preserves a special atmosphere.

EXCURSION

Galgenberg. – *4 km - 2½ miles.* Leave Hildesheim by ② on the road to Goslar. Turn right after having crossed the railway and follow the sign.

The Galgenberg offers a pleasant walk through its wooded hills. From Bismarck's Column there is a nice view of Hildesheim and the surrounding countryside.

The HOHENLOHE

Michelin map **206** 1, 11

The Hohenlohe Plain, lying between the heights of the Swabian Forest and the Tauber Valley which is followed by the Romantic Road, remains a traditional and profoundly rural area. Even German visitors sometimes have difficulty in understanding the local speech.

Small sleepy towns, castles with the typical German Renaissance round carved pediments – a dozen are still owned by the House of Hohenlohe – valleys, planted with a few vines and watered by the rushing, twisting Jagst or the calmer Kocher, invite a return to the past.

① FROM HEILBRONN TO SCHWÄBISCH HALL
by the Jagst Valley, Neuenstein and Waldenburg
97 km - 60 miles – about 4½ hours – Local map below

Heilbronn. – *Description p 149.*

Neckarsulm. – *Description p 195.*

Bad Wimpfen**. – *Excursion of 5.5 km - 3½ miles – from Bad Friedrichshall. Description p 259.*

Neudenau. – Gracious Marktplatz overlooked by houses with wooden walled gables.
The appearance of Möckmühl belfry and tower adds considerably to the area between Neudenau and Jagsthausen in the lower Jagst Valley.

Jagsthausen. – The Götzenburg, a castle completely restored in the 19C and now a hotel, was the birthplace of the knight, Götz von Berlichingen (1480-1562), who was immortalised in Goethe's drama *(see also p 195)* of the same name. Open air performances are given in July and August.

Schöntal. – *6 km - 3½ miles – from Jagsthausen.* The town lies entirely within the precincts of an old Cistercian abbey built in a rustic setting in the Jagst Valley. Go through a covered way to the inner courtyard. *To visit, apply to the caretaker or the sacristan.*

The **church*** (1727) is in the style of a Baroque hall-church, although the free-standing pillars give the whole a Gothic sweep. Four precious 17C alabaster **altarpieces**** (Alabasteraltäre) stand against the pillars closest to the transept crossing.

The oustanding sight on the tour of the old abbey buildings is the abbot's antechamber, known as the **Orders' Room*** (Ordensaal) since it is entirely faced with small panels painted to show the 300 religious and military orders extant in the 18C.

The road crosses the bridge dividing the Jagst and the Kocher Valleys before rising to the level of the Hohenlohe Plain proper. The three Waldenburg towers soon appear on the left.

Öhringen. – *Tour: ¼ hour.* The late 16C Gothic hall-type **church*** serves as a necropolis for the House of Hohenlohe. Enter through the cloister. Note in the chancel a monument to Philip of Hohenlohe (d 1606), son-in-law of William of Orange. At the base, high reliefs depict scenes from the Netherlands' War of Independence. The **St. Margaret altarpiece*** (Margarethen-Altar), in the large north chapel, is a delicate late 15C work.

Neuenstein. – *Open 1 March to 30 November, 8am to noon and 1.30 to 6pm; the rest of the year, 10am to noon (except Saturdays and Sundays) and 1.30 to 4pm; time: 1 hour; 3DM.*
The best view of this heavy 16-17C castle with its scrollworked Renaissance gables is from the entrance to the town coming from Öhringen.
A visit gives an impression of daily life in a small German court – in this case that of the Hohenlohe's. Bacchic curiosities (a precious tankard in the form of a stag made in Augsburg in 1580), richly encrusted furniture, glass, ivories are much in evidence. The mediaeval kitchen has a corner for slaughtering animals for the table.
The panoramic ascent to Waldenburg is succeeded by the woods over the Waldenburg hills.

Waldenburg. – The fortified town of Waldenburg, sited at the top of a spur of the low ranges of the Swabian Forest (Schwäbische Wald), enabled the Hohenlohes to command the plain. The town has three distinct fortified centres separated by moats.

In the final descent, the view extends across the Schwäbisch Hall Plain and its many villages.

Schwäbisch Hall**. – *Description p 229.*

The HOHENLOHE

② *FROM SCHWÄBISCH HALL TO BAD MERGENTHEIM
by Langenburg and the Jagst Valley
64 km - 40 miles – about 3 hours – Local map p 151

Schwäbisch Hall**. – *Description p 229.*

If you arrive in Langenburg from the south, you will see the castle, in all its magnitude, dominating the Jagst Valley.

Langenburg. – The fortified town of Langenburg has been built round a crest encircled, at its base, by a bend in the Jagst and crowned by the castle of the Hohenlohes. From the terraced gardens to the left of the avenue of approach, there is a view of the valley to the south.

Castle open from Easter to 15 October, 8.30am to noon and 1.30 to 6pm; 2DM. Brochure in English.

Go through to the **inner courtyard*** (Innenhof), the heart of the 15C fortified castle which was enlarged in the 17 and 18C. The courtyard, framed by ornamental pediments with scrollwork, and overlooked by tiered galleries, has a heavy Renaissance appearance overall which is nevertheless impressive. The wing dominated by the original keep of 1575 is embellished with three balconies with pierced balustrades.

The apartments open to visitors contain Hohenlohe mementoes.

The drive below Langenburg in the Jagst Valley is delightful when the fruit blossom is out (early May). The covered bridge at Unterregenbach is succeeded by the fortified house in the form of a tower which dominates Buchenbach, then by Jagstberg, built in green surroundings at the top of the left side of the valley.

Stuppach. – *Description p 178.*

Bad Mergentheim*. – *Description p 178.*

HOHENZOLLERN Castle *
Michelin map **206** 15 – 5 km - 3 miles – south of Hechingen – *Local map p 240*

Hohenzollern Castle, tall and bristling with towers on its hill separated from the main Swabian Jura Massif, looks, from whichever side you approach it, like a legendary fortress.

The Cradle of the Hohenzollerns. – Few in Germany can count such a tremendous rise in their family fortunes. The Zollerns were originally Swabian overlords, who through marriage became the Burgraves of Nuremberg and soon took the grander name of Hohenzollern. From this root sprang several branches which were to suffer diverse fortunes.

In 1415 the Emperor gave the Frankish line the hereditary title to the march of Brandenburg which brought its holder also the dignity of Elector. The Margraves of Brandenburg, who from 1618 were also the rulers of Prussia, gained even greater influence in the Empire and abroad. From the time that they were crowned Kings of Prussia in 1701 they worked for the unification of Germany and succeeded in re-establishing a German Empire in 1871 under Wilhelm I. The glory was brief, however, since it lasted only half a century – Kaiser Wilhelm II abdicated in 1918.

The name lives on today in the Hohenzollerns of Prussia and Sigmaringen. Prince Ludwig Ferdinand of Prussia, grandson of the Kaiser, is the present head of the family.

Ascent to the castle*. – *3 km - 2 miles – from road no 27 – plus 1 hour sightseeing.* The **site***** even more than the castle, which was completed in 1867, justifies its fame.

A mini bus provides transport between the car park and the castle; 1DM.

Entrance to the castle: 3DM. Guided tours of the chapels and apartments, 8am to 6pm (5pm in winter). The castle courtyard is reached by a fortified spiral ramp.

The two chapels are particularly interesting: the 12C Catholic Chapel of St. Michael, the only authentic feudal part of the castle that remains, possesses the oldest stained glass windows in Germany. The Protestant chapel in the north wing contains, since 1952, when they were moved from Potsdam, the tombs of the King-Sergeant *(p 66)* and Frederick the Great. Precious mementoes of Frederick II – uniforms, decorations, flutes and tobacco jars – may be seen in the treasury (Schatzkammer).

Before leaving the castle, make a tour of the ramparts, beginning left of the drawbridge so as to see the **panorama*** below of the Neckar depression and the Swabian Jura.

HOLSTEINISCHE SCHWEIZ *
Michelin map **987** 5, 6 – northwest of Lübeck

Holsteinische Schweiz or the Holstein Lake or Swiss District (highest point: the Bungsberg, 168 m - 550 ft) lies only a few miles from the Baltic beaches and has only one thing in common with the Alps: its moraine formation. The gently undulating wooded landscape, scattered with lakes often separated by only a narrow ridge of land, has made it popular with tourists.

The traveller will remember the trees which often form a green vault above the road.

Plön*. – The town lies beside the **Great Plön Lake*** (Grosser Plöner See), the biggest lake in Holsteinische Schweiz. It has all the air of a tourist centre with its Fegetasche beach – departure point for many boat trips – and its massive castle. Several famous Frenchmen, including La Fayette and the Duke of Liancourt, sought refuge in Plön or nearby localities at the end of the French Revolutionary period.

Leave the car on the Marktplatz, near the church, and walk up a paved alley to the castle terrace where there is a **view*** of the Great Plön Lake and its islands. Continue beyond the old stables to the Princes' Pavilion (Prinzenhaus), a fine Baroque building of brick to which two wings were inharmoniously added in the 19C.

Eutin*. – The old kernel of this town with its buildings all of brick has retained an 18C character and appeal. The moated **castle**, dating from 1723 *(guided tours: 15 May to 30 September at 11am, 3 and 4pm; closed Mondays; 3DM)* is surrounded by a landscaped park which extends to the shores of the Great Eutin Lake (Grosser Eutiner See). Strollers enjoy the long avenue of limes. Opera is given in the open air theatre during the summer season, thus honouring Eutin's most illustrious son, Karl Maria von Weber (1786-1826 – *p 28*).

Malente-Gremsmühlen. – A wooded isthmus in the heart of the lake region is the **setting*** for this resort, Malente-Gremsmühlen, which makes a good departure point for boat trips (motorboat trips of the "Five Lakes" westwards and the Kellersee, eastwards).

HOMBURG VOR DER HÖHE, Bad ★

Michelin map **204** 5 – *Local map p 242* – Pop 53 000
Town plan in Michelin Red Guide Deutschland

Bad Homburg lives at the peaceful pace of all medium sized German spas. It lies near the Taunus woods and is a favourite outing for Frankfurt citizens.

Castle. – *Open 10am to 5pm, 4pm from 1 November to 28 February; closed Mondays; 1DM.*
The main buildings, overlooked by the tall White Tower, which is a reminder of the old fortified castle, were the residence of the Landgraves of Hesse-Homburg from 1680 to 1866.
A visit evokes the memory of Frederick II (1633-1708), the Prince of Homburg in Kleist's drama. The great warrior appears in high relief on the doorway of the second inner courtyard and as a bust (by Andreas Schlüter – *p 26*), in the vestibule. A particularly well known exhibit is the Landgrave's wooden leg, known as the "silver leg" as the joints are of silver.

Castle Park (Schlosspark). – The White Tower can be seen from the edge of the pool.

Spa Park★ (Kurpark). – The park is the spa centre: monumental buildings containing the springs are dispersed over shady lawns.

EXCURSION

Saalburg★. – *6 km - 3 miles – by ④, the Usingen Road, plus 1 hour sightseeing (open 8am to 5pm; closed afternoons of 24 and 31 December; 1.20DM).*
The Saalburg Camp, reconstituted on the orders of Kaiser Wilhelm II, was built along the *limes* (fortified lines marking the northern limits of Roman occupation between the Rhine and the Danube) on the Taunus heights. Note the external trenches and, in the central courtyard, the buildings which now house the museum.

HÖXTER

Michelin map **987** 15 – *Local map p 256* – Pop 35 500

The Renaissance and the Baroque seem to unite in the gay, coloured washed houses of Höxter which also often have decorated wooden side walls. As in other towns in the central part of the Weser Valley the old roofs are covered in soft pink limestone tiles.

■ **SIGHTS** *time: ½ hour*

Deanery★ (Dechanei). – *To the right of St. Nicholas'.* This twin gabled house dates from 1561; a polygonal oriel stands out from the façade.
Return to the Markstrasse and go in the opposite direction to the main crossroads.

Westerbachstrasse. – Several picturesque **half-timbered houses★** line the start of the street on the right. No 4 has highly decorative woodwork.
Take the Weserstrasse on the left to reach the town hall (Rathaus).

Town Hall. – The staircase tower and an oriel window break the lines of the façade.

St. Kilian's. – The church, which dates back to the 11C in its oldest parts, has a high façade flanked on either side by much pierced towers. In the chancel stand a font dating from 1610 and an outstanding Renaissance **pulpit★★** adorned with rare alabaster motifs.

EXCURSION

Corvey. – *2 km - 1 mile – plus ½ hour sightseeing.* Leave Höxter by the Bahnhofstrasse which continues as the avenue leading to Corvey.
The only part of the original Carolingian **abbey building** that remains is the impressive west façade. The lower parts go back to the 9C *(see Romanesque Art, p 23). Church open April to October, 9am to 1pm and 2 to 6pm; November to March, 10am to 1pm and 2 to 4pm; 0.70DM.*
Enter through a Carolingian pre-nave, a low hall with five aisles known as the crypt. Above is a square church, two storeys high on to which the so-called Emperor's gallery opened. The remainder of the church is Baroque as are the former abbatical buildings.
The **château** *(open 1 April to 31 October, 9am to 6pm; 2DM)*, is converted into a museum. The 1st floor is devoted to the history and folklore of Corvey. The poet Hoffmann von Fallersleben who wrote the German national anthem, worked here the last 14 years of his life as librarian. Folklore, prehistoric art and natural history are on the second floor.

HUSUM

Michelin map **987** west of 5 – Pop 25 000

Husum, a small fishing port and the sailing point for ships going to the Halligen Islands, is also a market town known to all German copers for its horse and farm animal fairs.
Husum is the birthplace of **Theodor Storm** (1817-88), a writer and regional poet.

North Friesland Museum★ (Nordfriesches Museum). – *Open weekdays 10am to noon and 2 to 5pm (4pm in winter); Sundays 10am to 5pm (4pm in winter); closed Saturdays in winter; 2DM.*
The display on the 1st floor shows the geographic regions (Geest, Marsch, etc.) of the German coast *(p 128)*, the cataclysms of 1362 and 1634, the different phases in the war against the sea and the reclamation of the land by polders – known as Köge (singular: Koog). There are models of different kinds of farms and windmills.

EXCURSIONS

The Halligen Islands★. – *For boat times apply to harbour information office.* This archipelago of small and flat islands scattered in the North Sea, is worth a boat tour *(binoculars are recommended)*. Created, re-formed or destroyed during the past centuries by the high tides, these islands contain small villages of thatched cottages with about 400 inhabitants: fishermen as well as farmers whose isolation has just recently ended. To keep them company are cattle, salt-pasture sheep, seals and an infinite variety of sea birds (under rigorous protection). On the largest of the archipelago islands, **Langeness** (about 1 000 ha - 2 470 acres), salt is the main staple.

Friedrichstadt. – *15 km southwards - 9 miles – plus ½ hour sightseeing.* This small town, bearing the name of its protector, was founded in 1621 by Dutch Protestants, who were given hospitality by the Duke Friedrich III von Holstein. Attractive **scenes,** reminiscent of 300 years age, show uniform lines of houses with curvilinear gables, bordering straight streets and canals.

IDAR-OBERSTEIN

Michelin map **203** 7 – Pop 38 000

Oberstein lies in a surprising enclosed site★ along the bottom of a gorge carved by the Nahe through layers of volcanic rock. The town forms a single built-up area with Idar which spreads out more expansively along the tributary of the same name.

Idar-Oberstein, whose surroundings once held many agate and mineral deposits, remains a centre for cutting and polishing precious stones and costume jewellery manufacture.

General View★. – Cross Oberstein by road no 41 in the direction of Saarbrücken–Bad Kreuznach to see in the distance the Church of the Rocks (Felsenkirche) set in the far rock face.

■ **SIGHTS** *time: 1½ hours*

Felsenkirche★. – ½ *hour on foot Rtn.* This 15C Protestant church is encased by a rock overhang in the cliff-face. Before starting to climb the 214 steps that lead from the Oberstein Marktplatz to the church make sure from the information panel that the church is actually open. *Open 1 April to 12 October, 9am to 6pm; 1DM.*

Precious Stone Museum★★ (Deutsches Edelsteinmuseum). – *At Idar, in the Diamond and Precious Stone Exchange, Hauptstrasse. Open 1 May to 30 September, 9am to 6pm (5pm the rest of the year); closed 24 and 31 December and Monday before Ash Wednesday; 3DM.*

A profusion of colour and form creates a fabulous atmosphere. Every stone known to man is exhibited: in their natural and remodelled state and classified by geographical location, artistic and learned references or industrial use. Note the dental instruments in agate.

New Castle. – At Oberstein. Ruins with a view of the Nahe Valley.

Local Museum (Heimatmuseum). – *On the Marktplatz below the Felsenkirche at Oberstein. Open 9am to 5.30pm (5pm in winter); 1.50DM.*

The museum contains collections of minerals and precious stones, notably Landschafts-achat, thin nearly transparent, agate flakes depicting phantasmagoric countrysides.

Gem Cutting Centre (Weiherschleife). – *At the outskirts of Idar; open 9am to noon and 1 to 5pm (4pm Fridays); Sundays. 10am to noon and 2 to 4pm; closed Saturdays, Sundays and holidays from October to Easter.*

In this mill, the grinders, still working in the old fashioned process, are seen lying on tilting trestles to press the rough stones against the mighty sandstone grinding wheels – the different stages of cutting the gems are shown. A room, at the end of the visit, contains works of art.

EXCURSION

Fischbach. – *10 km - 6 miles – by road no 41 – down the Nahe River.* Go through Fischbach and take a right turn towards Berschweiler. *Guided tours 1 April to 15 November, every hour from 10am to noon and 1 to 5pm; the rest of the year only Saturday and Sunday afternoons, 1 to 5pm; it is advisable to be warmly clad.*

Upon entering this former copper mine, exploited as early as at the time of the Romans, the visitor is shown, by wax figures, the successive stages involved in the extraction of ore.

INGOLSTADT

Michelin map **987** northwest of 37 – Pop 88 000
Town plan in Michelin Red Guide Deutschland

Once famous for its university (1472-1800), Ingolstadt became, in the 19C, one of the most powerful strongholds of Europe. Today it is an active Danubian town with a motor car factory, and five oil refineries supplied by three pipelines *(map p 16)* of which the most modern, the TAL from Trieste, has a diameter of one metre.

Our Lady of Victories★ (Maria-de-Victoria-Kirche). – *Ring for the sacristan. Open 9am to noon, 1 to 6pm (4pm October to February); closed Mondays; 1DM.*

This plain single aisled chapel was transformed in 1732 by the Asam brothers *(p 27)*.

The vast ceiling fresco shows the spreading of the Faith to the four quarters of the globe through the intercession of the Virgin. The perspective effect is extraordinary. The high altar is adorned with statues of Medicine, Theology, Law and Philosophy.

Basilica of Our Lady (Liebfrauenmünster). – Enter through the Flamboyant south porch. The interior is in the form of a Gothic hall, upsweeping in line. The fine 1572 **altarpiece★** (Hochaltar) on the high altar is a transitional Gothic-Renaissance work: the central panel shows the *Madonna of the Cloak*, the Virgin being the patron saint of Bavaria.

Castle (Herzogschloss). – A rough 15C castle which, when it has been restored, will house the Bavarian military museum. *Open 9.30am to 4pm; closed Mondays; 1.50DM.*

Kreuztor. – The Kreuztor is the finest remainder of the town's 14 and 15C fortifications.

The KAISERSTUHL

Michelin map **205** 16

The setting of the Kaiserstuhl, a small isolated volcanic hill in the centre of the Baden Rhineland Plain, gives it, in spite of its modest altitude of 559 m - 1 834 ft – a majestic air which justifies its name of the "Emperor's Throne".

The Kaiserstuhl Vineyards. – A hot dry climate makes the last slopes of the hill a perfect spot for fruit trees and vines. *Sylvaner, Riesling* and *Traminer* and the fuller *Ruländer*, are the most full-bodied of the local white wines. Red grape juice (from black grapes) is often fermented as a rosé wine as with *Weissherbst*, a pleasant wine which keeps its wonderful colour particularly well after a sunny autumn. The *Ihringen, Bickensohl* and *Oberrotweil* vintages are among the best known.

Breisach. – *Description p 87.*

Burkheim. – This still rustic wine growers' village rises in tiers away from the road up a gentle combeside. Three streets run parallel, giving access to the houses at different levels. The lowest street, the Markstrasse, is still delightful with its Rathaus complete with emblazoned doorways (1604), its bow-windowed red house and half-timbered houses.

Endingen. – The **Marktplatz** is surrounded by fine public buildings. Note the new Rathaus, an 18C former burgher's house with a forefront adorned with a balcony and topped by an elegant mansard roof. In the northeast corner of the square, the old 16C Rathaus has scrolled gables; the former Kornhaus (Granary), also 16C, is a long building with stepped gables.

KAISHEIM

Michelin map **987** 36 – 6 km - 4 miles – northeast of Donauwörth by road no 2 – *Local map p 215* – Pop 1 252

The village of Kaisheim lies near a former Cistercian abbey which is now a prison.

Church (Ehemalige Klosterkirche). – The church was built in 14C Gothic style. Outside, from the end by the apse, three separate elements can be clearly seen: an ambulatory, a raised chancel and a tower above the transept crossing in 18C Baroque.

Interior. – *To visit apply to a priest or the sacristan. Offering.* Round the chancel which is very pure in style lies the twelve sided **ambulatory★** (Chorumgang). It has ogive vaulting and is divided into two galleries, one to walk along, the other, which is raised, for altars.

KALKAR

Michelin maps **987** 13 and **202** north of 4 – Pop 10 800

This town in the Lower Rhineland Plain gained considerable wealth in the Middle Ages through trade. The market place is picturesque with its straight lines of brick houses, town hall (16C) with turrets at each corner, and the lime tree under which judicial cases were decided.

St. Nicholas' (Nikolaikirche). – *Open 1 April to 30 September, 10am to noon and 2 to 6pm (5pm in winter); closed Sunday mornings and Mondays.*

This 15C hall-church possesses extraordinary **Gothic furnishings★★**. The high altar has a huge altarpiece of the *Passion* carved in about 1500 with attention to the smallest detail.

The altarpiece of the *Seven Joys of the Virgin* (1490) composed with great delicacy of feeling, particularly in the scene of the Annunciation in the centre, may be seen on the right pillar in the chancel. Against the south wall stands the altarpiece to *St. Crispin* (1540) with a graceful Mary Magdalene between St. Peter and St. Paul – this work already betrays considerable Renaissance influence. The altarpiece of the *Seven Sorrows of the Virgin* (1520) in the south chapel, shows the mastery of the artist, Henrich Douvermann.

The *St. George* altarpiece (1480) on the north pillar in the chancel demonstrates a different technique, being a vast panorama and more in the manner of a painting.

KARLSRUHE

Michelin map **205** 2 – *Local map p 215* – Pop 285 000

Karlsruhe was one of a group of towns built to a geometric plan in the 18C by the prince-builders of southern Germany. Today it is a city much frequented by lawyers and technologists: the supreme courts of the Federal Republic (Court of Appeal and the Constitutional Court) stand next to the Technological High School. This, the oldest such institution in Germany, was founded in 1825 and gained renown from the presence of such men as Hertz, who discovered electro-magnetic waves in 1888, and Benz *(p 238)*, the motorcar pioneer.

Many industries, including the Michelin Tyre Company, have erected factories near the Rhine; the south Europe pipeline, starting from Lavéra, near Marseilles, feeds two local oil refineries. A nuclear research centre is being constructed north of the town.

KARLSRUHE
CENTRE

Am Stadtgarten	Z 3
Douglasstraße	Y 7
Durlacher Allee	Y 8
Erbprinzenstraße	Y 9
Finterstraße	Y 12
Hans-Thoma-Straße	Y 15
Kaiserstraße	Y
Karl-Friedrich-Straße	Y 18
Karlstraße	YZ
Karl-Wilhelm-Straße	Y 19
Kronenstraße	Y 22
Marktplatz	Y 25
Schwarzwaldstraße	Z 30
Werderplatz	Z

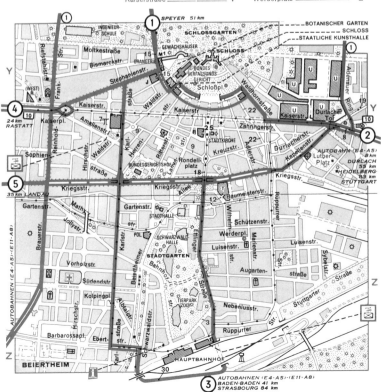

KARLSRUHE

The "Fan Town". – Karl Wilhelm, Margrave of Baden, abandoned Durlach (east of Karlsruhe), the family residence, after the devastations of 1689 *(p 146)*, deciding instead to build a castle further west among the trees of his favourite hunting grounds. The castle, whose foundation stone was laid in 1715, was to become the hub of a series of radiating roads: those to the north remained as hunting rides, those to the south outlined the scheme for future development. The plan reached fruition in the 19C when Karlsruhe, deeply marked by the Neo-Classical style, became the capital of the Grand Duchy of Baden in 1806.

The town hall, the Protestant church (Stadtkirche) and the modest pyramid of the founder's mausoleum combined to make the **Marktplatz**, from this date, the centre of the town.

Today the main street is the highly commercial Kaiserstrasse, the old road from Durlach to the Rhine.

■ SIGHTS *time: 2½ hours*

Fine Arts Museum (Staatliche Kunsthalle). – *Open 10am to 5pm; closed Mondays and some holidays.*

Go up the stairs to the first floor and turn left. The first galleries contain **German Primitives★★** (Gemälde Altdeutscher Meister). The Grünewald Gallery has as its focal point a terrifying *Crucifixion* by Grünewald himself.

There is a gallery of 19C painting – German Romantics, French Impressionists and their German contemporaries – in the wing at right angles to the Grünewald Gallery.

On the ground floor the **Hans Thoma Collection★** of paintings by the great Black Forest artist (1839-1924) includes *Mother and Sister of the artist, Children's Games* – one of the most popular of German paintings – *Rain in the Black Forest* and *Self-Portrait.*

Orangery (Y M¹). – The building, which now houses only contemporary works, includes Franz Marc's *Deer in the Forest.*

Castle. – The tall polygonal tower on the north side marks the centre of Karlsruhe's radiating system of roads. The castle now contains the Baden Regional Museum.

Baden Regional Museum★ (Badisches Landesmuseum). – *Open 10am to 5pm (10pm Thursdays); closed Tuesdays and some holidays.*

There are large collections of Egyptian, Greek and Roman Antiquities, folk crafts, popular Baden art, etc.

The first floor is devoted to the Margrave Türkenlouis *(p 205)* who reigned from 1677 to 1707. Rare items include war paraphernalia, the prince's insignia of command and particularly precious **trophies★★** (Türkenbeute), brought back from the campaigns against the Turks between 1683 and 1692: banners, dress harnesses, chased and inlaid arms, etc.

Botanical Gardens (Botanischer Garten). – The **glasshouses★** (Gewächshäuser) contain a magnificent collection of cacti. *Open April to September, 6am to nightfall; October to March 8am to 4pm (5pm Sundays).*

Stadtgarten (Z). – *Open April to March, 7am to 8pm; October to March, 8am to 5pm; 3DM.* This green space is balanced in the south by a zoo.

KASSEL ★
Michelin map **987** 15 – *Local map p 252* – Pop 203 000

Kassel, the economic capital of Hesse and a good centre from which to make excursions into the picturesque Waldeck countryside, is a long drawn out town stretching nearly 6 km - 4 miles – from east to west, from the business quarter, which has been entirely rebuilt on a terrace overlooking the Fulda, to the Wilhelmshöhe, the former princely residence at the foot of the wooded Habichtswald heights.

The centre of town exemplifies modern urbanism. Restricted to pedestrians only, one is tempted to just stroll. The main areas: Königsplatz, Königstrasse, and Treppenstrasse (Street of stairs), have all been very well rearranged.

As an economic centre, Kassel attracts conferences every year; as a cultural centre there are music and theatre festivals – the most renowned being the Documenta Exposition, where every four years (1981) contemporary art from all over the world is assembled.

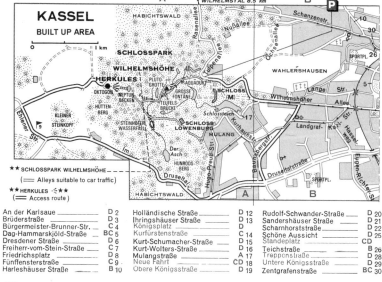

KASSEL
BUILT UP AREA

★★ SCHLOSSPARK WILHELMSHÖHE
(=== Alleys suitable to car traffic)
★★ HERKULES ⦰★★
(=== Access route)

The industrial tradition. – The Landgrave Karl of Hesse (1670-1730) had the idea of inviting to the town a group of French Huguenots whose knowledge would give impetus to local industry. From 1695 to 1707 he supported the exiled Frenchman, **Denis Papin**, in his research. The errant inventor performed before the prince in 1706, the first experiment in the use of steam power (fountain and commemorative plaque in the Natural History Museum – Naturkunde-museum – D **M³**).

Kassel's industries with their worldwide reputation for railway equipment, lorries and buses have therefore a tradition of research and technology.

The Brothers Grimm. – From 1805 to 1830 the brothers Jakob and Wilhelm Grimm (1785-1863 and 1786-1859), united by their philological work, histories of literature and their monumental German dictionary (1852-61), lived in Kassel and worked as court librarians. Impassioned folklorists, they gathered a harvest of stories from all over Hesse which were first published in Berlin in 1815 as the *Kinder- und Hausmärchen – Tales of Children and Home.*

■ WILHELMSHÖHE★★

12 km - 8 miles – from Kassel centre – plus 2½ miles of sightseeing.
The huge castle park (Schlosspark) which extends across the slopes of the Habichtswald Forest was commissioned by the Landgrave Karl of Hesse in 1701.

The Park★★. – *Time: 2 hours.*
Leave the car in one of the parks at the end of the Wilhelmshöher Allee. As you walk round the vast lawn shaded by rare trees look at the castle with the Hercules statue behind it. Finally nearby, amidst a Baroque group of temples, tombs and imitation grottoes, note the aqueduct, Pluto's Grotto and the Devil's Bridge (Teufelsbrücke).

The best time for a walk is when the **fountains are playing★** (Wasserkünste – *Ascension to September, Wednesdays and Sundays in summer at 3.30pm*). Go up to Neptune's Basin at the foot of the great cascade; wait until the first falls are in full flow then follow the water down to see the various features at their best: the Steinhöfer Wasserfall rocks, the Devil's Bridge (Teufelsbrücke), the ruins of the Roman Aqueduct and finally the Great Plume (Grosse Fontäne) of the castle's major pool *(fountains cease at 4.30pm).*

Go back to the car and turn round. Bear right, into the Baunsbergstrasse, then the Druseltalstrasse from which you again turn off right. At the mountain summit continue right.

The Hercules Statue★★. – *Climb (about ½ hour): 17 March to 15 November, 10am to 5pm; closed Mondays; 1DM.*
The gigantic statue, which is a copy of the Farnese Hercules in the Naples Museum, stands on a pyramid base which rests on a large pavilion, the Octogone.

The park's great water staircase which was laid out by the Italian architect, Guinero (1665-1745), begins at the foot of the Octogone. The steps are marked by grottoes, small falls, the Riesenkopf Basin, the Great Fall and Neptune's Basin.

From the base of the statue the **vista★★** extends across the park to the castle with the town of Kassel in the background.

Château (A). – *Open April to September, 10am to 6pm; March and October, 10am to 5pm; November to February, 10am to 6pm; closed Mondays and 24, 25, 26, 31 December and 1 January.*
This château, where Jerome Bonaparte, King of Westphalia, held a brilliant court from 1807 to 1813 and where Napoleon III was interned after the defeat at Sedan (1870), provides a focal point for tourists attracted by the view of the park crowned at its highest point by a colossal statue of Hercules.

Southern Wing. – Much of Louis XV and Empire furniture in the apartments bears a Parisian imprint recalling the period when Jerome Bonaparte ruled.

Ancient Greek and Roman Art★. – The Greek Classical Period (6C and 5C) shown (on the left upon entering) with Athenian vases painted with mythological scenes. Also from this same period are copies by Roman artists: *Apollo* and *Athena* by Phidias and a head of Apollo by Polyclitus. Displayed further on are marble sarcophagi, urns, busts, etc. evoking the cult of death so important during the Roman Empire. This section ends with Egyptian art: small statues of the various gods and sacred animals carved in bronze or stone.

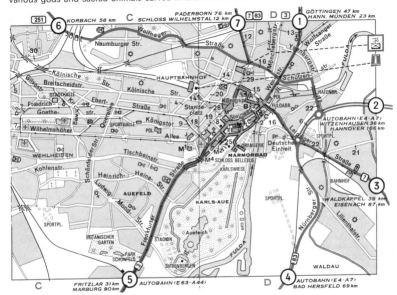

Painting Gallery★★★ (Gemäldegalerie). – While he was governor of Breda and Maastricht, Wilhelm VIII, began collecting paintings of the Dutch and Flemish masters.

1st floor. – In the central section **Rembrandt's** constant attention to light and shade and his feeling for humanity are exemplified in his self-portraits as well as *Portrait of Saskia, Winter Landscape, Jacob Blessing the Children of Joseph.* In contrast the happy-go-lucky genre paintings of Frans Hals: *The Children Singing, The Man with a slouched hat.* Among the larger canvases by the **17C Flemish masters** are the works of Rubens and Van Dyck: *Coronation of the Hero by the Victory* (Rubens), *Maria with Child and Saints as a refuge for sinners* (Van Dyck and Rubens) and *Sebastian Leerse with wife and child* (Van Dyck). In *The Engagement* by Jordaens, the artist depicts himself at his engagement celebration playing the lute.

2nd floor. – Jan Brueghel (end 16C-early 17C), a detailed still life and landscape painter is exemplified in his *Winter Landscape.* The variety among the Dutch masters is well displayed – compare Van Aelst, Brouwer, Van de Velde, Ruysdael's tumultuous *Water Fall* shows how the artist was able to grasp light and shade. The interior of the bourgeois house is carefully represented in *The Lute Player* by Metsu. Jan Steen paints a popular scene in *The King Drinks.*

3rd floor. – Exhibited here is *Leda with her Children* by Giampietrino once attributed to Leonardo da Vinci. Exemplifying Titian's style is a *Portrait of an Italian Nobleman,* a monumental composition based essentially on tonal colouring. Also exhibited are the Italians (Bellucci, Nogari, Damini), Spanish (Ribera, Murillo) and French (Poussin) masters of the 18C.

Löwenburg Castle (A). – *Same times of opening as for Wilhelmshöhe Château; 1DM.*
This castle which is a piece of pure late 18C architectural fantasy in the Romantic manner contains a valuable collection of arms and armour.

■ IN TOWN

From Königsplatz, descend the Untere Königstrasse to the Gothic **Church of St. Martin** (St. Martinskirche) (**DA**) *(to visit ask for the key at 5A Martinsplatz),* rebuilt in 1958; it contains the cenotaph of the Landgrave Charles and his wife. By taking Die Freiheit, passing by the **Markthalle** (**DB**) (the main wholesale produce market) built around a square courtyard (1580), one arrives at Brüderstrasse (on the right). The **Brüderkirche** (**DC**) (end 13C-early 14C) is all there is left of a Carmelite convent, on the north side of the chancel is the chapter house. Further down is the **Renthof** (**DC**), a Renaissance building, which had formerly housed the judiciary and finance, now a rest home. Opposite the Renthof, walk through the shaded An der Karlsaue to the **Staatstheatre** (**DT**), a modern theatre; continue up to the **Natural History Museum** *(description below)* and to the large square, Friedrichsplatz where is situated the **Fridericianum** museum *(being rearranged),* founded in 1799.

Starting from the east corner of the square stroll along the Schöne Aussicht, offering a nice view of the Fulda and the Karlsaue Park.

Karlsaue Park★ (**CD**). – The most popular parts of this 18C park are the sloping gardens below the Schöne Aussicht terrace and the artificial island of the Siebenbergen *(access: 0.50DM).*

The **Orangery Château** is under restoration until 1981, however it housed the Documenta Exposition in 1977 and several rooms are open to the public *(Easter to 15 October, Saturdays 1 to 5pm and Sundays 10am to 5pm; 0.50DM).* The Marble Pavilion (Marmorbad) which flanks the orangery is also open to the public (same conditions of opening). The **interior★★** is adorned with 17C reliefs and mythological statues.

Museums

Hesse Museum★ (**Hessisches Landesmuseum**) (**C M¹**). – *Open 10am to 5pm;closed Mondays and 25 December.*

On the ground floor the **Astronomy and Physics Room★★** (Astronomisch-physikalisches Kabinett) contains rare and old scientific instruments: a large planetary clock made in 1560 after plans by Landgrave Wilhelm IV, a celestial globe with an astronomical clock and calendar (1600) and a small 16C astronomical clock which functions by Copernicus's heliocentric theory.

The **Wall Hangings Museum★★** (Tapetenmuseum) on the 1st floor contains wonderful wallpapers, for example landscape scenes (1900) painted in Paris (Réveillon) or Kassel and embossed leather with Oriental influence. Workshops, reproduced the way they existed in the past, help relive the creation of wallhangings from the 16C to the present.

The 2nd floor is devoted entirely to decorative arts and folklore, note the Italian cupboard in ebony, encrusted in ivory made for the 1867 Paris Exposition. Also on display are exquisite porcelain, faience, glassware, jewellery, etc. A rural interior has been re-created with furniture, utensils and tools all relating to the Hesse farm.

New Gallery★ (**Neue Galerie**) (**D M⁴**). – *Open March to October, 10am to 5pm (4pm November to February); closed Mondays and 25 December.*

The collection includes works and styles from 1750 to the present. A special importance is placed on German painters: the artistic Tischbein family with its series of portraits and *The Woman in Blue,* the classical Nahl the Younger with his mythological scenes and Friedrich a member of the Nazarene Group (influenced by the Italian Primitives) with his religious painting. Not forgetting the Romantic German style exemplified by Bürkel, Spitzweg (the Munich School) and the Düsseldorf School. The Impressionist movement especially influenced: Liebermann, Trübner and Corinth *(Countryside at Walchensee, Woman with a Mask).* However, Heckel, Schmidt-Rottluff, Kirchner *(Café at Davos)* were followers of Expressionism.

The works of Warhol, Hamilton, Beuys *(The Hoard)* and Penck *(Standards,* where each bovine species is associated with car) puts the affluent society into question. Completing the collection are bronze, metal and cement sculpture, interpreting the "modern world".

Brothers Grimm Museum (Brüder-Grimm-Museum) (**C M²**). – *Open weekdays, 10am to 6pm (1pm Sundays); closed Mondays.* Portraits, manuscripts, letters, drawings and original illustrations recall the brothers' life.

Natural History Museum (Naturkundemuseum) (**D M³**). – *Open Tuesdays to Saturdays 10am to 4.30pm, Sundays 10am to 1pm.*

This museum is in the former Ottoneum, the first German theatre (1600).
The ground floor contains the zoology and anthropology section.
Displayed on the 1st floor is the development and evolution of species. There is also an important palaeontological (fossils of flora and fauna), geological, and entomological collection. A series of small boxes in the form of books, made from the wood of different trees, each containing the corresponding herb, flower or fruit that it produces.

EXCURSIONS

Château of Wilhelmsthal★. – *8.5 km - 5 miles by the Rosenallee, right to the château of Wilhelmsöhe or 12 km - 7 miles by ⑦ on the map and the château avenue (left). Guided tours 10am to 5pm (4pm November to February); closed Mondays; 1DM.*

Within an informal garden, where the basin is adorned with fountains and gilt statues, stands the château by François Cuvilliés. It is decorated with Rococo panelling. The painter Johann-Heinrich Tischbein the Elder, added, in accordance with the taste of the German princes of the time, a gallery of beauties. Delicate furniture (Roentgen), as is seen in the commode with mother of pearl inlay in the form of peacock feathers and Chinese porcelains, ornament the rooms.

Tour of the Hoher Meissner Massif★. – *Round tour of 150 km - 93 miles – ½ day.* Leave Kassel by ② for Witzenhausen and then turn right into road no 27.

As you leave Wendershausen you will see two fortified castles: the **Zweiburgenblick** site.

Bad Sooden-Allendorf. – *Tour of Allendorf: ½ hour.* The twin towns of Bad Sooden, a stylish spa, and Allendorf, a town that once gained wealth from salt refining, are separated by the River Werra. Allendorf, which was rebuilt in wood after the Thirty Years War, still has a number of 17C **half-timbered houses★** (Fachwerkhäuser): look, in particular, in the Kirchstrasse, the street between the bridge and the Marktplatz, at the **Bürgersches Haus★** (no 29) and the **Eschstruthsches★★** at no 59.

Eschwege. – The 16C château was the residence of the Landgraves. From the terrace is a view of the Werra. The market place with its fountain and 17C half-timbered houses evokes the past.

Turn round on the same road and after 7 km - 4 miles – turn left towards Frankershausen.

Beyond the town turn left into a road through the woods to the upper slopes of the Hoher Meissner. The Gasthof Schwalbental overlooks a **countryside★** bordered to the southeast by wooded hills, forerunners of the Thuringian Massif. By way of Hausen and Velmeden make for road no 7 and Hessisch Lichtenau where you turn left to Spangenberg.

Spangenberg. – *Tour: 1 hour.* Spangenberg's setting can be best appreciated from the castle terrace. The view along the village main street, the Klosterstrasse, is unusual.

Melsungen. – The town, washed by the waters of the Fulda, groups round its free standing **town hall★**, 16C **half-timbered houses★** (Fachwerkhäuser).

Leave in the direction of the motorway but pass beneath it and turn sharp right.

Heiligenberg. – *½ hour on foot Rtn.* Climb to the summit from the hotel. A **panorama** of the Eder Valley extends from Kassel (the Hercules Statue) to Fritzlar and Waldeck Castle. Turn and take the motorway back to Kassel.

KELHEIM
Michelin map **987** 27 – 28 km - 17 miles – southwest of Regensburg – Pop 12 600

The attractive small town of Kelheim, former residence of the Dukes of Bavaria, lies at the confluence of the Altmühl and the Danube overlooked by the Befreiungshalle.

Liberation Monument★ (Befreiungshalle). – *2 km - 1 mile – plus ½ hour. Open: 1 April to 30 September, 8am to 6pm; 1 October to 31 March, 9am to noon and 1 to 4pm; 1DM.*

It was Ludwig I of Bavaria *(p 183)* who first had the idea, on his return from a journey to Greece in 1836, of commemorating the liberation of Germany from the Napoleonic yoke with a monument. The huge rotunda was constructed between 1842 and 1863; the hall is upheld by eighteen buttresses each of which bears an allegorical statue of the people of a different German region. The wall coping, which partly hides the dome, is adorned with tall trophies. The interior beneath the dome (echo) has a certain nobility; in a circle round the marble paved gallery are 34 victory statues. Good **view** of the Altmühl from the gallery outside.

Weltenburg Abbey. – *Excursion of 6 km - 4 miles – by the Neustadt road, and off the by-road to Weltenburg, the abbey track on the right, plus ½ hour sightseeing.*

The only way to see the rocky Danubian defile (Donaudurchbruch) which gives the abbey its individual setting is by boat leaving from Kelheim: 1 May to 18 September departures 8.30, 9.30am and every ½ hour to 4.30pm; Sundays and holidays, 8, 9am and every ½ hour to 5.30pm. 19 September to 16 October, every 90 minutes from 10am to 4pm. In April 10.45am, 1 and 2.30pm; Sundays and holidays, 8.30, 9.30am and every ½ hour to 4pm; Rtn fare: 4.50DM.

The **church★** which was built by Cosmas Damian Asam in 1718 is divided into a narthex and a nave, both oval in form. The statue of St. George on the high altar lit by a "heavenly window" is immediately arresting *(illustration p 25)*. In the upper dome through an aperture in the lower dome a false relief composition by Asam depicts the Church Triumphant.

KIEL ★
Michelin map **987** 5 – Pop 258 500 – *Town plan in Michelin Red Guide Deutschland*

Kiel and its world famous shipyards, lies at the mouth of the sea canal linking the Baltic with the North Sea. A former naval base, it has been rebuilt and today is a new town, the capital of the Land of Schleswig-Holstein and a university city. The Holstenstrasse, bustling, trading and kept for pedestrians only, is a typical example of contemporary town planning.

The Roadstead★★ (Kieler Förde). – The shores of this deep bay are enlivened by a series of sheltered resorts – Strande, Schilksee, Schönberger Strand, Laboe and Heikendorf – between which you can make pleasant boat trips.

The "Kiel Week". – The regattas, held for the last eighty years in the northern part of the roadstead during June, and in which some 500 yachts take part, provide the setting for social, diplomatic and cultural exchanges. The Federal Republic President usually attends.

■ **SIGHTS** *time: 1 hour*

Hindenburg Quay★★ (Hindenburgufer). – The promenade extends for almost two miles affording **views★★** of the harbour on one side and shaded parks on the other. Liners and sailing craft provide a foreground to the tall Laboe memorial on the far bank.

Town Hall. – *Open Mondays to Fridays 9am to 3pm. Guided tours at 9.30, 10.30 and 11.30am from May to September. Apply to the Fremdenverkehrsamt, August-Viktoria-Strasse 16.*

The building, which was constructed from 1907 to 1911, is dominated by a tower 106 m high - 348 ft. From the upper platform there is an overall **view★** of the roadstead as far as the Laboe memorial; in the foreground are modern buildings, from which emerge the Church of St. Nicholas and the shipyards.

159

EXCURSIONS

Schleswig-Holstein Open Air Museum★★ (Freilichtmuseum). – *6 km - 4 miles by ② on the plan; then turn right and take the road B4 to Neumünster. Open 1 April to 15 November, 9am to 5pm (no tickets sold after 4pm); closed Mondays except in July and August. The rest of the year only open on Sundays; 2.50DM.* More than thirty farms and rural houses dating from the 16C to 19C have been rebuilt at Kiel-Ramsee. The dwellings are grouped in hamlets according to their geographical origin. The interiors of the Southern half-timbered farms, either painted or brick-designed, resemble those of Lower Saxony; the farms from North Friesland, all in brick, are more severe. The range of buildings includes the humble craftsman's house to the huge thatch covered barn whose roofs extends to the ground to the luxurious farm with carefully decorated rooms. The forge, the potter's workshop, the bakehouse and the looms are all operated by local craftsmen; the four mills are still working and animals are kept on the premises, meals are served at the heavily timbered inn, which dates back to the 18C.

Laboe★. – *20 km - 12 miles – about 2 hours.* Leave Kiel by the east along the Werftstrasse and by way of Heikendorf you will reach Laboe. The tower, 85 m tall - 279 ft – and in the shape of a ship's stern is the **German Naval War memorial★** (Marine-Ehrenmal). The **navigation museum★** in the lower gallery *(open 9am to 6.30pm, 4pm in winter; 2DM)* contains exhibits on German shipping since the Middle Ages, colonial history, submarine operations in the two world wars, and technical displays on the Kiel Canal, oceanography and naval construction.

There is an immense **view★★** from the top of the tower *(lift: 0.50DM)* of the entire roadstead lined with small sand beaches and, in clear weather, of the Danish archipelago to the north.

In 1943 **the submarine** (U-Boot) U 995 was launched in Hamburg to operate in the Norwegian and Barents Seas. *1DM.* Note the difference between the large space given to armament and engines as against the small space given to the crew and officers.

Prinz-Heinrich-Brücke. – *5 km - 3 miles – plus ¼ hour sightseeing. Come out of Kiel by the north, along the Holtenauer Strasse and leave the car in a park before reaching the southern end of the bridge.* The steel bridge overlooks the **Holtehau** locks which control the junction of the canal and the Baltic. There is a wide **view★** east as far as the Laboe monument.

KIEL Canal

Michelin map 987 5 between Kiel and Brunsbüttel

The maritime canal linking the North Sea and the Baltic (Nord-Ostsee-Kanal), which was opened by Wilhelm II in 1895, is the busiest in the world. In 1976, 60 323 ships from 50 nations passed through the canal – more than through the Panama, yet it ranks below this and when it was opened, of Suez, in the tonnage of goods transported.

Six iron bridges and the **Rendsburg road tunnel** cross the 100 km - 62 miles – of canal. Besides the Kiel **Prinz-Heinrich-Brücke** *(see above)* the most impressive undertakings are the **Rendsburg railway viaduct★** *(p 208)* and, on road no 204 (Itzehoe-Heide), the **Grünenthal Bridge**.

The greatest tourist attraction is the passage of the ships through the **Kiel-Holtenau locks** (Schleusen) *(access to the terrace on the north side of the canal; ticket vending machine; 0.50DM)* and the corresponding locks of **Brunsbüttell** into the North Sea.

KISSINGEN, Bad ★★

Michelin map 987 26 – Pop 22 300 – *Town plan in Michelin Red Guide Deutschland*

The spa of Bad Kissingen, which lies hidden in the Franconian Valley of the Saale (Fränkische Saale) at the foot of the last foothills of the Rhön *(p 216)*, is in full development.

The Cure. – The size of the thermal installations and the beauty of the Kurgarten, Rosengarten and Luitpoldpark parks are impressive.

EXCURSION

Aschach; Münnerstadt. – *Round tour of 44 km - 27 miles – about 2½ hours.* Leave Kissingen by the north along the Salinenstrasse. At Grossenbrach turn left towards the centre of Aschach.

Aschach. – *Castle tour: 1 May to 31 October, at 3, 4 and 5pm; closed Mondays; time: ¾ hour; 2DM.* The castle has a typical 19C interior enriched by **works of art★** (Kunstwerke) brought, in some cases, from the Far East. Return to the car and two miles before Bad Neustadt turn off to Münnerstadt.

Münnerstadt. – *Tour: ¼ hour.* The fortified walls encircling the town date back to the 13C. The church with its high Romanesque tower contains precious **works of art★**. In the chancel two panels which remain of an altarpiece carved by Tilman Riemenschneider in 1492 shows the communion and burial of Mary Magdalene; in the north aisle, five magnificent statues frame four panels painted by Veit Stoss telling the legend of St. Kilian.

The hilly roads nos 19 and 287, on the right, will bring you back to Kissingen.

KOBLENZ ★

Michelin map 204 14 – *Local maps pp 163, 181, 212 and 213* – Pop 119 000

Koblenz, as its name from the Latin *confluentia* indicates, stands at a confluence – that of the Mosel and the Rhine. The site is also the meeting point of four Rhine schist massifs.

Koblenz rose again swiftly after being three quarters destroyed in 1944. The summer festival which ends in the Rhine being set aflame with floating torches *(p 31)*, the open air concerts and the taverns in its "wine village" (Weindorf) (Y) attract many tourists.

The French at Koblenz. – The period of French influence in Koblenz began in 1789 with the arrival of emigrants and enemies of the Revolution, and continued until 1814. The leaders were the Counts of Artois and Provence, brothers of Louis XVI. Republican troops began to occupy the left bank of the Rhine in 1794; in 1798 Koblenz became the prefecture of the Rhine and Mosel Department. The prefect Lezay-Marnésia decided to embellish the town and in 1809 he gave it the Rheinanlagen (Y), a promenade along the river bank.

The Deutsches Eck★. – Only the base remains of a gigantic equestrian statue of Wilhelm I which once stood on the tongue of land marking the confluence of the Rhine and the Mosel. From the covered gallery at the top of the base *(107 steps)* there is a close **view★** of the town, the quarter on the right bank of the Rhine, overlooked by the fortress of Ehrenbreitstein which is flood-lit at night, the port and the Mosel bridges.

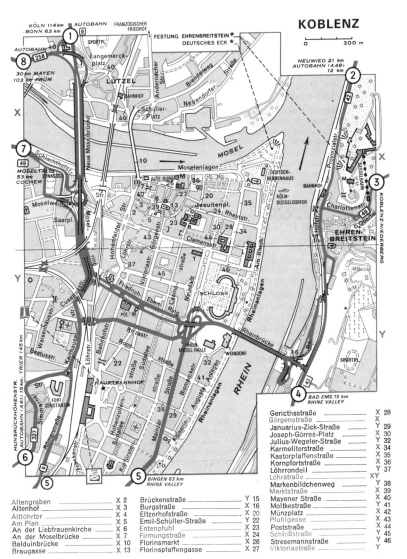

KOBLENZ

0   300 m

(Map of Koblenz with labels including:) KÖLN 114 km, BONN 63 km, AUTOBAHN, FRANZÖSISCHER FRIEDHOF, FESTUNG EHRENBREITSTEIN ★, DEUTSCHES ECK ★, AUTOBAHN 40, SPORTPL., Langemarck-platz, NEUWIED 21 km, AUTOBAHN (A48) 12 km, 30 km MAYEN 103 km PRÜM, LÜTZEL, BAHNHOF, Schüller-Platz, Andernacher Str., Neuendorfer Str., MOSEL, Moselanlagen, DEUTSCH-HERRENHAUS, KÖLN-DÜSSELDORFER, BAHNHOF, Charlottenstr., KOBLENZ-NIEDERBERG, MOSELTAL 53 km COCHEM, SYNAGOGE, Neue Moselbrücke, Moselweindorf, Saarpl., ALTE BURG, Jesuitenpl., Rheinstr., Clemensstr., EHRENBREITSTEIN, SCHLOSS, Neustadt, Rheinanlagen, Rheinbrücke, Rhein-Mosel-Halle, WEINDORF, RHEIN, HAUPTBAHNHOF, FORT CONSTANTIN, TRIER 145 km, HUNSRÜCKHÖHENSTR., AUTOBAHN (A61) 15 km, BAD EMS 15 km RHINE VALLEY, BINGEN 63 km RHINE VALLEY

St. Castor's (Stiftskirche S. Kastor) (X A). – This Romanesque church succeeded an earlier basilica in which the Treaty of Verdun was drawn up in AD 843 dividing Charlemagne's Empire. The nave and chancel, which are wide and somewhat squat, have a heavy fan vaulting. The furnishings are interesting: in the chancel are two archbishops' tombs at the back of multicoloured Gothic bays; in the south transept is a painted panel, once part of a rood-screen, with a picture of St. Castor (bottom left); in the north transept is a very old and, by the people of Koblenz, much venerated painting of the Virgin, the Brigitten Madonna.

Old Town. – The old town is centred round the Church of Our Lady.

Church of Our Lady (Liebfrauenkirche) (X B). – This Romanesque building was remodelled in the 13C, given a Gothic chancel in the 15C and Baroque belfries in the 17C. The carved keystones ornamenting the vaulting tracery are worth examining.

Jesuitenplatz (X). – The 17C Jesuit College is now the town hall. A fountain erected in 1941 in a corner where the Schlängelbrunne, the covered passageway, ends, is a reminder of the mischievousness of Koblenz urchins.

Middle Rhine Museum (Mittelrhein-Museum) (X M). – *Open weekdays 10am to 1pm and 2.30 to 5.30pm; Sundays 10am to 1pm; closed Mondays.*
The museum is in a 15C building in the Florinsmarkt, a delightful small restored square. On display are paintings by Januarius Zick (1730-99), Koblenz citizen by adoption.

EXCURSION

Ehrenbreitstein Citadel★ (Festung Ehrenbreitstein) (X). – *4.5 km - 3 miles – plus ½ hour sightseeing.* Leave Koblenz by ③, take the second street on the left after the church of Koblenz-Wiederberg. Car park beyond the covered passages leading to the ramparts. Go through the curtain wall to the esplanade.

This strategic position, commanding the confluence of the Rhine and the Mosel, was occupied from the 10C onwards by a fortress which was held by the archbishops of Trier until 1799 when it was destroyed by the French. Between 1816 and 1832 the Prussians, who had ruled the Rhineland from the time of the Treaty of Vienna in 1815, built the present powerful fortifications which, however, have never been used in war.

The **view★** from the terrace is extensive but you must go to the very end of the stronghold on the left for a more complete **panorama★★**. Beyond the town bristling with belfries, can be seen upstream, the first of the romantic Castles of the Rhine – Lahneck and Stolzenfels – then the wooded Hunsrück and volcanic Eifel Plateaux and, finally, the Neuwied and Andernach industrial basin.

KÖLN ★★★ – See Cologne p 95.

KÖNIGSLUTTER AM ELM

Michelin map **987** 16 – Pop 17 000

Königslutter, at the edge of the fine beech forests of Elm, charms visitors with the fresh greenery of its surroundings and the peace of its old abbey.

Abbey Church* (Ehemalige Abteikirche). – This is a Romanesque basilica with three aisles and five apses. The principal apse has a splendid, Lombard inspired, **carved decoration****: a frieze of acanthus leaves, brackets historiated with either masks or animal heads and, in the blind arcades, sculptured hunting scenes. The north doorway is original with three lobes upheld by two twisted columns supported by grimacing lions.

Cloister*. – The cloister north gallery consists of two Romanesque aisles with groined vaulting resting on elaborate, twisted, fluted, trellised and chevron columns. The capitals and abacci are as elegantly as they are variously decorated.

KREUZNACH, Bad ★

Michelin map **204** 16, 17 – Pop 44 000 – *Town plan in Michelin Red Guide Deutschland*

Bad Kreuznach lies 15 km - 9 miles – from the Rhine where the Nahe leaves the Palatinate mountains. It is known for its saline waters and its wine. The vineyards beside the Nahe allow tasters to enjoy the subtle differences, according to geographic origin, of the long-lasting freshness of the Mosel wines and the mellowness of the Rhineland Hesse wines. Among the best known vintages are *Schloss Böckelheim, Rotenfels, Brückes, Narrenkappe*, etc.

Badewörth Island. – The island, with its avenues and views of the river, is the life centre of the bathing resort. The downstream end is straddled by the **Old Bridge** (Alte Nahebrücke) whose piles support aged buildings which apparently defy the laws of gravity.

Karl Geib Museum. – *Open Mondays to Fridays, 9am to noon and 3 to 5pm, Sundays 10.30am to 12.30pm. Brochure in English.*

Excavations in the region have resulted in a prehistoric and geological collection. The most striking discovery is the **Gladiator Mosaic** (3C) where the central motif illustrates combat scenes. In the basement is assembled the Roman heating system, hypocaust, an open space below a floor to allow the passage of hot air and smoke to heat the room above.

EXCURSION

Bad Münster am Stein*. – *4.5km - 3 miles – by ④ on the plan, road no 48, plus 1 hour on foot Rtn.* Leave the car in one of the parks near the Kurhaus. Enter the **thermal park*** where one overlooks the delightful Salinental, then walk to the banks of the Nahe at the foot of the **Rheingrafenstein rocks**** (Felsenlandschaft), formerly the site of a castle.

Take the ferry across the Nahe *(February to October, 0.60DM round trip)* and from the Huttental café-restaurant climb to the top of the rock. There you will get a **view*** of the Bad Münster Basin and the Rotenfels porphyry cliff overlooking the upstream course of the Nahe.

In the **Ebernburg** quarter, once a wine producing village, is a 13C château rising from the top of a rock. Restored, it now houses a small museum and inn.

KRONACH

Michelin map **987** 26 – *Local map p 61* – Pop 12 000

Kronach has all the character of a small fortified Franconian mountain town. The Rosenberg fortress gives it a wild backdrop.

Rosenberg Fortress (Festung Rosenberg). – The approach ramp, which can be negotiated by car, begins in the upper town by the clock tower (Stadtturm).

Behind the fortress bastions are nobly designed 16-18C buildings. Terraces overlook the town (café) and the extensive wooded heights of the Frankenwald.

KULMBACH

Michelin map **987** 26, 27 – *Local map p 61* – Pop 30 000
Town plan in Michelin Red Guide Deutschland

The industrial town of Kulmbach, which is known for its strong beers *(Aechtes Kulmbacher, Bayrisch Gfrorns)*, has very varied art collections displayed in its Plassenburg Castle.

Plassenburg. – *Open 1 April to 30 September, 9am to noon and 1.20 to 5pm; 1 October to 31 March, 10am to noon and 1.30 to 3.30pm; time: ¾ hour; closed Mondays; 1DM.*

The castle is reached by car up a very steep ramp (Burgberg) which starts behind the east end of St. Peter's Church and comes out at a round platform which serves as a viewpoint over the town. St. Peter's has a square tower topped by a lantern tower.

The roughness of the original castle buildings, rebuilt in 1569, makes the surprise all the greater when one enters the **lovely Renaissance courtyard**** (Schöner Hof) surrounded on three sides by tiered galleries. Every square inch of the gallery exteriors, particularly the balustrades, is decorated with medallions, scrolls and low reliefs.

The apartments, which have been refurnished, contain the collections. The most attractive is that the **tin figurines*** (Zinnfigurensammlung) with more than 300 000 pieces grouped as dioramas. The battle scenes are the most successful.

KYLLBURG

Michelin map **203** 15 – Pop 1 300

Kyllburg is happily situated at the tip of a promontory encircled by a steep sided curve in the River Kyll.

Church. – The church, at the tip of the bend of the river in a lovely setting, is an old early 14C collegiate church built in a rose limestone covered here and there with patches of moss. The huge attached cloister is of the same period. The single aisle ends in a narrower chancel, pierced by two decorative niches, one containing a lavabo, the other the triple seat of the celebrant.

LAHN Valley

Michelin map **204** 3 4 14.

The sinuous course of the Lower Lahn announces with its wild scenery and wooded banks your arrival in Romantic Germany.

The valley, which separates the Westerwald and the Taunus Rhine schist massifs *(p 13)*, is, like all areas on the edge of a volcanic region, rich in mineral springs (Bad Ems, Fachingen).

The valley is much visited on account of the ruined castles (Nassau, Laurenburg, Balduinstein) and small towns such as Weilburg and Limburg which are often beautifully sited on a terrace or on the inner side of a river bend.

(After a photo by F.G. Zeitz)

Runkel – The castle and the old bridge.

FROM BAD EMS TO WETZLAR

89 km - 56 miles – about 4½ hours – Local map below

Bad Ems*. – The waters of Bad Ems are used principally to treat rhinopharyngeal affections. In the pavement opposite the Staatliches Kurhaus a flagstone, the Benedettistein, recalls the interview when the King of Prussia, Wilhelm I refused the request of French Ambassador to renounce "for ever" the claims of the Hohenzollerns to the Spanish throne. The king's dispatch relating the event to Bismarck was to precipitate the Franco-Prussian War of 1870.
The picturesque road along the Lahn starts above Bad Ems.

Nassau. – The small city of Nassau was the cradle of the Counts of Laurenburg who took the name of Nassau in the 12C. The Orange-Nassau branch has played a decisive role in the history of the Low Countries since the 16C and was the House of William of Orange, King William III of England (1650-1702). The family history is related at the château of Oranienstein in Diez.
The town was also the residence of the Stein overlords – Baron von Stein, a Prussian minister at the beginning of the 19C, was an ardent social reformer. There is a small commemorative museum (behind the town hall) in the tower of his natal home.

> **Arnstein Abbey.** – *Excursion of 2.5 km - 1½ miles – by a steep uphill road from the Obernhof Bridge.* The church of this former Premonstratensian monastery (Sacred Heart pilgrimage) stands alone on a wooded rock spike. The Romanesque west chancel contrasts with that in the east, which is Gothic.

The detour one has to make at Holzappel makes one appreciate, even at a distance, the site of Schaumburg Castle.

Balduinstein. – Ruins of a castle built in 1320 to rival that of Schaumburg by Baudouin of Luxembourg, Archbishop of Trier.

Schaumburg Castle. – *Open April to September, 8am to noon and 1 to 6pm; October and March, 9am to noon and 1 to 5pm; 2DM.*
Schaumburg Castle, a large-scale Neo-Gothic reconstruction, stands in one of the sunniest spots in the valley, the crenellated towers overlooking Balduinstein in its picturesque setting. The most interesting part of the tour is the **view** from the main tower.

Between Schaumburg Castle and Limburg, look out for the small town of Diez crowded together at the foot of a massively tall castle, now a youth hostel.

Diez. – In another part of the town, the château of Oranienstein (17C) preserves the memory of the Orange-Nassau House through its furniture and works of art. Queen Juliana of the Netherlands lived here during her official visit in 1971. From the garden a lovely view of the valley.

Army property, passport required. Guided tours 9.30 to 11.30am and 2 to 4.30pm; 1DM.

Limburg*. – *Description p 165.*

Runkel*. – The rough wall of the **castle***, which has been built into the rock face, stands like a shield above the old 15C village. The **setting**** of the village itself is one of the most picturesque in the valley and can be well appreciated from the bridge *(illustration above)* and from further away, on the uphill road to Schadeck (the Weilburg road from the village).

Castle open 1 May to 30 September: guided tours at 10.30, 11am, 2, 4 and 5pm; closed Mondays; 1.50DM.
There is a good **view** of the Lahn, the old bridge and Schadeck Castle on the far hillside from the upper terraces.

Weilburg. – *Description p 254.*
The sudden sight of Braunfels Castle immediately after the Usingen road fork on the Westburg–Wetzlar road is exciting.

Braunfels*. – *Castle open 15 March to 15 November, 2 to 5pm; Sundays, 10am to noon and 2 to 5pm; 2.50DM.*
The castle has a superb feudal outline. The perimeter wall encloses the whole village.

Wetzlar. – *Description p 257.*

LANDSBERG AM LECH ★
Michelin map 987 36 – Pop 16 000

Landsberg, which lies on the old Salzburg–Memmingen road, was a fortress town between Swabia and Bavaria in the Middle Ages, thus gaining wealth from tolls and trade.

Towers, fortified gateways and perimeter walls give it a most attractive mediaeval character.
The tiered **site*** of the town can be well appreciated from where the Karolinenbrücke (recommended parking place if the Hauptplatz – see below – is full) ends on the shaded walk on the left bank of the Lech.

■ **SIGHTS** *time: ¾ hour*

Hauptplatz*. – This, the main square, is triangular and is surrounded by a remarkable group of gaily coloured rough-cast houses.

The **St. Mary Fountain** (Marienbrunnen), in the centre, has a marble basin surmounted by a statue of the Virgin.

Town Hall. – The town hall was built between 1699 and 1702, except for its façade which was constructed in 1719 by Dominikus Zimmermann, one of the greatest artists of the Wessobrunn School *(p 256)*, who built the Church at Wies and was also burgomaster of Landsberg. The gable of this elegant town hall is ornamented with finely worked stucco.

In the far corner of the square stands the **Schmalztor**, commonly called the "Beautiful Tower", which enables you to reach the upper town. The 14C tower, which is crowded on all sides by houses, is topped by a lantern turret roofed with glazed tiles.

The Alte Bergstrasse climbs steeply to the Bavarian Gate.

Bavarian Gate (Bayertor). – This 1425 town gateway with its advanced porch flanked by turrets and sculptures is one of the best preserved of this period in all Germany.

The gateway outside the ramparts which continue on either wise is ornamented with carved and painted coats of arms and a Crucifixion.

LANDSHUT ★
Michelin map 987 37 – Pop 58 000 – *Town plan in Michelin Red Guide Deutschland*

Landshut, an elegant mediaeval city and former capital of the dukedom of the Lower Bavaria, on the banks of the Isar, is distinguished by the slender belfry of its Gothic church which rises high above the surrounding valleyed countryside.

The memory of the Ingoldstadt and Landshut branches of the House of Wittelsbach, who until the 16C outshone even their sumptuous Munich cousins, remains vividly alive. Every three years the town commemorates with great pomp the marriage in 1475 of the son of Duke Ludwig the Rich with Hedwige, daughter of the King of Poland *(see list of events p 31)*.

■ **MAIN SIGHTS** *time: ¾ hour*

St. Martin's*. – 14-15C. The **church**, built in red brick, has an outstanding elevation. The **tower****, which is square at its base, slims and becomes octagonal in shape as it rises to 133 m - 436 ft. Go round the outside of the church which is decorated with tombstones. Early Renaissance influences may be seen in the five Flamboyant doorways.

The interior is particularly well lit and uniform. The octagonal pillars, which look so fragile, support, in a single thrust, vaulting which rises 52 m - 170 ft.

There is a delicate *Virgin and Child* by Leinberger (1518) on the altar in the south aisle.

"Altstadt"*. – The most important monuments are to be found in this wide, slightly curved main street lined with 15 and 16C arcaded houses. Note the imagination of design and variety of the gables. Variety, though to a lesser degree, may also be seen in the house gables in the Neustadt, which runs parallel to the Altstadt, and Baroquised façades.

■ **ADDITIONAL SIGHTS**

Residence (Stadtresidenz). – *The German wing and the local museum, and the Italian wing are visited separately; open 9am to noon and 1 to 5.30pm; in winter 9am to noon and 1 to 4pm; closed Mondays in winter; 1.50DM for each tour.*

The palace, opposite the town hall, consists of two main buildings linked by narrow wings: the German one faces on to the Alstadt (18C furniture, decorations); the 16C Italian Renaissance one looks on to the courtyard (large rooms with painted coffered ceilings).

The German wing communicates with the museum (art and history).

Trausnitz Castle. – *Open 9am to noon and 1 to 5.30pm (4pm in winter); closed Mondays in winter; 1DM.*

Of the fortress embellished during the Renaissance with arcaded galleries, the chapel (Burgkapelle), remarkable especially for its Romanesque statuary, is open to the public as is also the Gothic hall known as the Alte Dürnitz, several rooms furnished or decorated in 16C style and the Buffoon Staircase (Narrentreppe), painted in the 16C with scenes from Italian comedy. There is an outstanding **view** of the town's rooftops and the St. Martin spire from a balcony (Söller).

LAUENBURG AN DER ELBE

Michelin map **987** southwest of 6 – Pop 11 000

Lauenburg, today a somewhat sleepy town, commands a section of the Elbe whose importance was formerly linked with the salt trade between Lüneburg and Lübeck *(p 170)*. The old sailors' houses are grouped at the foot of a steeply wooded slope, once a castle site.

Schlossberg. – Leave the road running through the town (the Hamburg–Berlin road) in the upper town to walk to the edge of the plateau. Take the round clock tower, sole relic of the castle, as your goal. Drop down from the tower to a terrace in the gardens: view of the Elbe, the bridge and the confluence of the Elbe–Lübeck Canal and the Elbe.

Lower Town. – *Follow the sign "Malerische Unterstadt".* The picturesque old houses of the old town are laid out along the Elbe.

LEMGO ★

Michelin map **987** 14 – Pop 40 000

During the 15 and 16C the Hanseatic town of Lemgo became prosperous due to its trading relations with Flanders and England. This wealth is still apparent: the well laid out plan of the comfortable private homes with their varied façades and frontons.

Tour. – *Time: 1 hour.* Start from the east gate (Ostertor) and make your way to the Mittelstrasse which forms the main street of the old town. Most of the houses date back to the second half of the 16C, in particular nos 17 (a wood carved house) and 36 (called house of Planets).

Town Hall★★. – It is composed of eight buildings placed side by side. Its oriel windows, gables and arcades are unique. The former pharmacy on the corner of the Marktplatz, with its elaborate façade shows, on the first floor, the sculptured portraits of the ten famous philosophers and physicians from Aristotle to Paracelsus. Under the central arcades, witchcraft trials took place in about 1670.

Bear left into the Breite Strasse.

House of the Witches Burgomaster (Hexenbürgermeisterhaus). – *19 Breite Strasse.* This patrician house (1568) has one of the most beautiful façades in the town. Inside, a **local museum** contains historical documents and instruments of torture *(open 10am to 7pm; closed Saturday afternoons and Mondays; 1DM)*.

St. Mary's (Marienkirche). – This Gothic building has a fine Renaissance organ.

Return to the Papenstrasse which you take to the right.

St. Nicholas' (Nicolaikirche). – The church is dedicated to the patron of merchants. Built at the beginning of the 13C, it shows both Romanesque and Gothic elements: a tympanum with three characters in the south aisle, stone triptych in the north aisle; frescoes and keystones. The pulpit and the font are late Renaissance (about 1600).

The Papenstrasse brings you back to the starting point.

LIMBURG AN DER LAHN ★

Michelin map **204** 4 – *Local map p 163* – Pop 29 000
Town plan in Michelin Red Guide Deutschland

The town of Limburg was owned by the counts of Lahngau until 1407 and by the electors of Trier from 1420 to 1803. Today it is the seat of a Roman Catholic bishop and an important cultural and economic centre of the Nassau region.

The outline of Limburg Cathedral, which is at the same time compact and lofty as it rises above the Lahn, puts in the shade everything else in the town.

The cathedral can be seen from the bridge over the Lahn *(see illustration)* or briefly from the motorway bridge.

■ **SIGHTS** *time: 1 hour*

Cathedral★ (Dom). – St. George's Cathedral stands in a picturesque **setting★★** on a spur of rock. It is also remarkable architecturally, being a classic example of the Gothic Transitional style which was widely current in Germany between 1210 and 1250

The exterior is still Romanesque and closely resembles the cathedrals of the Rhineland *(p 23)*.

The interior, disfigured by a multi-coloured decoration, the work of 19C archaeologists, is already Gothic and directly inspired by the Ile-de-France with superimposed galleries, triforium and upper windows; the crochet capitals are typical of the first Gothic period. The vaulting is on diagonal ribs; the transept crossing lies beneath a domed lantern tower.

(After a photo by Dr. Wolf Strache)

Limburg – The Cathedral.

From the **burial ground terrace** (Friedhofterrasse) on the north side of the church, there is a good bird's-eye **view★** of the river bed, the old bridge and the motorway viaduct.

Old Town (Altstadt). – South of the cathedral is an old quarter, crowded with half-timbered houses with festooned gables. From the centre of this quarter, narrow streets lead to the foot of the cathedral, some of which are stepped.

Diocesan Museum (Diözesan-Museum). – *Temporarily closed for reorganisation.*

The museum is in the old castle which belonged to the counts and was constructed in the 13C. From the courtyard there is a view of the cathedral apse. The 10C Byzantine reliquary-cross known as the Limburger Staurothek is the gem of this collection of religious art.

LINDAU ★★ (LINDAU IM BODENSEE)

Michelin map **206** 9 – *Local maps pp 42 and 103* – Pop 26 000

Visitors enjoy Lindau, a former Free Imperial City (1275-1802) which adds to the charm of its old streets an island setting, lights in the harbour and from the hotels at night and in the day a majestic panorama, sometimes obscured in summer by the haze from Lake Constance, the Swabian Sea.

Today, the Holiday Island (Ferieninsel) is attached to the mainland by a road bridge and a railway embankment and footpath. The town, which is the starting point of the German Alpine Road, became overcrowded with tourists, so a garden city (Gartenstadt) was developed on the lakeshore *(see general town plan in Michelin Red Guide Deutschland)* with a variety of sports and other facilities – beaches at Eichwald and Lindenhof, golf courses, tennis courts, sailing, horse-riding, etc.

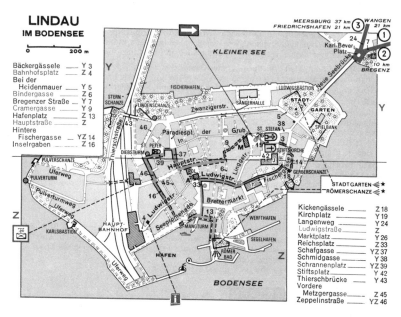

LINDAU
IM BODENSEE

Bäckergässele	Y 3
Bahnhofsplatz	Z 4
Bei der	
Heidenmauer	Y 5
Bindergasse	Z 6
Bregenzer Straße	Y 7
Cramergasse	Y 9
Hafenplatz	Z 13
Hauptstraße	Z
Hintere	
Fischergasse	YZ 14
Inselrgaben	Z 16

Kickengässele	Z 18
Kirchplatz	Y 19
Langenweg	Y 24
Ludwigstraße	Z
Marktplatz	Y 26
Reichsplatz	Z 33
Schafgasse	YZ 37
Schmidgasse	Y 38
Schrannenplatz	YZ 39
Stiftsplatz	Y 42
Thierschbrücke	Y 43
Vordere	
Metzgergasse	Z 45
Zeppelinstraße	YZ 46

■ SIGHTS *time: 1 hour*

When there is a lot of traffic we do not advise going to the island by car but suggest you leave it on one of the parks at the north end of the bridge (Karl-Bever-Platz).

Leave the Marktplatz on which stands, facing St. Stefan's, **Cavazzen House** – a lavish piece of Baroque bourgeois architecture (1729) which now houses the museum and the reading rooms for tourists.

Municipal Museum (Städtische Kunstsammlungen) (M). – *Open: weekdays, 9am to noon and 2 to 5pm; Sundays, 10am to noon; closed Mondays and from January to March; 2 DM.*

The museum contains old documents on the town of Lindau and also houses a gallery of painting and sculpture.

Go along the Cramergasse which comes out into the Hauptstrasse.

Hauptstrasse (Z). – This, the main highway of the old town, is lined with picturesque old houses and inns. Narrow façades, half-timbered and with the oriel windows characteristic of the Alpine Rhine Valley and the Vorarlberg, stand side by side with the stepped gables of Old Swabia. The old **town hall** (Altes Rathaus) **(A)** is a good example of this second style, it dates back to the 15C.

Bear right into the Schafgasse beyond the Brodlauben arcades, then left into the Schrannenplatz. Pass in front of the former Church of St. Peter, 11C and the oldest in the city and now a memorial to the 1914-18 War, and before the **Brigands' Tower** (Diebsturm), a well known Lindau silhouette with its crown of battlemented watch-towers. Turn left into the Zeppelin-strasse which continues as the Inselgraben and marks, in the west, the limits of the old fortification system on the island.

The Port (Hafen). – Tourists crowd the quays, not only to embark on large white Bodensee ships, but also to walk around enjoying the harbour life, and the views of the lake and the Alps.

A small lighthouse and the monument of the Lion of Bavaria (1856) command the entrance to the roadstead. Alone on the quay stands the 13C Mangturm, also formerly a lighthouse. A little further on, up a few steps, is the quiet shaded **Römerschanze★** terrace, a good viewpoint from which to pick out the Alpine landmarks of the "Bodan" – the old form of Bodensee – near the Rhine gap. These are Kanisfluh, Hoher Freschen, Drei Schwestern and, in Switzerland, Säntis and Altmann.

Make for the Ludwigstrasse, by way of the Reichsplatz which ends at the south façade of the former town hall, and turn right.

Ludwigstrasse. – This serves a pleasant popular quarter which is typically Vorarlberg in character *(see above)*.

Continue straight along by the Fischergasse which you leave to take on the right the narrow Kickengässele alley to the Hintere Fischergasse, a typical relic of the lesser old Lindau. The walk ends at the Bäckergässele, though some may wish to continue on to the **public gardens** (Stadtgarten) where there is once again a **view★** of the lake and the Alps.

To find a hotel or restaurant

look at the current Michelin Red Guide Deutschland.

LINDERHOF Castle ★

Michelin map **987** 36 – 14 km - 9 miles – west of Oberammergau – *Local map p 42*

Ludwig II had this small cream coloured palace built deep in the forest in one of the wild valleys of the Ammergau Alps, which the royal hunters of the House of Bavaria reserved for their own use. Linderhof charms, less through its fantasy and décor than its park.

Tour. – *About 2 hours. Castle, pavilion and grotto open 1 April to 30 September, 9am to 5pm (5.30pm June to August, Sundays and holidays, fountains playing every hour); 3DM. Castle open 1 October to 31 March, 9am to 12.15pm and 12.45 to 4pm; 2DM.*

The Castle. – Ludwig II, when he had the castle built between 1874 and 1879, hoped by interweaving the second Italian Renaissance and Baroque styles to achieve a certain intimacy. Thus inside are a state bedchamber surpassing in luxury even those of Versailles, a room of mirrors, painted cloth panels in imitation of tapestry, statues and pastels of Louis XIV, Louis XV, Madame de Pompadour, Madame du Barry and others.

The Park★★. – Pools, cascades and terraced gardens have been laid out in Italian villa style, on the slopes of the valley which forms a vista in line with the castle. The flower-beds are formal, with beech hedges and boxwood bushes trained in pyramids.

Climb up to the rotunda of the Temple of Venus, where the main viewpoint is above a large ornamental lake. Descend, keeping the castle on your right, to climb the opposite slope to the Moorish pavilion and the grotto. This displays the skill of the landscape gardener, Karl von Effner – plantations of oak, maple and beech have been placed before a dark background of pine trees.

Moorish Pavilion (Maurischer Kiosk). – A reminder of the Paris Exhibition of 1867, this building was used by Ludwig II whenever he decided to play the Oriental potentate.

The Grotto. – The entrance to this extravagant cavern is reminiscent of Ali Baba. On the lake, illuminated by the play of coloured lights, floats a boat shaped like a huge conch shell. The reason for this whim is to be found in the Venusberg episode in Wagner's opera *Tannhäuser*.

LÜBECK ★★

Michelin map **987** 6 – Pop 228 500

Lübeck, which has retained the air of an old Hanseatic town, is girdled by canals and crowned with towers. It has houses and monuments, often decorated with alternate red brick and glazed black brick courses. In the Middle Ages it was the business centre for northern Europe; today it is still the busiest Federal German port on the Baltic and a centre for heavy industry.

General View. – Enter the town over the St. Mary Bridge (Marienbrücke). From left to right may be seen the St. James' belltower, recognisable by the balls decorating the base of the spire, the twin towers of St. Mary's, the tower of St. Peter's with the platform flanked by pinnacles, and the two sharply pointed spires of the cathedral.

The Capital of the Hanseatic League. – Lübeck's power declined in the 14C, although it remained the capital of the **Hanseatic League** – that association of towns of northern Germany and the Netherlands which, from the 12 to the 16C, monopolised trade with Russia and Scandinavia. The port landed cargoes from Scandinavia which were then sent on by land to places as far as Hamburg *(p 136)*; it was also a base from which Germans colonised Scandinavia.

In the 16C shipping merchants and businessmen, after a long period of decadence, bestirred themselves again, thanks to the establishment of relations with the Netherlands and with France and the Iberian Peninsula, which sent shipments of wine. In the 19C the town suffered competition from the Prussian port of Stettin and from the opening of the Kiel Canal. The development of industry in the suburbs, the construction in 1900 of a canal connecting the town with the Elbe, the influx of nearly 100 000 refugees in 1945, give Lübeck its present status.

■ **THE OLD TOWN★★★** (Altstadt) *tour: 2½ hours*

Holstentor★★. – This fortified gate with its enormous twin towers was built in advance of the perimeter wall in 1477. The most carefully designed façade, that towards the town, has three tiers of blind arcades, plus ornamented ceramic friezes. The building houses the local municipal museum (**Museum im Holstentor** – *open 10am to 5pm, 4pm in winter; closed Mondays and holidays*) which displays a model of Lübeck in 1650.

Before going across the Trave Bridge look, on the right, at the group of 16 and 17C salt warehouses where formerly the salt from Lüneburg *(p 170)* was stored.

Go up the Holstenstrasse to the Marktplatz esplanade at the foot of the town hall.

Town Hall★. – The town hall was built from 1250 onwards and stands on two sides of the Marktplatz, its unusual buildings of dark glazed brick raised, in accordance with former municipal traditions *(see notes on town halls, p 24)* on arcades. The most typical features are the high protective walls, sometimes pierced with blind arcades or great gaping round openings strengthened by decorative slender turrets with pointed snuffer tops.

Superstructures on the north wing on the left contain the upper parts of Gothic blind arcades. In front of the wall a Renaissance façade has been added in ornately carved limestone. The east wing on the right is particularly interesting for its end main building, the Neues Gemach (1440), supported by an imaginatively pierced wall. Pass beneath to see, on the Breite Strasse, a stone staircase built in 1594 in the Dutch Renaissance style.

Go on round the Rathaus to the north face. This has kept its impressive original design with immense bays ranged in lines for almost its entire height.

St. Mary's★★ (Marienkirche). – The first plans in 1250 were for a hall-type church *(p 24)* without a transept, but the design was changed while work was in progress. Influenced by French cathedral architecture, the main vaulting supported by buttresses was raised to nearly 40 m - 130 ft – and two flanking towers were added to the façade on either side of the single original tower. The church, which was completed in 1330, was built for the burghers.

Before going inside through the south door, glance at the angular polygonal east end with the advanced Lady Chapel, built in 1440. Seen from the centre of the nave, the interior has grandiose proportions. Bear left to come to the end of the south aisle and the elegant early 14C chapel, the **Briefkapelle**, which is adorned with tall lancet windows similar to those of the Radiant Gothic period. The star vaulting rests on two slender monolithic granite columns.

Continue in a clockwise direction. The great organ, built in 1968, which stands inside the façade, is dedicated to the composer Buxtehude (1637-1707), organist at this church, whose reputation was such as to bring Johann Sebastian Bach and Handel to Lübeck in pilgrimage. The south tower, since 1945, has been a memorial to the German dead buried overseas.

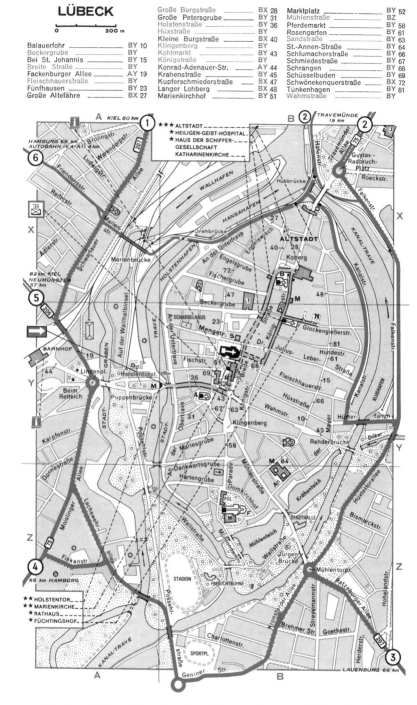

From beneath the north tower there is a striking view along the north aisle to the ambulatory bay at the turn of the apse. As you go round the ambulatory note Buxtehude's epitaph on the right of the chancel end wall at the height of the Dance of the Dead's organ.

The ambulatory vaulting in one sweep covers also the two radial apsidal chapels. The axial Lady Chapel (1444) contains an altarpiece to the Virgin made in Antwerp in 1518.

Come out of the church and go round the east end, walking through the arcade of the former chancellery of the town hall (15 and 16C). The Volksbank, on the square, now occupies the Baroque house, Buddenbrookhaus (**S**), which was made famous by Thomas Mann (1875-1955) in his novel *Buddenbrooks*. The author himself was born in the house.

Follow the Breite Strasse to the Koberg square and St. James' Church (p 169).

Seamen's Guild House★ (Haus der Schiffergesellschaft). The **interior★★** (now a restaurant) still has the furnishings of a seamen's tavern with rough wooden tables, pew benches with tall backs, copper lamps and lanterns and ships' models hanging from the beams.

Hospice of the Holy Spirit★ (Heiligen-Geist-Hospital). – From the end of the 13C this hospital *(being enlarged)* has stood upon the Koberg, its three aligned brick gables flanked by slender turrets reminiscent of the Rathaus. The gables mark the chapel aisles.

The **chapel** (1286), in the form of a wide Gothic hall with two bays *(open 9.30am to 5pm)*, is decorated with 13 and 14C wall paintings. Immediately beyond, in accordance with mediaeval tradition, is the great hospice hall (Langes Haus – *closed during alterations*).

St. Catherine's (Katharinenkirche). – The lower niches of the 14C façade contain modern statues* (Figurenreihe) of which the first three on the left are by Ernst Barlach.

The "Höfe" and the "Gänge". – Turn left by the corner of the church into the Glockengiesserstrasse on to which open the courts (Höfe) which are typical of Lübeck. These, set back from the street, are almost social amenities and were given by generous 17C personages. Successively along the streets are, at no 23, the delightful **Füchtingshof***, with a Baroque doorway dating from 1639 and buildings disposed round a shaded and flower adorned courtyard; at no 41, the **Glandorps-Gang**, a simple alignment of small houses along an alley and from no 49 to no 51, the **Glandorps-Hof** (N).

Return to the Königstrasse and bear right into the Schrangen (attractive glimpse of St. Mary's Church east end) to return to the town hall.

■ ADDITIONAL SIGHTS

Burgtor* (BX D). – This fortified brick gateway defended the small isthmus, formerly the only land approach to Lübeck. (The isthmus is now cut by a canal.) Seen from inside, the gateway is a fine example of 13-15C military architecture with a decorative design of superimposed tierce-point bays. Go through to look at the outer side.

St. James' (Jakobikirche) (BX B). – This small Gothic hall-church has dark furnishings and old Dutch style lighting and two 16 and 17C **organ lofts**** (Orgel) with magnificent woodwork. The first chapel on the north aisle is a memorial to the shipwrecked and contains a lifeboat said to be from the *Pamir*, the Lübeck training ship wrecked with all hands in 1957.

Mengstrasse (BY). – To some degree this street has kept its original character at its lower end. The line of brick gables illustrates the rivalry among former local notables. The two houses now occupied by the Schabbelhaus Restaurant have been carefully restored.

St. Peter's (Petrikirche) (BY A). – *Not open to the public.* Aerial view of the town, particularly the Holstentor, may be had from the tower platform *(lift, only in summer: 0.60DM)*.

Cathedral (Dom) (BZ F). – The original Romanesque building was transformed in the 14C when a vast Gothic chancel was added. A gigantic 1477 Christ by Bernt Notke stands on the glory beam.

St. Anne's Museum* (BYZ M). – *Open 10am to 5pm (4pm October to March); closed Mondays and holidays.* This museum in an ancient monastery is devoted to Old Lübeck. On the ground floor is a large collection of religious statuary; outstanding are the works of Bernt Notke, master sculptor of Lübeck in the 15C, and an **altarpiece of the Passion** painted by Memling in 1491.

Behnhaus (BX M). – This 18C mansion, now a museum *(open 10am to 5pm – 4pm October to March; closed Mondays)*, contains works by the Catholic painter Friedrich Overbeck (1789-1869), leader of the Nazarene Group and the Norwegian, Edvard Munch (1863-1944).

▆ LUDWIGSBURG ★
Michelin map **206** 12 – Pop 83 000 – *Town plan in Michelin Red Guide Deutschland*

An immense Baroque castle built at the beginning of the 18C by a Duke of Württemberg, dreaming of another Versailles, was the beginning of Ludwigsburg, a town with artificially dead straight streets. Visitors are more attracted by the park than the castle.

The Castle* (Schloss). – This quadrilateral monument has 452 rooms; 75 only are open.

Tour of the Apartments. – *Guided tours: end March to mid-October, 9am to noon and 1 to 5pm; the rest of the year, 10.30am and 3pm (Saturdays and Sundays, 10.30am, 2 and 3.30pm); time: 1¼ hours; 1DM. Brochure in English. Entrance: 1st courtyard on the right on the road from Stuttgart (access also through the park).* Inside the "fine floor" (first floor) of the New Building and the apartments decorated in the Empire style are arranged to illustrate life at court in the Baroque period. Through the Ancestors' Gallery (Ahnengalerie) and the Castle Catholic Church, adorned with luscious Italian stucco, you reach the Fürstenbau state apartments, the oldest and tallest part of the castle which closes the north side of the court.

Park*. – *Open end March to mid-October, 7.30am to 8.30pm; 3.50DM. Illuminations nightly.* In front of the new building to the south, formally patterned flowerbeds and Baroque green arbours, have been replanted; more rolling land north and east, landscaped.

Fairies Garden** (Märchengarten). – *Open 7.30am to 6pm.* Popular German folk-tales (taken from the Brothers Grimm) are performed by mechanical figures.

EXCURSION

Monrepos Castle; Markgröningen. – *10 km - 3 miles – about 1½ hours.* Leave Ludwigsburg by the Heilbronn road (no 27) 800 m - 850 yds after passing beneath the railway, turn right into the Monreposstrasse then left into the Monrepos Castle avenue.

Monrepos Castle. – *Open 1 March to 31 October, 9 to 11.30am and 2 to 6pm; 0.50DM.* This gracious Louis XV castle *(plan p 29)*, built in 1767 beside a pool, encircles a rotunda. Turn and, before the lower road, bear right for Markgröningen.

Markgröningen. – *Tour: ½ hour.* The 15C wooden **Rathaus*** is, by virtue of its impressive size and skilful construction, a monument to German half-timbering craftsmanship in this picturesque town, which still has many houses built of wood.

▆ LUISENBURG ★★
Michelin map **987** 27 – south of Wunsiedel – *Local map p 61*

This labyrinth (Felsenlabyrinth) of enormous granite blocks, eroded into round balls or piled up like plates, can be walked through along a pine shaded, hilly path. Viewpoints allow one to see the Fichtelgebirge.

Tour. – *About 2 hours.* The approach road branches off road no 303, south of Wunsiedel.

Leave the car in the Luisenburg car park. The footpath begins behind the open air theatre (well known festival). *When getting your ticket – 1DM – obtain a map showing the way.*

The way up is marked by blue arrows and the way down by red. The walk can be cut by an hour by turning right after the Grüne Wand site; this will bring you out at the Romantische Felsengruppe rocks on the return route.

Michelin map **987** northeast of 15 – Pop 65 000

Lüneburg, which is known for its brick houses, is built upon a salt deposit.

Salt. – Lüneburg thrived on salt in the Middle Ages when it supplied most of Scandinavia (the Baltic is not highly salted). Traffic passed along the old Salt Road via Lauenburg and Ratzeburg to the warehouses (p 165) and quays of Lübeck. Trade declined in the 16C.

A new port. – Since 1975 Lüneburg has been opened to river traffic with the new Lateral Canal which links Hamburg to Braunschweig industrial area. To the north of the town, an elevator can lift two barges (1 300 t each) in three minutes to a difference in level of 38 m - 125 ft.

Beim Benedikt						Y 21
Bleckeder Landstraße						X 22
Bockelmannstraße						X 24
Dahlenburger Landstr.						Y 25
Egersdorffstraße						X 27
Görgesstraße						Y 28
Grapengießerstraße						Y
Große Bäckerstraße						X 30
Im Wendischen Dorfe-						X 31
Kaufhausstraße						X 32
Kleine Bäckerstraße						Y 34
Kuhstraße						Y 35
Lüner Straße						X 38
Reitende-Diener-Str. -						X 40
Rosenstraße						X 42
Rotehahnstraße						X 43
Rote Straße						Y
Schröderstraße						Y 46
Vor dem Bardowicker Tore						X 47
Waagestraße						X 48

Altenbrückerdamm	X 2	An den Brodbänken	X 8	Bardowickerstraße	X 17
Altenbrückertorstraße -	Y 3	An den Reeperbahnen	Z 9	Bei der Abtspferdetränke	X 18
Am Markt	X 5	An der Münze	Y 10	Bei der St. Johanniskirche	Y 19
Am Sande	Y	Auf dem Kauf	X 12		
Am Schifferwall	X 6	Bahnhofstraße	Y 16		

■ MAIN SIGHTS time: 1 hour

Town Hall★★. – Guided tours: May to September 10, 11am, noon, 2.15 and 3.15pm; Saturdays and Sundays, 10, 11am and noon. October to April, Mondays, Tuesdays, Thursdays and Fridays, 10, 11.15am, 2 and 3.15pm; Wednesdays and Saturdays, 10 to 11.15am; Sundays 11am; 2DM.
The town hall is an assemblage of different buildings dating from the 13-18C.
Enter through the Gothic doorway on the Am Ochsenmarkt. The **Great Council Chamber★★** (Grosse Ratsstube), to the right of the entrance hall, is a Renaissance masterpiece (1566-84). The room is panelled and adorned with intricate wood sculptures by Albert of Soest: note the richness of expression of the small heads in the almost rhythmic frieze above the allegorical paintings, also the beautiful doorframes.
The Princes' Apartment (Fürstensaal), on the first floor, is outstanding. It is Gothic with lamps made from stags' antlers and a superb beamed and painted ceiling. The Hall of Justice, the Laube, has cradle vaulting and is decorated with Memling's and his pupils' paintings.

Am Sande★. – This town square, which is dominated on its east side by St. John's Church tower, extends between houses with scrolled or stepped gables. The twisting brick effects producing a cable-like appearance and rounded or tierce-point blind arcades are typical of Lüneburg and the region. Look particularly at nos 1, 6-7, 46 and 53.

■ ADDITIONAL SIGHTS

Walk through the Old Port (Wasserviertel) – Follow the tour indicated on the plan starting from the mill (Abtsmühle) on the left bank of the Ilmenau. From the second bridge across the millstream, there is a pleasant view of the galleried buildings overlooking the river on the left and the old 18C crane (Alter Kran) on the right.
The **Old Brewery★** (Ehemaliges Brauhaus), a gabled Renaissance building, decorated with twisted brick motifs and medallions, stands at the corner of the Am Werder square and the Am Werderstrasse. Further on, at the Lünertorstrasse and Kaufhausstrasse corner, is the Staatshochbauamt House (1574) with remarkable rusticated half-pilasters and cornice, and the Baroque gabled Kaufhaus, remains of a 1745 warehouse. Return to the mill.

WASSERVIERTEL

House no 14, Rotehahnstrasse (X D). – This house with its three half-timbered gables and rustic appearance is unexpected. Enter the courtyard shaded by a sycamore tree.

Reitende-Diener-Strasse (X 40). – The street is lined with low houses, all similarly designed with twisted brick cornices and medallions.

Grosse Bäckerstrasse (Y 30). – In this pleasant pedestrian street, the Raths-Apotheke (chemist's) and the house next door show fine twisted brick gables.

St. John's (St. Johanniskirche) (Y E). – *Open 9am (11.15am Sundays) to noon and 2 to 5pm (4pm October to March).*
The single robust tower, tall but inclined, shows efforts to counteract subsidence. The present church dates from the 14C. The wide interior has five aisles and two rows of side chapels and forms a perfect square overall closed at the east end by plain polygonal apses. The most precious of the furnishings is the high altarpiece with panels painted depicting John the Baptist, St. George, St. Cecilia and St. Ursula (1482).

EXCURSION

Lüne Convent (Kloster Lüne). – *2 km - 1 mile – by ① on the plan, plus 1 hour sightseeing. Open: May to September, weekdays from 9am to noon and 3 to 6pm; Sundays and holidays, 11.30 am to 1pm and 2 to 6pm; 2DM.*
The Gothic cloister and the fountain are the outstanding features of this old 15C abbey and its conventual buildings.

LÜNEBURG HEATH (LÜNEBURGER HEIDE)
Michelin map **987** 15, 16

Lüneburg Heath is remembered by many as the place in which Montgomery's caravan was situated at the end of the war, and to which the German High Command came to sign the treaty of unconditional surrender on 4 May 1945.
The heath is confined by the great sweeps of the Bremen–Hamburg motorway, the Aller Valley and the Brunswick–Lüneburg road. This rather bleak region is at its best in the second half of August when the heather flowers and the birches, pines and junipers are in leaf.

The Nature Reserve. – 200 m² - 77 sq miles round the Wilseder Berg have been classified as a nature reserve to prevent further agricultural encroachment. Flora and fauna are protected; cars have to keep to the through roads. Considerable effort is also being made to preserve the rural character of the Lower Saxony housing *(illustration p 30)*. Even outside the park the villages retain a rural charm (Müden, Visselhövede, Egestorf).

Notable Towns and Settings
directions for sights near the motorway, E 3-4, are given as from the motorway

Bergen-Belsen. – *Description p 65.*

Celle★★. – *Description p 92.*

Ebstorf. – *26 km - 16 miles – south of Lüneburg.* The Gothic cloister and the nuns' gallery (Nonnenchor), where an elegant statue of St. Michael in knight's armour (1300) and Romanesque and Gothic Virgins, are all that can now be seen of the former 14 and 15C Benedictine abbey *(summer only 10-11.15am Sundays and holidays – to noon and 2-3pm; Sundays and holidays – to 6pm; time: 1 hour; 2.50DM)*. Those interested in old maps will see a reproduction of a 13C **map of the world★** (Ebstorfer Weltkarte). The original was destroyed in the war.

Lönsgrab. – *8 km - 5 miles – from the motorway (Fallingbostel exit) by the Walsrode road and the route marked Lönsgrab (right on leaving Honerdingen), plus 1 hour on foot Rtn.*
The tomb and monument of the poet Hermann Löns (1866-1914), who sang the beauties of the heath with extravagant lyricism, stand in a bare setting of junipers.

Lönsstein. – *½ hour on foot Rtn.* Halfway between Baven and Müden, leave the car to follow a line of birch trees up towards the Lönsstein, another monument to the poet Löns *(see above).* Junipers, birches, pines and heather grow on the site.

Suhlendorf: Mills Museum (Mühlenmuseum). – *15 km - 9 miles – to the east of Uelzen by the B 71. Open 10am to 8pm; closed Tuesdays; 2.50DM.*
Collection of some thirty models of wind and water mills from Europe, Africa and Asia. The main attraction is the reproduction of the well-known Sanssouci mill at Potsdam, whose noise, it was said, disturbed Frederick II's sleep.

Undeloh★. – *8 km - 5 miles – from the motorway (Egestorf exit) by Egestorf.* Undeloh, an attractive **village★** where the houses shelter beneath huge oaks, sees the start of the 4 km - 2 mile road *(horse-drawn vehicles only – no cars)* to Wilsede, a village in the reserve kept apart from mechanical civilisation.

Walsrode: Ornithological Park★★ (Vogelpark). – *3 km - 2 miles – from the motorway E 71, exit Walsrode-West. Open 21 March to 31 October, 9am to 7pm (sunset in mid-season); 3.50DM.* Follow the itinerary sign "Rundgang". In a 15 ha - 37 acres – park decorated with flowers, 4 600 birds (900 species from all over the world) are to be found very often wandering freely in natural surroundings. There is a large quantity of stilt birds and web-footed birds, among those are flamingoes, cranes, ibis, etc. Two ostriches attract much attention as well as their neighbours: emus and penguins. In a bird hall (3 000 m² - 3 588 sq yds and 12 m - 39 ft high) you can observe tropical birds flying. The collection of budgerigars and parrots, one of the largest in the world, is striking both for its sound and visual effects. In the "Paradieshalle" the world of birds and tropical flora are well represented, note also birds from Europe. A big playground is reserved for children.

Wienhausen★. – *Description p 92.*

Wilseder Berg★. – *7 km - 4 miles – from the motorway (Bispingen exit), plus 2 hours on foot Rtn.* Leave the car in the Ober-Haverbeck park. Turn right into the wide sandy track to Wilsede. Leave this where it enters a wood and bear left, remaining on the heath but making for the point of the wood from which an uneven path leads to the summit. From the top (low post, alt 169 m - 554 ft) a vast wood and heath **landscape★** is visible. The spires of the churches of Hamburg can be seen quite distinctly, through glasses, 40 km - 25 miles – to the north.

MAIN Valley

Michelin map **987** 25, 26, 27

The Main, which will form part of the Rhine-Danube waterway system *(p 105)* and thus be linked to Nuremberg, is to Germany in its east-west flow and contact a symbolic frontier. The "Main equator" is often considered to be the boundary between northern and southern Germany – a valid distinction at least gastronomically *(p 33)*.

Tour of the Valley. – Motorists cannot follow the whole 524 km - 326 miles – of twists and bends of the valley; we therefore suggest that they at least see the valley vineyards round Würzburg *(p 263)* and that they go down the last defile between Spessart and Odenwald *(alternative approach road to Rothenburg described p 217)*.

MAINZ ★

Michelin map **204** 6 – Pop 190 000

Mainz, formerly the episcopal seat of the influential prince-electors, was promoted capital of the Rhineland Palatinate in 1949. This town, built at the confluence of the Rhine and the Main, is the largest wine market in Germany and the setting for a carnival famous for its fun and buffoonery *(p 31)*, which is televised nationally. **Gutenberg** *(c 1395-1468)*, the father of modern printing, is the native hero of Mainz.

General View. – The restaurant, An der Favorite, at the top of the **Stadtpark** (DZ), affords a general view of the town lying on either side of the Rhine.

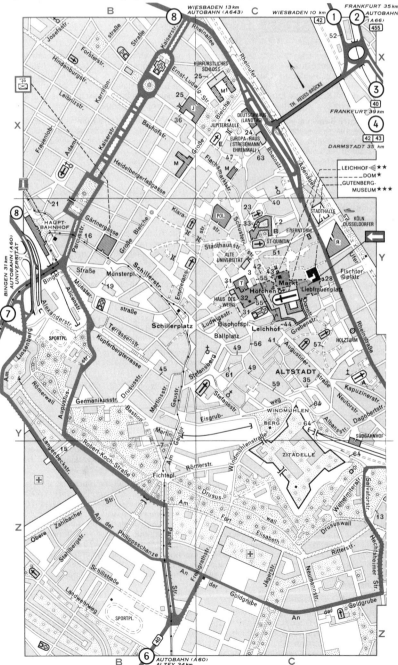

■ MAIN SIGHTS

time: 2 hours

Walk down the Domstrasse and left round the cathedral. The **whole building★★** can be seen from the Leichhof square; the west chancel and transept rising loftily, their complicated ridge roofs overlooked by the lantern tower which crowns the transept crossing. This tower on a Romanesque base showing Lombard influence has an 18C top of mixed Gothic and Baroque design.

The adjoining square, known as the Höfchen, is extended southwards by the Gutenbergplatz (statue of

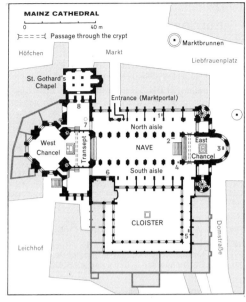

MAINZ

Gutenberg, theatre and Wine House) and northwards by the Markt which is embellished with a **Renaissance fountain** (Marktbrunnen). From the Markt a walk down the Korbgasse brings one to an old quarter with a lovely 15C statue of the Virgin on the corner of the Fledergässchen, where Gutenberg had his workshop.

Enter the cathedral by the doorway on the Markt.

Cathedral★ (Dom). – The cathedral is a huge reconstructed Romanesque edifice. Inside one appreciates the size of this basilica with two chancels, one in the west preceded by a wide transept whose crossing is lit by a fine Rhineland dome, and the other in the east of a simpler architectural style.

The church contains, fixed to the massive Romanesque pillars, a collection of archiepiscopal **funerary monuments★** (Grabstätte der Erzbischöfe).

Turn left into the aisle, on entering. In the second chapel (1) there is a pathetic late 15C Entombment. A multi-coloured Gothic funerary monument is fixed to the pillar (2).

Descend to the crypt below the east chancel to see upon the altar the **modern gold reliquary** (3) of the saints of Mainz.

A multi-coloured Gothic funerary monument attached to the pillar (4) is surrounded by statuettes of Sts. Benedict, Catherine, Maurice and Clare.

Enter the **cloister★** (Kreuzgang) through the door off the south aisle. In addition to the many tombstones there is a statue (5), remodelled in 1783, of the mastersinger, Heinrich von Meissen who was buried by the burgesses of Mainz in 1323.

Fine statues adorn the doorway (6) of the former 15C chapter house which is built in an elegant Rhineland style. Go into the transept and cross below the west chancel, to the south arm opposite. Note a pewter font (7) dating from 1328 and delicately ornamented with figures. A Romanesque doorway (8) leads to the Romanesque Chapel of St. Gothard.

Gutenberg Museum★★★. – *Open 10am to 1pm and 3 to 6pm; closed Sunday afternoons and Mondays. Brochure in English.*

Books are displayed in rotation. Gutenberg's hand press is in the basement among the reconstructed early printing workshops. In a strong room on the first floor is the museum's prize possession: the Gutenberg Bible of 1452-5 with 42 lines to the page *(film showing, daily at 11.15am, time: 18 minutes)*, other rooms show the development of bookbinding (collections of tools and book covers).

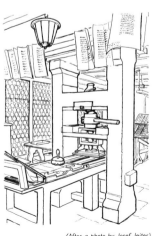

(After a photo by Josef Jeiter)

The Gutenberg Press.

173

MAINZ*

- **ADDITIONAL SIGHTS**

The Roman German Museum* (Römisch-Germanisches Zentralmuseum) (CX M¹). – *Open 10am to 6pm; closed Mondays.*
The museum in the former 15-17C Electors' Palace has collections concerning Mediterranean civilisations, prehistory and the Barbarians.

Mainz Museum of the Central Rhineland* (Mittelrheinisches Landesmuseum Mainz) (BX M).
– *Open 10am to 1pm and 3 to 6pm; closed Sunday afternoons, Mondays and some holidays.*
The department of antiquities tells the story of Rhineland civilisation, and especially that of Mainz, from prehistory onwards. Jupiter's column (Jupitersäule), the most precious relic of Roman colonisation, is on display – a copy stands on the Deutschhaus Platz (CX).

Schillerplatz and Schillerstrasse (BY). – The restored Baroque mansions now house the Land's ministries and the French Institute.

Old Town (Altstadt) (CY). – The picturesque Kirschgarten square lined with half-timbered houses opens off the Augustinerstrasse, the main street through the more or less complete old quarter. The Kapuzinerstrasse (a few houses with limestone doorways and Rococo door panels) leads to the Church of St. Ignatius.

St. Ignatius (Ignazkirche) (CY A). – A somewhat theatrical group of the **Crucifixion*** (Kreuzigungsgruppe) by Hans Backoffen (16C) stands outside the church.

Old People's Home (Altersheim) (CY B). – These modern buildings grouped round a garden have been fortunately placed in the centre of the town near such reminders of the past as the Church of St. Quintin and a Renaissance house with an oriel window.

██ MANDERSCHEID ★
Michelin map ███ 5 – *Local map p 116* – Pop 1 300

Manderscheid commands a wild section of the Lieser in the centre of the volcanic Eifel Massif. It is a tourist centre well situated for visiting numerous ruins and belvederes.

The Setting*. – The Oberburg, and, lower down, the Niederburg keeps, emerging from the forest which invades the narrow Lieser Valley, add a romantic touch to the scene.

Kaisertempel. – $\frac{1}{4}$ *hour on foot Rtn.* On the Niedermanderscheid road below the town, 100 yds after the Aral petrol station, take a hillside path on the left marked Oberburg, which leads to the pavilion. There is a **view**★★ of the Oberburg and Niederburg ruins.

Niederburg*. – Go down by car to Niedermanderscheid. The entrance to the ruin is beyond the arch on the left *(ask for the key from Herr Steffens, house no 1 – 0.60DM).*
From the top of the keep, reached by walking up and round the curves in the defensive system, there is a view of the village, the Oberburg and the Lieser Valley.

EXCURSION

Mosenberg. – *4 km - 2½ miles – plus 1 hour on foot Rtn.* Leave Manderscheid by the westerly Bettenfeld road. Cross a deep valley to the plateau where you turn back left into a field track. Leave the car at the Mosenberg path on the right. The most obvious relic of this volcano with its classic crater – rare in the Eifel – is the Windsborn crater lake.

Museums in Germany are usually closed all day Monday and on Sunday afternoons.

██ MANNHEIM
Michelin map ███ 8 – *Local maps pp 65 and 215* – Pop 320 000

Mannheim, at the confluence of the Rhine and the Neckar, was founded by the Palatine Electors after the sacking of Heidelberg in 1689 *(p 146)*; it soon became a home of the arts where the theatre especially flourished – Schiller's plays were first performed there.
Mannheim, together with Ludwigshafen which lives chiefly by its chemical industry, is the second largest **river port**★ in Europe. *Motorboat trips of the port start from the Kurpfalzbrücke (the bridge over the Neckar) May to September, Tuesdays and Thursdays at 10am, noon, 2.30 and 4.30pm; time: 1-2 hours; 6.50DM.*

The Squared Town* (Quadratstadt). – Mannheim was conceived as a fortified residential town and follows a strict plan: the centre forms a chessboard of 144 residential blocks each known only by letter and number according to its position.

- **SIGHTS** *time: 2¼ hours*

Fine Arts Museum★★ (Städtische Kunsthalle). – *Open: weekdays 10am to 1pm and 2 to 6pm; Saturdays, 10am to 1pm and 2 to 5pm; Sundays, 10am to 5pm; closed Mondays and some holidays.*
There are good 19 and 20C collections. Paintings are on the first floor; on the right are the Impressionists – with, in the French room, the famous *Execution of Maximilian of Mexico* by Manet and Cézanne's *Pipe-Smoker*. On the left is the large collection of Slevogts, Expressionists, with several Beckmanns, a delicate *Woman Asleep* by Heckel, a still life by Ensor and a lovely *View of Amsterdam* by Kokoschka. The department of modern sculpture on the ground floor has several Lehmbrucks, Barlachs and Rodins.

Reiss Municipal Museum*. – *In the Arsenal (Zeughaus). Open: weekdays 10am to 1pm and 2 to 5pm (Wednesdays also 8 to 10pm); Sundays, 10am to 5pm; closed Mondays and some holidays.*
The museum is chiefly devoted to the decorative arts and municipal history.
Fine collections of porcelain manufactured locally (Frankenthal) are displayed on the first floor. In the municipal history department on the second floor there is a copy of the first velocipede made in 1817 by Baron Drais and known as a *draisine.*

Autobahn (E12-A6)
SAARBRÜCKEN 132 km

Autobahn (E12-A6)
FRANKFURT 81 km

Autobahnen (A656), (E12-A6)
HEIDELBERG 18 km
KARLSRUHE 70 km

SCHWETZINGEN 14 km

Brückenstraße _____ CX 7
Dalbergstraße _____ BX 12
Heidelberger Str. _ CY
Kaiserring _____ CY
Kunststraße _____ CY
Kurpfalzstraße _____ CY
Planken _____ CY
Schanzestraße _____ BX 15
Schimperstraße _____ CX 19
Seilerstraße _____ BY 21
Waldhofstraße _____ CX 22

Castle (BCY). – *Guided tours: 1 April to 31 October, 10am to noon and 3 to 5pm; closed Mondays; 1 November to 31 March; open Saturdays, Sundays and holidays only; time: 1 hour; 1DM.*

This is the biggest Baroque palace in Germany. Building began in 1720 and ended in 1760.

Two wings at right angles to the main building enclose a deep courtyard of honour and end, to the right, in a church and to the left, in what was once a library.

Inside, the main castle staircase looks far down the Kurpfalzstrasse, the street that crosses the town from one end to the other. The most original apartment is the green and rose Rococo library adorned with panelling, stuccowork and camaïeu painting.

The **church**, a plain rectangular hall, has a curved ceiling painted by Cosmas Damian Asam.

Marktplatz (CY). – The town hall and the parish church (Untere Pfarrkirche) (CY B), attached on either side of the same tower, symbolised traditionally the union of the sacred and the profane.

Jesuit Church (BY A). – The church was founded at the same time as the castle. The façade is Classical with the three orders superimposed. The interior is light faced with imitation marble.

National Theatre (DY T). – The theatre was rebuilt in 1957.

MARBURG AN DER LAHN ★★

Michelin map **987** 25 – Pop 70 000

Marburg was formerly one of the great pilgrimage centres of the West, the crowds being drawn by the relics of St. Elizabeth of Hungary. Since the Reformation, the town, which retains the magnificent Gothic cathedral dedicated to its patron, has become through its University a centre for Protestant theology. The visitor, as he wanders through the twisting and climbing alleys of the old quarters, on the castle hill, is still likely to meet, particularly on market days (Wednesdays and Saturdays), country people in traditional local costume.

St. Elizabeth (1207-31). – Princess Elizabeth, daughter of the King of Hungary, and the intended bride of the Landgrave Ludwig of Thuringia, was brought, at the age of four, to the court of Thuringia at Wartburg Castle. She became known early for her kindness to the unfortunate. In 1227 her husband, the Landgrave Ludwig died of the plague. Elizabeth resolved to withdraw from the world and went to live at the foot of Marburg Castle in a house next to the hospital for incurables of which she took charge. She died of exhaustion at 24.

She was canonised in 1235; in the following year her body was exhumed to be placed in St. Elizabeth's. In 1527 the Landgrave **Philip the Magnanimous**, a descendant of the saint, was converted publicly to Protestantism. He decided to abolish the cult of the relics and removed the bones of his ancestor for burial in a nearby cemetery.

■ MAIN SIGHTS *tour: 2 hours*

St. Elizabeth's★★ – *Open Easter to 30 September, 9am (11am Sundays) to 6pm; 1 October to Holy Saturday, 10am (11am Sundays) to 6pm; time: ¾ hour; 1DM.*

This, the first Gothic church to be built in Germany, was erected from 1235 to 1283. Its typical German character derives from its three aisles of equal height – making St. Elizabeth's the first hall-church *(p 24)* – and the homogeneity of the chancel and transepts each terminating in an apse. Typical also of Hesse are the transverse roof timbers covering the side aisles. The towers, surmounted by stone spires, rest on powerful buttresses.

Enter through the main doorway. The chapel beneath the tower immediately on the left contains the tomb of Field-Marshal von Hindenburg (1847-1934).

The nave. – Note the following:

(1) St. Elizabeth's statue (c 1470).
(2) Openwork Gothic rood-screen with finely decorated consoles: on the altar, on the nave side, modern Crucifix by Barlach.

Chancel and Transept. – *1DM.*
Among the outstanding **works of art★★★**:

(3) Altarpiece to the Virgin (1517); 1360 *pietà* before the predella.
(4) St. Elizabeth's tomb (after 1250). The 14C low relief on this sarcophagus is of the Entombment.
(5) The remains of the frescoes in the niches are 14 and 15C. Right, a scene evoking Elizabeth's charitable life (the Landgrave sees in his imagination Christ in the bed in which Elizabeth had placed a sick man); solemn disinterring of 1236.
(6) **St. Elizabeth's Shrine★★** (Elisabethschrein) in the old sacristy. This masterpiece of the goldsmith's skill was completed by a Rhineland craftsman in about 1250. Scenes of the saint's life are on the casket's sloping panels.
(7) This window to St. Elizabeth made from 13C medallions, depicts the parable of the Good Samaritan.
(8) A statue of St. Elizabeth as the personification of Charity crowns the priest's former seat. The work dates from 1510 and is said to be by Juppe, a Marburg artist.
(9) "The Landgraves' Chancel" (south transept), the necropolis of the Landgraves of Hesse who were the descendants of St. Elizabeth. Note the tomb of Wilhelm II (d 1509), father of Philip the Magnanimous, which has all the macabre taste of the Renaissance, with the corpse below the prince's statue being eaten by worms (carved by Juppe).

ST. ELIZABETH'S CHURCH

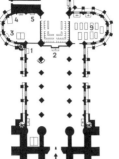

Go into old Marburg by way of Steinweg, a curious rise on three levels which continues as the Neustadt and then the Wettergasse. Turn right into the Marktgasse.

Marktplatz★. – Only the upper part, the Obermarkt, still has old half-timbered houses; outstanding among them the Red Stag House (no 19) (**A**) and no 21 dating from 1560. Students meet round the Market Fountain which is dedicated to St. George.

Rathaus. – A Gothic building dating from 1524. A fine carving by Juppe above the door in the staircase tower shows Elizabeth bearing the arms of her own house of Hesse-Thuringia.

Go by the Nicolaistrasse past the former Ossuary (Karner) to the forecourt of the late 13C Church of St. Mary (Marienkirche). From the terrace there is a wide view.

Descend through a passageway to the Kugelkirche, a late 15C Gothic church. Go up the Kugelgasse. Bear right, before the Kalbstor doorway, into the Ritterstrasse (no 15 was the house of the legal historian Friedrich Karl von Savigny – **B**) which comes out in the Marktplatz. At the upper end take the narrow Schlossteig alley on your left to return to the Wettergasse.

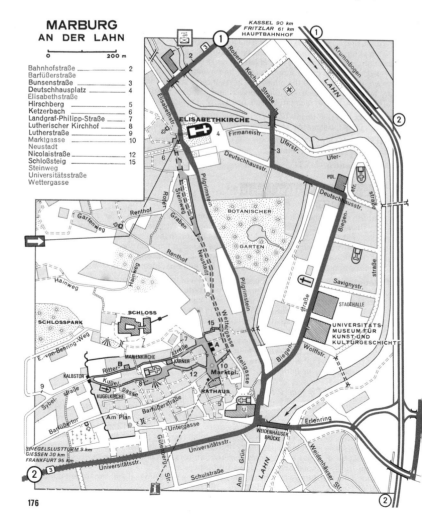

MARBURG AN DER LAHN

0 _____ 200 m

■ ADDITIONAL SIGHTS

Castle*. – Access by car up the Barfüssertor, Sybelstrasse, Lutherstrasse and the E. von Behring-Weg *(steep rises and hairpin bends). Open 16 April to 15 October, 10am to 1pm and 2 to 6pm; 16 October to 15 April, 11am to 1pm and 3 to 4pm; closed Mondays, holidays and, in winter, Sunday afternoons; 0.50DM.* From the 14 to 17C the castle was the residence of the Landgraves of Hesse, descendants of St. Elizabeth. From the terrace lining the first entrance esplanade on the south there is a view along the Lahn Valley to the Taunus. On a tour of these historic 13 and 14C buildings, one sees the Landgrave's study, the small Gothic chapel with its ceramic pavement and the Knights' Hall, a Gothic chamber with two aisles.

History of Art and Civilisation Museum* (Universitätsmuseum). – *Open 10am (11am in winter) to 1pm and 3 to 5pm; closed Monday afternoons.* Precious art objects from St. Elizabeth's Church are on display (stained glass fragments, 15C tapestry).

EXCURSION

Spiegelslustturm. – *9 km - 6 miles.* Leave by ⑦, the Universitätsstrasse going towards Frankfurt; bear left to cross the Lahn over a big modern bridge (Konrad-Adenauer-Brücke) and make for the large modern university buildings on the plateau. 2 km - 1 mile after entering the university quarter bear left into the forest road signposted Spiesegaststätte Spiegelslust. **View*** from the belvedere-tower in the distance of Marburg and the Upper Sauerland.

■ MARIA LAACH Abbey ★
Michelin map **203** northeast of 4 – *Local maps pp 115 and 213*

The vast crater lake beside which the abbey stands seems to increase the monumental air of solidity and poise of the group of Maria Laach buildings. Benedictines from Beuron *(p 251)* have lived in the monastery since 1892 *(high mass with the Gregorian chant Sundays at 8.15am, weekdays 5.30pm; vespers at 7.30pm in the week and 5.30pm on Sundays).*

Abbey Church* (Abteikirche). – *Tour: ½ hour.* Built largely in the 12C, this Romanesque basilica has three aisles and is reminiscent in design of the cathedrals of Worms, Speyer and Mainz. Basalt is used for the Lombard columns and blind arcades. The cloister type entrance portico, added in about 1220, has intricately worked capitals; note those in the doorway.

The interior, which is sombre and bare, was restored and provided with modern stained glass windows in 1956. The altar is surmounted with a bizarre 13C hexagonal baldachin which perhaps shows a certain Moorish influence. The triple aisled crypt *(to visit apply at the porter's lodge to the abbey to join a guided tour)* is the oldest part of the building.

■ MAULBRONN ★★
Michelin map **206** 12 – Pop 5 100

This was one of the earliest Cistercian foundations in Germany. The many abbey buildings, which are well preserved, and the outbuildings are all enclosed within a perimeter wall. The school, which, since the Reformation (1556), has been established here, counted among its pupils such German literary talents as Hölderlin and Hermann Hesse.

The Old Abbey**. – *Tour: about ¾ hour. Open April to September, 7.30am to 12.30pm (Sundays 7.30 to 9am and 11.15am to 12.30pm) and 2 to 6.30pm; the rest of the year, 9.30am (Sundays 11.15am) to 12.30pm and 2 to 5pm; 1DM.* The abbey, founded in 1147, became Protestant at the Reformation and thus escaped any Baroque transformation.

Church* (A). – It was consecrated in 1178.

The early 13C porch (Paradies – a) is the first German example of the transition from Romanesque to Gothic.

Inside, the fan vaulting of the nave and south aisle, which was added in the 15C, spoils the original Romanesque unity. The nave of ten bays is divided into two parts, one for the Fathers, the other for the Brothers, by a Romanesque rood-screen (b) of pure design with a dog-toothed frieze. Before the screen stands a large Crucifix dating from 1473. The chapels off the transept are all that remain of the original church. Note

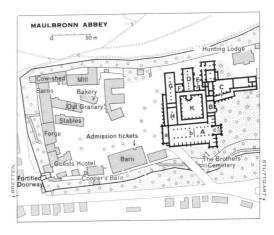

MAULBRONN ABBEY

a beautiful 14C Virgin to the left of the high altar (c).

Cloister** (Kreuzgang) (K) and **Monastery Buildings**** (Klosterbauten). – The south gallery, which runs between the church and the close, has slender columns grouped in large clusters as in the church porch and the fathers' refectory.

Opening off the east gallery are the 14C chapter house (B) whose groined vaulting springs from central pillars, and the parlour gallery (C) with fan vaulting.

The early 13C fathers' refectory (D) is flanked by the calefactory (E) and the kitchen (F). The monumental refectory gives an impression of being crushed low beneath the early Gothic vaulting with its heavy ribs even though these rest on tall, ringed columns. Facing the door, a delightful **lavabo**** (Brunnenkapelle) with quadrilobed blind arcades, dating from about 1350, juts out into the cloistral garden.

From the west gallery enter the brothers' refectory (restored) where groined vaulting lies low over the two aisles (G) and the store-room (H) which has square ribbed vaulting.

MEERSBURG ★

Michelin map **206** 18, 19 – *Local map p 102* – Pop 5 000

Meersburg, the native city of the painter Stefan Lochner *(p 27)*, is a delightful place with a stylish **upper town★** (Oberstadt) and a panoramic view over Lake Constance. To appreciate fully the perched site and the palace façades go out in a boat or ferry on the lake.

Marktplatz★. – The Rathaus backs on to this square, the meeting point of three streets each affording delightful vistas: the street by which you arrive, lined with houses covered with climbing plants, the street to the church and especially the Steigstrasse.

Steigstrasse★. – This street plunges between two lines of half-timbered houses. Walk along it, climbing the gallery on the right which serves the ground floors of the houses, rising ever higher as it proceeds. Stay on the highest paved rise: from the top of the stone stairs (left) there is a good view of the Old Castle.

Return to the Marktplatz, take the passageway beneath the Rathaus to come out on an esplanade, which is the Bishops' New Castle (1712-41).

Go round this by the right, and if the grille is open, up a stairway facing the bridge to the Old Castle, to the New Castle terrace: **view★** of the lake and the Säntis Massif.

MEERSBURG

Burgweg	3
Kirchstraße	4
Marktplatz	
Schloßplatz	6
Seestraße	
Seminarstraße	7
Steigstraße	
Unterstadtstraße	
Vorburggasse	8

Old Castle (Fürstenhäusle). – *Open 1 March to 31 October, 9am to 6pm; 3DM.*
This ancient castle is interesting with its typical keep with four stepped gables. There are frightening oubliettes (secret dungeons), an exhibition of mediaeval knights' tournament helmets and the apartments where the great poet Annette von Droste-Hülshoff (1798-1848) spent her last years.

Känzele. – **Belvedere★★** overlooking the lake and the Alps.

MEMMINGEN

Michelin map **987** 36 – Pop 36 000 – *Town plan in the Michelin Red Guide Deutschland*

Memmingen, established as an imperial town in the Allgäu foothills, still has a few traces of its earlier fortifications and mediaeval gateways crowned with helmet-shaped roofs.

Old Quarter (Altes Viertel). – The quarter lies beside the canal in the centre of the town. Old houses such as the **house of seven roofs** (Siebendächerhaus), formerly the tanners' house, give it its character. The Marktplatz is surrounded by interesting buildings: the **Steuerhaus** which dates from 1495 has arcades leading to the ground floor; the **town hall**, built in 1589 and remodelled in the Rococo style in 1765, is curiously designed with three oriel windows on different floors, crowned with rounded belfries.

St. Martin's. – This Gothic style church had its chancel elegantly remodelled at the end of the 15C. The **stalls★** (Chorgestühl), dating from 1507, are intricately carved with figures of the prophets, sybils and the church donors.

Kreuzherrnkirche. – *On the Hallhof Square.* The final octagon on the 1617 bell tower surpasses the town's other towers in the subtlety of its decoration.

MERGENTHEIM, Bad ★

Michelin map **987** eastern edge of 25 – *Local maps pp 151 and 217* – Pop 19 800

The old town of Bad Mergentheim which lies in the Tauber Valley on the right bank of the river is a stage on the Romantic Road. It has a dual function: as an ordinary town and as a spa.

Castle of the Teutonic Order (Deutschordensschloss). – This religious and military order began with a hospitaller community founded in the Holy Land in 1128 to assist German pilgrims. After the collapse of the Kingdom of Jerusalem, the knights returned home to fight the Slavs, conquer Prussia and the Baltic States. In 1525, the grand master of the Order, a Hohenzollern, on Luther's advice, dropped the religious tenets of the Order and converted the community's patrimony into a principality which became the cradle of the future states of Prussia. Those knights who remained faithful Catholics grouped themselves under the See of Mergentheim. This situation continued until 1809 when Napoleon dispossessed the order. The Order has resumed the functions of a religious and charitable body.

Tour. – *Open 1 March to 31 October, 2.30 to 5.30pm (Sundays 10am to noon; the rest of the year, Sundays 10am to noon); closed Mondays from 2nd week of Advent to mid-January; 1.50DM.*
The present building dates from 1565 and was partly remodelled in about 1780. Above the main doorway, which was richly decorated in the 17C, are the arms of the Order.

The corner towers in the inner courtyard contain spiral Renaissance staircases. A historical museum on the Teutonic Order adjoins the local historical museum.

The **park** (Schlosspark) has been relaid in the English style of the late 18C.

EXCURSION

Stuppach. – *6 km - 4 miles – by the Schwabisch Hall road – plus ½ hour sightseeing (7.30am to 6pm April to September; 8am to noon and 1.30 to 5pm October to mid-March); 1DM.*
The village church has inherited the central panel showing the Virgin and Child (1519) of the Grünewald St. Mary of the Snows **altarpiece★★** *(pp 52 and 126)*.

MICHELSTADT

Michelin map **987** 25 – south of Aschaffenburg – Pop 14 000

Michelstadt, with its gracious houses, stands in the depression which divides the rolling agricultural western Odenwald from the wooded eastern Odenwald. It attracts large numbers of tourists.

■ **SIGHTS** *time: ¼ hour*

Marktplatz*. – The square is a delight, with half-timbered houses, an ornamental 16C fountain, the town hall and, in the background, the church tower.

Town Hall* (15C). – The pointed roof rises on a scaffolding of wooden posts, flanked by two symmetrical oriel windows with candle-snuffer roofs.

The Local Stores (Städtische Kellerei). – Leave the square and follow the street which runs beside the town hall. Turn right into the Einhardtsporte alley to come out in the shaded courtyard of the stores which once belonged to the local count. The courtyard is framed with half-timbered buildings.

EXCURSIONS

Eulbach Park*. – *9 km - 5 miles – plus ½ hour sightseeing (8am to 6pm – 5pm in winter; 2DM).* Romantic park (pool, ruins, Roman stone fragments); European bison reserve.

Fürstenau Castle. – *2 km - ½ mile – by road no 47 going north – plus 1 hour sightseeing (9am to noon and 1 to 6pm, 5pm in March and October, 4pm November to February); 0.50DM.* The castle with its courtyard ending in an impressive archway stands in a green setting near the bridge over the stream at the end of the valley.

MILTENBERG ★

Michelin map **987** 25 – 40 km - 25 miles – southeast of Aschaffenburg – *Local map p 217* – Pop 9 700

Miltenberg lies along the outside of the final bend of the Main, which here runs between the wooded slopes of the Spessart to the north and the Odenwald to the south. The main and only large street of the town, the Hauptstrasse, which runs parallel to the quay, is lined with a series of most unusual houses with wood superstructures.

Marktplatz**. – The square is triangular in shape with the apex towards the hillside. The Renaissance fountain is surrounded by half-timbered houses among which, on the right, is Clausius' House with a polygonal oriel, and, on the left, the Miltenberg House.

Half-Timbered Houses* (Fachwerkhäuser). – Go up the Hauptstrasse between the Marktplatz and the Gasthaus Riesen, and you will see a wooden Renaissance house in the shape of a ship's prow at a road fork.

Mildenburg. – The approach, on foot, is from the Marktplatz. From the top of the tower: **view** of Miltenberg in its characteristic setting on the Main bend.

MINDEN

Michelin map **987** 15 – Pop 84 000 – *Town plan in Michelin Red Guide Deutschland*

Minden is an important junction at the exit to the **Porta Westfalica**, the last point on the Weser before the river, the railway and the road branch out across the wide North German Plain. Below the town, the canal's (Mittellandkanal) engineering works which extend across the valley are especially interesting.

■ **SIGHTS** *time: 1 hour*

Leave the car in the Cathedral Square or in one of the adjacent car parks.

Cathedral** (Dom). – The Cathedral stands in the centre of the town, its beautiful Romanesque façade preceded by porch and fretted by delicate blind arcades. The belfry wall rises out of this great west front *(p 23)*.

The interior, lit by modern windows in Gothic frames, has rounded Westphalian style vaulting over the transept and tiered Romanesque blind arcades in the Rhineland tradition in the chancel. The church contains two major works of art: an 11C **Romanesque Crucifix**** on the left hand pillar of the transept crossing, and at the altar in the chancel, a picture of the Crucifixion dated 1480 painted by a Westphalian master. The Apostles frieze (1250), now in the south transept, formerly surmounted the rood-screen.

Return to the car; leave the town by the Marienstrasse in the direction of Bremen. Immediately beyond the canal bridge bear right and go round the main harbour basin, crossing the Great Lock. When over the bridge leave the car in one of the visitors' car parks.

Great Lock** (Schachtschleuse). – *Access: 0.30DM.* The lock, which is 84 m long and 10 m wide – 276 x 33 ft – links the canal with the Weser which lies 13 m - 43 ft – below. It takes about 7 minutes to fill or empty.

Return to the car and continue round the harbour. From the exit to the tunnel beneath the canal, one can climb on to the embankment and the aqueduct towpath.

Aqueduct* (Kanalbrücke). – This 375 m long - 410 yd – aqueduct obviates the necessity for any more locks on the 211 km - 131 miles – of canal separating Münster from Hanover.

Return to town along the Werftstrasse.

EXCURSION

Porta Westfalica*. – *10 km - 6 miles – plus 1 hour walking and sightseeing.*
Leave Minden by ④, road no 61, which enters the Weser gap. Cross the river at the foot of the enormous statue to the Emperor Wilhelm, on the right, and go up the right bank. Bear left at Hausberge Church and, keeping left, go up to the Bismarck Tower.

Bismarck Tower. – From the top of the tower *(138 steps)* there is an interesting **view*** of the heavy road and rail traffic going through the Porta Westfalica.

Porta Belvedere (Porta-Kanzel). – *½ hour on foot Rtn.* The access road continues to the **belvedere*** which lies nearer the end of the promontory.

MITTENWALD ★

Michelin map 987 37 – Local map p 44 – Pop 8 300

Mittenwald, an old frontier town on the Augsburg–Verona trade route by way of the Seefeld and Brenner Passes, today suffers from heavy traffic. The motorist, as he travels slowly down the main street, has time, therefore, to look at the painted houses lining the pavements, the church's striped tower, the jagged peaks of the Karwendel and the sharply pointed teeth of the Viererspitze.

Mittenwald's popularity with holidaymakers is easily explained: the Kranzberg district, which joins the Wetterstein chain to the west, provides enjoyable walks; pleasant bathing in the lakes (Lautersee, Ferchensee and Wildensee) and, in winter, good skiing. In addition, the Karwendel range, formerly open only to mountaineers, is now accessible by way of the teleferic up to the Karwendelspitze (upper station alt 2 244 m - 7 825 ft).

Colour and Music. – If Mittenwald is a "living picturebook", as Goethe described it, the town has, for the past 200 years, also played a part in the expansion of musical culture. At the foot of the church a monument honours the memory of Matthias Klotz (1653-1743), born in Mittenwald, who, on his return from Cremona in 1684, introduced the making of stringed instruments to the country despite the fact that it was then in the midst of an economic depression. A dozen artisans, a technical school (on the Garmisch–Partenkirchen road) and a museum today uphold this fine tradition.

■ **SIGHTS** *time: 1 hour*

The Painted Houses★★ (Bemalte Häuser). – The **Obermarkt★** is lined with painted houses – the best of which have prominent eaves – and ends at the church where the tower is also vividly painted from top to bottom. Beside more modern decorations such as the Bozner Weinstuben stand the façades of the Neunerhaus (opposite the Post Hotel), the Pilgerhaus (crowned by a bell turret) and the Alpenrose Inn, painted by local artists in the 18C. Take the path beside the church to the old quarter, Im Gries.

The Church. – The church, built from 1738 to 1749, was designed by a decorator and architect of the Wessobrunn school, Josef Schmuzer, which explains the fine quality of the stuccoes on the vaults. The mural paintings (scenes from the life of St. Peter and St. Paul, patron saints of this church) are the work of Matthäus Günther. An imposing Christ Crowned, dating from the end of the 14C, is in the north side-chapel. Among the insignia of the different trade corporations along the main aisle, are those of the stringed-instrument makers.

Stringed-Instrument Museum (Geigenbau-und Heimatmuseum). – *Ballenhausgasse 3. Open: weekdays 10am to noon and 2 to 5pm; Sundays and holidays 10am to noon; closed 16 April to 14 May; 1.50 DM.* The museum is devoted to the evolution of stringed instruments and to old Mittenwald. In the surroundings of a traditional workshop of a master violin maker, a craftsman describes the different phases in the making of a violin.

MÖLLN

Michelin map 987 6 – Pop 15 700

Mölln, a stopping point on the old Salt Road *(p 170)*, is much appreciated by lovers of the open air for its local woods and series of **lakes★** (Seelandschaft). The Romantic **Schmalsee★**, which is within walking distance of Kurhaus Waldhalle, is the loveliest.

St. Nicholas' (Nikolaikirche). – The church, built of brick in the 13 and 15C, raises its stocky tower from a terrace overlooking the half-timbered houses on the Markt and the stepped gable of the 14C Rathaus. This is adorned with pierced arcades in the Lüneburg fashion. At the foot of the church tower may be seen the 16C tombstone of **Till Eulenspiegel** who died in Mölln in 1530. Another memory of Till *(p 90)* is to be found in the modern fountain on the Markt below. Touching his thumb, it is said, brings good luck – and the thumb bears witness to the fact that every visitor is superstitious.

MONSCHAU ★★

Michelin map 203 12, 13 – Local map p 114 – Pop 11 800

This small Eifel town, massing its slate roofs at the end of a winding gorge of the Rur, has to be approached from the north by road no 258. Stop at a **belvedere★★** on the left of the road from Aachen. Go down to the town where you will find **half-timbered houses★★** (Fachwerkhäuser) overlooking the stream and twisting streets.

■ **SIGHTS** *time: 1½ hours*

General View. – Leave the Markt by the Unterer Mühlenberg rise to the right of the Kaulad café. When you come to a bend, take the Kierberg on the right which brings you out by a chapel (Friedhofkapelle) beyond the cemetery. There is a **view★** from the chapel terrace of Monschau, the castle and the ruined "Haller" tower.

Return to the Markt down a stony path cut by steps.

Walk in the Town. – Bear left across the road bridge over the Rur and climb the stairway opposite. Walk along the Kirchstrasse, on the left, through the oldest quarter of the town. Continue to no 33, the old wooden house facing the church.

Turn and go back, bearing right, along the Kirchstrasse, which is lined with fine houses. At the end of the Holzmarkt look across at the Troistorff House in the Laufenstrasse.

Troistorff House. – *No 18 Laufenstrasse.* A solid house built by a linen weaver in 1783. Glance inside at the **staircase★** (Treppe) which rises in a single sweep.

Continue, right of the house down the Laufenstrasse, and almost immediately turn off left.

Red House (Rotes Haus). – The house, dating from 1752 and originally inhabited by a prosperous cloth merchant, has been preserved with its full 18C **interior decor★** which forms part of the local museum now installed inside. *Open 1 March to 30 November, 10am to 1pm and 2 to 5pm. Admission: 1DM.*

Take an alley to the left of the Red House which soon affords a **view★** on the right, of the houses lining the enclosed course of the Rur and an old mill wheel.

The street continues, skirting terraced gardens and beyond the Rur-café to become the delightful Eschbachstrasse.

Cross the bridge and turn right into the Austrasse, skirting the church to the Markt.

MOSEL Valley ★★

Michelin maps **203** 5 to 9, 17 to 19 and **204** 14, 15

The Mosel and the Lower Saar *(description p 224)* flow between the Eifel and Hunsrück Massifs. The open, luminous valley with deep curves, planted on its slopes with wonderful vineyards, is in sharp contrast to the short harsh span of the Rhine Gorge. At least drive along the Bernkastel-Cochem section.

Wines. – The three Valleys of the Mosel, the Saar and the Ruwer which radiate from Trier, produce dry white wines mostly from Riesling stock. The wines are light, slightly harsh, with a delicate bouquet and often a suspicion of the taste of an unripe grape. The wine becomes more acid and colder the further north it grows. The schist soil plays an important part in the maturing of the bunches of grapes: the broken rocks absorb heat during the day and give it off at night.

The wines, mounted on props sometimes 3 m - 10 ft high, follow the contours of the greatest slope. On the steepest hillsides carts, sprayers, etc. are pulled by ropes on winches.

The harvest is late and sometimes continues until the feast of St. Nicholas (6 December). All along the proposed itinerary are **caves** or cooperatives where tasting is available.

The Canalised Mosel. – 1964 saw the opening of the joint undertaking by Germany, Luxembourg and France to improve the 270 km - 168 miles – of the lower course of the Mosel, from Thionville to Koblenz. The navigable Mosel in Germany consists of 12 sectors. The locks beside the dams take barges of up to 1 500 tons and can accommodate towed convoys of 3 200 tons. The levelling of the river bed and of the embankment have spoilt the valley to a certain degree but the low-lying damworks add a modern touch to the scene.

Boat Services. – *From mid-May to mid-October, daily Rtn service between Trier and Bernkastel-Kues and between Koblenz, Cochem and Bernkastel-Kues. Other services between Basel, Rotterdam and Trier. Apply at the landing stage offices or telephone the Manager of Köln – Düsseldorfer, 15 Frankenwerft, Cologne (☎ 2 08 81).*

1 FROM TRIER TO BERNKASTEL-KUES

60 km - 38 miles – about 1½ hours – Local map p 182

Trier★★. – *Description p 245.*

Neumagen-Dhron. – The town is known for its Roman discoveries which have been transported to the Rhine Museum in Trier. At the east end of a chapel is a copy of the famous *Vessel charged with wine.* After Dhron the road climbs through vineyards. There is a good bird's-eye **view★** from a belvedere on the left of the road.

Bernkastel-Kues★. – *Description p 79.*

2 ★★FROM BERNKASTEL-KUES TO KOBLENZ by the Valley

135 km - 84 miles – about ½ day – Local map below

The curves sharpen – notably the Zell bend – and the valley becomes steep and wild. It is the area where the most famous vintages grow.

Bernkastel-Kues★. – *Descriptions p 79.*
One magnificent vineyard follows another. Note the sundials (Sonnenuhr) fixed to the rocks which have given their names to some of the vintages Wehlen, Zeltingen.

Ürzig. – Go into this village where the wooden houses shelter beneath tall gables.

Kröv. – Along the road beside the Mosel you will see fine 17 and 18C houses.

MOSEL VALLEY

0   10 Km

LAHN VALLEY

RHINE VALLEY

EIFEL MASSIF

LOWER SAAR VALLEY

Enkirch. – *Tour: ½ hour*
Leave the car in the main street on the Marktplatz, and walk along the Wein-gasse – on the mountain side – noting the amusing street signposting. Turn right after the first half-timbered house with a corner oriel window and take the Königstrasse, opposite. In this street, on the left, in a niche, is the cage once used for punishment in public. Opposite is the Drillestrasse which brings you back to the main street.

Starkenburg. – *5 km – 3 miles – from Enkirch.* The village is remarkably built upon a long and narrow crest. From the terrace just before the Gasthof zur Schönen Aussicht: **view★** of the Traben-Trarbach bend.

MOSEL Valley**

Pünderich. – The market town's very old streets provide a colourful scene.

Zell. – A town extending along the Mosel. Get an overall view of it from the far bank *(the itinerary road)* with its houses aligned along the embankment and guarded by the old fortifications. The ride halfway up the hillside above Kaimt affords good **views**✶✶ of the vineyards.

Marienburg. – The old convent stood in a remarkable **setting**✶✶, adjoining the Zell bend. From the restaurant terrace, there is an impressive **view**✶✶ of the valley and its vineyards.

The road goes through the deepest part of the valley which here is cut through limestone. Cross the Mosel by the Senheim Bridge.

Beilstein. – The minute fortified market town of Beilstein, whose last overlord was Chancellor Metternich, stands crowded at the feet of its vast church and castle, Burg Metternich. View✶ of the valley curve from the castle ruins *(½ hour walk Rtn from Liesenich road)*.

Cochem. – *Description p 94.*

Although the valley winds less there are still many castles on its slopes; the Coraidelstein ruins on the left bank are succeeded by those of Treis and Wildburg on the right.

Treis-Karden. – *Tour: ¼ hour.* The stunted **Church of St. Castor** represents a stage in the transition from Rhineland Romanesque (the "dwarf gallery" in the apse) to Gothic (pointed vaulting). Inside are a 1420 high altarpiece of the Magi Kings in carved wood, tombstones against the walls, a Baroque organ loft and in the chapel on the left of the chancel, a small wooden Gothic shrine to St. Castor of 1490.

> **Eltz Castle**✶✶. – *10 km - 6 miles – from Hatzenport by Münstermaifeld and Wierschem, plus 1½ hours walking and sightseeing.*
> The powerful fortress rises, bristling with towers and pinnacles, above the trees in an awe-inspiring **site**✶✶ at the end of the wild Eltz Valley.
> There are period furnishings inside as well as weapons and armour. *Open 1 April to 31 October, 9am (10am Sundays and holidays) to 5.30pm; 4DM. Brochure in English.*

Note soon the fine outline of Thurant Castle with two towers, commanding the Alken.

Kobern-Gondorf. – The road goes twice through a vast 15-17C castle. The stylish small town is overlooked by the ruins of two castles, each of which enhances the other. The upper castle, consisting of a plain square keep, adjoins the polygonal Romanesque Chapel to St. Matthias.

> **Alternative route to Koblenz by way of Ehrenburg Castle and the right bank of the Mosel (road no 49).** – *Extra distance: 5 km - 3 miles – reckon on an extra hour.* Cross the Mosel by the Hatzenport or Löf ferries. Take the Boppard road at Brodenbach and after 3 km - 2 miles – turn off right to the **Ehrenburg** Castle *(tour: ½ hour)* which has impressive towers.
> Return to Brodenbach where you take no 49 going to Koblenz.

Koblenz✶. – *Description p 160.*

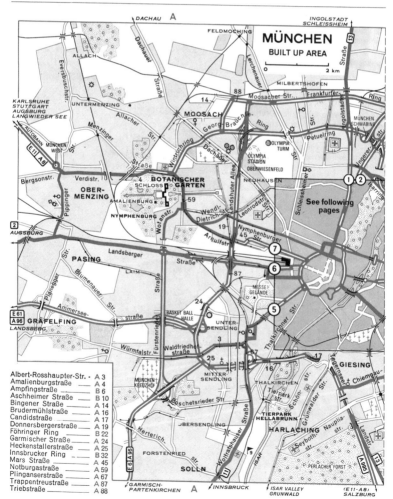

MUNICH ★★★ (MÜNCHEN)

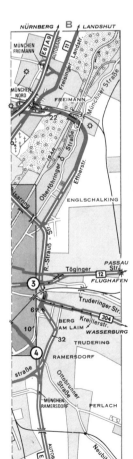

Michelin map **987** 37 – Pop 1 315 300

Munich, a cultural centre, the capital of Bavaria, is also the largest centre for industry and commerce in southern Federal Germany. Energetic reconstruction has eliminated most traces of the Second World War so that the town has recovered its former prosperity and appearance.

A large force of workers is employed by many different branches of industry: manufacture of cars, locomotives, carriages and machine tools; factories for rubber, chemicals, electrical appliances, optical and precision instruments; printing and publishing houses and breweries. Exhibitions such as the Fair of German Craftsmanship speak for the vitality of industries.

Olympic Village. – Munich was host to the XX Olympic Games which were held in the summer of 1972. Located at Oberwiesenfeld, northwest of the city, the television tower (Olympiaturm) erected in 1968, standing 290 m - 951 ft high has a terrace (190 m - 623 ft) with panorama, which offers an exceptional **view****** on the city and the Bavarian Alps *(lift: 2.50DM)*.

Built also for the occasion were swimming pools, gymnasiums, an open air theatre, a stadium, which holds 80 000 people, training fields, a cycling track and an artificial lake, which has made this complex a sports centre of the highest standing. *(Guided tours available; closed 1 November to 28 February; 5DM; time: 2 hours).*

HISTORICAL NOTES

Foundation of the Town. – A small village, established in the 9C near a Benedictine abbey, took the name of its monks – in German *Mönche*, High German *Munichen*. For this reason the town's emblem is a little monk (Münchner Kindl).

In 1156 the Emperor Frederick Barbarossa, to break the power of the Babenbergs, ceded a part of Bavaria to Henry the Lion, Duke of Saxony *(p 90)*. In 1158 Henry the Lion decided to monopolise the salt trade taxes which had formerly been levied by the Bishop of Freising, and in order to do so destroyed the bridge, warehouse and customs house set up some 6 miles from Munich, and built a new bridge, forcing all commercial transactions into the town. Duke Henry's action legalised by the Emperor Frederick Barbarossa, proved to be the beginning of a long and flourishing history for Munich, then only a cluster of houses.

Rise of the Wittelsbachs. – In 1180, Duke Henry the Lion was deprived of his titles and banished from his lands in southern Germany. Frederick Barbarossa replaced him with the Palatine Count Otto von Wittelsbach, and from then on the House of Wittelsbach became closely linked to Bavaria. In 1255, Munich became the ducal residence. In 1314, one of the Dukes, Ludwig the Bavarian, became King of Germany and in 1328 Emperor. With the demise of the Wittelsbachs of Landshut in 1503, the town became the unique capital of Ducal Bavaria, rivalling, as a business centre, both Augsburg and Nuremberg.

In 1623, Duke Maximilian I exercised the function of a Prince-Elector, and during the Thirty Years War made Munich the bastion of German Catholicism. During the 17 and 18C, the town was enriched by many new religious and civic buildings – the Theatine Church, the Nymphenburg, the Church of the Holy Spirit, the Church of the Asam brothers, and the Ducal Theatre – the ramparts were torn down and gardens laid out, the finest of which is the English Garden.

The Kings of Bavaria. – It was in the 19C that Munich reached its artistic zenith. The Prince-Elector of Bavaria and the Palatine, **Maximilian IV Josef** (1799-1825), remained neutral in the conflict in which France was opposed to the rest of Europe. In 1806, an alliance with Napoleon earned him the title of King of Bavaria, under the name of Maximilian I.

Maximilian's son, **Ludwig I** (1825-48), put everything into trying to make his capital one of the most beautiful in Europe. Through his artistic taste and his love of Italy and Greece, he attracted architects, painters and sculptors. Munich was enriched by the Old and New Pinakotheks, the University, the Glyptotheque (**CU**) (Museum of Ancient Sculpture) and the Propylaea. He constructed Ludwigstrasse and enlarged the Residence. In 1848, in face of the revolutionary movement caused by the scandal of his liaison with the Spanish dancer, Lola Montez, Ludwig I abdicated in favour of his eldest son, Maximilian. His second son, Otto, had become King of Greece in 1832. **Maximilian II** (1848-64) founded the Bavarian State Museum in 1855.

Ludwig II (1864-86) occupies a place apart in the Wittelsbach dynasty. This eighteen-year-old king, beloved by his subjects, drew the composer, Richard Wagner, to his court. Of a romantic and restless temperament, quickly depressed by political set-backs – the defeat of the Austro-Bavarian alliance at Sadowa in 1866 by the Prussians, whose king, Wilhelm I, became Emperor of Germany in 1871 – Ludwig II, in search of peace, decided to build three extravagant castles: Neuschwanstein, a feudal castle; Linderhof, in Rococo style, and Herrenchiemsee, a replica of Versailles. His tragic drowning has added to the legend.

The death of Ludwig II, without an heir, posed a problem of succession. Ludwig II's brother Otto was mentally deranged and it was the son of Ludwig I, **Prince Luitpold**, who assumed the Regency. The highly capable Prince-Regent laid out the great thoroughfare that bears his name (Prinzregentenstrasse), facilitated the creation and construction of the German Museum, the ethnographical museum, the zoological gardens and the new City Hall and the **Wittelsbach fountain** (1895) by Adolf von Hildebrand on the Maximiliansplatz.

His son, crowned under the name of **Ludwig III** (1912-8), experienced the end of the monarchy in the defeat of Germany. On 7 November 1918, Ludwig III was forced to abdicate under pressure from a workers' revolutionary movement.

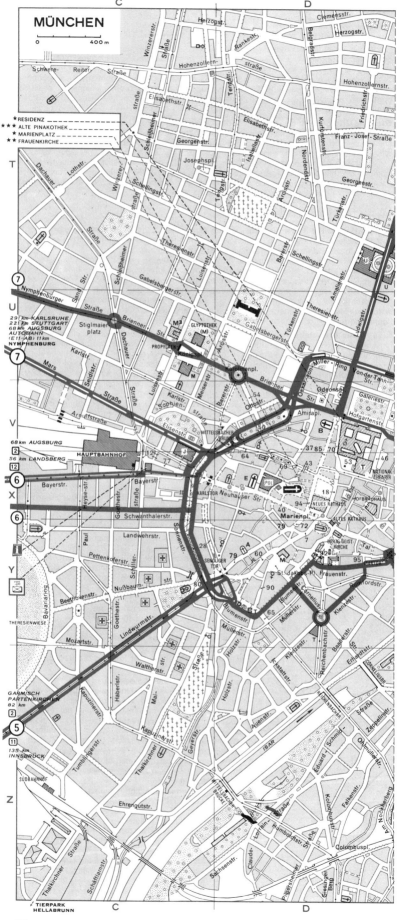

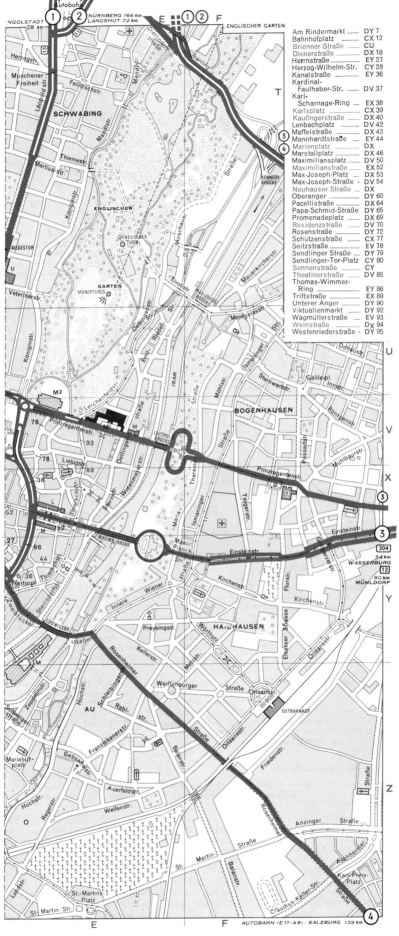

MUNICH★★★

Between the Two Wars. – The months that followed the end of hostilities were full of strife and anarchy. In January 1919, the National Socialist Party set up its headquarters in Munich, and on 14 February 1920 Adolf Hitler made known his party's programme at a large meeting held in the Hofbräuhaus. In 1923, Hitler and Ludendorff provoked an uprising, but after its collapse the Nazi Party was dissolved and Hitler imprisoned. Released before he had completed his sentence, Hitler reorganised his German Workers' National Socialist Party *(p 22 – The Rise of Hitler)*. In 1938 it was Munich that Hitler chose for the meeting with Mussolini, Chamberlain and Daladier at which it was agreed to let Germany annex the Sudetenland.

LIFE IN MUNICH

While the main life of the town is concentrated along Neuhauser Strasse and Kaufingerstrasse, between the Karlsplatz (or "Stachus") – where it is maintained German speed records are set up – and the town hall, the elegant shopping centre is on Maffeistrasse, Pacellistrasse, Promenadeplatz and Brienner Strasse. The antique shops are grouped in Ottostrasse near the Maximiliansplatz and the art galleries under the arcades of the Hofgartenstrasse. The Schwabing quarter (ET), with the Leopoldstrasse as its main street, was famous at the turn of the century as an intellectual and artistic centre. It is still one of the most entertaining places in Germany with its terrace cafés and night clubs.

Among the best known Munich specialities are the white sausages, known as *Weisswurst,* roast knuckle of pork. *Schweinshaxen* and *Leberkäse,* meat or offal *pâté* which can be bought in hot slices at the butchers in the early morning. *Steckerlfisch* are skewered fish roasted or grilled and best eaten in the open air. Cut and salted radishes, *pretzels* and Munich *Salzstangen* – small salt rolls – often accompany beer.

Beer and Breweries. – Munich beer is drunk in considerable quantities in the great beer halls (Hofbräu, Löwenbräu, Spatenbräu, Hackenbräu, Augustinerbräu and Pschorrbräu and Paulaner-Thomasbräu). A foreign tourist should visit at least one of these establishments of which the most celebrated is the **Hofbräuhaus** (DX).

Built at the end of the last century, this building is the heir to a long tradition going back to 1589. The brewery has ceased to function as such, but whole barrels are consumed each day, drunk from one-litre (1¾ pints) blue glazed jugs or glasses. In the many rooms and shaded courtyards, bands play lively tunes, often accompanied by the singing of the drinkers. The smells of sausage and stale tobacco mix in the thick overheated air. In the great vaulted hall on the ground floor, under the vigilant eye of chuckers-out, an extraordinary atmosphere reigns. Equally spectacular is the vast banqueting hall, on the second floor.

Popular Holidays and Religious Feast Days. – Carnival, *Fasching,* a German tradition, is celebrated in Munich with tremendous popular merry-making, masked and fancy-dress balls.

During the season of strong beers, which begins in March a few weeks after the end of carnival, special beers carry the suffix "-ator". Others are brewed for the celebrated October Festival (**Oktoberfest**), which goes back to 1810 and which perpetuates the great celebrations marking the engagement of Crown Prince Ludwig and Princess Theresa. About 4 000 000 litres - 880 000 gallons of beer are produced by the Munich breweries and brought to town in drays for this huge fair, which goes on for sixteen consecutive days on the Theresienwiese (Theresa's Meadow) (CY) at the foot of the colossal Bavarian statue. Visitors pause at the booths and eating places, where two oxen are roasted on the spit daily.

Corpus Christi is the greatest religious holiday of the year. An immense procession winds its way along the beflagged streets, decorated with bunches of young beech leaves. A huge crowd preceded by the clergy and members of all the religious orders, the leading Roman Catholic personalities and the different trade guilds take part.

■ MAIN SIGHTS

Marienplatz★. – The Marienplatz is the crossroads where the life of the town is concentrated. The two big streets of the business district coming from the Karlstor and the Isartor, former gates of the old city, end there as well as the Weinstrasse, Dienerstrasse and Sendinger Strasse, all equally busy. Luxury shops, great cafés and restaurants abound.

The column to the Virgin (Mariensäule), city patron, stands at the centre of the Marienplatz.

On this square, near the Old Town Hall (Altes Rathaus), with its stepped gables crowned by bell turrets, built from 1867 to 1908 in the Gothic style, is the **New Town Hall** (Neues Rathaus). Its outline and carillon (Glockenspiel), the largest in Germany, celebrated for its enamelled copper figures, is one of Munich's attractions.

Old Pinakothek★★★ (Alte Pinakothek). – This vast building, destined to house the paintings gathered by the Wittelsbachs from the beginning of the 16C, was built from 1826 to 1836 in the Venetian style of the Renaissance. After Duke Wilhelm IV had commissioned pictures from the most famous artists of the time – Altdorfer and Burgkmair – his great grandson, the Elector Maximilian I, founded a picture gallery, the Kammergalerie. Under Ludwig I numerous other acquisitions made it one of the finest in Europe.

Open 9am to 4.30pm, and also 7 to 9pm on Tuesdays and Thursdays; closed Mondays; 2.50DM.

First Floor Galleries

Gallery I. – **Albrecht Altdorfer** (1480-1538), master of the Danube school, succeeded in *Alexander's Victory* (1529) in showing in incredible detail the thousands who took part in the battle.

Gallery IIa. – *Virgin and Child* by Lucas Cranach the Elder (1472-1553).

Gallery II. – A remarkable **Albrecht Dürer** (1471-1528), *Birth of Christ;* also the masterly composition of the *Four Apostles* painted by the artist when he was at his greatest in 1526; and the *Lamentation over the body of Christ* where the background is painted with great care and is lit by a sunset which would make a picture in itself.

Good portraits of Andreas Ligsalz and his wife by the Munich painter, **Hans Muelich** (1516-73).

Gallery IIb. – *Susannah Bathing and the Chastisement of the Calumniators* by Altdorfer, a candid and careful work. Among the seven Dürers is the famous *Self-portrait in a fur-lined coat.*

Gallery III. – Hans Burgkmair's (1473-1531) *Crucifixion* and especially his *St. John at Patmos* show Italian influence.

Lucas Cranach the Elder (1472-1553) reveals with his *Christ on the Cross* his power of harsh and pathetic realism and with his *Cardinal Brandenburg in Prayer at the Foot of the Cross*, a deep knowledge of portraiture.

The *Death of Lucretia*, also by Cranach, is a much repeated theme with Renaissance painters.

Gallery IV. – This is a wonderful collection of Flemish and Dutch Primitives: good altarpiece by **Quentin Metsys** (1466-1530) of the *Holy Trinity and the Virgin and Child*.

An extraordinary triptych by **Roger van der Weyden** (1400-64) is known as the *Altarpiece of the Three Kings*. It was painted in about 1460 for the Church of St. Columba in Cologne. The clear and precise drawing, the composition, the emotion displayed by the different personages and the symphony of colour make it a remarkable work. *St. Luke Combing the Virgin's Hair* is by the same artist.

Thierry Bouts the Elder's (*c* 1415-75) *Taking of Christ* contrasts the resigned expression of Jesus with the anxiety of others against a lowering sky. An amazing *Danaë* is by the Flemish painter, **Jan Gossaert** (1478-1533). *The Seven Joys of the Virgin* is by **Hans Memling** (*c* 1435-94).

Gallery V. – Two Rembrandts (1606-69): the *Sacrifice of Isaac* and the *Holy Family. The Plain* by Philips Koninck and *Still Life with Silver* by Barent van der Meer.

Galleries VI and VII. – These house some fine paintings by **Rubens** (1577–1640), in which his great talent appears in compositions as different as: the huge *Last Judgment*, the biggest picture in the gallery; *The Drunkenness of Silenus*, full of truculence; *Helen Fourment and her eldest son Francis*, fine colouring and graceful attitudes; *Helen Fourment in her Wedding Dress*, in which the artist has painted the magnificent brocaded robe in detail; *Isabelle Brant and the artist in a Honeysuckle Arbour*; a *Crucifixion* of overwhelming feeling; *Christ and the Repentant Sinners*.

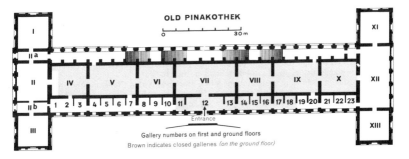

Gallery VIII. – A **Van Dyck** (1599-1641) gallery: *Susannah Bathing*, two *Descents from the Cross* and a *Young Girl Playing the Viol*.

Gallery IX. – An *Adoration of the Magi* by Tiepolo (1696-1770).

Gallery X. – Perugino's (1445–1523) *Vision of St. Bernard* distinguished for its painting of light: Botticelli's (1444-1510) *Lamentation of Christ* is overwhelmingly moving; also a *Holy Family* by Raphael (1483–1520) and an *Annunciation* by Fra Filippo Lippi (1406-69).

Gallery XI. – Two **El Greco** (1548–1625) paintings show intense feeling: *Saint Veronica* and *Christ Despoiled*. A **Murillo** (1618-82), *Children Playing Dice*, and a Velazquez (1599-1660), *Young Spaniard in Black*.

Gallery XII. – Tintoretto's (1518-94) warm toned *Vulcan Surprising Mars and Venus*, a good Titian (1490-1576), *Portrait of Charles V* and a *Crowning with Thorns*.

Gallery XIII. – This is devoted to 17C French painting. Excellent *Portrait of Turenne* by Philippe de Champaigne (1602-74), two canvases by Claude (1600-82), *The Repudiation of Agar* and *Agar and Ismael in the Desert* and a Poussin (1594-1665), *Daphne and Apollo*.

First Floor Rooms

Rooms 1 and 2. – A diptych by **Hans Memling** of the *Virgin and a Rosebush*, a *Virgin and Child* by **Lucas van Leyden** (1489-1533), an altarpiece known as the *Pearl of Brabant* by **Thierry Bouts the Younger** (1448-90); the *Adoration of the Magi*, which occupies the central panel, is of exceptional quality. By the **Master of Moulins**, a fine portrait of *Cardinal Charles of Bourbon*.

Rooms 3-6. – A series of scenes of the Passion and a self-portrait by **Rembrandt** hang beside works by the great Dutch landscape painters – Ruysdael and Van Goyen.

Room 9. – *Young Girl in Love*, a languorous girl being examined by an old doctor is by the Dutch painter, **Jan Steen** (1626-79), well known for his pictures of bourgeois life.

Room 11. – Peasant scenes by the Flemish painters, **Adriaen Brouwer** (1605-38) and **Teniers the Younger** (1610-90).

Room 13. – Sketches by Rubens of the paintings commissioned by Maria de' Medici for the Luxembourg Palace in Paris and now in the Louvre.

Room 15. – A portrait of *Don José Queralto* by Goya.

Rooms 16 and 17. – French 18C works – **Chardin's** (1699-1779) *Turnip Scraper* and **Boucher's** (1703-70) *Young Girl Resting*.

Rooms 22 and 23. – Italian 15C paintings: a series by **Fra Angelico** (1387-1435), a pure *Virgin and Child* by **Fra Filippo Lippi** and other Virgins by Masolino and Leonardo da Vinci.

Ground Floor Galleries

Only a part of the ground floor is given over to pictures. The east wing and the corresponding galleries contain 16C German and Dutch Mannerists (artists painting in the transitional years between the Renaissance and Baroque periods); the west wing is devoted to German Primitives.

The position and numbering of the galleries corresponds with the first floor (plan above).

Gallery I. – By **Willem Key** (1520-68), *Mourning for Christ*; by Van Hemessen (1504-75), masterly compositions of the *Calling of St. Matthew* and *Isaac Blessing Jacob*.

Gallery IIa. – Contains the well known *Country of Cockayne* by **Pieter Brueghel the Elder** (*c* 1525-69) – and also a *Head of a Peasant Woman*.

Gallery II. – The gallery is arranged round the *Venus* of **Lucas Cranach the Younger** (1515-86). There are also excellent portraits of the merchant princes of Augsburg by Christoph Amberger (1500-61).

Gallery III. – *Portrait of a Man with a Ruff* by Pourbus the Younger (1569-1622).

Rooms 1-3. – These contain the smaller pictures of **Jan Brueghel the Elder** (1568-1625): *Jesus preaching in the Port*; the *Great Fish Market*; the *Fire of Troy* and *Sodom and Gomorrah*.

Gallery XI. – An altarpiece by **Michael Pacher** (1435-98) depicts the *Fathers of the Church*.

Gallery XII. – The Wettenhausen altarpiece by **Martin Schaffner of Ulm** (1478-*c* 1547) has fine scenes from the *Life of the Virgin*, showing Flemish and Italian influences. Two series of panels from the Kaisheim altarpiece by **Hans Holbein the Elder** (1465-1524) show in gentle melting colours scenes from the *Passion* and *Life of the Virgin*.

Gallery XIII. – There is a fine painting on wood by the Master of the Altar of St. Bartholomew, a German painter of the second half of the 15C: central panel – St. Bartholomew is between St. Agnes and St. Cecilia with the donor on his knees nearby.

Room 22. – a *Holy Family* by Martin Schongauer *(c* 1430-91).

Church of our Lady★★ (Frauenkirche). – Built from 1468 to 1488 in late Gothic style by Jörg Ganghofer, architect of the Old Town Hall, the Church of Our Lady of Munich (**DX**) has, since 1821, been the metropolitan church of Southern Bavaria. In 1944 the church was severely damaged by air raids but has now been rebuilt. The edifice of dull red brick is striking in its sobriety. Only the side doors and the tombstones embedded in the outside of the church break the monotony of its high rectilinear walls. The onion domes, which since 1525 have topped the two symmetrical towers, 99 m high - 325 ft – on the western façade, are the symbol of Munich.

Interior. – The nave, of dazzling whiteness, is striking for its simplicity and its height. Octagonal pillars support the reticulated vault and that of the equally high upward sweeping aisles. On entering, one is struck by the perspective of the nave and the choir: the pillars form a continuous line, hiding the aisles, which are lit by tall stained glass windows.

The works of art and old furnishings which survived have been returned and stand in marked contrast to surroundings resolutely modern – the pulpit, for example, and 24 carved wood busts of the Apostles, the Saints and the Prophets attributed to the early 16C sculptor Erasmus Grasser have been placed on top of the modern stalls in the chancel.

The axial chapel in the apse contains a fine *Madonna with a Cloak* and the chapel to the south (Chapel of the Holy Sacrament) has a 15C altarpiece of the *Crucifixion* and scenes from the life of Christ. The original stained glass windows (Medallion of the Annunciation, 1392) have been restored to the north chapel which also contains an altarpiece painted in about 1510 of which the central panel by Michael Pacher shows the *Baptism of Christ*, and the side panels are by Jan Polach, the greatest Munich painter of the Gothic period. The crypt *(staircase to the left of the choir)* has a chapel of modern style as well as the burial vaults of the Cardinals of Munich and the Princes of the House of Wittlesbach.

Beside the south tower is the mausoleum of Emperor Ludwig of Bavaria (early 17C). There is a good **view★** of the town from the top of the south tower *(lift: 1DM)*.

The Palace★ (Residenz). – The Dukes of Wittelsbach who resided in Munich gradually extended their castle from the 14C onwards until it became a veritable palace with no less than seven inner courts. Although damaged in the war it has now refound much of its past glory, two periods primarily being represented – the Renaissance with the Kaiserhof buildings and the Residenzstrasse façade, erected between 1611 and 1618 in the reign of Duke Maximilian I, and the Neo-Classical with the Festsaalbau and the Königsbau recalling the reign of the patron king, Ludwig I.

Treasury★★ (Schatzkammer). – *Open weekdays 10am to 4.30pm; Sundays 10am to 1pm; closed Mondays; 1DM. Same ticket for visit to museum: 2DM.*

The valuable items – crowns, diadems, illuminated prayer books, ciboria, cameos and relics – are well set out. One is halted by a magnificent chased Cross executed at the beginning of the 11C for Queen Gisela of Hungary, and the dazzling example of goldsmith's work showing St. George transfixing the dragon (1590). Beautiful Crucifixes in ivory, swords with pommels encrusted with rubies and diamonds, vases and plates of jasper, agate and lapis lazuli, and exotic works from Turkey, Persia and Mexico.

Palace Museum★ (Residenz-museum). – *Open daily 1 April to 30 September, 10am to 12.30pm and 1.30 to 4.30pm (4pm in winter); Sundays 10am to 1pm; closed Mondays; 1DM.*

To see the entire collection successive morning and afternoon guided tours have to be made.

From the general effect the following stand out:

Morning tour. – The gallery of the Wittelsbach ancestors – where Charlemagne occupies the place of honour – a magnificent room decorated by gilded stuccoes; the Antiquarium, oldest part of the palace (1570), an immense room with marble floor and ceiling painted with frescoes, containing busts of Roman Emperors; the State Rooms (Reiche Zimmer), executed by Effner and Cuvilliés in the French Rococo style.

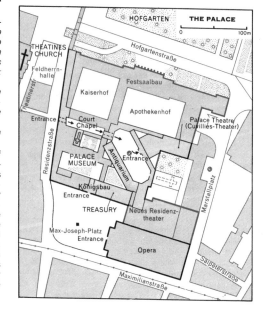

Afternoon tour. – The Porcelain Rooms, containing masterpieces from Meissen, Nymphenburg and Sèvres (Bird Service of 1759).

The 17C Hofkapelle (Court Chapel) has a fine compartmented ceiling. On the first floor is the strongroom containing the Wittelsbach Chapel treasure (outstanding Passion shrine) and 16-18C pieces of gold and silver plate.

Palace Theatre* (Altes Residenztheater). – *Open weekdays 2 to 5pm; Sundays 10am to 5pm; 1DM.*

Built by Cuvilliés from 1751 to 1753, this fine court theatre has four tiers of boxes, each different from the other in its shape and decoration, that of the Prince-Elector being the most elegant in the richness of its hangings, marbles and stuccoes.

Opera (Bayerische Staatsoper). – *The only way of seeing inside the opera house is to go to a performance.*

The National Theatre, built in 1811, was formerly one of the great music centres of the world. It went up in flames in an air raid in 1943 but has been rebuilt to its original plan. It was officially reopened on 22 November 1963 with a performance of Wagner's opera, *The Mastersingers of Nürnberg.*

English garden (Englischer Garten). – The 18C garden lies, with its lakes and pavilions, such as the Chinese building, near the centre of Munich. View* of the belfries of the old town from the Monopteros Temple (ET).

■ ADDITIONAL SIGHTS

Museums

National Museum of Bavaria** (Bayerisches Nationalmuseum) (EV M¹). – *Open 1 April to 30 September, 9.30am (10am Sundays) to 4.30pm; 1 October to 31 March, 9am (9.30am Sundays) to 4pm; closed Mondays; 2DM. Brochure in English.*

The museum was created in 1855 by Maximilian II in honour of the artistic and historical riches of Bavaria. Popular art is represented on the ground floor (cradle collection). On the first floor 47 rooms offer a complete picture of skilled crafts from the time of the invasions to the early 19C: religious gold and silver plate and statues, tapestries, furnishings, altarpieces and stained glass windows.

The Italian Renaissance is represented by bronzes, china and pewter, clothes, jewellery. On the second floor are large collections of china, glass and gold plate.

City Historical Museum* (Münchner Stadtmuseum) (DY M). – *Open 9am to 4.30pm; closed Mondays and holidays; 1.50DM (free on Sundays).*

The museum, originally devoted only to Old Munich, has been enlarged with departments on the theatre and marionettes, on musical instruments, photography and the cinema and on brewing.

On the first floor, the **Moorish Dancers*** (Moriskentänzer), ten carved wooden figures, gilded and painted in 1480 by Erasmus Grasser, must be seen.

German Museum* (Deutsches Museum) (EYZ M). – *Open 9am to 5pm; closed some public and religious holidays; 2DM.*

This museum, one of the most important devoted to science and technical subjects, is housed on an island in the Isar. Dioramas, scientific conspectuses and the reconstruction of different scientific instruments make things comprehensible to even the least knowledgeable visitor.

New Pinakothek and New State Gallery Collections (Staatsgalerie Moderner Kunst). – *In the Haus der Kunst buildings (EV M²). Open 9am to 4.30pm (and 7 to 9pm Thursdays); closed Mondays; 2DM.*

The main rooms on the ground floor display a **collection*** of 19C French paintings highlighted by two Daumiers *(The Drama* and *Don Quixote),* a satisfying group of Impressionists including a *Bridge At Argenteuil* by Monet and three Cézannes – one a self-portrait. Compare the collection with the German Expressionist painters *(p 31)* in the adjoining galleries.

Villa Lenbach Collections (Städtische Galerie) (CU M³). – *Open 9am to 4.30pm; closed Sundays, Mondays and Tuesdays during Carnival; 1.50DM.*

Many pictures by Lenbach (1836-1904) show the certain talent of the portrait-painter *(Bismarck).* The tumultuous and fecund period preceding the 1914-18 War is represented by works of the Blue Knight Movement *(p 27)* and includes a number of paintings by Kandinsky when young (1866-1944).

Churches

Church of St. John of Nepomuk or of the Asam Brothers* (Asamkirche) (DY A). – This church, built in 1733, is best known under the name of the Asam Brothers, its constructors: Cosmos Damian specialised in the frescoes, and Egid Quirin in the sculptures and stuccowork. Its unity of style is due to the fact that the Asam Brothers totally designed, directed and executed its construction and decoration.

The interior lines are of a remarkable harmony. A convex balcony overlooks the chancel, the nave and the organ loft; above, a second gallery, supported by pillars, is decorated with stuccoes and statues of angels and cherubim; the frescoed ceiling, lit by windows concealed behind mouldings, shows episodes in the life of St. John of Nepomuk.

Church of the Theatines (Theatinerkirche) (DV B). – The church, which was built from 1663 to 1688, its façade being added almost a century later by François Cuvilliés, is a synthesis of Renaissance and Baroque styles.

Church of St. Michael (Michaelskirche) (DX E). – This church, built for the Jesuits between 1583 and 1597, resembles the Gesù, the Society's church in Rome, and equally recalls the Italian Renaissance. Each tier of the façade is decorated with pilasters and niches filled with statues of the Bavarian sovereigns most devoted to the Catholic cause. The single aisle with its high cradle vaulting resting on the massive piles abutting on the walls, inspired many masterpieces of the Vorarlberg school *(pp 24, 25)* in the Baroque period.

The tomb of Eugène de Beauharnais, Napoleon's stepson, is in the north transept; Ludwig II of Bavaria lies buried in the crypt.

EXCURSIONS

Nymphenburg *see plan p 183*

Botanical Gardens★★ (Botanischer Garten). – *Main entrance: Menzinger Strasse. Open April to September, 9am to 7pm; October to March, 9am to 4pm; 1.50DM (1DM in winter). Between April and September a gate is opened to allow one to go through to the Nymphenburg Park (see below).*

The flowerbeds in front of the main building, the rhododendrons shaded by conifers, the Alpine rock garden and the hothouses are the outstanding features of the gardens.

Nymphenburg Castle and Park★. – The oldest part of the castle, the one-time summer residence of the Bavarian rulers, is the five-storey wing begun in 1664 in the style of an Italian palace – Max-Emmanuel, Prince-Elector from 1679 to 1726 added four lateral pavilions linking them by arcaded galleries to the central edifice which he transformed to the then current style, accentuating the vertical lines by the addition of pilasters. The outbuildings were constructed in a semicircle in further resemblance to Versailles during the period of his successors, Karl-Albrecht (1726-45) and Maximilian III Josef (1745-77).

The park was enlarged in 1701 by Carbonet and Girard, pupils of Le Nôtre. The formal gardens date from this period as well as the pavilions not far from the Grand Canal: Pagodenburg (1719), Badenburg (1721), Magdalenenklause (1728) and Amalienburg (1739).

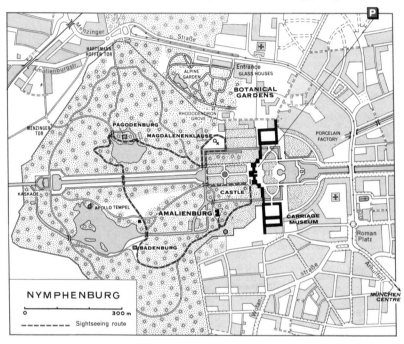

The Castle★. – *Open in summer, 9am to 12.15pm and 1 to 5pm; in winter, 10am to 12.15pm and 1 to 4pm; closed Mondays; 2.50DM – the ticket is also valid for the park pavilions and the carriage museum.*

The banqueting hall was decorated by Johann Baptist Zimmermann and his son with stuccoes of Rococo style and with richly coloured frescoes. The walls are pale green, white and gold. The north wing (Nordflügel) in the main building has a suite of rooms decorated in the French style with painted panels and carved woodwork: ante-chamber, drawing-room, bedchamber, and study are decorated with tapestries and pictures and the north gallery (Nördliche Galerie) with paintings showing the castle and park at the beginning of the 18C. The south wing (Sudflügel) contains an attractive Chinese lacquer room. The south gallery (Südliche Galerie) has views of the castles belonging to the Wittelsbachs. In the south pavilion (Südlicher Pavillon) the apartments of Queen Carolina contain the *Gallery of Beauties*, which King Ludwig I conceived by commissioning the portraitist Stieler (1781-1858) to paint the most beautiful women of the time.

The Park★. – *Open 8am to 7pm (5pm in winter). Follow the route marked on the plan above. Get separate tickets to each pavilion if no general castle ticket has been obtained.*

Most of the park can be seen from the castle steps. Beyond the large flowerbed, ornamented with gods and vases in white marble, the Grand Canal stretches away into the distance.

Amalienburg★★. – *Open 9am to 12.30pm and 1.15 to 5pm (10am to 12.30pm and 1.15 to 4pm in winter); closed Mondays; 1DM.*

This hunting lodge by Cuvilliés is one of the most successful of the many country mansions which delighted the courts of 18C Germany. The simplicity of the exterior is in vivid contrast to the rich decoration within. Beyond the unexpected "kennel" – a panelled central room surrounded by niches for hunting dogs – are the blue room and the panelled bedchamber decorated in silver on a background of lemon-yellow. Further on is the circular **Hall of Mirrors** in shades of blue and silver, panelling framing the mirrors and delicate stuccoes decorating the ceiling.

The Room of the Chase, the Pheasant Room and the kitchens (walls lined with Delft china), complete this masterpiece of Bavarian Rococo.

Badenburg. – *Open 10am to 12.45pm and 1.30 to 5pm; closed in winter and Mondays in season; 0.50DM.* This bathing pavilion, besides a luxurious pool with a painted ceiling representing mythological scenes, has a dressing-room and an ante-chamber serving as a games' and rest room.

Pagodenburg. – *Open 10am to 12.45pm and 1.30 to 5pm; closed in winter and Mondays in season.*
The Pagodenburg, octagonal in design with Chinese motifs, is typical of the period. A drawing-room, a Chinese room and a boudoir occupy the first floor of this tea pavilion.

Magdalenenklause. – *Open 10am to 12.45pm and 1.30 to 5pm; closed in winter and Mondays in season.*
A "hermitage" dedicated to Mary Magdalene.
After visiting the park and the pavilions, return to the castle and go to the south wing.

Carriage Museum (Marstallmuseum). – Besides splendid 17 and 18C harnesses, there are broughams, coaches, carts, sledges and sedan-chairs used in the 18 and 19C by the Wittelsbach family, also the coronation coach of Karl VII and the gala carriage and incredibly luxurious sledges of King Ludwig II.

Other Excursions

Hellabrunn Zoo★ (Tierpark Hellabrunn) (A). – *6 km - 4 miles. Open 8am to 6pm (9am to 5pm in winter); 3.50DM, children: 1.50DM. See plan p 182.*

Schleissheim Castle★. – *15 km - 9 miles – plus 1 hour sightseeing.* Come out of Munich by ①, the Ingolstadt road, which you leave on your right after 9.5 km - 6 miles. Continue straight on until you come to a crossroads where you bear left. Leave the car in the park immediately to your left beyond Schleissheim Castle.
Walk left round the castle to the central spur to buy entrance tickets.
Open 10am to 12.30pm and 1.30 to 5pm (4pm in winter); 2DM; closed Mondays.
The New Castle or Neues Schloss, which was built from 1701 to 1727, extends majestically for 330 m, its length harmonising with the formal gardens designed by the Frenchmen, Carbonet and Girard. The great staircase leads to the state apartments on the first floor: a large banqueting hall in dazzling white and a Hall of Victory gleaming with gold stucco. The princely apartments and galleries, now hung with paintings (16 and 17C Dutch and Flemish masters) and the Great Gallery are open to the public.
Another picture gallery is open on the ground floor beyond the music room.

Valley of the Isar. – *Round tour of 9.5 km - 6 miles.* Leave Munich to the south by Grünwalder Strasse. Soon you get views of the wooded Isar Valley. In Grünwald, take the road on your right. From the bridge crossing the Isar, there is a good **view** of the deeply embanked valley, laid out with pleasure gardens. The road then rises on the left bank of the river.

MÜNSTER ★ (WESTPHALIA)
Michelin map **987** 14 – Pop 260 000

Münster, the historical capital of Westphalia, where the local lords used to reside in winter, lies in the centre of a wooded plain studded with castles and manor houses. The local taste for the past has shown itself in the post-war rebuilding of the inner town on the old model. Münster is a large agricultural market, a university centre and a Catholic bishopric.

The Peace of Westphalia. – The Peace, which was proclaimed at Münster on 24 October 1648, ended the Thirty Years War *(p 20)*. Preliminary negotiations over five years had established the plenipotentiaries of the Emperor and the Catholic states (France and Spain) in Münster, while the negotiators for the Emperor and the Protestant states (Sweden and the Protestant states of the Empire) were in Osnabrück *(p 201)*.
The treaty resulted in the reorganisation of Europe through the carving up of Germany and considerable loss of prestige for the Emperor while the Peace of Westphalia gave France Alsace and the three Bishoprics, Metz, Toul and Verdun, and guaranteed the independence of the Netherlands and Switzerland. It favoured the development of Prussia.

■ MAIN SIGHTS *tour: 1½ hours*

Prinzipalmarkt★. – The Prinzipalmarkt is the most historic and once again the busiest street in town. The elegant houses with Renaissance gables, which have been so cleverly restored, were formerly the residences of rich burghers; arcades invite the stroller. North, the Bogenstrasse, an extension of the Prinzipalmarkt, has the same characteristics as the Prinzipalmarkt (halfway up the street is the well known statue of the pedlar with his basket, the Kiepenkerl).

Town Hall. – The late 14C gabled façade, adorned with delicate fanlights and pinnacles, is one of the finest examples of Gothic civic architecture.

Peace Hall★ (Friedenssaal). – *Open weekdays 9am to 5pm (4pm Saturdays); Sundays, 10am to 1pm; 1DM.*
The former council chamber has become the Hall of Peace in memory of the treaty.
Its Gothic and Renaissance woodwork is original and intact. At the end small symbolic or grotesque scenes mask doors to the archives cases. The councillors' pew backs on to fine panels, carved with niches containing figures and a frieze with includes many burghers' heads. The paintings are of the sovereigns of the countries which signed the treaties – the Emperor Ferdinand III, Philip IV of Spain, the young Louis XIV of France – and their delegates.
Beautiful 1520 wrought iron chandelier.

Cathedral★ (Dom). – This low lying cathedral with two chancels and two transepts is in the 13C transitional Westphalian style typified by the early use of the hall design *(p 24)*.
Enter through the 16C south porch. The inner doorway is surrounded by 13C statues and overlooked by a Christ in Judgment. A 16C statue of St. Paul, patron saint of the church, looks down from the pier.
Go anti-clockwise round the interior. The ample nave with wide bays is covered with rounded vaulting. **The altarpiece of St. John**, dating from 1520, stands in the south transept crossing. In the ambulatory there is a 1540 **astronomic clock★** (Astronomische Uhr) with striking jacks. Tom Ring the Elder painted, high up, a gallery used by spectators. Go through the north transept to the 14C cloister where there is a large 13C bust of St. Paul.
The Chapel of the Holy Sacrament, on the left of the entrance to the cloister, has rich **furnishings★**, notably a silver tabernacle made by an Augsburg silversmith in the 18C.

Castle★ (Residenzschloss) (AY). – This Baroque castle of the former prince-bishops is now a part of the University. The elegant façade is in three sections; the variegated limestone facings on the pink brick take away any monotony of design. At the back, surrounded by water, lies a park (Schlossgarten) off which is a botanical garden. South of the castle, the greenery is bordered by the Rampart Walk (Wallpromenade) with a view of Lake Aa.

MÜNSTER
(WESTFALEN)

0   200 m

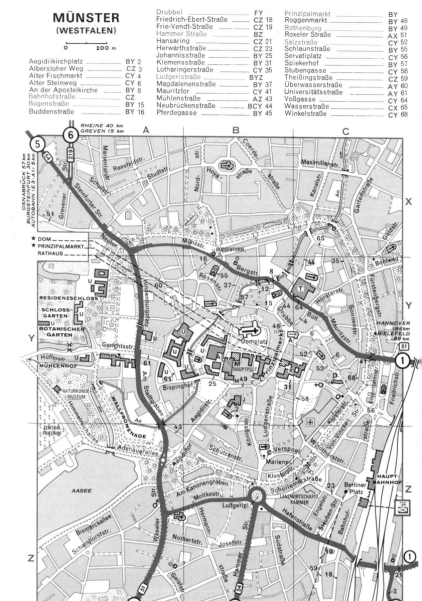

■ ADDITIONAL SIGHTS

Fine Arts Museum★ (Landesmuseum für Kunst- und Kulturgeschichte) (BY M). –*Open 10am to 6pm; closed Mondays.*

The revival of mediaeval Westphalian art is due to the Gothic statuary of Münster cathedral and churches, a collection of stained glass windows and sculptures by Johann and Heinrich Brabender. Outstanding **altarpieces★★** by Konrad von Soest, Koerbecke and the Masters of Liesborn and Schöppingen. Flemish influence is noticeable through the works of the family Tom Ring: Ludger Tom Ring anticipated still-life painting. Interesting portraits of Luther and his wife by Lucas Cranach.

A section of the museum evokes the Thirty Years War.

St. Lambert's (Lambertikirche) (BY A). – St. Lambert's is a Gothic hall-church with a pierced 99 m high - 325 ft – spire built in the 19C to top the tower in which hang three iron cages. These cages were used to exhibit the bodies of the Anabaptist leaders – a revolutionary sect believing in adult baptism – after their revolt had been crushed in 1536.

Church of St. Leger (Ludgerikirche) (BZ C). – **Modern stained glass windows** (1961) depicting the life of Jesus have been placed in the well lit Gothic chancel.

Erbdrostenhof (CY D). – The 1757 Palace has an imposing concave façade and a triangular forecourt.

Mill Open Air Museum (Mühlenhof). –*Signposted by the Hüfferstrasse (west of the plan – AY – south of the Schlossgarten). Open March to November 9am to 5.30pm weekdays, 10am to 6pm Sundays and holidays; in winter, 1pm (11am Sundays) to 4pm; closed 20 December to 5 January; 2DM.*

In a peaceful setting on the banks of Lake Aa, a large Westphalian farm (1619) and a windmill (1748) are surrounded by traditional rural buildings: a forge, a chapel, barns, an oven, a well.

EXCURSIONS

The Wasserburgen Country★. – *Round tour of 190 km - 118 miles – about ⅓ day.* Built in the Middle Ages, surrounded by moats or ponds, the château of the Munsterland (Wasserburgen) were transformed from the Renaissance to the 18C into residences. This explains, in part, the large variety seen in these buildings: being either brick or stone, fortresses or magnificent palaces.

Leave Münster by the Roxeler Strasse (west of plan **AX** – north of the Schlossgarten).

Château of Hülshoff. – Large square towers with the main building a manor house (small museum), create a pleasant setting, where in 1797 Annette von Droste-Hülshoff *(p 178)* was born.

Return and take the road to Havixbeck, then Nottuln and Dülmen, bear right towards Borken. 6 km - 4 miles – outside of Merfeld (red and white barriers) begins, on the left, the way to Merfelder Bruch, marked "zur Wildbahn".

Merfelder Bruch. – *Access: 1 March to 31 October, Saturdays, Sundays and holidays, 10am to 6pm; 2DM.* A mile from the road, some 200 horses may be seen roaming wild in a 500-acre enclosure (traditional rodeo in May – *see p 31*).

Go to Borken and take road no 57 towards Coesfeld. Shortly after taking the right fork for Coesfeld, go past the brick church in Gemen and bear left into the castle avenue.

Château of Gemen. – *Interior not open to the public.* This 15C castle, which was remodelled in the 17C, stands reflected in beautiful shaded waters.

Turn and at Borken take the Raesfeld road. In Raesfeld follow the sign "Schloss Raesfeld".

Château of Raesfeld. – The castle stands surrounded by 17C brick outbuildings including even a small church. The main castle building (1643-58) now consists only of two wings adjoining a tower. *Parts of the castle are now a restaurant.*

In the centre of Raesfeld take the Dorsten road, no 224. Leave this after 10 km - 6 miles – to bear left towards Münster; 5 km - 3 miles – along the road turn off left to Lembeck Castle.

Château of Lembeck. – *Open 1 April to 31 October, 9am to 5pm; time: ½ hour; 0.50DM outside (all the year round), 3DM to go inside.*

The long drive makes a striking approach to the castle with its series of Baroque doorways and roofs. The building is less impressive from the park. A few apartments are open.

Continue along road no 58 to Ludinghausen.

Château of Vischering. – *Open March to October, 9.30am to 12.30pm and 2 to 5.30pm; November to February, 10am to 12.30pm and 2 to 3.30pm; closed Tuesdays; 1DM.*

An island, a flowing circle with red tiles harmonising with the stone, makes up the graceful Vischering château. The interior displays furniture of the period: carved chests and cupboards especially in the bedroom and drawing room, under which is the prison. Note also the elegant chimneys framed in faience. In the large hall are impressive wooden beams.

Return to Münster by Nordkirchen. The 18C **château,** known as the Versailles of Westphalia, is now a School of Finance. From Ascheberg the motorway leads back to Münster.

Telgte; Freckenhorst. – *31 km - 20 miles – 2 hours.* Leave Münster by ①.

Telgte. – A Baroque chapel houses a *Pietà* (1370). Nearby, the local museum (Heimathaus Münsterland) contains a **veil of Hunger★** (Hungertuch, 1623) as well as other Westphalian folk art.

Take road no 64 towards Rheda and turn right in Warendorf.

Freckenhorst. – The **collegiate church★** (Stiftskirche) is an excellent example of Pre-Romanesque German architecture *(p 23)*. Inscribed on the outstanding **baptismal fonts★★** (north aisle) is the date of the church's consecration, 1129.

MÜNSTEREIFEL, Bad ★

Michelin map **203** 3 – *Local map p 115* – Pop 15 600

Tour. – *About ¾ hour.* Leave the main square, in which stands the red rough-cast town hall, and follow the Heisterbachstrasse on the left (mountain side) to reach the well preserved 13C **fortifications★** (Stadtbefestigung). Go left round the inside of the walls. At the first gateway turn left into the Orchheimer Strasse; no 23, the **Windeckhaus★**, a fine half-timbered house with a tall gable and oriel windows, is decorated with masks and roses.

You come out on the spotless flowered Marktplatz. Go up the Delle rise, to the right of the Jesuit church, as far as the entrance to the **Burg** (view of the abbey church). From there go down a road which passes through a Renaissance doorway to reach the Wertherstrasse. Follow the brook downstream and pass through the perimeter wall by the north gate. Return to the town centre through the next gate along and the Langenhecke street on the left.

Church of St. Chrysanthus (St. Chrysanthus und Daria). – This outstanding abbey church, recalling St. Pantaleon in Cologne *(p 99)*, has an early 11C Romanesque façade, and is flanked by partly round, partly octagonal towers. It is interesting to observe how well the modern stained glass windows harmonise with the austere interior.

MÜNZENBERG ★

Michelin map **987** 25 – 13 km - 8 miles – north of Bad Nauheim – Pop 7 000

The feudal castle of Münzenberg, together with Gelnhausen and Büdingen *(p 132)*, defended the Wetterau, an open depression between the Vogelsberg and Taunus Massifs.

Castle Ruins★ (Burgruine). – *Apply to Mr. Debus, 6309 Münzenberg 2, Burgweg 12; 0.50DM.*

The basic areas are remarkably well defined and preserved: the perimeter wall with its bastions emerges from the greenery: the two keeps planted proudly at the east and west ends; the living quarters with detailed Romanesque ornament clearly visible in the windows and the gallery. From the top of the east tower, there is a circular **view** over the Wetterau Depression.

Arnsburg★. – *Excursion of 6.5 km - 4 miles – plus ½ hour sightseeing.* Go towards Lich via Eberstadt. Beyond Eberstadt leave the Lich road on your left as you take the abbey avenue straight ahead. The old abbey consists now of a church in ruins and Baroque abbey buildings.

Cloisters. – These have been turned into a military cemetery. The adjoining chapter house is a fine example of early Gothic architecture.

Church★. – *Guided tours (apply at the "Freundekreis des Klosters Arnsburg" in the abbey offices); 0.50DM.* The church, which is in ruins, is on the Cistercian plan with a flat east end. Massed columns with Romanesque capitals still mark the transept crossing.

From the south transept stairs lead to the former monks' Gothic dormitory.

MURRHARDT

Michelin map **206** 2 – Pop 14 000

The town is well situated amidst the wooded heights of the Schwäbischer Wald.

Church (Stadtkirche). – The **St. Walterich Chapel★**, a small limestone building, Romanesque in style and as meticulously constructed and ornamented as a shrine, abuts on the north tower on the 15C church. Note the doorway and apse window ornament.

NAHE Valley

Michelin maps **203** 6, 7 and **204** 16, 17

The turbulent Nahe runs down the hills and follows a sinuous course, calming itself in the narrow valley (which widens after Idar-Oberstein). The river crosses beautiful vineyards, throwing itself into the Rhine at Bingen. Along its journey it crosses forests and vines from the Rhineland-Palatinate to the **Hunsrück**, a schistous massif whose far reaching woodland is dominated by game.

ROUND TOUR STARTING FROM BAD KREUZNACH

185 km - 115 miles – about ½ day – Local map below

The proposed itinerary goes up the Nahe before entering the Hunsrück region.

Bad Kreuznach★. – *Description p 162.*

Disibodenberg. – *At the entrance to Odernheim, turn right, after several yards, park the car and continue on foot.*
Here one discovers the extensive ruins of the Disibodenberg Abbey founded in the 7C. The chancel and the nave of the church are still visible. On the remains of the pillars carved figures can still be seen. A fortified wall encloses the abbey. Returning south, there is a beautiful view of the vine covered hills.

    Meisenheim. – *8.5 km - 5 miles – from Odernheim up the Glan.*
Half-timbered houses (16-18C) and the ruins of fortifications (gate of the town) give this small town a certain charm. In the château's church, with its pinnacled bell tower is an elegant Rococo pulpit and the "starred vaulting", intricately entwined groined vaulting forming a large star.

Monzingen. – The village, peaking out of the vineyards, has been known for its wine ever since the Romans. Old houses (one dating 1589), narrow, winding alleys and a 15C church, all help to create a picturesque scene.

    Dhaun. – *2.5 km - 1½ miles – by Hochstetten, after leaving route no 41.*
The route starts through the wooded valley before climbing up towards the castle with its remarkable **site★**. Built on a crag, it dominates the valley, lying verdantly at its feet. *Open April to October, 9am to 6pm; November to March, 10am to 5pm; 0.50DM.* One can still pick out the home, kitchen and old knights hall. On the esplanade, behind the statue, stairs lead to the underground passages.

NAHE VALLEY

Idar-Oberstein. – *Description p 154.*

Continue along route no 41 as far as Birkenfeld, take route no 269 towards Morbach for a couple of miles, then take a left turn on route no 422 towards Thalfang.

Erbeskopf. – From the highest peak of the Hunsrück (816 m - 2 675 ft), wooded paths make for wonderful walks. There is a lovely **view** of the rolling and verdured countryside from the wooden tower (near a military camp). In winter one can ski and toboggan.

After Thalfang follow route no 327 known as **Hunsrück Höhenstrasse★** or the mountain ridge road. There are beautiful views onto the valley: wooded hills and houses covered in slate. One then drives by an old Roman watchtower.

Kirchberg. – This small village, perched on a hill, has half-timbered houses especially around the market place, note the pharmacy. The foundations of the Church of St. Michael date back to the pre-Romanesque period whereas the present building is of the 15C.

Ravengiersburg. – *4 km - 2½ miles.* Leave route no 50 in the direction of Mengerschied. Ravengiersburg, a small village, lying at the bottom of the valley, exposes on a hill, a church, which is Romanesque on the exterior and has an imposing west façade with two towers. Note the richly carved cornices and the "dwarf gallery"; above the portal there is a Christ enthroned.

Simmern. – The agricultural centre of Hunsrück, Simmern was founded in the 9C and became part of the Palatinate duchy in the 15 and 16C. Behind the Church of St. Stephen (Stephanskirche) is a hill where one finds the old quarter. In the church note the "starred vaulting" *(see Meisenheim above)*, as well as the tombstones of the dukes, in the Renaissance style.

Stromberg. – From here one can take many pleasant walks through the Soonwald Forest. On the hills, which surround the village, are the ruins of the Château of Gollenfels (12C) and Fustenburg.

NAUHEIM, Bad ★★

Michelin map **204** east of 4 – Pop 27 000

Since 1910 spa activity in Bad Nauheim has centred on a group of monumental buildings erected round a central court where three springs rise. The spa, with a magnificent thermal park (Kurpark), has increased its prosperity with the development of medical institutions.

The Neckar, main artery of Swabia, flows, below Heilbronn, along a valley which runs parallel to that of the Rhine through a gentle landscape of orchards and vineyards. The river's lower course, cutting across the limestone Odenwald Massif, passes through a wilder wooded setting of castle crowned slopes.

The Lower Neckar has been opened to Rhine shipping, and up to Stuttgart provides a scene of dense and varied river traffic.

Another picturesque section of the Valley, Besigheim to Stuttgart, is described on p 248.

*FROM HEILBRONN TO HEIDELBERG

89 km - 55 miles – about 4 hours – Local map below

Heilbronn. – *Description p 149.*
Vineyards characterise this first, widely open section of the valley.

Neckarsulm. – *Museum open March to November, 9am to noon and 1.30 to 5pm; 2.50DM.* The German Motorcycle Museum (Deutsches Zweiradmuseum) is in the old castle of the Teutonic Order. Nearby stands the NSU factory, the first to manufacture and develop motorcycles in Germany.

Bad Wimpfen★★. – *Description p 259.*

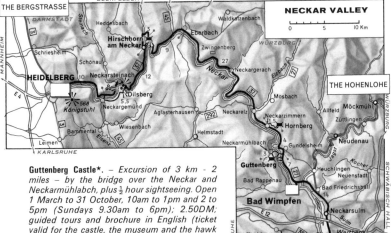

Guttenberg Castle★. – *Excursion of 3 km - 2 miles – by the bridge over the Neckar and Neckarmühlabch, plus ½ hour sightseeing. Open 1 March to 31 October, 10am to 1pm and 2 to 5pm (Sundays 9.30am to 6pm); 2.50DM; guided tours and brochure in English (ticket valid for the castle, the museum and the hawk house which is open from 9am to 6pm; 4DM).* The castle, defended on its mountain front by an impressive wall, contains unusual **archives and art objects★**. Look out for the wooden library, an 18C herbarium in which the plants were enclosed in 92 trick wooden boxes. The keep commands a **view** of the Neckar.

The beautiful Gothic chapel (Burgkapelle – signposted) alone at the foot of the hill, contains a 16C altarpiece of the Mantled Virgin and a 15C group of the Apostles.

Hornberg Castle. – *Excursion of 1.5 km - 1 mile – starting from Neckarzimmern, plus ½ hour sightseeing.*
The castle standing at the top of a vine covered hill and now partly in ruins can be recognised from far away by its round keep. The annexes are now a hotel. Those interested in history can see the armour of Götz von Berlichingen *(p 164)* who ended his days (d 1562) in the castle (now in a museum: *open 1 March to 31 October, 9am to 5pm; 2DM; brochure in English*).

Zwingenberg Castle *(guided tours from May to September, 2 to 4pm on Tuesdays, Fridays and Sundays; 1DM; brochure in English),* standing high above the road, marks the first of the Lower Neckar defiles.

In Hirschhorn am Neckar leave road no 37 for a while to bear right towards Beerfelden and right again up the approach road to Hirschhorn Castle.

Hirschhorn am Neckar★. – *Tour of the castle ¼ hour.* The castle stands on the summit of a fortified spur. From the terrace (bar) on the tower *(ascent: 0.20DM – 121 difficult steps)* there is a majestic **view★** downstream over the Hirschhorn bend and the wooded Neckar Valley.

Neckarsteinach. – The town known for the four castles which dominate its setting.

Dilsberg. – *Excursion of 6.5 km - 5 miles – starting from Neckargemünd, plus ½ hour sightseeing.* Leave the car outside the walls at Dilsberg. Follow the signs ''Burgruine'' to the castle ruins *(open in summer, 8am to noon and 1 to 6pm; in winter, 9am to noon and 1 to 5pm; 0.50DM)* and climb the tower *(97 steps)* for a **panorama★** of the Neckar bend.

You approach Heidelberg along the **right bank**, and arrive splendidly, opposite the castle.

Heidelberg★★★. – *Description p 146.*

NENNIG Roman Villa
Michelin map **203** 18 – 3 km - 2 miles – southeast of Remich

The Roman Villa of Nennig, rediscovered in 1852, must have been a large palace, judging by its 140 m façade - 459 ft. The choice of its site in the Mosel Valley is easily appreciated.

Access and Tour. – *On leaving Nennig follow the signs ''Römischer Mosaikfussboden''. Open 1 April to 30 September, 8.30am to noon and 1 to 6pm; 1 October to 31 March, 9am to noon and 1 to 4.30pm; closed Mondays. 0.50DM. Guided tours in English.*

The splendid reception hall **mosaic★★**, now under cover, has intricate geometric motifs framing pictures of Roman games.

NERESHEIM

Michelin map **987** north of 36 – *Local map p 217* – Pop 6 700

The huge white buildings of the 18C Abbey of Neresheim stand out in the predominantly undeveloped landscape which lies to the east of the Swabian Jura.

Church* (Klosterkirche). – The church was begun in 1745 under the direction of Balthazar Neumann *(p 26)* and was the great Baroque architect's last work. The bell tower with its many horizontal lines and levels dates from 1626 and is the oldest part of the building.

Inside, the painted decoration of Martin Knoller (1775) goes well with the unusual feeling of space which is further enhanced by free standing twin columns only being used to support the central dome. At the communion table, turn towards the organ for one of the best perspective views of the church.

The stuccoes and altarpieces are Neo-Classical *(p 26)*.

NIEDERALTEICH Abbey

Michelin map **987** 28 – 14 km - 9 miles – southeast of Deggendorf – *Local maps pp 59, 105*

Niederalteich Abbey stands with its two towers close together overlooking the Danube and is now occupied by Benedictines.

Church* (Klosterkirche). – The present church is the result of the Baroque transformation of a Gothic hall-church of which only the twenty pillars were used again. The new chancel was built in 1726 beneath low vaulting.

The height of the aisles is cut by galleries strangely pierced with lantern openings which afford surprising views of the upper vaulting.

NÖRDLINGEN ★

Michelin map **987** 26 36 – *Local map p 217* – Pop 17 500

The fortified town of Nördlingen lies along the Romantic Road in the Ries Basin *(p 218)*.

St. George's*. – *Tour: ¼ hour.* The **tower*** of this late 15C hall-church, built of volcanic stone, rises majestically in all its Flamboyant decoration.

The interior is covered by a magnificent fan vaulting; the Baroque organ gallery (1610), adorned with hanging keys, supports a loft with shutters painted overall; the late 15C pulpit has a graceful corbelled staircase. The walls are covered with 16-18C funerary medallions and epitaphs.

The Baroque altarpiece at the high altar has replaced the original one by Friedrich Herlin which has been moved to the museum, although the carved group of the Crucifixion, the statues of St. George and **Mary Magdalene***, which were part of the first altarpiece remain.

The Perimeter Wall* (Stadtmauer). – The wall is reinforced by fortified gateways and towers of which the most elegant are topped by helmet-shaped roofs (Reisturm, Löpsinger Tor, Deininger Tor). You follow the parapet walk from the Berger Tor to the Alte Bastei and the Reimlinger Tor.

Museum*. – *Guided tours, 9 (except Saturdays and Sundays), 10 and 11am; 2, 3 and 4pm (except Saturdays and Sundays); closed Mondays and in November; 1DM.*

The museum includes the old altarpiece from St. George's with panels painted by Friedrich Herlin, a citizen of Nördlingen, from 1462 to 1477. The work, which is dedicated to St. George, consists of scenes in deliciously fresh colours. Note the group of women donors at prayer.

NÖRDLINGEN

0 — 400 m

Baldinger Straße	
Bauhofgasse	3
Bei den Kornschrannen	4
Beim Klösterle	5
Brettermarkt	6
Bürgermeister-Reiger-Straße	7
Deininger Straße	8
Eisengasse	9
Hafenmarkt	12
Hallgasse	13
Judengasse	14
Kreuzgasse	15
Luckengasse	16
Marktplatz	17
Mittlere Gerbergasse	18
Münzgasse	20
Obstmarkt	22
Polizeigasse	23
Reimlinger Straße	24
Rothahnengasse	26
Salvatorgasse	27
Schäflesmarkt	28
Schrannenstraße	29
Vordere Gerbergasse	31
Waisengasse	32
Wemdinger Straße	33
Würzburger Straße	35

The NÜRBURGRING

Michelin map **203** 4 – *Local map p 115*

The open car circuit lies in wooded and hilly country. It has taken its name from the romantic Nürburg ruin *(p 114)* which stands within its northern loop, which is 22.835 km long - 14.17 miles. The car and motorcycle races with professional drivers and riders attract such crowds that it could be said that the track has led to the rediscovery of the Eifel by the Germans.

Practical Information. – *Apart from actual race-meetings and training days, the track is open to tourists from 8am (9am in winter) to nightfall. One-way driving only.*

Access is at three control points: Nürburg ("Start und Ziel" point where the stands are), Breidscheid and Müllenbach. Pay attention to the parking and turning regulations. Follow the directions given by the officials. *Charge: 9DM for the car; motorcycles, 4.50DM.*

NUREMBERG ★★ (NÜRNBERG)

Michelin map **987** 26 – Pop 491 400 – *Built up area plan in Michelin Red Guide Deutschland*

Nuremberg was one of the most beautiful mediaeval cities of Germany. Many of the half-timbered burghers' houses with historiated gables, which formed part of the setting for the Nazi party's spectacular annual rallies in September, were completely destroyed during the war.

The old bronze casters' and gold beaters' town is now, with its neighbour Fürth, one of the industrial centres of south Germany, manufacturing cars (lorries and tractors), electrical and electronic equipment, motorcycles, typewriters, sewing machines, pencils, toys, etc.

Gourmets will enjoy the *Bratwurst* (small grilled sausages) and the carp, fried or poached in wine. As mementoes they can take away boxes of *Lebkuchen*, a fragrant spice bread.

The Golden Age. – The 15 and 16C were Nuremberg's greatest period: the city was at the crossroads of commercial routes and was the capital of Franconian craftsmanship, rivalling Augsburg. Nuremberg's glory derived from the vitality of its flourishing arts, literature and science. In 1526 Melanchthon founded in the town the first German science university; the workshops of the bold sculptor Veit Stoss *(c 1445-1553)*, of Peter Fischer (1460-1529), talented bronze caster, of Michael Wolgemut (1434-1519), created for the town a renown that Albrecht Dürer *(p 27)*, pupil of Wolgemut, confirmed with his creative force and original genius. The Nuremberg Mastersingers *(p 28)* gave a new impetus to German poetry.

Nuremberg was the scene in 1945 of the International Military Tribunal at which the major German war criminals were tried and following which nine of them were hanged.

■ **MAIN SIGHTS** *tour: 2 hours – additional hour for tour of the ramparts by car*

Tour of the Ramparts★ (Stadtbefestigung). – Go round the outside in a clockwise direction to see, on the right, the town's fortifications (Stadtbefestigung), which are unique. The mediaeval perimeter was completed in 1452 and, from the inside outwards, consists of a main wall with a parapet walk, lists, a second wall and moats where the surrounding boulevards now run (Graben). The most massive constructions, apart from the castle, are the gates where the towers were reinforced in the 16C by enormous round cannon-proof stonework.

Dürer's House★ (BY). – *Open March to October, 10am to 5pm (Saturdays 9pm); the rest of the year, 1 to 5pm (Saturdays 10am to 9pm, Sundays 10am to 5pm); closed Mondays; 1.50DM.*

Dürer bought this 15C gabled house (restored) with jutting eaves in 1509 and lived in it at the base of the fortifications until his death in 1528.

The museum has a double interest: historical in the arrangement of the rooms, artistic in the exhibits (original drawings or copies of important works executed in this house).

St. Sebald's Church★ (St. Sebaldus-Kirche) (BY). – The building is largely 13C Gothic. The west face, which is plain with two Romanesque doorways framing the projecting chancel, contrasts with the huge 14C east chancel which is intricately worked and adorned with statues.

Inside, the Romanesque and Transitional Gothic (west) sections are easily distinguishable from the Radiating Gothic style of the chancel and ambulatory in the east.

Works of art★★

(1) St. Peter Altarpiece painted on a gold background in the Wolgemut studio.
(2) Bronze font with a hearth.
(3) St. Catherine (1310).
(4) St. Sebald (1390).
(5) The Emperor Heinrich II.
(6) The Virgin with a Halo.
(7) Tomb of St. Sebald: the shrine is incorporated in a pierced bronze monument, the famous work of Peter Vischer (1519). The bronze is adorned with crowds of figurines (note on the smaller sides, the artist in his working clothes and St. Sebald).
(8) Crucifixion group by Stoss (1520).
(9) Also by Stoss: above – Christ and the Virgin in sorrow; below – The Last Supper, the Garden of Olives and Taking of Christ in the Garden (1499).
(10) The Bearing of the Cross by Adam Kraft (1506).
(11) (Outside) Funerary monument of the Schreyer Family: the Passion and the Resurrection by Adam Kraft.

A fine series of 14 and 15C stained glass windows embellish the chancel.

The Beautiful Fountain★ (Schöner Brunnen) (BY). – This 14C Gothic fountain is the town's best known sight. The figures round the base are the seven Electors and nine heroes of the Old Testament or the Middle Ages; those at the top (19 m - 63 ft) are the Prophets round Moses.

St. Lawrence's Church (St. Lorenz-Kirche) (BY). – This Gothic church was given its "hall-chancel" in the 15C. The rose window makes the façade outstanding.

Inside *(enter by the south door)*, in the nave are two outstanding works of art: the 1420 Crucifix on the glory beam, medallions adorning its extremities and the 1517 **Annunciation★★** (Engelsgruss) by Veit Stoss, suspended from the chancel vaulting. The group of the Virgin and the Angel is surrounded by six medallions of the other Joys of the Virgin after the Annunciation. Left of the high altar a Gothic ciborium by Adam Krafft shows the artist supporting the balustrade. In the ambulatory, look at the windows, in particular the Tree of Jesse made in 1437.

■ **ADDITIONAL SIGHTS**

German National Museum★★ (Germanisches Nationalmuseum) (BY M¹). – *Open 9am to 4pm (also 8 to 9.30pm Thursdays); closed Mondays; 2DM.*

This huge museum is centred on a former Carthusian monastery. The outstanding exhibits are of fine arts and German craftsmanship only.

Castle (Kaiserburg) (BY). – The buildings, in which burgraves and emperors lived from the 11 to the 15C are of less interest than the different views of Nuremberg and its belfries. For example, stand on the eastern approach terrace at the foot of the **Sinwellturm** keep (BY D) or climb to its top for a more extensive **panorama★**. In the nearby courtyard there is a fascinating **covered well★** (Tiefer Brunnen) (BY F).

If you go inside the buildings (at the end of the courtyard – *open 1 April to 30 September, 9am to 5pm; 1 October to 31 March, 10am to noon and 1 to 4pm; 2DM*) look particularly at the two storey Romanesque **Imperial Chapel (BY K)** with its gallery for the Emperor.

ST. SEBALD'S CHURCH

The Marriage Doorway
Entrance
0   20m
5
3   6
*1 ○2   4   7   8
10   9
11
Doorway of the Last Judgment
Doorway of the Three Kings

NÜRNBERG
CENTRE

0 ___ 300 m

Temporary diversions due to construction of Underground

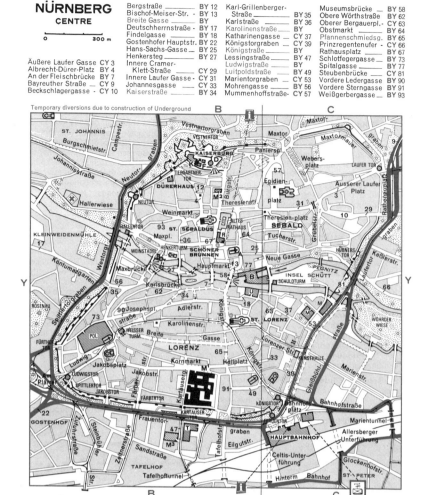

Fembo Municipal Museum (Stadtmuseum Fembohaus) (BY M²). – *Open weekdays 10am (1pm in winter) to 5pm; Saturdays 10am to 9pm, Sundays and holidays 10am to 5pm; closed Mondays; 1.50DM.*

This museum in the Fembo Renaissance mansion has exhibits on old Nuremberg.

Church of Our Lady (Liebfrauenkirche) (BY A). – This Gothic church, so fortunately sited in the Hauptmarkt, attracts visitors at midday when the jacks of its clock appear as the seven Electors coming to swear allegiance to the Emperior Karl IV.

Hospital (Heilig-Geist-Spital) (BY B). – The hospital, built on two arches, straddles an arm of the Pegnitz; its graceful corbelled tower can be seen from the Museumbrücke.

The building dates from the 14 and 15C. The central courtyard (go round to enter from the island upstream) with wide arcades built of limestone, surmounted by wooden galleries, gives an idea of what the mansions of Nuremberg used to be like.

The banks of the Pegnitz. – Some of old Nuremberg can be seen along the banks. From the bridge (Maxbrücke) (BY) there is an attractive **general view** of the half-timbered wine hall (Weinstadel) flanked by a tower, and of the Henkersteg covered footbridge.

Transport Museum (Verkehrsmuseum) (BY M³). – *Open 10am to 5pm (4pm October to March); closed Sunday afternoons and some holidays; 1.50DM.*

Large railway section of which the outstanding exhibits are the reconstruction of the historic train that ran on the Nuremberg–Fürth line – the first line to be opened in Germany (1835), a train circuit and a postal section of interest to philatelists.

EXCURSION

Round tour in the Hersbrucker Alb. – *109 km - 68 miles – about 3 hours.* Leave Nuremberg by ②; after 9 km - 6 miles – take the motorway in the direction of Bayreuth. Leave the motorway at the Plech exit to go along the Neuhaus road.

Neuhaus an der Pegnitz★. – Suddenly you come on the town in its **setting★** overlooked by the tall tower of Veldenstein Castle.

Go as far as Hersbruck down the enclosed Pegnitz Valley over which, here and there, tower tall needle-shaped rocks.

Hersbruck. – Former fortified and now a very bustling town at the spot where the Pegnitz Valley begins to open out.

From the bridge over the Pegnitz (going towards Happurg) look back for a characteristic view of the Wassertor gate and the neighbouring old roofs.

Return to Nuremberg by road no 14.

OBERAMMERGAU ★

Michelin map **987** 36, 37 – *Local maps pp 42 and 44* – Pop 4 900

The wooded foothills of the Ammergau Alps, from which rises the Kofel peak, surround the attractive little town of Oberammergau with its many painted houses.

The **church** was decorated with stuccoes by Joseph Schmuzer in the 18C and also furnished with Rococo altarpieces.

Besides many wood-carving workshops, employing some 500 people, Oberammergau is known for its Passion Play, which is performed every ten years *(next performance 1980)*.

The Origin of the Passion Play. – After a terrible plague epidemic in 1632, which miraculously stopped just short of Oberammergau, the people of the village vowed to give a presentation of the Passion of Christ every ten years. The first of these took place in 1634. The 17C text was rewritten in 1750 and again in 1850 to meet contemporary taste.

In 1970 some 530 000 spectators witnessed the 102 performances given by the inhabitants of Oberammergau from May to September. The roles are arduous, each presentation lasting all day, with a short intermission for the midday meal. The 1 700 amateur actors prepare for their parts a long time in advance and it is not unusual to see men with the long hair and beards of the Apostles in the village streets months before the Passion Play festival begins.

OBERMARCHTAL

Michelin map **206** 6 – Pop 1 300

The former monastery of the Premonstratensians, which stands to the north of the town on a terrace overlooking a small gorge of the Danube, has formed a Baroque ensemble since the 17C. Marie-Antoinette was received at the monastery in 1770 when on her way from Vienna to Paris.

Former Abbey★ (Ehemaliges Kloster). – *To visit the sacristy and the abbey buildings, apply to Mr. Adolf Hornung, Obermachtal, Hauptstrasse 10.*

Abbey Church. – This building, which was begun in 1686, was one of the first to be completed by the Vorarlberg school. The more or less symmetrical nave and chancel on either side of the transept are typical with heavy pilasters built into the side walls *(see plans, p 25)*.

The rigidity of this still unevolved Baroque architecture is accentuated by the heaviness of the furnishings; only the Wessobrunn *(p 256)* stuccoes lighten the overall effect. The monumental high altarpiece is lit in a strange way from the sides.

In the sacristy is a chasuble, which may be seen on request, made from the satin mantel worn by Marie-Antoinette at her wedding.

Abbey Buildings. – The refectory, decorated with frescoes and pieces of mirror originally intended to increase the size of the hall, is overpoweringly grandiose.

OBERSTDORF ★★

Michelin map **987** 36 – *Local map p 40* – Pop 11 800

Oberstdorf, the most developed resort of the Upper Allgäu, is situated in the higher basin of the Iller but without any overall plan. Upstream, a number of mountain valleys, such as the Stillachtal, the Trettachtal, the Oytal and the Kleinwalsertal, give access to the foot of the main crests of the limestone Alps of the Allgäu, a massif much sought after by German climbers and, since 1968, an official centre of mountaineering training. Winter affords skiing on the Söllereck crest which faces north and is served by a chairhoist.

EXCURSIONS

Walks – *local map below*

Nebelhorn★★. – About 1½ hours of which 30 minutes are by cableway and chairhoist *(every 8 minutes from 8.30am to noon and 1.20 to 5pm; inclusive Rtn fare: 4DM)*. A chairhoist linking with the cableway at an altitude of 1 932 m - 3 058 ft – ends at the summit, crowned with a cross. The **panorama★★** extends from the Zugspitze to the Säntis (the Swiss Appenzell Alps) and, in clear weather, even to the snows of the Bernese Oberland, which is set off, in the foreground, by the bold outlines of the Allgäu Alps (Hochvogel).

Breitachklamm★★. – 6.5 km - 4 miles – plus 1½ hours on foot Rtn. Tours from 8am to 5pm (a run especially recommended in wet weather and in mid-winter when the ice produces a drapery-like effect); 1.60DM. Leave Oberstdorf by the Sonthofen road; turn left immediately after the bridge and, still following the torrent, go on to the attended car park for the gorges. After a quarter of an hour's walk, the galleries will lead you down to a cutting which has been worn 100 m - 300 ft – deep by a turbulent stream. An easier path is to turn at the foot of the long stairway into the upper gorge, which is less surprising and varied.

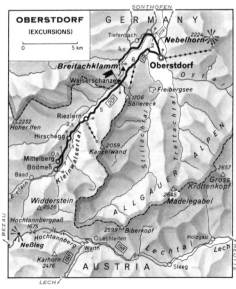

Walkers can leave the gorges by the exit at the top of the steps; this way (abandoning the gorge path) they will come to the Walserschanze, on the Kleinwalsertal road *(see below)*, which has a frequent bus service to Oberstdorf.

OBERSTDORF**

The Kleinwalsertal★ – *17 km - 10 miles – about 1½ hours – Local map p 199*

The Kleinwalsertal, a high valley of the Breitach, forming a tiny mountain area of about 100 km² - 38 sq miles, was settled in the 13C by emigrants of Germanic origin from the Upper Valais – the **Walsers**. Like other regions of the Vorarlberg (Grosswalsertal and Hochtannberg) cleared by these hardy workers, small dark wood houses scattered on the slopes follow the traditions of their grim individualism, forming a striking contrast to the unexciting cube-shaped farms of the Allgäu.

Until the modern road (1930) was built, the inhabitants were able to live their patriarchal way of life and keep their curious custumes; today, however, these are worn mostly at weddings and in the procession on Corpus Christi.

By feudal ties, the Walsers established here passed under the sovereignty of the Habsburgs in 1453, so that they found themselves Austrians when the national frontiers were fixed. Cut off from the rest of Vorarlberg by the peaks of the Allgäu Alps and oriented solely towards Germany in the commercial field, the district has had a special status from 1891.

Remaining under Austrian sovereignty, the Kleinwalsertal is today economically part of Germany. Because of this, there are only German Customs officials on the road from Oberstdorf although it is the Austrian constabulary who maintain law and order. The postal vans which serve Mittelberg from Oberstdorf are German, but locally issued postage stamps are Austrian. (They are paid for in Deutschmarks, the only means of payment for commercial transactions, including hotel bills.)

A number of hotels have been built since the Second World War in the Kleinwalsertal Valley where the three resorts of **Riezlern, Hirschegg** and **Mittelberg** share the tourist trade.

The excursion from Oberstdorf to Mittelberg provides the best general view of the Kleinwalsertal particularly between Riezlern and Hirschegg, where the church of Hirschegg stands out in the foreground against the rocky peak of the Widderstein. At the entrance to Mittelberg take the little road that drops sharply and leads to the hamlet of Bödmen, which is interesting for its traditional Valaisian chalets. Turn round.

OBERWESEL

Michelin map **204** 15 – *Local map p 212* – Pop 5 000

Oberwesel stretches out along the left bank of the Rhine at the beginning of a curve which ends downstream at the Loreley. The Schönburg dominates the town which still has 18 watchtowers. Among these the Ochsenturm, crowned with a turret, now serves as a semaphore.

Church of Our Lady★ (Liebfrauenkirche). – *Tour: ½ hour.* The church, south of the village, is recognisable from its red roughcast. Enter through the cloister. This Gothic church contains a number of **altarpieces★** (Flügelaltäre) and funerary monuments including the 1506 altarpiece to St. Nicholas in the south chapel; the curious 1510 triptych in the north aisle depicting the fifteen cataclysms ending the world; and, at the end of the south aisle, the funerary monument to a canon who died in 1515, and gave the greater part of the works of art in the church, and beside this, a Gothic altarpiece with a charming Nativity.

EXCURSION

Burg Schönburg★. – *2 km - 1 mile – by the uphill road next to the Church of Our Lady, plus ½ hour sightseeing. Go round the parapet path on the defence wall and the Gate Tower (Torturm).*

The burg consists of three castles protected by a wall. Each fortress had a keep; the oldest is seven-sided, the second, round and the third, square. The main terrace commands the Rhine and Oberwesel and its towers. Upstream the **view** extends to Kaub and the fortified island of Pfalz.

OLDENBURG

Michelin map **987** 14 – Pop 134 700 – *Town plan in Michelin Red Guide Deutschland*

Oldenburg is a widespread, airy town whose business interests lie chiefly in agricultural shows and processing food, supplied by the fertile hinterland where market gardening and flower growing, cattle raising and horse breeding are much in evidence.

■ **SIGHTS** *time: ¾ hour*

Castle Park★ (Schlossgarten). – The mild and humid coastal climate fosters the growth of magnificent trees and shrubs such as tulip trees and rhododendrons. From the weeping willows on the shores of the lake there is an attractive view of the towers of St. Lambert's Church.

Regional Museum (Landesmuseum). – *In the Grand Dukes' Castle. Open 10am to 1pm and 3 to 5pm; closed Sunday afternoons and Mondays.*

The museum gallery contains a pleasant series of **small pictures★** (Idylls) by Johann Heinrich-Wilhelm Tischbein (1715-1829), the best known of the painters of this name thanks to his picture of Goethe in the *Roman Countryside* which is at Frankfurt *(p 120).*

OPPENHEIM

Michelin map **204** north of 7 – Pop 5000

Below Worms, the Rhine ceases, for a short distance, to curve through the alluvial plain, and, far from towns and buildings, runs through the Rhineland Hesse Hills which are covered with such famous vineyards as the Nierstein. In these lovely surroundings stands Oppenheim, crowned by a Gothic church with beautifully carved stonework.

St. Catherine's Church★ (Katharinenkirche). – *Open April to September, 8am (11am Sundays) to 6pm; October to March, 9am (11am Sundays) to 5pm; 0.50DM (1DM for guided tours).*

The building's chief interest lies in its 14C Gothic façade on the south side. All the pierced surfaces have richly designed bays: note especially, as an example of Gothic art at its best, the tall windows with quadrilobed tracery, and the wide intermediate windows incorporating two superb rose windows. The gables above the tall windows, the pinnacles, baldachins and decorative blind arcades on the buttresses complete the decoration.

OSNABRÜCK

Michelin map **987** 14 – Pop 158 800 – *Town plan in Michelin Red Guide Deutschland*

Osnabrück, which lies between the Teutoburger Wald and Wiehengebirge heights, developed round two centres: in the 9C an Old Town grew out of the episcopal quarter and the market town and from the 11C onwards, a New Town spread around the Church of St. John. When they united within a single city wall in about 1300, Osnabrück became an important commercial centre.

Its former linen trade has been replaced by metal products (cables, car-bodies) and paper.

The Prologue to the Peace of 1648. – It was in Osnabrück that the preliminary talks before the Treaty of Westphalia were held by representatives of the Emperor and the Protestant belligerents (Sweden and the German Lutheran princes). The Emperor treated with the Catholics at Münster. When the news that peace had been concluded in Münster *(p 191)* was announced to the Osnabrück crowds on 25 October 1648, they were at first incredulous and then burst into hymns of thanksgiving.

■ **SIGHTS** *time: 1½ hours*

Town Hall. – *Open 9am to 5pm (3pm in winter); Saturdays and Sundays 10am to noon; closed holidays.*

The early 16C town hall had to be rebuilt after the war; it has a Gothic look beneath a large pavilion roof. The Peace of 1648 was declared from its steps. The statue of Charlemagne above the entrance, is accompanied by the statues of eight emperors.

Peace Chamber* (Friedenssaal). – The chamber in which the preliminary peace talks were held is decorated with portraits of the heads of state and negotiators. The floor and ceiling have been rebuilt; the carved wooden seats and the chandelier are authentic and date from 1554.

The Council Chamber next door has a fine Renaissance fireplace (1618).
Among the gold plate in the **treasury** is the precious 14C Kaiserpokal goblet.

St. Mary's Church (Marienkirche). – This 14C Gothic hall-church, with its elegant transverse gables, closes the north end of the Marktplatz. Its most remarkable work of art is the early 16C **altarpiece of the Passion*** originating from Antwerp.

St. Peter's Cathedral (Dom). – This 13C Transitional Gothic style building has a squat outline distinguished by large towers which differ in size and design. The northern side has a fine Romanesque decoration of blind arcades and cornices.

The interior is unusual with a flat ended square ambulatory. The ogive vaulting in the nave is definitely rounded; from the triumphal arch hangs an early 13C crucifix.

The chapels off the ambulatory are adorned with a few works of art, in particular a 16C carved wood altarpiece. From the asymmetrical Romanesque cloisters (enter from the south aisle) there is a good view of the cathedral towers.

Church of St. John (Johanniskirche). – This 13C Gothic hall-church served as the parish church of the New Town. It is an example of reduction to the basic in architecture and ornament. The dark wood **altarpiece** of the Passion at the high altar dates from 1512. The elongated cloister serves as a burial ground.

EXCURSION

Tecklenburg*. – *23 km - 14 miles – about 1½ hours.* Leave Osnabrück by ⑤ on the plan and, once out of the town, bear obliquely left towards Lengerich. At Lengerich turn right towards Rheine and, after 3 km - 2 miles – right again.

Leave the car in the park at the entrance to Tecklenburg, a picturesque town with half-timbered houses on the crest of the Teutoburger Wald. Make for the main square and then head west, passing through the Legge gateway, towards the oldest quarter at the foot of the **castle**. Of the castle there remain only a monumental Renaissance gateway and a belvedere tower. The fortress site is now a park with an open air theatre.

When visiting London use the Green Guide **"London"**

–Detailed descriptions of places of interest
–Useful local information
–A section on the historic square mile of the city City of London
  with a detailed fold out plan
–The lesser known London boroughs – their people, places and sights
–Plans of selected areas and important buildings.

OTTOBEUREN ★★★

Michelin map **987** 36 – Pop 7 000

Ottobeuren Abbey, a jewel of German Baroque architecture, stands surrounded by hills to which the Alpine foothills of the Allgäu form the background.

The Climax of the Baroque Style. – Founded in 764, the Benedictine Abbey of Ottobeuren prospered from the start when its patron, Charlemagne, gave it extensive rights. The early 16C saw one of the first printing presses functioning here and, a little later, the establishment of a school whose fame spread beyond Bavaria.

In the 18C the Abbey was completely transformed into the current Baroque style in which the influences of Salzburg (rounded transept arms), Rome (domes), and the Vorarlberg school (dividing columns) were all mingled. From 1748 Johann-Michael Fischer, the great architect of southern Germany, put the finishing touches to what was to be his masterpiece. With him must be associated in the Rococo decoration the names of the Zeillers for the frescoes and Johann-Michael Feichtmayr for the stuccoes and statues; under their direction a number of German and Italian artists helped to decorate the interior of the church.

Secularised in 1802, the abbey became a priory once again in 1834, but in 1918 regained its former standing in the Benedictine Order.

OTTOBEUREN★★★

■ **ABBEY★★★** (Kloster) *tour: ½ hour*

Abbey Church★★★ (Klosterkirche). – The squat appearance of the church gives no hint of its actual size, the largest of its style to exist in Germany, with towers 82 m high, a nave 90 m long and transept 60 m wide – 270 ft, 295 ft and 200 ft. It is, in fact, a huge construction, 480 m long - 1 575 ft – but entirely in scale from the towers of the façade to the last outbuilding.

It is, also, at Ottobeuren that once can test the theory of some German art critics, according to whom the exterior of Baroque churches has no value of its own but simply reflects in size the powerful influence exercised by the interior.

Once inside, the visitor is struck by the luminosity of the nave. The church is built north–south, contrary to the traditional custom of Christianity, and the light effects are sometimes remarkable, particularly early and late in the day.

The colours are harmonious: half-tints of pink, yellow, ochre and violet predominate, while the frescoes are in the vaults are of warmer tones. In the relatively shadowed chancel, more sombre colours blend with gold and the patina of the woodwork.

The Transept Crossing★★★ (Vierung). – The crossing gives an impression of immense strength. The transept could, in fact, be a church in itself. All the architecture is based on the flattened central dome.

Johann-Michael Fischer has skilfully laid out the crossing with canted piers. One notes here the altars of St. Michael, patron saint of the Ottobeuren region and of the Empire, the Saintly Guardian Angels, St. Joseph and St. John the Baptist. The pulpit, and opposite, the group of the Baptism of Christ which surmounts the baptismal font (sculptured by Joseph Christian) are the best works. The paving designed by Johann-Jakob Zeiller, shows the motifs of the Cross, the circle and the star. Zeiller

Ottobeuren – View of the church interior.

also painted the grandiose composition on the cupola: *The Miracle of Pentecost.*

Chancel★★ (Chor). – The small altar of the Holy Sacrament, which marks the entrance, is surmounted by a much-venerated Christ of the 12C, surrounded by stars which symbolise the kingship of the universe.

The high altar glorifies the Holy Trinity. At the foot of the columns of the altarpiece are statues of St. Peter and St. Paul, St. Ulrich, Bishop of Augsburg and patron saint of Swabia, and St. Conrad, Bishop and patron saint of the nearby diocese of Constance. The walnut **stalls★★** (1764) form, with the chancel organ, a single overall furnishing scheme. Their high backs are decorated with gilded limewood low reliefs by Joseph Christian (scenes of the life of St. Benedict and Biblical scenes).

Karl-Joseph Riepp (1710-75), pupil of Silbermann, who worked for a long time in Burgundy (churches of Dijon, Beaune and Besançon), made the **chancel organ★★** (1766), whose instrumental and decorative proportions, already large, were supplemented in 1957 with a new Organ of the Virgin, set up in the same organ loft.

Abbey Buildings (Klostergebäude). – *Open 10am to noon and 2 to 6pm (4pm December to February); 1DM.*

The buildings which were erected between 1711 and 1731 include an abbatical palace (Prälatur) with such usual state apartments as the Emperor's Hall and also a magnificent library and theatre.

PADERBORN

Michelin map **987** 15 – Pop 104 000 – *Town plan in Michelin Red Guide Deutschland*

Paderborn, at the source of the Pader, was an important stage on the Hellweg, the former commercial and strategic highway between Flanders and Saxony. The town, at the threshold of the Teutoburger Wald *(p 242)*, marks the last stage of the road (now Federal Road no 1) which went straight as the crow flies from belfry to belfry across the Westphalian Plain.

Paderborn is one of the oldest episcopal sees of Westphalia. Charlemagne had a meeting with Pope Leo III in the town in 799 at which the union of the Papacy and the Western Empire was sealed. Each year in July, festivities commemorate the return from Le Mans in 836 of the relics of St. Liborius, patron saint of Paderborn.

■ **SIGHTS** *tour: 2 hours*

Cathedral★ (Dom). – *Brochure in English.* The massive tower pierced with many Romanesque bays is the town's emblem. The present monument essentially goes back to the 13C. Outside on the Domplatz may be seen the 13C remains of the former carved doorway to the transept (the Wise Virgins, the Childhood of Christ, a frieze of animals taken from the fables of Antiquity).

The entrance porch (Paradies) is on the north side. Flanking the door are somewhat heavy statues of bishops, saints, and on the pier, the Virgin (c 1250). The door panels bear the older statues of St. Liborious (right) and St. Kilian (left).

Inside, a low hall built in the 13C shows the evolution from the Romanesque style in the west to Gothic in the east – the development is apparent in the capitals. The church contains important funerary sculptures. The crypt, which is reached from the transept, houses the relics of St. Liborius. The atrium, a small chamber with three equal aisles, and some arches dating back to 1000, opens to the north off the chancel.

Cloister. – The cloister, reached through the atrium, has two unusual features: the funerary chapel of the Westphalian Counts which contains a graceful Gothic altarpiece of 1517 and, visible only from outside, the amusing "three hares window" for which the artist drew only 3 ears. Reproductions are sold as souvenirs.

St. Bartholomew's Chapel (Bartholomäuskapelle). – The chapel is a Romanesque hall built apart to the north in 1017 by Byzantine masons summoned by the bishop of Paderborn. The slender columns with ornately worked capitals in a late Corinthian style, support a domed vaulting.

At the north side of the cathedral, excavations have revealed the remains of Charlemagne's castle.

Diocesan Museum (Diözesanmuseum). – *Open 10am to 5pm; closed Mondays; 1DM.*

This museum of sacred art is particularly rich in sculpture, the masterpiece being the **Virgin of Bishop Imad★** (Imadmadonna) dating from about 1050.

The treasure of the cathedral is in the basement. The most remarkable exhibits on display are Roger von Helmarshausens' small portable altar dating from about 1100 and the 1627 shrine of St. Liborius.

Town Hall. – The monumental town hall dating from 1616 has three gables decorated with late Renaissance ram's horn scrollwork reminiscent of the Weser school of architecture *(p 141)*.

Source of the Pader (Paderquellen). – More than 200 springs rise in the lower part of the town at the foot of the cathedral. The waters at once unite to form streams which are sufficiently powerful to drive water-wheels.

The park is pleasant and affords **views★** of the nearby church towers.

PASSAU ★

Michelin map **987** north of 38 – *Local map p 59* – Pop 50 000

Passau, a frontier town between Bavaria and Austria and known as the Town of the Three Rivers, lies in a marvellous **setting★★** at the junction of the Inn – 300 m wide – the Danube (Donau) and the small River Ilz.

The wooded rocks of the Danube's left bank, crowned by the fortress of Oberhaus, and the heights of the right bank of the Inn, with the church of Mariahilf, frame the narrow tongue of land where the town has developed. At the foot of the cathedral, the towers of the old fortifications, the Baroque churches and the aristocratic houses crowd close together.

HISTORICAL NOTES

A Powerful Bishopric. – St. Boniface, the Apostle of Germany *(p 129)*, was born in Devon of a noble Anglo-Saxon family, and was authorised in 1718 by Pope Gregory II to preach the gospel to the pagans of Germany. The Bishopric of Passau was founded by him and rivalled that of Salzburg in power and influence when, in the 13C, the town became a Free Imperial City and its bishop a Prince of the Empire. The vast Passau diocese included all the Danube Valley area in Austria and – until the 15C – Vienna also. It was at this time that the bishops of Passau, following the example of the bishops of Salzburg, who had built an almost impregnable fortress at Hohensalzburg, built their Oberhaus stronghold on the wooded hill of Georgsberg. Its successive defence systems allowed the castle to withstand long sieges and imposed respect for episcopal authority on the rebellious burghers.

A Commercial Calling. – The flow of the waters of the Inn almost doubles the volume of the Danube, which at Passau becomes a really large river. From the Middle Ages an important source of commercial activity on this river was the storing, in Passau, of cereals brought from Hungary by trains of barges. Today barges can go up river as far as Regensburg. Passau remains the starting point for regular passenger services down the Danube to Vienna.

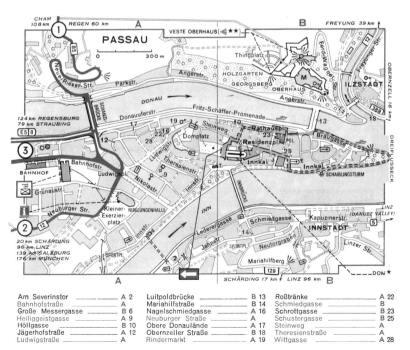

PASSAU★

■ **GENERAL VIEW**★★ *4 km - 2 miles – plus ¼ hour sightseeing*

From the Oberhaus Fortress (Veste) which is easily reached by car along a road branching off no 85 (north on the plan by ①) you come to the belvedere marked "zur Aussicht" near the car park, also a tower inside the perimeter *(payment on entry)* which affords a circular panorama. The striking **view**★★ shows the rocky promontory dividing the Inn from the Danube, with the town's churches and houses jumbled close together upon it. Some of the houses, following a former Inn Valley tradition, have ridge roofs behind façades – masking the many sloping angles from street level.

■ **SIGHTS** *time: 1 hour*

Start at the Domplatz.

Cathedral★ (Dom). – A fine late Gothic *(p 23)* building dedicated to St. Stephen, the cathedral was largely destroyed by a fire in the 17C and was, from 1680, reconstructed in the Baroque style.

The majestic west façade is framed by two symmetrical towers in which the fourth storeys are octagonal in design, producing a light note in an otherwise severe overall effect.

The vast interior is unfortunately spoilt by an over abundance of decorative stuccoes and frescoes, but this does not apply to the remarkable paintings of the chapels off the ambulatory. These, which are by the Austrian, Johann-Michael Rottmayr (1654-1730), show great technical skill: outstanding in the first chapel on the right of the ambulatory is the *Beheading of John the Baptist*, in the chapel opposite, the *Conversion of St. Paul* and, in the chapels nearest the organ-loft, *St. Sebastian being tended by St. Irene*, and the *Martyrdom of St. Agnes*.

Go to the Residenzplatz to see the **east end**★★ (Chorabschluss) of the cathedral: it is a remarkable work in Flamboyant Gothic, whose slender outline is lengthened by the domed belfry which tops the transept cupola.

The **Residenzplatz**, with the Renaissance buildings of the former bishopric and the fountain of the Wittelsbachs, and the streets near the cathedral, contain a number of arcaded houses with corbelling and ridge roofs.

St. Michael's Church (B E). – This 17C church on the left bank of the Inn was built by the Jesuits and over richly adorned with Baroque stuccoes and gilding in about 1720. The chancel with its flat east end is masked by a painted altarpiece by Carlone.

Walk to the River Junction (Dreiflusseck). – On leaving St. Michael's, make for the Inn quayside and follow it to the junction. The Inn, fast and torrential at times, runs at the foot of the Schaiblingsturm, a tower of 1481 which formed part of the town's defensive system. From the terrace laid out as a promenade at the end of the promontory, there is a good view of the Georgsberg and the Oberhaus Fortress. At the junction of the two rivers the waters of the Danube and the Inn can be seen flowing downstream side by side for some time before they intermingle.

Follow the Danube quayside: the river, whose water is browner than that of the Inn, carries a large river fleet.

On the **Rathausplatz**, one of the most picturesque squares in Passau, flanked by a high tower, stands the 14C **town hall** (R) with a painted façade.

Return to the Domplatz by way of the Höllgasse.

With this guide use the Michelin maps (scales 1:1 000 000 and 1:200 000) shown on page 9.

PIRMASENS
Michelin map **204** 20 – Pop 60 400 – *Town plan in Michelin Red Guide Deutschland*

Named after St. Pirmin, who was supposed to have preached Christianity here in the 8C. A garrison town in the 18C, belonging to the Landgrave of Hesse and in 1924 the centre of the Palatine independence movement. The town was heavily damaged during the last war. Today it extends over several levels and has been the capital of the shoe industry since the 19C.

Local Museum. – *Altes Rathaus, Hauptstrasse 26. Guided tours every hour Thursdays 3 to 6pm, Sundays 10am to 1pm; 1DM.*

The painting gallery is devoted to the works of the 19C painter, Bürkel, a native of the town. In the rooms, on the street side, paintings, engravings and military equipment recall the life of Pirmasens during the time of the counts of Hesse and as a garrison town. The prehistoric objects are from excavations done in the area. The **shoe section**★ is fascinating with its presentation of the history and progress in this industry. Oriental babouches with mother of pearl inlay, slippers (India), street walkers' shoes on "stilts" (Japan), Gaucho and Eskimo boots as well as the incredible mules made with human hair and ostrich feathers (Australia) and the shoes of Chinese women, with the reproduction of a stunted foot. Note also the reconstruction of a shoe maker's shop evoking a disappearing craft.

PYRMONT, Bad ★
Michelin map **987** 15 – Pop 22 500

The spa town of Bad Pyrmont stands among the green hills of the Upper Weser.

■ **SIGHTS** *time: ¾ hour*

Spa Park★ (Kurpark). – The park is magnificently planted with trees, particularly palm trees, of which there are hundreds and many species, and is the home of birds and squirrels. There are well conceived vistas of which the best is the Bombergallee which is cut by the main alley, and a picturesquely bordered pool.

Dunsthöhle. – *Open October to March, 2 to 5pm; 1DM.*

An accumulation of carbon dioxide in the bottom of this old quarry enables two classic and amusing physics' experiments to be demonstrated: soap-bubbles suddenly stop in their descent, and candles die on reaching the gas level.

RASTATT

Michelin map **205** 2 – *Local map p 81* – Pop 41 000
Town plan in Michelin Red Guide Deutschland

Rastatt has never refound the prestige it enjoyed at the beginning of the 18C when ruled by the Margrave Ludwig of Baden (1655-1707), known as **Ludwig the Turk** *(see Baden-Baden and Karlsruhe)*. The enterprising captain, under the threat of invasion through the political ambitions of Louis XIV, abandoned the ruins of Baden-Baden and turned the town into a stronghold. He also built a castle in accordance with his ambitions, basing the overall plan on Italian models.

The town was the seat of two congresses between the Holy Roman Empire and France: the resulting treaties provided, in 1714, for the ending of the War of the Spanish Succession and in 1797 for the enforcement of the Peace of Campo Formio, but the latter came to nothing as two of the French plenipotentiaries were murdered two years later.

■ **SIGHTS** *time: 1 hour*

Castle. – This enormous red limestone castle was designed by Rossi, architect to the Viennese court, at the command of Ludwig the Turk. It had only just been completed when the prince died. The building is now used as administrative offices and to house the local and historical museums.

Military Museum (Wehrgeschichtliches Museum). – *Open Easter to 15 October, 10am to noon and 3 (2pm Sundays and holidays) to 5pm; closed Mondays (except Monday holidays).*

The museum is the German Military Museum and displays through the largest collection in existence, Western Germany's military history.

Pagodenburg. – Attractive polygonal pavilion built by the Margravine Sibylla Augusta in 1722 in the centre of a terraced garden which is now open to the public.

The landscape is completed by the **Chapel of Our Lady of the Hermits** (Maria Einsiedeln) built in 1715. The façade with its intricately cut out Baroque gable is all the more beautiful for its position at the top of the main stairway.

EXCURSION

The Favourite's Castle★. – *5 km - 3 miles – plus 1 hour sightseeing.* Leave Rastatt by the Murgtalstrasse (southeast on the plan). Immediately after passing beneath the motorway bear obliquely right towards the castle.

Open 1 March to 30 November, 8.30 to 11am and 2 to 5pm; closed Mondays, December, January and February; 1.50DM.

The small castle built in 1711 and imbued with the memory of the Margravine Sibylla Augusta, widow of Ludwig the Turk, has an interesting interior: floors of *scagliola* – stucco imitating marble – brilliant as glass, mirror decorations – (mirror room) and Chinese decors; a Florentine room lined with miniatures and enriched with hard stonework; mosaics; collections of china (Frankfurt, Delft and Strasburg) and porcelain (Meissen, Nymphenburg, Chelsea) and kitchens.

RATZEBURG ★

Michelin map **987** 6 – Pop 13 000

The island town of Ratzeburg stands attractively in the centre of a **lake★**, the largest of the stretches of water which lie in the morainic hills between the Elbe and Lübeck. The **setting★**, enhanced by the squat outline of the cathedral, is best seen from the top of a polygonal **belvedere tower** *(access: 0.50DM)* which rises out of the woods (continue along the line of the embankment which crosses the lake to the east before bearing left into the Hindenburghöhe avenue).

Cathedral★. – This 12C Romanesque brick building stands in parkland at the north end of the island. The porch over the south doorway has a finely decorated gable, and forms one of the cathedral chapels. *Open April to September, 10am to noon and 2 to 6pm (4pm October to March); closed Mondays. Brochure in English.*

Enter through the door beneath the tower *(guided tours possible: 1DM)*.

At the high altar is an outstanding **altarpiece** (Hochaltarbild) **of the Crucifixion★** dating from 1430. Beautiful old gold embroidered sacerdotal ornaments may be seen in the chapel off the south transept.

Barlach Memorial (Ernst-Barlach-Gedenkstätte). – *In the centre of the town, beside a church. Open: 9.30am to noon and 3 to 6pm; closed Mondays; 1DM.*

Works by the sculptor, Ernst Barlach (1870-1938), one of the leaders of the Expressionist movement in Germany: the *Singer,* the *Avenger,* the *Man in Doubt,* etc.

RAVENSBURG

Michelin map **206** 8 – *Local map p 40* – Pop 43 900

Ravensburg has remained to this day an old Swabian town of many towers surrounded by a well preserved rectangular wall. Enter beneath the Obertor (at the end of the Wangen road), a gateway with stepped gables, near the Mehlsack *(see below)*. At the end of the Marktstrasse stands a group of old buildings, the Rathaus and the Blaserturm, a square tower with a polygonal coping.

The Sack of Flour (Mehlsack). – The burghers of the town, in order to see better what the constables of Veitsburg were doing on the hill, erected this 50 m - 164 ft – high greyish tower. From the top *(difficult climb: 240 steps; April to October, 3rd Sunday every month, 10am to noon)* the **view** extends to the Weingarten Church.

Church of Our Lady (Liebfrauenkirche). – This 14C building has been entirely modernised. Its best known work of art is a **copy of the Virgin of Ravensburg★★** (original in the Dahlem Museum in Berlin), a moving 15C sculpture of the Virgin in a Mantle, which stands on the altar in the south aisle.

You will find a selection of touring programmes on pp 34-37. Plan your route with the help of the map of principal sights and tourist regions on pp 4-8.

REGENSBURG ★★

Michelin map **987** 27 – *Local map p 105* – Pop 134 000

Regensburg, once known as Ratisbon, was originally a Roman garrison town guarding the natural frontier of the Danube at its most northerly point. The centre of the town has not been touched by war since 1809, when Napoleon was wounded beneath its walls (plaque at the corner of the Hemauerstrasse and Dr-Martin-Luther-Strasse), and has striking religious buildings of all styles. Standing cheek by jowl with these are the 13 and 14C Italian style towers erected by prosperous merchants. The development of commercial navigation on the Danube, which extends at present as far as the Regensburg quays, is helping to revive the town's economy.

Arriving by the old **Stone Bridge** (Steinerne Brücke) you will get a good view of the cathedral rising above the substantial houses which line the Danube: in the foreground a salt warehouse with a vast roof flanks the fortified gateway (Brückturm).

The "Diet" Town. – Regensburg, once a Free Imperial City, had the rare privilege of being the seat on occasion of the plenary sessions of the Imperial Diet (Reichstag) which was charged with keeping internal peace and external security for the immense and confused federation of states which formed the Holy Roman Empire. The founding of the Duchy of Austria in 1156 and the handing over of Bavaria to the Wittelsbachs *(p 183)* were two out of the majority of great events in German history solemnised in the city. From 1663 Regensburg became the seat of a perpetual diet, the first indication of a permanent German parliament. This same diet, sitting in the town hall, agreed in 1803 to the territorial reorganisation of Germany ordered by Napoleon *(p 21)*. This act presaged the dissolution of the old Empire which became effective on the abdication of Franz II in 1806.

■ **MAIN SIGHTS** *tour: 1½ hours*
Follow the route marked on the map below

St. Peter's Cathedral★ (Dom). – The present Gothic edifice with non-apparent transepts dates from the 13C. The spires were added only in the 19C.

The façade, flanked by two Flamboyant towers, is original especially in its central doorway with a triangular porch. St. Peter is at the pier; lovely statues, especially the meeting of the Virgin and St. Elizabeth, stand in the niches. Enter through the south door.

Inside, the high Radiating Gothic style nave is supported by aisles encircled by a gallery resting, on the south side, on fine carved consoles. Statues of the Archangel Gabriel and an Annunciation, masterpieces of Regensburg Gothic statuary of about 1280, stand before the west transept pillars. The three chancel windows are adorned with beautiful 14C **stained glass★★** (Glasgemälde). Come out of the cathedral by the door to the left of the chancel.

Cloisters. – *Tours with the sacristan (bell: Glocke-Mesner): April to October, 9.30am (11.45am Sundays) to 7pm; November to March, 9.30am (11.45am Sundays) to 6pm.*

The cloisters are divided into two by a central gallery paved with tombstones. To the right of the gallery stands the Romanesque **All Saints Chapel** (Allerheiligenkapelle) on whose walls are traces of frescoes. Opposite the entrance may be seen the Alter Dom, the old 11C cathedral with its empty saint's confessional altar pierced with small openings.

Parish Church (Niedermünster). – *Guided tours for the excavations, Fridays at 5pm. Admission: 1DM. Groups only.*

REGENSBURG

0 _____ 500 m

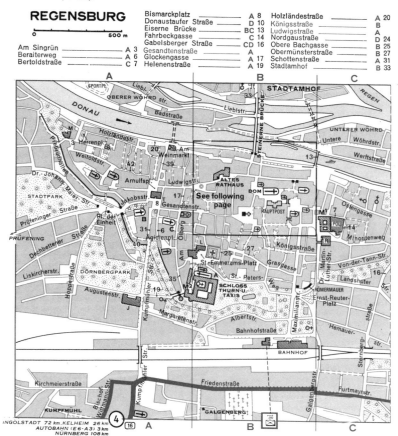

Alter Kornmarkt★. – On the northwest side of the square stands the square Romanesque tower, the Römerturm, which is linked by a covered passage to the Romanesque Ducal Palace (Herzogshof).

The Old Chapel★ (Alte Kapelle). – This originally Romanesque building was later entirely redecorated in the Rococo style: vaulting covered with false relief, galleries overlooking the chancel glazed, and a monumental altarpiece and elegant tall windows to light the gilded stucco on the ceiling, added.

Coming out of the Lady Chapel, which lies outside the main chapel to the south, turn left into the Kapellengasse, and then right into the Schwarze-Bären-Strasse.

St. Cassian's. – *Enter by the west door.* This Romanesque building was given a new ceiling and Baroque remodelling in the 18C. A Gothic low relief of the Visitation stands on the left.

Neupfarrkirche. – This Protestant church stands on a terrace foundation in the centre of the Neupfarrplatz. Go round clockwise by way of an external gallery and enter by the south door. Fine Renaissance interior with cradle vaulting.

Hinter der Grieb. – This ancient alley way is lined with old houses and affords a good view, right, of the cathedral spire.

Bear right, out of the Haidplatz (Fountain of Justice, 1656), into the Neue-Waag-Gasse.

Am Spielhof	4	Kapellengasse	21	Rote-Hahnen-Gasse - 30
Am Wiedfang	5	Krauterermarkt	22	Silberne-Kranz-
Brückstraße	9	Maximilianstraße		Gasse — 32
Drei-Kronen-Gasse - 12		Neue-Waag-Gasse — 23		Viereimergasse — 34
Eiserne Brücke	13	Neupfarrplatz		Weiße-Hahnen-
Goliathstraße		Rathausplatz	28	Gasse — 36
Haidplatz		Residenzstraße	29	Weiße-Lamm-Gasse - 37

Old Town Hall. – The Gothic façade includes a gabled doorway and, upon a pedestal, a slender oriel window which lights the Imperial Hall *(p 208)*.

Take the vaulted passageway on the left, which, by way of the Silberne-Kran-Gasse, brings you to the Keplerstrasse where you turn right. Note the St. George Fountain, known as the Fischbrunnen, in the small Fischmarkt square, where a fish market is held each morning.

Go through an alley (left) to the Danube, crossed at this point by the old stone bridge.

Viereimergasse	B 33
Waffnergasse	A 34
Weißgerbergraben	A 39
Wiesmeierweg	A 40
Wollwirkergasse	A 42

Follow the Goldene-Bären-Strasse on the left. The Historische Wurstküche (curious dining-hall, the oldest cooked sausage house in Germany, which every traveller famous or unknown who comes to Regensburg visits, is beyond the gabled house.

Bear right to return to the cathedral.

■ **ADDITIONAL SIGHTS**

St. James' (St. Jakobskirche) (A B). – The church was founded in the early 12C. The **Romanesque north doorway★** is famous for its decoration: on the tympanum, Christ is between Sts. John and James, above on the frieze, Adam and Eve stand on either side of Christ and the Apostles.

Museum★ (C M¹). – *Open: 10am to 1pm and 2 to 5pm (4pm October to March); closed Sunday afternoons, Mondays and some holidays; 2DM.*

The now deconsecrated Minorite monastery, church and cloister, house a museum. Lapidary collections are in the cloister; on the second floor are paintings by Albrecht Altdorfer and other masters of the Danubian school *(p 104)*.

St. Emmeramus' Church★ (B A). – *Open weekdays 10am to noon.*

The church was formerly the abbey to a Benedictine monastery. Go through the Gothic doors on St. Emmerams-Platz and across a close to the huge 12C porch and the two doorways cut through one-time niches.

Romanesque carvings that are among the oldest in Germany may be seen on the doorway walls.

Ask to see the **tombstone★★** (Grabmal) of the pathetically sad looking Queen Emma who was executed in 1280.

Thurn and Taxis Castle (B). – *Guided tours: weekdays at 2 and 5.15pm; Sundays at 10 and 11.15am; closed Saturdays; 1.50DM.*

The Thurn and Taxis family, which until 1867 held the German postal monopoly, owns the old St. Emmeramus' Abbey buildings. The great Gothic cloister and the halls *(1.50DM)* and the large **vehicle museum★** (Marstallmuseum – A M² – 1DM) are visited separately.

Dominican Church (A C). – *To visit apply in advance.* Severe and bare Gothic church.

Carmelite Church. – (K *on plan on p 207*). Baroque building in which 18C altarpieces, which were at one time in the cathedral, have been placed in the altar niches.

Imperial Hall (Reichssaal) in the Old Town Hall. – *Guided tours every hour weekdays from 9.30 to 11.30am and 2 to 4pm, Sundays from 10am to noon; 2DM.*
The Imperial Diets sat in this large Gothic hall. The dungeons are open to the public.

Porta Praetoria. – (E *on plan on p 207*). Remains of a Roman gateway built with huge archstones.

Ostentor (D F). – 14C fortified gate.

EXCURSIONS

Walhalla★. – *11 km - 7 miles – by the road marked in the northeast on the plan above, the Donaustaufer Strasse – plus ½ hour sightseeing Description p 253.*

Kallmünz. – *27 km - 17 miles – northwest of Regensburg.* Kallmünz, a semicircle at the foot of a steep promontory, the site of a ruined castle commanding the confluence of the Naab and the Vils, attracts artists and anglers.
To reach the castle *(¾ hour on foot Rtn)*, leave the village by the Amberg road. After the last house, climb up the hillside following a path and across the field to the ruins. From the plateau edge there is a **view★** of the village roofs and the confluence of the rivers.

REICHENHALL, Bad ★★

Michelin map **987** 38 – *Local map p 41* – Pop 14 500
Town plan in Michelin Red Guide Deutschland

Bad Reichenhall, which lies at the point where the last defiles of the Saalach lead into the open, is famous for salt. The thermal installations are used to treat respiratory maladies.
The spa itself extends for 2 km - 1 mile along the busiest section of the **Ludwigstrasse**, the main street between the Church of St. Zeno and the Saalach Bridge.

A Salt Metropolis. – Bad Reichenhall has been developing its salt industry since Celtic times for domestic purposes – it has the most highly concentrated (maximum of 24%) and the most abundant salt waters in Europe. The salt derives from springs, not from brine from mineral rocks as at Berchtesgaden or mines as at the Salzkammergut.
Until 1958 the waters passed through a 79 km - conduit (Soleleitung – 49 miles) to the extraction and refining factories of Traunstein and Rosenheim; now they and the Berchtesgaden brine are treated in new saline works (Neue Saline) in the town itself.

■ SIGHTS *time: ¾ hour*

St. Zeno's. – *On the street cutting across the northern part of the town.* This late 12C church, remodelled in the 16C and later Baroquised, corresponds, on the north side of the Alps, to the well known Romanesque church dedicated to the same saint in Verona. Lombard influence can be seen in the design and decoration of the main doorway which has archstones of alternating tones and slender end columns resting on couched lions. The tympanum depicts the Virgin and Child between St. Zeno, invoked in the Alps against flooding, and St. Rupert, first Bishop of Salzburg.
The high altarpiece was made up in 1962 from a group carved by the Inn Valley school in 1520, which had as its theme the Coronation of the Virgin.

Old Salt Works (Alte Saline). – *Guided tours of the Salt Springs building (Quellenbau): 1 April to 31 October, 10 to 11.30am and 2 to 4pm; in winter 2pm Tuesdays and Thursdays; 3DM; protective clothing is provided.*
Ludwig I of Bavaria had the works constructed in the troubadour style which accorded with the taste of 1834. One enters the large machine room where two immense paddle wheels work the pumps; the scene looks like an old engraving. Marble galleries and caverns lead to different catchment rooms where some of the old and archaic plant still stands, for example the 103 m - 113 yd long transmission arm which, thanks to five connections, works the pump at the Karl-Theodor spring.

RENDSBURG

Michelin map **987** 5 – Pop 34 300 – *Town plan in Michelin Red Guide Deutschland*

Rendsburg occupied one of the strategic points of northern Germany where the main highway from Denmark (now in the E 3) crossed the Eider, the old natural frontier between the Duchies of Schleswig and Holstein.
The town plan is interesting: the pleasant old town on a former island in the Eider, tightly packed around its 16C town hall and the 13C Church of St. Mary, is now hemmed in on either side by fortified quarters erected in one swift period at the end of the 17C to defend the ends of the bridge.
The Neuwerk quarter in the south, between the Kiel Canal and the old town, is typical with its immense central esplanade (Paradeplatz) from which diverging streets radiate, as in the citadels constructed by Vauban, the 17C French military engineer.
The opening of the Kiel Canal began the town's rapid industrial development (metallurgy, textiles, fertilisers) but proved a considerable obstacle to communications. This was only overcome by constructing a railway bridge and, in 1961, a road tunnel. Moreover a new bridge was constructed in 1972, it allows the motorway to cross the canal.

Railway Bridge★ (Eisenbahnhochbrücke). – This metal bridge crosses the canal at 42 m - 138 ft – and has a central span of 140 m - 153 yds. The descent at the town end is achieved down a loop road. A **transporter-bridge** still functions below the central superstructure.

Canal Tunnel (Kanaltunnel). – The road tunnel passes 20 m - 66 ft – beneath the canal and is 640 m long - 700 yds. A second parallel tunnel for pedestrians has escalators 1 278 m long of which 801 m are underground – ¾ and ½ mile.

RHINE Valley ★★★ (RHEIN)

Michelin maps **204** 5, 6, 13 to 16 and **203** 1 to 3

The Rhine, 1 320 km - 820 miles – long and one of the axes of civilisation, flows through four countries, and has often been a source of controversy between riparian neighbours. Below Basle, for example, no town has ever completely straddled the river. At the same time it has always been a unique highway for commercial, intellectual, artistic and religious exchanges.

The Rhine Legends. – There is not along the whole length of the Rhine a castle, an island, a rock without its tale of chivalry or its legend. Lohengrin, the knight of the Swan, appeared at the foot of Cleves Castle; Roland escaped from Roncesvalles to arrive too late before the Island of Nonnenwerth, where his fiancée, inconsolable at the rumour of his death, had taken the veil – Roland in despair withdrew to the neighbouring Castle of Rolandsbogen; at Loreley, Lore's rock, the enchantress bewitched boatmen with her song, allowing their boats to perish. The outstanding tale, however, is the legend of the Nibelungen which has proved an inexhaustible source of inspiration and on which Wagner drew for his sequence of operas known as *The Ring*.

The Nibelungen Legend. – This, the best known of all German epic tales, was composed probably towards the end of the 12C and enjoys fame beyond the Rhineland.

It tells of the splendour of the Burgundian Court at Worms in the 5C and of the passions in the hearts of the heroes. When the proud Brünhilde, wife of Gunther, King of the Burgundians (the Nibelungen), learned from her sister-in-law Krimhilde that it was not Gunther but Siegfried, Krimhilde's husband, who had broken his troth to her and won her for Gunther by deception, she swore vengeance. She found a ready ally in Hagen who treacherously slew Siegfried while out hunting.

Fearing that Krimhilde, through munificent gifts, would dissipate the Nibelungen treasure *(p 29)*, the wedding present of Siegfried to Krimhilde and that by her gifts she would find friends to avenge the death of Siegfried, Hagen threw the treasure in the Rhine. For thirteen years Krimhilde planned her revenge. To achieve her end she married Etzel (Attila), King of the Huns, and invited the Nibelungen to make the long journey down the Danube to Etzelburg in Hungary. As soon as they arrived the Nibelungen saw the trap into which they had fallen; a merciless struggle began with the Huns which ended in a general massacre. Hagen, decapitated by Krimhilde with Siegfried's sword, took with him the secret of the treasure's burial place.

GEOGRAPHICAL NOTES

An Even Flow. – The Rhine at first is a characteristically Alpine river with little water in winter and a full flood in summer when the glaciers melt. Lake Constance, the lakes of the Swiss Plateau whose waters flow into the Aar, a tributary which exceeds the Swiss stretch of the Rhine in length and volume, moderate the flood-waters.

In the 125 miles below Mannheim, the Rhine receives its two large German tributaries, the Neckar and the Main, and even more substantially, the Mosel. The more regular flow of these rivers tends to even out that of the main stream so that its variations do not impede shipping. The barges are delayed, however, by ice on average for about two weeks a year round the Loreley and in the Waal arm in the delta.

Undertakings on the Upper Rhine. – As it leaves Lake Constance, which is where the kilometric signposting of the river begins, the Rhine hurls itself against rock banks which are the outcrops of the Black Forest and Jura foothills. Below Schaffhausen the valley narrows. The stream runs more tempestuously and the river rampages through the rocks, producing the famous Rhine Falls *(see Michelin Green Guide Switzerland)*. Further on, other limestone stretches engender rapids (Laufen), which gave rise to the local town names of Laufen and Laufenburg. These inequalities in the course and flow of the river have proved insurmountable obstacles to shipping, but on the other hand, have allowed the river to be developed hydroelectrically and power stations to be constructed. At Basle, the Rhine sharply changes direction to follow and fertilise the cleft formed by the subsidence that divides the Vosges and the Black Forest. No towns grew up along its banks for fear of flooding; 19C works to regulate the flow and embank the shores have reduced this danger but accelerated erosion of the river bed. This, in turn, has exposed rocks that jeopardise shipping. The French solution, adopted in 1920, proposed the construction of a canal from Basle to Strasbourg which would draw off a large part of the river water as it passed through Alsace. The plan was modified while work was in progress: the canal waters are returned to the river below the Vogelgrün power station facing Breisach. From this point to Strasbourg, the canal is fed only from power station dams.

The Heroic Rhine. – The Rhine, after skirting the hillsides of the Rheingau and Rhineland Hesse, turns at Bingen to cut northwest through the Rhineland schist massif, forming what is popularly known as the Rhine Gorge. The dangerous whirlpools and impressive escarpments of this section are determined by the harshness of the rock, particularly the quartzites which lie exposed in the Loreley area. The medley of vineyards, woods, rock outcrops and ruins perched on rock spurs, produces a romantic fresco.

RHINE Valley***

The Rhine Plain. – The valley opens out for the first time in the Neuwied Basin, below where the Mosel and the Lahn join. After a pleasant passage at the foot of the Siebengebirge, the river enters another world which is typified by the industrial scenery of Duisburg *(illustration p 108)*. Beyond Duisberg the river makes for the sea across the green and peaceful plain.

LIFE ON THE RHINE

Shipping in the Rhine Gorge. – The term "Rhine barge" conjures up the idea of enormous loads towed by huge craft (1 500 tons) in procession. Modern development, however, is giving ever more importance to motorbarges (1 000 and 2 000 tons) and tugs pulling 2, 4 or 6 barges of 1 500–2 000 tons.

Ships going upstream signal instructions to those coming downstream although, in fact, those sailing downstream have the added difficulty of holding course in the swiftly moving current. Passing is usually on the port side but if this is not possible the ship going upstream flies a blue flag on her starboard side and when the order has been confirmed by a similar signal, the ships cross on the starboard side. Where it is impossible to see round the bends, signalling stations use flags (near the Loreley) or lamps (Ochsenturm to Oberwesel) to indicate the amount of traffic descending and allow ascending traffic to manoeuvre accordingly. The most important control post is on the Mouse Tower at Bingen *(p 79)* which gives clearance for the difficult **Binger Loch** reach of formerly redoubtable rapids and reefs. Beside the Binger Loch is a second navigable channel which is usually kept for ascending traffic.

Pilots are not compulsory but in accordance with tradition are taken on for the more difficult waters. There are pilot stations at Bingen, St. Goar and Bad Salzig.

Commercial Shipping. – The flags flying on ships are mostly those of Germany, the Netherlands, Belgium, France and Switzerland. A comparison of the traffic on German-Dutch and German-French frontiers is interesting: in 1969 for every 1 000 tons going through these points the Dutch carry respectively 514 and 179 tons, the Germans 307 and 567 tons, the Belgians 111 and 59 tons, the French 29 and 58 tons, the Swiss 41 and 131 tons, and other nations 5 and 3 tons. The French fleet which uses a considerable proportion of propelled craft and the Swiss with its motorbarges are the most modern. Most of the passenger-carrying ships are German.

The Rhine river traffic which was for so long closely dependent on German heavy industry has developed considerably since the end of the war. International commerce registered at the German-Dutch frontier, which in 1938 represented half the total Rhine traffic, by 1967, when it had reached a total of 250 million tons, represented only two-fifths of the total. This difference indicates the growing importance of commerce among the countries bordering the Middle Rhine (Germany, France, Switzerland) and among the German ports themselves.

Since 1938 it is noticeable, on the stretch of river between the sea and the Ruhr, how cargoes of overseas minerals have increased and those of Ruhr coal for abroad have decreased. On the German-French frontier traffic going upstream is largely Ruhr coal and hydrocarbons for Switzerland; downstream come hydrocarbons for Germany, construction materials, fertilisers (Alsatian potash) and semi-finished industrial products.

A refining industry supplied by oil pipelines *(see map p 16)* has sprung up all along the Rhine. This has resulted in a considerable increase in trade in refined oil products, but only over relatively short distances.

In 1972 among the 319 million tons of goods transported on the German canals and rivers, 181 million were conveyed on the Rhine between the Swiss and Dutch borders. The Rhine ports in descending order of their importance are Duisburg-Ruhrort (the most important river port in Europe, *p 108)*, Mannheim-Ludwigshafen, Cologne, Wesseling and Karlsruhe.

TOUR

Rhine Cruises. – *Services run daily between Easter and mid-October by the "Köln-Düsseldorfer Deutsche Rheinschiffhart" (Cologne Office: Frankenwerft 15; ☎ 208 81).*

The most popular and most frequent services are those between Bingen (or Rüdesheim) and Koblenz (downstream: 3 hours; upstream: 5 hours). The same company also runs cruisers from April to October from Rotterdam to Basle – 2 to 5 days depending on direction and time of year.

The Tourist Roads. – The most popular is along the left bank between Koblenz and Bingen, although heavy lorry traffic and a general lack of parking space do not make the run easy. The road along the right bank is less busy but some of the bigger castles are then out of reach. Between Mainz and Koblenz ferries enable one to cross to the opposite bank.

The Golden Road Along the Rhine (Rheingoldstrasse). – Certain small roads, often narrow and steep, running along the side of a valley and affording, here and there, impressive bird's-eye views of the Rhine, have been linked to form a tourist road known as the Rheingoldstrasse (signposts displaying a castle and a glass of wine). The main part of this route, of which the most interesting section lies between St. Goar and Bacharach on the left bank, sometimes entails long detours into the hinterland. The map on p 212 locates the best placed viewpoints.

① *FROM WIESBADEN TO RÜDESHEIM by the right bank

35 km - 22 miles – about 2½ hours – Local map p 212

The road crosses the vine covered hills of the Rheingau, an open countryside. The southern aspect of the vineyards permits cultivation high on the Taunus foothills.

Wiesbaden★★. – Description p 258.

Kiedrich. – *Tour: ½ hour.* The 15C church in this wine growing town used to draw many pilgrims who came to invoke St. Valentine against epilepsy. The Gothic style nave contains precious Flamboyant **furnishings★★** (Ausstattung). *To visit, apply to the sacristan at the small house situated at the east end of the nearby funeral chapel.*

The **pews★★** (Kirchengestühl), which were carved early in the 16C, have been preserved intact, complete with their multicolouring and curious Gothic inscriptions. Note especially those with inscriptions in spirals – Spiral of Justice. The venerable organ was installed in the 16C. The 14C **Kiedrich Virgin★** beneath the rood-screen shows French influence.

Eberbach Abbey. – *Open 1 April to 31 October, 10am to 5.30pm; time: ¾ hour; 1DM.* This former Cistercian abbey, dating from 1135 and sister to Clairvaux, was built at the vineyard's upper limit in a green Taunus valley.

The 1345 chapter house, in accordance with the order's rule, opens off the cloister of which only two Gothic galleries remain. In the chapter house the sixteen ribs of the vaulting fuse to rest upon a single central pillar.

A magnificent collection of **old presses**★★ (Keltern), their columns well decorated, may be seen in the vaulted refectory formerly used by the lay brothers.

On the same floor as the fathers' building is the **former dormitory** ★ (Mönchsdormitorium), an impressive 14C room, with two aisles 72 m - 236 ft – in length.

The **abbey church** which, in accordance with the early Cistercian tradition, has a flat east end and low rectangular side chapels, was completed in 1186. This Romanesque building has an austere grandeur, particularly when viewed from

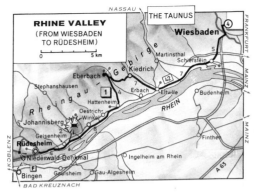

the north aisle. This is doubled by a second Gothic side aisle with sharply pointed arches.
The road, now running for long stretches beside the Rhine, by-passes several picturesque towns (Winkel, Geisenheim) which have returned to their former tranquillity.

Johannisberg Castle. – *Excursion of 2 km - 1 mile – from the Rhine by Johannisberg village beyond which you bear right repeatedly.* This long yellow 18C castle was offered to Prince Metternich in 1816 and has remained in the possession of the famous chancellor's family. From the part of the terrace open to the public, on the far right of the building, there is a **view** of the vineyard which has made the castle famous *(wine available in a Weinausschank).* The panorama extends to the Rheingau hills and the Rhine Plain, from Mainz (gasometer) to Bingen and the Niederwald Monument.

The Niederwald Monument on its hill marks, from afar, the entrance to the Rhine Gorge.

Rüdesheim★. – *Description p 222.*

② ★★FROM RÜDESHEIM TO KOBLENZ by the right bank
75 km - 47 miles – about 4 hours – Local map p 212

This is the wildest and steepest bank, wih the Loreley as its most famous landmark. There are views of the castles on the opposite bank.

Rüdesheim★. – *Description p 222.*

The road winds below the terraced vineyards over which tower the ruins of Ehrenfels Castle. This was built by the Bishops of Mainz as was the Mouse Tower on the opposite bank *(p 79)*, to collect river tolls. You continue and come to the first shaded and impressive section of the valley before passing through the trim little village of **Assmannshausen**.

Alternative road★ by the Niederwald Monument. – *Extra distance: 4km - 2 miles. Follow the itinerary described on p 222 as far as Assmannshausen.*

Three castles succeed each other on the left: Rheinstein, built in line with the cliff-face, Reichenstein and Sooneck, stepped against the sky. The crenellated tower of Fürstenberg on the wooded slopes facing Lorch marks the beginning of more open road.

Lorch. – Go over the railway track. In the first street running parallel with the Rhine, there stands, opposite the church, the Hilchenhaus, a mansion typical of the first German Renaissance where the stepped gable is adorned with small rounded pediments and scrollwork. The Gothic **church** has a 1483 carved altarpiece to St. Martin with painted panels, and, on the high altar a great Romanesque **crucifix**★.
Bacharach can be distinguished clearly on the left: its vines and its towers showing unevenly at the foot of Stahleck Castle. Pfalz Castle comes into view soon after Lorchhausen.

Kaub. – Kaub, overlooked by the restored ruins of Gutenfels and one of the outstanding landmarks in the valley, lies huddled on either side of a picturesque main street, the Metzgergasse (walk along it). The town tower stands at one end.

Pfalz. – *Boat trip of about 1½ hours starting from Kaub. Open April to October, 9am to 12.30pm and 2 to 6pm; November, 10am to 12.30pm and 2 to 6pm; 15 January to 31 March, 10am to 12.30pm and 2 to 6pm; 2DM.* This toll castle rises out of the centre of the river bed, its powerful five sided keep encircled by a turreted castle wall. The curve round the next spur marks the beginning of the wildest part of the valley. To the left is a **panorama**★★ of Oberwesel whose towers succeed one another along the river bank at the foot of the Schönburg.

Loreley★★★. – This legendary rock has an outstanding **site**★★★ on the Rhine and an honourable place in German literature.

St. Goarshausen. – A town interesting particularly for its position at the foot of the **Katz** (the Cat), a castle in which the round keep abuts on restored buildings ending in two projecting turrets overlooking the valley *(not open)* and a view of Rheinfels Castle *(p 225).*
The town of Katz, whose name derives from its builders, the Counts of Katzenelnbogen is said to have been constructed to counter the Mouse Tower (**Maus**) built a little further downstream. There are pleasant walks to be made beside the Rhine at both St. Goarshausen and St. Goar.

Leave St. Goarshausen by the road marked "Loreley-Felsen". As you come out of the town there is a good view of the Mouse Tower. After 2.5 km - 2 miles – turn right and leave the car in one of the parks before the hotel "auf der Loreley".

Loreley Belvedere★★. – ¼ hour on foot Rtn. The **view**★★ plunges down into the gorge from several accessible spurs below the hotel.

Turn and rejoin the Rhine road.

Wellmich. – The plain 14C country church shows traces of 15C wall paintings (restored). In the upper part of the nave are the Crucifixion and, on either side, the last agonies of the 12 Apostles; below are Christ in a mandorla and the Last Judgment. In the Gothic chancel may be seen the legend of Mary the Egyptian.

The hill slopes are once more wild. Beyond Kestert are the two fortresses of Sterrenberg and Liebenstein, traditionally linked to the legend of two rival brothers.

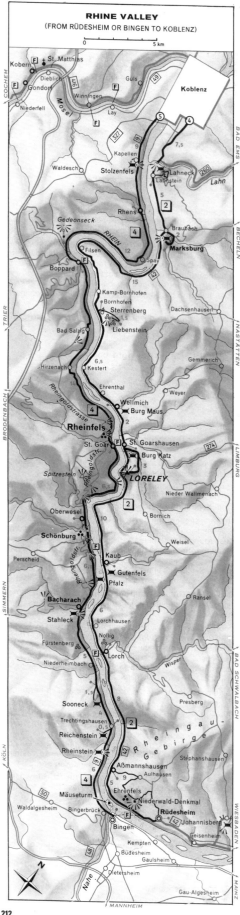

RHINE VALLEY
(FROM RÜDESHEIM OR BINGEN TO KOBLENZ)

0   5 km

The Hostile Brothers. – *Excursion of 1 km - ½ mile – by a narrow road that is also steep as it plunges into the valley behind the Bornhofen pilgrimage church, plus ½ hour on foot Rtn.* The road *(leave the valley floor after 1 km - ½ mile – and bear right)* ends beneath the Liebenstein ruin from which there is a good view of Sterrenberg and the valley. Descend the spur to the Sterrenberg ruins where the **view★★** is more open.

The landscape becomes less wild in the Boppard bend. Soon you see straight ahead the promontory on which stands the Marksburg fortress. Go up to the fortress from Braubach, taking the Nastätten road on the right and bearing right again into the castle rise.

Marksburg★. – *Open 16 March to 14 November, 8am to 6pm; the rest of the year, 11am to 4pm; 3DM.*

The castle, the only one on the Rhine never to have been destroyed, belongs to a Society which endeavours to preserve castles on their original **sites★★** and in their mediaeval aspect. The Great Battery, whose guns are pointed at the Rhine, and the Knights' Hall are remarkable. A tour all round the castle by way of the upper lists (Oberer Zwinger) affords many differing views of the valley.

North of Braubach, the **view★** back to Marksburg is impressive.

Lahneck. – *Excursion of 3 km - 2 miles – from Oberlahnstein by the Becheln road and the castle approach, left, when you reach the plateau, plus 1 hour sightseeing (Easter to October, 9.30am to 6pm; 2DM).* A fortress, reconstructed in the 19C, whose tower commands a **view** of the Lahn confluence.

The bridge over the Lahn affords a good view of Lahneck and, on the far side of the Rhine, of the Castle of Stolzenfels.

Koblenz★. – *Description p 160.*

③ FROM KOBLENZ TO BONN by the left bank

61 km - 38 miles – about 2 hours – Local map adjoining

Fertile, populated basins and industrialised areas break the continuity of the picturesque Rhine landscape. This route, however, brings you to the country of the small Siebengebirge Massif, magnificent when the setting sun catches the Drachenfels ruins. Byron described the scene in Childe Harold's Pilgrimage.

Koblenz★. – *Description p 160.* As far as Andernach the road travels through the rich fruit growing Neuwied Basin.

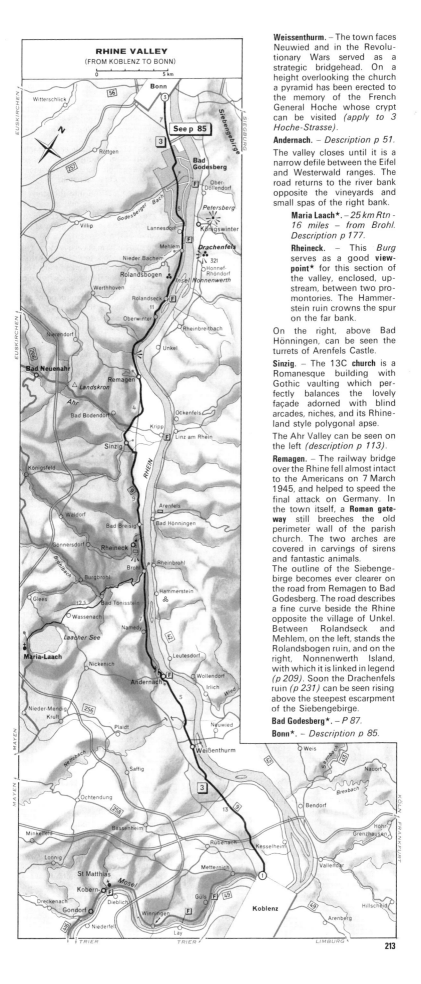

RHINE VALLEY
(FROM KOBLENZ TO BONN)

0   5 km

Weissenthurm. – The town faces Neuwied and in the Revolutionary Wars served as a strategic bridgehead. On a height overlooking the church a pyramid has been erected to the memory of the French General Hoche whose crypt can be visited *(apply to 3 Hoche-Strasse).*

Andernach. – *Description p 51.*

The valley closes until it is a narrow defile between the Eifel and Westerwald ranges. The road returns to the river bank opposite the vineyards and small spas of the right bank.

Maria Laach*. – *25 km Rtn - 16 miles – from Brohl. Description p 177.*

Rheineck. – This *Burg* serves as a good **viewpoint*** for this section of the valley, enclosed, upstream, between two promontories. The Hammerstein ruin crowns the spur on the far bank.

On the right, above Bad Hönningen, can be seen the turrets of Arenfels Castle.

Sinzig. – The 13C **church** is a Romanesque building with Gothic vaulting which perfectly balances the lovely façade adorned with blind arcades, niches, and its Rhineland style polygonal apse.

The Ahr Valley can be seen on the left *(description p 113).*

Remagen. – The railway bridge over the Rhine fell almost intact to the Americans on 7 March 1945, and helped to speed the final attack on Germany. In the town itself, a **Roman gateway** still breeches the old perimeter wall of the parish church. The two arches are covered in carvings of sirens and fantastic animals.

The outline of the Siebengebirge becomes ever clearer on the road from Remagen to Bad Godesberg. The road describes a fine curve beside the Rhine opposite the village of Unkel. Between Rolandseck and Mehlem, on the left, stands the Rolandsbogen ruin, and on the right, Nonnenwerth Island, with which it is linked in legend *(p 209).* Soon the Drachenfels ruin *(p 231)* can be seen rising above the steepest escarpment of the Siebengebirge.

Bad Godesberg*. – *P 87.*

Bonn*. – *Description p 85.*

4 ★★★FROM KOBLENZ TO BINGEN by the left bank

63 km - 39 miles – a good day's ride – Local map p 212

The route affords one the chance of seeing some of the pleasantest townships in the Rhine Valley and of visiting the most impressive castles.

As you leave Koblenz *(p 160)*, you will see on the right the Castle of Stolzenfels, built against the slope, and on the other bank, Lahneck Tower commanding the confluence of the Lahn.

Stolzenfels. – *Excursion of ½ hour on foot Rtn, plus 40 minutes sightseeing (open 9am to noon and 1 to 5.30pm; closed December and Mondays; 1.50DM).*
This huge castle was reconstructed with a considerable bonus of crenellations by Friedrich-Wilhelm IV in 1836 in a Neo-Gothic style inspired by English country houses and Spanish castles. The sumptuous interior is now a museum. From the keep there is a good **view** ahead of the Lahn confluence and Lahneck and, left, of Koblenz and Ehrenbreitstein.

Rhens. – Delightful town with half-timbered houses. The town hall juts out into the street.
On the left is the attractive outline of the Marksburg perched on an isolated hill.

Gedeonseck. – *Excursion of 1 hour Rtn of which 20 minutes are in a chair-hoist (Easter to 10 October: 9am to 5.30pm – 6pm in summer; Rtn fare: 4DM). The lower station is at the north end of Boppard.* View★ of the rounded convex curve of the Boppard.

Boppard. – This residential town lies in a relatively open site where several small valleys meet. The **Rhine Promenade** (Rheinallee) makes a particularly pleasant walk in this town. The Gothic Carmelite church (near the quay) with its single tower contains numerous works of art: 15C choir-stalls, several statues of the Virgin and, notably, in the chancel, a fine Renaissance funerary monument depicting the Eternal Father receiving the dead Christ.
The two ruins of the Hostile Brothers (Feindliche Brüder – *p 211*) mark the beginning of the Rhine Gorge. Beyond Hirzenach the road follows the bank until it reaches the Mouse (Maus) Tower, soon counterbalanced by the Cat (Katz) Tower, standing above St. Goarshausen. As you come to St. Goar you see the start of the rock-strewn Loreley passage.

St. Goar. – *Visit to Burg Rheinfels recommended. Description p 225.*

Soon, on the opposite bank, the legendary Loreley rock *(p 212)* narrows the passage dangerously and turns the waters into deep whirlpools. The banks continue steep and wooded as far as Oberwesel, whose approach is signalled by the appearance of the Schönburg.

Oberwesel. – *Description p 200.*

The amazing stone nave of Pfalz rises from the middle of the river while on the east bank Gutenfels Castle raises a solid crenellated tower to command the valley.

Bacharach★. – *Description p 54.*

The ruined towers of Nollig and Fürstenberg mark the end of the grandiose stretch of the valley. From here onwards it is less winding, running between the steep right bank where a few vines grow, and the cliffs of the left bank. The road on this side passes at the foot of castles whose sites are ever more audacious, from Sooneck to Reichenstein and finally, Rheinstein.

Sooneck. – *Excursion of 1.5 km - 1 mile – by a partially asphalted road, from Niederheimbach embankment, plus 1 hour sightseeing (open in summer 9am to 1.30pm and 2 to 5pm, 4pm in winter; closed Mondays; 1.50DM).* Much restored fortress, tiered to suit the terrain; a maze of staircases, platforms and terraced gardens.

Reichenstein. – *Excursion of 500 m - ½ mile – from Trechtingshausen, plus 1 hour sightseeing (open: 10am to noon and 1 to 5pm; 4pm in winter; closed December, January and Tuesdays in winter; 2.50DM).* Neo-feudal castle well situated at the mouth of a rural valley; collection of arms and hunting trophies.

Rheinstein. – *Excursion of ¼ hour on foot Rtn beside the Rhine along the road from the car park (open April to October, 9am to 6.30pm; November to March, 10am to 6pm; 3DM).* The castle is balanced on a perpendicular rock commanding the Rhine; from the foremost watchtower there is a bird's-eye view★★ of the river.

The colourful village of Assmannshausen, stretched out along the far bank, comes at the end of the narrow gap. The Mouse Tower (Mäuseturm) on its tiny island, the Ehrenfels ruin standing amidst terraced vineyards and the Niederwald Monument mark this final widening.

Bingen. – *Description p 79.*

5 LOWER RHINE VALLEY

75 km - 47 miles – about 4 hours

To the northwest the plain and the meadows recall that the Netherlands are not far away, making agriculture and especially cattle-breeding the main economic resources of the region. The Rhine, itself, is used a great deal by barges, between the Ruhr Basin and the Netherlands.

Xanten. – *Description p 265.*

Kalkar. – *Description p 155.*

Cleves (Kleve). – Being 14 km - 9 miles – south of the Dutch border, Cleves is an attractive resort town. It is the native town of Anne of Cleves, the fourth wife of Henry VIII.
The former ducal castle of the Cleves, Swans' Castle (Schwanenburg) associated with the legend of Lohengrin (the Knight of the Swan) and immortalised by Richard Wagner was built in the 11C on a hill in the centre of town. From the tower *(open 1 May to 31 October and Easter, 10am to noon and 2 to 6pm; 1DM)* is a very nice **panorama**. Then make your way to the Collegiate Church which contains funerary chapels and tombs of the House of Cleves.

Emmerich. – The last port and bridge on German soil, Emmerich's life is turned entirely towards the Rhine. Opposite the town hall, the Rhine museum (Rheinmuseum) displays interesting navigational documents. Note the Church of St. Aldegundis for its ancient sculpture and the Church of the Holy Ghost (Heilig-Geist) with its abstract architecture and altar.

Anholt★. – *Open 1 April to 30 September, 10am to 6pm (1 to 6pm the rest of the year), closed Mondays, 2DM.* This château (12-17C) with its moat and interior courtyard is within a large informal garden. Inside note the massive oak staircase, the knights' room with a portrait gallery, the reception room decorated with Flemish tapestries, the Japanese and Chinese porcelains and a painting gallery, consisting mainly of works from the Dutch School.

Bocholt. – Due to its textile industry, Bocholt is a prosperous city. One must admire the town hall (Rathaus) of brick and stone with Renaissance decoration (1620) as well as the large hall church, St. George (15C) containing several Gothic works of art.

The mountains of the Rhineland-Palatinate are a continuation of the northern Vosges. Like these the region has a wooded aspect broken by escarpments and red limestone rocks.

The Forest Lands. – The rolling and romantic **Wasgau** landscape stretches between Alsace and the Pirmasens – Lindau road. In this piecemeal region, wooded hilltops crowned by ruins (Trifels, Dahn) or spikes beloved by rock climbers, are succeeded by villages lying in cleared hollows.

The Palatinate Forest (**Pfälzer Wald**) extends further north, an almost unbroken wooded massif with few inhabitants and which, with the Wasgau, is a large (175 000 ha - 645 sq miles) nature reserve (Naturpark). It provides tourist facilities, particularly for walkers.

To the east, the edge of the mountain massif whose cliff face drops steeply to the Rhine Plain, is known as the **Haardt**. The peaks reach an altitude at Kalmit of 673 m and 687 m - 2 208 ft and 2 251 ft – in the small isolated volcanic massif called the Donnersberg.

The Palatinate Wines. – The Palatinate is the most extensive wine growing region of Germany and produces almost one-third of the total output. A long reach of good vine growing country, calcareous, protected, facing the sun, extends along the foot of the Haardt.

The almost flat land permits cultivation in the traditional way on fairly low cordons. The grapes are harvested late so that they may get riper and produce fruity red and white wines of rather high alcoholic content but still sweet to the taste. The white wines are the best known; the most famous vintages come from Bad Dürkheim, Wachenheim, Forst and Deidesheim.

The German Wine Road (**Deutsche Weinstrasse**) begins at Schweigen on the French frontier at a monumental gateway (Weintor) and ends west of Worms at Bockenheim. A bunch of grapes is depicted on most of the signposts. The itinerary below from Worms to Bergzabern goes along a considerable part of the Weinstrasse.

① FROM WORMS TO BAD BERGZABERN by the Wine Road hills

87 km - 54 miles – about 2½ hours – Local map below

Worms★★. – *Description p 261.*

After a run across the plain, covered by vineyards beyond Dirmstein, the Haardt barrier looms up.

Freinsheim. – A large wine town behind encircling ramparts. The town hall, beside the 15C church, is a graceful Baroque mansion whose roof overhangs an outside stairway.

The road, overlooked by ruins and enlivened by busy villages, continues, climbing one vine covered hill after another.

Bad Dürkheim. – *Description p 108.*

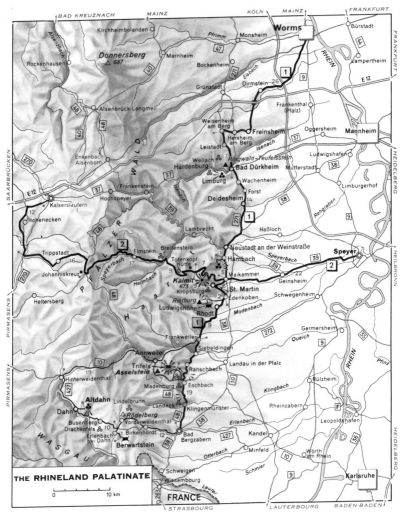

THE RHINELAND PALATINATE

0   10 km

Deidesheim. – Deidesheim is one of the most prosperous of the wine towns along the Wine Road.

Neustadt an der Weinstrasse. – The town, nestled at the foot of the Haardt mountains with its market place and 16C town hall, is a wine centre. On the north side of the church is an amusing fountain.

Hambach Castle. – *Excursion of 1 km - ½ mile – from Hambach town. Open March to September, 9am to 6pm. Access to the tower: 0.50DM.* The large fortress which fell into ruins in 1688 is famous for the demonstration in 1832 during which the liberal minded but militant patriots raised, for the first time, the black, red and yellow pennant which was adopted as the national flag of Germany in 1919 and again in 1949.

The **Kalmit★** *(see below)* belvedere summit can be visited as an excursion from Maikammer. South of Maikammer go round to the pretty little village of St. Martin which is dominated by the Kropsburg.

Ludwigshöhe Castle. – *Excursion of 2 km - 1 mile – from Edenkoben. Not open to the public.* The castle was built by Ludwig I of Bavaria in the Italian villa style popular in the 1850s. Take the chair-lift up to the Rietburg, 1 805 ft. *Every day from Easter to November; 9am to 6pm; 4DM round trip. A pleasant walk in a natural setting.* The **view★** extends over the vineyards to the Odenwald in the distance.

Beyond the foot of Ludwigshöhe hill, the road becomes more winding and the countryside more hilly.

Rhodt. – The wide and often sculptured carriage gateways indicate the house owners' prosperity. After the Leinsweiler Hof mansion, between Ranschbach and Eschbach you get one of the best long distance views of the last part of the drive.

Alternative route★ across the Wasgau, by way of Annweiler, Trifels Castle and Dahn. – *Extra distance 52 km - 32 miles – 4 hours.*

Annweiler. – *Description p 247.*

Trifels Castle. – *Description p 247.*

Dahn. – *Tour 1 hour.* Rock encircled country resort on the edge of the forest. Go by car along the Schloss-Strasse to the base of the rocks then climb to the **ruins★** (Burgruinen) of three separate castles (Altdahn, Grafendahn, Tanstein) all protected by the same perimeter wall. There remain troglodyte halls shored up on monolithic columns and two towers. You get good **views★** of the Wasgau as you walk round.

The character of the **rocky landscape★** of the Wasgau is at its best as you leave Dahn. Look back to see the wall behind which stand Dahn's semi-troglodyte castles and, on the right, to the rock and the Drachenfels ruin which form a double prong; beyond is Berwartstein Castle.

Berwartstein Castle. – *Excursion of 1 km - ½ mile – from the Erlenbach access crossroads.* Take the rise out of Erlenbach town to the castle which was formerly the retreat of the "pillaging knighthood" and has since been restored to serve as a restaurant. Casemates and rooms hewn out of the living rock may still be seen. *Open March to October, 9am to 6pm (Sundays 8am to 7pm); the rest of the year only Saturdays and Sundays 1 to 5pm; 1.50DM.* Above Vorderweidenthal tower the Rödelberg rocks with the Lindelbrunn ruin appearing like a pendant, below.

At Birkenhördt you join road no 427 to go to Bad Bergzabern.

② FROM KAISERSLAUTERN TO SPEYER by way of the Kalmit

83 km - 52 miles – about 3 hours – Local map p 215

The road between Kaiserslautern and Maikammer crosses the heart of the Palatinate Forest (Pfälzer Wald). Motorists often stop at the Hohanniskreuz or Totenkopf crossroads and go for a walk beneath the trees.

Kalmit★. – ¼ *hour on foot Rtn.* Go up to the Kalmithaus terrace to get a clear **view★★** of the Rhine Plain, Landau, Speyer Cathedral and Ludwigshafen and its factories. There are panoramic views throughout the descent from the Kalmit to Maikammer.

Speyer★. – *Description p 234.*

The RHÖN

Michelin map **987** 25

The Rhön, vestige of an immense extinct volcano, raises domed summits above the harsh moorland landscapes which clothe its sides at 1 000 m - 3 000 ft. The range, which lies southeast of Fulda, is known among sportsmen, as the cradle of gliding. Two resorts, Bad Brückenau and Gersfeld, attract many tourists.

The spa resort of **Bad Brückenau★** groups thermal establishments in a park below Brückenau. The Fürstenhof pavilion, built in 1775, gives character to the best view.

Gersfeld, the nearest country resort to the centre of the Rhön, has a Protestant **church** dating from 1792 with interestingly placed furnishings. The organ, the pulpit and the altar form a compact group symbolising liturgically the Lutheran reform.

The peaks

Kreuzberg★. – *6 km - 4 miles – from Bischofsheim – about ¾ hour – by a steep uphill road (1 in 7).* Leave the car at the Franciscan convent – traditional stopping place for a beer. Walk up to the Calvary (alt 932 m - 3058 ft). The **view★** expands to embrace the peaceful heights of the massif including the Wasserkuppe.

Wasserkuppe★★. – ¾ *hour on foot Rtn.* The access road branches off road no 284 between Gersfeld and Wüstensachsen. Leave the car near the gliding centre and walk to the summit (alt 950 m - 3 118 ft) by following the fencing on the left. The **view★★** extends towards Fulda and the Vogelsberg. The landscape is most uneven to the south and east.

The ROMANTIC ROAD ★★

Michelin map **987** 25, 26, 36

The Romantic Road links the River Main and the Bavarian Alps by way of peaceful valleys and a rolling countryside between Würzburg, Donauwörth and Füssen.

The romantic nature of the road is to be found in its gentle and poetic quality – it has no surprises but provides a serene journey through history which evokes the great periods of the old mediaeval towns, the religious sensitivity of such artists as Tilman Riemenschneider (p 272), the prestige of Teutonic chivalry, the sumptuously Baroque character of the episcopal courts and such Imperial Towns as Würzburg and Augsburg.

FROM WÜRZBURG TO ROTHENBURG

100 km - 62 miles – about 4 hours – Local map below

Würzburg★★. – *Description p 263.*
Road no 27 drops down towards the Tauber Valley which it enters at Tauberbischofsheim.

Bad Mergentheim★. – *Description p 178.*

Weikersheim. – *Description p 254.*

The picturesque section of the run in the narrow part of the Tauber Valley begins above the attractive town of Bieberehren. The road rises and falls as it runs over the slopes covered, sometimes with natural woodland, sometimes with orchards, above the willow bordered river banks. Occasionally the stream forms a loop to feed a sawmill or a watermill. This countryside is at its loveliest in springtime.

Creglingen. – Take the Blaufelden road to reach within a mile the isolated **Chapel of Our Lord** (Herrgottskirche). *Open 1 April to 30 September, 8am to 6pm; 1 October to 31 March, 1 to 4pm (also 11am to noon Sundays); 0.50DM.*

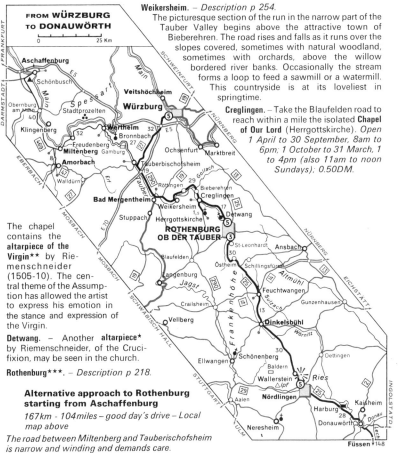

The chapel contains the **altarpiece of the Virgin★★** by Riemenschneider (1505-10). The central theme of the Assumption has allowed the artist to express his emotion in the stance and expression of the Virgin.

Detwang. – Another **altarpiece★** by Riemenschneider, of the Crucifixion, may be seen in the church.

Rothenburg★★★. – *Description p 218.*

Alternative approach to Rothenburg starting from Aschaffenburg

167km - 104miles – good day's drive – Local map above

The road between Miltenberg and Tauberischofsheim is narrow and winding and demands care.

Aschaffenburg★. – *Description p 51.*

Schönbusch Park. – *Tour: 1 hour. Description p 52.*
On the Obernburg am Main to Miltenberg road you will see Klingenberg in a setting of steeply sloping vineyards which produce highly esteemed red wines.

Miltenberg★. – *Description p 179.*

Amorbach★. – *Excursion of 16 km Rtn - 10 miles – from the Main Valley road. Description p 50.*

The landscape beyond Miltenberg becomes wilder but includes such occasional attractive scenes as Freudenberg village and the Stadtprozelten towers in the wooded defile of the Main.

Freudenberg. – The village lies thinly drawn out between the Main and the hill. There are many examples to be seen of popular piety: statues along the main road and steles leading to the cemetery, carved with the Stations of the Cross (as you leave to go towards Wertheim).

Stadtprozelten Castle. – The ruins of the two square towers rise close by on the far bank of the Main.

Wertheim★. – *Description p 255.*

The road follows every turn of the Lower Tauber Valley, which is lighter and wider than the Main Valley and has preserved its deeply rural charm.

Former Abbey of Bronnbach. – *Open: 1 April to 30 September, 9am to noon and 1 to 6pm; 1.50DM.*
The late 12C **church★** has kept its Romanesque design and, in particular, its groined vaulting above the nave especially designed to enable tall, deeply pierced windows to be constructed and provide far more light in the building than was usual for the period.
From the Gothic cloister, which has bays with treble blind arcades, there is a good view of the south wall of the church and the tiered roofs above it. The **Josephssaal** (1720) has all the sumptuousness of an Austrian style Baroque state apartment.
An old humpback bridge makes one slow down at the foot of Gamburg Castle standing on a promontory circled by its access road.
From Tauberbischofsheim follow the route described above, the Romantic Road to Rothenburg.

217

The ROMANTIC ROAD★★

FROM ROTHENBURG TO DONAUWÖRTH

101 km - 63 miles – about 4 hours – Local map p 217

Rothenburg★★★. – *Description below.*
The first few miles should be taken slowly so as to enjoy looking back occasionally at Rothenburg. Beyond Östheim lies the watershed between the Rhine and the Danube (signpost).

Feuchtwangen. – Small town proud of its Roman **cloister**, near the Café am Kreuzgang, and of its **museum** (Heimatmuseum) of Frankish folklore *(open 10am to noon and 2 to 4pm; 2DM)* in a 17C peasant's house with rustic furniture, regional pottery and costumes.

Dinkelsbühl★. – *Description p 106.*

After much green rolling countryside which is often cut by streams and is typical of the Feuchtwangen and the Dinkelsbühl region, you reach Nördlingen and the arable land of the **Ries** Basin. This almost treeless circular depression 20 km across and 220 m deep - 12 miles and 650 ft – lies in the centre of the Swabian Jura and is possibly the result of a gigantic volcanic explosion.

Wallerstein. – $\frac{1}{4}$ *hour on foot Rtn. Go up to the Fürstlicher Keller building from the crossroads at which stands a Virgin on a column. Leave the car after passing beneath an arch and walk through a wooden barrier to reach the foot of the rock.* A path and steps leads to the top of the rock from which there is a **panorama** over the Ries depression, dominated in the west by the bare summit typical of the Ipf and the solitary Baldern Castle. Among many villages which come into view, Nördlingen, with its tall belfry, is easily picked out.

Nördlingen★. – *Description p 196.*

Harburg Castle. – *Guided tours 9 to 11.30am and 1.30 to 5.30pm (4.30pm in October); closed 1 November to 15 March; 5DM (excluding the collections); groups between 2 to 15: 3DM.* Large fortified castle whose buildings, considerably enlarged and remodelled in the 18C, overlook a pretty village closely packed along the bank of the Wörnitz.
There are rich **collections★** (Sammlungen – *6 or 4DM*) of sculpture (fragment of a Riemenschneider altarpiece), illuminated manuscripts, incunabula and engravings.
The Wörnitz Valley, commanded by Harburg Castle, finally twists and peters out, allowing the Ries to communicate with the Danube.

Donauwörth. – Donauwörth, on a hillside running steeply down to the Danube, is dominated by its **Holy Cross Church** (Heiligkreuzkirche) which stands in the centre of a shaded burial ground. The large 1720 Baroque building with concave galleries inside, is adorned with Wessobrunn stuccoes. The crypt *(stairs opposite the entrance on the right)* contains on the north altar, a relic of the True Cross.

FROM DONAUWÖRTH TO FÜSSEN

148 km - 92 miles – a full day's drive – Local maps pp 217 and 42

This drive along the ancient Via Claudia, a most important commercial artery in the Roman Empire, is of interest less on account of the road itself, which follows the course of the splayed out Lech Valley, than of the towns and historical events evoked – **Augsburg★★** *(p 52)*, **Landsberg★** *(p 164)*, **Wies Church★★** (worth the slight detour – *p 257)* and the famous **Royal Castles★★★** *(p 221)*. The Steingaden–Füssen section is common also to the German Alpine Road and described in the opposite direction on pp 42-43.

▐ ROTHENBURG OB DER TAUBER ▌ ★★★
Michelin map ▐987▌ 26 – *Local map p 217* – Pop 12 500

Rothenburg, protected by its ramparts, commands the winding course of the Tauber and is one of the oldest towns to be crossed by the Romantic Road. Visitors seeing its paved streets, old houses, fountains and street signs are plunged into the atmosphere of the 16C.

HISTORICAL NOTES

A Happy Mediocrity. – The Burggarten spur, whose steep sided promontory overlooks an enclosed bend in the Tauber, had been a Franconian strongpoint according to tradition, since the time of King Pharamond.
It is certain, however, that from the 12C onwards two castles – the first an Imperial residence, the second belonging to a count – stood successively upon the terrace placed so commandingly above the valley. At this time the town upon the plateau was still small: the outline of the first circle of rampart walls can be seen together with two towers (Markusturm and Weisser Turm) in the semicircle formed by the Judengasse and Alter Stadtgraben.
In the 13C the town expanded and extended its boundary; the castles disappeared, destroyed in an earthquake in 1356. From this time forwards the ambitions of the eminent were to raise and subsequently embellish public monuments such as the town hall, St. James' Church and burghers' houses with their series of gables which may be seen particularly well in the Herrngasse.
The town turned Protestant and then failed to recover from the wasting depression brought on by the Thirty Years War *(p 24)*. Reduced to the status of an obscure regional market, it vegetated ingloriously during the 17 and 18C, too poor to expand beyond its walls.
Hardship first, followed by the strict preservation orders which have operated since the end of the 19C, have thus kept for today's tourists a typical 16C town unit including streets lined with houses and tall gables with steep roofs – inherited from the Gothic period – staircase turrets and corner oriel windows. Half-timbering above a stone base is the general rule, but usually roughcast hides the beams; near the hospital, however, the beams have been left exposed on many lovely old houses.

A Magisterial Bumper of Wine (Meistertrunk). – Every year on Whit Sunday and Monday all the citizens of Rothenburg take part in the Grand Hall of the Town Hall in a historical pageant *(see list p 31)* of which the principal theme is as follows.
During the Thirty Years War the Protestant town of Rothenburg was unable to resist the onslaught of the Imperial Army commanded by **Tilly** who was determined to raze the town. All pleas for mercy failed until the burgomaster, on the advice of his cup-bearer, offered a cup of the best local wine to the general. It worked the miracle: Tilly was moved. He agreed to spare the town provided a well known person could empty in one draught a 6 pint tankard of the self-same wine. The former burgomaster, Nusch, performed the feat.

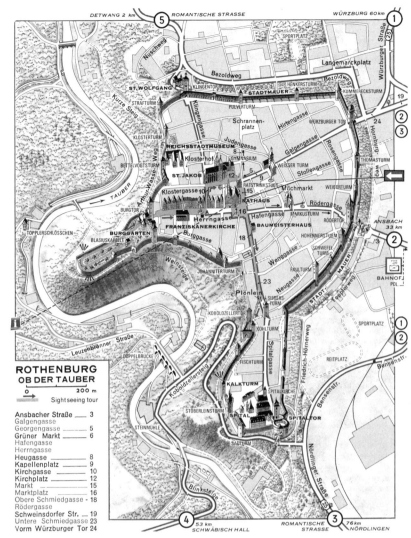

ROTHENBURG OB DER TAUBER

0   200 m

Sight seeing tour

■ THE OLD TOWN*** (Alte Stadt) tour: 3 hours

Town Hall*. – This fine town hall was built at two different periods: the Gothic section with its gable topped by a belfry dates from the 14C, whilst the part facing the Marktplatz is Renaissance. It is completed by a rusticated doorway dating from the 17C. The restored Gothic Imperial Hall, the vaulted galleries (Historiengewölbe), now a museum, and the belfry are open to the public *(Easter to 30 September, 8am to 6pm; 0.50DM; the last steps are difficult)*. There is a striking **view**** from the top of the tower of the roofs and walls of Rothenburg in the shape of a wine glass.

North of the Marktplatz can be seen the gable of the old Ratstrinkstube tavern whose clock jacks enact *(at 11am, noon, 1, 2, 3, 9 and 10pm)* the famous bumper of wine legend.

Descend the Obere Schmiedgasse which continues as the Untere Schmiedgasse.

Baumeisterhaus. – On the first floor, the statues of this Renaissance house represent the seven cardinal virtues, on the second, the seven deadly sins.

Plönlein*. – This picturesque corner is formed by the juncture of two streets, one level the other descending and both ending at a fortified gateway.

Leave the town by the Koboldzell Gate, on the right and turn to walk back, right, along the path which, at some distance, runs parallel to the wall. On the valley floor a remarkable fortified mediaeval bridge, two tiers high (Doppelbrücke), crosses the Tauber.

Burggarten*. – Of the two united fortified castles there remain only the St. Blasius Chapel (now a war memorial) and the fortified gateway (Burgtor). The area has been turned into a public garden overlooking the bend in the Tauber in which one can see the two tier bridge, the Topplerschlösschen, a tower bizarrely topped by living quarters, and the village of Detwang.

Herrngasse. – The mansions of formerly well known personages line this busy commercial street. Those interested should look into some of the courtyards, for instance no 15 (**A**) where the half-timbered gallery rests on embossed wooden pillars.

Go to St. James' Church by way of the Kirchgasse on the left.

St. James' (St.-Jakob-Kirche). – *Open 1 April to 31 October, 9am (10.30am Sundays) to 5.30pm; 1 November to 31 March, 10am (11.30am Sundays) to noon and 2 to 4pm (closed Monday mornings and Tuesdays); 0.50DM.*

The 1504 Riemenschneider **altarpiece**** known as the *Altarpiece of the Holy Blood*, which is in the south aisle, is the church's principal work of art. The Last Supper, which forms the main group is originally designed: Judas, the most striking character, is shown from behind, facing Christ. The expressions are tense and perplexed except for Christ's which is gentler, emanating compassion. The east chancel overlooks a square on which stands the 1593 Renaissance building of the former college (Gymnasium). Return to the Marktplatz.

■ ADDITIONAL SIGHTS

Hospital★ (Spital). – This picturesque group of buildings – mostly 16 and 17C – occupies the excrescence of the southern part of the perimeter which is known as the "peak of the cap" (Kappenzipfel). The most memorable items are the works of art in the Gothic chapel (Spitalkirche) and in the centre of the court, the design of the Hegereiterhäuschen, a graceful pavilion with pointed roof and turrets.

Go through the hospital courtyards to walk up to the **Kalkturm** (also accessible from outside), a **viewpoint★** over the monuments in the centre of the town, and on to the watch path linking the Stöberleinsturm and the Sauturm.

The Ramparts★ (Stadtmauer). – These 13 and 14C ramparts stand undamaged today complete with towers. In the hospital area, the south entrance to the town is defended by the **Hospital Gate★** (Spitaltor), a strong 16C bastion containing two oval inner courtyards.

On the northeast side between the Würzburger Tor and the Klingentor one can walk along the **watch path** (Wehrgang).

St. Wolfgang's Church. – *Open 15 March to 31 October, 10am to noon and 2 to 4pm; 15 December to 6 January, 10am to noon; 0.50DM.*

This curious late 15C fortified Gothic church, standing to the north of the Klingentor, forms part of the barbican which supported the gate as a defence. The casemates and the parapet walk can still be seen.

Franciscan Church (Franziskanerkirche). – *Open 1 April to 31 October, 10am (11.30am Sundays) to noon and 2 to 4pm; 0.20DM.*

This Gothic church has its original rood-screen which, like the nearby pillars and walls, is decorated with fine 15 and 16C sculpture, mostly funerary. Note also on the left, above a bay, the 1400 Creglingen Virgin.

Museum (Reichsstadtmuseum). – *Guided tours at 10 and 11am, 2 and 3pm; 1.50DM.*

The museum is in a former Dominican convent (1258-1544), which has kept its old character. On view are the mediaeval kitchens and, among the rooms with beamed ceilings containing the exhibits, the original tankard used by Burgomaster Nusch *(p 218)*.

RÖTTELN Castle ★

Michelin map **205** 18 – 4 km - 2 miles – north of Lörrach – *Local map p 84*

Rötteln Castle ruins stand in tiers on a wooded ridge which lies separated from the Black Forest and slightly inclined towards the Wiese Valley (Wiesental) where it approaches Basle.

Ascent to the Castle★. – *1.5 km Rtn - 1 mile – plus ¾ hour sightseeing.* A steep and narrow road signposted "Röttler Schloss" begins just before the entrance to Haagen on the road from Rötteln (road along the right bank of the Wiese); it ends at the car park at the foot of the ruins.

Tour. – *March to November, 10am to 6pm (9am to 8pm Sundays) when fine only; 0.50DM.*

Ramps, a bridge and covered passageways lead to the Oberburg, the fortress's defensive kernel. The Green Tower (Grüner Turm), which dominates all, has been rebuilt and made into a belvedere. From the upper platform (viewing table) the **view** includes the Wiese Valley which ends on the outskirts of Basle, the wooded Blauen Massif (Basle Jura), the rounded heights of the Black Forest and, on the horizon, the Swiss Alps.

ROTTWEIL ★

Michelin map **205** 6 – Pop 24 000

Rottweil is a small attractive fortified town, well sited between the Black Forest and the Swabian Jura on a spur surrounded by a river bend in the Upper Neckar. Its particularly lively carnival procession includes a spectacular cavalcade of buffoons (Narrensprung).

■ SIGHTS *time: ¾ hour*

Leave the car near the gate (Schwarzes Tor) which commands the entrance to the upper town and where the Oberndorf and Schramberg roads meet.

Hauptstrasse. – The Hauptstrasse, lined with houses with triple sided oriel windows, drops down towards the Neckar – giving an idea of what the old city must have looked like.

The **vista★** is attractive, extending to the limits of the Swabian Jura on the horizon.

Turn left by the town hall.

Church of the Holy Cross (Heiligkreuzmünster). – This much restored Gothic church is entered by the south door which has a Neo-Gothic porch. Numerous **altarpieces★** adorn the side chapels.

The Gothic fountain of St. George on the Münsterplatz esplanade, includes three delightfully natural sculptures of the Virgin, St. George and St. Catherine.

Go to the side of the church furthest from the square and turn right. Walking beside another church you will finally come out at St. Lawrence's Chapel which was built on the rampart wall.

St. Lawrence's Chapel (Lorenzkapelle). – *Open 10am to noon and 2 to 4pm; closed Saturdays; 1DM.*

Nearly 200 Gothic sculptures from neighbouring churches have been assembled in this former burial chapel. Among the masterpieces of this **collection★** (Plastiken-Sammlung) of Swabian art are the Holy Women of Eriskirch and the statues from Ehingen (St. Elizabeth, the Holy Family).

Bear right out of the St. Lorenzgasse to regain the Hauptstrasse which you walk up, beside the Kapellenkirche, to the town's main crossroads. This is adorned with a frail looking Renaissance fountain, the Marktbrunnen.

Kapellenkirche. – The **tower★** of this Gothic church is a glorious Flamboyant Gothic construction outside and Baroque inside. The square base, quartered with graceful staircase turrets, has as part of its façade, a rarely designed and finely pierced loggia. The upper part of the tower, with two octagonal tiers, is pierced with windows covered wit a fine tracery. The three doorways have their original carved Gothic decoration – the Last Judgment on the west face, and the "knight's betrothal" on the right corner turret are outstanding.

EXCURSION

Dreifaltigkeitsberg*. – *20 km Rtn - 12½ miles – about ½ hour*. Leave Rottweil by the Schwenningen road and bear obliquely left for Tuttlingen.

At Spaichingen, turn left into the small road leading to the Dreifaltigkeitsberg pilgrimage church, on the edge of the Swabian Jura. A wide **panorama*** spreads out from the church approach over the Baar Depression to the dark line in the distance of the Black Forest.

ROYAL CASTLES *** (KÖNIGSSCHLÖSSER)

Michelin map **987** 36 – 4 km - 2 miles – east of Füssen – *Local map p 42*

The use of the term Königsschlösser is often limited in tourist literature to the Hohenschwangau and Neuschwanstein Castles. This compliment which concerns particularly the extravagantly Romantic Neo-Feudal Neuschwanstein building should not allow the other royal residences of Upper Bavaria to be forgotten, examples of the unfortunate Ludwig II's passion for historic reconstruction as at Linderhof and Herrenchiemsee *(pp 167 and 93)*.

HOHENSCHWANGAU* AND NEUSCHWANSTEIN**

about 3 hours walking and sightseeing – Local map below

Leave the car in a car park at Hohenschwangau.

Go round the wooded spur crowned by Hohenschwangau Castle and make for the shaded **Pindarplatz** spur on the north shore of the **Alpsee*** where there is a **belvedere*** which looks out over the lake, pine encircled and dominated by the Säuling cliffs. Take the alley on the right to the castle.

Hohenschwangau Castle*. – *Open 1 April to 30 September, 8.30am to 5.30pm; 1 October to 31 March, 10am to 4pm; 4DM.*

Between 1832 and 1836 Maximilian II of Bavaria, then Prince-Regent, had this castle constructed from the ruins of what had been a large fortress.

The Neo-Gothic style, strongly influenced by the English manor-house plan, satisfied the current taste for troubadour Romanticism. In these surroundings Ludwig II dreamed away his youth.

ROYAL CASTLES (KÖNIGSSCHLÖSSER)
OF HOHENSCHWANGAU AND NEUSCHWANSTEIN

(map showing: Füssen 4 km, Steingaden 21 km, Neuschwanstein, Pöllatfall, Marienbrücke, Hohenschwangau, Pindarplatz, Alpsee, Gassenthomaskopf 1366, Pöllat, Road, Closed)

Compared to Neuschwanstein and in spite of its many extravagances – obsessive repetition in the décor of the swan motif, accumulation of ponderous objects of art given by Bavarian communities to the Royal Family – Hohenschwangau still has the warmth of a palace that was once lived in, which it was for many years by Queen Marie, mother of Ludwig II. The visitor, sated by the Gothic mania for decoration, particularly gruelling in the Radiating style ceilings, will appreciate the Biedermeier furniture *(p 26)* in light cherry and maple wood. The place given to Oriental art is completely compatible with the chivalrous atmosphere which is also apparent in the vast mural paintings, taken from cartoons by Moritiz von Schwind, of heroes of mediaeval verse chronicles. On the second floor the old music room contains moving examples of the king's admiration for Richard Wagner, including letters and the piano which both played. Fantasy is again to be seen in Ludwig II's bedchamber where the ceiling is painted to look like the sky at night – the stars could be made to light up. From his window the king could see through a telescope work progressing at Neuschwanstein.

Return to the car park and walk up a wide path to Neuschwanstein.

Neuschwanstein Castle**. – *Open: 1 April to 30 September, 8.30am to 5.30pm; 1 October to 31 March, 10am to 4pm; 3DM.*

The fortress, a formidable mass of cold grey granite bristling with towers and pinnacles, rises from a spur cut at its eastern end by the Pöllat Gorge. Building began in 1869. As at Hohenschwangau, a theatrical decorator and not an architect drew the first sketches, which explains the dream-like atmosphere.

(After a photo by Fr. Wirth)

Neuschwanstein Castle.

ROYAL CASTLES★★★

The tour of the interior where marble, gilded panelling and heavy tapestries are in abundance confirms this impression of unreality. King Ludwig II stayed at Neuschwanstein only for 102 days, and it was here on 10 June 1886 that he learnt from the Governmental Commission hastily sent from Munich that he had been deposed. He died three days later *(details p 235).*

The most revealing rooms are on the third floor. These include the artificial stalactite grotto with a small adjoining winter garden that recalls the Tannhäuser legend, the Great Chamber whose décor has for its theme the legend of Lohengrin – new invasion of swans – and the unfinished throne-room which is a veritable Romanesque-Byzantine sanctuary, whose apse was to have sheltered the royal throne. From this room, one enters an outside gallery from which there is an unforgettable **view★★★** of the wooded mountains of the Füssen district and its lakes, the largest of which, the Forgensee, is formed by a dam on the Lech. On the left you can see the Pöllat waterfall (Pöllatfall). The Singers' Hall (Sängersaal) with its fine coffered ceiling occupies practically the whole of the fourth floor. It contains many fine candelabra and chandeliers. The architect here was influenced by Wartburg Castle, the Thuringian fortress in which is said to have taken place in the early 13C the legendary poetical contest recalled in Wagner's opera *Tannhäuser.* The castle was later made famous by the visit of Luther. Richard Wagner, who was a guest at Hohenschwangau, never stayed at Neuschwanstein, Linderhof or Herrenchiemsee.

At the end of the visit, tourists who are not tired can walk up the Pöllat Gorge to the Marienbrücke which spans the ravine *(allow another hour for this walk).* At night, Ludwig II sometimes came to this bridge to contemplate the castle, silent and empty, but for the lights in the Singers' Hall.

Turn and go straight down to Hohenschwangau by the roads shown on the plan, *p 221.*

RÜDESHEIM AM RHEIN ★
Michelin map **204** 16 – *Local maps pp 212-213* – Pop 10 000

Rüdesheim, at the spot where the Rheingau vineyards cease and the Bingen Gap opens – the beginning of the Rhine Gorge – has become a busy tourist centre with amateur wine-tasters hastening to visit the local industry (spirit distilleries, cellars of sparkling wines). *To visit, apply to the Verkehrsamt, Rheinstrasse 16; ☎29 62.*

Drosselgasse. – The wine bars are usually full in this very lively, narrow and picturesque street.

Brömserburg. – This cubic fortified castle, commanding the downstream exit to the town, is now a **wine museum** *(open May to September, 9am to noon and 2 to 6pm; October to November, 2 to 5pm; closed Mondays, December and January; 1DM).* The outstanding exhibits are 21 old presses and a rich collection of amphores or vases which served as storage jars or bins for transporting wine.

EXCURSION

Niederwald Monument. – *Round tour of 14 km - 9 miles – about 1¼ hours.* Leave Rüdesheim by the Niederwald road at the top of the town. Turn left after one mile.

From the terrace at the foot of the Germania statue, erected to commemorate the re-establishment of the Empire in 1871, there is a **view★**, from left to right, of the Johannisberg vineyards, Bingen and Bingen Castle, the Nahe confluence and the opening of the Bingen Gap.

Descend by a steep road by the Hotel Jagdschloss Niederwald to Assmannshausen where you rejoin the Rhine. Bear left to return to Rüdesheim by way of the end of the Bingen Gap and the foot of Ehrenfels Castle.

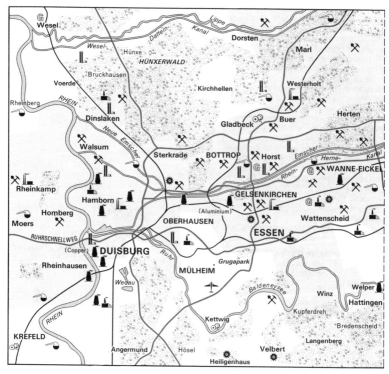

The Ruhr, testimony to the technical genius and spirit of enterprise which made Germany a world power in the 19C, and still the greatest single industrial area in Europe, has a population of 5 600 000 inhabitants, of whom 1 million work in industry.

The basin at present is in a state of change. A development plan was put into operation in 1968, including among other matters the introduction of new industries.

Town reconstruction after 1945 had already brought a more even distribution of the built-up areas and better road traffic conditions. The old road no 1, major artery through the basin, has now been converted into an expressway (Ruhrschnellweg).

Further, although the Ruhr has never presented the appearance of a "black country" – it is still possible to photograph a flock of sheep or a ploughed field before a background of blast furnaces – it has been found necessary to take definite measures to ensure nature conservation. Seven north–south green belts (Grünzage) limit the spread of the industrial zone between Duisburg and Dortmund, with parks, woodlands and farmland.

The vitality of the Ruhr is shown more than ever in its social, cultural and sporting activites, marked on the spot by the number of modern theatres and art museums, stadiums and swimming pools, sports palaces and congress halls, etc.

GEOGRAPHICAL NOTES

The hillsides of the Ruhr Valley, where coal outcrops occurred, have now been abandoned as production areas. Instead metal workshops distinguish the countryside, indicating it as being the widely scattered industrial area of the southern Bergisches Land. Without being idyllic, this half-industrial, half-forest region makes a welcome stopping place.

The middle zone between the Ruhr and the Emscher, which began to be developed in 1850, is still the main steel area and that where the coal mines, which are relatively shallow (rarely more than 400 m - 1 300 ft – deep), are closest together. The proliferation of works and factories and industrial towns has completely submerged old towns and market villages, resulting instead in a built-up area more than 50 km - 30 miles – in extent between the Rhine and Dortmund. While Oberhausen, Gelsenkirchen and the banks of the Emscher here and there afford somewhat sombre and oppressive industrial scenes, Duisburg, Essen, Bochum and Dortmund have little of the Black Country about them with their airy modern quarters, bustling trade and administrative offices, as well as their parks and stretches of water.

The New Basin (Neues Revier) between the Emscher and the Lippe, is a 20C feat. The mineshafts are further apart and are sometimes more than $\frac{1}{2}$ mile deep; equipped with the latest machinery the mines are producing, but at a high cost, more than 1 million tons of coal a year. In this area the chemical industry is larger than steel. The landscape has as yet no individual characteristics; towns remain separate, divided by areas of wood or arable land.

Heavy Industry. – The heavy industry of the Ruhr depends in great measure on coal.

The coal deposits are exceptionally well situated: seams run straight with few faults, dropping gently from south to north and increasing in both richness and variety. All types of coal are present from anthracite and slack to coal containing gas. Present-day rationalisation demands the concentration of production in the best equipped mines and in 1969 a single development company was founded to regroup the existing mining companies. This policy and improved techniques have resulted in an increase in production from 488 000 tons per mine in 1913 to 2 200 000 tons in 1975, while in the same interval the number of pits in operation has dropped from 175 to 35 and the production per miner tripled between 1957 and 1966 (nearly 3.5 tons per shift now). As elsewhere the total tonnage produced is now dropping considerably as competition increases with other sources of power.

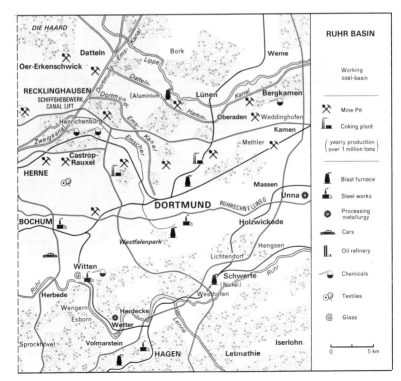

Steel production too is being concentrated in vast works marking the three production stages: smelting, steel production, semi-finished products.

The non-ferrous metal industry (copper, nickel, aluminium), the extraction of coal-tar and its by-products, the production of sulphuric acid and the chemicals for petroleum chemistry and the glass industry, complete the range of the chief industries of the Ruhr Valley.

A Few Figures. – The contribution of the Ruhr to the Federal Republic's economy is 82% of the coal, 63% of the smelting metal, 60% of the steel, more than 87% of the coal gas and ammonia and 64% of the industrial electric power produced from coal.

A FEW MUSEUMS IN THE RUHR AND THE BERGISCHES LAND

Villa Hügel*. – *Essen. Description p 117.*

Mining Museum* (Bergbaumuseum). – *Bochum. Open 8.30am to 5.30pm; closed Mondays, Sundays and holidays, 9am to 1pm; 2.50DM.*

Models on the ground floor trace the history of mining; collections of tools illustrate the improvements in equipment. Below ground a mine-museum has been constructed with $1\frac{1}{2}$ miles of galleries in a disused mine to display coal extraction, transport and the safety problem.

Blade Museum* (Klingenmuseum). – *Solingen-Gräfrath. Description p 233.*

Folkwang Museum**. – *Essen. Description p 117.*

Icon Museum** (Ikonenmuseum). – *Recklinghausen (Kirchplatz). Open 10am to 6pm; Sundays and holidays, 10am to 1pm and 3 to 6pm; closed Mondays and 1 May; 1DM.*

The icons are classified by theme in four galleries: iconostases separating the sanctuary from the rest of the church are painted with the Holy Trinity and the heavenly hierarchy – a theme rich in symbolism – then of the Virgin, and finally that of the Saints and their feast days.

Von der Heydt Museum* (Städtisches Museum). – *Wuppertal-Elberfeld. Description p 262.*

Ostwall Museum. – *Dortmund. Description p 107.*

Karl-Ernst Osthaus Museum. – *Hagen, Hochstrasse 73. Open Tuesdays and Wednesdays 11am to 8pm; Thursdays 11am to 10pm; Fridays 11am to 6pm; Saturdays 9am to 6pm; Sundays 11am to 5pm; closed Mondays.* Paintings by Christian Rohlfs (1849-1938).

SAAR, Valley of the Lower

Michelin maps ███ 23 and ███ 17, 18 or ██ 5

The Valley of the Saar in Germany is far from remaining throughout its length the corridor of industry that the Volkingen and Dillingen steelworks sector presents so strikingly. Below Merzig, the river cuts into the crystalline Hunsrück Massif, winding through a defile so narrow that it can be seen only from the top of its steeply sloping sides.

FROM MERZIG TO TRIER

53 km - 32 miles – about 2 hours – Local map below

Mettlach. – The Baroque façade in red limestone of the old abbey, now the offices of a ceramic works, stands out amidst the greenery. In the nearby park *(open to the public)* downstream, deep in the trees, stands an octagonal edifice, a funerary chapel dating from the 10C, the Altar Turm. A steep climb through the trees leads to the plateau. Leave road no 51, bearing left at the entrance to Orscholz to go up the Cloef.

Cloef**. – $\frac{1}{4}$ *hour on foot Rtn from the car park.* From the **belvedere**** high up, there is a view of the Montclair loop encircling a densely wooded promontory.

Rejoin the main route near Freudenberg, a village crowded upon a spur behind a ruined castle commanding the Leukbach depression.

Kastel-Staadt. – *3 km - 2 miles – plus $\frac{1}{2}$ hour's walking and sightseeing.* Cross the town of Kastel-Staadt to come out, at the end of the road, on the abrupt edge of the plateau. Enclosed on all sides by the parish graveyard, stands a Gothic church containing a modern bronze of the Resurrection. From the adjoining military cemetery, the **view*** sweeps down the Saar Valley which widens out into the Saarburg Basin, entirely covered in vineyards. Slightly below, perched upon its rock, can be seen the Hermitage Chapel (Klause), a place venerated in the valley since the Middle Ages. *Access through a fortified gate. Open February to December, 9am to noon and 2 to 5pm; the rest of the year 10am to noon and 2 to 4pm; closed Mondays; 0.70DM.* The chapel was rebuilt in the 19C to contain the tomb of John the Blind, King of Bohemia and Count of Luxembourg, killed at the Battle of Crécy in 1346. The hero's last remains now rest in Luxembourg Cathedral.

Alternative route by way of Saarhölzbach. – *Shortening of drive: 1 km - $\frac{1}{2}$ mile.* The road follows the bed of the wooded valley dominated by rock escarpments on which stand the Taben and Kastel chapels. The arrival at Saarburg is attractive.

Saarburg. – The setting of this small town is characteristic of the final section of the valley which is carpeted with vineyards. Good general view of the castle garden.

In the centre of the old quarter, near the Markt, a cascade (*usually dry in summer except on Saturday afternoons and Sundays*) falls between houses built on the rocks. Waters from the power station turn the mill wheel.

The juncture of the Mosel and the Saar opens out the countryside still further.

Trier**. – *Description p 245.*

VALLEY
OF THE **LOWER SAAR**

SAARBRÜCKEN

Michelin map **203** 9 – Pop 204 000 – *Town plan in Michelin Red Guide Deutschland*

Saarbrücken is a big industrial town lying in a coal basin where pit shafts have been sunk all over the wooded hills. The town, sometimes French, sometimes German has profited from the efforts of both nations to increase its prosperity and has learnt how to recover quickly from destruction.

St. Louis' Church (Ludwigskirche). – The church is part of the unified Baroque design of the Ludwigsplatz implemented by Stengel. He built this Protestant church on the Greek cross plan, added an octagonal tower and windows surmounted by oculi.

St. Arnual's Church. – *Access by the Talstrasse and the Saargemünder Strasse in the southeast.* A Gothic church of the 13 and 14C with bare pillars without capitals. The porch is surmounted by a Baroque tower. Funerary monuments, among others those of the Nassau-Saarbrücken family, adorn the interior; note the 15C tomb of Elisabeth of Lorraine in the chancel and that of Johann III, between his two wives, in the north transept.

Saarland Museum. – *St. Johanner Markt 24. Open 10am to 2pm (6pm Sundays and New Gallery); closed Mondays.* 18C decorative art; 19 and 20C painting and sculpture.

German-French Park (Deutsch-Französischer Garten). – *1.50DM.* It was created by landscape architects from the two countries. There are fountains and pink flamingoes.

EXCURSION

Homburg: Roman Open Air Museum. – *36 km - 22 miles.* Leave Saarbrücken by ③ on the plan – motorway direction Mannheim – exit at Homburg – take road no 423 in the town to Schwarzewacker. *Open in summer, 9.30 to noon and 1.15 to 5.30pm (6pm Sundays); in winter, Wednesdays 9.30am (noon Saturdays) to 4.30pm; 1.50DM. Brochure in English.*

Excavations have clarified the plan of a Celtic-Roman country town: two streets of residential and commercial buildings with pavements. Behind the columns stood closely packed houses: they generally had a yard surrounded by the living and sleeping quarters, one room of which contained the hypocaust, the Roman heating system.

SÄCKINGEN ★

Michelin map **205** 19 – Pop 14 800

Säckingen is a small town lying on the edge of the Black Forest beside the Rhine where the river forms the frontier with Switzerland. The lay architecture shows Swiss influence.

Church of St. Fridolin★ (Fridolinsmünster). – This 13C Gothic church was remodelled in 1752. It shows procedures used in Baroquisation: pointed arcade arches link directly with semicircular arcs (graceful bays letting in light between columns), low vaulting for easier decoration (Rococo stuccowork from the Wessobrunn school – *p 256*), tall windows transformed into rounded bays.

The **treasure** *(to visit, apply to Herr Ulmer, Fischergasse 9)* contains St. Fridolin's shrine, a magnificent 18C Augsburg work in the form of a carriage chest.

ST. BLASIEN

Michelin map **205** 18 – *Local map p 84* – Pop 4 100

The majestic domed Church of St. Blaise comes as a surprise at the end of a wooded Hotzenwald Valley in the southern part of the Black Forest.

Church★ (Dom). – *Round tour: ¼ hour.* The church, in accordance with a plan much in favour in the Baroque period, is surrounded on four sides by the former abbey buildings. The building's interest lies entirely in its design and proportions. Inside the dome, which is lit by deeply embrasured windows, is a false cupola suspended within the true dome; the weight is only borne in appearance, therefore, on the columns of the central rotunda. The chancel, which has cradle vaulting, lies behind the high altar and is where the Benedictines themselves worshipped.

EXCURSIONS

Bernau. – *Round tour of 42 km - 26 miles – about 2 hours.* Leave St. Blasien by the road that goes first to Todtmoos. Continue towards Freiburg. Beyond a pass (Weissenbachsattel) the road drops down to Präg where you turn right for St. Blasien. The fine Bernau farms, nestling close to the ground in a pastureland combe, are grouped in hamlets. At Bernau-Dorf follow the signs "Hans-Thoma-Museum" to the town hall where there is an exhibition of paintings by Hans Thoma *(p 156)*, a son of the Bernau region (1839-1924). *Open 9am (10am Sundays) to noon and 2 to 6pm; closed Sundays 15 October to 15 December; 2DM.* Return to St. Blasien.

Waldshut; the Alb Valley (Albtal). – *Round tour of 61 km - 38 miles – about 2½ hours.* Leave St. Blasien by the Waldshut road described on p 84.

After Waldshut, go down the Rhine Valley by road no 34, which you leave at Albbruck to go up the Alb Valley on the right towards St. Blasien. The road rises and soon overlooks the rocky defile at the bottom of which, but out of sight, runs the stream. *Corniche* sections and tunnels increase in number. 11 km - 7 miles – from Albbruck, turn left into the Wolpadingen road which ascends again to the Hotzenwald plateau and continue through hills to St. Blasien.

ST. GOAR

Michelin map **204** 15 – *Local map p 212* – Pop 3 500

St. Goar looks down from the foot of the Rheinfels Castle, the strongest fortress on the Rhine until dismantled in 1797, on the Loreley. On the far bank is St. Goarshausen.

Burg Rheinfels★★. – *1 km Rtn - ½ mile – along the signposted road "zur Burg Rheinfels", plus ¾ hour sightseeing (open April to September, 9am to 6pm; October 9am to 5pm; 2DM).*

This 13C castle, which was remodelled in the Renaissance style in the 16C by the Landgraves of Hesse, resisted assault by Louis XIV but fell later to the French in 1794.

From the keep you get an overall view of the castle and the Valley of the Rhine and, on the far bank, the Cat and Mouse Castles. A visit to the great vaulted hall is also worth while (50 yds beyond the clock tower). More time is needed to enjoy a walk through the maze of towers, gates, courts and casemates, which make up the castle system.

Church. – Enter through one of the side doors into the galleried 14-15C Gothic hall-church. Delicately coloured 15C frescoes decorate the north aisle; look also at the pulpit.

ST. WENDEL

Michelin map 203 8 – Pop 27 300

This small Saarland town, in a rustic setting, is said to have been founded in the 6C by St. Wendel, a king's son who became a shepherd and whose relics are greatly venerated locally.

Church. – The Gothic church with an unusual façade of three abutting 15C towers, contains, at the entrance to the chancel, St. Wendel's tomb, a fine, somewhat naive 14C work. The recumbent figure is modern.

Tholey; Schaumberg. – *Excursion of 13 km - 8 miles – 1 hour – westwards by the Tholey road.*
The 13C Gothic abbey church has been restored by the monks who returned in 1949. Inside are an outstanding series of modern stained glass windows, designed by a Benedictine.
Turn and as you come out of Tholey, take the left road which circles the Schaumberg mountain. From the top, where a chapel is to be built, there is a vast **panorama** of the wooded hills of the Saar region as far as the Vosges.

SALEM Abbey *

Michelin map 206 18 – Local map p 102

This Cistercian abbey reached its peak under Abbot Anselm II (1746-78), the builder of Birnau (*p 80*). After secularisation (*p 20*) the monastery's riches passed to the House of Baden-Baden. Part of the buildings are occupied by a private school which was founded by Dr. Kurt Hahn and attended before the war by the Duke of Edinburgh. Dr. Hahn later came to the United Kingdom and founded Gordonstoun.

Abbey Church*. – *Guided tours: 1 April to 31 October, 9am (11am Sundays) to noon and 1 to 5.15pm; time: ¾ hour; 2.50DM. Brochure in English.*
Outside, the severity of the walls is relieved by the slender Gothic bays which light the east and west gables, the decorative latticework applied to the buttresses supporting the façade, and especially by the radiating tracery in the clerestory on the south gable.
Inside there is a vivid contrast between the sobriety of the architecture and the richness of the decoration. Typically Cistercian Gothic is the plain design of a large chancel with a flat east end, high vaulting and side aisles supporting the nave by walls abutting on wide arcades and against which the side altars stand.

Abbey Buildings* (Schloss). – *Same times as for the church.*
The buildings were reconstructed at the beginning of the 18C in the Baroque style; the stuccowork was entrusted to artists of the Wessobrunn school.

Oratory (Betsaal). – The room, the former summer refectory, still has its Wessobrunn stucco ceiling. The 1735 porcelain stove is decorated with lively illustrations showing the monks' seasonal activities and scenes from the Old Testament.

Library. – Superb basket-handle vaulted ceiling.

Emperors' Hall (Kaisersaal). – This great Baroque hall of state was the first to be built in a German abbey. The carved decoration includes imperial statues and papal medallions.

The Abbot's Apartments (Prälatenquartier). – Note among these discreetly charming apartments, the green Rococo study with its swan motif, the emblem of Abbot Anselm II.

Lower Gate House (Untertor-Haus). – Between the pilasters, of this strikingly elegant entrance, the decorative window lintels have a different design on each storey.

The SAUERLAND

Michelin map 202 9, 10, 18 to 20

The Sauerland, which forms the hinterland to the Ruhr Basin, is the most mountainous, if not the most elevated region of the Rhineland Schist Massif (*p 13*).
The Upper Sauerland, particularly the Rothaargebirge, forms the tourist area.

The Dams. – Many reservoirs are built in the Sauerland Valleys. The Möhnesee and the Sorpesee with their artificial lakes, are among the most popular.

☐ FROM SIEGEN TO SOEST by the great dams

131 km - 81 miles – about 4 hours – Local map p 227

After Siegen (*p 231*) road no 54 goes up an industrial valley. As you cross Krombach note the bronze beer fountain which flows with beer at a special festival held every four years. The road between Olpe and Attendorn looks down on the Bigge lake and dam.

Bigge Dam* (Biggetalsperre). – The biggest dam in Westphalia.

Attahöhle*. – *Open 15 April to 15 October, 9am to 5pm; the rest of the year, 9.30am to 4pm; closed 8 days around Christmas; 2.50DM. The way is signposted, "Tropfsteinhöhle", as you come out of Attendorn.* The galleries are decorated with long and sometimes translucid rock draperies and a cascade of stalactites.
There are some remarkable rock passages in the valley below Attendorn.
The crossing of the Lennegebirge, between the Lenne Valley and the Sorpe artificial lake, affords some good brief views, particularly on either side of the dividiing pass.

> **Luisenhütte.** – *Alternative route resulting in 11 km - 7 miles – extra distance. The approach road branches off between Balve and the "Sans Souci" crossroads, just before a road passes beneath a railway (coming from the south). Open May to October, 10am (11.30am Sundays) to 6pm; closed Mondays; 1DM. Apply at the Luisenhütte Inn (Gaststube).* The oldest blast furnace (1732) in Germany in perfect condition, though not alight, is on view.

Sorpe Dam (Sorpetalsperre). – Large watersports centre.

Arnsberg. – The old town rises in tiers up a spur overlooking a bend in the Ruhr. To the north, the clock tower commands the approach to the Schlossberg ruins; to the south lies the former abbey quarter where a superb Rococo gate, the Hirschberger Tor, still stands.
There is a very good view of Arnsberg to be had from road no 229 which rises as it leaves the town. Beeches, birches and larches are all to be found on the wooded Arnsberg Massif. Arrival on the Westphalian Plain is marked by the vast Möhne lake.

Möhne Dam* (Möhnetalsperre). – The **reservoir*** reaches back for 10 km - 6 miles – from the dam wall 650 m long by 40 m high - 711 yds by 131 ft. The wooded southern end has remained wild, whilst the north bank has been developed with beaches and hotels.

Soest*. – *Description p 232.*

② *TOUR OF THE ROTHAARGEBIRGE, starting from Siegen

179 km - 111 miles – about 5½ hours – Local map below

This round trip can be made equally well starting from Winterberg, the busiest winter sports centre of the Upper Sauerland.

Siegen. – *Description p 231.*

West of Siegen, one begins by crossing a green and wooded region which, with its lovely villages, well reveals the Siegerland's charm. From Freudenberg it is possible to make a detour to see Crottorf Castle.

Crottorf Castle*. – *11 km - 7 miles – starting from Freudenberg, by the Waldbröl road; bear right after 10 km - 6 miles. Open April to October, 10am to 6pm; 2DM. The interior is closed.* This vast moated 16C Castle standing isolated in the valley, is circled by two successive defence ditches. The castle site is best appreciated by following the boundary line on the right as you come from Freudenberg.

Later, when on the Olpe road, make a point of looking north at the new artificial lake at Bigge.

Bigge Dam* (Biggetalsperre). – *26 km Rtn - 16 miles – about ½ hour starting from Olpe. Description p 226.*

A small mountain road, which begins at Bilstein, leads first to a pass from which there is a view eastwards over the Upper Valley of the Lenne and on to the summit of the Hohe Bracht.

Hohe Bracht. – *Tour: ¼ hour.* From the belvedere tower (alt 584 m - 1 916 ft) *(ascent 0.50DM)* there is a panorama which reaches across the rounded hill ranges of the Rothaargebirge to the Kahler Asten.
The countryside of the Lenne Valley, passed through by the road, has a rural charm at first.

Grafschaft. – Attractive village with wooden walled houses.

Oberkirchen. – Beautiful village with white houses and black half-timbering.
The settings become more mountainous and wilder above Oberkirchen. The **road*** next climbs towards the Kahler Asten in a hilly beech-covered region.

Nordenau. – A typical mountain village of the Upper Sauerland, its slate clad houses standing perched upon a spur.
There is a fine panorama from **Altastenberg**, a village in a bare setting on the plateau.

Kahler Asten. – *Tour: ¼ hour.* The Kahler Asten is the highest peak (alt 841 m - 2 759 ft) in the Sauerland. From the belvedere *(ascent: 0.50DM)* there is a vast but monotonous circular panorama: to the east lies the resort of Winterberg.
The drive continues through a region of slate quarries.

Berleburg. – A severely dignified mountain town with its streets darkened by the slates facing the houses. Go through the upper town for a closer look at the 16 and 18C castle. The return road by Erndtebrück and Hilchenbach has a curious section beyond Lützer when it suddenly plunges from the shallow high pastoral combe of the Eder to the deep wooded valleys of the Sieg tributaries.

SCHLESWIG ★

Michelin map **987** 5 – Pop 32 000 – *Town plan in Michelin Red Guide Deutschland*

Schleswig, an old maritime town of many white houses, was built on low-lying banks at the end of an arm of the sea, the Schlei. Arrival in Schleswig is most memorable from the south, particularly late in the afternoon. The car park beside European Road no 3 affords a **view★** of the old town at the foot of the cathedral on the far shore of the Schlei.

The Town's Foundation. – A village, Sliesthorp, in the southern area of the Schlei is mentioned in the 9C annals of the Frankish Empire. It stood at a remarkable crossroads of the old north–south Jutland road and the east–west road along which light loads were carried across the isthmus to speed their transport between the Baltic and North Seas. The Vikings, who named the place **Haithabu** – the town in the heather – made it their commercial and trading metropolis. A vast defence system was constructed of which there remain the semicircular Haithabu entrenchment (access by ③ on plan), an archaeological site on the banks of the Haddebyer Noor Pool (access by ②) and stones with runic carvings such as the Busdorder Runenstein (access by ③). Further remains may be seen in Gottorf Castle.

At the end of the 10C the townspeople, seeking better defences against Scandinavian tribes, crossed to the north bank of the Schlei to found the old town (Alstadt) of Schleswig.

■ **SIGHTS** time: 1½ hours

The Nydam Ship★★★ (Nydam-Boot). – *Open 1 April to 31 October, 9am to 5pm; 1 November to 31 March, weekdays 10am to 4pm; Sundays and holidays, 9.30am to 5pm; closed Mondays; 1DM.*

The ship is displayed in a building west of Gottorf Castle.

This, the oldest ship of any considerable size to be left us by the Germanic civilisations, was discovered in 1863 in the Nydam marshes, in Danish territory. She dates from approximately the 4C and her oak hull, which is 23 m long by 3 m wide - 75 by 10 ft – is elegant with beautiful lines. 36 men were needed to man the oars.

In the same building are mummies, garment pieces, shoes and arms buried with her.

Gottorf Castle (Y). – *Same times of opening and same ticket as for the Nydam Ship (see above)*. The 16 and 18C castle, which was the cradle of the Holstein-Gottorp family, which in 1762 became the Imperial House of Russia, now houses two huge museums.

Schleswig-Holstein Museum★★. – Rich art, handicraft and folklore collections. Note especially the Gothic Hall (mediaeval religious art), the furnished rooms and the **Renaissance chapel★★** which has been left as it was, including the ducal loggia.

Prehistorical Museum★. – Exhibits of prehistory to Viking civilisations.

St. Peter's Cathedral★ (Dom) (Z A). – *Open 1 April to 30 September, 9am (1pm Sundays and holidays) to 6pm; 1 October to 31 March, 10am (1pm Sundays) to 4pm; 0.50DM.*

The brick cathedral is of the Gothic hall-church type with a fine spire.

Enter by the south, St. Peter's doorway, which is of stone (carved tympanum dating from 1170). Inside on the right stands a large statue of St. Christopher. The outstanding work of art is the 1521 **Bordesholm altarpiece★★** in the chancel.

Northwest of the transept lies the 14C cloister with decorative motifs on the vaulting.

Holm (Z). – This is the old fishermen's quarter. The low houses crowd round a quiet **square★** (Friedhofplatz) containing a burial ground and chapel.

SCHLIERSEE ★

Michelin map **987** 37 – *Local map p 45* – Pop 6 200

Schliersee, in a wonderful setting in the Bavarian Alps, gets its name from its lake, a small sheet of water in beautiful surroundings.

The town's tourist facilities are complemented by those of neighbouring Fischhausen, Neuhaus, Joseftal and Spitzingsee *(access p 46)*.

■ **SIGHTS** time: ¾ hour

Parish Church★ (Pfarrkirche). – This old collegiate church, which was a dependent of the Frauenkirche chapter of Munich *(p 188)*, was rebuilt in the Baroque style in 1712. The interior, which is bathed in light, is a feast for the eyes, with walnut altarpieces where the natural colour of the wood highlights the gilding. The painting on the roof and the delicate stuccowork are by J. B. Zimmerman (1680-1758), brother of the architect of Wies *(p 257)*.

The seated statue of St. Sixtus, patron of the church, in the chancel to the left of the high altar, is typical of the early Renaissance in Bavaria *(c 1520)*. Opposite, attributed to Erasmus Grasser (1480), is the poignant group of the Throne of Grace (Gnadenstuhl) – the Eternal Father presents Christ descended from the Cross. Beside this is the *Virgin in a Mantle* painted by Jan Pollack in 1494. The collaboration of these two artists, who both worked for the Frauenkirche, recalls the link between this church and the great Munich chapter.

Town Hall. – This 15C law court with many picturesque details – turret, arcades, oriel windows – was remodelled in a pleasantly sumptuous fashion suitable to its new municipal dignity. A few minutes away, towards the mountain, stands the Weinberg with St. George's Chapel providing a viewpoint over the lake.

SCHORNDORF

Michelin map **205** 3 – Pop 32 900

Schorndorf, which, before the Thirty Years War, was the small political capital of the Duchy of Württemberg, is now a busy industrial town (woodworking, electrical engineering), proud of having preserved its traditional appearance.

Oberer Marktplatz★. – This large square with its off-centre flower decked Rococo fountain has a pleasing monumental unity. The façades, usually with pointed gables and wooden walls, are attractively varied.

Church (Stadtkirche). – This is a Flamboyant Gothic building: note the groined vaulting in the form of a Tree of Jesse in the northeast chapel.

SCHUSSENRIED
Michelin map **206** 7 – Pop 5 869

The old abbey buildings (now a psychiatric hospital) and church owe their sumptuous Baroque appearance to Premonstratensian abbots.

■ **ABBEY** *tour: ½ hour*

Church (Ehemaliges Kloster). – The church has a Romanesque plan, Gothic vaulting and a Baroque arrangement. In the chancel, the top panels of the highly decorated choirstalls (1717) are separated by 28 upright statuettes of the men and women founders of religious orders.

Abbey Library* (Klosterbibliothek). – *Open in summer, 9am to noon and 1.30 to 5pm; in winter, 9am to noon and 2 to 4pm; closed Mondays; 0.60DM.*
The library, built between 1755 and 1766, has a huge painted ceiling and winding gallery with a Rococo balustrade supported by twin columns. The column pedestals are adorned alternately with hilarious cherubim in burlesque costumes and effigies of Fathers of the Church.

SCHWÄBISCH GMÜND
Michelin map **206** 3 – Pop 56 600 – *Town plan in Michelin Red Guide Deutschland*

By tradition Schwäbisch Gmünd is a centre where precious metals are worked and its silver cutlery is seen on many German tables. The town makes a good excursion centre since it lies near the **Kaiserberge** whose three conical summits, Hohenstaufen, Hohenrechberg and Stuifen, stand out clearly and are characteristic of the landscape of the northern borders of the Swabian Jura.

■ **SIGHTS** *time: ¾ hour*

Cathedral of the Holy Cross* (Heiligkreuzmünster). – The cathedral was built in the 14C by the Swabian master Heinrich Parler whose descendants went as far afield to design cathedrals as Prague, Vienna and Milan. Surprisingly it has no towers. The exterior tracery, balustrades and pinnacles are Flamboyant. Gothic decoration is delicately worked to form a grid on the west gable, and the chancel doors are carved beneath their porches which were once also decorated overall. The two-tier east end is harmoniously designed.
The interior is a perfect hall *(p 24)*. The chancel, which has the same plan as the nave, is distinguished by more intricately decorated ribbed vaulting. The early Renaissance choirstalls and the radiating chapels are rich in statues; note especially, in the axial chapel, the early 15C Holy Sepulchre watched by the three Marys.

Marktplatz. – This large square has a Baroque character which is emphasised further by the prosperous looking houses standing round it and the fountain to the Virgin with a double statue. A few half-timbered houses, the Grät Mansion (former town hall) and the hospital, however, recall the town's mediaeval period.

EXCURSIONS

Hohenstaufen*. – *14 km - 8½ miles – plus ½ hour on foot Rtn.* Leave Schwäbisch Gmünd by the Rechbergstrasse, south on the plan. Bear obliquely right at Strassdorf. Leave the car on the central esplanade in the village of Hohenstaufen.
Walk to the two churches at the top of the town and to the mountain top by the shaded paths. Nothing remains of the castle, the cradle of the Hohenstaufens, but there is a **panorama*** of the two other Kaiserberge in the distance and, on the horizon, of the Swabian Jura.

Hohenrechberg. – *12 km - 7½ miles – plus 1 hour on foot Rtn.* Leave Schwäbisch Gmünd by the Rechbergstrasse, south on the plan. Continue straight on up from Strassdorf crossroad. Park the car at the central crossroads in Rechberg.
Walk in the Hinter-Rechberg direction and beyond the transformer, turn right into the castle's surfaced rise. The castle ruins overlook a vast **horizon**. Walk round the watchpath or the crests of the walls that have been made into a footpath. Hohenstaufen stands in the foreground.

SCHWÄBISCH HALL ★★
Michelin map **206** 1 – *Local map p 151* – Pop 31 300

This old town, built in tiers up the steep flank of the Kocher Valley, grew round salt springs that were known as far back as Celtic times. In the Middle Ages the town became famous for the imperial silver coins which were minted there, the Häller or Heller.
The most colourful local festival is that of the Salt Boilers (Kuchenfest). *See list on p 31.*

General View*. – Make for the banks of the Kocher for a good **overall view*** of the old town with its roofs stepped one above the other at the foot of St. Michael's Church and the Büchsenhaus *(see below)* pierced all over with windows and dormer lights. Go to the Mauerstrasse, the quay on the left bank, from where you will see, from near the Löwenbrauerei, the attractive roofed wooden bridges which cross the arms of the river in the foreground.

■ **MARKTPLATZ★★** *tour: ¾ hour*

The sloping Marktplatz is dominated by the monumental stone steps to St. Michael's Church, where on summer evenings actors perform the Schwäbisch Hall festival in which world famous theatre forms the repertoire. Only the typical alignment of half-timbered gables on the south side on the right, spared by the fire of 1728, remains to remind one of what the square must have looked like in the 17C.

Town Hall*. – The town hall is an elegant Baroque building (1730-5), its simple decoration confined to the window frames and pilasters. *Open only by arrangement with the tourist office.*

Fountain (Marktbrunnen) (B). – The fountain, which dates from 1509, stands against a decorative wall adorned with statues of Samson, St. Michael and St. George. The square design, which is unusual in such a Gothic ornament, includes within it the old pillory post.

St. Michael's Church (Pfarrkirche). – *Open 1 April to 31
October, 8.30am to noon and
1.30 to 5pm; closed Sunday
mornings and Mondays; 0.50
DM.* The church is con-
siderably enhanced by its
position at the top of 53 steps.
The octagonal porch opening
beneath a Romanesque tower
with a Renaissance top, has a
statue of St. Michael before its
central pillar.

Interior★ (Inneres). – The
building, which was originally
Romanesque, was transformed
into a Gothic hall-church in the
15C and had a Flamboyant
chapel added in the 16C.
The Dutch influenced
altarpiece at the high altar dates
from the 15C while several of
those in the radial chapels are
16C. In a chapel on the south
side of the chancel is a 1510
altarpiece to St. Michael with a
fine Christ in Sorrow above it.

■ **ADDITIONAL
SIGHTS**

**Walk through the Old
Town.** – The route marked on
the plan *(about ½ hour starting
from the Marktplatz)* takes you
through a picturesque quarter
in the upper town. Note the
huge Büchsenhaus or
"Neubau" building (1527)
which was once the arsenal.
Several old 15 and 16C half-
timbered houses may be seen
in the parallel Obere Herrn-

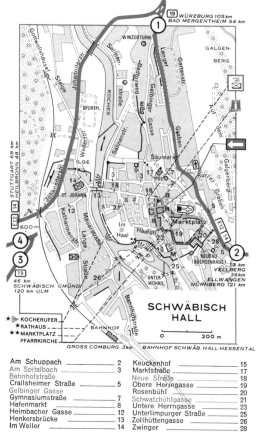

SCHWÄBISCH
HALL

0   200 m

★≋ KOCHERUFER
★ RATHAUS
★★ MARKTPLATZ
PFARRKIRCHE

GROSS COMBURG 3km   BAHNHOF SCHWÄB. HALL-HESSENTAL

gasse and Untere Herrngasse streets which are linked by steps. The half-timbered house on the
corner of Obere Herrngasse, no 11, is made even more attractive by a Renaissance balustraded
terrace.

Keckenburg Museum (M). – *Open 1 April to 30 September, 9am to noon and 2 to 5pm; the
rest of the year, 10am to noon and 3 to 5pm; closed Mondays; 3DM.* This historical museum is a
tall Romanesque tower ten storeys high, which was formerly inhabited. It contains mementoes of
Schwäbisch Hall's past as an industrial salt town and a mint and of the region generally.

Gräterhaus (E). – This lovely half-timbered house dating from 1605, which is so finely
ornamented, stands in the town's northern suburb.

Henkersbrücke (C). – There is an attractive **view** from this bridge, or even better from where the
Am Spitalbach street comes out on the quayside (Salinenstrasse), of the mass of half-timbered
buildings of the Ilge quarter and their reflection in the waters of the Kocher and also of the east
end of the old Church of St. John.

EXCURSIONS

Gross Comburg★. – *3 km - 2 miles - plus 1 hour sightseeing. Open April to September, 9am to
noon and 1.30 to 5pm; closed Mondays; 0.50DM.* Leave Schwäbisch Hall by the Bahnhofstrasse, south on the plan; cross Steinbach suburb from one end to the other at the foot of the old
and impressive fortified abbey of Gross Comburg and then turn almost backwards left into the
rise to the fortress.
    The buildings and furniture dating from the Romanesque period are particularly interesting.
    The third **entrance door★** to the abbey (Romanisches Klostertor), which is Romanesque and
12C, is distinguished by its gallery of blind arcades and twin towers. Higher up on the left stands
the late 12C hexagaonal Chapel of St. Ehrard, which is encircled by an arcaded gallery and
probably served at one time as an ossuary.
    Three Romanesque towers still crown the **abbey church** (Klosterkirche), the tall west one
dating from the end of the 11C. The rest of the building was reconstructed in Baroque style in
1715 and inside takes the form of a Baroque hall.
    A Romanesque **chandelier★★★** (Leuchter) made in 1130 in the form of a crown in iron then
copperplated and gilded, hangs from the vaulting. With those of Aachen and Hildesheim, it is one
of the most precious in the West. The **altarfront★** before the high altar is of the same period; the
copper of which it is made is again gilded, and also beaten to depict Christ among the Apostles.
The surrounding framework is in *cloisonné* enamel or filigree.

Vellberg. – *13 km - 6 miles - about ¾ hour.* Leave Schwäbisch Hall by ② and follow the
Ellwangen road on the right to the Vellberg road branching off to the left.
    One can still walk over some of the bastions of the double fortification system which remains
from the 15C. To get a good overall **view★** go up to St. Martin's Church on the Steckenburg
height at the north end of the valley.

The Michelin Red Guide **Deutschland** *lists hotels and restaurants
serving good meals at moderate prices.
Use the current annual guide.*

SCHWETZINGEN ★★

Michelin map **204** 9 – Pop 18 500

Asparagus lovers flock to Schwetzingen in the season. In the 18C the town was the summer residence of the Palatine Electors *(p 146)*. A park which is full of surprises extends behind the very ordinary castle building – rebuilt after the Orleans War.

The Castle Park★★ (Schlossgarten). – *Tour: 1½ hours. Enter through the castle: 1.50DM.*

The park was landscaped in two periods after 1758. It now combines the formal French style – the main vista – with the natural greenery popular at the end of the 18C inspired by the "spectacle of nature" to which were added symbolic monuments – imitation ruins, temples, etc. The whole is the work of the Lorraine architect, Nicolas de Pigage (1723-96).

The main vista begins with a semicircle of more or less graceful buildings and a round garden with fountains. Behind the buildings on the right is the lovely 1752 court **theatre** which is still used each summer. Walk through the thicket on the right and beyond the group of stags, to the small winding stream leading to the "bird-bath". Bear obliquely left and through another thicket you will come on the Temple of Apollo. Hidden near this rotunda is a delightful Bath Pavilion (1773). Birds perched, in a setting of green, dart streams of water at a central basin – the whole, in fact, a false perspective in the form of a diorama painted in the receding back of an arbor. Return to the main alley which ends shortly at the lake. Climb to the top of the "ruin" of the Temple of Mercury on the left to get a full view of the lake and the minarets of a "mosque".

SEEBÜLL ★

Michelin map **987** 4 – 15 km - 7 miles – north of Niebüll

The painter Emil Hansen (1867-1956), better known as **Nolde**, lived in a house in Seebüll which he designed and had built in the centre of the marsh after the 1914-18 War.

Access and Tour. – *15 km - 7 miles – from Niebüll – about ¾ hour. The approach is difficult, therefore follow the signposts "Nolde-Museum". Open 1 March to 30 November, 10am to 6pm; 3DM. The paintings are exhibited in rotation.*

The 1927 house, which stands alone surrounded only by flowers, is now a **museum★** (Nolde-Museum). Anxiety and religious emotion dominate Nolde's work, often expressed in a paradoxical juxtaposition of the sacred and the burlesque – see the religious works exhibited in the painter's old studio – and by thick, aggressive, incandescent colours which totally destroy all form.

SEGEBERG, Bad

Michelin map **987** 5 – Pop 14 600

The Kalkberg spike, emerging unexpectedly from the almost flat Holstein countryside, heralds Bad Segeberg, a resort famous since 1952 for its Karl May festival.

Karl May (1842-1912), the author of many adventure stories, is still popular with young Germans who enjoy the valorous exploits of the Apache Chief Winnetou.

Kalkberg. – The mound, eroded by gypsum mining, is now preserved by the town – in 1645 its altitude was 111 m - 364 ft, today it is 91 m - 298 ft. There is a belvedere at the top and the underground grottoes are open. The old quarry has been turned into an open air theatre which at the time of the festival forms an appropriate setting for galloping Bedouins and Indians.

The SIEBENGEBIRGE ★

Michelin map **203** 2 – southeast of Bonn – *Local maps pp 115 and 213*

The Siebengebirge (Seven Mountains) mountain range, overlooking the Rhine and facing Bad Godesberg, is a group of rounded volcanic hills whose average height is about 400 m - 1 300 ft. The seven characteristic summits *(local map p 85)* were, in nearly every case, crowned at one time by a castle; today they are covered with thick forests which soften their outlines. The whole massif forms a national park of 42 km² - 10 400 acres.

This is the most northerly point in Germany at which vines are cultivated; the best known local vintage is the Drachenblut (Dragon's Blood). The Siebengebirge is a focal point for Rhineland Romanticism, the jagged Drachenfels ruins its popular symbol.

Königswinter, at the foot of the range, is the busiest tourist centre and the departure point for excursions to Drachenfels and Petersberg. There are flower bordered walks beside the Rhine and a swimming pool, the Lemmerzbad, above the town.

Car Tour. – *19 km - 12 miles – about 1 hour. Follow the itinerary marked on p 85.* An ascent by car of the **Petersberg** summit (331 m - 1 096 ft), crowned by the huge hotel *(temporarily closed)* where Queen Elizabeth II and the Duke of Edinburgh stayed on the state visit to Germany in 1965 can be added to the tour marked on the map as well as the visit to Konrad Adenauer's house (**M**) *(open Tuesdays to Sundays, 10am to 4.30pm)* at **Honnef-Rhöndorf**.

Drachenfels Ascent★. – *About 1 hour Rtn – 15 minutes by rack railway from Königswinter; departures every ½ hour, 9am to 8pm in summer; Rtn fare: 5.50DM.*

The rock owes its name to the dragon which once haunted it: legend has it that Siegfried, hero of the Nibelungen *(p 209),* killed the dragon and bathed in its blood to become invincible.

There is a **panorama★★** from the terrace at the foot of the ruined tower: from left to right are the Westerwald and Eifel plateaux, Bad Godesberg, Bonn and Cologne (the cathedral is visible in clear weather) and below of the unceasing procession of Rhine shipping.

SIEGEN

Michelin map **204** 1 – *Local map p 227* – Pop 121 500
Town plan in Michelin Red Guide Deutschland

Lying in the valleyed Siegerland region south of the Sauerland, Siegen has become the industrial heart of the Sieg Valley, a town dominated by ironworks. It was Rubens' (1577-1640) native town, his parents living there in exile from Holland.

The town has a distinctive **setting** on a slender promontory overlooking the confluence of two rivers. It can best be seen from the terrace of the castle (Oberes Schloss).

Below Siegen an exceptionally big bridge – 1 km long and 104 m high (½ mile x 345 ft) – has been constructed to carry the Sauerland motorway (Sauerlandlinie) over the Sieg River.

St. Nicholas' (Nikolaikirche). – *On the Neumarkt.* This 13C Romanesque church has an extraordinary domed nave. A galleried ambulatory with groined vaulting surrounds the central hexagon.

SIGMARINGEN ★

Michelin map **206** south of 16 – *Local map p 240* – Pop 15 200

The strong defensive position of Sigmaringen – a rock rising out of the valley at the mouth of the Upper Danube gap *(description p 239)* – made the town the minor capital of the principality of the Swabian and Catholic branch of the Hohenzollerns *(p 152)*. Only its position and overall appearance testify to the castle's feudal history. The buildings and particularly their interior decoration are a Renaissance pastiche.

■ THE CASTLE AND ITS ANNEXES *tour: 1 hour*

The approach begins at the highest point in the street cutting across the loop of the Danube (leave the car in front of the Rathaus). *Take tickets at the castle's fortified gateway. Tours are guided, therefore if you have to wait, begin by going to the museums or the church; groups for tours are called by loud-hailer.*

Castle. – *Open 8am to noon and 1 to 5pm; 2.50DM.*
The state apartments adorned in 16C style with coffered ceilings and tapestries (Royal Bedchamber, Ancestral Hall, etc.) will be of most interest to those well versed in the family ties of European royalty. There are rich **collections of arms and armour.**

Church. – The church, luminous with Rococo stuccowork, clings to the castle rock. A shrine in a transept chapel on the left, contains the cradle of St. Fidelio of Sigmaringen (1577-1622), first Capuchin martyr and patron of the order and local protector.

Museums. – *Open same hours as the castle.*
Collections of paintings (Swabian Primitives) and vehicles (Marstallmuseum).

SINGEN (HOHENTWIEL)

Michelin map **206** 18 – *Local map p 102* – Pop 49 000
Town plan in Michelin Red Guide Deutschland

The name of Singen, a large metallurgical and food processing centre, is linked with that of the Hohentwiel Fortress which overlooks the town. The **setting★★** with this enormous volcanic spike crowned with ruins is particularly striking when seen against the late afternoon sky as you approach from Radolfzell.

Ascent to Hohentwiel. – *About 1½ hours walking and sightseeing. Open April to September, 8.30am to 6pm; October to March, 9am to 4pm; 1DM.* Leave the car on an esplanade at the end of the Hohentwielstrasse.
Since the fortress was dismantled on the orders of Napoleon in 1801, the remains are of no interest monumentally, although a walk through open doorways up staircases and across barrack rooms and ruined magazines is worth while. The **views★** from the bastions and ramparts vary widely: the Hegau spikes *(p 101)*, the two reaches of Lake Constance, the Allgäu Alps and the Rätikon (Vorarlberg), the Swiss Alps from Säntis to the Jungfrau.

EXCURSION

Hilzingen. – *5 km - 3 miles – by ④ on the map, plus ¼ hour sightseeing.*
The village church gives a good idea of the full joy of Rococo.

SOEST ★

Michelin map **202** 10 – *Local map p 227* – Pop 43 000

Soest, an agricultural market for the Westphalian Plain, has remained a mediaeval town with its circle of walls enclosing almost village style buildings and gardens haphazardly lining the twisting streets. **Pumpernickel**, the wholemeal rye bread which is baked for 24 hours and whose black slices are to be seen on many German breakfast tables, is made in the town.

■ MAIN SIGHTS *tour: 1½ hours*

Leave the car on the Markt where, among the half-timbered houses, may be seen the double gabled Im Wilden Mann (restaurant) (Y **X**). Walk along the Marktstrasse. The 16C **Zur Rose Haus** (**Z C**) decorated with multicoloured woodwork in the shape of a fan, stands at the corner of the Rosenstrasse. Go down the narrow Petristrasse on the left to the square on which stand the cathedral, the town hall and St. Peter's Church.

St. Patroclus' Church★ (Patroklidom). – The interest in this massive 11 and 12C Romanesque building lies entirely in the **west end★★** (Westwerk – *see p 23*) and the square **tower★★** which is perfectly balanced and is decorated only with blind arcades and blind rose windows. The two tiers of arcades which lighten the tower correspond to two series on the cubic base to the porch where the lower arcade has gracefully slender columns.
Walk along the north side of the cathedral and enter through the door opening on to the small Am Vreithof square. The **interior** has been completely restored: the frescoes in the chancel were repainted to the old Romanesque design in 1950; those in apse of the north transept (Mariechörchen) have been preserved. A fine 15C Crucifix stands upon the altar.
Cross the Vreithof, a picturesque market, to reach the shady banks of a pool (Grosser Teich). Go round this to the right and enter a small public garden (Theodor-Heuss-Park) which lies on the west bank. Return to the market and drive along the winding Walburger Strasse and the Ritterstrasse on the right to the Church of Our Lady of the Pastures.

Our Lady of the Pastures★ (Wiesenkirche). – The nave of this very light 14C Gothic hall-church is almost a perfect cube. The Virgin and Child, at the pier in the south doorway, is late 14C.

Interior. – *Open April to September, 9am to noon and 2.30 to 5.30pm; October to March, only on request, 10am to noon and 2 to 4pm; closed Sunday mornings and Mondays; apply to the sacristan: Herr Tomaschewski, 477 Soest, Widumgasse 1.* The 1520 window of the Last Supper above the north door gave the artist the opportunity of depicting local specialities – boar's head, ham, small jugs of beer and little rye loaves. On the same side the late 15C window nearest the apsidal chapel is of the Virgin appearing to St. Patroclus. The most important work of art is the 1525 **Aldegrever altarpiece★** of the Virgin between St. Agatha and St. Antony in the south apsidal chapel.

SOEST

Am Loerbach	Y 4	Hohe Gasse	Y 14	Magazingasse — Y 23
Am Vreithof	Y 6	Hospitalgasse	Z 15	Markt — Y
Bischofstraße	Z 7	Jakobitor	Z 17	Marktstraße — Z 24
Brüderstraße	Y	Katzengasse	Y 18	Nöttentor — Y 25
Damm	Z 10	Kolkstraße	Z 20	Oestinghauser Str. - Y 26
Am Großen Teich		Grandweg	Z	Kungelmarkt — Y 22	Petrikirchhof — Z 27
Am Kützelbach	Z 3	Grandweger Tor	Z 13	Lentzestraße	Y 22	Petristraße — Z 28

Propst-Nübel-Str.- Z 30
Puppenstraße — Z 31
Rathausstraße — Z 32
Ritterstraße — Y 33
Schültinger Straße - Y 34
Teichmühlengasse - Y 35
Thomätor — Z 36
Waisenhausstraße— Y 38
Walburger Straße— Y 39
Walburgertor — Y 40
Westenhellweg — Z 41
Wiesenstraße — Y 43
Wildemannsgasse - Y 45

■ ADDITIONAL SIGHTS

Church of St. Mary on the Hill (St. Maria zur Höhe) (YB). – This bizarre squat church of Romanesque origin has a flat chancel and a north apsidal chapel that is slightly out of line with the main building. It was converted into a hall in the 13C. Cross the old cemetery and enter through the north door; immediately on the right is the baptistery half hidden by short thick columns. The walls and roof are painted all over: look particularly, in the chancel, at the Virgin in Majesty surrounded by angels with wings stylised in the form of flames – a work painted at the time the church was built.

St. Nicholas' Chapel (Nikolaikapelle) (ZA). – *Apply to the cathedral presbytery to visit, Probst-Nübel-Gasse 1.*

In the chancel of this double-aisled chapel is the **St. Nicholas altarpiece★**, painted on a gold background in about 1400 by Konrad von Soest, a great name in Westphalian art *(see Bad Wildungen, p 259)*. St. Nicholas is shown as the patron of merchants and mariners.

Museum (Burghofmuseum) (ZM). – *Open: weekdays 10am to noon and 3 to 5pm; Sundays 11am to 1pm; closed Mondays.*

History and geography of the region.

Osthofentor (Y). – 16C fortified gateway, now isolated, with fine Gothic ornament.

SOLINGEN

Michelin map **202** 16 – Pop 172 000 – *Town plan in Michelin Red Guide Deutschland*

Solingen, whose knives and scissors are world famous, is one of the capitals of Europe for fine metalwork, an industry nowadays embracing much precision work.

The Blade Museum★ (Deutsches Klingenmuseum). – *North of the town in the Gräfrath suburb (by ① on the plan), Wuppertaler Strasse 160. Open 10am to 1pm and 3 to 5pm (8pm Fridays); closed Mondays; 0.50DM.*

The museum traces the history of side-arms (wonderful dress swords), table cutlery, surgical instruments, scissors, candle-snuffers and razors. Current designs are displayed on the first floor.

EXCURSION

Burg an der Wupper★. – *8 km - 5 miles – plus 1 hour sightseeing.* Leave Solingen by ③ on the plan; follow the Remscheid road for 2 km - 1 mile. Turn right. After crossing the enclosed Wupper Valley turn right and back towards Burg castle on its outstanding perched **site★**.

This former residence of the Dukes of Berg, who gave their name to the region, was rebuilt in the 19C and now houses the **Berg Land Museum** (Bergisches Museum). *Open 9am to 5.30pm (4.30pm 1 November to 15 March); closed Mondays 9am to 1pm and all Mondays in winter; 2DM.* Go round in the direction suggested and come out on to the parapet walk which leads to the keep. From the top there is a **view** deep down into the Wupper Valley where lies the closely compact and attractive village of Burg. The usual souvenir from the visit, which is a popular local excursion, is a giant pretzel which one hangs round one's neck.

SPEYER ★

Michelin map ██ 9 – *Local map p 215* – Pop 44 500
Town plan in Michelin Red Guide Deutschland

Speyer can be recognised from afar by its belfries, picturesquely grouped when seen from the Heidelberg road. The town stands on the banks of the Rhine where embanked arms of the river circle small islands or form crescent shaped points.

Speyer is in such an exposed position on the plain that few buildings have escaped damage by war over the years. As the town where the Diet *(p 206)* and the Imperial Council sat, it was annihilated by Louis XIV's troops in 1689. However, some idea of its past may be gained from the group of buildings formed by the tall tower of the Altpörtel, an old town gateway, the Maximilianstrasse and the Emperors' Cathedral.

The "Protestants". – The Edict of Worms of 1521 *(p 261)* was never enacted. In 1529 the Diet of Speyer confirmed the declarations of the Edict which caused the Lutherans to make a solemn protest – a fact commemorated at Speyer early this century with the building of the Neo-Gothic church, the Gedächtniskirche on the Bartholomäus–Weltz-Platz. The name "Protestant" derives from the Lutheran protest. The next year the followers of the Reformation drew up a profession of their beliefs at Augsburg *(p 52)*.

■ **SIGHTS** *time: 1½ hours*

Cathedral★★ (Dom). – *Open 1 April to 30 September, 9am to 6.30pm (Sundays 1.30 to 4.30pm); 1 October to 30 March, 9 to 11.30pm and 1.30 to 4.30pm (closed Sundays); 0.50DM. Guided tours, 9 to 11.30am and 1.30 to 4.30pm; apply to the chapter house, Dom-Platz 3; 1DM.*

The cathedral, which was founded by Konrad II in 1030 and remodelled at the end of the 11C, is a Romanesque basilica with four towers and two domes. Walk round the outside. There is an interesting view★★ of the east end from the approach to the Pagan Tower (Heidentürmchen).

Exterior. – An elegant dwarf gallery *(p 23)* runs round the nave and transept just below the roof; the finely carved capitals show a wide variety of motifs on the east side (park side) of the apse. Note on a half column of the blind arcades, in the centre, a worn 11C relief illustrating the Kingdom of Peace. The arches above the windows in the east transept show Lombard influence and, on the south side especially, are richly decorated with scrolls and palm leaves.

Interior. – Go in through the door in the west face which was rebuilt in the 19C. The statue of Rudolph of Habsburg stands on the right in the porch. The huge and well lit nave has groined vaulting with hammer beams. The main columns are engaged in pillars and are cut halfway with heavy capitals. The aisles with groined vaulting are even plainer. There is a good vista of the interior from the stairs in the south transept.

Transept★★ (Querschiff). – The transept is a masterpiece of unity and balance. Note the lantern tower and the octagonal dome on squinches. The lack of ornament brings out the natural decoration of the architecture, further enhanced by the materials used in its construction.

The Chapel of the Holy Sacrament (St. Afra Chapel), to the left before the north transept, is adorned with 15C sculpture: the Carrying of the Cross, the Annunciation.

The baptistery (St. Emmeramus' Chapel) before the south transept is square; eight groined vaults surround a two tier central rotunda.

Crypt★★★. – *Enter from the south aisle; 0.50DM.* This is the finest and the largest Romanesque crypt in Germany. Beneath the chancel and the transept, whose crossing is marked by four columns with splendid square capitals, Romanesque groined vaulting spreads out like a net supported by archstones cut alternately of pink and white limestone.

The 13C tombstone of Rudolph of Habsburg stands at the entrance to the impressive vault of the German Roman Emperors.

Palatinate Museum (Historisches Museum der Pfalz). – *Open 9am to noon and 2 to 5pm; closed 24 December to 1 January; 1DM.*

In gallery 5 is the "golden hat" of Schifferstadt dating from 12C BC and the most precious treasure in the Palatinate's historical collections.

A portrait of Liselotte, the Princess Palatine *(p 146)*, hangs on the stairs. The collections on the first floor cover the 16 to 19C and include outstanding Frankenthal porcelain (1755-99).

Wine Museum. – *In the cellars.* In the round room there is a bottle of still liquid wine from the 3C.

STADE

Michelin map ██ south of 5 – Pop 45 000

Stade has remained a small port handling wood, linked to the Elbe estuary by a navigable channel. When the town was under Swedish rule from 1648 to 1712 it was turned into a strongpoint and from those days it retains moats still filled with water. The two north-westerly bastions (left as you leave to go to Stadersand) now provide pleasant green open spaces.

The flat **Altes Land** beside the Elbe between Stade and Buxtehude is a countryside of cherry and apple orchards and lovely when the blossom is out *(10 May for the apple trees)*.

St. Cosmas Church (Cosmaekirche). – Enter by the east end. The 13 and 15C building with its heavy Baroque spire complete with onion bulb, rises above a picturesque old quarter where the wooden houses are bricked between the beams.

Inside, the 17C furnishings – organ, pulpit, copper chandeliers – are intact. The iron grilles in each doorway, which were wrought in 1670, were designed with imagination.

Walk a little beyond the church façade to the Hökerstrasse and follow it to the right where it twists to the Fischmarkt and the bridge (Hudebrücke) over the old port.

Old Port (Alter Hafen). – A winding basin is now almost deserted, leaving only a nostalgic scene of still water and rusting iron. The quay on the far side (Wasser West) has fine buildings upon it: the stone house at no 23 is Renaissance, the brick granary dates from 1700.

EXCURSION

Altes Land★. – *51 km - 32 miles – about 2 hours. Narrow twisting paved roads.* Leave Stade by the Hamburg road (no 73) from which you branch off left for the centre of Buxtehude.

Come out of Buxtehude by the **Jork** road which runs beside the winding Este embankment. After the picturesque village of Estebrügge turn left in Königreich towards Jork which you go right through to discover at the far end a series of thatched **farm houses★** (Bauernhäuser) with gables adorned with decorative brickwork. Stay on the right bank of the canal at Mittelnkirchen and cross the stream further down on the small weighbridge at Steinkirchen. Return to Stade.

STAFFELSEE

West of Murnau (Michelin map **987** west of 37) – *Local maps pp 42 and 44*

Set at the limit of the Alps and the Bavarian Plateau, the Staffelsee, with its deep bays, promontories and wooded islands, offers a striking picture of the upheavals caused by the moraines of the last glacial invasions. The motorist will get good views of this small lake by following the shore as closely as possible along the road from Uffing to Murnau.

The busy crossroads township of **Murnau** has two beaches laid out along the Staffelsee.

STARNBERGER SEE

Michelin map **987** 37 – *Local map p 40*

Starnberg Lake, which is also known as the Würmsee from the name of the river, the Würm, which drains out of it, stretches out over 20 km - 12 miles – in a setting of wooded banks interspersed by villas, castles and small resorts.

The Lake's Surroundings. – The popular road along the west shore, between Starnberg and Seeshaupt, goes through some trim little towns; brief views increase first of the lake whose banks are bordered with rushes and, later, in the Feldafing area of the Alps. Further south, the former Bernried monastery fits harmoniously into the landscape.

It was in **Berg** Castle (5 km - 3 miles – southeast of Starnberg – *not open to the public*), that the deposed Ludwig II of Bavaria was sent to pass his last hours *(p 221)*. However, the day after he arrived he went for a row on the lake and threw himself overboard, at the same time drowning the doctor who had accompanied him (13 June 1886).

Starnberg, with a pleasant lakeside promenade, stands at the foot of a former castle of the Dukes of Bavaria. **Tutzing** has a good view of the Alps and is more rural in character.

STEINAU

Michelin map **987** 25 6 km - 4 miles – south of Schlüchten – Pop 6 300

The Brothers Grimm, sons of a magistrate, grew up in Steinau. The walks they took as boys in the surrounding countryside influenced their tales *(p 157)*.

Castle. – *Open 10am to noon and 1 to 5pm (4pm November to February); closed Mondays; 1DM.*

The castle, a picturesque fortified group with two inner courts well defended by towers, has a square keep and three-storey oriel window. Inside is a memorial to the Brothers Grimm.

Tribunal (Hanauisches Amtshaus). – *No 80, Brüder-Grimm-Strasse.* The massive tribunal house in which the Brothers Grimm lived from 1791 to 1798 stands back attractively in a courtyard.

STEINHAUSEN

Michelin map **206** 7 – Pop 2 173

Steinhausen church, which was built by the Abbot of Schussenried *(p 229)* in the centre of a hamlet in Upper Swabia, bears the imprint of the great architect Zimmermann *(p 26)*.

Pilgrims' Church★ (Wallfahrtskirche). – *Tour: ¼ hour.* The building conceals a single oval aisle which is prolonged by a small chancel, again oval in shape. A crown of pillars supporting the inner shell of the vaulting mark the edge of a gallery which circles the building – pause a moment beneath the organ-loft to appreciate the sweeping lines. Stand in the centre of the aisle and you will have the illusion of being in a church of classical design with straight aisles.

The capitals, cornices and window embrasures are carved with birds and insects or flowers with heavy corollas. The overall impression is of an artist with an intimate knowledge of nature.

STEINHUDER MEER

Michelin map **987** 15 – 31 km - 19 miles – northwest of Hanover

This lake extending over 3 000 ha but nowhere deeper than 3 m attracts sailing enthusiasts (11½ sq miles and 10 ft). A nearby ridge, the Rehburger Berge which the Loccum–Berg-kirchen–Wunstorf road follows more or less along its crest, enables you to see the lake from end to end. In the centre is the man-made island on which stands the Wilhelmstein Fortress, built by the Count Wilhelm of Schaumburg-Lippe *(p 92)* in 1757 and the seat of a military school famous in the early 19C as the training centre of Prussian officers.

One can walk beside the lake in the town of Steinhude. With its pleasure harbour and fishing grounds it attracts many visitors who also come to taste the local smoked eel.

STRAUBING

Michelin map **987** southeast of 27 – Pop 45 000

Straubing, a small and still agricultural market town in the Gäuboden, the granary of Bavaria, is washed by the Danube as it winds on its course.

Stadtplatz★. – In the centre of the main square stands an original 13C tower topped by five pointed turrets – last reminder of a town hall. This tower also closes the vista which begins on the Theresienplatz side with gabled houses, a lovely Renaissance fountain and the column of the Trinity adorned with swirling statuary. The whole effect reminds you that you are nearing Austria.

St. James' Church (Jakobskirche). – This huge hall-church was built of brick near the Stadtplatz in the 15C. Slender round pillars support the arches which meet but have no rib tracery, above the nave. Rare in Bavaria is the almost total lack of Baroque decoration.

The shuttered altarpiece at the high altar, bought in 1590, comes from a Nuremberg church; within it are 16C statuettes including, in the centre, the Virgin, and on the far left, Mary Magdalene. In the first chapel to the left of the axial chapel is the admirable tomb of Ulrich Kastenmayr (1430) wearing the uniform of a magistrate of the town.

St. Peter's Church. – *1.5 km - 1 mile – plus ½ hour sightseeing.* Leave by road no 20 towards the Danube; turn right just before the bridge. St. Peter's is the second church.

The old burial ground surrounding the Romanesque church contains numerous funeral crosses made of wrought iron of which Straubing was once a manufacturing centre. Ask the caretaker to open *(1DM)* the Chapel of the Dance of Death and that of **Agnes Bernauer**, a touching and popular figure in Germany. Agnes, a young commoner from Augsburg, was married secretly to the son of a Duke of Bavaria but fell a victim to the vindictiveness of her father-in-law who had her condemned for sorcery and thrown into the Danube in 1435.

Stuttgart, since the 15C, has gradually supplanted the old towns of the Staufen patrimony, Cannstatt, Waiblingen and Esslingen, and spread across the depression which opens to the northeast on to the Neckar. The capital town has an undulating **site★★** which is highly original. Beyond an encircling belt of trees lies its large suburb and overlooking all is a densely wooded plateau. The city is proud of the vineyards on the slopes overlooking the business quarters; grapes are harvested within 250 m of the main railway station.

The town, where historical monuments occupied only a small space even before the last war, was rebuilt in the fever of economic recovery.

Although the Mercedes star lights up the city sky the car industry and its affiliated industries absorb only a part of the city's life and energy. Stuttgart, which lies on the canalised Neckar and acts as a terminus for the great fleet of Rhine barges, is also a book metropolis and a centre of production for electrical, photographic and optical equipment.

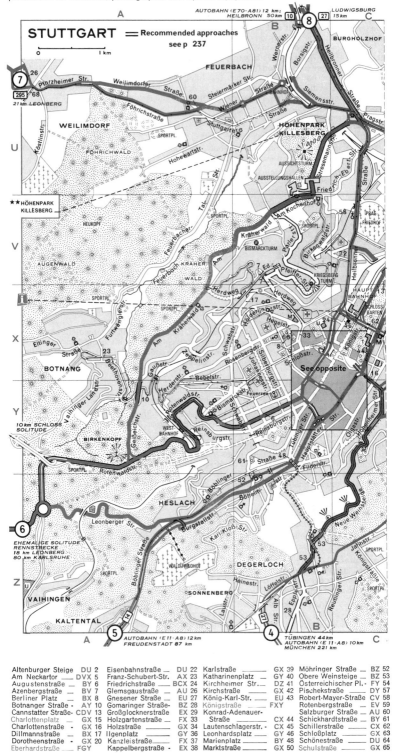

Altenburger Steige	DU 2	Eisenbahnstraße	DU 22	Karlstraße	GX 39	Möhringer Straße	BZ 52
Am Neckartor	DVX 5	Franz-Schubert-Str.	AX 23	Katharinenplatz	GY 40	Obere Weinsteige	BZ 53
Augustenstraße	BY 6	Friedrichstraße	BCX 24	Kirchheimer Str.	DZ 41	Österreichischer Pl.	FY 54
Azenbergstraße	BV 7	Glemsgaustraße	AU 26	Kirchstraße	GX 42	Pischekstraße	DY 57
Berliner Platz	BX 8	Gnesener Straße	EU 27	König-Karl-Str.	EU 43	Robert-Mayer-Straße	CV 58
Botnanger Straße	AY 10	Gomaringer Straße	BZ 28	Königstraße	FXY	Rotenbergstraße	EV 59
Cannstatter Straße	CDV 13	Großglocknerstraße	EX 29	Konrad-Adenauer-		Salzburger Straße	AU 60
Charlottenplatz	GX 15	Holzgartenstraße	FX 33	Straße	CX 44	Schickhardtstraße	BY 61
Charlottenstraße	GX 16	Holzstraße	GX 34	Lautenschlagerstr.	CX 45	Schillerstraße	CX 62
Dillmannstraße	BX 17	Ilgenplatz	GY 36	Leonhardsplatz	GY 46	Schloßplatz	GX 63
Dorotheenstraße	GX 20	Kanzleistraße	FX 37	Marienplatz	AY 48	Schönestraße	DU 64
Eberhardstraße	FGY	Kappelbergstraße	EX 38	Marktstraße	GX 50	Schulstraße	GX 65

RECOMMENDED APPROACHES *(see the routes on the map)*

-approaching from the west along the motorway (driving from Karlsruhe, Strasbourg, etc.). – At the "Stuttgart triangle" (Autobahndreieck Stuttgart) fork, take the Heilbronn road; leave the motorway immediately at the Stuttgart-West-Leonberg exit. The road through the woods brings you in by the Rotenwaldstrasse (**AY**);

-approaching from the south. – If possible take the road from Tübingen (Stuttgart-Süd-Degerloch exit from the motorway) which, after Degerloch, drops down into Stuttgart by the Neue Weinsteige (**BZ**), a *corniche* road which runs above a vineyard;

-approaching from the north. – Follow the line of the Killesberg Park *(p 238)*, before descending to the centre. The Eduard-Pfeiffer-Strasse, at the foot of the Kriegsberg Tower (**BV**) affords a bird's-eye view of the station area.

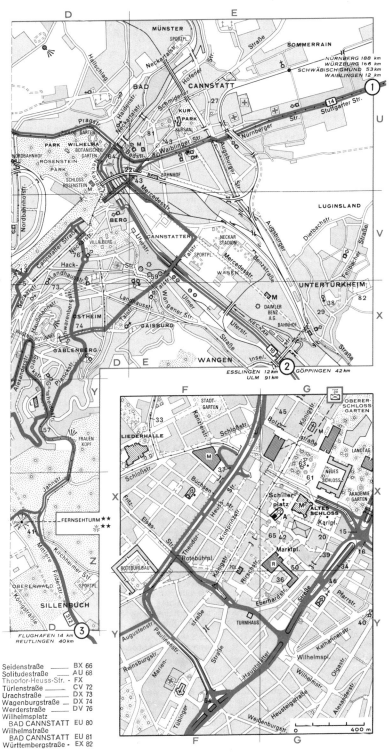

Seidenstraße	BX	66
Solitudestraße	AU	68
Theodor-Heuss-Str. -	FX	
Türlenstraße	CV	72
Urachstraße	DX	73
Wagenburgstraße	DX	74
Werderstraße	DV	76
Wilhelmsplatz BAD CANNSTATT	EU	80
Wilhelmstraße BAD CANNSTATT	EU	81
Württembergstraße •	EX	82

237

HISTORICAL NOTES

The Princes of Württemberg, who rose successively from counts to be dukes and kings, left the mark of their subtle and sagacious temperaments upon the rise in political power of a state which began as the Swabian heritage of the Hohenstaufens, situated between the Neckar and the Danube. Under Napoleon the creation of the Kingdom of Württemberg in 1886 helped to transform the former duchy into a truly independent region. The State (Land), formed in 1951 by uniting Baden-Baden and Württemberg, is one of the most stable in Federal Germany today with Stuttgart, the capital, contributing largely to its prosperity.

Two Major Figures in the Automobile World. – **Gottlieb Daimler** (1834-1900), an engineer who lived in Bad Cannstatt *(see below)*, pioneered the adaptation of the petrol engine to vehicular propulsion. Collaboration with the brilliant engineer, Wilhelm Maybach, enabled him to develop a vertical-type engine in 1883.

Carl Benz (1844-1929), unlike Daimler, was more interested in producing a motor with a universal application than a new engine. Born and brought up in Karlsruhe, he envisaged a whole constructive unit, a complete motor vehicle which he worked out himself in every detail at Mannheim and was able to begin manufacturing in series. In 1899, Benz sold his 2 000th car and thus became the world's leading car manufacturer.

In 1901 Daimler put on the market a car christened Mercedes, the name of the daughter of its most important foreign agent. The name was worth a fortune.

Daimler and Benz amalgamated in 1926.

■ **MAIN SIGHTS** *tour: 3 hours*

Television Tower★★ (Fernsehturm). – *Lift: 2.50DM.*

The tower rises out of the woods which stand south of the town, on the edge of the plateau. The hollow concrete shaft has thin walls: 10 m - 30 ft – above the ground they are 30 cm thick and higher still less than 20 cm – 11¾ and 8 inches. They support a glazed "basket", a restaurant, at 150 m - 446 ft. The tips of the antennae reach 217 m - 692 ft.

The visitor on the upper platform stands some 400 m - 1 300 ft – above the centre of the city. In clear weather this **aerial view★★** is completed by a panorama of the heights of the Swabian Jura.

Killesberg Park★★ (Höhenpark Killesberg). – *Open April to October, 8am to midnight; 1.50DM.*

Circle the park on a height to the north of the town in the miniature railway before walking beside the pools, the brilliant flowerbeds and ascending the belvedere tower.

■ **ADDITIONAL SIGHTS**

The Heart of the Old Town (GX). – The old town of the Dukes of Württemberg has as its centre the **Schillerplatz**, named after the statue of Schiller (1839) by Thorwaldsen which stands upon it. The square looks as it used to do since the restoration of the Old Castle and the Collegiate Church whose east end faces on to it.

Old Castle (Altes Schloss) (GX). – The quadrilateral building flanked by round towers was largely built in the 16C. It encloses a Renaissance courtyard around which are three tiers of galleries resting on fluted pilasters. It houses the Württemberg Regional Museum.

Württemberg Regional Museum★ (Württembergisches Landesmuseum) (M²). – *Open 10am to 4pm (8pm Wednesdays); closed Mondays.*

In the **prehistoric and ancient history section★★** a map shows the Roman occupation and the fortified border line, the *Limes (p 19)*. Among the mediaeval art objects are seven Stations of the Cross carved in 1515 by Jörg Syrlin the Younger for Zwiefalten Church *(p 266)*.

Collegiate Church (Stiftskirche) (GX A). – The best feature is the fine 1490-1531 belfry-porch with superimposed polygonal copings. When the church was rebuilt, the nave and the aisles were united in a single chamber and covered with a panelled ceiling. On the left in the chancel is the commemorative monument erected in 1580 by Duke Ludwig III in honour of his ancestors who appear in armour against a Renaissance background of arcades and terminal figures.

Stuttgart State Gallery★ (Staatsgalerie) (CX M¹). – *Open 10am to 4pm (9pm Tuesdays and Thursdays); closed Mondays.*

The collection consists of old masters (14 and 16C Swabian painters, Italian and Dutch masters) and a rich modern art department of modern French paintings, German Expressionists and Bauhaus *(p 26)*. Look at the canvases of Willi Baumeister (1889-1955) and Oskar Schlemmer (1888-1943) who helped to make Stuttgart, their native city, a town of art. There are also huge sketches (1929) by Schlemmer for wall paintings which were destroyed by Hitler in his crusade against what he condemned as "degenerate art".

Liederhalle★ (FX). – *To visit phone 29 13 67. No visits in July and August.*

The most outstanding feature of this 1956 asymmetrical block of buildings is the exterior, where the coldness of the basic concrete has been brightened by the use of glazed brick, quartz and mosaic. The Liederhalle consists of three concert halls equipped with the latest acoustic devices. Three different events can be held simultaneously without disturbing each other acoustically (conferences, balls, banquets, recitals, etc.).

Birkenkopf (AY). – ¾ *hour on foot Rtn.* Leave the car at the junction of the Rotenwaldstrasse and the Geisseichstrasse *(car parks)* and climb to the top by a wide spiral rise. The height has been raised by adding debris from the wartime ruins of the town: the summit, on which stands a commemorative Cross, consists of a heap of stone blocks amongst which lie the carved cornices from destroyed official buildings. The **panorama★★** shows clearly the centre of the town, the new tower blocks and the unbroken green belt round Stuttgart.

Wilhelma Park (DU). – *Open 7am to 6pm September to April, 8am to 4pm; 3.50DM.* This zoological and botanical garden also has tropical plant **hothouses★** (Gewächshäuser).

Bad Cannstatt Spa Park★ (Kurpark) (EU). – The old town of Bad Cannstatt has become a suburb of Stuttgart but has retained its functions as a spa. Its abundant mineral springs provide cures and fill three swimming pools. The park lies behind the casino (Kursaal).

Daimler-Benz Automobile Museum (EX M). – *Temporarily closed for rearrangement.*

The museum is in the main Stuttgart-Untertürkheim factory. The history of the firm and the early cars and engines occupy the ground floor. The first floor shows the various purposes since their amalgamation in 1926 which Daimler-Benz motors serve: cars, ships, aeroplanes and railways. The second floor contains the prizes of nearly 60 years of car racing – a phase only ended in 1955 when "Mercedes" decided to abandon the sport.

EXCURSIONS

Solitude Castle*. – *10 km - 6 miles. Temporarily closed, being restored.* Leave Stuttgart by the Solitude road (west on the plan) (**AY**); bear right after 9 km - 6 miles.

The central oval building of the castle stands on an arcaded base, which gives it height and majesty in relation to the outbuildings which lie in an arc around it. The building, whose oval plan was in accordance with prevailing taste *(see details of country houses on p 25)* and discreet pomp was inspired by ancient Greek architecture, was erected from 1764 to 1769 under the aegis of the French court architect, La Guépière. The décor of the central rotunda chamber (Weisser Saal) and the small marble room are in the Neo-Classical tradition. The other apartments are panelled and have a French-style Rococo decoration.

Friedrich I of Württemberg's desk, hollowed out because of the stoutness of its owner, whom Napoleon ridiculed cruelly, is on view.

From the rooms just below the dome, one can see clearly the 14 km alley - 9 mile – running dead straight across the now divided plain from the Solitude to Ludwigsburg Castle.

Neckar Valley*. – *Round tour of 71 km - 44 miles – about 4 hours (excluding a tour of Ludwigsburg). During the season (daily from May to mid-October) this excursion can be made in a day by pleasure steamer (embarkation at Wilhelma, Bad Cannstatt). Information at the Neckar–Personen–Schiffahrt, ℡ (0711) 54 10 73, 54 10 74.*

Leave Stuttgart by ⑧, the Ludwigsburg road.

Ludwigsburg*. – *Description p 169.*

At the end of the main street in Ludwigsburg turn left and follow road no 27 towards Heilbronn. Where this road crosses the Enz below Besigheim, you get a view of Ludwigsburg town on its height.

Besigheim. – *Tour:* ½ *hour.* The old town is packed tightly between the two massive round towers which formerly marked its boundary on the crest separating the Enz and Neckar Rivers which meet soon afterwards.

Leave the car on a square at the foot of the lower tower, and climb the former main street along the crest to the Marktplatz which is adorned with a 15C half-timbered town hall and a fountain. The street continues to the church which has an interesting Gothic chancel and 1520 altarpiece dedicated to St. Cyriacus.

Coming out of Besigheim, leave road no 27 when it reaches the valley floor and bear right up the Neckar Valley which runs through vineyards on its way to Hessigheim – this is where the very pleasant Württemberg red wines come from. 500 yds before reaching this village bear left and after 500 yds turn into a rising surfaced vineyard road. Leave the car at the foot of some steps.

Hessigheim Rocks* (Felsengärten). – ½ *hour on foot Rtn.* The edge of the plateau lies at the top of the steps. Walk left until the cliff breaks away into individual rock pinnacles.

View* *(access: 0.20DM)* of the Neckar bend, the outer bank covered with vineyards.

Return to the road through the valley as far as Pleidelsheim where you turn left towards Steinheim. 3 km - 2 miles – from Pleidelsheim turn right towards Marbach.

Marbach am Neckar. – *Museum open all the year round, 9am to 5pm; closed 24, 25 and 26 December; time:* ¾ *hour; 1DM.*

This small town cultivates the memory of the poet Schiller *(p 32)*, its most illustrious son. The huge **Schiller National Museum*** rises, like a castle, above the valley. Portraits, casts, engravings, manuscripts and first editions are on display not only of Schiller (1759-1805) but also of many other Swabian writers who lived between the 16 and the 19C.

This literary pilgrimage may be completed by a visit to Schiller's **birthplace** (Schiller-Geburtshaus), a modest half-timbered house *(open April to September, 8am to noon and 1 to 6pm, the rest of the year, 9am to noon and 1 to 5pm; 0.80DM),* where the Schiller family lived.

Leave Marbach by the Ludwigsburg road to return to Stuttgart.

The SWABIAN JURA ★ (SCHWÄBISCHE ALB)
Michelin maps **987** 35, 36 and **206** 3 to 5, 15 to 17

The high limestone plateaux of the Swabian Jura, lying between the Black Forest and the crystalline massifs of the Bohemian ranges, form the "roof" of southern Germany as they follow the watershed line between the Rhine (Neckar Basin) and the Danube.

The Swabian Jura drop 400 m - 1 300 ft – to the Neckar Basin at their northwest. Mountains detached from the main block and themselves forming natural fortresses were chosen as castle sites by families that were to acquire great glory and dynastic status, such as the Hohenstaufens and the Hohenzollerns. The hinterland's rugged reputation was based on the barrenness of the countryside, the harshness of the climate and the scarcity of water; it is now less valid since the land has been improved or afforested. Vast horizons and subterranean beauty afford possibilities for tourist development.

An Ingenious Race. – As in many mountain regions the long winters gave rise in the Swabian Jura to many cottage industries. In the 19C under the influence of pastors, philanthropic teachers and small inventors, the northern fringe of the massif sprouted factories and workshops: cotton at Reutlingen, hosiery at Tailfingen and Burladingen, turbines and hydraulic transmission gear at Heidenheim, precision balances at Balingen and Ebingen, cutlery at Geislingen, toys at Göppingen and Giengen an der Brenz and harmonicas and accordions at Trossingen.

Tour. – Under the insignia of the common thistle (Silberdistel), a **Swabian Jura Road** (Schwäbische Albstrasse) has been built from Trossingen (south of Rottweil) and Tuttlingen to Nördlingen (or Aalen). The road is marked by blue-green arrows and in the Reutlingen area particularly has numerous car parks which serve as belvederes as well as lay-bys. The itineraries below follow certain parts of this road.

① ★FROM TUTTLINGEN TO SIGMARINGEN by the Danube River
48 km - 30 miles – about 2½ hours – Local map p 240

Mühlheim. – To get a general view of this attractive fortified market town aligned along a terrace with a small white castle with domed towers as its final outpost, go round the town by the north, taking, at first, the by-road towards Kolbingen.

Knopfmacherfelsen**. – ¼ *hour on foot Rtn.* Leave the car in the car park near the Knopfmacher Hotel (Berghaus) and make your way down to a belvedere placed at the tip of a spur. The **view****, on the left, extends along the valley as far as Beuron Abbey. On the right Bronnen Castle stands on the summit of curious breached rocks.

Beuron Abbey. – *The abbey buildings are not open to the public. The meadowland basin attracted the builders of the abbey to this spot, which is now also a small but busy tourist centre.*

The flourishing Benedictine congregation at Beuron contributed greatly to the revival of monastic life, liturgy and especially the Gregorian chant in Germany (high mass at 11.15am on weekdays, 10am Sundays and holidays; vespers at 6pm on weekdays, 3pm Sundays and holidays). Pilgrims make for the chapel (Gnadenkapelle) abutting on the Baroque abbey church. The chapel is in the Beuron style, a late 19C school of ecclesiastical architecture influenced by Byzantine art.

Wildenstein Castle. – *7 km - 4 miles – by the Worndorf road which you leave after 1 km to bear left for Leibertingen. From here there are signposts along a good road to Wildenstein.*

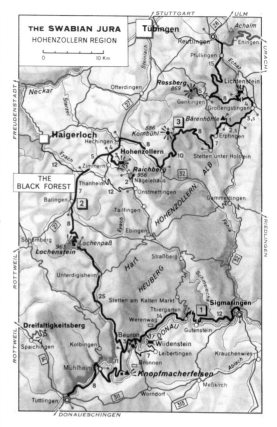

THE SWABIAN JURA
HOHENZOLLERN REGION

Two moats and a forward defence system consisting of two towers linked by a long wall on the plateau side, protected this small citadel commanding the Danube. Below Beuron the road follows the **valley*** past the foot of the Wildenstein and Werenwag fortresses which are built upon the rock.

As you approach Sigmaringen, the cliffs give place to rock needles providing an extraordinary landscape between Thiergarten and Gutenstein.

Sigmaringen*. – *Description p 232.*

② FROM BEURON TO HOHENZOLLERN CASTLE
51 km - 32 miles – about 2 hours – Local map above

Beuron Abbey. – *Description above.*

The road cuts right across the Grosser Heuberg, a bare, rolling plateau where the Swabian Jura reach a height of nearly 1 000 m - 3 000 ft. The road descends through the Lochenpass, into the Balingen-Hechingen Depression arriving at the foot of the Hohenzollern Castle.

Lochenstein*. – *½ hour on foot Rtn.* Leave the car in the Lochenpass car park. Climb up left (west) to the Lochenstein summit which is surmounted by a Cross. From the rock edge there is a **view*** of the Balingen and Hechingen Depression with Hohenzollern Castle away on the horizon.

> **Haigerloch**.** – *12 km - 7½ miles. Description p 135.*
>
> **Raichberg*.** – *14 km - 8½ miles – plus ½ hour on foot Rtn.* Turn left at Onstmettingen into the road signposted to the Nägelhaus Hotel. Leave the car at the hotel and walk past a stone tower on your right, straight across the fields to a clump of pines which marks the edge of the plateau from where there is a **view**** of the downward sweep of the Swabian Jura and, in particular, of Hohenzollern Castle, slightly below and some two miles away.

Hohenzollern Castle*. – *Description p 152.*

③ FROM HOHENZOLLERN CASTLE TO REUTLINGEN
73 km - 47 miles – about 3½ hours – Local map above

The drive across the plateau provides an opportunity to visit some caves, Lichtenstein Castle and, on the Genkingen-Pfullingen section of the road, to discover the north face of the Swabian Jura, cut into promontories and preceded in the plain by such foothills as the Achalm.

Hohenzollern Castle*. – *Description p 152.*

Kornbühl. – *¼ hour on foot Rtn.* The 16C pilgrimage chapel, on one of the mounds (alt 886 m - 2 907 ft) which rise from the Heufeld plateau, overlooks a wide, peaceful **countryside***.

> **Bärenhöhle.** – *1 km - ½ mile, plus ½ hour sightseeing (15 March to 30 October, 8am to 6pm; 1 November to 14 March, only Sundays 9am to 5pm; 2DM).* The main chamber in this Bear Cave contains well preserved concretions.

Lichtenstein Castle. – *Open 1 April to 31 October, 8.30am to noon and 1 to 5.45pm; 1 November to 31 March, only Saturdays and Sundays 9am to noon and 1 to 5pm; time: ½ hour; 1.50DM.* Lichtenstein Castle, built on a rock spur defended by a natural cleft, is one of the most popular castles in Württemberg. It was completely redesigned in the "troubadour style" in 1842. Before crossing the bridge and passing through the entrance bear right and make first for two belvederes: one overlooks the Echaz Valley, the other the castle.

> **Rossberg*.** – *5 km - 3 miles – plus ¼ hour sightseeing.* From the belvedere tower on this height *(access from the hotel)*, there is a remarkable **view*** of the Swabian Jura range from the Achalm foothill (above Reutlingen) to Hohenzollern Castle.

④ *FROM REUTLINGEN TO THE MOTORWAY (Mülhausen access road)

60 km - 37 miles – about 3 hours – Local map below

The hilly road takes one over the Swabian Jura.

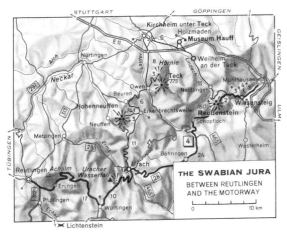

Urach Waterfall. – $\frac{1}{4}$ *hour on foot Rtn.* The falls are attractive, less on account of their volume which is insignificant in summer, than their "end of the world" setting.

Leave the car some 100 m beyond a log-built bus shelter (Reutlingen-Urach side of the road) and make for a belvedere signposted "Aussichtspunkt 350 m" at the top of a cliff. To reach the top of the fall *(somewhat strenuous walk going up – 1½ hours on foot Rtn)* leave the belvedere path to take the path marked "Wasserfall" through the woods.

Continue to a shaded esplanade (rustic café).

The rapid descent to Urach affords a bird's-eye view of the town, deep in the Erms Valley.

Urach. – In this pleasant but tightly enclosed town, the visitor will find, especially around the **Marktplatz**, the half-timbered houses which are so rare on this plateau.

Reussenstein Castle*. – $\frac{3}{4}$ *hour on foot Rtn from the itinerary road from Schopfloch (from the alternative route: bear right in the pass dividing Neidlingen and Wiesensteig).*

Leave the car on the edge of a wood (car park) and make for the escarpment edge to see the austere **setting**** of Reussenstein Castle dominating the end of the Neidlingen combe. From the belvedere built into the castle ruins, there is a **view*** of the combe and the Teck Plain.

> **Alternative route by way of Kirchheim unter Teck.** – *Extra distance: 16 km - 10 miles (excluding the access roads to Hohenneuffen and Teck).*
>
> **Hohenneuffen.** – *3 km - 2 miles – from Erkenbrechtsweiler, plus about ½ hour walking and sightseeing.* This fortress (alt 743 m - 2 438 ft), although dismantled in 1802, still has the monumental appearance of a 17C citadel.
>
> **Teck Castle.** – *3 km - 2 miles – from Owen to the Hörnle car park, plus ½ hour on foot Rtn.* An inn and a tower belvedere have been erected on the scarcely extant remains of the castle which has been in ruins since the 16C. From the tower top *(0.50DM; closed Tuesdays)*, the **panorama*** includes the three Kaiserberge *(p 229)*, the Black Forest and the Odenwald.
>
> **Kirchheim unter Teck.** – The half-timbered **town hall** (1724) stands at the main crossroads.
>
> **Holzmaden.** – *Follow the arrows to the Hauff Museum (tour: ½ hour).* The **Hauff Museum*** *(open 9am to noon and 1 to 5pm (4pm weekdays November to February); closed Mondays; 2DM)* contains extraordinary fossilised saurian skeletons embedded in layers of schist which date from approximately 140 million years ago. Outstanding are two ichthyosauri and some immense sea lilies belonging to the animal world.
>
> **Weilheim an der Teck.** – The beautiful Gothic Protestant **church** is abundantly ornamented with mural paintings, some of which are early 16C. The artistic value is unequal but all have a fresh character. The intricately worked pulpit dates from 1500.

Wiesensteig. – This market town crowds its half-timbered houses below the motorway.

SYLT Island ★★

Michelin map 987 4

The Frisian Island of Sylt, the most northerly point of German territory.

The landscape is varied: round Kampen, Westerland and Morsum the agricultural appearance of the countryside reveals its Geest origin *(p 128)*, increased in area to the southeast by the Marschen which have been reclaimed from the sea. On the seaward side of the island, an immense beach of fine sand runs for miles, passing, between Kampen and Wenningstadt, at the foot of small cliffs (Rotes Kliff) to join the continuous line of dunes south of Westerland. The whole island is a holiday setting where sea, sand and light reign supreme. Nudist camps have been established on certain beaches.

The towns and roads on the island are not accustomed to motor traffic (regulated in certain areas) and driving speed should therefore be considerably reduced.

Access by Rail. – Train car ferries leave Niebüll and cross to the island on the Hindenburgdamm causeway. *Frequency of service: 6 to 16 departures according to the season (no advance booking). Fare: from 35DM single for the car; free for the passengers.*

Access by Car Ferry. – Boat ferries ply between Havneby (Danish Island of Römö – accessible by road) and List at the north end of Sylt.

Frequency of service: 11 to 16 crossings a day in summer, 8 to 10 in winter; Rtn fare 31 to 39DM for the car plus 4.50DM per person. Information and reservations: Havneby (Denmark) ☎ (00454) 73 53 03; in Germany: Navis, Spaldingstrasse 1B, Hamburg, ☎ 24 81 41.

Westerland**. – This is the largest and perhaps most elegant German seaside resort. The Kurpromenade, a mile along the seashore, is always lively with people while below the sea beats magnificently at its foundations.

Keitum. – Keitum remains an old Friesland village. Walk behind the "Louise-Schröder-Heim" institute towards the coast and a low cliff (bench) – the pleasantly shady **site*** of the **Keitumer Kliff**. The horizon is lost in mud flats and the sea between the island and the mainland.

The TAUNUS *

Michelin map 204 4, 5

The Taunus, which is limited in extent but at the Grosser Feldberg reaches a greater height, 880 m - 2 887 ft – than any of the other Rhineland Schist Massifs (p 13), is wrapped in wonderful forests. The mineral springs which have been developed into spas on the massif's periphery (Bad Ems, Wiesbaden, Bad Homburg, Bad Soden, Bad Schwalbach, Schlangenbad) and its proximity to Frankfurt have promoted its development as a recreational centre.

*FROM BAD HOMBURG TO WIESBADEN

58 km - 36 miles – about 3½ hours – Local map below

Bad Homburg★. – *Description p 153.*
The great attraction of this drive lies in the density of the oak and beech woods of the Upper Taunus, particularly lovely during the climb from Oberursel to Sandplacken.

Grosser Feldberg★★. – *Tour: ¼ hour.* Leave the car in one of the parks near the summit. The Grosser Feldberg is an important telecommunications centre. From the belvedere tower *(ascent: 0.40DM – 167 difficult steps)* there is an immense **panorama★★**, northwest to the Westerwald, northeast to the Wetterau Depression whose course is followed by the Hamburg Motorway and south to the Lower Main Plain cut into by Frankfurt (the Henninger brewery tower is

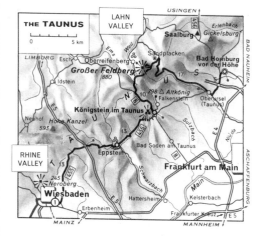

discernible) and its satellite towns. Feudal ruins – Oberreifenberg and Königstein – add character to the foreground.

Königstein im Taunus★. – *Tour: ¾ hour.* Leave the car in the centre of the town in the town hall square *(parking fee). Castle open: 8am (9am in winter) to 7pm (4pm in winter); 1DM.*
The Königstein **fortress★** (Burgruine), standing on a height well isolated from the main Taunus slope, is a feudal ruin with impressive lower quarters – 16C round bastions and 17C projecting defences. The grass covered terraces invite one to linger, as does the twisting path, through the fortifications to the keep. Climb the keep *(154 steps)* to get a bird's-eye **view** of the small town. In the distance can be seen the Henninger Tower – a Frankfurt landmark. The Falkenstein tower stands out on the mountainside as do the many towers and antennae on the Grosser Feldberg.

Eppstein. – The town is in a boxed and wild setting. Go to the centre and take the narrow main street, where there is a **perspective★** of the surroundings from the tower of the fortified castle.

Wiesbaden★★. – *Description p 258.*

The TEUTOBURGER WALD

Michelin map 987 14, 15

The Teutoburger Wald heights and the parallel line of the Wiehengebirge hills bound a fertile depression which extends from Detmold to Osnabrück.

The raised mass itself separates two plains – the great German-Polish Plain to the north and the Westphalian Plain to the south – giving an impression of height greater than the actual 500 m - 1 500 ft – of the hills.

The Teutoburger Wald near Paderborn and Detmold is thickly covered with fine deciduous trees and includes two popular sights: the Externsteine Rocks and the Arminius or Hermann Monument.

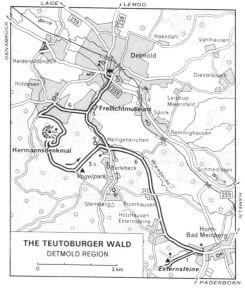

The Victory of Arminius. – In early Christian times the Roman legions stationed in Germany were under the command of Varus, a man schooled in Syria, who undertook to control the area by the brutal methods he had used so successfully before. The local people gathered round Arminius, the son of one of their chiefs. Arminius (or Hermann), who was Roman by culture and upbringing, succeeded in the difficult task of uniting the tribes living in what are now the areas of Westphalia and Hesse. He decided against meeting the enemy in open battle but drew the Roman army into the inner fastnesses of the Teutoburger Wald where he annihilated it in AD 9.

In the 19C with the dawn of German nationalism, Arminius was named a hero, the liberator of his country from foreign oppression and, above all, the precursor of German unity.

■ SETTINGS AND SIGHTS

Open Air Museum* (Freilichtmuseum). – *Open 1 April to 31 October 10am to 6pm; closed Mondays; 2DM.*

Here are grouped farms of southern Germany. The main house where peasants and animals lived together *(see illustration and text p 30)*, staff quarters, and dependencies have all been rebuilt and equipped with furniture, utensils and tools – a rural atmosphere of the past reigns.

Arminius Monument* (Hermannsdenkmal). – *See approach roads on the map on p 242; some have one-way sections. Tour: ¼ hour.*

The sword of vengeance can be seen from afar, brandished by the hero on the monument which was completed in 1875 and stands on a natural wooded elevation near the spot on which the battle is presumed to have been fought. A round colonnaded building forms the base for the gigantic statue, made of beaten copper, of the armed Arminius (statue height: 16 m plus a further 7 m for the sword – 52 ft and 23 ft).

There is a **panorama*** of the surrounding forest, the town of Detmold and the Weser hills (Weserbergland), from the gallery *(75 steps – access: summer, 8.30am to 5pm; winter, 9am to 4pm; 0.50DM)*.

The narrow winding road leads to an **ornithological park** (Vogelpark) where birds live in cages and at liberty. *Open 1 April to 1 November, 9am to 6pm; 2.50DM.*

Externsteine*. – *Tour: about ½ hour; 0.50DM.*

This group of limestone rocks, isolated in a lovely forest **setting*** beside a lake, was, in ancient times, a place of worship of the German people and later, in the Middle Ages, a Christian pilgrimage.

In the 11C a replica of the Holy Places of Jerusalem was constructed for the benefit of the pilgrims. The most extraordinary sight is the 12C **low relief**** of the Descent from the Cross which was carved into the living rock – the largest on the right (1). This relief is a rare example in Germany of Byzantine influenced Romanesque sculpture. To the right of the low relief is the lower troglodyte chapel (2), an evocation of St. Helen's Chapel or the Chapel of Adam beneath Golgotha. It was consecrated in 1115.

On the left, on the other side of the opening, at the foot of a thinner

(After a photo by Klocke Verlag)

The Externsteine.

rock, is an open air pulpit. The staircase (3) beside the pulpit leads to the upper chapel (4), which presumably was constructed as a copy of the Calvary Chapel on the Golgotha heights.

At the end of the path beside the water, a single block of stone, hollowed out in the form of a tomb, is intended to represent the Holy Sepulchre. A hermit's cell has been burrowed out of the rock above.

Tecklenburg*. – *Access and description p 201.*

TIEFENBRONN ★

Michelin map 206 13 – Pop 3 500

The Gothic village church contains precious works of art.

Church (Pfarrkirche). – *April to October, 9.30 to 11.30am and 1.30 to 5pm, Sundays 11am to noon and 1 to 4pm; the rest of the year, apply at the presbytery, 9.30 to 11.30am and 1.30 to 3.30pm, Sundays 1 to 3pm; 0.50DM.*

The whole church is worth looking at carefully with its 15 and 16C altarpieces and the tombstones placed in the chapels. The oustanding item is the 1431 **Lucas Moser altarpiece**** in the south aisle.

The master himself only painted the outside of the doors. The whole piece, however, has perfect unity. It illustrates the legend of Mary Magdalene: on the tympanum is the Feast at Bethany; in the centre, the crossing of the Mediterranean from Palestine to Provence with Martha, Lazarus, Maximinus and Cédoine, then the stay at Marseilles where the saints had no lodging and Mary Magdalene appeared before the town governor in a dream and, finally, the Magdalene's last communion. On the predella Christ is depicted between the Wise and the Foolish Virgins.

TITTMONING

Michelin map 987 38 – Pop 1 995

Tittmoning, built on the left bank of the Salzach, which marks the frontier between Germany and Austria, preserves the remains of its mediaeval fortifications and a castle which was once the residence of the prince-bishops of Salzburg.

Main Square (Stadtplatz). – Two old fortified gateways provide access to this big street-square surrounded by houses with ridge roofs masked by perpendicular copings *(p 204)*. Some of the painted house façades are decorated with gilded figures. Wrought iron signs, oriel windows, emblazoned fountains give the square considerable style.

If you want to find
a placename or other item by name
look at the Index at the end of the guide.

TÖLZ, Bad ★

Michelin map **987** 37 – *Local map p 44* – Pop 12 200

The twin towns of Bad Tölz, which lie on either side of the rushing Isar River, are completely different in character: the picturesque old town faces a modern spa with wide streets which has been repeatedly embellished since it was decided, in 1845, to exploit the richest iodised waters (41·5 mg per litre) in Germany. Those suffering from heart or circulatory maladies who come to the spa for cures benefit also from being able to explore, to the south of the town, the delightful Isarwinkel region which, in turn, provides access to the Karwendel Massif.

The traveller with little time should, at least, cross the bridge over the Isar. The fragile Calvary Chapel, rising out of the greenery downstream, gives the setting individual character.

■ SIGHTS *time: ½ hour*

Marktstrasse★. – This street more than most, and in spite of its many alterations, with its wide curve and steep slope giving it a plunging view (go up as far as the statue of the Warrior bearing a Lance), evokes Old Bavaria. Beneath the broken line of gables with overhanging roofs are painted façades, the most brilliantly coloured being those on public buildings (Rathaus).

Calvary (Kalvarienberg). – Walk up the Kalvarienbergweg, bordered by the Stations of the Cross, to a height crowned by two chapels. The smallest dates from 1743 and is dedicated to St. Leonard whose cult has remained popular among both Austrian and Bavarian peasants. The Limousin hermit is here invoked not only as the deliverer of prisoners (note the chain round the building) but also as the guardian of horses. On the saint's day on 6 November, a solemn procession of country carts drawn by horses in magnificent harness files slowly past.

The **view** from the terrace before the chapels runs pleasantly over the wide Valley of the Upper Isar to the first foothills of the Karwendel.

EXCURSION

Isar Valley (Isarwinkel). – *22 km - 13½ miles – about 1½ hours.* Leave Bad Tölz by the Lenggries road to the south, leaving on your right the modern road no 2074 which avoids all towns.

The Isarwinkel region is very attractive with flower surrounded farmhouses dispersed among clumps of trees. Crosses surmount the gables on the farmhouses, and great covered Crucifixes stand at the roadside.

Lenggries. – This town is the tourist centre of the Isarwinkel. A cable-car ascends to the Brauneck (1 535 m - 5 036 ft), a viewpoint over the lower Bavarian region where the Isar can be seen winding on its way. In the near foreground are the summits of the Karwendel.

Sylvenstein Dam or **Sylvenstein-Staudamm.** – This earthen dyke with a watertight core of clay which was completed in 1959 entailed displacing more than 1·1 million cubic yards of soil. The dam regulates the alarming Isar floodwaters and supplies an underground power station, besides forming the huge and ramifying lake, the Sylvenstein-Stausee.

It is possible to continue the drive from the Sylvenstein Dam across the Austrian frontier *(customs formalities)* to either the Eng site in the heart of the Karwendel *(35 km – 21½ miles – about 3 hours)* or the steep shores of the Achensee, the biggest mountain lake in the Tyrol *(22 km - 13½ miles – about 1 hour).* For further details refer to the Michelin Green Guide Austria.

TRAVEMÜNDE ★

Michelin map **987** 6 – *Town plan in Michelin Red Guide Deutschland*

The resort of Travemünde, as its name indicates, was built at the mouth of the Trave. It has developed into Lübeck's beach and playground and now has something of the air of an international seaside resort. A thriving casino (roulette and baccarat) and a pleasure harbour attract many visitors. Travemünde is the embarkation point for many sea services linking Germany and Scandinavia, and many Scandinavians like to stay in the resort.

A ferry runs between the resort on the left bank of the river and the Priwall Peninsula, where the beach forms an enclave in East Germany and is more crowded. On this side lies the port where is moored the *Passat,* a former three-masted training ship.

North of the town the beach narrows until finally the sea no longer laps sand but steep cliffs. These are the small unstable **Brodtener Ufer** which rise no higher than 20 m - 65 ft – but afford wide views over the Baltic. They end at the north, at the popular seaside resort of **Timmendorfer Strand**.

TRIBERG ★

Michelin map **205** 6 – *Local map p 82* – Pop 7 000

Triberg, a watch and clockmaking industrial centre, is in the heart of the Black Forest, near the great diagonal highway from Strasbourg to Constance and the Schwarzwaldbahn, the railway, which by the unusual means of a series of loops manages after some considerable effort to cross the massif crestline.

■ THE WALK TO THE FALLS★ (Wasserfall) *1 hour on foot Rtn*

Leave the car in the park off the main road, near the bend (bridge) at the bottom end of the valley. Follow the tourist path *(access in summer: 7am to 7pm – 1.50DM),* keeping to the right branch of the stream (left as you go up). The Gutach Falls cascade down in shaded surroundings, dropping in all 162 m - 531 ft.

■ ADDITIONAL SIGHTS

Local Museum (Heimatmuseum). – *Open: 1 May to 30 September, 8am to 6pm; 1 October to 14 May, 9am to noon and 2 to 5pm; 2DM. Brochure in English.*

The museum is devoted to the traditions of the Black Forest and gives pride of place to old local costumes and regional crafts: watch and clockmaking, cooperage, ceramics and wood carving. There are also a mechanical organ which plays away gaily and a working model of the Schwarzwaldbahn railway.

Church of Our Lady of the Fir-Trees (Wallfahrtskirche Maria in der Tannen). – *Inside the first hairpin bend of the Schönwald road.* This pilgrimage church, which dates from 1705 and is one of the most popular in the Black Forest, contains Baroque **furnishings★** (Ausstattung), carved and painted with a peasant vivacity. The pulpit is the best item.

TRIER ★★

Michelin map **203** 17 – *Local maps pp 181 and 224* – Pop 100 000

The venerable episcopal city of Trier whose ecclesiastical electors ruled a territory which extended as far as Koblenz, is the first town reached by the Mosel in Germany. It is also the native town of Karl Marx (1818-83) whose house *(Brückenstrasse 10)* is now a museum. The philosopher is buried in England at Highgate *(see Michelin Green Guide to London)*. Trier has the character of a frontier town, but even more of the capital of Roman Antiquity in Germany, and, pleasing in the richness and variety of its works of art, is an essential stopping place for travellers in the Mosel region.

HISTORICAL NOTES

Trier was a meeting point for the Celtic, German and Latin cultures which evolved to form Western civilisation.

The Treveri and the Romans. – Legend has it that Trier was founded in 2000 BC by Trebeta, son-in-law of the fabulous Semiramis, Queen of Assyria. History, more soberly, attributes the foundation to Augustus in the 1C BC after the conquest of the Treveri, a Celtic tribe from eastern Gaul. Craftsmanship, trading and intellectual activity were considerable at that time, as may be seen from the many exhibits in the Rhineland Museum. But Trier, founded purely as a civil and residential town, and grown prosperous with the years, was unable to resist and fell before German assault in the 3C.

The Second Rome. – The reorganisation of the Roman Empire under Diocletian, at the end of the 3C, promoted Trier to the position of capital of Gaul and an imperial residence. The advent of Constantine as ruler (306-37) opened another period of prosperity.

Trier extended and became transformed. In 310 an orator proclaimed "I see this town, where every wall is rising again and which is now so beautiful that it must rejoice in having had ruins to rebuild". Constantine commanded ramparts to be built, of which the Porta Nigra is part, and magnificent religious and civil edifices to be constructed between the cathedral and what is now the Südallee. In 313 the Edict of Milan put an end to Christian persecution and Trier became, on an equal footing with Rome, a Christian metropolis of the west. The first bishopric to be founded in Germany was established in the city in 314.

Soon, however, Trier was supplanted by Byzantium and Arles. In the 5C the Frankish invasion confirmed its downfall.

■ MAIN SIGHTS *tour: 4½ hours*

Porta Nigra.★★ – *Open 9am to 1pm and 2 to 6pm (5pm 1 October to 31 March); closed Mondays (except holiday Mondays) and in December; 1DM.*

This wonderful gateway is the finest Roman relic in Germany. It owes its name to the dark patina which has formed over the limestone blocks which were built up without mortar, held only here and there with iron crampons. These the Germans removed in places, damaging the lower part of the edifice. The double arcade of the central building, defended on either side by towers, leads to an inner court in which assailants found themselves exposed on all sides to attack from the defenders. Every detail of military architecture has been attended to, including piercing the blind arcades only on the two upper storeys.

In the 11C this gateway fortress was transformed into a two-storey church. The Romanesque apse can be seen on the east side, and as you walk along the galleries inside on the different floors, traces are evident of additional alterations such as the Rococo decoration. Good view of the town from the tower terrace.

In 1804 Napoleon restored the monument to its original appearance.

Make for the Hauptmarkt by way of the Simeonstrasse.

Hauptmarkt. – Walk to the centre of the square where stands a Cross which was erected in 958 when the right to hold a market was granted to the town. From the centre, the square appears as a synthesis of all the greatest moments in Triers' history – typical monuments stand on all sides: to the north, the Porta Nigra; to the east, the Romanesque cathedral; to the south, the Gothic Church of St. Gangolf whose 15-16C tower symbolises the ambitions of mediaeval burghers; and finally westwards, a group of burghers' houses, some with Baroque gables, others older and half-timbered. The Steipe (**BX D**), an old 15C municipal mansion, bears the proud inscription: "Trier lived for 1300 years before Rome even came into being".

Go left along the Sternstrasse to the corner on which stands the former Walderdorff Palace adorned with a Virgin and Child.

Cathedral★ (Dom). – Seen from the forecourt (Domfreihof) the cathedral looks like a fortress. A rounded apse juts forward from the austere and massive façade which, with its squat square towers crowned with turrets, is a good example of early Romanesque architecture.

Walk forwards to the left of the cathedral along the Windstrasse from where the different stages of its construction are plainly visible. The central part crowned with a pediment is the square Roman heart of the building and dates from the middle of the 4C; the part on the right, the west end, which includes the façade and overlooks the parvis is the first Romanesque addition and is 11C; on the left, the east end, dating from the 12C, includes a polygonal chancel adorned with a dwarf gallery *(p 23)* – this chancel was unfortunately spoilt in the 18C by the juxtaposition of a Baroque axial chapel covered by a dome. It stands almost outside the main building, and was intended to hold the cathedral treasure.

The cathedral interior is Baroque and contains interesting altarpieces. In the west chancel stands the Gothic funerary monument of Archbishop-Elector Baudoin of Luxembourg; in the south aisle, a fine Romanesque **tympanum★** depicts Christ between St. Peter and the Virgin, and in a chapel covered in stucco, to the right of the chancel, there is a graceful 16C Virgin.

The cathedral **treasure★** contains precious works: ivories, goldwork exemplified by the case holding the Holy Nail (10C), the portable altar of St. Andrew decorated with enamel, illuminated evangelistaries, and a 12C Russian ornamented reliquary with vermeil filigree work. There are also invaluable relics: part of St. Peter's chain and Christ's Holy Tunic (rarely displayed).

Cloister. – The Gothic cloister affords an attractive **view★** of the cathedral and the adjoining Church of Our Lady. In the northwest corner stands the lovely 15C Virgin of Malberg.

Return to the cathedral forecourt and turn sharp left to enter the Church of Our Lady.

Church of Our Lady★★ (Liebfrauenkirche). – This was one of the earliest Gothic churches to be built in Germany and dates from 1235 to 1260. It was directly inspired by a church in Champagne and is in the form of a Greek cross. Between each of the four apsidal chapels, two chapels, each with three sides, have been built, producing an almost circular building which is highly original.

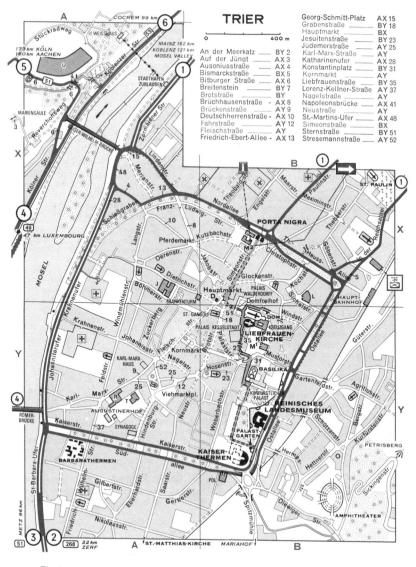

The tympanum, at the west porch, shows St. Mary enthroned, The Annunciation and Adoration of The Three Kings, the Massacre of the Innocents and the Presentation in the Temple. The statues of the archivolts represent the hierarchy of the church. At the north porch, the only entrance to the church, there is a representation of the Coronation of the Virgin Mary surrounded by the heavenly host and an admirable decoration of foliage and floral ornaments.

The interior has an incomparable elegance, enhanced by the rings of foliage carved round the pillars, the lines of the public galleries and the high central vaulting with four small arches.

There is a fine 17C **statue**★ (Grabmal Metternichs) on the tomb of Canon Metternich (north chapel), one of several funerary monuments in the church.

Take the Liebfrauenstrasse on the left as you come out of the church. This passes beneath an arcade surmounted by a Crucifix which formerly marked the boundary of the episcopal quarter. Go left round the ancient Roman civil basilica.

Basilica (Basilika). – Constantine the Great built the imperial palace in 300. Only the "Aula Palatina", the basilica, survived. Many alterations were done through the centuries, however, in the 19C the basilica was restored and handed over to the Protestant community as their place of worship. The interior, restrained in decoration, is overwhelming in size.

Palace Gardens★ (Palastgarten). – This park includes pools, flowerbeds and Baroque statues.

Rhineland Museum★★ (Rheinisches Landesmuseum) – *Open 10am to 1pm and 2 to 5pm; Sundays and holidays, 9am to 1pm; closed some holidays.*

This museum is one of the most varied archaeological museums in Germany. In gallery 3 there are "flaked" tools from the Lower Palaeolithic Age. Pottery, bracelets, and daggers were discovered in the tombs dating from the Bronze Age. During the Iron Age, a certain degree of ornamentation was mastered, exemplified in the gold jewellery found also in tombs.

There is a remarkable Roman antiques department in the basement and on the ground floor. Priceless marble sculpture is shown – note especially the Bacchus and the Diana. The **mosaics** reveal a highly developed craftsmanship: the figures have an eloquence of gesture and expression; the motifs, geometric in nature, are intricate and varied, examples are the famous Dionysus mosaic; the Muses, several by Monnus and a "rosary" mosaic. Among the Neumagen discoveries *(p 181)* is exhibited the sculpture of the ship loaded with wine. On the carving is the sailor with a broad grin known as the "gay mariner". Another form of expression displayed are the bas-reliefs. The glassware section is made up of several unique pieces: coloured cups and flasks, glasses decorated with fish and shells, and a diatrus cup *(see Cologne, Roman-Germanic Museum p 97)*. In the basement are sarcophagi and other funerary objects.

Imperial Baths★★ (Kaiserthermen). – *Open 9am to 1pm and 2 to 6pm (5pm 1 October to 31 March); closed Mondays (except holiday Mondays) and in December; 1DM.*

These baths were among the largest in the Roman Empire after those of Caracalla and Diocletian in Rome.

They were constructed under Constantine and were constantly remodelled in Roman times, but would appear never to have been used.

The walls pierced with wide windows formed part of the apses of the rooms containing hot water baths (caldarium); the alternate courses of stone and brick are typical of Roman architecture. The tepid (tepidarium) and cold water bathrooms (frigidarium) and finally the gymnasium court (palestra) follow.

A tour of the two floors below ground where the water heating and circulation machinery were installed is particularly evocative.

Return by the same route to the Porta Nigra.

■ ADDITIONAL SIGHTS

Episcopal Museum★ (Bischöfliches Museum) (BY M²). – *Guided tours 10am to noon and 3 to 5pm; Saturdays 10am to noon; Sundays and holidays, 10am to 1pm; 1DM.*

The 4C **frescoes★★** (Deckenmalerei) which were discovered in Constantine's Palace beneath the cathedral are the most precious exhibit. The figures portrayed are said to be St. Helen and Fausta, the mother and wife respectively of the emperor. The colours are extraordinarily fresh and the technique highly skilled.

Almost all the first floor is devoted to mediaeval statuary and includes the original figures of the west door to the Church of Our Lady.

St. Paulinus' Church★ (St. Paulin) (BX). – The church, which was completed in 1754, is the work of Balthazar Neumann *(p 27)*. It is plain and upward sweeping with a single aisle lit by tall windows. The upper parts are Rococo in style; the frescoes on the ceiling depict the martyrdom of St. Paulinus.

Amphitheatre (BY). – *Same times and price as for the Imperial Baths.* The theatre, which was built on a hillside and could accommodate a seated audience of 20 000, is an example more of terracing than of building. In the Middle Ages the stone tiers were stolen and removed to such a degree that by the 18C vines were being cultivated on the site. The cellars below ground house theatrical equipment.

St. Barbara's Baths (Barbarathermen) (AY). – *Same times of opening as the Imperial Baths.* These baths were constructed in the 2C and were used for several hundred years. They are now somewhat battered.

Municipal Museum (Städtisches Museum) (BX M²). – *Open 9am to 5pm; Fridays 1 to 9m; 0.50DM.*

These galleried Romanesque buildings are grouped round the courtyard of the former **Convent of St. Simeon** beside the Porta Nigra. The exhibits refer to the town's history.

St. Matthias Church. – *By the Saarstrasse (south on the plan).* St. Matthais' reliquary, the only tomb of an apostle to lie north of the Alps, has made the church a place of pilgrimage. The façade presents a juxtaposition of Romanesque and Baroque architectural styles with curious effect.

TRIFELS Castle
Michelin map **204** 20 – *Local map p 215*

Trifels Castle stands on the summit of one of the Wasgau heights on a superb **site★**.

Access. – *7 km - 3½ miles – from Annweiler – plus 1½ hours walking and sightseeing. Open 1 April to 30 September, 9am to 1pm and 2 to 6pm (5pm 1 October to 31 March); closed Mondays, Tuesdays (if Monday a holiday) and 1 December to 20 January; 1DM.*

The road to the castle begins in the town of **Annweiler** where a copy of the crown of the German Emperors, in memory of the crown jewels kept at Trifels in the 12 and 13C, may be seen in the town hall *(to see the copy apply to the Verkehrsamt)*. The road rises steeply and passes beside the **Asselstein★**, an isolated limestone rock, before running at the feet of the slopes once crowned by the Scharfenberg and Anebos Castles, now insignificant ruins.

Castle. – This is one of the castles in Germany most deeply steeped in history. It was an imperial residence and housed the royal treasure, a fact which gives credit to the poetic tradition that it also once contained the Holy Grail. Richard Lionheart, as he returned from the 3rd Crusade, was captured and held prisoner in the castle by Emperor Heinrich VI in 1193 and freed a year later on payment of an enormous ransom.

The castle, which is built into the rock, was reconstructed in 1937 in the style of the Romanesque palaces of the Hohenstaufens. From the chapel tower (Kapellenturm) there is a **panorama★** southwards of the Wasgau region with, here and there, hills crowned with rocks (Asselstein) and ruins.

TÜBINGEN ★★
Michelin map **206** 14 – *Local map p 240* – Pop 73 600

Since the University of Tübingen was founded on the banks of the Neckar in 1477, students have hurried along the narrow streets and enlivened the town as did their predecessors, the great poets of olden times, Hölderlin, Mörike and Uhland, the more recent philosophers, Hegel and Schelling, and learned men like the astronomer, Kepler.

■ MAIN SIGHTS *tour: 2 hours*

Eberhardt Bridge. – The **view★★** upstream from the bridge is picturesque with the Hölderlin Tower rising above weeping willows. Go down to the Platanenallee.

Platanenallee★★. – This avenue of plane trees on a manmade island is known throughout Germany. It is a pleasant place for a stroll on a summer evening when students, in lantern-lit boats, row gently on the river to the accompaniment of traditional songs and with the lights of the old town as a backcloth.

Return to the Eberhardt Bridge and follow the Neckargasse as far as the Holzmarkt.

TÜBINGEN★★

Collegiate Church of St. George (Stiftskirche). – The church, which was built in the 15C, is divided by a Flamboyant rood-screen. The elegant **pulpit★** (Kanzel) covered with a baldachin dating from 1490, is also Flamboyant; it is adorned with statues of the Virgin surrounded by the four Fathers of the Church.

The **chancel** *(open Easter to 1st Sunday in October, on Saturdays, Sundays and holidays, 1 to 5pm; 0.50DM)* is the necropolis of the Württemberg princes. Among the funerary monuments are, at the end, that of Eberhardt the Bearded, founder of the University, and, near the entrance, the Renaissance **tombs★★** (Grabtumben) of Duke Ludwig (died 1593) and his wife, ornamented with delicate alabaster reliefs.

From the top of the **tower** *(open Easter to 30 September only, Sunday and holiday afternoons)* there is an interesting **view★** of the Neckar, the castle promontory and, on the horizon, the blue line of the Swabian Jura.

Go along the Kirchgasse to the Marktplatz.

Marktplatz★. – This asymmetrical old square is always lively and particularly so on market days (Mondays, Wednesdays and Fridays) when peasants in regional costume come into the town. In front of the town hall is a lovely Renaissance fountain of Neptune.

Town Hall★. – The 15C building has been frequently restored; the painted decoration on the façade dates from 1876. Eberhardt the Bearded can be seen beneath the 1511 astronomical clock.

Mount the Wienergässle and then, on the right, the rise to the castle (Burgsteige).

Castle. – The present edifice was built on 11C foundations during the Renaissance. It now houses several departments of the University.

The successive **entrance gateways★** imitate the triumphal arches of Antiquity; the first is surmounted by a large medallion bearing the arms of the House of Württemberg and the riband of the Order of the Garter. The Garter motif and the maxim "Hon(i) soit qui mal y pense" recall the honour bestowed in 1597 by Queen Elizabeth I upon Duke Friedrich of Württemberg, the builder of the gateway. (The investiture took place in the Church of Stuttgart in 1603.)

Attractive **views** of the Neckar and the roofs of the old town may be seen from the bastion terraces and the gardens laid out before the monumental doorway.

The **cellars** contain an 850 hl - 18 700 gallon vat of 1548 and prison cells *(tours temporarily suspended)*.

Walk back into the town; at the end of the Burgsteige turn right into the Klosterberg steps and follow the signs, "Hölderlinhaus". Go first to the far end of the Protestant seminary then to the University Bursa where the terraced street affords a view of the Neckar.

The sign "Hölderlinhaus" will lead you to the riverside path. On the right, recognisable from its tower, stands the house of Hölderlin, the poet – now a memorial museum.

Return along the Neckar to the Eberhardt Bridge.

TÜBINGEN

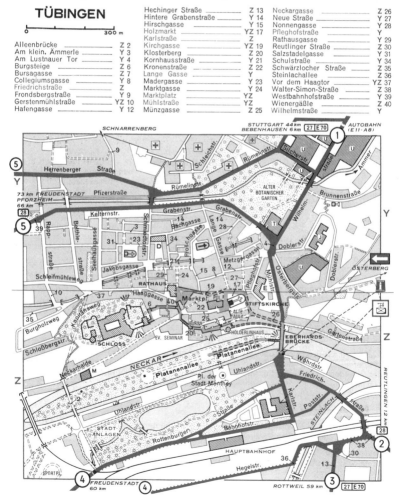

■ ADDITIONAL SIGHTS

Bebenhausen Hospital (Bebenhausener Pfleghof) (YZ E). – This former tithe barn of Bebenhausen Abbey *(p 62)* was built in the 15C. Go through to the courtyard where a three-storey dormer window, through which the grain was handed into the barn, juts out from the main roof.

Fruchtschranne (Y D). – Now the Albert Schweitzer College (Realschule). The roof of this 15C building with wooden walls is most unusual, since it has four storeys each with mansards. The building was constructed as the ducal granary.

ÜBERLINGEN ★

Michelin map **206** 18 – *Local map p 102* – Pop 17 500

The ancient stone buildings of the old town of Überlingen combine well with the modern leisure facilities, including promenades, built on the shores of Lake Constance.

■ MAIN SIGHTS *tour: 1½ hours*

Start from the square with the coloured houses, the Hofstatt, and make for the Münsterplatz.

Münsterplatz. – The "Münster", the north face of the Rathaus or town hall, the Renaissance building that was formerly the municipal chancellery (Alte Kanzlei), give the square its character.

Town Hall. – The hall stands to the left of the church. Enter through a turret on the right of the building and walk up to the first floor. Ring. *Open 9am to noon and 2.30 to 5pm; closed Saturday afternoons and Sundays.*

The **Council Chamber★** (Ratssaal) is decorated overall with considerable delicacy in the Gothic manner: the panelled walls are adorned with projecting arches while the ribbed wooden ceiling is slightly rounded. The statuettes, which add to the general effect, are late 15C.

Go left round the church and enter through the west door.

Christophstraße	2	Klosterstraße	7
Franziskanerstraße	3	Lindenstraße	8
Gradebergstraße	4	Luziengasse	9
Hochbildstraße	5	Marktstraße	10
Hofstatt		Münsterstraße	
Jakob-Kessenring-Straße	6	Pfarrhofstraße	13
		Schulstraße	15

Minster★ (Münster). – The church has a vast interior with five aisles, each shouldering the other and covered in Gothic fan vaulting. The side chapels contain several altarpieces, while in a chapel off the south aisle, the St. Elizabeth Chapel, there stands a graceful Virgin of the Crescent Moon, a Swabian work of 1510.

Continue to follow the itinerary marked on the map to the moat bottom.

The Moat Walk★★ (Stadtbefestigungsanlagen). – The route through the western sector, including the moat (Westanlagen), makes a delightful walk in the height of summer. On the town side the soft yellowish sandstone escarpment support fortifications, notably the massive round tower known as the Gallerturm.

Walk to the lake shore and continue along the **Seepromenade★**, before turning ninety degrees left to go along the Mantelhafen Quay.

Bear left into the Münsterstrasse to re-enter the town and return to the Hofstatt.

■ ADDITIONAL SIGHTS

Local Museum (Städtisches Museum) (M). – *Open weekdays, 9am to noon and 2 to 5.30pm; Sundays (except in winter), 10am to noon; closed Mondays; 1.50DM.*

The museum is in a late 15C mansion from whose terraced garden there is a view of the town, with its old roofs and churches and the Überlingen Lake and Mainau Island.

The cribs (Krippen), among the collections, display 18C wood carvings in the popular tradition, of scenes in the life of Christ.

Municipal Gardens (Stadtgarten). – Flourishing cacti testify to the mild climate.

EXCURSION

Salem Abbey★; Heiligenberg. – *21 km - 13 miles – about 2½ hours.*

Leave Überlingen by the Salem road. Bear right when you reach the village of Andelshofen.

Salem Abbey★. – *Description p 226.*

Return to the car; turn left at Stefansfeld into the Heiligenberg road.

Heiligenberg. – *Castle open 1 April to October, 8am to noon and 1 to 5pm; time: ½ hour; 2DM; Brochure in English.*

This castle, although transformed in the second half of the 16C by the Fürstenbergs into a Renaissance style residence, retains its original heavy and impressive character.

Inside, the Knights' Hall has a magnificent late 16C coffered ceiling and windows on all four sides. From these there is a pleasant view of the lake.

A short walk in the park (iron grille on the right as you come out) will bring you to the terrace on the edge of the plateau, a **viewpoint★** over the lake towards the Swiss Alps.

ULM ★★

Michelin map **206** 5 – Pop 99 000

Ulm's situation, at the point where the great Stuttgart–Munich highway, newly descended from the Swabian Jura, crosses the Danube increased by the inflow of the Iller, explains its commercial bent. Albert Einstein, the physicist, was born in Ulm in 1879.

General View★★. – A walk along the right bank of the Danube **(Jahnufer)** (Z) provides a view, on the opposite bank, of the gabled houses of the Butchers' Tower (Metzgerturm) and the cathedral.

ULM

		König-Wilhelm-Str.	Y	32
		Kornhausgasse	Z	33
		Kramgasse	Z	34
Adenauerbrücke	Y 2	Kronengasse	Z	35
Allgäuer Ring	Y 3	Ludwigstraße	Y	37
Augsburger-Tor-Pl.	Y 4	Marienstraße	Z	38
Bahnhofstraße	Z	Marktplatz	Z	39
Basteistraße	YZ 7	Memminger Tor	Y	41
Bismarckring	Y 10	Michelsbergstraße	Y	42
Blaubeurer Straße -	Z 12	Münsterplatz	Z	43
Blaubeurer Tor	Y 13	Neue Straße	Z	
Dreiköniggasse	Z 16	Platzgasse	Z	
Ehinger Tor	Y 17	Römerstraße	Y	49
Eythstraße	Y 18	Salzstadelgasse	Z	50
Fischergasse	Z 19	Schuhhausgasse	Z	52
Fischerplätzle	Z 20	Schweinemarkt	Z	54
Glöcklerstraße	Z 23	Schwilmengasse -	Z	55
Herdbrücke	Z 24	Schwörhausgasse	Z	56
Herdbruckerstraße -	Z 25	Seestraße	Y	57
Hermann-Köhl-Str. -	Y 27	Stadtmauer	Z	58
Hindenburgring	Y 28	Talfinger Straße	Y	60
Hirschstraße	Z	Wagnerstraße	Y	61
Illerstraße	Y 29	Zinglerstraße	Y	62

■ THE CATHEDRAL★★★ (Münster) *tour: ¾ hour – excluding the ascent of the spire*

The spire is the tallest in the world and seems about to shoot the whole Gothic building upwards into the sky with its 161 m - 528 ft – thrust. The sweeping vertical lines and the lightness of the pierced architecture are very beautiful. Although the foundation stone of the cathedral was laid in 1377, the two towers and the spire were only erected in 1890.

A beautiful porch with three arcades precedes the two Renaissance doors at whose pier stands a moving statue carved in 1429 by Hans Multscher of *Man in Sorrow.*

Interior. – *Open 1 April to 30 September, 8am to 6.45pm; the rest of the year, 9am to 5pm; no visit during services; 0.50DM; 1DM including the ascent of the spire.* The upward sweep of the nave with sharply pointed arches is emphasised by the absence of a transept which also concentrates interest in the chancel.

A series of graceful early 15C consoles are supported by the pillars of the nave. The pulpit is surmounted by a 1510 sounding board above which is a kind of second pulpit for the Holy Ghost, the invisible preacher. A Flamboyant ciborium, in the same style, stands to the left of the entrance to the chancel. The four aisles are covered, also in the Flamboyant style, with fine fan vaulting.

Choir-stalls★★★ (Chorgestühl). – This splendid example of wood carving, executed by Jörg Syrlin the Elder between 1469 and 1471, places face to face two series of personages, those of the Bible, and those of pagan Antiquity.

Men are grouped on the left, women on the right. The upper gables are devoted to the Church's apostles and martyrs, the tall backs to the stalls to the great figures of the Old Testament. The most expressive sculptures are carved into the sides of the stalls and include, on the left, busts of Greek and Latin philosophers and writers (Pythagoras, Cicero, etc.), and on the right, sibyls. The **priest's triple throne** behind the altar completes the whole.

Ascent of the Spire. – *768 steps.* **Panorama★★** from either the tower platform or the spire balcony, of the town, the Danube, the Swabian Jura plateaux and the Alps.

(After a photo from the Langewiesche Bücherei)

Cathedral Stalls –
A Sibyl.

■ ADDITIONAL SIGHTS

Fishermen's Quarter★ (Fischerviertel) (Z). – Start from the Fischerplätzle, a small square shaded by a lime tree. Take an alley on the left that goes over a culvert. The picturesque **Schiefes Haus** building has subsided curiously over a tanners' canal.

Return to the foot of the ramparts which you climb by a stairway. Follow the rampart crest round to the left within sight of some old houses, their gables all turned towards you. It was here, in 1805, before the swift flowing Danube, that the Austrian garrison capitulated to Napoleon. Continue to the Butchers' Tower (Metzgerturm) before returning.

Ulmer Museum★ (Z M¹). – Open 1 July to 30 September, 10am to 5pm; the rest of the year, 10am to noon (1pm Sundays) and 2 to 5pm; closed Mondays.

The museum is in a house which once belonged to an influential citizen. The fine arts section is the most interesting; on the ground floor are works by the Masters of Ulm: Hans Multscher (Bilhafingen Virgin), Jörg Syrlin the Elder (reliquary bust), Daniel Mauch (Virgin and Child) and Martin Schaffner (Portrait of Eitel Besserer).

Town Hall (Z R¹). – This elegant Gothic and Renaissance building has pierced gables and façades painted and richly decorated in false relief. An astronomic clock adorns the west face.

The **Fischkasten**, a fountain whose twisted stem was made by Jörg Syrlin the Elder in 1482, stands in the nearby Marktplatz.

Church of the Holy Spirit (Heilig-Geist-Kirche), southwest of the plan, by the Romerstrasse. – This modern church, whose campanile in the shape of a finger singles it out from afar, stands on a fine panoramic site above the town.

EXCURSIONS

Blaubeuren★. – 18 km - 11½ miles – about 1¼ hours. Leave Ulm by ⑤, the Reutlingen road. In Blaubeuren, a Swabian village known for its beautiful rock surroundings, follow the "Blautopf-Hochaltar" signs. Leave the car in a park near the abbey's monumental entrance.

Blautopf. – ¼ hour on foot Rtn. This deep blue pool was formed by a natural embankment of glacial origin. The deeply shaded approaches have been arranged as walks.

Former Abbey. – Tour: ½ hour. Follow the "Hochaltar" signs. The abbey includes a picturesque group of old wooden walled buildings.

In the chancel of the church (open 1 April to 31 October, 9am to noon and 2 to 6pm; the rest of the year, only weekends 10am (10.30am Sundays) to noon and 2 to 5pm) stands the Blaubeuren **altarpiece★★** (Hochaltar), a cooperative work by the principal studios of Ulm in the 15C. The themes portrayed are the Passion, the Life of John the Baptist and the Virgin with the Saints.

Lonetal★; Charlottenhöhle. – Round tour of 67 km - 42 miles – about 3 hours. Leave Ulm by ①, the Heidenheim road (no 19). One mile beyond Hausen ob Lontal, turn right towards Niederstotzingen.

After Bissingen the road enters the Lone Valley (Lonetal). Fork left to follow the valley floor through a deserted countryside.

Charlottenhöhle. – Tour: 1 hour. Open 1 April to 30 September; if the guide is absent apply to Giengen Town Hall; 2.50DM.

The 532 m long gallery shows well the effects of subterranean erosion and also displays a covering of delicate concretions.

Turn left on reaching the outskirts of Hürben to join road no 19 which brings you back to Ulm.

■ VIERZEHNHEILIGEN Church ★★

Michelin map **987** 26 – northeast of Bamberg

This pilgrimage church dedicated to the Fourteen Saints of Intercession, or Auxiliary Saints, stands on an open hillside in the Upper Main Valley, facing Banz Abbey (p 58). The interior reveals the bold concepts of Balthazar Neumann, the master of Baroque architecture.

The Pilgrimage. – In this spot in 1445 and 1446 a herdsman was blessed with visions of which the last was identified as being that of the Infant Jesus among the "Fourteen Saints of Intercession". The cult of this pious cohort of saints, which was actively fostered by German Dominicans and Cistercians, must be seen in the context of the mystical atmosphere prevailing at the beginning of the 15C when visions were frequent – the "voices" heard by Joan of Arc (born 1412) were those of St. Catherine and St. Margaret, two of the intercessionary group. For a long time this devotion to the holy helpers remained alive amongst the people and attracted crowds of pilgrims to a chapel which, in the 18C, was superseded by a sumptuous Rococo church.

Tour. – ½ hour. The church, built from 1743 to 1763 in fine ochre coloured stone, has a façade framed with domed towers which are unusually tall for a Baroque building. This façade has an admirable vigour of design, with jutting cornices which emphasise the arrangement in tiers of the pilasters and columns and the sinuous lines of the convex frontal building. In accordance with Rococo taste, this façade is not just a covering as at Ottobeuren (p 201), but an adornment reminiscent of the castles of the period with four lines of windows, some wide and spacious, others small as for a mezzanine or attic room. The broken pediment is surmounted by statues, which were once gilded, of Christ between Faith and Charity.

Interior. – Illustration p 25. The interior arrangement is ordered by a succession of three oval bays framed by colonnades and covered with low inner cupolas. The centre of the church is the bay containing the altar to the Saints of Intercession, to the detriment of the transept crossing which is invaded by the bay's colonnade. Circular domes cover the transepts. All these geometric subtleties create an overall perspective and carry out the ideal of a central focal point, which haunted 18C architects who had become tired of the endless succession of straight sided bays.

The precious Rococo decoration in this church will surprise many visitors by its subtlety and elegance; outstanding are the clear colours of the painting on the domes, the lightness of the stuccowork, the richness of the gold outlines which highlight the woodwork of the galleries and the grace of the putti which surmount the confessionals and the cornices.

Altar to the Fourteen Saints of Intercession★★ (Nothelfer-Altar). – The altar, where all the lines are convex or concave, was constructed in 1764, a Rococo pyramid with a pierced baldachin, by the stuccoworkers of the Wessobrunn school (p 256). It stands on the spot where the visions occurred.

VIERZEHNHEILIGEN Church★★

The Statues

Balustrade: (1) St. Denis. (2) St. Blaise. (3) St. Erasmus. (4) St. Cyriacus (deliverer from the devil in the final hour).

Altar Niches: (5) St. Catherine, patron saint of the learned, of students and girls wishing to get married (the model of Christian wisdom). (6) St. Barbara, patron saint of miners, artillerymen and prisoners (the grace of a noble death).

Buttresses: (7) St. Acacius (the agony of death). (8) St. Giles, the only intercessor who did not suffer martyrdom (to obtain the grace of a true confession). (9) St. Eustace (converted by the vision of a stag with a Cross between its antlers). (10) St. Christopher, patron saint of travellers.

Top of the Baldachin: (11) St. Guy (epilepsy). (12) St. Margaret (intercession for the forgiveness of sin). (13) St. George, patron saint of peasants and their possessions. (14) St. Pantaleon.

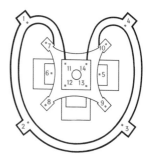

PLAN OF THE ALTAR

Those who enjoy unusual views should climb the slopes above the church from where they will see Banz Abbey in line with the ridge of the church roof and between its towers.

WALDECK Region ★
Michelin map **987** 15, 25

This small region, lying on either side of the lower course of the River Eder, lived under the tutelage of the Waldeck Princes and was more than half forgotten by the world until 1918.

Today its deep forests, the magnificent stretch of water behind the Eder Dam and the spa resort of Bad Wildungen make it one of the busiest tourist regions of central Germany.

★FROM FRANKENBERG TO KASSEL
109 km - 68 miles – about 4½ hours – Local map below

Frankenberg an der Eder. – The upper town contains a fine group of 16C houses built of wood and often protected with a slate overcovering; decoratively arranged bricks pattern the areas between the beams. The two central squares, the Obermarkt and the Untermarkt, grain their main appeal from the half-timbered **town hall★** which bristles with turrets.

Go a little higher up to the crest where stands the 13 and 14C **Church of Our Lady** (Liebfrauenkirche). The **Lady Chapel** (Marienkapelle), an asymmetrical polygon abutting on the south transept, was built in the middle of the Gothic period. It contains a stone altarpiece, which now lacks its statues but has a rare decorative perfection.

Haina★. – *Tour: ¾ hour.* The former Cistercian Abbey built in the heart of the woods was transformed by the Landgrave Philip the Magnanimous *(p 175)* into a mental hospital. *Open 10am to 5pm; apply at the hospital doorway. The church★* is a large, very plain Gothic hall. The flat east end, the small columns in the nave broken halfway up the historiated consoles, conform to the traditions of the Cistercian Order. The building still has its original red and yellow rough casting and, on the left, large fragments of monochrome stained glass. The six transept chapels are evidence of the first building undertaken in the Romanesque period. The cloister, on the south side of the church, shows a mingling of Romanesque and Gothic elements.

The road passes through the oak and beech woods of the tree covered Kellerwald range.

Bad Wildungen★. – *Description p 259.*

Fritzlar★. – *11 km - 7 miles – from Bad Wildungen by road no 253. Description p 129.*

The road comes out on the rock banks of the Eder Lake overlooked by Waldeck Castle.

Eder Dam★ (Edertalsperre). – *Tour ¼ hour (car park beside the lake).* This stonework undertaking, completed in 1914 and considered large at the time, retains 200 million m³ - 44 000 million gallons. Waldeck Castle, rising above the wooded shores, dominatees the **artificial lake★** and the dam which the RAF breached with a 4-ton bomb in 1943, blowing a gap in the stonework 70 m wide and 22 m high - 77 yds x 72 ft - resulting in catastrophic floods.

Waldeck★. – Leave the car beside the castle rise. The castle of the Waldeck Princes *(tour: ½ hour)*, which was abandoned in the 17C, has been transformed in part into a hotel. From the large terrace on the lake side *(free access)*, the **view★★** extends over the water until this finally disappears behind wooded hill crests. Inside the castle two galleries have been arranged as a museum *(open 1 April to 15 October, 10am to 5pm; 1DM)* in memory of the House of Waldeck. The Sorceresses' Tower (Hexenturm) contains three prison cells one below the other.

The drive ends in a rolling countryside, swelling here and there into a volcanic hill.

Naumburg. – *4 km - 2½ miles – from Ippinghausen.* A picturesque fortified town best appreciated in a general **view★** from above, as at the start of the Netze road.

Alternative route by Korbach and Arolsen. – *Extra distance: 36 km - 22 miles. Count on an extra hour's drive and ½ hour's sightseeing.*

Korbach. – The town was formed by joining together the two fortified centres of Altstadt (built round the Church of St. Kilian – without a spire) and Neustadt (built round the Church of St. Nicholas – with a spire). **St. Kilian's** is a Gothic hall wider than it is long which shows Westphalian influence (Church of Our Lady of the Fields at Soest). At the south door a fine group of statues depicts the Last Judgment on the tympanum, while the Virgin stands against the pier.

Korbach still has many wooden houses. In the main street of the old town (Stechbahn), between St. Kilian and the Rathaus, **house no 9** has a Baroque wood doorway which is amusingly rustic with reliefs in white against a green background.

Arolsen. – *Description p 51.*

Kassel★. – *Description p 156.*

WALDSASSEN
Michelin map **987** 27 – 70 km - 43 miles – east of Bayreuth – Pop 8 800

The glass and ceramic industries provide a living for Waldsassen, like its neighbours, Selb and Weiden, in the wooded region east of Bayreuth between the Fichtelgebirge and the Oberpfälzer Wald.

Former Abbey Church★ (Stiftskirche). – The church's interior is unduly narrow for its length of 83 m - 272 ft; more than a third of the floor space is occupied by the chancel, a reminder of the Cistercian plan. The building as a whole, which was completed in 1704, is an early example of the attempt to adapt the Italian Baroque style to German taste. Aisles and galleries provide a second storey of chapels which communicates vertically through a passage in the roof.

The choir-stalls, the high altar and altarpiece of the Annunciation incorporating a tabernacle in the form of a gilded globe, date from the same period as the church and were carved by local craftsmen.

EXCURSION

Kappel. – *6.5 km - 4 miles – plus ½ hour sightseeing.* Leave Waldsassen by the Schirnding road. After 5 km - 3 miles – bear left into the village of Münchenreuth and continue to the sanctuary.

The **church★** which stands isolated in a wide open pastoral **setting★★** within sight of the Cheb Basin in Czechoslovakia is dedicated to the Holy Trinity. It was constructed in 1689 by Georg Dientzenhofer in the shape of a trefoil rotunda, studded with three towers. Inside, three apses, each dedicated to one of the three Persons of the Trinity, radiate from a central triangular bay resting on three columns. Three altar niches have been hollowed out in each apse.

Join us in our never ending task of keeping up to date.

Send us your comments and suggestions, please.

Michelin Tyre Co Ltd.
Tourism Department
81 Fulham Road, LONDON SW3 6RD

WALHALLA ★
Michelin map **987** 27 11 km - 7 miles – east of Regensburg

This Doric temple seems strangely out of place in the Danube Valley. It was constructed in 1842 in an impressive **site★**, at the top of a long series of slopes rising above the river. Ludwig I of Bavaria, who built it, had in mind the construction of a memorial to the great and illustrious men of Germany – soldiers, artists, scientists, etc. (Walhalla or Valhalla, in Nordic mythology, was the final resting place for heroes' souls).

Access and Tour. – The rising access road begins at Donaustauf, branching off the road up the left bank of the Danube. *Open 1 April to 31 October, 9am to 6pm; 1 November to 31 March, 10am to noon and 2 to 4pm; closed 24 and 31 December; time: ½ hour; 0.50DM.*

Inside may be seen the busts of 118 German personages and, beneath the gallery, 64 commemorative plaques honouring older and more obscure heroes.

There is a good **view** from the peristyle of the bend in the River Danube, the ruins of Donaustauf Castle and the spires of Regensburg Cathedral.

WANGEN IM ALLGÄU ★
Michelin map **206** 9 – *Local map p 40* – Pop 23 300

Wangen, lying within sight of the first crests of the Allgäu Alps, is a typical colourful small Swabian town. The simplicity of its layout enables one to appreciate its charm at a glance.

Marktplatz★. – The square is at the crossroads of the towns' two principal streets. The Herrenstrasse, lined with houses with attractive signs, leads to the Ravensburg Gate (Ravensburger Tor or Frauentor). The square building with a 17C upper part, quartered with engaged towers, has a most elegantly fantastic ribbed roof. At right angles to the first, stands the St. Martin or Lindau Gate with a pyramid shaped roof. It is decorated with highly ornate gargoyles and, like the Ravensburg Gate, also with paintings.

WASSERBURG AM INN
Michelin map **987** 37 – Pop 7 000

Wasserburg owes its existence to its **site★**, a promontory encircled by a loop in the River Inn, and its name to the castle built upon it by the Wittelsbachs. The salt trade and shipping contributed to the town's rapid development in the Middle Ages.

A very pleasant **view** of the old town opens out from the bridge over the Inn, coming from the south. The high façades of the houses along the quayside, their flat roofs or ridged roofs behind copings or stepped gables, give the town the half-German half-Italian look typical of the Inn and Salzach Valleys.

■ **SIGHTS** *time: ½ hour*

Marienplatz. – The main square is lined with houses with arcades, ornamented in some cases, with oriel windows.

Town Hall. – The tall stepped gable is decorated with paintings in which religious subjects jostle armorial bearings. The façade has Renaissance windows.

A fine chamber next to the Banqueting Hall on the first floor may be visited on application to the caretaker *(9, 10 and 11am, 2, 3 and 4pm; closed Saturdays and Sunday afternoons; 0.80DM).* The walls are covered with 16C woodwork and painted panels; the ceiling, with carved beams, belongs to the same period.

Patrizierhaus Kern. – This lovely house has an outstanding façade, richly ornamented with stuccowork by J B Zimmermann, paintings and two-storey oriel windows.

Parish Church (Pfarrkirche). – The church stands back from the Marienplatz but can be easily distinguished on account of its massive outline and tall square tower. The interior is Gothic in style. The wooden pulpit, carved in 1638, is decorated with many statues.

EXCURSION

Rott am Inn. – *15 km – 9½ miles – plus ½ hour sightseeing.* Leave Wasserburg by road no 304 going towards Munich. After 4 km - 2 miles – bear left to Rosenheim, and after a further 9 km - 6 miles – right to the village of Rott am Inn.

Of an old 11C Benedictine Abbey, Rott retains only a **church**, Baroquised in the 18C.

A somewhat low basket handle arched porch, topped by the organ loft, leads to the main building roofed by three domes of which the centre one is vast. With Johann-Michael Fischer as architect, Johann-Michael Feichtmayr as master of the stuccowork which is very delicately executed, and Matthäus Günther as painter of the frescoes, great harmony was achieved.

■ **WEIKERSHEIM** ─────────────────

Michelin map **987** 26 – 20 km - 12 miles – south of Würzburg – *Local maps pp 151 and 217* – Pop 7 100

This small town on the Romantic Road developed round a castle built by the Hohenlohes *(p 151)* which is magnificently furnished. The architectural unity of the 18C still retained by the town is seen particularly well in the design of the Markt, which is semicircular on the palace side to provide a noble vista.

Castle. – *Open (tour: about ¾ hour) April to October, weekdays 8am to 6pm; November to March, 10am to noon and 2 to 4pm; closed Mondays in winter; 2DM.*

The castle was built between 1580 and 1680 beside the Tauber round an inner court overlooked by an ancient keep. The style is plain, uninfluenced as yet by the Baroque.

The remarkable collection of **furniture**★★ (Ausstattung) represents two hundred years of decorative art, from 1550 to about 1750.

The magnificent **Knights' Hall**★★ or Rittersaal (36 m long by 12 m wide by 9 m high - 116 x 39 x 30 ft) was completed in 1603 and is in a transitional style between Renaissance and Baroque. The coffered ceiling is painted with hunting themes. A monumental doorway balances the enormous chimneypiece, both being adorned with the sculptured figures of emperors and empresses.

Tapestries, glass, mirrors and china enrich the other rooms.

The view of the formally designed park (1710), peopled with statues in caricature in the taste of the small Franconian courts of the period, ends in the pretty pierced orangery.

■ **WEILBURG** ─────────────────

Michelin map **204** 3 – *Local map p 163* – Pop 14 000

The spur enclosed by a bend in the Lahn River, where the Counts of Nassau chose to build their residence, became in the 16C the **site**★ of a small Baroque town which developed compactly and picturesquely. The Marktplatz quarter is particularly well designed.

Castle. – *Tour: ¾ hour.* Leave the car at the top of the town on the Marktplatz, a square ornamented with a fountain to Neptune and overlooked by the castle church. Walk along beside the large orangery buildings to the Schlossplatz from which the covered way leads to the castle. *Open 1 March to 31 October, 10am to 4pm; the rest of the year, 10am to 3pm; closed Mondays; 1DM.*

The castle courtyard was the hub of the vast number of buildings that went to make up the former princely residence. The Renaissance buildings framing the court make a picturesque whole of which the most memorable features are the turreted clock tower and particularly, on the left, the elegant 1573 gallery where the arcade has twin Doric columns and is surmounted by a glazed gallery with Corinthian columns and an attractive transverse timbered roof.

On the ground floor several vaulted rooms are open to the public (guardroom, kitchens, judgment room, marble bath), and on the first floor a series of bedrooms and saloons whose chief interest lies in their fine state of preservation and homogeneity of arrangement.

Gardens (Schlossgarten). – The gardens drop by way of three series of terraces and flower borders from the Marktplatz to the town gate (Landtor) which stands at the start of the river curve on the Frankfurt road. The upper terrace is planted with lime trees and edged with a balustrade and decorative vases. At its far end it covers a pretty Louis XVI orangery which stands on the middle terrace and is now a café-restaurant.

Museum (Heimat- und Bergbaumuseum). – *On the Schlossplatz, opposite the castle entrance. Open April to October, 10am to noon and 2 to 5pm; closed Mondays and weekends in winter; 1DM.*

This Upper Lahn regional museum has mainly geological exhibits as well as memories of the princely House of Nassau and the early heroic days of flying and its personalities.

If you would rather plan your own itinerary
look at the map in this guide
of the principal sights and tourist regions (pp 4-8).

WEINGARTEN ★

Michelin map 206 8 – 4 km - 2 miles – north of Ravensburg – *Local map p 40* – Pop 21 500

Weingarten church, enhanced by its dominant situation and by its fine façade of bare sandstone, forms part of an abbey, rebuilt in the Baroque period to an ambitious plan which was never completed. The region was the cradle of the dynastic Guelph family *(p 90)* so that some of the 10-12C ancestors lie buried in the crypt.

■ THE BASILICA★★ *tour: ½ hour*

The church, which was consecrated in 1742, competes in size (102 m long, 44 m wide at the transepts - 335×144 ft) with Ottobeuren as the largest Baroque church in Germany.

The façade, framed by two towers which are short but elegant with fluted ribs, is rounded. The position of the towers and the construction above the transept crossing of a dome on a drum with wide window-openings, betrays an Italian influence transmitted by way of Salzburg. The chief architect was Gaspard Moosbrugger who was famous in Switzerland as the architect of Einsiedeln Abbey. Colossal Order pilasters applied to the stonework rise from a high base.

The vistas inside are amplified by the openings pierced through the dividing piles in a manner typical of the Vorarlberg school *(p 25)*. The side galleries are reduced to the narrowness of footbridges, curving in a graceful design which leaves uninterrupted the upward sweep of the columns towards the vaulting in the roof. Turn on reaching the transept to look back at the 1750 organ whose loft is pierced and allows the light to pass through it. The altar at the transept crossing holds the shrine of the Precious Blood which attracts many pilgrims.

The relatively circumspect painted and stucco decoration was entrusted to the great masters of the period. Cosmas Damian Asam painted scenes full of virtuosity upon the vaulting: note the perspective in the *Glorification of St. Benedict* (central bay in the nave) where painted pilasters and decoration exactly reproduce the stone architecture and stucco.

WERTHEIM ★

Michelin map 987 25 – *Local map p 217* – Pop 20 500

This pleasant town groups together its closely overlapping half-timbered houses along winding streets at the spot where the Main and Tauber Rivers meet. The perimeter towers, the Spitzturm rising up at the head of the city, and the castle whose ruins stand out red against the promontory's wooded slopes, give the town an already Rhineland appearance.

■ MAIN SIGHTS *tour: 1 hour*

Leave the car on the quay beside the Main and enter the town through the square and battlemented Main Gateway (Maintor). Go along the Maingasse to no 26, a fine **house** dating from 1573 with a carved frieze.

Marktplatz. – Among the half-timbered houses, the Zobel-Haus (bakery), a 16C building, juts forward from the aligned façades.

Angels' Well (Engelsbrunnen). – The well, a 1574 Renaissance monument in limestone, adorns the picturesque crossroads, at the church end of the Marktplatz. Above the curb two crossed stone arcs surmounted by two cherubim support the town's arms.

Church (Stadtkirche). – Enter through the small Gothic porch beside the tower. The church contains a precious **group of tombs★** (Grabdenkmäler).

The chancel *(it is not possible to walk round the tombs)* is the necropolis of the Counts of Wertheim. The **Renaissance monument to the Count of Ysenburg★★** (Isenburgsches Epitaph), on the north side, which was erected about 1590, is easily recognised from the figure of the countess in a flared robe, her gloves in her hand.

St. Kilian's Chapel. – On the far side of the church square stands this late Gothic building, a good example of a two-storey or double-ossuary chapel – now a museum.

Go to the far end of the church square and up the steps which join the rising approach to the castle. At the foot of the castle walls, take the steeper ramp on the left over a bridge to the fortified entrance to the 18C castle.

Castle. – Go beyond the castle café (Burgschenke) terrace to reach the crest of a defensive wall which juts out over the valley. From the narrow terrace with its Gothic balustrade, the view plunges down to the town and back over an impressive ruin with gaping windows.

Next ask at the café for the key to enter, higher up, the close in which the earlier castle stands isolated. Of this feudal castle there remain the old courtyard with a spiral staircase turret with a Renaissance doorway and the keep. From the platform, there is an attractive **panorama** of Wertheim and the river confluence. The horizon is darkened by the wooded heights of the Spessart in the north and the Odenwald in the west.

Return to the Main quayside by going all the way down the castle ramp.

■ ADDITIONAL SIGHT

Left Bank of the Tauber (Linkes Tauberufer). – Start for the left bank preferably from the Angels' Well, continuing by the Friedleinsgasse and the Tauber footbridge.

Walk upstream below the railway, until opposite the Kittstein Gate (Kittsteintor), on the far bank. A fine round tower enables the gate to be pinpointed from a distance. Attractive **view★** of this corner of the town overlooked by the church belfry and the castle ruins.

WESER Upper Valley ★

Michelin map 987 15

The Weser, 470 km long - 292 miles – begins at Hann. Münden from the junction of two already full rivers, the Werra and the Fulda. It first runs through the tree covered limestone mountains of the Weserbergland and then, emerging from the Porta Defile *(p 179)*, enters the plain.

It is possible to go up or down the river, which is controlled by dams between Hann. Münden and Hamelin – there are even two paddle-steamers on the run. *There is a regular daily service from May to September which takes one day downstream, two up. Also regular service between Vlotho and Minden.*

★FROM HANN. MÜNDEN TO HÖXTER

65 km - 40 miles – about 2 hours

Hann. Münden★★. – *Description p 142.*
The valley between Hann. Münden and Karlshafen has neither railway nor industry, appearing silent and at times deserted in its wooded setting. Small groups of French Huguenots, collected together by the Landgraves of Hesse, erected villages in the 18C to which they gave such symbolically pious names as Gottstreu – Constant in God.

Wahlsburg-Lippoldsberg. – *Excursion of 3 km - 2 miles – from Gieselwerder.*

The **old abbey church★** (Ehemalige Klosterkirche) of the 12C Benedictine Monastery was one of the first vaulted Romanesque churches erected in Germany. The small columns of the low narthex seem as numerous as those of a crypt.

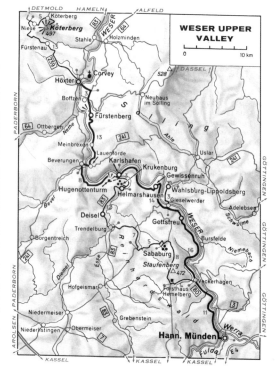

WESER UPPER VALLEY

0   10 km

Go to another Huguenot village **Gewissenruh** – meaning "peaceful conscience" – to see the minute temple (1779) and the inscriptions in French upon the houses.

Alternative route★ by Sababurg Castle. – *Extra distance 9 km - 6 miles – and ½ hour on foot Rtn. Close the gates across the forest roads described below.*
The road from the Hemelberg forest hut (Forsthaus) and Sababurg Castle goes through the Reinhardswald, one of the finest oak forests in Germany.

Sababurg. – *0.50DM.* This small and partly ruined castle (inn), is believed locally in Hesse to have been the Grimm Brothers' inspiration for the Sleeping Beauty's castle.

Deisel. – The town, like Helmarshausen, contains typical Diemel Valley peasant cottages.

Krukenburg. – *½ hour on foot Rtn.* Leave road no 83 on the outskirts of Karlshafen and then turn left into the Graseweg. Leave the car at the mountain top and walk up a surfaced path to the Krukenburg castle ruins. The most interesting are those of the Romanesque rotunda chapel.

Karlshafen. – The town was founded in 1699 at the confluence of the Weser and the Diemel round a shipping basin connected to the Weser, by the Landgrave Karl of Hesse and peopled with Huguenots. The regular plan and uniform buildings produce a monumental effect.
View★ down on to the town from the **Huguenot Tower** *(1 hour's walk Rtn by a steep path starting from the Diemel Bridge).*
The road crosses to the right bank and climbs **Fürstenberg** hill where, since 1747, the castle-factory has been making famous porcelain. *Guided tours of the porcelain museum, every hour from 9 to 11am and 1 to 4pm (Sundays 10 and 11am); closed Sundays 1 October to 30 April; 1DM.* Corvey towers in the distance mark the approach to Höxter.

Höxter. – *Description p 153.*

Köterberg★. – *18 km - 11 miles – from Höxter – by the Detmold road and, on the right, the road through Köterberg village to the summit.* **Panorama★** of the Weser winding through the rolling Weserbergland countryside. The Porta Westfalica *(p 179)* gap can be recognised on the horizon to the northwest and the Arminius Monument *(p 243)* to the west.

WESSOBRUNN Abbey ★

10 km - 6 miles – northwest of Weilheim (Michelin map 987 36, 37) – Local map p 40

The Benedictine Abbey of Wessobrunn has undergone many vicissitudes. Secularised in 1803 and cut off from its mother church in 1810, the abbey is now used as a rest home.
In the 17 and 18C many artists employed their talent in the corporative and family framework known as the School of Wessobrunn. Among these artists of Baroque genius, who were in no way specialists, the names of the Schmuzers and the Feichtmayrs stand out brilliantly in both Bavaria and the Tyrol. But the most celebrated of the group was Dominikus Zimmermann, architect and decorator of Wies Church *(p 257)*.

Church. – The church has been rebuilt near the old abbey church, of which only the 13C clock tower, covered by a saddle-back roof, remains. The present building, now the parish church, is striking for the elegance of its **interior decoration★** (Ausstattung), the freshness and softness of the coloured frescoes, the harmonious furnishings.

Monastery Buildings (Klostergebäude). – *To visit the buildings apply to the porter's lodge, from 9 to 11am and 3 to 5pm; closed Monday mornings.*
On the first floor, a magnificent gallery known as the **Fürstengang★** (Gallery of Princes) is decorated with stuccoes. Painted medallions decorate the vault, which is covered with a profusion of stuccoes where acanthus leaves, heads of cherubim and other motifs mingle.

As late as the beginning of last century, Wetzlar was still a town of lawyers and clerks, a seat of one of the Law Courts of the Holy Roman Empire (1693-1806); the old cathedral quarter – particularly the squares known as **Eisenmarkt** and **Kornmarkt** – recalls this period. The town's reputation today rests on its production of items as varied as metal pipes and cameras: it is also the birthplace of the 35-millimetre film.

Prelude to Werther. – In the spring of 1772, the young lawyer Goethe came for session to the Wetzlar tribunal. While in the town he got to know **Charlotte Buff** – Lotte – the fiancée of the diplomat, Kestner. Goethe's violent passion for the young girl could only result in the betrayal of his sincere friendship for Kestner and he resolved, therefore, to return to Frankfurt. There, he learnt not long afterwards of Kestner's suicide from a broken heart.

Two years later Goethe produced his immortal work *The Sufferings of the Young Werther*, a brilliant transposition of his own sorrowful experience and association with the tragic suicide.

■ **SIGHTS** *time: 1½ hours*

General View. – From the new Lahn Bridge (Neue Lahnbrücke) which lies above the two older bridges and affords a crossing to the Siegen–Frankfurt and Weilburg–Siegen roads, there is a view of the collegiate church whose limestone tower overlooks a mass of slate covered houses.

Collegiate Church (Dom). – The outside of the building is interesting. On the west side the construction of a Gothic work has apparently been rudely interrupted with bizarre effect. Of the 12C Romanesque edifice there remains the north tower of the façade – recessed on the left – built in basalt and a dark limestone. The construction of a new Gothic façade in the 14C was never completed – only the fine Flamboyant south tower in red limestone. The central doorway, whose decoration – the Coronation of the Virgin – was finished, opens on nothing. Work on the nave and chancel, in light stone, was ultimately completed in 13C Gothic style.

Local Museum (Städtisches Museum) and **Lotte's House*** (Lottehaus). – *Open 9am to noon and 2 to 5pm; closed Sunday afternoons and Mondays; 1DM.* The museum and house are in a former commandery of the Teutonic Order *(p 178)* which is reached from the collegiate church by way of the Pfaffengasse on the right. As the local museum it contains interesting documents on the history of the town as a judiciary centre and the Revolutionary wars; also works by Johann-Georg Wille (1715-1808), engraver to the king in Paris.

Lotte's parents' house recalls Charlotte's personality and her family setting with furniture and showcases of mementoes: first editions of *Werther* and the 30 translations of the novel.

EXCURSIONS

Starting from Giessen *(town plan in Michelin Red Guide Deutschland)*

Castle of Krofdorf-Gleiberg. – *6 km - 3½ miles.* The village perched upon a promontory, just out of the plain. From the top of the feudal castle's keep *(open April to October 10am to 6pm; closed Mondays; 0.50DM)*, there is a **panorama*** which extends as far as Vogelsberg to the east. The knights' hall serves as a restaurant.

Schiffenberg Monastery. – *7 km - 4 miles – by Bismarckstrasse and Schiffenberger Weg.*
From the Romanesque basilica (12C), belonging to the Augustinian Order, there remains standing the nave, the west façade and the priory. From here one can take pleasant walks through the surrounding countryside.

WIES Church ** (WIESKIRCHE)
Michelin map **987** east of 36 – *Local map p 42*

Wies Church, an amazing realisation of Bavarian Rococo art, stands amid the forests, peat-bogs and meadows that characterise the last slopes of the Ammergau Alps, between the Lech and the Ammer.

The Masterpiece of Dominikus Zimmermann. – It was in 1746 that Dominikus Zimmermann, a brilliant member of the Wessobrunn school *(p 256)*, was given the task, on completing Steinhausen Church *(p 235)*, of designing a pilgrimage church, to be called "in der Wies" (in the meadows). This was to be dedicated to Christ Scourged.

Dominikus Zimmermann, aided by his brother, Johann Baptist, a painter at the Bavarian court, completed this work between 1746 and 1754. Taking the plan of Steinhausen, he raised an oval cupola calling for the painted decoration which gives to the nave an overall impression of Rococo style.

Unwilling to leave the scene of his masterpiece, Zimmermann spent the last ten years of his life in a little house near the church.

TOUR *about ½ hour*

The simplicity of the exterior contrasts with the glowing richness of the oval bay beneath the cupola and the deep and narrow chancel which prolongs it. Wood carvings, gildings, stuccoes and frescoes stand out from the whitewashed walls, while the abundant light coming from the windows, whose elaborate design is characteristic of Zimmermann, is an essential factor of the decoration both inside and outside.

The most striking aspect is the impression of unity and perfect harmony which is achieved by a close adaptation of the decoration to the architecture. This was made easier by the building being completed within eight years.

The lower parts – the walls and paired pillars defining the ambulatory in the usual manner of pilgrimage churches – are deliberately sparsely decorated, for in the mind of the decorator they symbolise the Earth, while the upper parts, symbolising the Heavens, are thick with paintings, stuccoes and gilded work. The immense fresco on the dome shows Christ Returned, the Gate to Paradise and the Last Judgment before the Judge has arrived.

The choir has an unparalleled decoration: columns, balustrades, statues, gilded stuccoes and frescoes, make up an extraordinary symphony of colour.

The organ and its loft and the pulpit mark the height of Rococo art in southern Germany by the delicacy and richness of their carvings.

Michelin map **204** 5 – *Local maps pp 211 and 242* – Pop 253 400

Wiesbaden, which is a very large spa, has above all the appearance of a residential city well situated at the foot of the wooded slopes of the Taunus near the Rhine.

The National Opera sets the tone for the entertainments provided, which are many, and of a high standard: the most brilliant occur during the May Festival when the best foreign theatrical companies play in the evening and horse racing takes place by day. Wiesbaden is one of the centres of the German film industry and many artists in all fields find the atmosphere congenial.

The 27 hot springs which are recommended for rheumatism, rise either in the spa hotels (Badhäuser) or in the public establishments of which the largest is the Kaiser-Friedrich-Bad.

Wiesbaden, which was created in Roman times round the thermal springs, began to develop extensively in the 18C when the Nassau princes took up residence in the town. Court life combined with the cure seasons gave the spa its style. In 1841, in addition to the 18C Biebrich Castle, a new ducal palace was built in the centre of the town. Since 1945, when Wiesbaden was chosen to be the capital of the Land of Hesse, this new palace has been the seat of government.

Bath Quarter★★ (Kurviertel). – The quarter lies round the Kurhaus and the Wilhelmstrasse promenade. The Kurhaus is primarily an international meeting place. On either side of the esplanade, two colonnaded buildings extend the vista: to the north, the Brunnenkolonnade, which contains the thermal fountain concert and exhibition halls; to the south, the theatre.

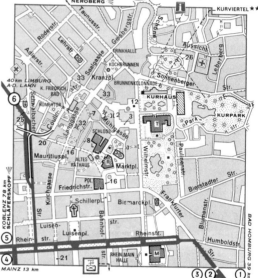

WIESBADEN CENTRE

0   500 m

An den Quellen	2
Bahnhofstraße	
Burgstraße	3
Friedrichstraße	
Goldgasse	7
Grabenstraße	8
Kaiser-Friedrich-Flatz	12
Kirchgasse	
Langgasse	
Luisenstraße	
Marktstraße	16
Michelsberg	20
Moritzstraße	21
Platter Straße	25
Prinzessin-Elisabeth-Straße	26
Wagemannstraße	32
Webergasse	33
Wilhelmstraße	

Spa Park★ (Kurpark). – The park, a shady spot, in which some of the trees are more than 100 years old, has an attractive lake. It stretches half a mile northwards along roads known as Kuranlagen which end at the Sonnenberg residential quarter.

EXCURSIONS

Neroberg. – *4 km - 2½ miles – about ½ hour.* Leave the town centre by the Taunusstrasse (northwest on the plan) and bear right into the Nerobergstrasse which leads uphill to the **Greek Orthodox Chapel**. This, complete with gilded onion domes, was built in 1855 to contain the tomb of a Russian princess who married a duke of Nassau *(open 10am to 5pm; closed Sunday mornings; 1DM).* Continue uphill, keeping left, to get to the Neroberg summit. There is a good **view** of the town from the rotunda.

Schläferskopf. – *5 km - 3 miles – by ⑤ on the plan, road no 54 – and the Schläferskopf road on the left just after a railway bridge.*

From the tower belvedere *(access: 0.40DM – closed Tuesdays except in July and August)* there is a panorama of Wiesbaden, Mainz, the Rhine Valley and the Taunus foothills.

Michelin map **987** 14 – 36 km - 25 miles – southwest of Bremen – Pop 13 000

This small town in the Oldenburg plain lies near the most important prehistoric remains in Germany, the Visbeck megalithic monuments.

In the immediate vicinity of the town along the Pestrup road, one can also see a bumpy landscape containing several hundred tumuli (Pestruper Gräberfeld).

St. Alexander's Church. – This Romanesque church benefits from a green **setting★**, reminiscent of many country churches.

Visbek Megalithic Monuments★ (Steindenkmäler). – *Excursion of 17 km - 10½ miles.* Leave Wildeshausen by the Cloppenburg road. Immediately before the access road to the motorway, turn left into signposted roads, "Visbeker Braut".

The Betrothed Woman★ (Visbeker Braut). – The monument is, in fact, a group of granite rocks, set in the form of a rectangle 80 m by 7 m – 260 x 23 ft – in a clearing.

Continue towards Cloppenburg but bear left at Alhorn towards Visbek. After crossing the motorway leave the car at the Engelmannsbäke Inn and walk to the Visbeker Bräutigam.

The Betrothed Man★ (Visbeker Bräutigam). – *½ hour on foot Rtn.* You pass a dolmen, which is thought to have served as a sacrificial table (Opfertisch), before reaching the alignment which is like the previous monument only larger. The rectangle consists of 80 blocks. At the extreme west end an elongated funeral chamber, made from upright granite blocks covered with heavy stones, is perhaps a replica of contemporary prehistoric houses.

WILDUNGEN, Bad ★

Michelin map 987 25 – Local map p 252 – Pop 15 500

The waters of this spa, used for maladies of the kidneys and gall bladder, are now also the source of a thriving industry in bottled mineral waters. The most impressive bathing installations, which extend to the first of the Kellerwald woods lie on either side of the Brunnenallee, along the Kurpark and end in the horseshoe buildings of the Georg-Viktor spring. Many Dutch people visit the spa which is the busiest tourist centre in the picturesque Waldeck region.

Protestant Church (Evangelische Stadtkirche). – The church's beautiful 14C tower rises above the old town (Niederwildungen). Enter through the south door on the car park side.

The 1403 **altarpiece★★** (Wildunger Altar) on the high altar by Konrad of Soest *(p 232)* is one of the earliest landmarks in German painting. The sense of depth, the elongation of the highly idealised figures and the delicacy of the reds, pinks and mauves are remarkable.

The paintings depict the Life and Passion of Our Lord. On the outer sides of the door panels are St. Catherine, John the Baptist, St. Elizabeth (the Visitation) and St. Nicholas.

WILHELMSHAVEN

Michelin map 987 south of 4 – Pop 102 500 – *Town plan in Michelin Red Guide Deutschland*

Wilhelmshaven, which stands on the Jade Bay (Jadebusen), was the great naval port of Germany between the wars and as such a target which was largely destroyed in the last war.

In 1956 German ships, this time belonging to the Federal Republic, once more entered the harbour of the town. The construction of an oil pipeline 400 km long - 249 miles – from the port to the Ruhr Basin has brought about specialisation in the handling of oil and made it Germany's third most important port on the North Sea after Hamburg and Bremen.

Town Hall. – This is a large modern (1927) brick building whose tower forms a **viewpoint** over the town, the harbour and the bay. *Access: Mondays to Thursdays 8am to 4pm (3pm Fridays); Saturdays, Sundays and holidays between 15 May to 10 September, 10am to 4pm; 0.50DM.*

Coastal Museum (Küsten-Museum). – *City-Haus (facing town hall). Open 10am to 1pm and 3 to 6pm; closed Saturday afternoons and Mondays.*

The museum is devoted to the formation of the coasts of the North Sea due to the rivers and tides. The Frisian Islands and Jade bay, the peat bogs, varied scenery of the area, the mode of life beginning with the prehistoric ages (the result of excavations) are explained and illustrated. With models of ships and of the town, one can follow the development of the port.

Aquarium. – *Open in summer 10am to 7pm; in winter 10am to 1pm and 3 to 6pm; 2DM.*

The aquarium which is beside the bay, near the "green beach" (Südstrand), displays the fauna and flora of the North Sea: starfish and anemones, hermit crabs, crustaceans, sea urchins, shellfish, edible fish and, the chief attraction, a delightful family of seals.

EXCURSION

Gödens-Varel-Rodenkirchen. – *47 km - 29 miles – plus 1 hour sightseeing.* Take the road to Oldenburg. Just after Sande bear right towards Neustadt–Gödens.

Château of Gödens. – In the middle of a superb park is a 17C castle surrounded by a moat, built in brick and stone, which recalls those of Münsterland *(p 193)*. Enter through a Renaissance doorway into an open courtyard, with an elegant octagonal staircase.

Return to the road to Oldenburg and bear left on the road to Varel.

Varel. – The church of the old château (Schlosskirche) fortified in granite, contains several works by the sculptor **Ludwig Münstermann** (beginning of the 17C): note the baptismal fonts, the pulpit and the Last Supper above the altar, where the expressive characters and tormented attitudes foreshadow the Baroque movement.

Follow route no 437 to Rodenkirchen.

Rodenkirchen. – This village bordering the lower Weser also has a fortified church were the altar and pulpit (around 1630) are by the same sculptor, Münstermann.

WIMPFEN, Bad ★★

Michelin map 206 11 – *Local maps pp 151 and 195* – Pop 6 000

The fortified town of Wimpfen, the imperial residence in the 13C of the Hohenstaufens, is today, with its picturesque network of streets lined with half-timbered houses, a worthwhile stopping place for any traveller. It looks down on a bridge over the Neckar, from which there is an attractive view of the town.

Along the foot of the hill extend the Ludwigshalle
Saltworks – salt brought prosperity to this entire region –
and the built up area of Bad Wimpfen im Tal, grouped
round a former collegiate church.

■ **THE UPPER TOWN★★** (Bad Wimpfen am Berg)

tour: 1 hour

Start from the Marktplatz and walk behind the Rathaus to the last remains of the imperial palace which are scattered at the end of the spur on which the town is built.

Imperial Palace   remains (Kaiserpfalz). – Standing isolated, behind the Rathaus, is the **Blue Tower** (Blauer Turm) **(A)**, the tallest building in the town. The Neo-Feudal top dates from the 19C. Climb the tower, occupied as heretofore by a watchman, for a panoramic view of the town and the valley *(access April to September 9am to noon and 1.30 to 5pm; closed Mondays; 0.50DM).*

Further on is the Romanesque Steinhaus **(B)**, which had a stepped gable added to its façade in the 16C.

Go down 4 steps from the panoramic terrace preceding the Steinhaus to the foot of the wall to see on the right, the Romanesque blind arcades with small twin columns through which light entered the gallery in the old palace. The decorative intricacy of the arcade demonstrates the building genius of the Hohenstaufens under whom Romanesque civil architecture reached its peak *(see also Gelnhausen, p 132).*

Continue along the wall until you come to some steps on the right which you climb to reach the tip of the spur and the foot of the **Red Tower** (roter Turm) (**C**), the fortress's last defence. The belvederes on the spur afford views of the Neckar Plain and the river bend.

(After a photo by R. Schuler)

Bad Wimpfen – The upper town.

Return towards the centre but bear left immediately to drop down towards the town's main street which you reach by going through the Hohenstaufen Gateway (Hohenstaufentor) (**D**), the principal entrance to the castle in mediaeval times. Bear right for the Lion Fountain (Löwenbrunnen) (**E**) crossroads where you turn first left then right along the Klostergasse.

Klostergasse★. – This street, which has a considerable rustic charm, contains some half-timbered houses standing in their own gardens. On the left are the former bath-houses, which can be recognised by their exterior galleries. Higher up, on the right, house no 10 dates from 1451.

Return to the Langgasse crossroads and go down a very narrow alley opposite, which leads to the Hauptstrasse which you follow left. Almost immediately on the left, at no 45, is the courtyard of the former hospital (Spitalhof), a half-timbered building and one of the oldest in Wimpfen.

Return up the Hauptstrasse with its many picturesque signs. On the right, a bit beyond the beautiful 1576 Eagle Fountain (Alderbrunnen) (**K**), can be seen, through the Badgasse alley, an unusual small house narrowly drawn up to an extraordinary height. Return to the Marktplatz by way of the Salzgasse.

■ ADDITIONAL SIGHT

St. Peter's Church (Stiftskirche). – *At Bad Wimpfen im Tal. Open 10am to noon and 3 to 5pm on weekdays; Sundays and holidays, 11am to noon and 3.30 to 5pm; closed Saturdays; apply to the porter's lodge in the monastery.*

This collegiate church was a dependent of the priory which, since 1947, has been reoccupied by Benedictines. The 13C Gothic church has kept, from an earlier Romanesque building, a west face *(p 23)* which is strikingly rough and bold.

The **cloister★★** (Kreuzgang) shows the Gothic style slowly evolving towards aridity. The east gallery, which is late 13C, is an example of Gothic at its height with purity of line displayed in the tri- or quadrilobed bays and the carved decoration. The north gallery, which dates from about 1350, and where the design is already more angular, marks the transition to the style of the west gallery, built at the end of the 15C where the style is thin and cold.

BAD WIMPFEN

0   200 m

HEIDELBERG 53 km   HEILBRONN
MOSBACH 20 km   16 km
VALLÉE DU NECKAR   vers 27

NECKAR

Hauptstraße	5
Kirchgasse	6
Langgasse	7
Marktplatz	8
Marktrain	9
Neutorstraße	10
Rappenauer Straße	12
Salzgasse	13
Schwibbogengasse	15
Spitalhof	17

Badgasse	2
Biberacher Straße	3
Burgviertel	4

■ WOLFENBÜTTEL ★

Michelin map **987** west of 16 – Pop 54 000 – *Town plan in Michelin Red Guide Deutschland*

For three centuries, until the court transferred to Brunswick in 1753, Wolfenbüttel was the residence of the Dukes of Brunswick and Lüneburg. The exact and spacious **plan** of this small town, with straight streets ending in vast symmetrical squares, gives it great unity.

It is one of the most successful examples of Renaissance town planning in Germany.

The local style of half-timbering is very elegant. Lining the Lange Herzogstrasse and the main square (Stadtmarkt) are houses with splayed upright beams filled in with pink bricks.

■ MAIN SIGHTS tour: ½ hour

Stadtmarkt★. – This square owes its character to the surrounding early 17C wooden houses of which a well coordinated group form the town hall (north and west sides of the square). Picturesque weather vanes creak in the winds from the plain. The philologist **Schottell,** inventor of the semi-colon, and known as the father of German grammar, lived in the square in about 1650.

The statue to Duke Augustus (1635-66) honours one of the most cultivated princes of the House of Brunswick and Lüneburg.

Church of St. Mary (Hauptkirche). – St. Mary's, built as a Protestant church in 1608, on the Kornmarkt, is Gothic in design with very tall windows and pointed vaulting, but it also has features characteristic of the late Renaissance. Note the lateral gables whose swollen pediments with niches and columns have a thick decoration of curiously twisted scrollwork. The massive tower with a Baroque roof resembles that on the castle.

■ ADDITIONAL SIGHTS

Castle. – The castle is reached by an attractive narrow arcaded street, the Krambuden.
This old 12C castle, captured by Henry the Lion *(p 90)*, underwent alterations and rebuildings before becoming the present Baroque residence, adorned with pediments and overlooked by a fine Renaissance **tower★**.

Open 9.30am to 12.30pm (1.30pm Sundays) and Wednesdays also 3 to 5pm; closed Mondays.

The 16 and 17C saw several ducal patrons as local rulers and the castle as a centre of literature, letters and sacred music. Lessing, the precursor of the German theatre, spent ten years (1770-81) at Wolfenbüttel as the duke's librarian, writing among other things at this time his *Nathan the Wise.* His last home was a building with a mansard roof **(Lessing-Haus)** at the north end of the esplanade *(open: in summer, 10am to noon and 3 to 5pm; in winter, 10am to noon and 2 to 4pm; closed Mondays and some holidays)*. Right of the Lessing-Haus is the **Arsenal** (Zeughaus), a vigorous Renaissance building of 1613.

Trinity Church (Trinitatiskirche). – *Apply for information to Frau Arnold, Kannengiesser-strasse 16.*

The church, which closes the Holzmarkt at its east end, was built in 1719, utilising a twin towered city gate as part of the construction – hence the unusual flat outline. The interior, which is oval, is encircled by two tiers of galleries.

At the back, a deconsecrated burial ground has been turned into a romantic **public garden.**

WÖRISHOFEN, Bad ★
Michelin map 📕987📕 36 – *Local map p 40* – Pop 10 800

Wörishofen has become unique among the Bavarian-Swabian villages on the plateau in this last century through the impulse of its priest, Father **Sebastian Kneipp** (1821-97). This priest, a passionate believer in natural cures, perfected his treatment here – applying hydrotherapy and diets tending towards vegetarianism, to a wide variety of maladies. Many Germans have always believed in and given active support to such cures and the priest's village thus became a large spa. Cures are conducted in hotels but the unbeliever can see the external evidence by taking a walk through the Kurpark, shaded by birches and pines, where he will find the characteristic pools (Wassertretanlagen).

WORMS ★★
Michelin map 📕204📕 8 – *Local map p 215* – Pop 77 000

Worms was, like Speyer and Mainz, an Imperial residence on the banks of the Rhine, a town with a legendary past, a town of history and prestige. Today it extends along the river which irrigates the rich vine growing Palatinate Plain. The Church of Our Lady (Liebfrauenkirche) which stands in the northern suburb amidst the vines has given its name to the famous "Liebfrauenmilch" (milk of Our Lady).

Luther before the Diet. – In 1521 Rome promulgated a bull against all that Luther believed. Thereupon the young Charles V convoked the Imperial Diet at Worms and invited Luther to appear before it. He went "as though going to his death" although without hesitation, held back by the anxiety of his friends but acclaimed by enthusiastic crowds. He refused to retract his beliefs and was banned from the Empire *(p 20)*.

■ MAIN SIGHTS *tour: ¾ hour*

St. Peter's Cathedral★★ (Dom). – *Open March to October, 8am (noon Sundays) to 6pm; November to February, 9am (noon Sundays) to 5pm; 0.20DM.*

The cathedral is a Romanesque edifice with two apses quartered by four round staircase towers. Outside, the west chancel, completed in about 1230, is one of the best examples of Romanesque architecture in Germany with two dwarf galleries superimposed in the Rhineland manner *(p 23)*. Enter through the Gothic south doorway, on whose tympanum may be seen the Coronation of the Virgin. On the reverse side is a splendid 12C Christ. In the first chapel on the right as you enter, a very old carving shows Daniel in the Den of Lions.

The east chancel, on the right, is the oldest and has pointed vaulting. The transept crossing is admirable with the Rhineland cupola mounted on squinches. Eight Imperial tombs rest beneath this chancel *(access: 0.10DM)*.

The Romanesque nave, which has five bays with vaulting on diagonal ribs, is decorated with blind arcades whose ever more intricate carving recalls the style's development.

The west chancel, the last to be built, is elegant with a chequered frieze, arches to its blind arcades and rose windows.

A series of five **Gothic sculptures★** (Reliefs aus dem Leben Christi), the Annunciation, Nativity, Entombment, Resurrection and Tree of Jesse adorn the north aisle.

Luther Monument (Lutherdenkmal) (Y). – The monument, which was inaugurated in 1868, commemorates Luther's appearance before the Diet *(see above)*. Luther, in the centre, is surrounded by the precursors of the Reformation, Pietro Valdo, John Wycliffe, John Hus and Savonarola; at the four corners stand, at the back, Reuchlin and Melanchthon, Protestant theologians, and in front of the Landgrave of Hesse (Philip the Magnanimous, *details p 175*) and the Elector of Saxony, both Luther's patrons. Seated women between the figures symbolise the towns of Augsburg, Speyer and Magdeburg.

■ ADDITIONAL SIGHTS

Jewish Cemetery★ (Judenfriedhof) (Z). – Worms was one of the old centres of Jewish culture in Germany. The ancient cemetery, which has been in use since the 11C, bristles with more than 1 000 ancient steles carved in Hebrew. View of the cathedral towers.

St. Martin's (Y A). – The Romanesque west door of this church is flanked by eight columns with crocheted capitals. The interlacing of vine stems and leaves on the tympanum is highly decorative. The interior plan is identical with that of the cathedral.

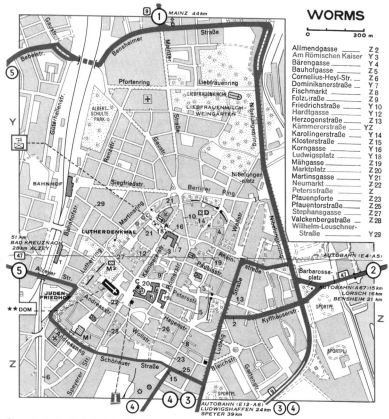

Church of the Holy Trinity (Dreifaltigkeitskirche) (Z C). – *Open April to October, 9am to noon and 2 to 5pm; November to March, 10am to 4pm; 0.30DM. Brochure in English.*

Only the Baroque façade and tower remain of the 18C building. The interior has been remodelled to commemorate the Lutheran Reformation.

Synagogue (Y D). – *Open 10am to noon, 2 to 4pm.* This, the oldest synagogue in Germany, was founded in the 11C and rebuilt in 1961. Nearby, the Karolingerstrasse passes beneath a doorway, a fragment of the mediaeval perimeter wall.

Municipal Museum (Museum der Stadt Worms) (Z M¹). – *Open April to September, 9am to noon and 2 to 5pm; in winter, 10am to noon and 2 to 4pm; 1DM.*

The prehistorical and historical collections are in the Romanesque cloister of a former monastery. The church contains sacred art.

Heylshof Museum (Kunsthaus Heylshof) (Z M²). – *Open 10am to noon and 2 to 5pm (4pm in winter); closed Mondays; 1DM.*

The collections include 15 and 16C stained glass, Frankenthal and Ludwigsburg porcelain and, in the basement, ceramics and glass.

WUPPERTAL

Michelin map 202 16, 17 – Pop 406 000 – *Town plan in Michelin Red Guide Deutschland*

Wuppertal was the name given in 1930 to a vast built-up area which has spread along the Wupper Valley and whose prosperity derives from the textile industry.

The area consists of two centres, Barmen and Elberfeld, lined by an **overhead suspension railway*** (Schwebahn), a 13 km long - 8 mile – monorail, which follows the course of the river. This ancestor to the modern monorail has been in existence since 1900.

Von der Heydt Museum*. – At Wuppertal-Elberfeld, Turmhof 8. Open 10am to 5pm (9pm Tuesdays); closed Mondays.

The museum offers a panorama of German painting from 1850 to the present. The collection includes works by Hans von Marees (1837-87), a native of the town.

Contemporary art is shown through acquisitions and recent gifts.

WURZACH, Bad

Michelin map 206 7, 8 – Pop 4 000

Wurzach stands somewhat isolated in the centre of the hills of Upper Swabia which give place in this region to vast Rieds, or peat bogs studded with birches and conifers. A Baroque castle with a presumptuous staircase remains as a monument to its past.

Church* (Pfarrkirche). – This was completed in 1777. The interior, which is bathed in light, reveals a happy compromise between the style of Louis XVI and German Neo-Classicism. High pilasters with Ionic capitals decorated with garlands, are all that divide the discreetly decorative hall. The demands for symmetry which were all powerful at that period, explain the dummy pulpit with a Christ in Sorrow facing that intended for the preacher.

Bad Waldsee. – *Excursion of 13 km - 8 miles.* This small Swabian Town is tightly massed on a narrow isthmus between two lakes. The larger **lake*** to the east reflects the town roofs rising one above the other and the twin white towers of St. Peters' (walk round the lake: ½ hour on foot Rtn).

WÜRZBURG ★★

Michelin map **987** 26 – *Local map p 217* – Pop 127 000

Würzburg, which stands beside the Main in a setting of vineyards at the foot of the episcopal citadel of Marienberg, acquired its plan and appearance between 1650 and 1750 under the supervision of three prince-bishops who were members of the Schönborn family and who built the town's Baroque churches and the Residence Palace.

The Master of Würzburg. – This was the name given to **Tilman Riemenschneider** (1460-1531), the sculptor who came to live in the town in 1483 and remained faithful all his life to the Gothic ideal. Decoration counted little with him. His interest centred entirely on people whose faces, hands and clothes served as the means to express emotion and sensitivity. His work has a melancholy gravity. The splendid altarpieces at Creglingen and Rothenburg, the Würzburg statues, the tomb at Bamberg, are among the treasures of Franconian art.

■ THE RESIDENZ★★ *tour: 1 hour*

Residence open: 1 April to 30 September, 9am to 5pm; 1 October to 31 March, 10am to 4pm; closed Mondays; 2DM.

The Residenz is one of the biggest Baroque palaces in Germany and one of the most successful. It was begun in 1720 under the aegis of Balthazar Neumann and was completed in 1744 when it became the residence of the prince-bishops in succession to the Marienberg citadel.

The **grand staircase★** (Treppenhaus), with a double flight of stairs, ends on the left of the spacious vestibule which is one of Neumann's masterpieces. The vaulted ceiling is decorated with a large fresco of the *Triumph of the Prince-Bishop Karl-Friedrich von Greiffenklau* painted by the Venetian, Tiepolo, in 1753.

The **imperial hall★★** (Kaisersaal) on the first floor is a splendid room. It is oval in shape but its outstanding feature is its decoration. **Tiepolo's paintings** illustrate episodes in the town's history: the marriage of Frederick Barbarossa and Beatrice of Burgundy, the bishops' homage to the Emperor. Note the artist's skill in passing, in accordance with Baroque taste, from sculpture imperceptibly to false relief painting.

Church★★ (Hofkirche). – The architectural fantasy and audacity displayed by Neumann in this building are amazing – the complex positioning of oval arching, the brilliance of gold highlighting the colours of the Byss frescoes. Two paintings by Tiepolo have pride of place on the side altars: *The Assumption* and *The Fall of the Angels*.

Gardens★ (Hofgarten). – The gardens' terrace design and elegant approaches, to the east, was determined by the stepping of former bastions. From this side you can see clearly the palace's 167 m long - 183 yd – façade and the elegance of the main central building.

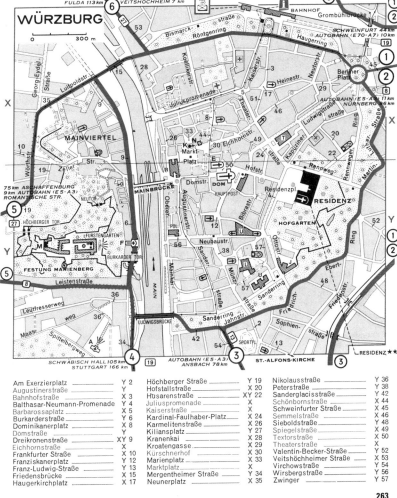

Am Exerzierplatz	Y 2	Höchberger Straße	Y 19	Nikolausstraße	Y 36
Augustinerstraße	X 3	Hofstallstraße	X 20	Peterstraße	Y 38
Bahnhofstraße	X 3	Husarenstraße	XY 22	Sanderglacisstraße	Y 42
Balthasar-Neumann-Promenade	Y 4	Juliuspromenade	X	Schönbornstraße	X 44
Barbarossaplatz	X 5	Kaiserstraße	X	Schweinfurter Straße	X 45
Burkarderstraße	Y 6	Kardinal-Faulhaber-Platz	X 24	Semmelstraße	X 46
Dominikanerplatz	X 8	Karmelitenstraße	X 26	Sieboldstraße	X 48
Domstraße	Y	Kiliansplatz	X 27	Spiegelstraße	X 49
Dreikronenstraße	XY 9	Kranenkai	X 28	Textorstraße	X 50
Eichhornstraße	X	Kroatengasse	X 29	Theaterstraße	X
Frankfurter Straße	X 10	Kürschnerhof	X 30	Valentin-Becker-Straße	Y 52
Franziskanerplatz	Y 12	Marienplatz	X 33	Veitshöchheimer Straße	Y 53
Franz-Ludwig-Straße	Y 13	Marktplatz	X	Virchowstraße	Y 54
Friedensbrücke	X 15	Mergentheimer Straße	Y 34	Wirsbergstraße	Y 56
Haugerkirchplatz	X 17	Neunerplatz	X 35	Zwinger	Y 57

263

■ ADDITIONAL SIGHTS

Cathedral of St. Kilian (Dom). – Rebuilt after 1945, the cathedral has preserved its Romanesque exterior. The interior, however, is marked by several different centuries: the austere yet harmonious Romanesque nave, with its false ceiling; the Baroque stucco decoration of the upper half of the chancel which contrasts with the unique altar (1967). On the right side of the transept there are three sculptures by Riemenschneider (16C) which blend well with the decoration by H. Weber (1967). Against the pillars in the nave are the tombs of the prince-bishops lined up side by side.

Zum Falken House★ (X N). – The graceful façade with Rococo decoration of this house was reconstructed after the war.

Old Bridge★ (Mainbrücke) (Y). – This 15C bridge is adorned with the statues of eleven saints, monumental in size and Baroque in concept.

St. Mary's Chapel (Marienkapelle) (X K). – This fine Gothic hall-church with its lovely upward sweeping lines, was built by the town burghers in the 14 and 15C. The beautiful Annunciation over the north door dates from about 1420.

Inside, note at the back of the façade a 1502 tombstone carved by Riemenschneider and, on a pillar on the right, a commemorative plaque to Balthazar Neumann.

Neumünster (XY E). – The **façade★** of this 18C church is a fine example, said to be by Dientzenhofer, of Baroque architecture. The general line of the twin superimposed gables depends on the depth of the doorway's curve.

The main part of the interior, which is divided into three and is the heritage of an earlier Romanesque church, is preceded by a vast bay covered by a dome. In niches beneath the cupola are a Virgin and Child attributed to Riemenschneider and a strange 14C figure of Christ with folded arms. The west crypt contains the shrine of St. Kilian, apostle and patron of Franconia, whose relics are venerated in the adjoining cathedral (canonised: 1967).

Lusamgärtlein (XY E). – This small garden lies on the north side of the Neumünster where the 12C cloister used to stand and of which a gallery still remains. A modern funerary monument has been erected in honour of the minstrel-poet Walther von der Vogelweide *(p 28)* who died in 1231 and is said to be buried in this garden.

Outside the centre of the town

Marienberg Fortress (Festung Marienberg) (Y). – *Guided tours 1 April to 30 September, 9am to 5pm; 1 October to 31 March, 10am to 4pm; time: 1 hour; 1DM; closed Mondays.*

The fortress occupies a commanding position above the town. The stronghold, a residence of the prince-bishops from the end of the 12C, became, in the 17C, an Imperial fortress.

The old castle forms a rectangle around a courtyard in which stand a circular 13C keep, a Renaissance well building and the **round Lady Chapel** (Marienkirche). The chapel is paved with bishops' tombstones and covered by a lovely cupola decorated with Baroque stuccowork.

The terrace of the **Princes' Garden** (Fürstengarten) provides a **view★** of Würzburg.

The Franconian Museum of the Main★★ (Mainfränkisches Museum). – *Open 10am to 5pm (4pm from 1 November to 31 March); 1.50DM; Brochure in English.*

The entrance is on the right in the first courtyard on Marienberg Castle. Among the displays of art and local crafts in the Arsenal galleries (Zeughaus) may be seen sculptures by Riemenschneider (1st floor, gallery 3): *Adam and Eve*, the *Virgin and Child* and statues of the apostles.

The magnificent rooms and vaulted cellars of the Echterbastei contain statues, religious gold and silver plate and Franconian popular art. The former wine store is particularly interesting since it includes some old presses.

Käppele (Y A). – This well situated Baroque pilgrimage chapel with curious rounded domes consists of a central chapel adorned with frescoes by Matthäus Günther and Rococo stuccowork by J. M. Feichtmayr to which abuts a miraculous chapel. The terrace affords the most interesting **view★★** of the town and the River Main. The Marienberg Fortress, can be seen in the foreground, rising from surrounding vineyards.

St. Burkard's Church (Y F). – This Romanesque and Gothic church stands picturesquely on the left bank of the Main. The chancel bestrides the street (covered way).

St. Alfonso's Church★. – *Go by the Franz-Ludwig-Strasse (southeast on the plan) and after passing beneath the railway, turn sharp right into the uphill Keesburgstrasse Avenue.* The church, which was built in 1954, is an example of the Renaissance in ecclesiastical architecture of the Würzburg diocese. Inside the vigorous composition on the chancel wall by the painter Meistermann, depicts in flamboyant colours, *Creation's Glorification of the Deity.*

EXCURSIONS

Veitschöchheim★. – *7 km - 4½ miles – plus 1 hour sightseeing.* Leave Würzburg by ⑥, road no 27. On arriving at Veitschöchheim, turn left opposite the main entrance to the park and leave the car beside the Main.

Park★. – The prince-bishops of the 18C were constantly improving the park so that it ended up as an entirely Rococo garden. The formal south end includes vistas of clipped limes and hornbeams and green arbors peopled with small Rococo statues. In the centre of the great lake stands the superb Parnassus group carved in 1766 (Pegasus, the Muses and Apollo).

Castle. – *Open 1 April to 30 September, 9am to noon and 1 to 5.30pm; closed Mondays; 1DM.*
Fine Rococo (gaming tables) and Empire furnishings.

The Main Valley Vineyards★. – *Round tour of 98 km - 61 miles – about 4½ hours.* Leave Würzburg by ⑤ and follow road no 13 along the right bank of the Main.

Sommerhausen. – Small enclosed town, the home of vine growers. The pinnacled gable of the 16C town hall and even more that of the castle, dominate the main street.

Ochsenfurt. – *Tour: ½ hour.* Cross the Main, to enter the town through one of the gates in the encircling **ramparts★** best seen from the promenades on the west side. From the bridge make for the corner of the Brückengasse and the main street, the Hauptstrasse, to see the half-timbered houses adorned with old signs or statuettes. Sightseers gather beneath the clock with striking jacks on the 15C **New Town Hall** at whose corner stands a lovely statue of the Virgin (1498).

Frickenhausen. – Beautiful Renaissance door with ramshorn scrollwork.

Markbreit. – *Tour: ¼ hour.* The main gate (Maintor), dating from 1600, at the end of the bridge across the Main, together with the town hall, which is a little older, form a Renaissance **group of buildings★**. Two Baroque houses with corner oriel windows complete the picture.

Sulzfeld. – Go into this fortified town where you will find that the 17C **town hall** has a gable ornamented with scrollwork and pinnacles.

Turn right at Kitzingen towards Nuremberg. Soon the walls of Mainbernheim come into sight on the left. Turn left for Iphofen, 3 km - 2 miles – further on. Continue through Rödelsee and Rüdenhausen (avoid roads that take you on to the motorway) to Wiesentheid.

Wiesentheid. – At least see the **church**, decorated in false relief paintings in the Italian style (1728) and the park of the Castle of the Counts of Schönborn.

Prichsenstadt. – *Tour: ½ hour.* From the west, pass through two gates in succession to reach the **main street★** (Hauptstrasse) where the houses, some stone, some half-timbered, are decorated with trelliswork.

Go into an adjacent alley (sign "Alfons Hyna – Pferde und Viehhandlung") to see the Freihof, one of the most attractive houses in the town which is decorated with wood carvings.

Leave the town by the same gate but turn right into the road which, beyond Laub, will bring you on to the return road to Würzburg (no 22).

Dettelbach. – *Tour: ¼ hour.* Go through the perimeter wall and the upper town to the plateau beyond, where, on the right, you will come to the **pilgrimage church** (Wallfahrtskirche). This building with its detailed construction clearly marks the transition between Flamboyant Gothic and Renaissance art. The 1626 **pulpit★** (Kanzel) in limestone and alabaster, is carved to look like the spreading Tree of Jesse.

XANTEN

Michelin map **202** 4 5 – Pop 15 600

Xanten, originally a Roman town, honours equally St. Victor, martyr of the Legion of Thebes and Siegfried, hero of the Nibelungen saga *(p 209)* who, according to legend, was born in the town. Traces remain of the mediaeval fortifications, such as the **Cleves Gate** (Klever Tor) which was built in 1393.

St. Victor's Cathedral★ (Dom). – *The south doorway is being restored.*
This is one of the finest Gothic buildings in the Lower Rhineland. A Romanesque church was erected in the 12C on the site of an earlier church founded by St. Helen to guard St. Victor's relics. The west end and towers, although damaged by the war, remain standing. The Gothic cathedral was begun in 1263; the nave with five aisles was completed in the 16C.

The high altar, where St. Victor's shrine stands, has a fine altarpiece by Barthel Bruyn the Elder (1530) illustrating the lives of St. Helen and St. Victor. The altarpiece of the Virgin (1536) in the south aisle, with the intricately worked predella is by Heinrich Douvermann, the Master of Kalkar *(p 155)*; the outer panels of the altarpiece to St. Antony (1500) in the north aisle were painted by Derick Baegert. The Gothic **cloister** is 16C.

Cathedral Museum (Dom-Museum). – *Entrance off the end of the first south aisle. Open 10am to noon and 2 to 5.30pm (5pm November to March).* The cathedral treasure is in the museum.

Local Museum (Regionalmuseum). – *Open 10am to 6pm (7pm Sundays); closed Mondays; 0.50DM. Brochure in English.*
Prehistoric, Roman and Celtic eras are exhibited on the ground floor. Temporary exhibitions on the 1st floor.

The ZUGSPITZE ★★★

Michelin map **987** 36, 37 – southwest of Garmisch-Partenkirchen – *Local map p 42*

Highest peak on German territory, the Zugspitze is the northwest pillar of the limestone massif of Wetterstein, whose range forms a magnificent background for Garmisch, Ehrwald and Lermoos. In keeping with its position, the panorama it offers, and the extensive ski-fields which can be used to the end of spring in the mountainous amphitheatre of the Schneeferner, the summit is well served with tourist arrangements. It can be reached by cableway either from the Schneefernerhaus, terminus of the cog-railway from Garmisch, or direct from the Eibsee, or from the Zugspitzkamm station in Austria, terminus of the cableway from Ehrwald.

■ ASCENT OF THE ZUGSPITZE★★★

From the Schneefernerhaus (Bavarian side). – *Access p 132 – 1 to 2 hours Rtn, according to crowds.*
The underground train trip ends at an altitude of 2 650 m - 8 691 ft – at the Hotel Schneefernerhaus. As long as good snow conditions continue (October–June), the bottom of this amphitheatre, known as the Zugspitzplatt, provides a skiing area of about 7·5 km² - 3 sq miles (numerous ski-lifts) – between 2 300 m and 2 800 m - 7 500 to 9 800 ft – which can be reached from the hotel by a short descent by cableway. By an inside lift to the fifth floor, one reaches the departure station of the cableway for the Zugspitze summit ("Gipfelbahn" – departures at least every ½ hour between 8.15am and 5.15pm – Rtn fare: 5DM).

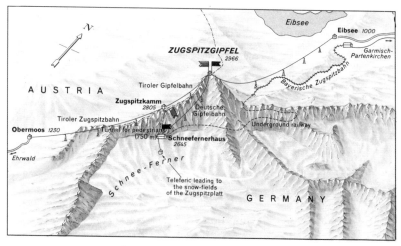

Plan of climbing arrangements on the Zugspitze

From the Eibsee (Bavarian side). – *Access by the road leaving Garmisch: see local map p 131. Cableway departures at least every ½ hour. Fare: 23DM Rtn Eibsee–Zugspitzgipfel.*

From the Zugspitzkamm (Tyrolean side). – *See Michelin Green Guide Austria. Take your passport or identity card.* The cableway from Ehrwald is linked to the "Zugspitzkamm" station *(transfer from one car to another)* by a cableway which also goes to the summit. *Departures at least every hour from 8.15am to 5.30pm; Rtn fare: 150 Schillings from the lower station.*

Finally it is also possible to leave Zugspitzkamm and, by a steeply descending glacial tunnel 800 m long, come out on the Bavarian side at the Schneefernerhaus *(descent: 20 minutes; toll; 0.50DM or 3.50S. – customs formalities).*

■ THE ZUGSPITZE SUMMIT★★★ (Zugspitzgipfel)

The summit is occupied by several edifices which are linked by terraces and lie in the following sequence across the frontier *(customs formalities)*:

– **On the German side** (east) beside the eastern peak, on which a cross has been planted (alt 2 961 m - 9 715 ft) stand the upper terminals of the Gipfelbahn (belvedere terrace at 2 966 m - 9 735 ft) and the Eibsee cableway. Next come the Müncher Haus refuge and the observatory.

– **On the Austrian side** (west – alt 2 963 m - 9 721 ft) stands the upper terminal of the Zugspitzkamm cableway.

The **panorama**★★★ to the south reveals the forward bastions of the Kaisergebirge, the Dachstein and the Karwendel, the glacial summits of the High Tauern (Grossglockner, Gross Venediger), the High Alps of the Tyrol (Zillertal, Stubai and Ötztal Alps), of the Ortler and Bernina. Nearer, towards the east, the Arlberg mountains stand before the Säntis in the Appenzell Alps and beyond the mountains of the Allgäu and the Ammergau. To the north are the Bavarian lowlands and the large stretches of water of the Ammersee and the Starnberger See.

■ CROSSING THE ZUGSPITZE★★

By combining the various railways and cableways on the Zugspitze several round tours are possible. Of these the most popular is: by railway from Eibsee to Schneerfernerhaus – cableway to the summit – cableway return direct to Eibsee. *Fare: 25DM.*

ZWIEFALTEN ★

Michelin map **206** northwest of 6 – Pop 2 800

This village on the Danubian edge of the Swabian Jura has a remarkable Baroque church.

Church★★ **(Ehemalige Klosterkirche).** – This former Benedictine abbey church, which became an object of pilgrimage, was remodelled in the Baroque style from 1741 onwards. Inside is a striking profusion of colours, movement and exuberance in the very free decoration.

The best view of the church is from the grille dividing the porch from the nave. Gold and brown predominate in the décor. The paintings on the ceiling are devoted to the Virgin; above the organ the theme is *Salve Regina*; the dome exalts the Queen of all the Saints; the pendentives represent the four quarters of the globe.

The pulpit illustrates the vision of Ezekiel; out of the tree of sin rises the hollow pulpit where man's suffering and his redemption through the Instruments of the Passion are shown symbolically. The Tree of Life ends in the Cross of the Redemption at Christ's Coronation.

The less ornate chancel is divided from the nave by the altar to the Virgin which is surrounded by superb grilles dating from 1757. The choir-stalls are richly carved and gilded. The 1753 altarpiece at the high altar is a vigorous composition illustrating the Vision of Isaiah.

Before leaving look at the extraordinary confessionals constructed to look like grottoes.

ZWISCHENAHN, Bad ★

Michelin map **987** north of 14 – Pop 22 600

The resort of Zwischenahn has been developed along the shores of the **Zwischenahner Meer.** The lakeside banks between the harbour and the church have been made into public gardens and planted as a rhododendron **park**★ (Parkanlagen). A typical local Ammerland hamlet has been constructed in the park complete with windmill and thatched cottages.

Preceded by a bell tower which serves also as the porch, the **church of St. John** has a fascinating fresco of 1512 (the Last Judgment) and a large altarpiece depicting the Passion (around 1480). The pulpit and the stalls were installed after the Reformation

INDEX

Swabian Jura . . . . . Towns, beauty spots, sights and tourist regions

Weser (Mountains) . . . . Other towns or places referred to

Königswinter . . . . . . The bistre underlining indicates that a town is

Schwalmstadt . . . . . . mentioned in the Michelin Red Guide Deutschland (hotels and restaurants)

Luther . . . . Main references to historical events, persons and particular

Jugendstil . . . . . . terms appearing in the text

Rüdesheim am Rhein
→ Koblenz . . . . 211 } Route from Rüdesheim to Koblenz described on p 211

The Province (Land) is given in brackets after the town, see abbreviations below :

Baden-Württ. : Baden-Württemberg　　　　　Rhine.-Pal. : Rhineland-Palatinate
L. Saxony : Lower Saxony　　　　　　　　　Rhine-Westph. : Rhine-Westphalia
　　　　　　　　　　　　　　　　　　　　Schl.-Holst. : Schleswig-Holstein

(EF 5)

MANUFACTURE FRANÇAISE DES PNEUMATIQUES MICHELIN
© Michelin et Cie, propriétaire-éditeur, 1978
Société en commandite par actions au capital de 700 millions de francs
R.C. Clermont-Fd B 855 200 507 (55-B-50) — Siège Social Clermont-Fd (France)
ISBN 2 06 015 030 - 2

Printed in Great Britain by Jarrold & Sons Ltd of Norwich